AMERICAN GOVERNMENT

AMERICAN GOVERNMENT
CONFLICT, COMPROMISE, AND CITIZENSHIP

Christopher J. Bosso
Northeastern University

John H. Portz
Northeastern University

Michael C. Tolley
Northeastern University

Westview PRESS **A Member of the Perseus Books Group**

To our teachers, and to our students

Photo credits:
p. 2: © Ellen Senisi, The Image Works; 4: © George Bellerose, Stock Boston; 8: © Les Stone, Corbis Sygma; 23: © Wesley Hitt, Liaison Agency; 28: © Bill Greenblatt, Liaison Agency; 29: © Reuters/Blake Sell, Archive Photos; 42: © John Giordano, Saba; 50: © Archive Photos; 55: © Hulton Getty Picture Library, Liaison Agency; 61: © Hulton Getty Picture Library, Liaison Agency; 71: © U.S. Senate/CNP, Archive Photos; 86: © Matthew Neal McVay, Stock Boston; 94: © Wally McNamee, Sygma; 97: © Ralf-Finn Hestoft, Saba; 106: © Daemmrich, The Image Works; 110: © Corbis/Bettmann; 134: © Tim Barnwell, Stock Boston; 145: © Russell Lee/Hulton Getty Picture Library/Liaison Agency; 152: © Paoni/Contrasto, Saba; 160: www.stormfront.org; 162: © Daemmrich, The Image Works; 167: © Fugliano, Liaison Agency; 183: © A. Ramey, Stock Boston; 187: © Ira Wyman, Corbis Sygma; 187: © Reuters/T. Bochatey, Archive Photos; 187: © B. Kraft, Corbis Sygma; 187: © Darren Carroll, Liaison Agency; 194: © Archive Photos; 199: © Steven Rubin, The Image Works; 208: © Reuters/Donald Winslow, Archive Photos; 231: © Bob Daemmrich, Stock Boston; 247: © Hulton Getty Picture Library, Liaison Agency; 258: © Daemmrich, The Image Works; 279: © John Mantel, Sipa Press; 286: © Corbis/Bettmann; 290: © Ken Hawkins, Corbis Sygma; 294: © Alain McLaughlin, Impact Visuals; 298: © Joseph Fitzgerald, Sipa Press; 310: © James Nubile, The Image Works; 326: © Jeffrey Markowitz, Corbis Sygma; 328: © Matthew Borkoski, Stock Boston; 340: © A. Lichtenstein, Corbis Sygma; 349: © Reuters/Mark Wilson, Archive Photos; 362: © Senate Pool, Saba; 374: © J. L. Atlan, Corbis Sygma; 376: © Clark Campbell, Sipa Press; 386: © Archive Photos; 387: © J. L. Atlan, Corbis Sygma; 389: © Agence France Presse, Archive Photos; 409: © Wally McNamee, Corbis Sygma; 421: © Dion Ogust, The Image Works; 423: © Gregg Mancuso, Stock Boston; 425: © Greg Smith, Saba-Pool; 430: © Richard Ellis, Corbis Sygma; 435: © L. Kolvoord, The Image Works; 439: © Sheppard Sherbell, Saba; 453: © Daemmrich, The Image Works; 466: © Pixel by Pixel; 469: © David James, Kobal Collection; 478: © Reuters/Steve Jaffe, Archive Photos; 482: © Corbis Sygma; 486: © Hulton Getty Picture Library, Liaison Agency; 491: © Meyer Liebowitz/New York Times Co., Archive Photos; 508: © McLaughlin, The Image Works; 512: © Jacksonville Journal-Courier, The Image Works; 518: © Gyori Antoine, Corbis Sygma; 521: courtesy Project Vote Smart; 522: © Wade Goddard, Corbis Sygma; 526: © Dion Ogust/The Image Works; 530: © Jim West, Impact Visuals

Published in 2000 in the United States of America by Westview Press, 5500 Central Avenue, Boulder, Colorado 80301-2877, and in the United Kingdom by Westview Press, 12 Hid's Copse Road, Cumnor Hill, Oxford OX2 9JJ.

Find us on the World Wide Web at www.westviewpress.com

A CIP record for this book is available from the Library of Congress.
ISBN 0-8133-6871-5

The paper used in this publication meets the requirements of the American National Standard for Permanence of Paper for Printed Library Materials Z39.48-1984.

10   9   8   7   6   5   4   3   2   1

CONTENTS

TABLES AND ILLUSTRATIONS

Primary Source Readings

PREFACE

Any decision to add to the towering pile of textbooks on American government and politics is either a sign of simple lunacy or, believe it or not, because we had an overriding sense of purpose. Although you do have to be a little crazy to take on such a daunting task, we did approach this project with several goals in mind.

A Convenient Length   Our first goal was to design a text that would occupy a middle ground between the massive hardback texts that traditionally have been used in college courses on American politics and the short, almost terse, *basics* texts that offer little more than a litany of facts. For many of us—students and teachers alike—the big texts are too long: you often don't get to use all of the textbook because you run out of time, no matter how long the school term is. These books cost a lot, so many students simply didn't buy them. And they included so much information that both teachers and students had a hard time deciding what was *important*—in general, not just for the final exam—and what was merely *interesting* to diehard politics junkies. These books are excellent sources, but they have real shortcomings for classroom use.

The shorter *basics* texts are, to be charitable, often sketchy and uninteresting. More than one of our students, when asked about the one or the other of these texts, typically responded with a single word: boring. Now, we don't presume that every text—even this one—is a literary classic, but being boring is a major indictment.

Thus, our first goal was to try to offer the essential information about and analysis of American politics without being boring. OK, so we may not always succeed— you may not be as excited as we are about discussing the structure of the federal bureaucracy—but we try to keep the reader in mind. We also tried to keep the length of the text within reasonable limits so that it can be used either as a core text, particularly for shorter terms (such as quarter systems, summer sessions, or evening courses), or as one of several books in a semester system course.

A Focus on Core Questions   The goal of keeping the text's length within reasonable limits forced us to think hard about what was fundamental versus what is merely interesting. For example, in chapter 6, we don't spend a lot of time discussing the organizational dimensions of political parties, but instead ask two fundamental questions: Why do parties exist? Why is the American political system dominated by two large parties? If you come away from this course just understanding the answers to those two questions, then you understand the essence of political parties in American politics. The same consideration of *core questions* runs through each of the chapters.

A Theme That Works   We also wanted to explain American politics by using a theme that didn't leave the reader confused, alienated, or cynical. To be blunt about it, some texts rely on themes that are so complicated that only a trained political scientist can understand them, or are so subtle that students never quite get the point. Some themes are so *radical* that too many students automatically turn off their brains when confronted by an *alien* perspective. This tendency is not exactly a sign of intellectual openness, to be sure, but it happens too often to be ignored. And, frankly, some themes describe politics in ways that leave the impression that none of this is worth studying in the first place.

We disagree, and use a theme of *conflict and compromise* throughout this text to show, first, how politics is a natural part of any free society and, second, that the end result of politics frequently is some sort of compromise, some mutually beneficial outcome, that leaves most people satisfied that some progress was made. This is not always true, mind you, but it happens enough to make us believe that, in a democracy, compromise is the norm, not the exception.

More important, the theme is a hopeful one. It is not naive: we don't assume that everyone is always honest, good, or even very smart. But neither do we begin with the assumption that politics is dirty, politicians are crooks, and voters are morons. It isn't, and they aren't, and the sooner we get away from such shallow assumptions the better off we'll all be in the end. After all, politics is important: it is the process by which we try to transcend our conflicts in a peaceful manner. The alternatives are far worse.

So count us among the believers who think that politics is too important to be dismissed as irrelevant or stupid. We don't expect that students will come away from this book wanting to become activists, politicians, or, even, political scientists—although we might like it—but we do hope it will make them think more about their role in the American political system.

THE ORGANIZATION OF THIS TEXT

Each chapter of this text is organized in the following manner. Our overriding goals were clarity of organization, integration, and ease of use.

Objectives   These are intended to act as organizing features for the chapter, and to give the reader a preview of the major questions we intend to focus on.

Case Study   Each chapter begins with a short discussion of a case that illuminates the major theme in the chapter. This case can be used as a basis for class discussion, in particular, the question, *What would you do?*

Boxed Material   Each chapter contains two or three boxes on issues that bear on the themes in the chapter. Some of the boxes focus on historical perspectives, whereas others present contemporary issues that can be used as the basis for class discussion. We also provide a number of tables and charts to illuminate issues raised in the text, but we try to keep them to a minimum in order to avoid clutter.

Chapter Summary   Each chapter ends with a restatement of the chapter objectives and short summary of the major points addressed in the text. This summary is intended to reassert the themes that we think are critical to remember.

Questions for Review and Discussion   Here we pose four or five questions that bear on major themes in the chapter. These questions can be used for class discussion or for essay exams.

Terms to Remember   A list of the major terms and concepts posed in the chapter. These terms are put in bold face at the point in the chapter at which they are discussed.

Web Sources   A short list of useful web sources relevant to that chapter, selected to enable the reader to obtain additional information on the topics raised in the chapter. We also chose sources that are still likely to be valid when you read this text.

Suggested Readings   An annotated bibiography of books, some classic and some contemporary, that are worth examining if you want to dig more deeply into the issues raised in the chapter.

Primary Source Readings   Finally, at the very end of each chapter, we've provided excerpts from relevant original sources on the themes presented in the chapter. These readings will give students a flavor of the original language and intentions of the writers or speakers—something that can't be done by summarizing events and goals.

A NOTE ON THE COLLABORATIVE PROCESS

There are three authors behind this project for two reasons. First, even a relatively short textbook is a massive project, and the lead author (Chris Bosso) would never have been able to finish the book without his colleagues.

Second, three authors, like three heads, are better than one in that the three of us bring different areas of scholarly and teaching interest to bear on the project.

Chris Bosso is a specialist on American institutions and public policy process, with a particular scholarly focus on Congress. He also studies interest groups and environmental policy.

John Portz is a student of state and local government as well as a scholar of education policy. Moreover, Portz is an elected official serving on the town council of Watertown, Massachusetts, a position that gives him a better understanding of the process of politics, not to mention elections.

Michael Tolley is a student of constitutional law, federalism, and civil rights and liberties. He also studies the development of constitutional law in other countries, in particular the United Kingdom and South Africa. His breadth of knowledge was of immeasurable value to the entire project.

Our diverse talents were brought to bear throughout this book. As lead author, Chris Bosso wrote most of chapters 1, 2, 5, 6, 7, 8, 9, and 12, and generally ensured that all chapters followed the same structure and writing style. John Portz wrote most of chapters 3 (federalism) and 10 (the bureaucracy), and Michael Tolley wrote most of chapters 4 (civil rights and liberties) and 11 (the judiciary). Portz and Tolley also contributed to the development of various boxes, tables, charts, and other resources throughout the text, and provided feedback to Bosso on the draft chapters as we proceeded.

So this truly was a collaboration, and we think the book is stronger for it. Let us know what you think.

ACKNOWLEDGMENTS

Authors incur debts. In this case the lead author, Chris Bosso, wants to thank his wife, Marcia Goetsch, for her patient support and companionship throughout all of the years it took to translate a vague idea to what you hold in your hand. Anyone who writes a book simply dreads to hear the question, *How is it coming?* Marcia was gracious enough not to ask. She just assumed it would get done.

Other debts: to Leo Wiegman, executive editor at Westview Press, our gratitude for taking on this project. Thanks also go to the other professionals at or working with Westview Press: Tom Kulesa, Michelle Mallin, and the staff of Professional Book Center. In this regard we owe a special debt to our development editor, Carolyn Smith, whose critical eye, vast experience, and quick green pen made this a better book than it sometimes had a right to be.

Throughout the development process, this text benefited greatly from the careful readings of our professional colleagues. For their comments and suggestions, we would like to thank, Carol Sears Botsch, University of South Carolina, Aiken; Gary Keith, University of Texas, Austin; Matthew Kerbel, Villanova University; John C. Kuzenski, The Citadel; Roger J. Moiles, Michigan State University; Mark P. Petracca, University of California, Irvine; Craig Rimmerman, Hobart and William Smith Colleges; Barbara Segnatelli, University of Maryland; Sandra Wood, University of North Texas.

Finally, as the dedication page says, we thank our teachers. All of them, from first grade through graduate school. We became college professors because we had teachers who inspired us, shaped us, moved us. They are too many to mention individually, but they know who they are.

And we thank our students, from whom we learn more than we can ever say. They keep us honest, they keep us young, and they remind us that it is up to future generations to continue the hard task of making democracy work.

Carpe diem. Sieze the day.

Christopher J. Bosso
John H. Portz
Michael C. Tolley

AMERICAN POLITICS

Transforming Conflict into Compromise

OBJECTIVES

❑ To understand that conflict is natural in human society and that "politics" is about how a group of people tries to transform conflicts into mutually acceptable compromises

❑ To examine the societal contexts that shape American politics: the size of the nation, its physical diversity, the diversity of its population, social and economic changes, the impacts of new technologies, and broad trends occurring throughout the world

❑ To understand the core values that define the American political culture and how these values affect the ways in which Americans look at the world

A typical older school building. Many of the nation's schools were constructed decades ago, and today need expensive reconstruction or replacement to meet the demands of today's teaching methods and educational technologies, such as the Web. To do this requires a lot of money. Who pays is a political question.

In 1993 the Supreme Court of the State of New Hampshire ruled that the state has a legal duty to educate its children. The ruling came in response to a lawsuit, brought by over two dozen of the poorest school districts in the state, charging that New Hampshire's almost exclusive use of local property taxes to finance public education prevented these districts from providing their children with the "adequate" level of education required by the state constitution. The court agreed and ordered state lawmakers to come up with a new way to pay for public education.

Few issues are more important to average Americans than public education. The United States has a long and proud tradition of providing free public education for everyone regardless of income, race, ethnicity, or religion. In this respect, the public school is an important symbol of American democratic values as well as a vehicle for ensuring economic well-being and social mobility for all Americans.

Thus, it is never a minor issue when parents complain about the quality of public schools. Almost every generation of parents seems to criticize the skill level of teachers, the adequacy of the curriculum, and the availability of special programs such as music, art, or even sports. These concerns are magnified when parents compare the quality of their children's schools to those in neighboring communities. Some schools offer a lengthy list of optional courses, small class sizes, computer labs, and extensive extracurricular activities; others seem to offer only a basic curriculum with large class sizes and few after-school events. These disparities usually stem from the different levels of financial support the taxpayers in the districts are able or willing to provide. Parents in the less well funded school districts get upset by these disparities, particularly if they stem from the simple fact that some communities are more affluent than others. Parents contact their local, state, and federal representatives seeking what they see as a more equitable distribution of financial support. They may even go to court to force their lawmakers to act.

The conflict concerns a key question: How *should* we fund our public schools? Today approximately 90 percent of the funding for the typical American public school comes from state and local governments, and most is in the form of local property taxes. This is the source of the funding disparity between communities and the basic conflict in New Hampshire. A town's property tax fund is based on the value of homes, office buildings, factories, and other commercial property in a community. A community with expensive homes and a healthy commercial base can spend more on its schools. One with less-valuable homes and scant commercial development has a far smaller base from which to generate funds for schools.

Let's go back to New Hampshire. In 1993 residents of Allenstown paid a property tax rate of about $20 per $1,000 of the value of their property. That is, someone with a house valued at $100,000 paid $2,000 in property taxes. This is a very high property tax rate compared to most other communities in the nation. At the same time the residents of Newington paid a tax rate of only $2 per $1,000, so the taxes on a $100,000 house in that town came to only $200. Yet Allenstown, a poorer residential area, could only provide $3,400 per pupil. Newington, a more affluent town with a strong commercial base, could afford more than $10,000 per pupil despite having a far lower tax rate. As a result, Newington's schools were much better equipped.[1]

This kind of gap caused a great deal of conflict among New Hampshire residents and led to the lawsuit that eventually overturned the way schools were funded. New Hampshire was only one of dozens of states in which this conflict arose. Today getting a good education is far more important to a person's economic future than it might have been a generation or two ago, when many high school graduates took high-paying jobs in factories rather than go to college. Parents know that the quality of public schools will directly affect their children's ability to compete for the best career options. They wanted more financial support from the state to make up for the gaps between the richer and poorer districts.

States have responded to these pressures by developing funding formulas to allocate money to school districts across the state, but these responses have provoked their own conflicts. If some parents are concerned about the inequities that result from the property tax, others argue just as strongly that the property tax should remain the primary source of school funding. Why, they argue, should some communities be penalized just because they have high property values and can afford more school funding? Still others argue that because the state has an overall legal responsibility for education, all school districts, regardless of their property values, should receive state support. Nevertheless, almost no one wants to raise state taxes to cover these expenses.

State lawmakers usually try to put together some kind of compromise solution to address as many of these competing demands as possible. In some states, such as Massachusetts, the state government will provide additional state money, generated by either state income taxes or sales taxes, to bring communities with lower property values up to some minimum level of support. Other states, such as Georgia, use state lottery proceeds to provide supplemental funding. Wealthier communities naturally will get less state funding, but sometimes states will provide those school districts with a minimum level of support based simply on the number of students in the dis-

A resident speaks at the annual Weybridge, Vermont, town meeting. Such "direct democracy" is increasingly rare, even in New England, as town populations grow larger and the demands on government become more complex. In many cases, town meetings are replaced by elected town councils and mayors.

trict. Such formulas ensure that every district gets at least some state support—a strategy designed largely to reduce opposition to any state funding for poorer areas.

However, some states, such as Vermont, have gone even further and created programs that openly transfer money raised in a wealthy community to schools in poorer ones. Not surprisingly, such open transfers are hotly opposed by residents in communities where property values are high. On one side is a local district's right to finance the level of education its residents want to provide if they can afford it. On the other side is the state's responsibility to ensure that all of its residents, rich or poor, can enjoy comparable levels of educational quality.

What would you do? This isn't an easy question to answer, as we will see throughout this text. How to resolve these kinds of conflicts and how to balance competing needs are political matters. They involve efforts by concerned citizens and government officials to resolve a problem peacefully and, ideally, to the benefit of everyone. As we will see, conflicts such as these are a normal part of American politics.

EVERYDAY POLITICS

Let's start with a simple question: Why study politics? A "civics course" answer might be that citizens *should* know how their government is organized and how their political system works. To study politics is the first responsibility of citizenship in a democracy.

OK, but what is a **democracy**? The term comes from the Greek words *demos* ("people") and *kratein* ("to rule"). So "democracy" literally means "rule by the people." However, there is some disagreement over what exactly is meant by government "by the people." For some, it is a system in which every person votes directly on every single issue, with a simple vote total determining what is going to be done. Such a direct form of democracy exists to some degree in many small towns, particularly in the New England states.

So far so good. It is relatively easy for the 1,500 residents in a rural Vermont town to vote to spend $25,000 to buy a new pickup truck for the town's maintenance workers. It is a far different matter for the 270 million citizens of the United States to vote directly on each one of the thousands of items contained in the $1.8 trillion federal government budget. The logistical challenges are mind-boggling. Indeed, direct forms of democracy do not exist on a national level. Nations simply may be too large and complex to be run by a direct vote of the people. Thus, in a strict sense *no* nation is a democracy.

That being said, we tend to agree that a nation can be regarded as "democratic" so long as the people in that nation can select other people to represent their views, and so long as the government itself pays attention to citizens' needs and views. This is called representative government or, more precisely, a **republic,** a term derived from the Latin *res publica* ("affairs of the public"). Another term with the same meaning is "representative democracy."

The United States of America is a republic. So are Canada, France, Japan, Costa Rica, and many other nations with democratic political systems. We are somewhat lenient about using the term democracy in such cases because a republic requires that "the people," average citizens, have some control over how government works. They exercise this control through various mechanisms: sitting on town councils or school boards, joining political parties, becoming a member of an activist group, signing petitions, marching in a protest, voting in elections, or just paying attention to political events and affairs. How much *effective* control citizens have on any given day is a matter of debate, but for our purposes the idea that they *should* have such control is a good place to start.

If democratic government involves some kind of rule by the people, it should be clear that the essential health of any kind of democratic government requires that the people be informed and active. Democracy depends on the **citizen,** a French term (*citoyen*) that conveys a sense of independence and activism that is distinguished from the British notion of a **subject,** a more passive notion of the individual. So democracy depends on active and informed citizens. This may seem unfair, as most people have to work for a living and may have limited time to get involved in public life, but democracy demands that citizens play a part in their government.

Given this reality, citizens cannot keep the government honest or responsive if they don't understand the basic structure and rules of their governmental system. For example, in any election citizens must make choices among competing candidates and campaign promises. In doing so, citizens must be able to compare people and ideas, a task that requires some basic knowledge about the major issues at hand, some capacity to assess the potential leadership qualities of the candidates, and even to assess the likelihood that campaign promises can actually be fulfilled. Those who do not understand politics will have a harder time making reasoned judgments, but democratic government depends on citizens who can make such judgments.

BOX 1.1.
THE NEW BABY BOOM

A CLOSER LOOK

In 1998 the number of Americans younger than 18 years of age grew to 70.2 million, surpassing the previous peak of 69.9 million in 1966. So the children and grandchildren of the famous Baby Boom (those born 1946–1964) now outnumber their parents and grandparents. This fact comes as a great surprise to a great many people.

What are the consequences? Schools left empty during the "baby bust" of the late 1970s and 1980s are now overcrowded and taxpayers are being asked to fund new school buildings and expanded education programs. Consumer goods related to children—from toys to computer games, children's magazines to clothing—increasingly dominate the market, and purchases of a wide array of "adult" goods ranging from minivans to meals at restaurants are influenced by the presence of children. Some observers estimate children now spend or influence the spending of $500 billion a year.

The new baby boom is also influencing American politics in arenas as varied as funding for public schools, how to improve education, the sale of cigarettes to minors, health care, or the future of social security. Politicians of all political views are devoting increasing effort at wooing the parents of young children, particularly mothers, who, unlike during the Baby Boom generation, are likely to work.

The so-called Millennium generation also looks very different from the Baby Boom generation. First, many more of them are the children of immigrants, particularly those from Spanish-speaking countries, and Hispanic Americans soon are expected to surpass African Americans as the largest minority group in the United States.

Second, unlike during the Baby Boom generation where virtually every home had children, today there are far more households with no children at all. This is particularly true for senior citizens, who as a group bore the burden for the Baby Boom and now are faced with increased demands for new schools and, as a result, more tax money. Conflicts between older and younger Americans over spending priorities are likely to intensify.

In general, the Millennium generation is going to reshape American politics. The great question is *how*. Nobody knows, but everyone has a stake in the answer.

Source: Dale Russakoff, "Millennium Generation Is Shaping Trends," *Washington Post*, June 29, 1998, p. A1.

But that's the civics course argument. A simpler and more relevant reason to study politics is that it *matters*. Every part of our daily lives is affected in some way by politics (see Box 1.1). We are born in hospitals in which doctors are licensed by state health agencies. We go to public schools run by local boards whose legal authority is derived from state and national laws. Politics dictates whether we need a blood test to get married, where our children can attend school, whether a neighbor is allowed to store junked cars in his backyard, how much we pay in sales taxes, even whether we can legally buy a beer. Whether we know it or not, every aspect of our lives—work or play, in our homes or in public places—is influenced in some way by politics, by the activities of people and institutions around us, some of them close at hand and others far away—even in other nations. We go to war, and might even die, because of politics. In short, politics is woven into our lives.

Look again at the case of funding public schools discussed earlier in the chapter. You or someone you know probably went to a public high school whose quality was affected by how well it was funded. And no doubt this issue has been the subject of intense local conflict, but probably also attempts at reaching a compromise. These results don't just happen by themselves, however. They come about because of politics, because those involved have been willing to try to get beyond their conflicts and work out their differences.

Of course, as we will see, there are plenty of examples in which no compromise was reached, or in which one side in a conflict simply overpowered the other side through its superior resources, numbers of supporters, or control over important government positions. Some conflicts, such as those occurring throughout the former Yugoslavia or the Middle East or Northern Ireland, have been bloody ones. Conflicts can degenerate into open war.

Short of actual war, however, politics is very much about how people struggle to resolve their conflicts in constructive ways. This fact makes it critical for citizens to understand the factors and forces that shape politics in their communities, their nation, and the world. The citizen must be able to understand why some groups seem to have a lot of influence, why some issues are more controversial than others, or why some problems are more difficult to solve than others. An informed citizen may be a more thoughtful, more rational one who is more likely to participate in politics, even if only to vote. That citizen is less likely to be persuaded by superficial arguments or antidemocratic leaders or causes.

Thus we come back to the civics answer. Politics matters in everyday life, and studying politics is an act of citizenship. No democracy can survive, much less thrive, without informed, involved, and active citizens. Without such citizens, all that might remain are elections that don't mean much, institutions that have no purpose, and government that lacks legitimacy. This government is a "democracy" in name only.

THE NATURE OF POLITICS

Because **politics** is so important, we need a clear notion of what politics is. This is a lot more important in practical terms than it might seem at first. After all, how we define a concept shapes the discussion that follows. Think for a moment about "welfare," an issue we will examine more closely in chapter 5. Is welfare "help" for people in need or "a handout" to the lazy? Which image of welfare we accept as "truth" shapes the policies we actually pursue—assuming that we believe the poor should get any help at all. Definitions are important.

Conflicting views over whether the House of Representatives should vote for articles of impeachment against President Bill Clinton in December, 1998. In a democracy, one is supposed to be free to express one's views without fear of persecution by government. As a result, conflict is natural in a democracy.

In the same way, how we define politics shapes the way we interpret each event, trend, or person who plays a role in politics. Or, as political scientist E. E. Schattschneider once wrote, whoever "determines what politics is about runs the country."[2] Just deciding what politics is all about affects the kinds of activities we think should be allowed or prohibited, the kinds of people we elect or do not elect to office, and the kinds of policies we find acceptable or unacceptable.

Political scientist Harold Lasswell defined politics as the process of deciding "who gets what, when, and how."[3] Lasswell's definition makes a lot of practical sense, since much of everyday politics revolves around how people decide to divide up resources, impose costs, or distribute burdens. How to fund the public schools is one such political conflict. But a subtle problem with Lasswell's definition is that people can end up thinking that politics is always about money, or only about economic selfishness or "making deals." This definition can have negative connotations, particularly in an era in which so many Americans seem so cynical about government and, especially, politicians. If politics is only about "deals," every action by government is merely another rip-off of the taxpayer and every politician little more than a liar or crook. Politics defined this way can seem pretty dismal.

CONFLICT

Each of us undoubtedly regards *some* actions by government at *some* time as bad or wasteful. And certainly some politicians *are* liars or crooks, if not worse. Sadly, so are more than a few regular people. There are few angels in any area of life. Yet to say that all politics is "dirty" and that all politicians are crooks is simplistic and frankly wrong. More often than cynics admit, politics is about generally decent people trying to do what they think is right. Some people, for example, want to ban all abortions. Their personal values lead them to believe that abortion is wrong. These people disagree passionately with other generally decent people who, because of their personal values, want to keep abortions legal. The problem is not that either side is necessarily "evil," although there is always a temptation to depict the other side in such stark terms. The problem here is that these groups sincerely disagree on this difficult issue.

Such is the nature of **conflict.** The root causes of conflict can be material, such as with financial support for the schools, or, as with abortion, can stem from deeply held religious values, cultural beliefs, or basic ideals about how people should behave. Conflicts also arise because of ethnic, racial, or gender differences. In fact, conflicts arise simply because most of us live in communities of some kind. We are not hermits, each living in a separate cave. As communal beings we are doomed to disagree. The seeds of conflict thus are sown in human nature—envy, greed, anger, fear, bigotry, pride. Many conflicts are relatively trivial—how loud car speakers can be or whether you can hang out in the mall—but some, such as whether we should execute people who commit murder or go to war against other nations, are deadly serious.

COMPROMISE

So conflicts are inevitable. Much of what we call politics is simply the process of trying to find some way to get beyond our conflicts, to keep them from getting out of hand before someone gets hurt.

Depending on the issue, most conflicts are resolved in some way, and more often than not this resolution involves some kind of **compromise**—a "deal." This is the "politics" part. In a compromise, nobody gets everything they want, but nobody loses everything either. Ideally, everybody involved at least comes away satisfied that they got *something*. Is this a dirty deal? No. Sometimes a compromise is all that is possible at a particular time or place, especially when the only alternative is more conflict—even bloodshed. Politics in this sense is about trying to work out mutually acceptable outcomes in difficult, even dangerous situations.

Do compromises always occur? Are they always possible? Of course not. Sometimes one side wins outright because it is bigger or richer, has better access to those who make the decisions, or simply has the law on its side. If a major corporation wants to build a factory against the wishes of a group of local residents, it is safe to assume that the company has more resources to ensure that it gets its way. It can promise jobs for local residents, contribute funds for new roads and schools, advertise in local papers to persuade residents to favor its position, or hire better lawyers in case of a court battle. Even here, however, the citizens' group might get the company to make a few concessions, such as creating a new park between the factory site and the adjacent neighborhood, if only because the company doesn't want to make any more enemies than it has to.

Sometimes a conflict cannot be resolved. The struggle over abortion is a good example. It is hard to imagine that people who believe that abortion is equivalent to murder will compromise on their core religious or moral values. People who believe that the death penalty is morally wrong also are hard-pressed to compromise on their beliefs. In such cases, a conflict can persist without apparent resolution. Not surprisingly, these are the most difficult conflicts to resolve.

For our purposes it is useful to think of politics as the process of *trying to transform conflict into compromise*. Viewed in this way, politics is more than deciding who gets how much government funding or who pays how much in taxes, although these issues dominate many political debates. Almost everyone wants benefits for themselves and their communities, but nobody wants to pay for these benefits if they can avoid it. That's human nature. But politics is also infused by strong ideas about how the world should work, about the intrinsic nature of humanity, and about the desirability of change. It is fueled by hidden fears, keen hopes, and idealistic dreams. It is not simply about money. It is not solely about who gets to make the "big" decisions, or even who has "control." Politics can be about material survival, but it also can be about virtue, dishonesty, honor, loyalty, hatred, or even love.

Thinking about politics as the process of trying to transform conflict into compromise also helps us understand situations in which no compromise occurs. It helps us understand when one side simply overwhelms the other, and it helps us understand when neither side is able or willing to find some middle ground on a contentious issue.

The Greek philosopher Aristotle argued that man by nature is a political animal.[4] Just so, politics is about how people—not just "politicians"—go about trying to hold together their families and communities. Politics is a human activity. It is a means of achieving common goals, even one as deceptively simple as just being left in peace. It is about how people who have to live with one another try to resolve their conflicts without resorting to violence. It is about how people try to improve their lives, whether in their immediate neighborhood or in the world as a whole.

POWER AND AUTHORITY

Thinking of politics inevitably raises the issues of power and authority. **Power** is a concept that suggests the capacity of one side in a conflict to overcome another simply because it has superior resources, numbers, or even weapons. The company trying to build its factory can be said to have power over the local residents because of its wealth or because of its ability to hire better lawyers. The police force can be said to have power because it can compel people to obey laws by threatening lawbreakers with arrest. A nation displays power when it forces other nations to do what it wants because of its military might. In general, power is about being able to *compel* others to act in ways you want.

Authority, by contrast, is the legal capacity to do something. A police officer might be able to compel you to obey the law because that officer has a weapon, but whether the officer can arrest you for a crime hinges on the officer's legal authority to do so. That is, the law itself, not the fact that the officer is armed, grants the officer the authority to compel you to obey. As we will see, the notion of law, of the legal authority to do something, is the basis for a legitimate government. Power is not the same as authority.

GOVERNMENT

The term **government** is used here to refer to the formal structure of laws and procedures under which we live. In a democracy, the people theoretically grant to government the authority to create and enforce the laws under which they have agreed to live. Government also can be thought of as the set of authorized institutions and processes within which people engage in politics. That is, government is a set of authorized rules and procedures that help manage conflict and enable people to resolve their conflicts peacefully. As we'll see, that's why we have constitutions, legislatures, and courts, not to mention elections and other procedures for choosing those who will govern on our behalf. In many ways it is good to think of government as the *arena of politics*, the place where we fight out our differences without violence and according to specific rules of the game. Government thus is a mechanism for managing conflict.

Government is created by politics. Its rules, institutions, and goals are all products of political decisions. This was true even in the making of the United States Constitution, as we will see in chapter 2. How any nation sets up elections, why it has a legislature, or which kinds of powers it grants its leaders reflect political decisions. More often than not, these decisions are the result of hard-won compromises worked out by people with strong beliefs about right and wrong. Finding some minimal common ground is what politics is all about.

So here we define politics as the art of transforming conflicts into compromises. At its heart, it requires that people who strongly disagree with and maybe even dislike one another find ways to resolve their conflicts peacefully. The alternative is a society in which one side wins simply because it is more powerful, which is hardly a prescription for a healthy democracy. Politics is also not the same as war. War is not simply "politics by other means," as one famous military strategist put it.[5] War is the result when politics fails.

THE CONTEXT OF AMERICAN POLITICS

To restate: Politics is about how people try to transcend their conflicts and reach some kind of compromise. This characterization sounds a bit mushy. So is real life, filled as it is with ambiguities about which answers are right or wrong. Sometimes people lie, but more often they honestly disagree about what is "true," and sometimes an action that once seemed reasonable now looks pretty stupid. Perfection eludes us all.

Everyday politics is all about ambiguities and possibilities. At any given time some activities are allowed and others forbidden because of societal norms or prevailing values. For example, anyone who advocates slavery today is seen as a crank, if not worse, even though slavery was common once in the United States. The history of homosexuality in America is another example of how changing values have altered the political dimensions of an issue. In the 1970s, it was rare to find openly gay people in elected office. Today it is more common—though not everywhere in the country and not for all offices. People in one part of the nation may elect an openly gay person to the U.S. House of Representatives even as people elsewhere pass laws barring equal benefits for homosexual couples. So where a gay or lesbian resides has an effect on the opportunities open to that person at a particular moment.

The point here is that politics does not take place in a vacuum. Far from it. Conflicts are generated and compromises sought within identifiable and powerful societal contexts. Politics is affected by these contexts: by what kind of country we live in, what kind of people we are, what kinds of beliefs we hold, which issues we care about.

However, contexts do not *determine* what kinds of conflicts occur or which kinds of compromises are reached. This is an important, if subtle, distinction. To argue that context determines outcome is to take the human element out of politics. Politics is not an automatic process. In real life we need to allow for the very real impacts of changing societal norms, new technologies, the varied roles played by individuals, temporary mass hysteria, or the capacity of humans to change their minds. As a result, politics can be an unpredictable activity.

Some contexts are common to all nations. Every nation grapples with poverty, racism, pollution, and countless other sources of conflict. Every nation tries to maintain social peace, economic strength, and national security. Most nations have a formal plan of government based on a written constitution (see chapter 2); many have lively and honest elections; and all have bureaucracies with varying degrees of power. In this sense at least, the United States shares features with many other nations.

However, how each nation addresses its conflicts or how its politics works at any given moment will vary to some degree. Despite common conflicts and similar kinds of institutions, there are broad societal contexts that give American politics a distinctive direction and flavor. Some contexts are enduring, whereas others change rather quickly. Some have easily observable impacts on everyday politics, and others have effects that are not as immediately obvious. But all contexts matter. In this section we will explore some of the major societal contexts that affect American politics.

THE SIZE OF THE NATION

Americans take for granted the sheer physical size of the United States, the fourth largest nation in the world after Russia, Canada, and China (see Table 1.1). If you drive the 3,000 miles from Boston, Massachusetts, westward on Interstate 90 to Seattle, Washington, you will cross thirteen states and three time zones. But you will remain within the boundaries of one nation.

TABLE 1.1.   HOW THE UNITED STATES COMPARES WITH SELECTED
             OTHER NATIONS

	Size (in square miles)	1998 Population (in millions)	Rank	People (per square mile)	Gross Domestic Product (in dollars per capita, 1995)*
Brazil	3,265,061	169,807	5	50	$4,084
Canada	3,560,219	30,675	33	8	19,000
China	3,600,930	1,236,915	1	339	2,303
Columbia	401,042	38,581	30	93	2,107
Egypt	384,344	66,050	16	169	746
France	210,668	58,805	20	278	26,290
Germany	135,236	82,079	12	622	26,190
India	1,147,950	984,004	2	843	348
Indonesia	705,189	212,942	4	297	931
Israel	7,849	5,644	100	719	17,070
Japan	152,411	125,932	9	826	41,160
Mexico	742,486	98,553	11	133	2,521
Nigeria	351,649	110,532	10	314	946
Poland	117,571	38,607	29	328	5,404
Russia	6,592,817	146,861	6	22	4,478
Singapore	241	3,490	125	14,487	-na-
United States	**3,539,227**	**270,312**	**3**	**76**	**27,550**

Sources: United States Bureau of the Census, *Statistical Abstract of the United States, 1998* (Washington, D.C.: Government Printing Office, 1998), pp. 827–829, 835. See also http://www.census.gov/prod/3/98pubs/98statab/.

* Gross Domestic Product is a statistic that reflects the total value of all the goods and sevices produced by the country in a year. The per capita figure is the total GDP divided by the population. The figure for Japan, for example, reflects the high value of its industrial production compared to a relatively smaller population. Not all Japanese are rich, of course.

By contrast, if you were to drive 3,000 miles from Lisbon, Portugal, northeast through Europe into Russia—which you cannot do easily or quickly—you would cross at least 10 different nations, each with its own ethnic makeup, language, history, and political system. No wonder the average American tourist thinks Europe is small and crowded, or that generations of European visitors to the United States have marveled at its vast and comparatively empty spaces.

The size of a nation matters. How so? First, it is not easy for Americans, even with television and air travel, to keep an eye on or participate in a national government hundreds, even thousands of miles from home. For citizens in the western

United States—Alaska and Hawaii in particular—the government in Washington, D.C., seems remote, run by distant politicians whom they probably will never meet in person. Imagine, by contrast, the citizens of Luxembourg, a European nation smaller than the smallest state in the United States, Rhode Island. For them the government is close to home, easy to get to, and run by people whom they probably know.

Second, size makes it difficult for any government official to meet personally with citizens or to know what is going on throughout the nation. Even with modern communications, those who govern are hard-pressed to keep an eye on all possible conflicts within the society or to gauge the priorities and demands of citizens a thousand miles away. The size of some American states themselves—such as California or Texas—presents similar problems to residents and officials alike.

Third, the size of the nation affects the basic organization and operation of government. It requires that government's everyday functions—education, public services, law enforcement, and so on—to be decentralized so that they can be performed by governments closer to the people. The United States, as we will discuss further in chapter 3, has a *federal* system of government in which some responsibilities are left to the national government and others are in the hands of state governments. As the example of public school funding discussed at the beginning of this chapter shows, subnational governments play far greater roles in the everyday lives of Americans than is the case in smaller nations. The same is true in other large nations, such as Canada and Brazil, suggesting that size by itself affects how government is organized and how it works.

This tendency toward decentralization has political impacts. National officials may have a harder time overseeing, much less controlling, what goes on in the nation. This is not an entirely bad thing if one is worried about a few people having too much power, but it does make it harder to ensure that national policies are working as intended. Decentralization can also produce great variation in the types and quality of services available in different places, whether it be the quality of education provided to children or the types of penalties imposed for certain crimes. These variations can create great inequities among citizens whose only difference is place of residence.

Citizens of a large nation must deal with a great deal of complexity. They constantly need to figure out which level of government—federal, state, or local—is responsible for a particular decision or function. The physical remoteness of the national government also makes citizens wary of giving it too much power over their communities and families. Some of the sharpest American political conflicts have to do with which functions should be handled by government in Washington and which ones should be kept close to home, a topic we will cover more extensively in chapter 3.

PHYSICAL DIVERSITY

The physical diversity of the nation complicates the picture even more. The visitor who drives along Interstate 90 from Boston to Seattle encounters many climates, terrain, and natural features, as well as different patterns of living, work, and leisure.

The United States contains within its legal borders Alaska's arctic tundra and Hawaii's tropical islands, the swamps of Florida and the deserts of New Mexico, the vast treeless plains of the Dakotas and the staggering majesty of the Rocky Mountains as they slice downward from Idaho to Arizona. One nation, but many distinct places.

The scholar H. G. Nicholas, a native of England, once observed in the United States "a natural harmony between New England Puritanism and the rocky rigours of its terrain, between Californian eclecticism and a climate which is for all seasons, between the tempo and tempers of Louisiana politics and the enervating languors of the bayou."[6] We shouldn't overstate the degree to which a region's climate or terrain by itself creates conflicts or determines local political customs, but there is little doubt that the nation's physical diversity has produced a corresponding variety in local lifestyles, cultures, and, as a result, politics. Maybe the intense localism of New England politics was shaped a bit by the region's harsh winters and rocky soil. Maybe, as Nicholas suggests, only a disciplined, religious, and community-oriented people could endure such conditions. Maybe the rugged individualism so celebrated in the West grew out of that region's vast spaces and corresponding need for individual self-sufficiency. Maybe Louisiana's famously relaxed lifestyle is shaped just a little by the heat and swamps characteristic of the Mississippi Delta. Whatever the reason, politics in Louisiana certainly seems more freewheeling and passionate than it does in the chillier climes of Wisconsin!

We shouldn't overdo this, of course. The climate and physical characteristics of an area do not determine how people there will behave. But it is useful to keep in mind that physical diversity does affect politics. People from different regions of the country have different political views and cultural values. These differences in themselves are sources of conflict.

RESOURCES

Some of these conflicts stem from the unequal distribution of resources from one region to another. The United States is a rich nation, although not all Americans are rich—an important distinction to keep in mind. The nation has some of the world's best farmland, greatest river systems, and deepest seaports. For generations it was able to meet most of its own needs for raw materials, whether oil from Texas, cotton from Mississippi, iron ore from Minnesota, timber from Maine, beef from Nebraska, or coal from West Virginia. These industries once dominated the economies of whole regions, which in turn affected local, state, and national politics.

Why does this matter? The sheer wealth of the land, Nicholas argues, enabled American democracy to grow by allowing Americans to avoid the kinds of economic and social class conflicts that were common in the Old World.[7] Once the native tribes were pushed aside, and with free land available to anyone willing to farm it, the frontier was wide open to settlers seeking a new life. There was less need to fight over land or resources when all the energetic settler had to do was move westward, first to Ohio, then to Illinois, and later to California. Free land and abundant resources obliterated social classes and made it possible for poor people to start over and improve their condition. This possibility had immense appeal for immigrants, who flocked to the new nation from throughout the world. Abundance more than any-thing else made American society more open, less bound by social class distinctions.

Abundance also was a societal safety valve. It meant that most political battles were over dividing what seemed to be an ever-expanding pie, not about taking a piece of that pie away from one group to give it to another. Dividing up the wealth is a bit easier to do when resources are plentiful and growing, as the obvious solution is to give everybody a share—though how much of a share is what everyone ends up fight-ing about. In this sense, the great civil rights battles, whether for racial minorities or for women, were over the right to be included at the table, to be allowed to share in the nation's abundance. Not surprisingly, these battles became more difficult as the frontier closed up and Americans began to perceive limits on their nation's resources. We will discuss this aspect of civil rights in chapter 4.

REGIONALISM

The size and physical diversity of the land produces a nation that is best thought of as an amalgam of distinct regions, each with its own social, economic, cultural, and po-litical needs and characteristics. The legendary rowdiness of Texas politics stems to some degree from its long dependence on the notoriously rough and fickle oil indus-try. The politics of the Southwest is shaped by lack of water, whereas in West Vir-ginia it still reflects the legacy of the coal industry, with its isolated company towns dominated by powerful mine owners. And of course, the traditions of southern poli-tics are rooted in the "peculiar institution" of black slavery, which itself grew out of the region's dependence on a labor-intensive cotton industry.[8]

Single industries no longer dominate any region the way they did in the past, and the more obvious regional distinctions have been blurred by the effects of modern telecommunications, travel, and common consumer patterns. After all, a Gap Store in a mall in Columbia, South Carolina, is pretty much the same as a Gap Store in a mall in Dubuque, Iowa, and pretty much everyone anywhere in the country can watch *Dawson's Creek* if they want to do so. Even so, regionalism remains a potent factor in American politics. More often than not, national policies are products of compromises hammered out among representatives from the various regions. In fact, as we will see in chapter 8, actions by the U.S. Congress on issues such as air pollu-tion, civil rights, agriculture, defense, or health care often are little more than balanc-ing acts among important regional economic and political interests. The "national interest"—what is best for the nation as a whole—sometimes can be overwhelmed by the conflicting tugs of local demands and often reflects whatever can be gained through compromises among those representing the various regions. This dynamic may be more practical than pretty, but sometimes it is all that is possible.

A DIVERSE POPULATION

John Jay, one of the framers of the U.S. Constitution, wrote in 1787 that Ameri-cans were "one united people—a people descended from the same ancestors, speak-ing the same language, professing the same religion, attached to the same princi-

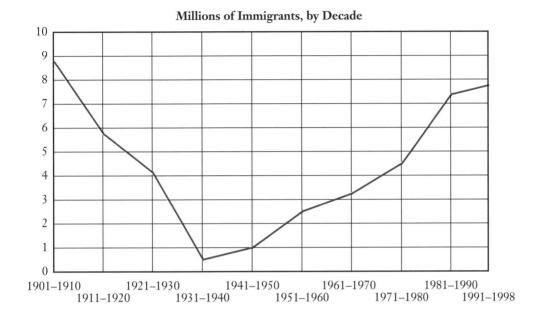

FIGURE 1.1. IMMIGRATION TRENDS, 1990–1998

Source: Statistical Abstract of the United States, 1998 (Washington, D.C.: Government Printing Office, 1999), p. 10.

ples of government, very similar in their manners and customs."[9] Indeed, at the time most citizens were of English or Scottish descent, and most were Protestants. Jay's observation did not include people of German, Dutch, French, or Irish descent, many of them Roman Catholics—even a few Jews—not to mention a large population of black slaves and native Americans. Still, John Jay's America seemed remarkably homogeneous.

American society today definitely does not describe Jay's "one united people." Americans may be one *citizenry* with common political ideals, but they are not necessarily one *people*. As the Italian journalist Luigi Barzini once wrote, the United States "can be seen as an unpredictable loose conglomeration of heterogeneous people of different races, origins, cultures, religions, and values."[10] This "conglomeration" was shaped primarily by immigration. Between 1820 and 1990 more than 60 million people came to the United States from other countries, 25 million of them between 1880 and 1920 alone. And large-scale immigration continues: approximately 10 million new immigrants entered the nation legally during the 1990s (see Figure 1.1).[11]

Today the United States is a nation of 270 million people whose ethnic, racial, linguistic, cultural, and religious diversity defies easy understanding. American culture is a mosaic of many only partially overlapping subcultures. In the United States the answer to the question "What are you?" is likely to be a hyphenated one: Polish-American, African-American, Cuban-American, Japanese-American, Native-American, and so on. Many of these "hyphenated Americans" cling proudly to their ethnic traditions and values even as they also rush headlong into being accepted as simply "American" by those who were here before them. It is a balancing act familiar to generations of immigrants and their children.

The effects of this diversity on American politics are profound, whether the issue is public education, access to jobs, foreign policy—or immigration itself. The United States is not Japan or Sweden, where a shared ethnicity, language, and culture make it easier to govern simply because a homogeneous population contains within it fewer lines of sharp social conflict. Many of the characteristics that divide Americans—especially race, ethnicity, and religion—are sources of strong conflict, even bloody warfare, in other lands, as can be seen in the genocidal tribal wars in Rwanda and Burundi or the ethnic and religious conflicts that split the former Yugoslavia. Many immigrants to the United States fled their countries because of such conflicts.

Our history of immigration also has reinforced some of the regional and local differences discussed earlier. In the past it has meant an upper Midwest with a heavily Scandinavian population and cities such as Boston and Chicago where the Irish came to dominate public life. Today it is reflected in places such as the border between Texas and Mexico, an almost distinct binational, bicultural world of cross-border trade, employment, entertainment, and family ties. Or it reveals itself in cities such as Los Angeles, New York, and Miami, where many immigrant groups have their own distinct neighborhoods—Little Korea, Little Havana, Little Russia. This is nothing new, of course, as any visitor to San Francisco's Chinatown, Cleveland's Little Italy, or Pittsburgh's Polish Hill can attest.

So it is no surprise that such distinct differences among Americans produce conflicts, whether locally, on issues such as bilingual education in elementary schools, or nationally, on issues such as the nation's policy toward another country. Just as this huge land is fragmented into distinct regions, Americans themselves are fragmented into many distinct peoples. Politics in the United States reflects the obvious and always difficult need to build consensus out of a great many differing values, customs, and outlooks (see Tables 1.2 and 1.3, pages 19 and 20).

SOCIAL AND ECONOMIC CONDITIONS

The size of the United States, its physical features, and the diversity of its people shape the nation's politics in a broad sense. These features guarantee societal complexity, and they influence how public policies are made. But by themselves they do not determine what happens on particular issues at particular times. To understand politics we must also look at current economic and social conditions, such as the cost of consumer goods, the level of unemployment, or how much crime exists. These conditions, whether they are experienced directly or indirectly, affect what citizens

TABLE 1.2.   WHO WE ARE: AMERICAN SOCIETY IN THE LATE 1990S

| *Gender* | Male | 49% | *Median Age** | 34.9 years |
| | Female | 51 | | |

*Racial and Ethnic Background***		*Estimated Annual Household Income*	
White	74.8%	Less than $9,999	7.6%
Black	15.4	$10,000–14,999	6.1
Latino/Hispanic	11.0	$15,000–24,999	13.5
Asian	3.7	$25,000–34,999	13.5
Native American	0.9	$35,000–49,999	17.7
Other	2.9	$50,000–74,999	21.3
		$75,000 and over	20.3

Current Religious Preference		*Marital Status*	
Protestant	58.0%	Never married (single)	17%
Roman Catholic	26.0	Married, spouse present	53
Jewish	2.2	Married, spouse absent	5
Other	6.0	Widowed	11
None	8.0	Divorced	14

Size of Households	
One person	25%
Two persons	32
Three persons	17
Four persons	15
Five persons	7
Six persons	2
Seven or more	1

* The median denotes the halfway point. So half of Americans are below this age, half above.

**Total percentages exceed 100 because those of Latino or Hispanic background can be of either race.

Source: United States Bureau of the Census, *Statistical Abstract of the United States, 1998* (Washington, D.C.: Government Printing Office, 1998), pp. 14, 63, 72, 471. See also http://www.census.gov/prod/3/98pubs/98statab/.

TABLE 1.3.　WHO YOU ARE: THE CLASS OF 2002

Each year the Higher Education Research Institute at the University of California, Los Angeles, surveys incoming college freshmen on their personal characteristics and their attitudes about a wide range of issues. The survey results for 1998–99 were based on the reponses of 275,811 students in the class of 2002 at 469 two-year and four-year colleges.

Racial and Ethnic Background		*Estimated Annual Parental Income*	
White	82.5%	Less than $9,999	5.1%
Black	9.4	$10,000–19,999	7.6
Latino/Hispanic	4.5	$20,000–29,999	11.0
Mexican American	2.1	$30,000–39,999	11.4
Puerto Rican	1.0	$40,000–49,999	11.5
Other Latino	1.4	$50,000–59,999	12.0
Asian	4.0	$60,000–74,999	13.3
American Indian	3.1	$75,000–99,999	12.3
Other	2.3	$100,000–149,999	9.1
		$150,000–199,999	3.0
		200,000 or more	3.6

Current Religious Preference		*Parents' Status*	
Protestant	48.6%	Living with each other	70.2%
Baptist	16.8	Divorced or living apart	25.5
Other Christian	11.5	One or both deceased	4.3
Methodist	8.1	Mother a full-time homemaker	10.7%
Lutheran	4.3		
Presbyterian	3.9		
Episcopal	1.8		
United Church of Christ	1.9		
Seventh Day Adventist	0.3		
Roman Catholic	28.6		
Jewish	1.6		
Mormon	1.1		
Buddhist	0.6		
Muslim	0.5		
Eastern Orthodox	0.5		
Quaker	0.2		
Other	4.0		
None	14.5		

Source: "This Year's Freshmen: A Statistical Profile," *The Chronicle of Higher Education,* January 29, 1999.

worry about and the kinds of demands they make on government. For example, citizens who are worried about violent crime are more likely to support harsh criminal sentences, including the death penalty.

We also need to know whether these conditions reflect temporary phenomena or are evidence of long-term trends. For example, the conflict over abortion is shaped by broad trends such as the changing roles of women in society as well as by the religious beliefs of a great many Americans. To use another example, the politics of health care will be shaped as much by the aging of the post–World War II generation of Americans—the "baby boomers" born between 1946 and 1964—as by which political party dominates Congress or who is elected president.

Change   Among the most significant social conditions is change. Human societies never stand still, and a great deal of politics involves reacting to the impacts of change. Some changes are not obvious or dramatic, but evolutionary, and we adjust accordingly. An example is the ways in which public policy reflects changes in living and occupational patterns. Most Americans no longer work on farms, but instead live in suburban housing developments and work in office parks. Not surprisingly, farmers have less political clout today than they did even two decades ago. This loss of influence didn't happen suddenly; it evolved over time.

Other changes are sudden and sharp, confronting citizens and political officials with grave and unexpected challenges. A case in point is the economic, political, and social trauma that resulted from the "oil crisis" of the early 1970s, provoked when petroleum-producing nations banded together and sharply raised the world price of oil. Americans long accustomed to cheap and plentiful gasoline confronted prices that literally doubled and tripled overnight and, in some instances, actual gas shortages. Overall inflation rose dramatically as a result, boosting the cost of virtually everything. This created unease among middle-class Americans, which, in turn, magnified disenchantment with government and contributed to the defeat of President Jimmy Carter in the 1980 election. Consumers also began to demand automobiles with better gas mileage, which American auto manufacturers could not supply quickly or easily. So Americans rushed to buy more fuel-efficient imported cars, giving the Japanese auto industry a chance to establish a market in the United States. The American auto industry was forced to restructure, tens of thousands of autoworkers lost their jobs, and entire communities that depended on the auto companies were hurt badly. In this way, the actions of a few oil-producing nations had massive impacts on local, state, and national politics.[12]

Technology   Technological change lies at the heart of many economic and social transformations. For example, inexpensive computers, facsimile machines, the Internet, and other communication technology make it possible for anybody to communicate more easily with government officials thousands of miles away. This kind of access is a far cry from the days when citizens could only write letters to their representatives or talk with them only when the representatives came home from Washington. In many ways technology has made this huge nation a little smaller, shrinking the gap between the government and the governed. Airing sessions of the

U.S. Congress on television or posting proposed legislation on the Internet makes it easier for citizens to keep track of their legislators, who for their part are keenly aware that they are under constant scrutiny.

Technology also has a great impact on the nature of the problems we face, often creating new sources of conflict. Once, for example, it was relatively easy for the average person to maintain a degree of privacy. But with countless public and private computerized databases that keep track of every purchase, traffic ticket, and prescription, privacy is no longer a simple matter of drawing the curtains or moving to a less crowded area. Insurance companies may insist on drug and alcohol tests before issuing a new policy, and may even require genetic testing to screen for hereditary diseases. The technological ability to do these things makes it more likely that they will be done, raising a whole new set of legal, ethical, and political concerns. New technologies can mean new social conditions, and new conflicts.

Global Conditions   The United States is not insulated from the broader world, as can be seen in the case of the oil crisis of 1970s. Once the nation was rather remote from the world and almost self-contained in its vastness, but today it is woven into a global community—whether Americans like it or not. The line between "domestic" and "foreign" politics is blurred in an age where the flow of money, air pollution, manufactured goods, people, news stories, or ideas takes place on a global scale. American politics affects and is affected by world politics.

THE AMERICAN POLITICAL CULTURE

Our politics is shaped by the broad societal contexts just described, but for most people the impacts usually are indirect. The average person's political views and actions are not directly motivated by the size and diversity of the nation, broad economic trends, or technological changes. These factors generate conflicts, but they do not determine what we think or do. What matter more directly, at any moment and on any issue, are the values that people bring to the political arena. The society's core value system, the beliefs and biases that motivate citizens to act, is the most powerful immediate context in which politics takes place.

What Americans believe matters a great deal, and not only to American politics. The global influence of the United States is immense by any measure. It is the world's greatest economic and military power. The U.S. dollar is the world's dominant currency. The ideals embodied in the U.S. Constitution, especially the Bill of Rights (discussed in chapter 4), have found their way into global concepts of human rights. American popular culture, including rock music, basketball, Coca-Cola, blue jeans, McDonald's, and Mickey Mouse, is a major part of world culture. It comes as no surprise, then, that a great many people spend a lot of time trying to figure out what Americans think or what they will do at any given moment.

These core values make up what can be called the American political culture. **Political culture** can be defined as the complex set of beliefs, customs, attitudes, outlooks, feelings, and traditions that the majority of the citizens of a nation holds about their political system and about the world in general. It is composed of fundamental assumptions about what is right and wrong, good or bad—about what *should* (or should not) be. These ideas are abstractions that transcend divisions of race, ethnicity, and gender. They are ideals that Americans can share and still disagree when it comes translating them into actual policies or laws. Even so, these broad values serve to orient Americans of all types toward certain kinds of political attitudes and behavior, and away from others. Political culture can be described as a "tinted lens" through which Americans look at and interpret the world. Despite the globalization of communications, entertainment, travel, and work, Americans still interpret the world a bit differently from the way Greeks, Ugandans, or Pakistanis might.

American politics thus is profoundly affected by widely shared hopes, values, and beliefs. As with the other contexts discussed earlier, the elements of American political culture do not determine what will happen in our politics at any one moment, but these values and traditions certainly have a major impact on what Americans believe is or is not allowable, much less possible. Values shape the ideas or actions Americans accept as legitimate and the ones they regard as unacceptable. Common values create the *boundaries* for debate. Ideas or options that lie within those boundaries are regarded as acceptable, but those that lie outside the boundaries are rarely discussed. In the rest of this section, therefore, we take a close look at the core values of American political culture.

INDIVIDUAL LIBERTY

No value is more "American" than the belief in individual liberty, which Americans have traditionally defined as freedom *from* the constraints of government, or simply from one another. Americans hold that every person has basic political rights and liberties that cannot be taken away by government (see chapter 4). Individual liberty is, at its core, the freedom to be left alone.

Individual liberty also means that individuals should be able to determine their own destiny without government interference. Popular mythology, whether embodied in Clint Eastwood films or video games featuring the fictional Lara Croft, or in respect for "self-made men" such as Microsoft founder Bill Gates, reveres the individual, the person who stands out from the crowd, the one who takes risks.

FEAR OF GOVERNMENT POWER

Closely tied to the notion of individual liberty is fear of government itself, particularly with respect to the relationship between government and the individual. Fear of abuse of government power is woven throughout American history, and the core components of the political system reflect strong desires to protect the individual from the possibility of government tyranny (see chapter 2). This view of government is captured in the words of Thomas Paine, the great pamphleteer who roused the American colonists to rebellion: "Government, even in its best state, is but a necessary evil; in its worst state, an intolerable one."[13] Few Americans today would disagree strongly with Paine's view.

This cultural predisposition in favor of minimal government recurs throughout American history. Despite Emma Lazarus's invitation to the "huddled masses yearning to breathe free" in the poem etched on the pediment of the Statue of Liberty, the waves of immigrants to the New World were not attracted primarily by democracy. Most immigrants came for economic reasons.[14] This was, after all, the land of "milk and honey"—or, if you were Italian, *"pane e lavoro"* (bread and work). America offered a chance to start anew in a rich and uncrowded land. People came to seek their fortunes, not to get involved in politics. Equally important, most immigrants came from countries where government itself was equated with repression and corruption, class conflict, and inequality. These diverse peoples learned early on to trust one another, not government.

The practical effect of this fundamental value is that Americans are generally wary of giving government—any government—too much power. Few Americans, regardless of ideology or political party, readily accept the kind of active and powerful government that is common in other nations. They also, not surprisingly, extend their dim view of government to a general distrust of politicians, who tend to be kept on a relatively short leash, or altogether ignored.

FREE MARKETS AND PRIVATE PROPERTY

Linked to these beliefs in individual liberty and minimal government is a cultural bias in favor of a free-market economic system. Americans are far less likely than citizens of many other nations to approve of a direct government role in the economy. When government intervention is allowed, such as when the national government subsidizes shipbuilding or agriculture, support is often based on concern for "national security." Other cultures, such as the French or the Japanese, are less enamored of free markets. They may regard tradition or social cohesion as more important values. As a result, citizens of these nations are far more willing to accept, even demand, direct government involvement in the economy.

Intertwined with Americans' deep faith in individual liberty and free markets is an unshakable defense of private property rights. Private property is sacred, and "one's home is one's castle." To Americans the right to private property is at the heart of individual freedom: without the one, the other cannot exist. Thus, in a conflict between one person's property rights and the desires of the community, such as when a town zoning board seeks to restrict development in some areas, Americans almost instinctively side with the individual until they are convinced that restrictions on the use of private property make sense for the community as a whole. As a practical matter, it is hard for government in the United States to enact regulations to prevent suburban sprawl and the loss of fertile farmland, at least without being required to pay "fair compensation" to property owners. Such restrictions are far more common in Western Europe.

POLITICAL EQUALITY

In his observations of Americans in the early 1830s, the French aristocrat and philosopher Alexis de Tocqueville wrote, "Nothing can satisfy them except equality,

No trespassing. The right to own and control the use of private property is a bedrock principle in the American political culture and the nation's legal system. As a result, government cannot take away or restrict the use of one's property without "just compensation."

and rather than lose it they resolve to perish."[15] However, the attitude that Tocqueville admired had to do with political equality, the notion that all citizens are equal in the eyes of the law and in the polling booth. At no time in American history has equality ever meant equality of income, intelligence, achievement, or social status. The notion of equality is tied to the notion that everyone should have *equal opportunity*, but that's it. The rest is up to the individual.

As a result, Americans are likely to support policies that provide opportunity, such as public education, and just as likely to resist any program that is perceived to give another group an "unfair" advantage. The often fine distinction between equality of opportunity and equality of outcome pervades battles over civil rights, to give just one example. Groups seeking equal rights have an easier time gaining broad popular support when they are perceived as seeking equal opportunity. Few people today would argue that women or racial minorities should be barred from the right to compete for a job. As we will discuss in chapter 4, the uproar comes the moment individuals or groups are perceived, rightly or not, as seeking preferential treatment.

Related to equality of opportunity is the belief that achievement should be based on merit alone. The surest way to become wealthy may be to be born that way, but this fact matters little to those who are convinced that the American Dream is real.

The American Dream says that anyone, regardless of background, can become rich, anyone can succeed, anyone can become president. Even if this dream doesn't come true for everyone, there are enough real "rags to riches" stories in American history to reinforce the symbolic power of that belief. If you work hard and persevere, you will make it someday. Both Bill Clinton, the boy from a small town in Arkansas who grew up to become president, and Bill Gates, the college dropout who is now one of the wealthiest men in the world, would probably agree.

This belief in hard work, when tied to notions about equality of opportunity, also explains common attitudes toward those who are less lucky or less smart. Americans tend to regard the poor and others who fail as lazy and weak, both physically and morally, and therefore tend to oppose government programs that might be perceived as "handouts."

THE RULE OF LAW

Americans believe in the law, but in a contractual sense. At times the law seems to be the only thing that binds together such a diverse people. Americans do not assume that everyone shares the same values; thus rules governing relations among citizens must be written in the form of legal codes so that everyone knows what is allowed and what is forbidden. The law is a contract among the nation's citizens. Indeed, as we will see in chapter 2, the American political system itself is based on a supreme law, the Constitution, which is a form of contract. The legality of every action taken by government stems from that document.

As a result of this belief in the rule of law, American politics and society are highly legalistic, with legions of lawyers acting as translators of the law for the average citizen. The classic American response to any problem seems to be, "There ought to be a law against that." And often there is. But, despite the passage of laws to address all kinds of conditions and actions, Americans frequently distinguish between "good" and "bad" laws, even if the rationalization for those distinctions often border on the comical. Even generally law-abiding Americans might not stop for a red light at 3:00 a.m. if no one else is around, or may cheat a little on their taxes if they feel that the tax laws aren't fair—and if they believe that they can get away with a little dishonesty.

CIVIC DUTY

Despite their support for individual rights, Americans also believe strongly that citizenship is accompanied by responsibility. They join innumerable civic groups, give billions of dollars to private charities, and involve themselves in countless community functions. They believe that citizens have a duty to participate in public life, to serve on juries, to help run the schools, tend the parks, or fund the libraries—even if they are sometimes reluctant to pay higher taxes for these purposes out of fear that government won't spend their money effectively. Although some worry that fewer people today may have the time to volunteer for such community purposes, Americans still believe that average citizens should do so.

This notion of civic responsibility extends to voting. In most other countries citizens are automatically registered to vote by the government when they reach voting age, but in the United States citizens are expected to take that responsibility upon themselves. Americans believe that voting is a duty and that citizens who do not make the effort to register shouldn't be allowed to vote. Partly as a result, the United States generally has a lower level of voter turnout than other representative democracies, a matter that is fully discussed in chapter 6. Even so, Americans are wary of making it too easy to register, fearing that it would make it too easy for the uneducated and the easily swayed to show up at the polls at the last minute and vote for "irrational" reasons.

REASON AND PROGRESS

Americans traditionally have professed a strong belief in the capacity of rational thought to solve all problems. Indeed, they have an inordinate faith that all problems can be solved. All that is needed is better science, new technology, better organization, or more information. We went to the moon, so why can't we eliminate poverty? This faith in reason goes back to the founding of the nation and its structure of government. The Constitution itself was based on the belief that reasonable people can solve a vexing problem—how to achieve effective *and* representative government—through rational thought and discourse.

Tied to the idea of reason is a pervasive belief in progress. Throughout the nation's history progress has been linked to the abundant material rewards made possible by the transformation of a vast wilderness into farms and towns, the growth of towns into cities, and the steady rise in the nation's wealth and power. The closing of the western frontier hasn't entirely erased these feelings. Despite occasional yearnings for small town life—with its Main Street and white picket fences—Americans remain a highly restless and mobile people, always seeking greener pastures. If you don't like the way things are going, move, "go West," vote with your feet. This attitude is reflected in the classic line in *Huckleberry Finn* where Huck, at the end of his adventures with Jim, exclaims, "I reckon I got to light out for the Territory ahead of the rest, because Aunt Sally she's going to adopt me and civilize me and I can't stand it. I been there before."[16]

Americans' views on progress also extend to the belief that each generation should do better than the one preceding it, that the children should do better than the parents. And, indeed, each generation of Americans *did* seem to do better: they lived longer, were better educated, had better jobs, and were able to surround themselves with more and better material goods. Whether such intergenerational progress is still as possible today as it was for the generation born in the 1950s is unclear, as overall living standards may not improve much beyond their current levels. Still, Americans of all generations are driven by the belief that progress must occur. Their dream is shared by those who emigrate to the United States. Their children will do better. They know it.

FAITH

For all their belief in reason and progress, Americans as a people are also strikingly religious. From the beginning, the ideal of freedom of religion has been embedded in the nation's history and its legal system (see chapter 4). Even today, Americans have one of the highest rates of regular attendance at religious services among all Western

Church and state. Religion plays a major role in American politics. Here, Vice President Al Gore and his wife, Tipper, greet Pope John Paul II as he visits the United States. As a spiritual leader, the pope has tremendous influence with the nation's over 60 million Roman Catholics.

nations, and most Americans express the view that religion plays a role in their lives.[17] So, despite the "separation of church and state" reflected in the First Amendment to the Constitution, religion plays a major role in national politics. The United States is a secular society, but Americans are a highly religious people—perhaps the most religious among all the Western nations. This duality inevitably leads to conflicts over issues such as prayer in public schools or which books should be allowed in public libraries.

NATIONALISM

Americans are strongly nationalistic. They believe that the United States is a great nation, perhaps the greatest nation in human history. For most Americans, the United States is a noble democratic experiment founded in a desire for freedom from government tyranny. It rapidly became the world's wealthiest and most powerful nation, and it did so while espousing the values of freedom and democracy. It also backed up those values with the blood of its own people when it was necessary to do so.

Small wonder that Americans may be among the most nationalistic people in the world. Their faith is more than a simple belief in national power or cultural superiority. At its core is a thoroughgoing belief in the values that make up the American political culture. It includes belief in the nation's inherent moral goodness, particularly when compared to other nations. These values are especially strong among recent

New Americans pledge allegiance. To be an American is not a matter of ethnicity. It is defined by citizenship, a legal status that is conferred by birth (to American parents or on U.S. soil) or by naturalization. Thus, new Americans have all of the rights that longtime citizens enjoy.

immigrants, who are eager to display their love of their new country to any fellow American who might doubt their loyalty. If other peoples and other nations occasionally express resentment about the power and wealth of the United States, Americans seem not to care. They feel, perhaps arrogantly, that they earned it.

DEMOCRACY

Finally, Americans believe in the ideal of democracy, in "rule by the people." Most Americans could not imagine any other kind of political system, nor could they imagine not holding elections—even during wartime. Few Americans would support a military takeover of the nation, even during a major crisis, and few members of the armed forces could even imagine such a thing. This faith in democracy is important to its continued existence.

ON BEING "AMERICAN"

Taken together, these values impose clear boundaries on American politics. They shape the range of legitimate discussion on major social or political issues. In general, Americans have a deep faith in the people's ability to take care of themselves and to determine their own fates without being controlled by politicians or anybody else who claims to know better. The American political culture is hostile to unchecked governmental power and errs on the side of individual freedom, including the freedom to fail.

BOX 1.2.
WHAT MAKES A "GOOD" AMERICAN?

Americans hold strong views about what makes a "good" citizen. In a national poll conducted in 1998 by The Public Agenda, a nonpartisan, nonprofit organization, 801 randomly selected parents were asked what the United States "stands for and what schoolchildren should be taught about its history and other ideals." Here are their responses.

WHAT DOES IT MEAN TO LIVE IN AMERICA?

Respondents were asked, "Thinking about what it means to live in the U.S., which of these is most important to you personally?"

Personal freedom	61%
Prosperity and economic opportunity	25%
Political freedom	13%
Don't know	1%

WHO IS A "BAD" AMERICAN?

The numbers in parentheses represent the percentage of people surveyed who agreed with the sentiment that a "bad" American is someone

▶ who lives on government programs such as welfare even if they are able to work. (77%)

▶ who refuses to work "with people from different racial or ethnic backgrounds." (70%)

▶ who settles in the United States "but never tries to learn English." (60%)

▶ who "makes it a point never to stand up when the national anthem is played during public events such as ball games." (58%)

→

The political culture also affects what ideas are regarded as more acceptable or legitimate for debate at any given time. New ideas must be couched in terms that mesh, at least symbolically, with these dominant values. Those that clash with the dominant values are viewed as "un-American." Social Security thus is often described as an insurance program, not as a subsidized pension for the elderly. The image of hardworking Americans contributing to their own retirement fits long-established values, even though most retirees get more money out of the Social Security system than they ever put in (the rest is subsidized by younger generations of workers). Even so, the symbolic power of Social Security makes it a hard program to attack.

Cultural values are not absolute. There are always contradictions and exceptions, countervailing values that create conflicts, spark political debate and, on oc-

WHAT DO YOU THINK?

▶ who believes that communism, not democracy, is the "best political system." (56%)

▶ who avoids jury duty and is able to vote but never does. (50%)

▶ who has "no interest" in important issues facing the country. (48%)

▶ who knows "virtually nothing about America's history or founding fathers."(36%)

WHAT SHOULD THE SCHOOLS DO?

The numbers in parentheses represent the percentage of people surveyed who agreed that schools should

▶ teach new immigrants about "American values." (90%) This view was shared by those who came to the United States from other countries.

▶ teach students to "understand the common history that ties Americans together." (85%)

▶ teach "what it means to be an American." (80%)

▶ teach "about the holidays and traditions of different cultures." (70%)

What do you think?

Sources: The Public Agenda, *A Lot to Be Thankful For: What Parents Want Children to Learn About America*, November 1998, Web site: http://www.publicagenda.org/thankful/thankful.html. See also, Richard Morin, "What Makes a 'Bad' American," *Washington Post National Weekly Edition*, November 30, 1998, p. 35.

casion, prompt major political change. For all their belief in individualism, Americans also yearn for community and stability, and at times they will accept a great deal of government intervention in their daily lives. For example, most Americans accept restrictions on personal freedom, such as work-related drug testing, when fears of social disorder or crime overwhelm the desire to protect individual rights. At times this drive for stability and order can take on ominous overtones, as when freedom of speech is restricted for some citizens because their views are labeled as "radical" and, hence, contrary to shared ideas about what is or is not "American" (see Box 1.2).

The core values of the American political culture thus can conflict with one another. Individual liberty collides with belief in civic duty, of giving up something of yourself for your community. Belief in reason and progress can run up against strong religious values, as when a school district becomes embroiled in a conflict over which books should be in the high school library or whether the biblical view of creation should be taught alongside the scientific theory of evolution. Belief in limited government can be overtaken by nationalism, leading Americans to restrict the rights of fellow citizens whom they suspect of being disloyal. Belief in equality may run shallow, particularly when those who demand equality aren't very popular or attractive.

Contradictions and conflicts aside, the faithfulness with which Americans adhere to their core ideals means that alternative ways of seeing the world tend to be relegated to the margins of debate. Americans are so diverse in everything else that maybe the only thing uniting them is their citizenship, their legal status as Americans. To be Japanese or Finnish is more a matter of ethnicity, language, and culture, not legal citizenship or a particular form of government. The French can change their political system and still be French. But to be an American is to be a citizen under the Constitution. Ideas or values that conflict with the values of the American political culture thus are labeled "un-American" because they contradict what being "American" supposedly means. Political culture thus plays a central role in defining the nation's politics.

CONCLUSION

Politics is at the heart of all human endeavor. It is the process through which people try to transform their inevitable conflicts into some kind of compromise, assuming that they want to do so. Although sometimes it is difficult to overcome long-standing hatreds or fears, the process of politics is the effort to resolve conflicts without violence.

We also have seen that politics is affected by forces beyond the control of politicians and citizens. Economic trends, social change, and public values all impose boundaries for political discourse. They are the boundaries within which we try to transform conflicts into compromises.

However, the human factor still plays a role. Broad contexts help shape political dynamics, but what actually happens is affected by the actual people involved in any conflict. The mood of the electorate, the choice of candidates available to voters, and the eventual outcome of an election may all be influenced by broad social and economic conditions, but the campaign itself still matters.

For example, in the 1992 presidential election, George Bush's failure to win re-election could be traced to an economic recession that made voters uneasy about the future and about Bush's ability to improve matters. Bush may simply have been unlucky: Much of what happens in the economy is beyond the president's control.[18] Even so, Bush did not lose because of the economy. He lost because he faced two challengers: Bill Clinton, who seemed to understand better the fears and hopes of the voters, and H. Ross Perot, who fed voters' sense that it was time for a change in leadership. Broad social and economic factors created a context that was ripe for change, but without the possibility of a credible replacement the voters might well have stuck with Bush. Instead they elected Clinton, and reelected him in 1996 despite concerns about his personal character. We will examine these elections more closely in chapters 6 and 9.

So even within these broad contexts, *who* is involved in politics and *how* they are involved still matters. How Americans design their election system, who represents them in Congress or the White House, and by what rules they engage in political action all affect the outcomes of politics. The institutions of government are the formal arenas within which Americans fight their conflicts and seek their compromises, and processes such as elections are the formal "rules of the game" that determine who participates.

The institutions of government and the rules by which Americans engage in politics have their own impacts on the workings of politics in the United States. Institutions and rules are not neutral. They affect how easy or difficult it is for any group of people to achieve its goals. Not surprisingly, institutions and rules themselves are political factors. They shape politics and in turn are shaped by politics. To understand both of these dynamics it is best to go right to the set of rules that has the greatest impact on American politics: the Constitution of the United States.

SUMMARY

▶ Conflict is natural in any human society. It arises over economic issues, such as the allocation of resources, and it emerges out of moral, religious, ethnic, racial, or gender differences. Some conflicts seem to defy solution, for example, moral issues such as abortion. But most conflicts are open to compromise, some middle ground between the opposing sides. In this regard, we define politics as the process of trying to transform conflict into compromise. Politics is a complex, messy process through which people with differing views and needs seek to settle their differences peacefully. Of course, for this process to work, the alternative to compromise must be regarded as unacceptable.

▶ The politics of any issue is shaped to a great extent by broad societal contexts, and short-term events or problems. Broad societal contexts include the immense size and physical variety of the nation, its diverse population, and its technologically advanced economy. These contexts affect the problems American face and the resources available to face them. To understand politics, one must understand the contexts within which politics takes place.

▶ Americans do not have a common ethnic, racial, religious, and linguistic heritage, but they share a set of fundamental beliefs about how the world should work. The core elements of the political culture include a belief in individual liberty and a parallel distrust of government; support for free markets and the right to own private property; belief in the rule of law and civic duty; a tension between belief in reason and progress and strong religious faith; a pervasive nationalism; and a staunch support for the concept of democracy. These values strongly shape what Americans believe should or should not be done in a given situation.

▶ However, within these societal and cultural contexts, politics ultimately depends on the people involved, the institutions they work in, and the rules they agree to abide by. Government is the set of formal institutions and procedures through which the people seek to resolve their differences; in a democracy, the legitimacy of those institutions and procedures hinges on the support of the people.

QUESTIONS FOR REVIEW AND DISCUSSION

1. Is conflict inherent in human nature? Are conflicts natural in human societies?

2. Under what conditions is compromise more likely to occur? Under what conditions is compromise harder to achieve? Give examples.

3. How do a country's characteristics (size, resources, diversity of people) affect its politics? Answer by comparing the United States to another nation.

4. Discuss, using examples, how aspects of the American political culture affect political debate in the country.

TERMS TO REMEMBER

authority	democracy	power
citizen	government	republic
compromise	political culture	subject
conflict	politics	

WEB SOURCES

Center for Immigration Studies (www.us.net/org/). A research institute dedicated to the study of the social and economic impacts of immigration on the United States. The site includes extensive links to other immigration policy-related resources.

Statistical Abstract of the United States (www.census.gov/prod/3/98pubs/98statab). A treasure trove of statistical information on every aspect of the American society, economy, and population. Published by the U.S. Bureau of the Census.

Smithsonian Institution (www.si.edu). Lovingly called "the nation's attic," the Smithsonian was established by Congress in 1846 and today is best known for its extensive collections that offer a window into virtually every aspect of American life.

SUGGESTED READINGS

Benjamin R. Barber, *Jihad vs. McWorld: How Globalism and Tribalism Are Reshaping the World*. (New York: Random House, 1995). Barber examines the economic, social, and political forces shaping the world. In particular, he looks at the collision between consumer-driven capitalism, with its emphasis on private property, free markets, and individual choice, and the powerful communal impulses shaped by religion and ethnicity. Barber worries that these forces pose serious threats to the future of democracy everywhere.

Robert N. Bellah, et al., *Habits of the Heart: Individualism and Commitment in American Life* (Berkeley, CA: University of California Press, 1985). Bellah and his colleagues explore how Americans try to handle the difficult balancing acts between their desires for individual freedom and their yearnings for nurturing communities. Bellah is part of what is known as the Communitarian Network (see "Web Resources", chapter 12).

Samuel Huntington, *American Politics: The Promise of Disharmony*. (Cambridge, MA: Harvard University Press, 1983). A thought-provoking exploration of that set of ideals comprised by American political culture—what Huntington calls the "American Creed"—and the struggle over how Americans seek to apply those ideals to everyday life. Efforts at "reform," Huntington argues, almost always stem from an effort by Americans to make the real practice of politics adhere to how they think the world *should* work.

Richard Reeves, *American Journey: Traveling with Tocqueville in Search of Democracy in America* (New York: Simon and Schuster, 1982). Reeves traces the route taken in the 1830s through the young United States by the French aristocrat Alexis de Tocqueville. Both asked the same questions as they journeyed throughout the land: Who are these people, the Americans? How does American democracy work?

NOTES

1. John Milne, "NH Measure Halts Funding Schools with Property Taxes," *Boston Globe*, January 4, 1994, p. 20.

2. E. E. Schattschneider, *The Semi-Sovereign People: A Realist's View of Democracy in America* (Hinsdale, IL: The Dryden Press, 1960), p. 68.

3. Harold D. Lasswell, *Politics: Who Gets What, When, How* (New York: Meridian Books, 1958). See, especially, chapter 1.

4. See, for example, *Nicomachean Ethics*, Book I.

5. Karl Von Clausewitz, as cited in Michael Jackman, ed., *Crown's Book of Political Quotations* (New York: Crown Publishers, 1982), p. 236.

6. H. G. Nicholas, *The Nature of American Politics*, 2d ed. (London: Oxford University Press, 1986), p. 3.

7. Nicholas, *The Nature of American Politics*, p. 13.

8. Kenneth Stampp, *The Peculiar Institution: Slavery in the Ante-Bellum South* (New York: Vintage Books, 1956).

9. Alexander Hamilton, James Madison, and John Jay, *Federalist* No. 2, in *The Federalist Papers*, Clinton Rossiter, ed. (New York: New American Library, 1961), p. 38.

10. Luigi Barzini, "The Americans," *Harper's*, December 1981, p. 31.

11. U.S. Naturalization and Immigration Service, as reported in "Record Immigrant Flow Fuels U.S. Housing Market," *New York Times*, July 2, 1998, p. C9.

12. See Daniel Yergin, *The Prize: The Epic Quest for Oil, Money, and Power* (New York: Simon & Schuster, 1991).

13. Thomas Paine, *Common Sense* (New York: Doubleday, 1960; originally published 1776), p. 13.

14. Emma Lazarus, "The New Colossus" (1883). To understand why people traditionally immigrated to the United States, see Maldwyn A. Jones, *American Immigration* (Chicago, IL: University of Chicago Press, 1957).

15. Alexis de Tocqueville, *Democracy in America*, vol. 1 (New York: Schocken Books, 1961; originally published in 1835), p. 46.

16. Mark Twain, *Huckleberry Finn*, in Lawrence Teacher, ed., *The Unabridged Mark Twain*, vol. 1 (Philadelphia, PA: Running Press, 1979), p. 956.

17. The Gallup Poll has followed Americans' religious beliefs and practices for over four decades. See http://www.gallup.com.

18. See Bob Woodward, *The Agenda: Inside the Clinton Presidency* (New York: Simon & Schuster, 1994).

PRIMARY SOURCE READINGS

FRANCIS A. WALKER
"Restriction of Immigration"

Historian and economist Francis A. Walker (1840–1897) served as a general in the Union army during the Civil War, twice supervised the administration of the U.S. Census, served as U.S. Commissioner of Indian Affairs, and, finally, was president of the Massachusetts Institute of Technology. Compare the views expressed in this essay to the sentiments expressed in "The New Colossus."

Fifty, even thirty years ago, there was a rightful presumption regarding the average immigrant that he was among the most enterprising, thrifty, alert, adventurous and courageous of the community from which he came. It required no small energy, prudence, forethought, and pains to conduct the inquiries relating to his migration, to accumulate the necessary means, and to find his way across the Atlantic. To-day the presumption is completely reversed. So thoroughly has the continent of Europe been crossed by railways, so effectively has the business of emigration there been exploited, so much have the rates of railroad fares and ocean passage been reduced, that it is now among the least thrifty and prosperous members of any European community that the emigration agent finds his best recruiting-ground. The care and pains required have been reduced to a minimum; while the agent of the Red Star Line or the White Star Line is everywhere at hand, to suggest migration to those who are not getting on well at home. The intending emigrants are looked after from the moment they are locked into the cars in their native villages until they stretch themselves upon the floors of the buildings on Ellis Island, in New York. Illustrations of the ease and facility with which this Pipe Line Immigration is now carried on might be given in profusion. So broad and smooth is the channel, there is no reason why every foul and stagnant pool of population in Europe, which no breath of intellectual or industrial life has stirred for ages, should not be decanted upon our soil. Hard times here may momentarily check the flow; but it will not be permanently stopped so long as any difference of economic level exists between our population and that of the most degraded communities abroad.

But it is not alone that the presumption regarding the immigrant of to-day is so widely different from that which existed regarding the immigrant of thirty or fifty years ago. The immigrant of the former time came almost exclusively from western and northern Europe. We have now tapped great reservoirs of population then almost unknown to the passenger lists of our arriving vessels. Only a short time ago, the immigrants from southern Italy, Hungary, Austria, and Russia together made up hardly more than one per cent of our immigration. To-day the proportion has risen to something like forty per cent, and threatens soon to become fifty or sixty per cent, or even more. The entrance into our political, social, and industrial life of such vast masses of peasantry, degraded below our utmost conceptions, is a matter which no intelligent patriot can look upon without the gravest apprehension and alarm. These people have no history behind them which is of a nature to give encouragement. They have none of the inherited instincts and tendencies which made it comparatively easy to deal with the immigration of the olden time. They are beaten men from beaten races; representing the worst failures in the struggle for existence. Centuries are against them, as centuries were on the side of those who formerly came to us. They have none of the ideas and aptitudes which fit men to take up readily and easily the problem of self-care and self-government, such as belong to those who are descended from the tribes that met under the oak-trees of old Germany to make laws and choose chieftains.

Their habits of life, again, are of the most revolting kind. Read the description given by Mr. Riis of the police driving from the garbage dumps the miserable beings who try to burrow in those depths of unutterable filth and slime in order that they may eat and sleep there! Was it in cement like this that the foundations of our republic were laid? What effects must be produced upon our social standards, and upon the ambitions and aspirations of our people, by a contact so foul and loathsome? The influence upon the American rate of wages of a competition like this cannot fail to be injurious and even disastrous. Already it has been seriously felt in the tabacco manufacture, in the clothing trade, and in many forms of mining industry; and unless this access of vast numbers of unskilled workmen of the lowest type, in a market already fully supplied with labor, shall be checked, it cannot fail to go on from bad to worse, in breaking down the standard which has been maintained with so much care and at so much cost. The competition of paupers is far more telling and more killing than the competition of pauper-made goods. Degraded labor in the slums of foreign cities may be prejudicial to intelligent, ambitious, self-respecting labor here; but it does not threaten half so much evil as does degraded labor in the garrets of our native cities.

Finally, the present situation is most menacing to our peace and political safety. In all the social and industrial disorders of this country since 1877, the foreign elements have proved themselves the ready tools of demagogues in defying the law, in destroying property, and in working violence. A learned clergyman who mingled with the socialistic mob which, two years ago, threatened the State House and the governor of Massachusetts, told me that during the entire disturbance he heard no word spoken in any language which he knew,—either in English, in German, or in French. There may be those who can contemplate the addition to our population of vast numbers of person having no inherited instincts of self-government and respect for law; knowing no restraint upon their own passions but the club of the policeman or the bayonet of the soldier; forming communities, by the tens of thousands, in which only foreign tongues are spoken, and into which can steal no influence from our free institutions and from popular discussion. But I confess to being far less optimistic. I have conversed with one of the highest officers of the United States army and with one of the highest officers of the civil government regarding the state of affairs which existed during the summer of 1894; and the revelations they made of facts not generally known, going to show how the ship of state grazed along its whole side upon the rocks, were enough to appall the most sanguine American, the most hearty believer in free government. Have we the right to expose the republic to any increase of the dangers from this source which now so manifestly threaten our peace and safety?

For it is never to be forgotten that self-defense is the first law of nature and of nations. If that man who careth not for his own household is worse than an infidel, the nation which permits its institutions to be endangered by any cause which can fairly be removed is guilty not less in Christian than in natural law. Charity begins at home; and while the people of the United States have gladly offered an asylum to millions upon millions of the distressed and unfortunate of other lands and climes, they have no right to carry their hospitality one step beyond the line where American institutions, the American rate of wages, the American standard of living, are brought into serious peril. All the good the United States could do by offering indiscriminate hospitality to a few millions more of European peasants, whose places at home will, within another generation, be filled by others as miserable as themselves, would not compensate for any permanent injury done to our republic. Our highest duty to charity and to humanity is to make this great experiment, here, of free laws and educated labor, the most triumphant success that can possibly be attained. In this way we shall do far more for Europe than by allowing its city slums and its vast stagnant reservoirs of degraded peasantry to be drained off upon our soil. Within the decade between 1880 and 1890 five and a quarter millions of foreigners entered our ports! No nation in human history ever undertook to deal with such masses of alien population. That man must be a sentimentalist and an optimist beyond all bounds of reason who believes that we can take such a load upon the national stomach without a failure of assimilation, and without great danger to the health and life of the nation. For one, I believe it is time that we should take a rest, and give our social, political, and industrial system some chance to recuperate. The problems which so sternly confront us to-day are serious enough without being complicated and aggravated by the addition of some millions of Hungarians, Bohemians, Poles, south Italians, and Russian Jews.

Francis A. Walker, "Restriction of Immigration," *Atlantic Monthly*, vol. 77, no. 6 (June 1896), pp. 827–829.

EMMA LAZARUS
"The New Colossus" (1886)

Emma Lazarus (1849–1887) is best know for this poem, which is engraved at the base of the Statue of Liberty, located in New York Harbor. For tens of thousands of immigrants who entered by ship, the statue was one of their first images of the New World.

Not like the brazen giant of Greek fame,
With conquering limbs astride from land to land;
Here at our sea-washed, sunset gates shall stand
A mighty woman with a torch, whose flame
Is the imprisoned lightning, and her name
Mother of Exiles. From her beacon-hand
Glows world-wide welcome; her mild eyes command
The air-bridged harbor that twin cities frame.
"Keep ancient lands, your storied pomp!" cries she
With silent lips. "Give me your tired, your poor,
Your huddled masses yearning to breathe free,
The wretched refuse of your teeming shore.
Send these, the homeless, tempest-tost to me,
I lift my lamp beside the golden door!"

THE CONSTITUTION AS A POLITICAL DOCUMENT

OBJECTIVES

❑ To understand the political, economic, and philosophical reasons for the American rebellion against England, and the effects of the rebellion on the effort to create a new nation

❑ To examine the broad political contexts within which the framers of the Constitution operated and the compromises that were necessary to gain support for the new plan of government

❑ To assess the core elements of the American constitutional system, particularly as they affect the political process in the United States

Making a political statement. To many Americans, burning the flag is an unpatriotic act that should be outlawed by a constitutional amendment. To others, the right to burn the flag is as American as the Constitution itself.

On June 12, 1997, over two-thirds of the members of the U.S. House of Representatives voted to approve a proposed amendment to the U.S. Constitution that would allow Congress to pass laws banning physical desecration of the American flag. However, this vote was only one part of a very long process. According to rules set down in the Constitution, for the amendment to become part of the Constitution, it needed to be approved by a similar two-thirds vote of the U.S. Senate and then ratified by three-quarters (or 38) of the 50 states. In 1998 the amendment's backers tried to use upcoming congressional elections to put political pressure on the Senate to approve the amendment, but no further action occurred. The amendment died in the Senate, but its backers vowed to try again in 1999.[1]

The flag occupies an important place in American culture. To most Americans it is an object of respect, even veneration. By tradition—as well as law—it never touches the ground, is never dipped to flags or officials of other nations, and must be burned when it is no longer in any condition to be used. To war veterans in particular, it is a symbol of the supreme sacrifice made by a great many of their comrades. To other Americans, the flag is important as a symbol of democratic government and the freedoms guaranteed to citizens throughout the land.

The flag is also a potent symbol for protest. Critics at home and abroad focus on the flag as a symbol of all that they see wrong in American politics or foreign policy. Sometimes these protests result in a flag's being burned or otherwise defaced. Such acts are almost guaranteed to incur anger among Americans for whom the flag is the sacred embodiment of all that is good about the nation. So the flag isn't just a piece of cloth.

Many Americans want to make burning or otherwise defacing an American flag a crime. Many others want to defend anyone's right to burn or deface a flag if he or she wishes to do so as a reflection of the constitutionally guaranteed right to freedom of personal expression. To one side, the issue is one of patriotism; to the other, it is one of individual freedom.

Americans have been embroiled in conflict over the flag for decades. In the late 1980s Congress and some states passed laws prohibiting physical desecration of the flag, but the U.S. Supreme Court later declared that these laws violated the Constitution's guarantee of freedom of expression.[2] In 1995 the U.S. House of Representatives supported a constitutional amendment banning desecration of the flag, but the U.S. Senate fell three votes short of the required two-thirds vote. The House passed an amendment again in 1997, but the Senate never acted.

So the debate goes on. Those who support the idea that the Constitution should be amended to ban desecration of the flag will continue to work hard to achieve their goal. Those who fear that such an amendment will limit their constitutionally guaranteed freedom of political expression will work just as hard against passage. Even if the amendment becomes part of the Constitution, Congress and the federal courts will still have to determine what actually constitutes desecration. Given how the flag is used for all kinds of purposes, drawing that line is not going to be easy. After all, one can argue that it is just as disrespectful to use the flag in a commercial as to sew a flag patch on a pair of jeans. Passing a constitutional amendment may be the easy part.

THE CENTRALITY OF THE CONSTITUTION

In many ways the conflict over the flag is a conflict over the meaning of the Constitution. It also is a revealing example of the many ways in which the Constitution shapes American politics. The House of Representatives, one of the two chambers of the U.S. Congress, wants to amend the Constitution because the U.S. Supreme Court, the nation's highest court, has ruled that previous laws designed to prohibit flag burning violated the Constitution's guarantee of freedom of expression. Those prohibitions were therefore invalid. To remedy this situation, however, Congress and the states must proceed according to procedures set down in Article V of the Constitution.

The Constitution of the United States is the nation's formal plan of government and the government's legal basis. It was drafted in 1787, ratified over the next 18 months, and went into effect in 1789. The government it created has operated without interruption since then. It has endured deep divisions that provoked a bloody civil war. It has survived lengthy periods of disruptive social and economic turmoil, and it has weathered the strains brought on by U.S. involvement in the world wars of the 20th century. No other single national system of constitutional government has fared as well for so long. In fact, the U.S. Constitution is the oldest written constitution that remains in force today.

Americans have a deep pride in, and even reverence for the Constitution. To many, the Constitution is not just a simple blueprint for a government. It is, instead, an almost sacred embodiment of a great nation and its basic values. In this view, the Constitution is the only thing that binds together this huge nation and its staggeringly diverse population. As we saw in chapter 1, Americans lack a common ethnic, racial, or religious heritage, but they are a single citizenry. They are bound together by a national contract, the Constitution, that legally and literally defines what it means to be an American.

To be an American is not a matter of blood, religion, or language. An American is somebody who is either born in the United States or, having lived legally in the nation for a prescribed length of time and met certain requirements, is sworn in as a "naturalized" citizen. Both types of citizens are legally equal, with one exception: Naturalized citizens cannot be elected president. This constitutional restriction (Article II, Section 1) was rooted in the fear that foreign-born citizens might hold divided loyalties, perhaps unconsciously, on issues having to do with war with their homelands. However, naturalized citizens are not barred from other elected or appointed offices, which underscores the irony that an immigrant cannot be elected to the highest office in a nation populated by immigrants. This prohibition could be eliminated through an amendment to the Constitution, but so far, this hasn't happened.

Thus, to be an American is to be a part of a legal and political system defined by a document over 200 years old. No wonder scholars and citizens alike study the Constitution to figure out exactly what "the framers intended" in the same way that Jews consult the Torah, Christians the Bible, or Muslims the Koran. And, as befits its sacred stature, an original parchment copy of the Constitution is protected, alongside an original copy of the Declaration of Independence, behind thick glass and steel within the National Archives on Constitution Avenue in Washington, D.C.

A POLITICAL DOCUMENT

Americans' faith in their political system has been a source of tremendous social and political stability in an often unstable world. Without that faith, the system, and the nation, probably would not have survived very long.

Yet reverence can be overdone. The Constitution is not religious dogma. It does not demand unquestioning faith. It is a political document, the plan for a political system. It is a framework of rules and procedures under which citizens and their elected representatives engage in conflict and, where possible, transform that conflict into some workable compromise. In this sense any **constitution** is best understood as a compact among citizens that both empowers government and limits what it can do. It also provides the means by which citizens can change rules that no longer work. Nor is any constitution meant to be unchanging or eternal: It too is meant to change when it no longer serves the needs of the people.

The Constitution of the United States did not spring suddenly from the admittedly fertile minds of its drafters. Certainly it reflects the keen intellects of a uniquely gifted set of leaders—among them George Washington, James Madison, and Benjamin Franklin—but much of its direction and substance was the product of hard political experience, sharp economic and social conflicts, and pressing necessity. The Constitution's underlying political ideals and its formal structure of government are deeply rooted in the history of a people. The document reflects deep-seated beliefs about the rights and responsibilities of virtuous citizens, as well as acute fears about the inherent dangers of government left unchecked.

More than anything, however, the Constitution was a practical response to an immediate need: to create an effective and accountable form of national government.

This point is worth repeating. The challenge facing the framers of the Constitution was to create a government that was effective *and* remained accountable to the citizenry. This is more than a philosophical dilemma. Governments that are not effective may look good on paper, but they cannot provide social stability or national unity. Worst of all, weak governments cannot ensure justice; they cannot protect the weak from the strong.

By contrast, governments in which a few rule without meaningful participation by the people may be efficient in a narrow sense—things may get done quickly and without apparent conflict—but they are distant from citizens and lack concern for them. Such **authoritarian regimes** give citizens few real political rights and little individual freedom, so they often rely on coercion to maintain order or loyalty. They cannot ensure justice, as they themselves are the chief abusers of citizens' rights and liberties. Thus, neither weak government nor tyrannical government is a palatable choice.

It is important to keep this dilemma in mind when trying to understand the Constitution. Much of its design is aimed at making government effective. But just as much, if not more, of it is aimed at making government accountable. In this regard the Constitution is a balancing act, a compromise. It embodies what a select group of men thought was possible to achieve at a particular moment in the history. That this late 18th-century plan of government has endured so long is testimony to the framers' wisdom and to their capacity to balance effectiveness and accountability.

The Constitution's longevity is also testimony to the later generations of Americans who worked hard, fought, and even died to apply the Constitution to their own needs and wishes, to their own beliefs in the proper role of government in a free society. As we will see, the Constitution, for all its virtues, is only a framework for how Americans should govern themselves. It doesn't guarantee results. Without the willingness of each generation to abide by its rules and make them work, the Constitution would probably be yet another dusty relic of the past. If the framers gave the Constitution its birth, later generations of Americans have kept it alive.

THE LONG ROAD TO THE CONSTITUTION

The American colonies did not rebel against England simply to create a new nation. The rebellion came about because the colonists had grown tired of increasingly rigid and unresponsive English rule. By the 1770s most colonists wanted the English government to let them govern themselves as they saw fit. These feelings did not erupt suddenly in 1776, when the colonies formally declared independence. They developed slowly through years of growing tension between England and its American colonies.

At the root of the conflict was a fundamental disagreement about how the colonies were to be governed. In the 1760s the English made what they thought were reasonable efforts to reassert control over their North American colonies, which had been relatively free to govern themselves while England battled Spain and France for global supremacy. The colonists, having enjoyed a great deal of leeway, naturally opposed renewed controls by the English king and Parliament, which by this time held true power in England's system of limited monarchy.

The English also thought, with reason, that the colonists should help pay the huge costs of defending the colonies against France and its Indian allies during the Seven Years' War (1754–1763). But the passage of the Stamp Act of 1765, which imposed new taxes on the colonies, drew sharp protests against "taxation without representation." The colonies had no direct representation in Parliament, and as historian Jack Greene argues, they regarded the passage of the Stamp Act "as a violation of their inherited and customary constitutional right not to be taxed except by their own local representatives."[3] Parliament did eventually repeal the Stamp Act, but its actions stirred anger toward what the colonists saw as a remote and unaccountable government.

THE ROAD TO REBELLION

Matters worsened after the Boston "Tea Party" of December 16, 1773, in which a mob dumped three shiploads of English tea into the harbor to protest a new law that ordered colonists to buy their tea from a company supported by the English government. The mob included a number of prominent Bostonians whose businesses were threatened by the new law. The English reacted angrily to this illegal destruction of property by passing a series of Coercive Acts—which the colonists labeled Intolerable Acts—designed to force the rebellious Bostonians to obey English law. These acts imposed a British naval blockade on the port of Boston to prevent goods from being shipped into or out of the city and instituted military control over the Massachusetts Colony. Such harsh actions shocked other colonists, who feared that the same fate might befall them. As a result, in September, 1774, delegates from all the colonies except Georgia convened in Philadelphia to discuss the deteriorating relations with England.

The delegates to this First Continental Congress faced a great dilemma. On one hand, they were English subjects who had always deferred to the authority of the government in London. On the other hand, the colonists worried about the erosion of their freedoms. As English subjects, they believed that they had a basic right to have a voice in government decisions affecting them, and they had repeatedly petitioned the king and Parliament to address their complaints.

These efforts had failed because England was determined to control its colonial holdings and because by this time the English and the colonists held conflicting political values. The English retained a strong belief in the legitimacy of rule by the monarch and a hereditary land-owning aristocracy. In their view the colonists had little if any say in what Parliament did. However, the views of the colonists had been

TABLE 2.1.   THE ROAD TO THE CONSTITUTION: A CHRONOLOGY

1776	Declaration of Independence
	Drafting of Articles of Confederation
1777	Articles of Confederation submitted to states
1781	Battle of Yorktown, cease fire with Britain goes into effect
	Articles of Confederation fully ratified, becomes first American form of government
1783	Treaty of Paris with Britain, war officially ends
1786	Annapolis Convention calls for meeting to revise Articles.
	Shays's Rebellion
1787	Constitutional Convention held in Philadelphia
	Delaware becomes first state to ratify Constitution
1788	Constitution ratified by New Hampshire, goes into effect
1789	Congress convenes for first time under Constitution
	Congress approves 12 amendments to the Constitution
1791	First 10 amendments fully ratified, collectively become the Bill of Rights

shaped by their experiences in the New World, where hard work and innovation mattered above all else. Their experiences had made them more egalitarian, more unwilling to obey a remote ruling elite. They believed that Parliament had no right to pass laws affecting them without their approval.

The colonists had forged a separate identity, yet they were still reluctant to sever their ties with their home country. Indeed, the First Continental Congress tried once more to resolve the conflict peacefully. It adopted a Declaration of Rights and Grievances in which the colonies protested English actions and, more important, authorized a boycott on all English goods in an attempt to force the government in London to negotiate in good faith. However, this declaration only infuriated the English government, which now declared the colonies in open rebellion, restated Parliament's supremacy over colonial affairs, and tightened control over colonial political activities.

These actions hardened attitudes even among colonial leaders who still sought a peaceful way out of the conflict. Finally, on April 19, 1775, armed revolt erupted at Lexington and Concord, Massachusetts. A month later, as colonial militias surrounded English troops in Boston, a Second Continental Congress met in Philadelphia and approved the formation of a continental army headed by George Washington. At the same time, the Continental Congress once again petitioned King George III for a peaceful end to the conflict. But the English government either could not or would not give in to any challenge to the way it ran its vast empire. English generals were ordered to crush the growing rebellion. By 1776 all that remained for the colonies was to formally declare and win their independence from England (see Table 2.1).

THE DECLARATION OF INDEPENDENCE

The Declaration of Independence was approved by the Second Continental Congress on July 2, 1776. It was signed and announced to the public in Philadelphia on July 4, the date now celebrated as Independence Day. (The full text of the Declaration of Independence is included in the appendix.)

The Declaration of Independence was the work of a committee of delegates consisting of John Adams of Massachusetts, Benjamin Franklin of Pennsylvania, and Thomas Jefferson of Virginia.[4] Its content reflected resolutions that had been passed by the Second Continental Congress, as well as a number of compromises reached by the drafters as they worked on the document. Even so, much of its most memorable language came from the pen of the young and brilliant Jefferson. In his hands the Declaration became a powerful defense of the right of a people to part ways with their government when that government no longer safeguards their fundamental rights and liberties, and after all peaceful means to resolve the problem have failed. The Declaration was not a call for revolution, nor was it a plan for any specific kind of new government. It was a statement to colonists, the English, and other nations in defense of legal separation from England, which the colonists still hoped would happen peacefully.

In this regard, the Declaration of Independence makes most sense as a list of specific grievances involving the perceived abuses of power by an unaccountable government. Many of the same concerns about the proper limits of government power would emerge 11 years later during the drafting of the Constitution. For example, the complaint that the king "has refused his Assent to Laws, the most wholesome and necessary for the public good" is revisited in the Constitution's provision (Article I, Section 7) requiring that all bills passed by Congress but not acted upon formally by the president automatically become law after 10 days. In the same way, constitutional provisions that guard against executive (i.e., presidential) manipulation of judges' salaries and terms of office, ensure trial by jury, and establish firm dates for election to the House of Representatives have roots in complaints expressed in the Declaration of Independence.[5]

Of course, the Declaration of Independence is more than a list of grievances. It is also a philosophical treatise on the proper relationship between government and the people. Its justifications for separation from England were incorporated into the governmental system established under the Constitution and embodied in the guarantees of rights and liberties extended to Americans. These justifications were shaped by the colonial political culture, the set of values and beliefs embedded in the colonial mind. Although the colonists differed among themselves, according to regional and personal characteristics, as a group they professed two fundamental values that had a great impact on their decision to separate from England. These values were political equality and the concept of natural rights.

Political Equality   Jefferson's claim in the Declaration that "all men are created equal" was a breathtaking rebuke to the widely held European view that only some people—namely, aristocrats—enjoyed political rights or could take part in governing. Even many educated or more affluent colonists were skeptical about claims that people were equal in any way. But over a century of limited self-government in a rough and often hostile environment had led colonists to develop more egalitarian views about the intellect and resourcefulness of the average person.

Two cautions must be kept in mind in considering the colonial view of equality. First, equality was political, not social or economic. There will always be some people who are richer, smarter, or better looking than others. The colonists may have been more egalitarian than the English, but even they did not believe that everyone was equally well equipped to govern. Nevertheless, the colonists believed that every qualified member of a community should have political rights, such as the right to vote.

Second, even political equality did not extend to every colonial resident in the 1770s. It was extended solely to *qualified* individuals, which at the time usually meant males who owned some minimum amount of property. Keep in mind that the Declaration was written within a cultural context in which even white males without property frequently were barred from equal participation, where women were still legally subordinate to their fathers or husbands, and of course, where slaves were themselves property.

Slavery, particularly the forced importation of Africans, was a controversial issue during the debate over independence. Many colonists openly opposed the practice. Even Thomas Jefferson, a plantation owner who arranged for his slaves to be freed only at the time of his death, expressed dislike of the institution. In fact, Jefferson's original draft of the Declaration condemned England for establishing slavery. But this grievance apparently was omitted from the final draft after strong objections by delegates from colonies in which slavery was critical to the local agricultural economy.[6] These delegates threatened to withhold their support unless all references to slavery were deleted. This was not the last time the issue of slavery would be sidestepped for more immediate political concerns.

Even with these contradictions, in a world characterized by kings and nobility the Declaration's idealistic claim that "all men are created equal" was a revolutionary one. It offered a philosophical foundation for a set of rights and liberties that would be explicitly stated in the first 10 amendments to the Constitution, the Bill of Rights. As we will see in chapter 4, with such a foundation in the nation's supreme law, it would become increasingly difficult to deny these rights to groups that had been left out at the beginning.

Natural Rights   Not only are all men politically equal, the Declaration states, but "they are endowed by their Creator with certain unalienable Rights," and that among these are "Life, Liberty, and the pursuit of Happiness."

What do we mean by "unalienable" rights? The answer can be found in the *Second Treatise of Civil Government* (1689) by the 17th-century English philosopher John Locke (1632–1704), an essay that was widely read by educated colonists. According to Locke, all people were born "by nature free, equal, and independent" and there-

John Locke (1632–1704). The writings of the English philosopher influenced the American colonists at the time of the Revolution. In particular, Locke's views on "natural" rights shaped colonists beliefs in their "unalienable" rights to life, liberty, and happiness, as expressed in the Declaration of Independence.

fore had "natural" or "unalienable" rights.[7] In Locke's view, these were the rights to life, liberty, and protection of private property. It is interesting to note, however, that in the Declaration Jefferson changed the seemingly narrow right to own private property into a much broader right to pursue "happiness." This apparently was done to prevent anyone from claiming an inherent right to own "unnatural" forms of property—that is, slaves.[8] Even so, as we saw in chapter 1, Americans continue to link protection of private property with political liberty.

More important, Locke (and the American colonists) believed that these rights are not granted by a king or a parliament. They exist in nature or are granted by God. No person or body, not even a king or a parliament, has the authority to revoke what nature or God has granted. An individual's life, liberty, or property could not be taken away without just cause (such as breaking the law) or, in the case of property, without just compensation. Indeed, the movement toward independence gained momentum when colonists' beliefs about their natural rights as English subjects were challenged by actions of the English government.

Limited Government   The colonists defended separation from England at least partly on the basis of Locke's notions about limited government. Locke believed that most individuals are motivated by enlightened self-interest. In the positive sense, this meant that most people would not interfere with the natural rights of other individuals. To do so would be irrational, as it would give others "permission" to respond in kind. The result would be that no person's rights would be safe.

Locke's assumption that human nature is inherently rational is important. Rational individuals do not interfere with one another's natural rights, so there is little real need for government. However, Locke admitted, the picture is not perfect. Human nature may be rational, but it is also flawed. People are not saints, and even good people can fall into sin. Rational self-interest can at times degenerate into selfishness and greed. If left alone, some individuals might try to take away the natural rights of others. Rational people therefore will seek to prevent the tyranny of the strong over the weak by creating some kind of government, a framework of laws and institutions designed to enforce the rights of all when the laws of nature might prove inadequate.

Locke's views were popular in the New World. However, in England the views of an earlier English thinker, Thomas Hobbes (1588–1679), were more popular with the ruling class. Hobbes argued that most people are irrational and ill-equipped to govern. For Hobbes, life in the "state of nature" (that is, without a strong government) would be "solitary, poore, nasty, brutish and short."[9] The world would be a dismal place rife with anarchy, a "war of all against all" that could be prevented only by the strong hand of a king whose power came directly from God. Hobbes was no democrat—he argued that the average person had little capacity to govern—and neither were the aristocrats who dominated Parliament.

But Locke's views fit better with colonists' values and experiences. For Locke, government was not gifted by the authority of God but developed out of a contract among political equals. To the colonists, this idea of a contract was to be formalized in a written constitution that stated in explicit terms the role of government in safeguarding citizens' rights. Even more important, such a document would set clear limits on the power of government. Written agreements of this kind were well known in many of the colonies, going back to the Mayflower Compact of 1620. By 1776, then, the notion of explicitly limited government came naturally to colonial thinkers and leaders.

Such a contractual notion of government was uncommon in Europe. Even the English system, which by the early 18th century was marked by parliamentary supremacy and a limited monarchy, was regarded in the colonies as an inadequate check on the potential abuses of government power. The reason for this unease was that the English "constitution" was and still is an unwritten one, "an accumulation of *customary* practices, long-standing legal procedures and principles, and basic individual rights that had slowly taken shape over the centuries."[10] It is not a single document but a collection of traditions, customs, and laws dating back to agreements forged between the king and the nobles in the Magna Carta of 1215. What is more, in the English system Parliament, not a written constitution, is the ultimate source of law.

To the colonists, parliamentary supremacy was problematic. Parliament's word was supreme, but Parliament could change its mind. This perceived weakness in the system was worsened by the lack of meaningful colonial representation in Parliament, which made it harder to ensure that the rights of colonists were protected. This combination of parliamentary supremacy, lack of effective colonial representation in Parliament, and the apparent fragility of individual rights and liberties caused many colonists to conclude that the English system's lack of a written constitution was a fatal flaw. Put simply, the English view on parliamentary supremacy clashed with the emerging colonial view that only a written constitution could adequately check possible abuses of power by Parliament and by government in general.

Justifying Separation Finally, a contractual notion of government implies that people have a right to change or to abolish an existing form of government if it fails to safeguard their rights or, worse, if the government itself becomes the problem. In the Declaration Jefferson stressed that such an action was not to be taken lightly—that "prudence" dictates that an established government should not be changed "for light and transient causes." But, he added, a people can suffer patiently only so long, and there comes a time when "it is their right, it is their duty, to throw off such Government, and to provide new Guards for their future security."

The American Revolution was in many ways a "conservative" rebellion. Unlike the French Revolution of 1789, the American rebellion did not seek to demolish existing social institutions. Unlike the Bolshevik Revolution of 1917, it did not aim to remold society according to a powerful utopian ideology. Unlike the Iranian Revolution of 1978, it did not seek to install a theocracy, or government by religious leaders. The American rebellion was conservative in the sense that the colonists wanted to *conserve* their homegrown ways of self-government. They could no longer tolerate an English system that seemed so unresponsive and apparently without limits on its power. In essence, they rebelled because their ideas about natural rights and the proper role of government were no longer satisfied by existing arrangements.

THE ARTICLES OF CONFEDERATION

By late 1781 the fighting had all but ended and negotiations with England over formal independence would soon begin. At the same time, with the final ratification of the Articles of Confederation, the 13 colonies joined together into a loose partnership. First drafted in 1777, the Articles constituted a contract among the former colonies that spelled out the powers and responsibilities of a new national government with respect to the new "states." In a sense, the Articles established a "league of friendship" among 13 separate entities. This was the new nation's first national government.

The Articles placed strict limits on the new national government, reflecting the revolutionary generation's experience with English rule and their resulting fear of central government power. Most believed that no truly representative government could exist at the national level because the distances between citizens and their government were too great. A strong national government would become inevitably remote and tyrannical, producing the kinds of grievances that had sparked the rebellion in the first place.

Moreover, the new states did not trust one another. They had been allies against England but remained competitors on a wide range of economic and political issues. Each state in this huge but sparsely populated new country—already one of the largest nations in the world—also had a distinct history and local culture.[11] "In short, Americans did not know each other very well," notes Warren Burger, former chief justice of the United States, "and that made them distrustful of any distant government that put power in the hands of people they did not know."[12] They were eager to retain as much local control as possible. This view was reinforced by the reality that, even with independence, most people still saw themselves as citizens of their respective states, not of a nation. They were not yet "Americans."

The Structure of the Articles   The Articles of Confederation retained a revised version of the Continental Congress that had acted as the nation's government during the Revolution. Each state had one vote in Congress, regardless of its population, in line with each state's status as an equal legal entity. A simple plurality of the states (seven out of thirteen) was needed to pass routine legislation, but a vote of nine states was required to enact any law concerning the coining of money or treaties with other nations. This high standard was designed to force consensus on especially important issues, and in so doing to protect the rights of any single state from possible tyranny by a majority of the other states. Finally, a unanimous vote was required to change the Articles themselves.

The former colonists were so fearful of monarchy that the Articles did not provide for a separate executive in the new government. Any executive functions (such as negotiations with England) were to be carried out by a committee of Congress. There also was no provision for a separate and permanent national judiciary; any conflict between two or more states was to be arbitrated by a panel created by Congress for that dispute alone.

Limited Powers   Article II declared, "Each state retains its sovereignty, freedom, and independence, and every power, jurisdiction and right, which is not by this Confederation expressly delegated to the United States in Congress assembled." The Articles thus reserved virtually all power for the states. It gave the new national government limited power to make peace with other nations and to run a national post office, but any other powers were to be granted to the national government by the states through Congress.

The states' fears of centralized power made them reluctant to give the national government much power at all. It could not levy taxes against the states or citizens, for example. It had no control over the coining of money and could not by itself regulate "interstate" commerce, nor could it involve itself in any domestic problems unless expressly directed to do so by the states, acting through Congress. In short, the national government could do only what the states allowed it to do, which turned out to be very little.

Government under the Articles   If the rebellion against England grew out of hostility to remote and unaccountable central government, the Constitution grew out of practical experience with the apparent impotence of government under the Articles of Confederation. This government boasted some real achievements, chief among them peace with England, but it could not create national unity, domestic stability, or economic health.

The economic situation was serious. The economies of the former colonies had been devastated by the war, and the new nation owed massive debts to those who had loaned it money to fight for independence. Efforts to rebuild were hamstrung by the inability of Congress to institute the kinds of national policies (such as a common currency) that would convince merchants and lenders, including foreign ones, to take financial risks in the new nation. The states, for their part, settled back into old rivalries, including trade wars and even armed disputes over western frontierlands. Such rivalries undermined efforts to give Congress some authority to collect taxes on a national level, settle interstate boundary disputes, or regulate interstate commerce.

By the late 1780s the national government was weak, broke, and unable to prevent destructive disputes among the states. In their fear of centralized power, the former colonies seemed to have veered too far in the other direction. They avoided creating a government that was too strong but created one that ended up being too weak.

Many of the young nation's leaders, including George Washington, James Madison of Virginia, and Alexander Hamilton of New York, recognized these problems. They feared that continued economic and political instability might prompt some states to go their own ways or tempt foreign governments to meddle in the young nation's affairs. Only a stronger national government, they believed, could alleviate these problems and hold the nation together.

In September 1786 these leaders held a special convention in Annapolis, Maryland, to discuss interstate trade issues, but only five states sent representatives. Unable to proceed, they decided to try again but with a different agenda. A call went out to the states to appoint delegates to another special meeting to address specific ways to fix the problems of the Articles of Confederation, but again the idea was met with general indifference.

SHAYS'S REBELLION

The perceived need to revise the Articles gained wider acceptance during the winter of 1786–87, when thousands of Revolutionary War veterans in western Massachusetts, led by Daniel Shays, rebelled openly against the state government in Boston. Shays's Rebellion grew out of the veterans' frustrations with high state taxes, high interest rates, and low prices for their farm goods, whose combined effects forced many into poverty and indebtedness.

The revolt, aimed at the bankers and merchants who dominated the state's economy and government, produced similar unrest throughout New England. Neither the national government nor Massachusetts had the resources to stem the revolt. Finally the rebellion was stopped by a militia financed by bankers and merchants who were terrified that the rebellion might further "infect" the poor and cause them to rise up against the affluent.

Shays's Rebellion failed, but it had a powerful effect on the course of American history. The revolt, and the dire conditions that provoked the uprising in the first place, convinced many leading Americans of the need for a stronger national govern-

A scuffle breaks out during Shays's Rebellion in western Massachusetts (1786). Although the rebellion was eventually put down, its size and fury drove home the need for extensive changes in the system of government provided under the Articles of Confederation.

ment that could maintain civil order and economic stability. A few even agitated to make George Washington a king, an offer that he rejected. Congress, however, recognized its inability to deal with the rebellion or to address pressing economic and political problems, and in February 1787 the states were invited to send delegates to a convention in Philadelphia for the purpose of discussing changes in the Articles. This time, the states listened.

CREATING THE CONSTITUTION

The fifty-five delegates who convened in Philadelphia in May 1787 faced a major dilemma: how to bolster the obvious weaknesses of the national government under the Articles of Confederation without creating the government tyranny that had caused the Revolution. If national government under the Articles seemed too weak, all other forms of government known at the time seemed too strong and too remote from the people.

The challenge was to devise a system that was capable of governing effectively while ensuring that it would not abuse its power or destroy the natural rights and liberties of the governed. James Madison of Virginia stated the problem succinctly:

If men were angels, no government would be necessary. If angels were to govern men, neither external nor internal controls on government would be necessary. In framing a government which is to be administered by men over men, the great difficulty lies in this: you must first enable the government to control the governed; and in the next place oblige it to control itself.[13]

In short, those assembled at the Constitutional Convention in Philadelphia needed to devise a government that was both effective and accountable.

Americans often seem to believe that their form of government sprang fully grown from the mind of Madison, the "father" of the Constitution. This is not the case. Madison's contributions to the Constitution were important, but the Constitution is best understood as the product of many compromises reached by delegates who had been selected by their respective states primarily because of their political skills. These leaders, while often suspicious of one another's motives, were pragmatic enough to strive for compromise wherever possible.

In sum, the Constitution is a political document. Only the constant need to build compromises among diverging opinions and interests can explain the more complicated contrivances built into the system or account for the addition of an explicit Bill of Rights after the Constitution had been ratified by the states.

SOURCES OF CONFLICT

The most obvious problem was how to balance the vastly different political and economic needs of the various states within a political atmosphere marked by fear and distrust. In the New England states, many of the leading figures who had led the rebellion against England continued to oppose a strong central government. States with small populations (e.g., Delaware) feared that those with larger populations (e.g., New York) would dominate national politics. For their part, the more populous states wondered why sparsely populated states should have equal representation in Congress. States that depended on agriculture feared that their interests would suffer at the hands of states whose economies depended on trade or manufacturing—and vice versa (see Box 2.1).

Of course, the problem of slavery loomed ominously, ready at any time to rip the convention apart. By 1787 slavery was already being phased out in most of the northern states, and support for its complete abolition was strong even among southerners. But slavery was still too important to the agricultural economies of the five southern states for them to compromise on the issue, and it was clear from the beginning of the convention that any attempt to abolish slavery would provoke a fatal split between the states.

The blunt reality was that without the support of the slave states, no Constitution would have been possible. Without the Constitution, no nation or national unity would have been possible. As had happened with the Declaration of Independence, the issue of slavery was sidestepped in order to satisfy more immediate political needs. So intractable was the dispute over slavery that no political skill could resolve it, and eventually, it would take a bloody civil war to do so.

BOX 2.1.   **WHAT DO YOU THINK?**
WERE THE FRAMERS
MOTIVATED ONLY BY ECONOMIC
SELF-INTEREST?

The economic health of the new nation was an important issue to the delegates who met in Philadelphia in 1787 to craft the new constitution. After all, any nation that has a weak economy and cannot repay its debts will not establish economic stability or any faith in its government. But did the framers act on behalf of their own economic interests rather than the needs of the nation?

Some of the framers probably did have their own economic interests in mind. Many of the 55 delegates had their own farms or businesses, and all clearly would be affected by the nation's economic health. But an early 20th-century historian, Charles Beard, went even further. He argued that many of the delegates wanted a stronger national government for personal reasons. Many owned government securities—pledges to repay loans, with significant interest—that at the time were almost worthless because the government's inability to pay its debts. A stronger national government that had the power to levy taxes and generate its own revenues could pay off these debts, and those who held the securities would recoup their investments.

Was Beard onto something? It's hard to say. Some of the delegates no doubt acted partly out of personal desires for profit, or at least to avoid financial losses. However, other scholars concluded that Beard was being simplistic. Some of the most influential delegates, such as Madison, owned no securities at all. What is more, seven delegates who refused to sign the Constitution owned more securities than all the other delegates combined.

So was Beard entirely wrong? Not according to Michael Parenti, who argues that the framers may not have been motivated by the narrow issue of ownership of public securities but were influenced by their own class status. None of them were poor or uneducated. All were men of means, and some were quite affluent. Some owned slaves. Clearly, these were upper-class men in a society in which there were more than a few tenant farmers with no land or money to speak of, as well as a good number of people in prison because they could not repay their debts. The primary impetus to the convention itself had been Shays's Rebellion, in which debt-ridden Revolutionary War veterans threatened to take over the government of Massachusetts and enact laws to relieve their own economic woes.

To Parenti, the Constitution was an elitist document designed to protect the interests of a small class of property holders. At a minimum, it created a stronger national government, one that quickly used public funds to pay debts and open the way for economic expansion.

Was there any other choice? What do you think?

Sources: Charles A. Beard, *An Economic Interpretation of the United States* (New York: MacMillan, 1936); Forrest McDonald, *We, The People: The Economic Origins of the Constitution* (Chicago: University of Chicago Press, 1958); Michael Parenti, *Democracy for the Few*, 6th ed. (Upper Saddle River, NJ: Prentice Hall, 1995), ch. 4.

THE ROUTE TO COMPROMISE

The creation of the Constitution, argues historian John Roche, "was largely one of a masterful employment of political expertise by the Constitutionalists as against the bumbling, erratic behavior by opponents of reform."[14] Indeed, those who wanted to scrap the Articles and strengthen the national government—called "nationalists" or, later, "Federalists"—had the advantage from the moment the delegates began to arrive in Philadelphia.

The list of delegates to the convention underscores this point. On one hand, some of the most famous and passionate defenders of the Articles—such as Patrick Henry of Virginia, and Thomas Paine and Samuel Adams of Massachusetts—either were not chosen as delegates or refused to attend because they knew that their views would be in the minority. Thomas Jefferson, another staunch defender of the states, was in Paris as the American ambassador to France. On the other hand, the nationalists were represented not only by Madison, Hamilton, and Washington but also by such eminent men as Edmund Randolph of Virginia and Benjamin Franklin, James Wilson, and Gouverneur Morris of Pennsylvania.

However, even though the nationalists were better represented and better organized, they still needed to work with the large number of delegates who wanted to preserve the rights of the states. "We must make concessions on both sides," said Elbridge Gerry of Massachusetts. "Without these the Constitutions of the several States would never have been formed."[15]

The Virginia Plan   The nationalists had the advantage from the beginning because they submitted the first formal proposals for changes in the Articles. The **Virginia Plan,** so named because it was crafted by Virginians Edmund Randolph and James Madison, dominated the convention's agenda throughout the hot summer of 1787. Any discussion about reform thereafter was in reference to the Virginia Plan, putting those who opposed a stronger national government at a disadvantage.

The Virginia Plan was a radical attack on the Articles of Confederation (see Table 2.2). It called for a national government whose power and authority no longer depended on the approval of the states but instead came directly from a constitution. Under the Virginia Plan, Congress would have the authority to make laws in a broad range of areas (such as trade) in which national interests should prevail over state interests.

The structure of Congress would also change. Instead of a legislature in which states were represented equally—thus giving more leverage to less-populated states—the Virginia Plan proposed a **bicameral** (or two-chamber) legislature. In the first or "lower" chamber, the number of representatives from any state would depend on that state's population. These members would be selected directly by the people. The members of the second or "upper" chamber were to be nominated by the state legislatures and approved by the first chamber. This arrangement also gave more influence to the more-populated states, and it would make it harder for one or two small states to block legislation, which happened often under the Articles. Finally, under the Virginia Plan, the national government would have its own executive

TABLE 2.2. COMPARISON OF KEY ELEMENTS OF THE VIRGINIA PLAN, NEW JERSEY PLAN, AND CONSTITUTION

Key Elements	Virginia Plan	New Jersey Plan	Constitution
Congress			
Structure	Two chambers	One chamber	Two chambers
Representation	Both by population	Each state equal (1 vote per state)	House—by population Senate—equal representation (two senators per state)
Selection	By direct election	By state	House—direct election Senate—by respective states*
Executive			
Structure	One person	A committee	One person
Selection	By Congress	By Congress	By an electoral college
Removal	By Congress	By a majority of states	By Congress
Judiciary			
Jurisdiction	National	Hear appeals from state courts on violations of national laws	National
Selection	By Congress	Appointed by executive committee	Nominated by president, confirmed by Senate

* Actual method left to the states. Superseded by 17th Amendment (1913), which mandated direct election of senators.

branch, to ensure effective administration, and its own judiciary, to mediate disputes between states. However, Congress alone would select the people to run both the executive and judicial branches.

The Virginia Plan was a direct attack on the perceived weaknesses of the Articles. In the minds of its supporters, the future of the nation depended on a strong central government run by leaders whose inherent virtue would prevent them from governing in a tyrannical fashion. In their view, the purpose of the national government was to promote economic stability, social order, and national power. It would be the "energetic center" that would bind together a nation, foster its economic health, and promote its strength in international affairs.[16] Government under the Articles had been ineffective. What was needed was a strong national government that was able to overcome the normal divisions among the states.

The New Jersey Plan   Such a radical departure from the Articles of Confederation, however, was unlikely to gain the approval of the delegates who still supported the ideal of limited national government. Those who defended the powers of the states (later labeled by their critics as "anti-Federalists") were afraid that the Virginia Plan would give far too much power to the national government. Delegates from less-populated states also worried that under the Virginia Plan Congress would be controlled by the more-populated states.

Critics of the Virginia Plan proposed an alternative in the form of the **New Jersey Plan,** which was introduced by William Paterson of New Jersey. Supporters of this plan recognized the need to grant the national government some new powers, such as the capacity to impose national taxes and regulate commerce among the states. However, they opposed the Virginia Plan's design for Congress, which they felt gave too much power to the more-populated states, as well as its creation of a separate and more powerful executive office. The New Jersey Plan reserved more power for the states than the Virginia Plan did, and it left in place the single-chamber Congress in which each state was represented equally.

The limited changes proposed in the New Jersey Plan reflected its supporters' belief in the egalitarianism expressed by Jefferson in the Declaration of Independence. In their view individual freedom was the goal; a society of rational, self-sufficient individuals had no need for strong government. They firmly believed that government should be limited and decentralized, placed as close to the people as possible. For them, a strong national government risked tyranny over individual liberty, and thus over democracy itself.

These views had a great deal of popular appeal, and embodied values about individual liberty and decentralized government that are woven into the American political culture. But at the convention the cause of states' rights was undermined by the perceived failures of the Articles of Confederation, by the dire economic and social conditions facing the country, and by the superior organization of the nationalists. Realizing their disadvantages, the supporters of states' rights moved to ensure that clear limits on the power of the national government would be instituted somewhere in the new system. Because advocates of a new constitution needed their support, they were in a position to force compromises from the nationalists.

The Connecticut Compromise   After weeks of tough negotiations, with the fate of the convention in doubt, a committee of delegates came up with the **Connecticut Compromise** (also known as the Great Compromise), so named because of the pivotal role played by the Connecticut delegation. In the compromise plan, Congress still would have two chambers as envisioned by the Virginia Plan, but in the Senate (or upper chamber) the states would have equal representation. The nationalists conceded the need to protect the interests of the smaller states, but only on the condition that all taxing and spending bills originate in the House of Representatives (the lower chamber), in which representation was still based on population. Many nationalists opposed this scheme because they felt that the Senate would give the small states too much influence over national policy. On the other hand, many defenders of states' rights worried that the more-populated states still had too much influence in the House of Representatives. So great were these differences that even this compromise barely passed.

Forming a More Perfect Union. George Washington (standing, behind desk) presides over the final signing of the Constitution in 1787, while elder statesman Benjamin Franklin (seated, at center) looks on in approval.

Other Issues Many other differences had to be hammered out. The delegates worked out agreements on the scope of authority to be given to the federal judiciary, the lengths of terms for members in both chambers of Congress, and, at the very end, the means for selecting a president. The delegates agreed that the Constitution would be submitted directly to special state conventions for ratification, recognising that the state legislatures would oppose any plan that took away their power. Actual ratification of the new constitution would occur when at least nine of the thirteen states had approved the plan.

On the other hand, the delegates avoided some issues entirely because they could not reach a compromise. A good example was suffrage—the right to vote—which was essentially left up to the states because of sharp disagreements over whether women and freed slaves should be able to vote in national elections. As we will see in chapter 4, the conflict over the right to vote would endure far into the 20th century.

However, the issue of slavery could not be avoided entirely. Delegates did sidestep the core issue by agreeing that Congress would not interfere with the slave trade until at least 1808—at which time Congress banned further importation of slaves—but they fought over how to count slaves for the purpose of allocating seats in the House of Representatives. Opponents of slavery pointed out that if slaves were property, as defenders of slavery insisted, they could not be counted as persons for the purpose of determining representation. How could property also be people, they asked? But if this happened, the slave-holding states would have few House seats and little political power, because slaves made up a large portion of their populations.

Despite the contradictions in their argument, delegates from the slave-holding states demanded that slaves be counted as persons only for the purpose of allocating House seats. Opponents of slavery had no choice but to compromise: Without the slave-holding states there would be no constitution. The sides agreed that three-fifths of the slave population in each state would be added to the free population for the purpose of calculating representation in the House.

BOX 2.2.
THE FEDERALIST PAPERS

New York State was important in the conflict over ratification of the Constitution. A big state with a growing population and an important commercial center, New York also occupied a strategic geographic position at the center of the nation. Furthermore, New York City was the nation's capital at the time. Although the Constitution could be ratified without New York, both sides recognized the political significance of the state's vote.

Among the key Federalists supporting the Constitution was Alexander Hamilton, a young lawyer and skilled political operator who had been an aide to George Washington during the War of Independence. Hamilton knew that newspapers, the primary mass medium of the day, were important to the outcome of the ratification battle, so he commissioned a series of essays to attack the deficiencies of the Articles of Confederation and extol the virtues of the new plan. For this task he recruited two major allies: John Jay, the author of New York's constitution and one of the negotiators of the treaty of independence from Britain; and James Madison, a primary author of the Virginia Plan whose overall role at the convention later led to his title, "Father of the Constitution."

Together they produced the *Federalist Papers*, 85 essays that appeared in New York City newspapers between October, 1787, and August, 1788. The essays were published under a pen name, "Publius" (after the Roman writer of the same name), to conceal the authors' identities. Jay apparently wrote only five essays before becoming too ill to continue. Madison wrote 26 before heading back to Virginia to participate in his state's ratification battle, in which the essays also played a role. Hamilton wrote 51 essays, and collaborated with Madison on another three. →

After four months of debate, the delegates assembled on September 17, 1787, to take the final vote on the new constitution. The tone was set by the elderly Benjamin Franklin. Although he did not like everything in the new Constitution, he said, he would support it:

> For when you assemble a number of men to have the advantage of their joint wisdom, you inevitably assemble with those men, all of their prejudices, their passions, their errors of opinion, their local interests, and their selfish views. From such an assembly can a perfect production be expected? . . . Thus I consent, Sir, to the Constitution because I expect no better, and because I am not sure that it is not the best.[17]

The delegates did not vote directly on the Constitution. Instead, following a suggestion by Gouverneur Morris, they voted on a motion that would indicate the "unanimous consent" of the states (not delegates) present. This motion was designed to paper over the disagreements that still remained. It passed without opposition. Thus, after many compromises, the Constitution went to the states for ratification.

HISTORICAL PERSPECTIVE

Like the Constitution they promoted, the *Federalist* Papers reflected compromises among individuals with strong political views. Hamilton and Madison differed on major political issues and later became political enemies, but they joined together at this time because they both felt that the Articles of Confederation had been a failure. Hamilton is perhaps best known for his attacks on the Articles and his thoughts on the role of the federal judiciary (Essay No. 78). Madison's defense of a strong union to cure the "mischiefs of faction" (Essay No. 10) and his argument in favor of separation of powers as a check on the potential abuse of government power (Essay No. 51) are perhaps the two most famous of all the essays.

The *Federalist* should be regarded as part of an overall political campaign to convince New Yorkers to approve the Constitution, and in this regard it played only a small part in a vigorous battle of ideas. However, it has endured as the single most important explanation of the Constitution's design and intent actually written by any of the framers themselves. Despite its evident purpose as partisan propaganda, the *Federalist* is still a profound philosophical treatise on human nature, individual rights and liberties, and the proper role of government in a free society. Taken together the essays are regarded as a uniquely American contribution to the classics of political theory.

The best-known commentary on the *Federalist Papers* is provided in the version edited by Clinton Rossiter (New York: New American Library, 1960).

THE CONFLICT OVER RATIFICATION

The façade of unanimity presented by the final vote of the convention dissolved as soon as the Constitution went to the states for approval in late 1787. Opposition was particularly strong in New England and some of the less-populous southern states. Opponents of ratification argued that the Constitution gave the national government too much power. Such a government also would be too remote to be kept accountable and might develop into tyranny.

These arguments were persuasive. But the apparent failures of government under the Articles of Confederation, widespread fears of continued economic and political instability, and the inability of opponents to offer a credible alternative to the Constitution gave its supporters the advantage. What is more, promoters of the Constitution were led by the likes of Alexander Hamilton and James Madison, whose superior political skills made the difference in key states such as New York and Virginia (see Box 2.2).

The Final Compromise   Even so, the battle over ratification was closely fought, and the Constitution's supporters had to agree to one final compromise. This was the promise to add a bill of rights, a list of explicit limits on the powers of the national government, to the Constitution. Bills of rights were common in state constitutions by the late 1780s, and opponents of ratification argued that the Constitution must include a similar statement of limits on the power of the national government with respect to the states.

Nationalists such as Alexander Hamilton argued that an explicit bill of rights was unnecessary because the Constitution already contained significant protections against arbitrary government power. Worse, as he argued in *Federalist* No. 84, a specific bill of rights might be construed as leaving everything not explicitly stated open to federal government power.[18] Nevertheless, the opponents of ratification had enough political leverage in enough key states to persuade nationalists to agree to add a bill of rights to the Constitution after ratification.

The Constitution became the official plan for American government on June 21, 1788, after New Hampshire became the ninth state to ratify the document. As promised, one of the first actions taken by the new Congress when it convened in New York City in 1789 was to approve amendments that would constitute a bill of rights. Twelve amendments were sent to the states for approval, and ten of them became part of the Constitution in 1791 after being ratified by the required three-fourths of the states. (Another, dealing with the pay of members of Congress, was ratified in 1992, and became the Twenty-seventh Amendment.) These first ten amendments are collectively known as the **Bill of Rights.**

The guarantees embodied in the Bill of Rights were meant originally to limit the power of the national government with respect to the states. The rights and liberties of individual citizens were matters for state governments. Later, with the addition of the Fourteenth Amendment (1868), the limitations contained in the Bill of Rights would be extended to the state governments with respect to individual citizens (see chapter 4). In this sense at least, the Bill of Rights became an explicit defense of individual rights against government in general. In many ways, its addition made the Constitution complete.

CORE ELEMENTS OF THE CONSTITUTION

The core elements of the Constitution include the creation of a federal system of government, separation of powers, separate constituencies, distinct terms of office and means of selection, and an intricate web of checks and balances. Many of the specific provisions found in the Constitution are discussed in later chapters.

FEDERALISM

Under the Articles of Confederation the states were sovereign. They alone determined what laws applied within their own boundaries. Moreover, they determined the powers of the national government. The Constitution, by contrast, provides that the national (or federal) government is sovereign and that federal law supersedes state law in areas where the national government is granted explicit power (see Article VI in the appendix). These powers are not determined by the states.

In essence, the Constitution provides for separate spheres of influence and authority for the federal and state governments. It grants explicit legislative, executive, and judicial powers to the federal government, but it also reserves certain powers to the states, particularly in the Tenth Amendment. Moreover, the states were to play critical roles in the new system. Most laws that affected citizens' daily lives were state laws; states determined the right to vote and how elections would be run (see chapter 4), state legislatures initially appointed U.S. senators; and states, through the electoral college, were to be instrumental in electing the president.

Today the Constitution is generally interpreted as giving the federal government supremacy over the states; but this relationship is not etched in stone. Indeed, the history of American politics has been marked by conflicts over which powers and responsibilities are to be reserved for the states. The subject of **federalism,** the system that allocates separate spheres of action to the states and the national government, is covered more extensively in chapter 3.

SEPARATION OF POWERS

The notion of **separation of powers** refers to the division of governmental power and functions among distinct institutions. Separation of powers was not a new idea when the Constitution was being written. The notion of separate institutions responsible for making and executing the law has historical roots going back at least to the Roman Empire. Colonial ideas about assigning distinct functions to separate institutions were shaped more directly by the French thinker Baron de Montesquieu (1689–1755), whose book *The Spirit of the Laws* (1748) was widely read by colonial leaders. As political theorist Judith Shklar has observed, the colonists learned from Montesquieu "that the functional separation of governmental powers was the primary way to avoid concentrations of political authority in too few hands and the way to achieve the real end of constitutional government: political stability without the oppression of individuals."[19]

In the Constitution, separation of powers refers to the division of responsibility and power among the legislative branch headed by Congress, an executive branch headed by the president, and a judicial branch headed by the Supreme Court (see Figure 2.1). This tripartite (or three-part) design also recurs in state constitutions.

Sharing Power   "Separation of powers" is actually a misnomer. As presidential scholar Richard Neustadt reminds us, the Constitution provides for separate institutions with distinct functions that *share* power.[20] None of the three branches can govern unchallenged by the others. In particular, a great degree of cooperation and compromise between Congress and the president is necessary to pass laws. In this way neither branch would have too much power. Congress itself is split into two chambers for much the same reason: The House of Representatives and the Senate share legislative power.

FIGURE 2.1.   THE CONSTITUTIONAL SYSTEM OUTLINED

Legislative Branch (Congress)   *Executive Branch*

House of Representatives	*The Senate*	The president and vice president
2-year terms	6-year terms	4-year term
All up for election every two years	1/3 up for election every two years	Electoral college process 2-term limit
Initiates all taxing and spending bills	Confirms nominations and treaties	Removal through impeachment process
Impeaches (indicts) executive and judicial branch officials	Holds trials. Can convict and remove from office by 2/3 vote	Can veto legislation Negotiates treaties Appoints federal judges, executive branch officials

Can override presidential veto by 2/3 vote of both chambers
Regulates the jurisdiction of the federal courts
Initiates process of amending the Constitution

Judicial Branch (Supreme Court and other Federal Courts)

Nominated by the president and confirmed by the Senate
Serve for life terms
Removal through the impeachment process
Interprets laws and treaties
Decides constitutionality of laws and executive actions

The executive branch, headed by the president, was given the authority to implement laws passed by Congress, a role dictated largely by the need for government efficiency. As we will discuss in chapter 9, the president can negotiate treaties with other nations and is the leader of the armed forces in times of war. However, the Senate has the power to approve treaties, and Congress as a body declares war and must appropriate the funds to fight it. The third branch, the federal judiciary, was created primarily to ensure the uniformity of federal law under the Constitution, the nation's supreme law. It would also settle legal disputes between residents of different states, or between the states themselves when Congress was unable or unwilling to do so.

Separation of powers is a complicated way to organize a government, particularly if we are worried about efficiency or speed. The system's design makes more sense when we recall that its creators worried about giving too much power to any one part of government. The provision for a separate executive, which did not exist under the

Articles, certainly had administrative efficiency in mind, but it also reflected the framers' concern that legislative and executive powers should not rest with the same institution. Just as no one person should act as judge, jury, and executioner, no single institution should be able to make, implement, *and* interpret the law. To allow for such a concentration of power was to invite tyranny.

SEPARATE CONSTITUENCIES

Separation of powers would not, however, prevent the abuse of power if one branch were allowed to select members of the others. The drafters of the Virginia Plan had such an idea in mind in their proposal that an elected lower chamber would actually approve the members of the other chamber. Delegates representing the less-populous states opposed the idea precisely because it gave so much power to the majority. This fear, along with concern about ensuring adequate representation for as many different parts of society as possible, led the framers to design means of selection and terms of office in ways that they hoped would foster democratic accountability. As a result, American national government is a collection of separate institutions, each representing distinct and only partly overlapping groups of citizens (or "constituencies"), with none having total power.

House of Representatives   The impacts of these arrangements are best seen in Congress, where the House and Senate embody distinct notions about representation and were meant to represent different constituencies. The House of Representatives was designed to represent the majority of the people, wherever they lived. Article I, Section 2 of the Constitution specifies that the number of representatives per state will be based on that state's population and that there should be one representative for every 30,000 people, with each state having at least one representative. The larger its population, the more representation a state would have in the House. However, rapid population growth in the late 18th century meant that the number of representatives to the House also grew, so in 1929 its size the size was capped at 435.

Today, as we will discuss more fully in chapter 8, members of the House represent districts of approximately 650,000 people each. All are elected directly by voters in their districts, and all serve for a two-year term. Every two years they all face reelection, and it is theoretically possible that every House member could be replaced. Thus, the House acts as a barometer of public opinion, reflecting the "passions of the moment" of the majority. In a far-flung and largely agrarian nation, before public opinion polls and telecommunications, the House transmitted public attitudes to government. This function required frequent elections and relatively small constituencies, offering voters their most direct opportunity to influence government by retaining incumbents or replacing them with newcomers. By extension, legislation passed by a majority in the House of Representatives would reflect the wishes of the majority of the people.

The Senate   The Senate is a holdover from the Articles of Confederation. Defenders of less-populous states demanded this concession as one of their prices for supporting the new Constitution. Whereas the House represents "the people" or the majority, the Senate can be thought of as representing the needs of the individual states.

In the Senate each state is represented equally, regardless of population. Each state has two senators, so that today there are 100 senators in all. Only through equal representation could the interests of the less-populous states be balanced against those of the more-populous ones. Today the Senate's design serves to protect the political interests of the many states with relatively small populations, particularly those in the upper Midwest and Rocky Mountain regions. In doing so, it acts as a counterweight to the more urban and suburban majorities found in the House.

The Constitution originally decreed that senators would be selected by "the legislatures thereof," not by the people directly (Article I, Section 3). The "people" as such were already represented directly in the House. What is more, "the people" might have short-term political interests contrary to those of their own state governments. As we saw in Box 2.1, scholars such as historian Charles Beard argue that the Senate in particular (and the Constitution in general) was designed to protect powerful economic interests against the demands of the less-affluent majority. Whether this is true is a matter of some dispute, but it is clear that the original method of selection reflected the framers' fears about allowing the majority to govern unchecked. Sudden changes in public opinion would show up in the House every two years, a pace of change that was useful for taking the pulse of the electorate but unsuited for stable government—and stable government was seen as essential for economic stability. In this sense, the Senate exists to balance the demands of the mass public against the needs of the states, and by extension the nation.

Senators are no longer selected by state legislatures. The Seventeenth Amendment to the Constitution (ratified in 1913) requires that senators be elected directly by the people of the respective states. This change was prompted by the fact that in the late 1800s so many senators were openly controlled by powerful economic interests in their states. Direct election was seen as a way to ensure that senators represented the entire state, not just its more powerful residents.

Despite the change in the method of selecting senators, the Senate is not like the House. As the flag desecration case at the beginning of this chapter suggests, the Senate retains its status as a defender of the potentially unpopular views of the minority on some issue, as well as acting as a brake on rapid and potentially destabilizing change. One reason is the size and breadth of the states themselves, which encompass larger and more diverse constituencies than do the more compact and homogeneous House districts. As a result, senators tend to hold broader, less-localized views than do representatives.

More important are three rules affecting senatorial terms of office. First, senators serve for six years, a period equal to three House terms. This longer term is designed to insulate them somewhat from the momentary passions of the public and allow them to think more broadly about national needs. Second, each state's two senators are elected in different years. This ensures that the views or interests that led to the election of one senator will vary from those leading to the election of the other. It also explains why some states have senators from different political parties. Each Senate race is a distinct and independent event, so voters are assured that their two senators are unlikely to share the same views or partisan attachments. Finally, the election of senators is staggered so that only a third of the seats is up for election every two years. This provision makes the Senate a continuous and hence more stable body, whereas the House literally reconstitutes itself after every election.

Because of these differences, shifts in public opinion may not affect the Senate as directly or strongly as they affect the House. Voters cannot remove more than a third of the senators in any one election, nor are both senators from any single state vulnerable at the same time. These mechanisms enable a healthy minority to slow things down, at least in the short run. If change is to sweep through the Senate, it must stem from more than the passions of the moment: It must be long-term, maybe irreversible change. These essential differences between the two chambers of Congress have a major influence on the kinds of laws that can be enacted at any one moment.

The Presidency   Whereas the House represents the people (or majority) and the Senate represents the states, the president was meant to represent the nation as a whole. Selection of the president, who would serve for a four-year term, was not left up to Congress because such a procedure would undermine the separation of powers. However, the framers did not want the president to be elected directly by the people. They feared that the people would elect leaders whose goals were fueled by the passions of the moment or by the need to cater to public whims.

The Constitution therefore provided for the selection of the president by an **electoral college** made up of electors selected by the states. The framers did not specify how the states were to select the electors, although originally the task was usually left to state legislatures. These electors, who would be chosen ideally for their wisdom and virtue, would cast votes for two people whom they deemed best qualified to serve as president; the person who received an absolute majority (i.e., one more than half) of all the electoral votes would be named president. The second-place finisher became the vice president, who would preside over the Senate and would become president if the sitting president were to die, resign, or be removed from office. If nobody won the required majority of electoral votes, the names of the top five electoral-vote winners would go to the House of Representatives. There each *state* would have one vote, with the candidate receiving the most votes becoming president.

The electoral college worked as intended for a few elections, but the framers did not anticipate that the emergence of strong political parties would undermine the system. In 1800, Thomas Jefferson and Aaron Burr ran as the presidential and vice-presidential candidates of Jefferson's "Republican-Democratic" party (the predecessor of today's Democratic party), but they each received the same number of electoral votes. The electors had no way to indicate on the ballot which of the two men should be president, and out of party loyalty they refused to prevent a tie by voting for other candidates. The deadlock threw the election into the House of Representatives, which finally elected Jefferson after 36 ballots.

The Twelfth Amendment to the Constitution, ratified in 1804, sought to remedy the problem by having electors clearly designate their choices for president and vice president. If no candidate received the required majority of electoral votes, the names of the top three vote winners would go into the House, where each state still would have one vote.

Today the candidate who wins the popular vote in each state also wins its electoral votes. Nevertheless, the election of the president still depends on winning a majority of electoral votes. As we will discuss further in chapter 6, no one can be elected president without mounting a credible national campaign in order to win the popular vote in enough states to get the requisite number of electoral votes. The election of the president thus is a national event and requires a national majority.

The Federal Judiciary   Article III of the Constitution specifically creates a Supreme Court, leaving it to Congress to create lower federal courts as needed. The federal judiciary was created to try offenses under federal law, to resolve disputes between the states and between the states and the federal government, and, even, to settle legal disputes between Congress and the president. It was not viewed as a particularly important branch. However, as we will see in chapter 11, over time the Supreme Court evolved into an institution that serves to defend the Constitution against the momentary passions of the public and the political intrigues of elites. A system of governance based on a constitution ultimately requires someone to interpret the terms of that higher law, and the Supreme Court evolved to fulfill this role.

The framers tried to insulate the federal judiciary from public opinion. This is achieved through a selection process in which the president nominates the justices, who are then confirmed or rejected by the Senate. The House of Representatives, the barometer of public opinion, plays no direct role in selecting federal judges, indicating the degree to which the framers wanted the courts to be free from political influences. The Constitution also protects federal judges from political pressures by granting them terms of office for "good behavior"—that is, for life—and forbids Congress from reducing their salaries while they are in office. These provisions are intended to allow federal judges to act in defense of the Constitution no matter how controversial or unpopular their actions. Like presidents, federal judges can be removed from office only through the highly cumbersome process of impeachment, discussed in the next section.

RIGID TERMS OF OFFICE

Members of Congress and the president have rigid terms of office. House members serve for two years, senators for six, and the president for four. This means that presidents and members of Congress truly are stuck with one another for at least the two-year cycle of the House of Representatives. As noted earlier, the fact that federal judges have terms for life shows that the framers of the Constitution wanted to insulate the judiciary from everyday political pressures.

The Constitution originally did not limit the number of terms the president or any member of Congress may serve. However, the Twenty-second Amendment to the Constitution, ratified in 1951, limits presidents to two four-year terms (although a vice president who takes office upon the death, resignation, or removal of the president technically can serve up to 10 years). The impetus for this amendment was the four-term presidency of Franklin Roosevelt (who served from 1933 until his death in 1945), after which many Americans decided to put into law the tradition of two terms

The Senate impeach-
ment trial of President
William Jefferson Clin-
ton, February, 1999.
Chief Justice William
Rehnquist presides, the
House members prose-
cuting the case are to his
right, and the president's
attorneys are to his left.
Clinton was acquitted of
all charges brought
against him by the
House.

that goes back to George Washington. However, efforts to pass a constitutional amendment imposing term limits on members of Congress have not been successful, so members of Congress may serve as long as voters reelect them.

On the other side of the coin, Congress cannot remove a president who is merely unpopular or ineffective. Barring some kind of physical or mental disability (in which case a president can be relieved of office under the provisions set down in the Twenty-fifth Amendment), the only legal way to remove a president from office be-tween elections is through the process of **impeachment.** In this process, the House of Representatives passes articles of impeachment that accuse the president of "trea-son, bribery, or other high crimes and misdemeanors" (Article II, Section 4). The Senate then acts as a trial court, and the president can be removed from office if two-thirds of the senators present vote for conviction. The Senate has held such a trial only twice: in 1868, when it acquitted President Andrew Johnson of defying the will of Congress, and in 1999, when it acquitted President Bill Clinton of charges of per-jury and obstruction of justice (see chapter 9).

The framers made it difficult for Congress to remove a president, but they made it impossible for a president to remove members of Congress. Thus, Congress and the president are forced to work together. Compromise is the only alternative to stalemate, at least until the next election.

CHECKS AND BALANCES

To ensure further that governing power is kept in check, the framers devised a set of **checks and balances** that force the branches, particularly Congress and the presi-dency, to cooperate if anything important is to be done. In this way the Constitution actually institutionalizes conflict by giving each branch the limited capacity to block actions by the others. In doing so, it encourages friction among the branches, making it more difficult for any single branch or political faction to gain too much power.

This process is especially visible when it comes to lawmaking. No bill emerges from Congress unless it has been approved in exactly the same form by both chambers. And no bill passed by Congress can become law unless it is approved by the president. This ensures that the needs of the nation or the protection of minority rights are balanced against the possibly short-term imperatives of a legislative majority. What is more, the president can *veto*, or refuse to approve a bill, but this power is not absolute. A vetoed bill must be returned to Congress, which then has an opportunity to enact the bill into law by a two-thirds majority vote of both houses. The president cannot circumvent this process by not acting: If left unsigned, bills become law automatically after 10 legislative days, unless Congress has adjourned at the end of the two-year House session (see chapter 8).

The Constitution's balancing act does not end here. The federal judiciary has developed the power of *judicial review* (see chapter 11). This is the power to declare invalid—that is, without constitutional justification—laws passed by Congress or actions taken by the president if those laws or actions run contrary to the letter or spirit of the Constitution. In this way the courts can block a legislative majority or the political desires of a president. But decisions by the courts can also be counteracted. If Congress is dissatisfied with a court's interpretation of a statute it can pass a new one, thereby resolving the conflict over the law's meaning. However, in cases dealing with the fundamental meaning of the Constitution, Congress can respond only by proposing a constitutional amendment that, if ratified, would overturn the Supreme Court's ruling.

CHANGING THE CONSTITUTION

The Constitution is the supreme law of the land, but it was not meant to be immutable. The people, through Congress and the states, have the right to change their form of government as they deem necessary or desirable, particularly if the change makes for more effective and accountable government. But, as Jefferson warned in the Declaration of Independence, changes in the fundamental design of government must not be made in haste or too easily. To do so would be to invite rashness or tyranny. Thus, Article V requires that any amendment to the Constitution be added only after a complex and difficult process.

Proposing Amendments   Amendments to the Constitution can be proposed in two ways: (1) Congress can propose a constitutional amendment by a two-thirds vote of each chamber, or (2) two-thirds of the states can call for a constitutional convention to propose amendments. The second option has never been used, although in the late 1990s supporters of a constitutional amendment to require a balanced federal budget have come close to winning the approval of the minimum number of states necessary to call a convention. Whether such a convention will actually be called is anyone's guess. For one thing, in the 1990s Congress and the president worked together to balance the federal budget, which in 1998 showed a surplus for the first time in 30 years. This took some of the steam out of the effort to pass a constitutional amendment. What is more, history suggests that Congress often responds to repeated calls for a convention by passing the amendment in question. Such was the case with the Seventeenth Amendment, which mandated direct election of senators.

Ratifying Amendments Proposed amendments are sent to the states for ratification, either by the state legislatures or by special state ratifying conventions, whichever method Congress chooses. Congress can also specify a "reasonable" time limit for ratification: since the early 1960s a seven-year time limit has become the norm.[21]

Even so, an accident of history gave the Constitution the Twenty-seventh Amendment, ratified in 1992. This amendment, which regulates when pay raises for Congress can go into effect, was one of the 12 amendments originally sent to the states by Congress in 1789. Ten of those amendments were ratified by 1791 and became the Bill of Rights. But Congress imposed no time limit on ratification, so the Twenty-seventh Amendment became valid when it was ratified over 200 years later. Whether other similarly "lost" amendments might gain much-delayed ratification is unknown, but possible.

Amendments become part of the Constitution if they are ratified by three-quarters of the state legislatures or state ratifying conventions. Only the Twenty-first Amendment (1933), which repealed the prohibition of liquor mandated by the Eighteenth Amendment (1919), was ratified using state conventions. This came about because proponents of repeal knew that state legislatures were heavily influenced by groups supporting anti-liquor (or "dry") interests.

Impacts of the Amendment Process The amendment process is laborious, and only a few of the literally thousands of amendments suggested have ever been formally proposed, much less actually ratified. Most of the amendments that have been ratified since 1789 have either modified government processes (e.g., direct election of senators) or extended equal political rights to certain segments of society (e.g., adults under 21) that were not mentioned explicitly when the original document was approved. It is no surprise, then, that it is easier (and, for some, preferable) to "change" the meaning or application of constitutional provisions through new judicial interpretations than through the amendment process.

Critics argue that the difficulty of amending the Constitution prevents changes from being made when they are deemed necessary or desirable by a majority of the people. They point to the failure of the Equal Rights Amendment (see chapter 4) and various abortion-related amendments as evidence that the process allows entrenched minorities to veto the wishes of the majority. For their part, defenders of the amendment process argue that any changes in the supreme law of the land *should* have the support of a supermajority. They point out that the only amendment that was has ever been repealed—the one prohibiting the manufacture or sale of liquor—was itself a failed attempt to change social behavior through constitutional mechanisms.

That so few amendments have been ratified in over 200 years, and that most of them deal with procedures or political rights, testifies to the wariness with which the framers approached the issue of changing the form or nature of government. Their experiences with British rule and with the Articles of Confederation predisposed them to make it possible for citizens to change their government when it no longer governed effectively or protected the natural rights of the people. Changes in the Constitution, however, should not be made for frivolous or fleeting purposes, nor should it be easy for a simple majority or even a vocal minority to prevail on such important matters. Thus, without a broad consensus among many sectors of the public, it is unlikely that an amendment banning desecration of the flag, for instance, will be passed. To the framers of the Constitution, such a stalemate was preferable to the possibility of tyranny.

CONCLUSION

Americans wonder why Congress and the president always seem to be fighting. The answer is simple, if surprising: Conflict is built into the Constitution. "Ambition must be made to counteract ambition," wrote James Madison in *Federalist* No. 51. He was referring to the need for checks and balances to prevent Congress from enacting laws against the will of the people, and to prevent the president from behaving like a king.[22] The Constitution forces citizens with differing views to cooperate long enough to get things done. Conflict between the branches of government, and even between the two chambers of Congress, is guaranteed regardless of which political party controls Congress and the presidency.

By creating conflict, the Constitution also creates the need to seek compromise. As we will see in chapter 8, no law can pass through Congress, much less gain approval from the president, without compromises that balance the views of the majority with those who disagree. Of course, there are times when a decisive majority has the votes to overwhelm any opposition, but such situations are rare in American politics. So seeking compromise is the normal dynamic in American politics, one that is difficult even in the best of times. On especially divisive issues, such as abortion, it is almost impossible.

In a sense the constitutional system reinforces the natural differences of opinion or desires that separate groups of people. The framers were worried about the potential for tyranny by a majority, so in the Constitution they made it difficult to build and maintain a strong governing majority. The Constitution actually breaks up potential majorities into smaller and possibly less-dangerous pieces: Citizens are divided into states and congressional districts; Congress itself is split into two often-competing chambers; and separation of powers guarantees that no single branch of government can hold all power. Thus, a relative minority in the Senate can hold up legislation passed by the House, just as a president can veto a bill passed by Congress, or the Supreme Court can declare a law unconstitutional. In each case a minority has checked a majority, forcing the majority to negotiate if it wants to get anything done.

The framers instituted these safeguards because they were afraid that an unchecked majority might pass hasty or ill-considered laws. The short-term passions of the House were to be "cooled" by the more deliberate pace of the Senate; the possibly expensive or hasty demands of a congressional majority were to be moderated by the president's veto power; and even popular laws might be struck down by the courts if they went against the spirit or letter of the Constitution.

This whole process also slows the pace of change. The greater the change intended, the more controversial the issue at hand, the greater the framers' concern that change might disrupt the society or harm the basic rights and liberties of the people. Rapid change can cause insecurity and undermine social stability. Change cannot be stopped, but it can be slowed down in order to ensure that as many citizens as possible can play a part in shaping its direction and extent.

A government that runs according to consensus-building, not by simple majority rule, is a government that seeks stability. Change comes, but it is more evolutionary than revolutionary. Change might come more slowly than many might like, but when it does come it is likely to be more acceptable to more people, more likely to be seen as the legitimate will of the people rather than the whim of some momentary majority or the dictate of some remote elite.

For the citizen, then, the practical effects of the Constitution are these: In normal times, when there is no great crisis to mobilize the people behind a single cause, change in the American political system comes slowly. It is the product not of sweeping temporary majorities but of the often frustrating process of knitting together workable compromises from a great many competing interests. Without compromise, nothing gets done, especially on controversial issues, because the system makes it relatively easy for one group of Americans to stop others, even a majority, from getting their way easily or completely. The system itself forces Americans to work together.

SUMMARY

▶ The Constitution is the nation's supreme law. The form of government created by it reflects the values, fears, and experiences of a selected group of leaders at a specific time in history. Above all, the American constitutional system was based on the belief that people could analyze and solve a particularly difficult problem: how to achieve government that was both effective *and* remain accountable to the people.

▶ The Constitution is a product of many compromises. Some reflected longstanding political tensions between the more-populated states and the less-populated ones. Others reflected fundamental disagreements about the proper role of the national government versus the states. Still others, such as the dispute over the continuation of slavery, grew out of more basic economic needs or cultural biases. Overall, however, the Constitution's contents reflected the real need to find compromises that would help attain the ultimate goal: a workable national government.

▶ The Constitution shapes the workings of American government and politics. Through the concept of federalism, it grants explicit powers to the national government but reserves important powers to the various states. Through its formal separation of powers, it forces the branches of government to work together in order to accomplish anything. Through separate means of election and terms of office, it makes Congress and the president independent of each other, and thus forces them to cooperate. Through an array of formal checks and balances, it guarantees conflict and makes it difficult for any single group to control power with ease.

▶ Above all, the Constitution was meant to provide for a government that could work, but one that still preserved the basic rights and liberties of all the people. That fundamental tension between effectiveness and accountability is a perpetual one.

QUESTIONS FOR REVIEW AND DISCUSSION

1. Are written constitutions necessary to the maintenance of democratic government? Explain.

2. What were the political and philosophical issues at the heart of the rebellion against England?

3. Why did government under the Articles of Confederation fail?

4. What were the major political and ideological conflicts that marked the drafting and ratification of the Constitution?

5. Discuss the major features of the constitutional system, particularly federalism, separation of powers, and checks and balances.

TERMS TO REMEMBER

authoritarian regime	Connecticut Compromise	impeachment
bicameral	constitution	New Jersey Plan
Bill of Rights	electoral college	separation of powers
checks and balances	federalism	Virginia Plan

WEB SOURCES

Citizens' Flag Alliance (www.cfa-inc.org). A network of groups dedicated to persuading Congress to pass a constitutional amendment to allow for prohibitions against physical desecration of the American flag.

Library of Congress (www.loc.gov). The Library of Congress is the world's largest library. This site contains a wide variety of resources on every aspect of American society, history, and government, as well as links to the library's massive on-line catalog. A great place for any bibliographic research.

National Archives and Records Administration (www.nara.gov). The official site of the National Archives contains a wealth of historical information on the drafting of the Declaration of Independence and the Constitution, as well as images of the documents.

SUGGESTED READINGS

Michael Kammen, *A Machine That Would Go of Itself: The Constitution in American Culture* (New York: Knopf, 1986). A thought-provoking exploration of the sometimes surprising, and not always positive cultural impacts of the Constitution on American politics in the 200 years since its creation.

Pauline Maier, *American Scripture: The Making of the Declaration of Independence* (New York: Knopf, 1997). Shows how the Declaration was based in part on many previously enacted local declarations of independence, how its language was crafted, and how it eventually evolved into the "sacred" American text.

Forrest McDonald, *Novus Ordo Seclorum: The Intellectual Origins of the Constitution* (Lawrence: University Press of Kansas, 1985). A thorough examination of the political and economic turbulence of the 1780s, as well as an effective re-creation of the intellectual debates that marked the drafting of the Constitution.

Herbert Storing and Murray Dry, *What the Anti-Federalists Were For* (Chicago: University of Chicago Press, 1981). The final work by the preeminent 20th-century scholar on the anti-Federalists; states in brief the guiding principles of those who opposed the ratification of the new constitution, particularly their belief that power should be decentralized in order to avoid tyranny.

NOTES

1. "Plan to Ban Flag Desecration Wins Bipartisan Vote in House," *Congressional Quarterly Weekly Report*, vol. 55, no. 24 (June 14, 1997), p. 1380; "Legislative Review: Flag Desecration," *Congressional Quarterly Weekly Report*, vol. 55, no. 45 (November, 14, 1998), pp. 3116–3117.

2. *Texas v Johnson*, 491 US 397 (1989); *United States v Eichman*, 496 US 310 (1990).

3. Jack Greene, "The Origins of American Constitutionalism," in A. E. Dick Howard, ed., *The United States Constitution: Roots, Rights, and Responsibilities* (Washington, D.C.: Smithsonian Institution Press, 1992), p. 36.

4. Pauline Maier, *American Scripture: Making the Declaration of Independence* (New York: Knopf, 1997), p. 99.

5. Jack W. Peltason, *Understanding the Constitution*, 12th ed. (New York: Holt, Rinehart, and Winston, 1992), p. 7.

6. Maier, *American Scripture*, pp. 146–147.

7. John Locke, *The Second Treatise on Civil Government* (Indianapolis, IN: Bobbs-Merrill, 1952; originally published in 1690), pp. 4–11.

8. Merrill D. Peterson, "The Idea of a Written Constitution in the Thought of the Founders: The Organization of Consent," in Howard, ed., *The United States Constitution: Roots, Rights, and Responsibilities*, p. 48.

9. Thomas Hobbes, *The Leviathan*, J. C. A. Gaskin, ed. (New York: Oxford University Press, 1996; originally published in 1651).

10. Greene, "The Origins of American Constitutionalism," p. 23.

11. Richard B. Bernstein, with Kym S. Rice, Are We to Be a Nation? *The Making of the Constitution* (Cambridge, MA: Harvard University Press, 1987), p. 1.

12. Warren Burger, "Foreword," in Howard, ed., *The United States Constitution: Roots, Rights, and Responsibilities*, p. xii.

13. Alexander Hamilton, James Madison, and John Jay, *Federalist* No. 51, in Clinton Rossiter, ed., *The Federalist Papers* (New York: New American Library, 1961) p. 322.

14. John P. Roche, "The Founding Fathers: A Reform Caucus in Action," *The American Political Science Review*, vol. 55, no. 3 (1961), pp. 799–816.

15. As cited in Max Farrand, ed., *The Records of the Federal Convention of 1787*, 2d. ed. (revised edition, 1937; reprint, New Haven, CT: Yale University Press, 1966), vol. 1, pp. 404–405.

16. Bert A. Rockman, *The Leadership Question: The Presidency and the American System* (New York: Praeger, 1984).

17. As cited in Farrand, *The Records of the Federal Constitution of 1787*, vol. 2, pp. 641–643.

18. As argued by Alexander Hamilton in *Federalist* No. 84, p. 513.

19. Judith Shklar, "A New Constitution for a New Nation," in Howard, ed., *The United States Constitution: Roots, Rights, and Responsibilities*, pp. 131–132.

20. Richard Neustadt, *Presidential Power and Modern Presidents: The Politics of Leadership from Roosevelt to Reagan* (New York: Free Press, 1990).

21. Peltason, *Understanding the Constitution*, p. 155.

22. *Federalist* No. 51, p. 322.

PRIMARY SOURCE READINGS

JAMES MADISON

Federalist: No. 51: The Structure of the Government Must Furnish the Proper Checks and Balances between the Different Departments

From the New York Packet, *Friday, February 8, 1788.*

To the People of the State of New York:

TO WHAT expedient, then, shall we finally resort, for maintaining in practice the necessary partition of power among the several departments, as laid down in the Constitution? The only answer that can be given is, that as all these exterior provisions are found to be inadequate, the defect must be supplied, by so contriving the interior structure of the government as that its several constituent parts may, by their mutual relations, be the means of keeping each other in their proper places. Without presuming to undertake a full development of this important idea, I will hazard a few general observations, which may perhaps place it in a clearer light, and enable us to form a more correct judgment of the principles and structure of the government planned by the convention.

In order to lay a due foundation for that separate and distinct exercise of the different powers of government, which to a certain extent is admitted on all hands to be essential to the preservation of liberty, it is evident that each department should have a will of its own; and consequently should be so constituted that the members of each should have as little agency as possible in the appointment of the members of the others. Were this principle rigorously adhered to, it would require that all the appointments for the supreme executive, legislative, and judiciary magistracies should be drawn from the same fountain of authority, the people, through channels having no communication whatever with one another. Perhaps such a plan of constructing the several departments would be less difficult in practice than it may in contemplation appear. Some difficulties, however, and some additional expense would attend the execution of it. Some deviations, therefore, from the principle must be admitted. In the constitution of the judiciary department in particular, it might be inexpedient to insist rigorously on the principle: first, because peculiar qualifications being essential in the members, the primary consideration ought to be to select that mode of choice which best secures these qualifications; secondly, because the permanent tenure by which the appointments are held in that department, must soon destroy all sense of dependence on the authority conferring them.

It is equally evident, that the members of each department should be as little dependent as possible on those of the others, for the emoluments annexed to their offices. Were the executive magistrate, or the judges, not independent of the legislature in this particular, their independence in every other would be merely nominal. But the great security against a gradual concentration of the several powers in the same department, consists in giving to those who administer each department the necessary constitutional means and personal motives to resist encroachments of the others. The provision for defense must in this, as in all other cases, be made commensurate to the danger of attack. Ambition must be made to counteract ambition. The interest of the man must be connected with the constitutional rights of the place. It may be a reflection on human nature, that such devices should be necessary to control the abuses of government. But what is government itself, but the greatest of all reflections on human nature? If men were angels, no government would be necessary. If angels were to govern men, neither external nor internal controls on government would be necessary. In framing a government which is to be administered by men over men, the great difficulty lies in this: you must first enable the government to control the governed; and in the next place oblige it to control itself.

A dependence on the people is, no doubt, the primary control on the government; but experience has taught mankind the necessity of auxiliary precautions. This policy of supplying, by opposite and rival interests, the defect of better motives, might be traced through the whole system of human affairs, private as well as public. We see it particularly displayed in all the subordinate distributions of power, where the constant aim is to divide and arrange the several offices in such a manner as that each may be a check on the other that the private interest of every individual may be a sentinel over the public rights. These inventions of prudence cannot be less requisite in the distribution of the supreme powers of the State. But it is not possible to give to each department an equal power of self-defense. In republican government, the legislative authority necessarily predominates. The remedy for this inconveniency is to divide the legislature into different branches; and to render them, by different modes of election and different principles of action, as little connected with each other as the nature of their common functions and their common dependence on the society will admit. It may even be necessary to guard against dangerous encroachments by still further precautions. As the weight of the legislative authority requires that it should be thus divided, the weakness of the executive may require, on the other hand, that it should be fortified.

An absolute negative on the legislature appears, at first view, to be the natural defense with which the executive magistrate should be armed. But perhaps it would be neither altogether safe nor alone sufficient. On ordinary occasions it might not be exerted with the requisite firmness, and on extraordinary occasions it might be perfidiously abused. May not this defect of an absolute negative be supplied by some qualified connection between this weaker department and the weaker branch of the stronger department, by which the latter may be led to support the constitutional rights of the former, without being too much detached from the rights of its own department? If the principles on which these observations are founded be just, as I persuade myself they are, and they be applied as a criterion to the several State constitutions, and to the federal Constitution it will be found that if the latter does not perfectly correspond with them, the former are infinitely less able to bear such a test.

There are, moreover, two considerations particularly applicable to the federal system of America, which place that system in a very interesting point of view. First. In a single republic, all the power surrendered by the people is submitted to the administration of a single government; and the usurpations are guarded against by a division of the government into distinct and separate departments. In the compound republic of America, the power surrendered by the people is first divided between two distinct governments, and then the portion allotted to each subdivided among distinct and separate departments. Hence a double security arises to the rights of the people. The different governments will control each other, at the same time that each will be controlled by itself. Second. It is of great importance in a republic not only to guard the society against the oppression of its rulers, but to guard one part of the society against the injustice of the other part. Different interests necessarily exist in different classes of citizens. If a majority be united by a common interest, the rights of the minority will be insecure.

There are but two methods of providing against this evil: the one by creating a will in the community independent of the majority that is, of the society itself; the other, by comprehending in the society so many separate descriptions of citizens as will render an unjust combination of a majority of the whole very improbable, if not impracticable. The first method prevails in all governments possessing an hereditary or self-appointed authority. This, at best, is but a precarious security; because a power independent of the society may as well espouse the unjust views of the major, as the rightful interests of the minor party, and may possibly be turned against both parties. The second method will be exemplified in the federal republic of the United States. Whilst all authority in it will be derived from and dependent on the society, the society itself will be broken into so many parts, interests, and classes of citizens, that the rights of individuals, or of the minority, will be in little danger from interested combinations of the majority.

In a free government the security for civil rights must be the same as that for religious rights. It consists in the one case in the multiplicity of interests, and in the other in the multiplicity of sects. The degree of security in both cases will depend on the number of interests and sects; and this may be presumed to depend on the extent of country and number of people comprehended under the same government. This view of the subject must particularly recommend a proper federal system to all the sincere and considerate friends of republican government, since it shows that in exact proportion as the territory of the Union may be formed into more circumscribed Confederacies, or States oppressive combinations of a majority will be facilitated: the best security, under the republican forms, for the rights of every class of citizens, will be diminished: and consequently the stability and independence of some member of the government, the only other security, must be proportionately increased. Justice is the end of government. It is the end of civil society. It ever has been and ever will be pursued until it be obtained, or until liberty be lost in the pursuit. In a society under the forms of which the stronger faction can readily unite and oppress the weaker, anarchy may as truly be said to reign as in a state of nature, where the weaker individual is not secured against the violence of the stronger; and as, in the latter state, even the stronger individuals are prompted, by the uncertainty of their condition, to submit to a government which may protect the weak as well as themselves; so, in the former state, will the more powerful factions or parties be gradually induced, by a like motive, to wish for a government which will protect all parties, the weaker as well as the more powerful.

It can be little doubted that if the State of Rhode Island was separated from the Confederacy and left to itself, the insecurity of rights under the popular form of government within such narrow limits would be displayed by such reiterated oppressions of factious majorities that some power altogether independent of the people would soon be called for by the voice of the very factions whose misrule had proved the necessity of it. In the extended republic of the United States, and among the great variety of interests, parties, and sects which it embraces, a coalition of a majority of the whole society could seldom take place on any other principles than those of justice and the general good; whilst there being thus less danger to a minor from the will of a major party, there must be less pretext, also, to provide for the security of the former, by introducing into the government a will not dependent on the latter, or, in other words, a will independent of the society itself. It is no less certain than it is important, notwithstanding the contrary opinions which have been entertained, that the larger the society, provided it lie within a practical sphere, the more duly capable it will be of self-government. And happily for the REPUBLICAN CAUSE, the practicable sphere may be carried to a very great extent, by a judicious modification and mixture of the FEDERAL PRINCIPLE.

—PUBLIUS.

THE DECLARATION OF SENTIMENTS
Seneca Falls Conference, 1848

On July 19–20, 1848, nearly 100 men and women met in Seneca Falls, New York, to discuss the lack of political, social, and economic equality for women. Led by Elizabeth Cady Stanton (1815–1902), the conference drafted and approved a "Declaration of Sentiments" modeled openly on the Declaration of Independence. Compare the text here with that in the Declaration, located in the appendix of this book.

When, in the course of human events, it becomes necessary for one portion of the family of man to assume among the people of the earth a position different from that which they have hitherto occupied, but one to which the laws of nature and of nature's God entitle them, a decent respect to the opinions of mankind requires that they should declare the causes that impel them to such a course.

We hold these truths to be self-evident: that all men and women are created equal; that they are endowed by their Creator with certain inalienable rights; that among these are life, liberty, and the pursuit of happiness; that to secure these rights governments are instituted, deriving their just powers from the consent of the governed. Whenever any form of government becomes destructive of these ends, it is the right of those who suffer from it to refuse allegiance to it, and to insist upon the institution of a new government, laying its foundation on such principles, and organizing its powers in such form, as to them shall seem most likely to effect their safety and happiness. Prudence, indeed, will dictate that governments long established should not be changed for light and transient causes; and accordingly all experience hath shown that mankind are more disposed to suffer, while evils are sufferable, than to right themselves by abolishing the forms to which they are accustomed. But when a long train of abuses and usurpations, pursuing invariably the same object, evinces a design to reduce them under absolute despotism, it is their duty to throw off such government, and to provide new guards for their future security. Such has been the patient sufferance of the women under this government, and such is now the necessity which constrains them to demand the equal station to which they are entitled.

The history of mankind is a history of repeated injuries and usurpations on the part of man toward woman, having in direct object the establishment of an absolute tyranny over her. To prove this, let facts be submitted to a candid world.

He has never permitted her to exercise her inalienable right to the elective franchise.

He has compelled her to submit to laws, in the formation of which she had no voice.

He has withheld from her rights which are given to the most ignorant and degraded men—both natives and foreigners.

Having deprived her of this first right of a citizen, the elective franchise, thereby leaving her without representation in the halls of legislation, he has oppressed her on all sides.

He has made her, if married, in the eye of the law, civilly dead.

He has taken from her all right in property, even to the wages she earns.

He has made her, morally, an irresponsible being, as she can commit many crimes with impunity, provided they be done in the presence of her husband. In the covenant of marriage, she is compelled to promise obedience to her husband, he becoming, to all intents and purposes, her master—the law giving him power to deprive her of her liberty, and to administer chastisement.

He has so framed the laws of divorce, as to what shall be the proper causes, and in case of separation, to whom the guardianship of the children shall be given, as to be wholly regardles of the happiness of women—the law, in all cases, going upon a false supposition of the supremacy of man, and giving all power into his hands.

After depriving her of all rights as a married woman, if single, and the owner of property, he has taxed her to support a government which recognizes her only when her property can be made profitable to it.

He has monopolized nearly all the profitable employments, and from those she is permitted to follow, she receives but a scanty remuneration. He closes against her all the avenues to wealth and distinction which he considers most homorable to himself. As a teacher of theology, medicine, or law, she is not known.

He has denied her the facilities for obtaining a thorough education, all colleges being closed against her.

He allows her in church, as well as state, but a suborinate position, claiming apostolic authority for her exclusion from the ministry, and, with some exceptions, from any public participation in the affairs of the church.

He has created a false public sentiment by giving to the world a different code of morals for men and women, by which moral delinquencies which exclude women from society, are not only tolerated, but deemed of little account in man.

He has usurped the prerogative of Jehovah himself, claiming it as his right to assign for her a sphere of action, when that belongs to her conscience and to her God.

He has endeavored, in every way that he could, to destroy her conficence in her own powers, to lessen her self-respect, and to make her willing to lead a dependent and abject life.

Now, in view of this entire disfranchisement of one-half the people of this country, their social and religious degradation—in view of the unjust laws above mentioned, and because women do feel themselves aggrieved, oppressed, and fraudulently deprived of their most sacred rights, we insist that they have immediate admission to all the rights and privileges which belong to them as citizens of the United States. . . .

FEDERALISM

One Nation, Many Governments

THE NATURE OF FEDERALISM
A BALANCING ACT
A CONFUSING SYSTEM
A PRACTICAL SOLUTION
THE IMPORTANCE OF THE STATES
DIVIDING POWER AND RESPONSIBILITY

FEDERAL POWERS AND RESPONSIBILITIES
ENUMERATED POWERS
IMPLIED POWERS
INHERENT POWERS
FEDERAL GUARANTEES TO THE STATES
THE CONSTITUTION AND NATIONAL SUPREMACY

POWERS AND RESPONSIBILITIES OF THE STATES
CONCURRENT POWERS
RESERVED POWERS
RELATIONS BETWEEN STATES

THE STRUGGLE OVER FEDERALISM
STATES' RIGHTS AND NATIONALIST PERSPECTIVES
THE GROWTH OF NATIONAL POWER

AN EVOLVING PARTNERSHIP

BENEFITS AND COSTS OF FEDERALISM
BENEFITS
COSTS

OBJECTIVES

❑ To examine why the United States has a federal system of government and how federalism was a practical answer to the problem of providing effective and responsive government for such a large country

❑ To show how the Constitution allocates power and responsibility between the national government and the various states, and to understand that the framers left many controversial matters unsettled or vague, forcing later generations to struggle over the relative powers of the national and state governments

❑ To discuss the critical struggle over the meaning of federalism throughout American history, and to understand why the power of the national government increased during the 20th century

❑ To examine the benefits and costs of federalism

Burying radioactive waste. Like other unpleasant by-products of modern life, such waste must go somewhere. How such burdens are apportioned, and who will bear them, are major issues within the federal system.

When people think of radioactive waste, they usually conjure up images of spent uranium fuel rods immersed in huge pools beside nuclear power plants, or decommissioned warheads buried somewhere in the desert. Either way, they think of "high-level" radioactive waste, stuff that is so dangerous to human beings that governments must take considerable care in its processing and disposal.

Most radioactive waste, it turns out, has nothing to do with nuclear power plants or atomic warheads. Most of it is "low-level" waste generated by industries, hospitals, universities, and research centers engaged in all kinds of important commercial, medical, and academic work. Chances are that most people are regularly exposed to some kind of low-level radioactivity, if only an X ray during an annual dental exam. Whatever people think about nuclear power, few argue about the benefits society derives from products that leave behind low levels of radioactive waste.

These benefits of the nuclear age produce their own problems, chief among them the problem of disposal. For instance, old X rays are still radioactive and should not be tossed into the trash casually. This waste needs to be disposed of separately and with far greater care.

Before the 1980s most of this waste was handled by commercial haulers, which buried the waste in large trenches scattered around the country. By 1980, however, the volume of low-level radioactive waste was increasing dramatically at the same time that the number of available disposal sites had shrunk to only a few, located in South Carolina, Nevada, and Washington state. Concerns about the environmental and health risks posed by this waste grew, and residents of these states began to resist the idea of becoming dumps for the rest of the nation.[1]

State officials throughout the country disagreed about what to do. Some wanted the federal government to take total responsibility for the problem, arguing that only a national policy could resolve conflicts between the states over disposal standards and costs. Others argued that the states should continue to have primary control over the disposal problem. They wanted more direct control over waste disposal, especially if it involved waste from other states.

In 1980 Congress passed the Low-Level Radioactive Waste Policy Act. This law forged a compromise in which the federal government required each state to develop a policy for disposing of all radioactive waste generated within its borders but also granted the states primary control over the development of disposal facilities. States could go it alone, or they could form *compacts* (agreements) with other states in the same region. As an incentive, Congress allowed states that entered into a compact to keep out waste from states that were not part of the compact. Without this provision, states that established their own disposal sites might not be allowed to keep out waste from other states, because such unilateral action would violate constitutional prohibitions against interfering with interstate commerce—in this case, the trade in low-level radioactive waste.

Forming these compacts and establishing regional waste sites has proven to be difficult, time-consuming, and controversial. By 1985, 37 of the 50 states had entered into 7 separate compacts, but none of them were able to develop new disposal sites. Nobody wanted a low-level radioactive waste site in their area, no matter how much they were assured that the waste would pose no threats if handled properly.

Congress then amended the law and mandated that any state that did not identify a disposal site by 1996 had to assume full legal responsibility for all the low-level waste generated within that state. This provision was supposed to encourage the states to establish appropriate disposal facilities within their borders, but it only created more conflict. Eighteen states took the federal government to court, arguing that Congress did not have the authority to force them to keep all their own waste. The federal courts, which handle legal conflicts between the states and the federal government, agreed with the states and struck down the provision.

Today matters are pretty much at a standstill. Most of the interstate compacts have identified suitable disposal sites, but none have been constructed because of strong fear about possible environmental and health effects. Institutions that generate low-level radioactive waste continue to use existing disposal sites or store the wastes on their own property. A national policy exists, but it has proven difficult to implement. State compacts exist, but the states involved have found it hard to agree on appropriate sites, and no community wants a disposal site anyway.[2]

On the other hand, the volume of low-level radioactive waste has dropped significantly since the passage of the 1980 law, from nearly 4 million cubic feet in 1980 to about 400,000 in 1996.[3] Mounting concerns about the costs and potential dangers of disposal prompted most hospitals, universities, and businesses to reduce, reuse, or recycle their low-level radioactive materials as much as possible. Seeing this trend, many state officials question whether the nation needs a waste-disposal policy at all. In one sense at least, the conflicts among the states, and between the states and the federal government, may have produced the desired effect.

THE NATURE OF FEDERALISM

Look at the front of a one-dollar bill. Across the top is engraved in big letters, "The United States of America." The official name of the nation says a lot. Before there was *a* United States there were only the states, separate and often not united. The states distrusted one another, and they also feared a strong national government. As we saw in chapter 2, under the Articles of Confederation this condition undermined the government's ability to foster national unity or stability. The states' distrust of one another and their shared fear of national government power linger to some degree to this day. The case of low-level radioactive waste just discussed is but another version of political conflicts that are over two centuries old.

Few Americans fully understand the workings of federalism. The system is even more confusing to foreigners. The French aristocrat Alexis de Tocqueville, one of the more astute visitors to these shores, lamented the complexities of the American system:

> The first difficulty which presents itself arises from the complex nature of the Constitution of the United States, which consists of two distinct social structures, connected, and, as it were, encased one within the other; two governments, completely separate and almost independent, the one fulfilling the ordinary duties, and responding to the daily and indefinite calls of a community, the other circumscribed within certain limits, and only exercising an exceptional authority over the general interests of the country.[4]

Tocqueville was writing about the division of power and responsibility between the states and the national—or "federal"—government, a system devised by the framers of the Constitution (see chapter 2). In the 1830s, when he visited the United States, the nation had one of the world's more complicated systems of government. It still does. Moreover, American federalism is constantly changing. As we will see, in Tocqueville's day the national government was far more "circumscribed"—that is, limited—than it is today.

A BALANCING ACT

A federal system is an oddity. It isn't a **unitary system,** in which all power and responsibility are centralized in a national government. Tocqueville's native France was, and still is, a unitary system with power centered in the national government located in Paris, even though the specific type of government has changed from a monarchy to a republic.

Neither is federalism a **confederation,** in which power and responsibility are decentralized among many subnational governments, be they provinces, cantons, departments, or states. America under the Articles of Confederation was such a system. So was the Confederate States of America during the Civil War.

Federalism is a hybrid. It is neither pure centralization nor pure decentralization. In federalism neither the national government nor the states hold all power. In American federalism today the national government is supreme, especially in matters of national defense, but a great deal of power and responsibility remains in the hands of the states. Federalism thus is a system in which power and responsibility are divided among *and* shared by the national and subnational governments (see Box 3.1 on pages 90 and 91).

A CONFUSING SYSTEM

For citizens, this division of power and responsibility poses practical problems. Often it is not clear which government is responsible for which policy areas. In some areas, such as national defense, the federal government clearly runs the show, but in others there may be great variation from one state to another. For example, civil rights (such as ensuring the right to vote) typically are enforced on a national basis by the federal government. However, responsibility for primary education is in the hands of the states and, particularly, thousands of local school systems. In France, by contrast, all primary school curricula and rules are established by the national government. In a federal system, just knowing which government is in charge is a challenge.

Federalism also produces a confusing mixture of responsibility. Fighting crime, for example, generally is a responsibility for the states, yet today the national government also funds efforts to deter crime and determines the punishments for certain specific crimes. Some actions are crimes under state law, some under federal law, and in some cases both laws may apply. A person accused of assault (a state crime) can also be charged with a civil rights violation (a federal crime) if the assault was racially motivated. Furthermore, this mix of responsibilities and authority can change over time, depending on circumstances and demands by the public.

Compared to other systems, federalism is a complicated hybrid of national and state governments, each with its own powers and responsibilities (see Table 3.1, p. 91). The question is why any nation would develop such a system.

BOX 3.1.
FEDERAL, UNITARY, AND
CONFEDERATED SYSTEMS COMPARED

Federal: Power is distributed by a constitution between a national government and various subnational governments, such as states. The national government is not dependent on the states for its power, nor are the states subservient to the national government. Both enjoy a great deal of power and responsibility. For example, both have the power to tax and to spend money. The laws affecting citizens can vary quite a bit among the subnational governments but they generally stay within the boundaries provided by federal law. *Examples:* United States, Canada, Mexico, and Australia.

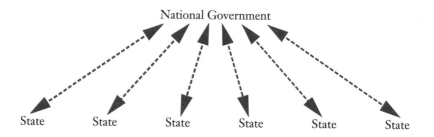

Unitary: Virtually all power and responsibility are in the hands of the national government. Subnational governments exist to carry out the mandates of the national government. They have limited power to tax and spend, and local laws affecting citizens are uniform throughout the nation. *Examples:* France, Japan, and Israel.

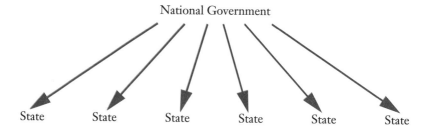

A CLOSER LOOK

Confederated: Power resides primarily with subnational governments, and the national government is kept highly constrained. Indeed, in a confederacy the national government may be dependent on the subnational governments for its powers and resources. The government under the Articles of Confederation, and the Confederacy during the Civil War period are American examples of confederation. *Example:* Switzerland.

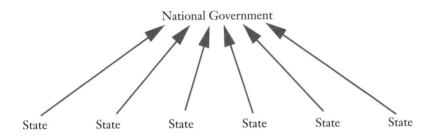

TABLE 3.1. NUMBER AND TYPES OF GOVERNMENTS IN THE UNITED STATES

Federal government	1
State governments	50
Local governments	
Counties	3,043
Municipalities (most of these are cities and towns)	19,269
Townships (mostly in Midwest; usually offer fewer services)	15,666
Special districts (entities such as sewer and water authorities, convention authorities)	33,131
School districts	14,556
Total local governments	86,693
Total number of governments	**86,744**

Source: Statistical Abstract of the United States, 1998 (Washington, D.C.: U.S. Department of Commerce, 1998).

A PRACTICAL SOLUTION

Suppose that the nation had emerged from its War of Independence without 13 separate states. Suppose that there had been no states at all in the 1780s. The course of American history might have been very different. The Civil War might never have happened. After all, the Confederate States of America—notice the name—seceded from the Union because people in the Confederate states believed strongly that individual states could negate or nullify laws passed by the federal government. However, people in the northern states believed equally strongly that the national government was supreme, and they fought to preserve the Union as they defined it. Other important issues, particularly slavery, were just parts of this fundamental conflict between defenders of "states' rights" and supporters of "national supremacy."

So American history might have been different. Even so, if states had not existed in 1781 when the War of Independence ended, the nation probably would have created them. In other words, the nation probably would still have a system in which power and responsibility are divided between a national government and some subnational governments.

One reason is straightforward. Even in the 1780s the nation was too big and spread out to be governed easily or effectively by a single government, especially one that was meant to be responsive to citizens. Means of communication and transportation were rudimentary and slow. Today the drive from New York to Philadelphia takes less than two hours, but in the 1780s the same journey took two days by stagecoach.[5] Federalism made it possible to govern this vast nation.

Today, even with modern telecommunications and transportation, size is still a factor. Look around the world. Regardless of whether they are considered democracies, large nations such as Russia, China, Australia, Brazil, Canada, Germany, and Mexico tend to have systems in which duties and powers are spread out among national and subnational governments. Despite its monolithic image, even the former Soviet Union—known formally as the Union of Soviet Socialist Republics—was divided into a number of subnational units. So in some respects the United States is not unique.

What does vary is the degree to which real decision-making authority is spread out. The 11 provincial governments of Canada have a great deal of autonomy from the federal government in Ottawa. In France, however, the "departments" historically have done little more than administer orders coming out of Paris. Such differences usually exist because every nation has its own history and culture. In a fictional America in which the nation existed before the states, maybe the states would have been created simply to administer national programs and policies, becoming more like the French departments than the Canadian provinces.

The second major reason that the new nation adopted a federal system is equally important: The states already existed. They *were* the nation under the Articles of Confederation.[6] As a result, federalism was a practical political solution to the founders' dilemma of how to establish a stronger national government without making the states subservient. As the scholar H. G. Nicholas writes:

The unique advantage of federalism is that it makes the United States possible. This great invention of the Founding Fathers squarely confronts the two greatest difficulties we have been examining—size and diversity—and, to a degree totally without precedent in history, provides a mechanism by which they can be accommodated within the framework of a single democratic government.[7]

Federalism balanced the virtues of nation-building promised by strong national government with the responsiveness promised by vibrant state governments. The benefits of a strong nation seem obvious, but effective and responsive state governments serve important ends as well. A government that is closer to the people of a particular place better reflects the cultural, economic, and social traits of that place. Oregon, for example, with its temperate climate, timber and fishing industries, and relatively homogeneous population, differs dramatically from the vast spaces, massive economy, and diverse population of Texas. The problem for government becomes even more evident when we multiply these differences. A government located thousands of miles away would be hard pressed to respond quickly or effectively to distinct local needs and desires.

Federalism thus was a practical answer to the framers' dilemma of how to create an effective and responsive government. It was, and remains, a balancing act between fostering national unity and ensuring sufficient local control. It is the central defining feature of the American system of government.

THE IMPORTANCE OF THE STATES

National law imposes boundaries on what we can and cannot legally do, regardless of where we live. State law, however, has a great deal to say about how long and where we go to school, at what age we can legally drive an automobile, how we get married (and maybe divorced), how we raise our children, the kinds of taxes we pay, when and where we buy liquor, the rules under which we run our businesses, the public services we receive, and even how and where we are buried.

Variations in laws from one state to another also affect our lives. These differences can be as minor as whether we can turn right at a red light, as irksome as the variations in regulations on setting up a small business, or as profound as whether the state permits the death penalty. As American citizens we may share basic constitutional rights and liberties (see chapter 4), but which state we call home still affects how we live. Moving from one state to another is not just a matter of changing addresses: It is a matter of changing the laws under which we live our daily lives.

In short, the states, individually and together, are important players in American politics. Even with the expansion of the national government's power, the states retain a significant amount of autonomy on a wide range of legal and policy matters. The states, not the national government, directly administer major federal programs such as Medicaid, the federal health care program for the poor, and states have some leeway in how they run these programs. Diversity thus exists even

President Bill Clinton addresses the nation's governors at the annual meeting of the National Governors Association. Just as state governments are key components in the American system, governors are important political figures. In fact, three of the past four presidents—Bill Clinton, Ronald Reagan, and Jimmy Carter—were governors.

within national policies. What is more, no national program—be it air pollution control, health care, or crime prevention—can gain approval in Congress without legislators first taking into account differences among states' needs, resources, and political values.

The states are important in other ways. Throughout American history the relationship between the states and the national government has been a source of considerable conflict. The early arguments about whether federal law supersedes state laws, the increasingly bitter disputes over "states' rights" that led to the Civil War, the long struggle over extending constitutional rights and liberties to all Americans, and the evolution of national policy on a wide range of issues all were, and still are, reflections of disagreements over the meaning of federalism.

Federalism made the United States possible. It allowed these diverse and mutually suspicious former colonies to form a workable government and build a nation. This will become clear in the next section as we examine how power and responsibility are divided between the state and national governments.

DIVIDING POWER AND RESPONSIBILITY

As we saw in chapter 2, delegates to the Constitutional Convention knew that they would have to grant more power and responsibility to the national government than it had enjoyed under the Articles of Confederation. The need to foster unity and social stability—indeed, to create a nation—had become paramount. Even so, the delegates knew that the states would retain a great deal of autonomy and authority. After all, the states already existed, and they were in no mood to surrender all their power to the central government.

The dispute was over how much and what types of power and responsibility would be granted to the national government. Even delegates who wanted a stronger national government feared unchecked power. Nobody wanted a king or an unrestrained parliament. Yet most also realized that certain matters were in the "national" interest—for example, defending the nation against foreign enemies, ensuring social peace, and maintaining a stable monetary system. Beyond that, agreement broke down. What other matters were exclusively national? What functions should be left to the states? How strong should national government be relative to the states or to the people? What government functions could the states perform better, if they should be done at all? Out of such questions came the fundamental disagreements that have divided "nationalists" and defenders of "state sovereignty" throughout American history.

Much of the blame for this historic tension must be laid at the feet of the framers themselves. As we saw in chapter 2, they fought and compromised with one another to shape a Constitution that stood a chance of being ratified. In doing so, they left many matters vague or unaddressed. If explosive issues such as slavery were left unsettled, it was because such disputes would have wrecked the convention and sent all the delegates home empty-handed.

Thus, although the framers fudged on a great many issues, they did what they thought was possible at the time. They devised language that suited the needs of both promoters of national power and defenders of state sovereignty. It would take later generations and a civil war to complete the process begun in 1787. In many respects, however, the conflict over the division of power and responsibility between national and state governments continues today, and will do so indefinitely.

FEDERAL POWERS AND RESPONSIBILITIES

The Articles of Confederation left it to the states, through Congress, to allocate power to the national government. Powers that were not explicitly granted to the national government were retained by the states. The states' unwillingness to grant power or money to the national government, and the national government's consequent inability to achieve national unity or stability, were among the failings that led to the drafting of the Constitution.

Unlike the Articles, the Constitution does not allow the states to determine the powers of the national government. Instead it grants to the national—or federal—government its own, separate powers. These powers are of three types, depending on the degree to which they were clearly stated in the Constitution: enumerated powers, implied powers, and inherent powers. Let's take a closer look at each.

ENUMERATED POWERS

The first type of power comes directly from the lists of responsibilities and powers granted exclusively to the three branches of the federal government. These powers are known as **enumerated powers** (also called *express powers*). They are spelled out relatively clearly, primarily in Article I, Section 8. Enumerated powers can be grouped into three broad areas: the power of the purse, the power to regulate commerce, and the power to declare war and raise armed forces.

The Power of the Purse   The federal government was granted the power to collect taxes, borrow money, pay debts, and spend money. The states retained their own "concurrent" powers of the purse (discussed later), but the national government would no longer depend directly on the states for revenues or for permission to spend money. What is more, only the federal government has the express authority to coin or print money and regulate the money supply. States could no longer have their own currencies, which had been a major source of economic and social instability in the period after the War of Independence.

It would be difficult to underestimate the importance of the purse as a basis for federal government power. The federal government has the unique capacity to collect and spend the kinds of funds necessary for massive projects such as the interstate highway system or the space program. It alone can coin or print money, so it has the sole capacity to manage the nation's currency or incur the level of debt necessary to finance the nation's defense, among other purposes. In these ways the federal government has become over time what "nationalists" such as Alexander Hamilton had sought: an "energetic center" able to promote national economic growth and national power.[8]

The federal power of the purse also has a direct effect on the power and autonomy of the states. Throughout the nation's history, Congress has committed the federal government to finance local and state projects when those governments were unable or unwilling to do so. Education, housing, transportation, health, and crime-fighting are just a few areas in which federal money has become important to states and localities. State officials, always leery of raising state or local taxes, are often glad to let the federal government pay for these programs and spread out the costs nationally. Of course, whoever pays the bills gets to make the rules. Federal money has strings attached to it. States or localities that do not abide by the rules do not receive the money.

The Power to Regulate Commerce   Congress has the sole power to regulate commerce with other nations, among the various states, and with "Indian Tribes" (Article I, Section 8). This power was intended to prevent the states from engaging in trade wars, or levying their own taxes on goods imported from other nations. A single, stable national economy required that the national government prevent states from interfering with the flow of goods, people, money, and ideas across state lines. It also required that the nation have a uniform law dealing with exports to and imports from other countries.

By extension, the federal government can also prohibit the movement of goods, services, or people into the country or across state lines when doing so is deemed to be in the nation's interest. Thus, in 1808 Congress banned the importation of slaves, although it took a bloody war to end slavery altogether. Today federal law prohibits the interstate movement of stolen goods and child pornography, among other things.

The face of interstate commerce at Denver International Airport. Airports offer a mix of state and federal government roles and responsibilities: The state government has primary authority over the airport itself, whereas the federal government regulates air traffic, airplane safety, and the security of air travel.

Combined with the notion of "implied" powers (to be discussed shortly), the reach of the "commerce clause" is potentially limitless.

The Power to Defend the Nation Only Congress can declare war on another nation, and only Congress can legally raise and equip armed forces. Congress also has the power to oversee the armed forces, although it shares these responsibilities with the president, who is the commander-in-chief of the armed forces. The states, as subnational entities, cannot engage in these kinds of activities. Even state National Guard units come under federal control during periods of war or national emergency.

Interpreting Enumerated Powers Although the enumerated powers just described seem straightforward, most are stated in rather broad terms. It would have been impossible for the framers to be precise; if they had tried they would never have completed the Constitution. Yet, the broad wording of many enumerated powers left the door open to later interpretation, particularly as changing circumstances or needs required new kinds of answers. For example, the federal government's power to regulate commerce now extends to situations and goods that nobody could have imagined 200 years ago, such as the sale of compact discs over the Internet. As a consequence, the range and scope of the federal government's powers have changed considerably. And from the perspective of defenders of states' rights, the changes always seem to be in the direction of increased power and responsibility for the federal government.

The **general welfare clause** is perhaps the best example of this phenomenon. After granting Congress the power to tax and spend, Article I, Section 8 of the Constitution empowers Congress to "provide for the Common Defense and General Welfare." At first glance this clause pertains solely to the power to tax and spend, but these powers alone give the federal government significant potential power to promote other goals or regulate other activities. After all, there are few practical limits if the government has the power to tax and spend for "the general welfare." The only limits are those imposed by citizens themselves.

So although Congress technically does not have the power to make any legislation it wants in order to provide for the "general welfare," over time the scope of that power expanded because the framers could not foresee the changing demands or needs of citizens. For example, providing for the "general welfare" can mean federal funding for a wide range of social programs (such as health care) that in the 1950s were under the jurisdiction of state governments—if they were performed by government at all.

IMPLIED POWERS

Although often vague and broadly stated, enumerated powers are relatively explicit. However, some powers of the national government are not stated clearly in the Constitution. These powers are "implied" because in most cases they are linked to or grow out of enumerated powers. For example, Congress has the implied power to establish a national minimum wage based on its enumerated powers to regulate commerce and provide for the general welfare. The founders simply could not think of every possible contingency, nor could they foresee future demands and needs, so over time the national government has assumed more power and responsibility based on the enumerated powers of the Constitution.

The notion of **implied powers** is often controversial. In a constitutional system the government can exercise new powers or take on new responsibilities only when its actions are based on legal authority; otherwise these actions are unconstitutional. In an ideal world such legal authority would be established by amending the Constitution, but as we have seen, the founders intentionally made it difficult to do so. An easier way to "change" the meaning of the Constitution is to rely on broader or entirely new definitions of already established powers and responsibilities.

Over time a great many of the federal government's powers have been inferred from its enumerated powers by Congress, the president, or the federal courts, although such interpretations have often been opposed by state governments. This expansion of powers has been accomplished through legislation, through federal court decisions, out of necessity during crises, or simply through gradual acceptance of new practices. As Chief Justice John Marshall noted in the Supreme Court's decision in *McCulloch v. Maryland* (1819; see Box 3.2, p. 100), the Constitution was "intended to endure for ages to come" and hence must be adapted to meet changing needs and challenges. The notion of implied powers was a major vehicle for such adaptation.

The Necessary and Proper Clause   The constitutional basis for implied powers rests primarily on the **necessary and proper clause** in Article I, Section 8. In it Congress is granted the power to "make all laws which shall be necessary and proper for carrying into Execution the foregoing powers and all other Powers vested by this

Constitution in the Government of the United States, or in any Department or Officer thereof." This clause, also referred to as the *elastic clause*, was designed to allow Congress to make whatever laws it deemed "necessary and proper" for the federal government to carry out its enumerated powers. On its face, this seems to be a rather limited grant of power. But as noted earlier, the vagueness and breadth of many enumerated powers left plenty of room for flexibility and growth.

Throughout U.S. history there have been arguments over whether "necessary and proper" should be interpreted narrowly or broadly. Defenders of states' rights usually argue that only powers that are deemed absolutely necessary should be inferred from the enumerated powers, leaving most duties and powers in the hands of the states. This view held sway through much of the 19th century. However, promoters of national power argue that "necessary and proper" should be interpreted more as "convenient and useful," in line with the Supreme Court's ruling in *McCulloch v. Maryland*. This "nationalist" view was especially prevalent in the second half of the 20th century. Indeed, as one constitutional scholar notes, to understand the full reach of federal power one should read the list of enumerated powers as if the "necessary and proper" clause were attached to each one.[9]

Coupling the "necessary and proper" clause to the commerce clause (Article I, Section 8) is a good example of this phenomenon. For a long time the commerce clause—which empowers the national government "to regulate commerce among the several states"—was applied rather narrowly to the movement of goods and services across state lines. Today its reach extends to any activity that can be construed as relating to commerce, such as communications. Indeed, together the "necessary and proper" clause and the commerce clause have been used to justify federal intervention in virtually every sphere of public and private life. The commerce clause was the basis for federal intervention in civil rights issues—for example, banning racial discrimination in public accommodations such as hotels or restaurants. It lay behind the creation of the Federal Bureau of Investigation, which was given the responsibility for pursuing felons who robbed federally chartered banks or crossed state lines with their loot. It also supported laws governing environmental protection, workplace safety, and consumer products, among many other things. It is no exaggeration to suggest that a broad reading of the commerce clause was a primary basis for the growth of federal government activity beginning in the late 19th century.

INHERENT POWERS

The federal government assumes some powers simply by virtue of being the national government. Even if it had not been granted the enumerated powers to declare war and provide for armed forces, these **inherent powers** would have existed anyway because the federal government has sovereign power. As the Supreme Court stated in a major decision, "The power to declare and wage war, to conclude peace, to make treaties, to maintain diplomatic relations with other sovereignties, if they had never been mentioned in the Constitution, would have vested in the federal government as necessary concomitants of nationality."[10] The national government alone engages the

BOX 3.2.
NATIONAL SUPREMACY AND *McCULLOCH V. MARYLAND*

The conflict between those advancing a "states' rights" interpretation of the Constitution and those who advocated a "national supremacy" view first came to a head in 1819 in the U.S. Supreme Court's decision in the case of *McCulloch v. Maryland.*

The state of Maryland had levied a tax against the Baltimore branch of the Bank of the United States, a national bank chartered by Congress. James McCulloch, the bank's head cashier, refused to pay the tax, arguing that the state had no power to tax an institution of the national government. The case went to the Supreme Court.

The attorneys for the state of Maryland were led by Luther Martin, a defender of state sovereignty who had left the Constitutional Convention after it became clear that the Constitution would grant more power to the national government. Martin argued that Congress had no explicit constitutional authority to create a national bank and that the "necessary and proper" clause in Article I, Section 8 did not apply because a national bank was not, strictly speaking, necessary for Congress to regulate the nation's currency. Even if Congress had the *implied* right to incorporate a national bank, he added, the state certainly enjoyed the power to tax this bank the way it taxed all others. After all, the power to tax was reserved to the states.

The federal government was represented by the great orator, Daniel Webster of Massachusetts. Webster admitted that Congress had no explicit power to create a national bank. However, he said, Congress did have the implied power to create the bank. The "necessary and proper clause" should be applied broadly because for Congress to create the bank was a *convenient* and *useful* means to carry out its express powers to tax, regulate currency, and so on. More important, Webster continued, Maryland did not have the right to tax an instrument of the national government. The power to tax certainly is reserved to the states, but the states cannot use their powers to undermine or harm the national government.

nation in war or represents it in peace. It alone has sovereign power. The states can conduct business with other nations, but their actions must conform with federal law.

Safeguarding the Nation   The greatest inherent power of the national government is the **war power.** As noted earlier, Congress has an enumerated power to declare war, but the concept of an inherent war power is much broader. It is based on the notion that the first responsibility of any nation is to protect its people and land from its enemies. Thus, over time the federal government, particularly the presidency, has asserted the power to do whatever is "necessary and proper" to preserve the nation's security.

The potential scope of this power is immense. For example, during World War II the federal government imposed wage and price controls, suspended certain civil lib-

HISTORICAL PERSPECTIVE

A unanimous Supreme Court, led by Chief Justice John Marshall, supported the nationalist argument on both counts. First, the Court found that the national government did have the implied right to create the Bank of the United States because it was a "necessary and proper" means to carry out the national government's express power to regulate the money supply and promote interstate commerce. As Marshall wrote, "Let the end be legitimate, let it be within the scope of the Constitution, and all means which are appropriate, which are plainly adapted to the end, which are not prohibited, but consist with the letter and spirit of the Constitution, are constitutional."

But did the state of Maryland have the right to tax this national bank? No, the Court said. Although the states do have the power to tax banks generally, and have the power to regulate commerce within state boundaries, they cannot tax an entity of the federal government. The power to tax "involves the power to destroy," wrote Marshall, so the states are forbidden to tax the federal government or its creations. Why? Because the national government, the "government of the people" is supreme. "If the right of the states to tax the means employed by the general government be conceded, the declaration that the Constitution, and the laws made in pursuance thereof, shall be the supreme law of the land, is empty and unmeaning declamation."

McCulloch v. Maryland was the first great legal battle over the issue of states' rights versus national supremacy. The nationalist view prevailed; but the issue was not settled, and it endures to this day. In fact, in a 1995 decision (*United States v. Lopez*) the Supreme Court ruled *against* an expansion of federal government power. This case concerned a 1990 law in which Congress prohibited the possession of a firearm in a school zone. Attorneys for the federal government argued that the law was constitutional under the commerce clause, but a majority of the justices disagreed. The Court held that the interstate commerce clause did not apply in this case and that the issue fell properly under state jurisdiction.

Sources: McCulloch v Maryland, 4 Wheat. 316 (1819); Jack W. Peltason, *Understanding the Constitution,* 12th ed. (New York: Holt, Rinehart and Winston, 1992), pp. 19–20.

erties, and generally did whatever was "necessary" to win the war short of actually usurping the Constitution. To cite another example, nowhere does the Constitution give the federal government the power to engage in espionage, but spying on other countries may be considered part of the nation's inherent right to survive. Thus, after World War II, Congress created the Central Intelligence Agency, part of what became a huge and permanent national security institution within the executive branch (discussed more in chapter 10).

FEDERAL GUARANTEES TO THE STATES

The Constitution also requires the federal government to do certain things with respect to the states. First and foremost, the national government must protect the states against foreign invasion and domestic violence, and it is required to preserve the integrity of state territory (Article IV). The Constitution also requires the national government to guarantee that all states have a republican—that is, representative—form of government (Article IV). New states are admitted to the Union only with the approval of Congress, which can make certain stipulations before it approves the state's admission. For example, Utah was not admitted as a state until the Church of Latter-Day Saints (the Mormons), whose adherents populated the territory, agreed to prohibit the practice of polygamy, whereby a man could have multiple wives. Beyond such provisions, the actual structure and operation of state and local government is left pretty much to the states.

The federal government—particularly Congress—is prohibited from favoring any state in regulating interstate commerce (Article I, Section 9) and must guarantee equal representation in the Senate for all states (Article I). In fact, the provision that each state is represented by two senators cannot be changed by constitutional amendment without that state's permission.

THE CONSTITUTION AND NATIONAL SUPREMACY

The cornerstone of the federal government's power is the supremacy clause (Article VI), which states that the Constitution and laws made by the national government "shall be the supreme Law of the Land." Over time and after many conflicts—chief among them the Civil War—the **supremacy clause** has become the basis for overruling state and local laws or actions that conflict with the Constitution, a federal law passed under the authority of the Constitution, or a treaty. As the Supreme Court ruled in *McCulloch v. Maryland,* the supremacy clause solves the problem of which law prevails when the laws that are in conflict are laws passed by Congress and laws passed by the state legislatures.

General acceptance of national supremacy does not mean that the conflict is over—far from it. In the view of those who favor states' rights, the supremacy clause should be limited to enumerated powers. In their view, the federal government should leave most matters to the states, which should have great discretion (if not sovereignty) within their own boundaries. Promoters of national supremacy reject this notion. In their view there is only one sovereign entity: the federal government. What is more, national unity and the demands of equal treatment for all citizens require national government supremacy. The powers of the national government thus should be construed broadly, and "the national government should not be denied power unless its actions clearly conflict with enumerated constitutional limits or clearly have no constitutional basis."[11]

In a broader sense, the framers sowed in the Constitution the seeds of national supremacy. Their often vague statements provided the foundations for the national government to meet the demands posed by unforeseen circumstances and a changing society. Most of these changes have been in the direction of as much federal government responsibility as Americans will tolerate.

POWERS AND RESPONSIBILITIES OF THE STATES

The states still retain a great deal of power and authority. Some of the powers exercised by the states are "shared" with the federal government. Others are "reserved" entirely to the states, at least on paper. As with the powers and responsibilities granted to the federal government, the powers of the states are often vaguely defined and subject to changing interpretations.

CONCURRENT POWERS

Discussions of federalism tend to focus on the differences between the powers granted to the national and state governments. This is not surprising: Those differences are the main sources of controversy and conflict. However, it is easy to forget that certain responsibilities of the federal and state governments are similar, and as a result both levels of government exercise those powers within their own separate spheres. These shared or **concurrent powers** affect citizens and businesses directly, but from different sources. In this section we examine some of the most important concurrent powers.

The Power to Tax and Spend   The federal and state governments have concurrent powers to tax. This is why citizens and businesses must pay both federal and state taxes (local governments derive their power to tax from state constitutions). However, a state's ability to levy taxes on individuals and businesses is limited—state taxes may not hinder interstate commerce or affect entities of the federal government. A state's power to tax may also be limited by its own constitution and laws.

Federal and state governments also have the power to spend. Federal spending tends to be for national purposes such as defense, but in recent decades there have been increases in payments to individuals (such as unemployment insurance or health care for the elderly) and for services that formerly were financed almost entirely by the states (such as education).

This expansion in federal spending has come about for two reasons. First, most states are too small to generate the revenues necessary to finance major programs on their own. They can finance projects such as highways by issuing bonds, but this can saddle their residents with huge debts. The second reason is more political: State officials seek federal funding to avoid raising state taxes—and risking voter unhappiness. Federal money often comes with strings attached, however. For example, federal funding for elementary education might be accompanied by stringent rules about the functions for which the money can be used. States that object to these rules can refuse to accept the funds, but giving up "free" money is rarely easy.

The Power to Take Private Property   The federal government has the inherent power of "eminent domain," that is, the power to "take" private property for national purposes, such as military bases and national parks. State governments—and, under state law, local governments—enjoy a similar power of eminent domain for state and local projects such as highways, schools, or sewage treatment plants. However, the Fifth Amendment mandates that whenever either the federal or state government takes private property it must provide "fair compensation" to property holders (see chapter 4). Of course, what is fair is often a matter of dispute and frequently ends up being determined by federal and state courts.[12]

Other Concurrent Powers   Federal and state governments have concurrent powers to establish courts, charter banks and corporations, pass and enforce laws, and protect civil rights. Federal law usually supersedes state law, although it has taken countless legislative battles and court decisions to lay out the precise lines between federal and state jurisdictions. As a general rule, state law operates within the boundaries imposed by national law. So long as this holds, and depending on the issue in question, variations among states can be significant. For example, state laws regulating business practices (such as retail store hours) vary widely, whereas on civil rights issues the federal government tends to keep a very tight rein on the states.

RESERVED POWERS

The basis for most state government power lies is the **reserve clause,** contained in the Tenth Amendment, the last of the 10 amendments constituting the Bill of Rights. Though only one sentence long, the Tenth Amendment is one of the most important statements of American federalism: "The powers not delegated to the United States by the Constitution, nor prohibited to it by the States, are reserved to the States respectively, or to the people."

In 1791, when it was ratified, this amendment seemed to restate what most Americans already assumed: The states would retain whatever powers were not delegated to the national government. Yet even the Tenth Amendment could not stop the eventual shift of power from the states to the national government. For example, it is vague about whether powers that are not *expressly* granted to the national government are reserved to the states. If the writers of the Tenth Amendment had been specific about the powers to be reserved to the states, the reserve clause might have curtailed the growth of national government power. But they were not specific, and as a result the expansion of federal action under the doctrine of implied powers began soon thereafter.

The **reserved powers** of the states thus are limited by current interpretations of the federal government's powers under the Constitution. The shape and extent of states' reserved powers have changed over time as the federal government was granted a greater range of functions and powers. The autonomy of the individual states is not as absolute as it was two centuries ago. Even so, the states retain considerable authority and leeway in four general areas: establishing local governments, running elections, police power, and intrastate commerce.

Local Governments   Local governments are created by the states. Their structures, operations, and range of powers are directed by state constitutions and statutes.
How local governments work thus can vary considerably from state to state and even
from region to region.

These differences usually stem from varied histories and experiences. The New
England states, for example, have a tradition of town government in which even the
most mundane expenses must be approved by a direct vote of townspeople at an annual meeting. County government is almost nonexistent in New England, but important in the Midwest and West. Many northern cities provide for a strong mayor,
while in the South and Southwest professional city managers are often hired by city
councils to administer municipal functions.

Elections   State governments have primary responsibility for setting the times,
places, and procedures for local, state, and in some cases, federal elections (Article I,
Section 4). As we will see in chapter 6, this provision had a profound impact on the
evolution of American political parties, which traditionally were federations of state
parties. However, beginning with the Fifteenth Amendment (1870), state election
laws and practices became subject to stricter federal constraints, largely to prevent
states from using election procedures to discriminate against voters on the basis of
race, length of residency, or party affiliation (see chapter 4). Even so, elections usually
are more state-centered than national in scope, and variations in state election laws
and traditions can make for fascinating study.

Police Power   **Police power** refers to the right of the states to regulate people
and property within their borders in order to promote public safety and welfare.
Even with the greater federal role in such matters as illegal drugs, almost all aspects
of criminal and civil law remain under the primary jurisdiction of the states. All local
ordinances, police procedures, and corrections systems come under state jurisdiction.
States also retain the power to maintain their own militias (now known as state National Guards) so as to preserve the peace and protect against public disorder,
whether the cause be a natural disaster or public unrest. But, here again, the president can call up a state's National Guard unit for national purposes, even if the state
governor objects.

Many of the rules that affect residents' daily lives grow out of states' police powers. Those powers are the basis for laws governing public health, such as the requirement that a couple take blood tests before they may obtain a marriage license. The
stated purpose of such blood tests is to prevent the spread of sexually transmitted diseases such as syphilis, and today, AIDS. Police powers enable the states to regulate
motor vehicle ownership and operation. They also have been used to protect "public
morality," for example, by regulating the sale of sexually explicit literature, subject to
prevailing interpretations of First Amendment guarantees of freedom of of the press
(see chapter 4).

Intrastate Commerce   The states retain considerable authority to regulate business within their own boundaries, so long as they do not interfere with interstate
commerce. However, the line between "intrastate" and "interstate" commerce is in-

Legally married, by authority of the state. State governments, not the federal government, regulate much of everyday life through their array of "police powers." Americans are born, go to school, work, sign contracts, are married, have children, die, and are buried under state law.

creasingly fuzzy in a world where *all* commerce is potentially interstate or international. For example, a state can regulate wine sales over the Internet if both the seller and buyer are located within the state, but it cannot do so if the purchaser is out of state.

Even so, there is still a considerable range of variation among states in a great number of matters related to commerce. The states still set the terms for the sale of liquor or for retail sales on Sundays. They determine the age at which people can legally buy cigarettes or guns. States inspect agricultural goods or foodstuffs produced within their boundaries. They set statewide building codes and guidelines for local zoning regulations. States require licenses for practitioners of law and medicine, both to maintain quality and to regulate the supply. For the same reasons, many states also license hair stylists, taxidermists, mortuary operators, and garbage haulers, to name but a few possibilities.

Such variety in state laws is not always welcome to businesses, which prefer the convenience of uniform national laws. Moreover, in instances such as the legal drinking age the national government has enacted policies that essentially create a national standard. Even with these pressures in the direction of uniform national laws, however, the states will continue to reflect the values and biases of their own residents, at least within the broad confines set by national law and general political attitudes.

RELATIONS BETWEEN STATES

Federalism is more than a relationship between the national government and the various states. It also governs how the states treat one another. One of the weaknesses of the Articles of Confederation was the inability or unwillingness of the states to cooperate on important interstate and national matters. Federal systems also can have such conflicts—for instance, our Civil War, or the current tensions between the French-speaking province of Quebec and the rest of Canada.

Competition among states is inevitable. Every state official wants to promote economic development, create new jobs, and attract new talent. Sometimes this means "stealing" businesses and residents away from other states. The Constitution does not prevent such competition, but it does try to keep it within boundaries. Relations among the states are covered in Article IV.

Every state must give *full faith and credit* to the laws, court decisions, and records of all other states. This provision refers largely to civil matters, such as when one person sues another in court over the payment of a debt. The loser in a civil lawsuit cannot move to another state to avoid paying the debt, because court decisions in any one state are respected in all the others. However, controversial issues can threaten cooperation among the states. In Hawaii, for example, a policy allowing "same-sex" marriages raised considerable debate in states where elected officials did not want to give legal recognition to these partnerships. These officials lobbied their members of Congress, which in January, 1996, passed a law denying federal benefits (such as Social Security) to spouses in same-sex marriages and allowed individual states to refuse to recognize these partnerships even though they are legal in other states.

Criminal cases can also cause controversy. Individuals who are wanted for or convicted of a crime in one state but who flee to another state generally are returned to the state in which the crime was committed. This process, known as *extradition*, involves a formal request by one governor to another to return a fugitive for trial or punishment. Extradition is usually routine, but it is not automatic. There have been cases in which governors have refused to return fugitives because of vast differences between state criminal laws and penalties. For example, a governor in a state that does not employ the death penalty might not wish to extradite an accused murderer who is wanted in a state that does employ the death penalty.[13]

Residents of any state are entitled to the same privileges and immunities that are enjoyed by all other American citizens. The **privileges and immunities clause** (Article IV, Section 2) was designed to prevent states from discriminating against residents of any other state. This clause, augmented by the equal protection clause of the Fourteenth Amendment (see chapter 4) is in many respects essential to fusing the residents of 50 separate states into a single citizenry.[14]

The Fourteenth Amendment does not prevent all possible disparities. States can mandate that people establish residency (that is, live in the state for a certain length of time) before they may vote in that state or be eligible for lower tuition rates at state universities. States can charge higher fees for nonresidents using state parks. Such requirements cannot conflict with federal law or the basic constitutional guarantees afforded to all Americans, and they must be "reasonable and suitably tailored"—that is, differences in the ways nonresidents are treated cannot be great.

Finally, the Constitution provides mechanisms by which states can cooperate if doing so is in their common interest. States can enter into *interstate compacts* subject to the approval of Congress. These arrangements, which have the force of law, generally are created in order to allow adjoining states to regulate shared waterways or public transportation systems, control regional pollution problems, or encourage regional economic development. Examples include the Port Authority of New York and New Jersey, which coordinates a wide array of ground, air, and water transportation activities in the New York City metropolitan area; the Colorado River Compact, a multistate agreement governing the rates at which respective states can draw water from the Colorado River; and, of course, the various compacts growing out of the Low-Level Radioactive Waste Policy Act discussed at the beginning of the chapter.

THE STRUGGLE OVER FEDERALISM

American federalism began as a system in which the states were strong and the national government had limited power, in many ways resembling the arrangement under the Articles of Confederation. Today, however, it is a system in which the states are decidedly weaker than the national government. The seeds for the expansion of federal power were sown in the array of enumerated, implied, and inherent powers contained in the Constitution. But this shift from state-centered to nation-centered federalism did not happen quickly or without tremendous conflict. Nor has it always been in one direction. Indeed, this conflict between defenders of states' rights and promoters of national power is an enduring feature of American politics.

STATES' RIGHTS AND NATIONALIST PERSPECTIVES

No conflict related to the core meaning of the Constitution has been more significant than the conflict over state sovereignty. Because the framers were vague in drawing the lines between state and federal power, later generations were left with the task of struggling over these divisions of legal authority. These were important decisions, often accompanied by intense conflict. They would determine, for example, whether the federal government could stop the spread of slavery to new states. More profoundly, they would determine whether a state could "nullify" or refuse to apply a national law to residents within its own boundaries. At issue was whether "the United States" was a plural or a singular, many separate states or one united nation.

The States' Rights View   The state-centered interpretation of federalism grew out of the view that the Constitution was a compact among the states. The states were to be equal partners and would hold power together when it came to domestic policy. The powers of the national government, by contrast, were to be explicit and narrowly interpreted.

To advocates of **states' rights** there would be no implied powers and few inherent powers available to the national government. When in doubt, the states should have their way, especially with respect to their reserved powers. The states' rights stance rested on the belief that state (and local) governments were closest to the people and, hence, more likely to reflect the desires of the majority. It also reflected the strong fear of central power that runs throughout American history. Contemporary defenders of states' rights, not surprisingly, see themselves as the true heirs of the nation's founders.

Out of this view of the Constitution evolved the concept of **dual sovereignty,** the idea that each government is sovereign within its own sphere. That is, state law would be supreme within state boundaries, whereas federal law would apply only to the enumerated powers granted in the Constitution, such as the coining of money or the management of foreign policy. This belief would give states the right to override, or *nullify,* decisions or laws of the national government. Dual sovereignty also promotes strict separation of functions. Matters of domestic policy were to lie primarily within the legal authority of the states. The federal government, for its part, was to stay relatively small and focus mostly on foreign relations and trade issues.

The Nationalist View   Nationalists deny the very premise on which advocates of states' rights base their views. To nationalists the Constitution was *not* a compact among the states, nor was the national government an agent of the states. Instead, the Constitution is the supreme law of the land based on a compact among the people, not the states. After all, the Constitution was ratified by the people meeting in special conventions within their states, and the preamble of the Constitution begins with, "We the people of the United States," not "We the States."

For this reason, nationalists argue, the national government represents all of the people equally, regardless of the state in which they reside. Nationalists reject the notion of dual sovereignty. There is only one sovereign government: the federal government. All other governments are "inferior" by definition. State laws and actions must conform to the Constitution and to federal law.

To nationalists, the very notion of dual sovereignty was a recipe for the instability and disunity that had undermined the Articles of Confederation. What is more, the federal government should be able to do whatever is "necessary and proper" to carry out its enumerated, implied, and inherent powers, which should be interpreted broadly. The needs of a growing population and an expanding nation demanded a national government that could foster westward expansion, create national economic stability, and provide for national defense.

THE GROWTH OF NATIONAL POWER

It is tempting to suggest that the nationalist view prevailed only because the Union won the Civil War, but this would be an oversimplification. The more complex truth is that the seeds of the eventual triumph of the nationalist position were sown in the language of the Constitution. As mentioned earlier, the general welfare, necessary and proper, commerce, and national supremacy clauses all embodied the potential for expansion of national government power. Add to this the failure of the Tenth Amendment to clearly limit the federal government to its enumerated powers, and all that was needed was for the Congress, the president, the Supreme Court—indeed, the American people themselves—to give these clauses the fullest possible meaning.

Alexander Graham Bell and the telephone. The story of Bell's invention is well known. Less so is the battle he subsequently went through to establish patent rights to his invention. With the federal patent in hand, Bell could reap the financial rewards of his invention.

Thus, the constitutional foundations for expansive federal power have always existed. But what specific factors prompted the growth of federal power? The reasons are many and varied, but most are linked to the transformation of the country from a collection of somewhat unconnected states into a true nation. The process of nation-building itself contributed to the growth of federal power, a process that may well have been inevitable. Let us look more closely at the factors that spurred the growth of the national government's powers.

Nationalization of the Economy   Perhaps the earliest factor in the expansion of federal government activity and power was the emergence of a true national economy as opposed to a collection of states with stronger economic links to England than to one another. Westward expansion and growing interstate commerce soon led to pressures for a more active federal government role in building roads and canals, managing the nation's money supply, and protecting domestic industries against foreign competition. Later came federal support for transcontinental railroads, the state land-grant universities, pure food and drug laws, antitrust statutes, and child labor regulations. Businesses seeking uniform and predictable national markets began to demand that the federal government supersede the patchwork of state laws. Meanwhile, those seeking to protect workers and consumers sought tougher federal action to prevent businesses from using state laws as loopholes. Today, of course, the federal government plays a vital role in virtually every aspect of an integrated economy that is increasingly international, not just national.

Technological Change   Contributing to the nationalization of the economy was a tremendous expansion in technological innovations with national and international ramifications. Early inventions, such as electricity, the telegraph, and the steam engine, transformed the way Americans worked, lived, and traveled. Indeed, they allowed Americans to spread themselves across the continent and communicate with one another along the way, which in the process helped to build the idea of the nation. The federal government fostered this innovation in its constitutional power to grant patents and copyrights that protected new innovations from unscrupulous copycats, which in turn safeguarded the initial economic investments in the new technologies. More recent technological advances such as cellular phones, the Internet, and genetic engineering have only expanded this role of the federal government.

Nationalization of Rights and Liberties   The Bill of Rights was added to the Constitution in order to place limits on the federal government's power to interfere with the rights of the states. The rights and liberties of citizens were covered by state constitutions and laws. But, as we will see in chapter 4, after the Civil War the guarantees embodied in the Bill of Rights began to be extended to citizens through the Fourteenth Amendment. This "nationalization" process ebbed and flowed during the next century, but gradually the states ceded their sovereignty over the rights and liberties of their residents. Today the nationalist position on rights and liberties generally prevails, with states largely unable to contradict federal laws or constitutional guarantees on such matters as racial or gender discrimination, freedom of speech and assembly, or the treatment of individuals accused of crimes. States can expand on these basic rights and liberties, but they cannot narrow or eliminate what the federal government has guaranteed.

Population Growth and Social Complexity   The nationalization of government accompanied the massive growth in the size and complexity of the nation's population. Westward expansion and a growing national economy required millions of workers, and waves of foreign immigrants eventually created a society more diverse than the framers could ever have imagined. The transformation from the farm to city, from small shop to the factory, placed strains on government that the states were hard-pressed to handle. Only the federal government seemed capable of addressing the needs of an ever-changing national population.

Nationalization of Problems   The problems confronting government also changed dramatically. Government once faced problems that were largely local in character. States were able to build roads, educate students, and regulate local businesses. Today, however, concerns such as air pollution, health care, the economy, and crime often cross state and national boundaries. No one state can solve its own air pollution problems if neighboring states do nothing—airborne pollution does not respect state borders. No one state can handle a national problem such as illegal drugs, or adequately regulate businesses whose manufacturing facilities and customers span the globe. Whether the national government can handle these problems is itself a subject of debate, but the nationalization of many problems has put state governments at a disadvantage.

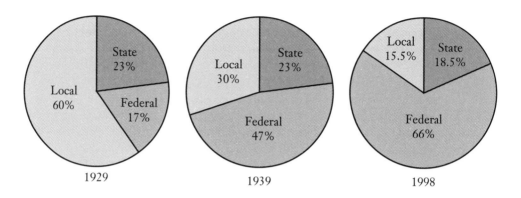

FIGURE 3.1. THE SHIFT TOWARD FEDERAL SPENDING

Source: Adapted from U.S. Department of Commerce, Bureau of the Census, *Government Finances* (Washington, D.C.: Government Printing Office, 1997).

Changing Societal Demands For many of the reasons suggested, Americans have come to demand a more active federal government (see Figure 3.1). Beginning with the election of Franklin Roosevelt in 1932, voters have tended to elect presidents who were committed to federal government involvement in economic growth and individual security. Voters have also favored members of Congress who promise to obtain federal assistance for their constituencies. Even advocates of states' rights, such as Richard Nixon and Ronald Reagan, could not "roll back the clock" in this respect, largely because of continued public support for a strong federal role.

War and Foreign Affairs The emergence of the United States as a world power has irrevocably altered the size and scope of the federal government. Throughout most of the 19th century the nation was a rather isolated republic with no real foes on its borders and only a modest military. Without an active role in world politics, it could afford a system of decentralized power and responsibility and did not have to spend much on national defense. The activity and power of the government had expanded during the Civil War and again during World War I because the needs of war require greater spending and more central planning. However, after those wars ended, the size and scope of government returned to close to prewar conditions.

But World War II was different. The United States emerged from that war as the world's most powerful nation, with new and somewhat unwelcome global responsibilities. More important, the United States embarked on a long and expensive "cold war" with its chief rival, the Soviet Union. The result was a permanent state of international tension that eventually endowed the U.S. federal government with unparalleled power and responsibility. National security became a rationale for enlarging the government's role in areas that had previously been the domain of the states. For example, the need to provide for a healthy and trained military led to federal nutrition and education programs; the need for effective transportation produced the interstate highway system; massive federal subsidies for private industry were needed to maintain the "arms race" and the "space race" with the Soviet Union.

In short, the federal government grew in order to meet the needs of a nation that was in a more or less permanent state of military readiness. This growth in national power occurred under Democratic as well as Republican, liberal as well as conservative presidents. It remains to be seen whether the end of the Cold War and a reduced emphasis on defense spending will translate into a reduced federal role in domestic policy areas.

Crises   Other crises have promoted a broader role for the federal government. The Great Depression of the 1930s, for example, left state and local governments with insufficient resources to aid citizens in distress. States and citizens alike turned to the federal government for help. Franklin Roosevelt responded with the New Deal, a slate of federal programs that marked a sharp break from decades of minimal federal action. Natural disasters also give rise to calls for federal help. The devastation caused in Florida by Hurricane Andrew in 1992 and in the Midwest by the vast Mississippi River floods of 1993 led state governments to call for federal assistance.

Together, these factors have the effect of making the federal government more prominent than the state governments in the minds of most citizens. These factors also can undermine the capacity of state governments to respond to pressing societal problems or citizen demands. Finally, state governments have been criticized for ignoring large sectors of their populations, particularly racial minorities. Thus, the dominant trends have been in the direction of greater national power and responsibility.

AN EVOLVING PARTNERSHIP

The apparent supremacy and activism of the federal government should not give the impression that states are little more than administrative adjuncts of the national government. States are still vital units in the political system. Members of Congress, particularly senators, are elected to represent the states. States are the primary unit for presidential elections (through the electoral college), and states must ratify amendments to the Constitution.

Most important, state law still has the most direct impact on the lives of citizens, whether through police power or regulation of intrastate commerce In this regard, states have dramatically improved their levels of professionalism and expertise. Many states have become known as innovators in delivering basic services and resolving complicated problems. For example, New Jersey led the nation in creating ways to handle toxic wastes, Kentucky restructured its public and secondary school systems, and Hawaii pioneered universal access to health care. Many of these innovations spread to other states or were adopted in some form by the federal government. The role of the states as policy innovators is especially important when the federal government is inactive or disinterested in a particular policy area at the moment.

BOX 3.3.
IMAGES OF FEDERALISM

Scholars have used different metaphors to describe the division of power and responsibility between the national and state governments. Interestingly, two of the most popular metaphors involve cakes!

Some scholars have compared American federalism to a *layer cake*. Like a layer cake, the national government and the states have their own distinct areas of responsibility. The national government, the top layer, is responsible for functions such as national defense, while the states are responsible for functions such as public education. Some scholars even portray local government as a third layer of the cake. In this view of federalism each "layer" of government has its own separate sphere, and none of the functions overlap. This was the dominant view of federalism throughout the 19th century and the early 20th century, and is closely associated with the concept of "dual sovereignty" advocated by proponents of states' rights.

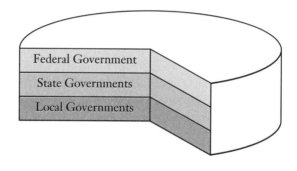

Federal Government
State Governments
Local Governments

"Layer Cake Federalism"

What has not changed is the historical tension between national and state governments as they divide, as well as share, government responsibilities (see Box 3.3). This partnership has both coercive and cooperative elements.

Coercive Federalism   **Coercive federalism** is the case in which the federal government requires states to go along with a national goal or program, often leading states to complain about **federal mandates.** These are federal laws, regulations, or court orders that require states to do something, such as cleaning up polluted waters, building more prisons, or providing new services for the disabled, but often do not give the states sufficient funds or much discretion in how to carry out these demands.

A CLOSER LOOK

This image still has its proponents, but it has largely been replaced by one that more accurately reflects the reality of American federalism today. This is the metaphor of federalism as a *marble cake* in which distinct policy-related ingredients are swirled together. In such an image national and state governments are still separate but work together to achieve shared policy goals. This image of federalism is more cooperative in nature. For example, the welfare system is a collaboration in which the federal government sets broad national guidelines and provides financial support while the states administer the actual programs and tailor their welfare systems to reflect local conditions and goals. As before, some scholars also include local governments in this metaphor, because cities and towns are important, distinct, ingredients in the marble cake. They are not always hidden within state or federal functions.

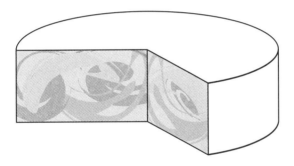

"Marble Cake Federalism"

Source: Morton Grodzins, "The Federal System," in *Goals for Americans: The Report of the President's Commission on National Goals, and Chapters Submitted for the Consideration of the Commission* (Upper Saddle River, NJ: Prentice Hall, 1960).

One variation of a federal mandate, known as a *crossover sanction*, is particularly coercive. In this instance the federal government gives states an "option" to comply with a policy, but states that decline to do so lose federal funding for related programs. In this way the mandate "crosses over" between different programs. The seat belt law is an example. In the 1980s the federal government wanted all states to adopt laws requiring seat belt use, especially by children. States were not technically required to pass such laws, but a state that did not comply would lose a portion of its federal highway funds. For states, this was not a real option: State officials could not afford to lose federal funds for their states' highway programs.

Mandates became controversial during the 1980s as the federal government sought to achieve national policy goals without further increasing an already large federal budget deficit. The states naturally resented being required to carry out federal mandates with state funds, especially because federal rules often left little flexibility for innovation or experimentation. Furthermore, state governments certainly did not want to raise taxes to pay for these mandates without having some say in how the programs were designed or implemented.

In 1995 Congress passed the Unfunded Mandates Relief Act to try to limit the ability of the federal government to consider new laws or policies that impose mandates on state and local governments. The law has forced Congress to think more openly about the relationship between the federal government and the states when considering new laws, but the debate continues. Those defending mandates argue that the states have often evaded their responsibilities and that the federal government should not be required to subsidize states that intentionally lag in such areas as education or pollution control while other states bear their fair share of the burden. Critics of mandates argue that the federal government should not impose programs on state and local governments without also paying for them.[15]

Cooperative Federalism   Another view of the relationship between the national government and the states is offered by **cooperative federalism.** Indeed, to a great extent the partnership between the national government and the states is based on cooperation. It is no longer a situation in which *either* the state *or* the federal government takes action in a certain policy area. More often than not, federalism today involves *both* state and federal activity. State and federal officials often work together to solve problems that cross state boundaries and cannot be addressed at only one level of government. Even the most ardent defenders of state sovereignty seek federal assistance. Even the strongest proponents of national government power admit that state government is more often responsive to residents than the federal government.

Many important government policies and programs are cooperative ventures. For example, welfare assistance to the poor is funded by both the federal government and the states. The federal government establishes broad rules for the program, but states have considerable flexibility to tailor the program to meet their own needs (see chapter 5). Highway construction and maintenance are also cooperative ventures in many instances, as is education, a policy area that has historically been under state control. Goals 2000, for example, is a federal program that provides assistance to states and local schools to develop innovative programs. It is voluntary, but most states take part in order to take advantage of the program's benefits.

Federalism thus remains a balancing act. The federal government is supreme, but its powers are not unlimited. For example, in the case of low-level radioactive waste discussed at the beginning of this chapter the federal courts ruled that Congress had overstepped its constitutional boundaries when it tried to force states to keep their own wastes.[16] Moreover, during the 1990s the U.S. Supreme Court was more active in using the reserve clause of the Tenth Amendment to put a check on the powers of the federal government when it tried to intrude into areas regarded as prerogatives of the states. A return to the kind of state-centered federalism characteristic of the 19th century is unlikely, but the states will continue to retain considerable power.

BENEFITS AND COSTS OF FEDERALISM

Federalism thus is a complex system of divided power and responsibility. It has evolved over time and will continue to evolve. Its tensions have defined American politics throughout the nation's history. Federalism is not going to disappear anytime soon, nor is there any good reason to wish for its demise. The alternatives might well be worse. Having said this, it is useful to examine federalism's benefits and its inevitable costs.

BENEFITS

In some ways federalism makes the United States possible. In a large and diverse country, federalism offers the advantages of decentralization through state and local governments while also providing some of the advantages of centralized systems, which are in a better position to achieve national goals. Federalism is a hybrid, one that remains relevant because it has been adapted to the nation's changing needs and conditions.

Federalism has additional virtues: It enhances citizen control, expands participation, promotes innovation, checks excessive power, and promotes diverse views.

Enhances Citizen Control   The decentralized nature of federalism brings government closer to the people. Maintaining state and local governments with effective decision-making power gives citizens greater control over their own affairs than would be possible if all power were concentrated in the national government. State governments, particularly in smaller states, are seen as more knowledgeable about and responsive to local needs. State governments thus best reflect the sentiments of the majority of their states' residents, which in turn protects diversity within the nation as a whole. In short, federalism promotes responsive government.

Expands Participation   Federalism also provides many avenues for access and participation. Having federal, state, and local governments enhances participatory democracy by giving citizens many more ways to express themselves than are available in unitary or confederated systems. For example, citizens can influence education policy by attending a meeting of the local school board, lobbying the state's educational policymaking body, or contacting the federal Department of Education personally or through their elected representatives. Some states allow citizens to enact or repeal laws directly through a petition and referendum process that places a law on the ballot for a vote. In 1998 California voters used the referendum process to ban the use of race or ethnicity as a factor in university admissions and limit bilingual education in public schools.

A federal system thus lowers the overall "cost" of participation. With federalism, citizens have more, and more varied, points of access to government. If they cannot obtain satisfaction from one set of officials, they can go to others. What is more, citizens usually don't need a huge party or group to have some impact. A few people who organize to make a complaint may be all it takes to get an answer from somebody. This is a relatively low-cost way of participating that cannot help but increase citizen participation in public affairs.

Promotes Innovation   Another advantage of federalism is that it diffuses governmental responsibility and thus promotes innovation. With one federal government and 50 state governments—not to mention countless local governments, school districts, and specialized authorities for such matters as waste disposal or airports—federalism provides many potential "laboratories" for nurturing new ideas or trying out new approaches.[17] States are small enough that the impact of new ideas can be measured more easily than if they were tried nationally. Ideas that don't work can be dropped with less difficulty; those that work in one state are often adopted by others. These new ideas may also be picked up by the federal government, though usually in a form adapted to the needs of all the states.

Perhaps it is no surprise that more than one-third of all American presidents have been former state governors. Indeed, three of the last four presidents—Bill Clinton, Ronald Reagan, and Jimmy Carter—had been governors. Local and state politics are training grounds for public officials who move into the national sphere through Congress or the presidency. Furthermore, the dynamism of state government often puts governors in close contact with new ideas or emerging ideals.

Checks Excessive Power   A key benefit of federalism is that it diffuses political power among many different levels of government. This, combined with separation of powers, makes it far more difficult for any single group of people to monopolize political power or dominate all parts of government. This works in several ways. First, a stronger national government enables national leaders to blunt the power of local majorities that may be violating the civil rights of others. For example, in the 1950s the federal government ended forced racial segregation of the public schools, first with the Supreme Court's decision in *Brown v. Board of Education of Topeka, Kansas* (1954), and soon thereafter with President Dwight Eisenhower's deployment of federal troops to Little Rock, Arkansas, to enforce the court's ruling (see chapter 4).[18]

The same goes for local elites. Local businesses wield tremendous influence on political actions, particularly if a local or state economy is dominated by a single industry. The federal government can act as a counterweight to local business or political elites. This is especially true when their actions run afoul of federal laws or constitutional guarantees, most notably in areas involving civil rights of minorities, consumer and workplace safety, and environmental protection. For example, the federal government has supported racial integration of public schools since the early 1950s, often in the face of strong resistance by local officials.

Promotes Diverse Views   In theory, federalism also helps ensure that the diversity of interests and values found throughout the land are recognized, even if they do not always prevail. After all, the dominant values and norms found in a state such as Utah, which is dominated by members of the Church of Latter-Day Saints (Mormons), can differ profoundly from the values and norms found in California, with its great diversity of people and lifestyles.[19] This diversity is also protected in Congress, particularly in the Senate, thus ensuring that minority voices are heard.

The merits of federalism that we have discussed combine to enhance the overall ability of government to meet the needs of its citizens. Unitary systems may be more efficient and can act more quickly than a federal system, but they also tend to become overwhelmed by their responsibilities. Because all decisions must be made at the center, problems can pile up. This frustrates citizens, particularly those with little political power, who may react with violence when their voices go unheeded. In pure confederations, by contrast, problems that are not addressed by state governments can lead to inequities among citizens of the same nation.

By diffusing power and responsibility and providing many avenues for citizen access, federalism actually reduces the overall burden on the national government and makes government more adaptive and responsive. Compared to unitary systems, the national government of the United States is actually rather small, with state and local governments taking on much of the responsibility. Many problems are dealt with locally, but the national government can provide help if necessary. This diffusion of power, though it may produce a more complicated system, may actually enhance the overall responsiveness of government. Such a government has greater legitimacy in the eyes of its citizens.

COSTS

Federalism does have a price. As H. G. Nicholas observes, many of the defects of American government are "no more than the inescapable consequences of the federal system."[20] Indeed, many of the virtues of federalism have their corresponding disadvantages.

Creates Complexity   One of those disadvantages is complexity. In the United States there are over 80,000 separate subnational governments, most of which have some power to tax.[21] There are states, counties, cities, towns, boroughs, villages, special authorities (airport, sewer, etc.), and school districts, not to mention the federal District of Columbia (Washington, D.C.) and areas controlled by Native American tribes, which are legally separate from the states. On election day Americans are often confronted by a large number of candidates for local, state, and federal offices. No wonder many people don't vote: Even well-informed citizens cannot keep up with all the offices and candidates. Neighboring states can have wildly divergent laws; one level of government may contradict another; and sometimes no one really knows who is responsible.

Not only is this confusing, but it makes for a lot of government. If the American national government is rather small and constrained compared to national governments in unitary systems, Americans nonetheless face a lot of government. Federalism does not necessarily reduce the overall size of government. It merely chops it up into more manageable pieces. This condition increases the effectiveness and responsiveness of government, but it does place a burden on citizens.

BOX 3.4.
COMPARING STATE SPENDING

There are plenty of ways to show differences among states. One is to show differences in spending on certain kinds of functions or programs. One of the examples shown here is based on spending per person, the other on total dollar amounts.

Per Pupil Spending on Elementary and Secondary Education, 1993

Top Five

New Jersey	$9,491
New York	$8,794
Connecticut	$8,170
Pennsylvania	$6,914
Vermont	$6,731

Bottom Five

Idaho	$4,025
Arkansas	$3,838
Alabama	$3,830
Mississippi	$3,390
Utah	$3,218

Source: Statistical Abstract of the United States, 1995, p. 168. Figures include local, state, and federal expenditures. They do not include Hawaii, Alaska, or the District of Columbia.

These figures show clear regional differences, but of what? Do states in the Northeast put more emphasis on education? Or are they just more affluent, and thus better able to afford higher spending? Or, are the differences due to the fact that the cost of living is higher in the Northeast, thus making everything more expensive? What do you think?

Here's another comparison, on the total expenditure on Medicaid by some states.

Allows Inequities   Another drawback is the potential for inequities among citizens. Federalism allows for a great deal of variation, which may perpetuate unequal treatment of citizens of the same nation depending on which state they reside in. On issues such as traffic laws the variations are minor, but on others, such as the death penalty, they can be profound. Add to this the fact that poorer states are unable to

WHAT DO YOU THINK?

Total Medicaid Expenditures, 1996

Top Five (dollars per student)

New York	$15,281,000,000
California	$8,692,000,000
Texas	$4,407,000,000
Pennsylvania	$4,213,000,000
Illinois	$4,070,000,000

Bottom Five

Delaware	$219,000,000
Montana	$217,000,000
Arizona	$209,000,000
Alaska	$187,000,000
Wyoming	$114,000,000

Source: U.S. Health Care Financing Administration.

In this case a crucial piece of data might be the size of each state's population. States with larger populations are likely to spend more on Medicaid, the federally supported program for health care for the poor (and, to some extent, the elderly). It might be useful also to know the degree to which each state's population fits the profile of the typical Medicaid recipient. In the case of New York, we have a large state population with a large share of poorer and older residents. Wyoming, by contrast, is a small state in terms of population. It *might* also spend less per person for Medicaid, but you cannot infer that from these data.

Which data might be more useful to policy makers? What problems are there with each kind of data? What do you think?

offer the kinds of services that are provided by more affluent ones, and the potential for inequity grows more evident (see Box 3.4). This situation raises important questions as to whether all Americans have a right to "equal treatment" regardless of the state in which they reside.

Another source of inequity has to do with political power. As noted earlier, federalism provides for government "closer to the people," but it also allows local elites and groups to acquire a great deal of power. A few individuals can wield more control over government at the local and state levels than they typically can in the much larger federal government. Such "minority" control can come at the expense of underrepresented majorities.

The legacy of discrimination against local black majorities in many southern states is a familiar example of this situation, but there have been similar kinds of inequities throughout the nation. For example, state legislatures were often controlled by rural politicians who tended not to care much about urban problems. These politicians had disproportionate power because over the years they and their predecessors benefited from state election laws that had the effect of diluting the power of more populous urban constituencies. Such biases have practical results: In this case, many states were very slow to respond to the growing problems of urban areas, contributing to the intense social unrest in the 1960s.

Today federal law and the federal courts tend to rein in the more outrageous abuses of power. Even so, state politics are still dominated by local elites, especially local businesses. The political power of business is particularly significant in smaller and poorer states, where a single business or industry may wield great influence over elected officials and citizens alike.

Ironically, for all its importance, state and local politics often do not attract the same level of interest as do national or international issues. Thus, while citizens—and the mass media—focus on Washington and other world capitals, local and state politics are often ignored. This inattention allows the relatively few individuals who care a lot about local and state politics to have influence far beyond their numbers.

Fosters Unhealthy Competition   Federalism also has the potential to foster unhealthy competition between the states. States compete vigorously for citizens, businesses, and jobs. Competition no doubt spurs innovation, but some argue that too much interstate competition is bad for the nation as a whole. Poorer states understandably want to entice businesses to locate there with promises of lower wages and more lenient regulatory environments. This in turn puts pressure on all states to try to attract business interests or individuals whose skills make them desirable. It is harder for workers to seek higher wages or better working conditions if businesses can simply move to another state. The natural temptation for businesses to "shop around" for the best deal also leads to criticism that states spend too much time and resources trying to swipe businesses such as professional sports franchises from one another.

Undercuts National Policymaking   Another disadvantage is the potential for inefficiency. Diffusing power and authority may help deter governmental tyranny, but it also makes it far more difficult to create and implement national policies. National policies often fall victim to local and regional needs represented in Congress, particularly the Senate. Forging national policy usually involves patching together support among the various states. The result is what some observers call "lowest common denominator policymaking," with Congress enacting only the policies that encounter the least resistance.

"Lowest common denominator" policymaking is inherently slow and piecemeal. Individual states may be innovators, but no state can be seen as too radical on policy matters. For example, states that pass tough air pollution laws may find themselves losing factories to states whose laws are more lenient. Attempts to pass national laws designed to "level the playing field" among the states get bogged down in Congress because of resistance from legislators whose states are opposed to any change at all, even if doing nothing runs counter to the national welfare.

Slow and incremental change is not inherently a bad thing. Often it is better to proceed slowly. At least any mistakes made will be small, and adjustments can be made before it is too late. But, critics say, the problems of contemporary government are increasingly national in nature and eventually require some degree of national government coordination or intervention. For them, federalism is an obstacle to effective national policy. Federalism may have made sense in the 19th century, when both problems and responses were localized, but whether it is suited to the challenges of the next century is sure to be a matter of great controversy.

CONCLUSION

Federalism dates back to the nation's founding and is one of the most important compromises in the history of the American political system. The failures of the Articles of Confederation prompted calls for a stronger role for the national government, but fears about potential tyranny limited the degree to which power could go entirely to the national government. Federalism was a compromise: It both divided and shared powers and responsibilities among the national and state governments.

The result, however, is a tension that continues to shape American politics. Under federalism, Americans accept the inevitable conflicts and compromises that come with this hybrid form of government. National and state officials frequently disagree over their respective roles, yet they continue to work together to provide governmental services. Our opening example on the national policy on the disposal of low-level radioactive waste captures both the conflicts and the compromises that emerge in a federal system. The national government, through its representative bodies, sets the overall direction, but the states and their local governments reflect the diversity of the nation's population and the localities in which they live.

Federalism also influences both the process and the style of politics in the United States. The effects of federalism can be as profound as having citizens of the same nation living under different sets of laws, depending on the state in which they reside. Policymaking under federalism requires a lot of hard work to hammer out compromises among the various states or ensure that national policies don't treat some states unfairly. Policy making under federalism is more difficult and time consuming than it might be in a unitary system, in which the national government has most of the power and responsibility.

But federalism also makes change more possible, even likely. Its multiple points of access give citizens many more places to seek redress of grievances or make changes in policy. Certainly the process of making new laws or creating new programs is more complicated, but citizens have many more opportunities to have an effect. The result is often loud and messy, but it ensures that the system does not stagnate. At any given time, somewhere in America, citizens are agitating for change, and federalism gives them more ways to have an impact on the future.

SUMMARY

▸ Federalism is a system in which governmental power and responsibility are divided between the national and state governments. Federalism was a practical response to the problem of creating a national government that would be capable of fostering national unity while at the same time maintaining the responsiveness promised by state government.

▸ The Constitution grants to the national government a range of explicit enumerated or express powers (Article I, Section 8). However, the national government also has grants of inherent power (such as the power to defend the nation) as well as a broad array of implied powers, that is, powers that are implied by extension from its enumerated and inherent powers.

▸ The states also possess a wide range of concurrent and reserved powers. Concurrent powers include the power to tax and spend, as well as the power to appropriate private property for public uses with proper compensation. Reserved powers, which are protected by the Tenth Amendment, extend to such areas as authority over local governments, and election laws.

▸ American federalism was initially characterized by state sovereignty and a limited role for the national government. Today the national government is far more powerful and active in virtually every aspect of law and policy. However, the states continue to have major impacts on national policy and on the lives of Americans, and the relationship between the national and state governments is always going to be a balancing act.

▸ Federalism imposes significant costs on the American system, but it also generates significant benefits. Federalism's costs include complexity and inequitable treatment of citizens based on state residency. Benefits include flexibility and innovation. However, whatever its flaws, federalism will characterize the American system for as long as anyone can foresee.

QUESTIONS FOR REVIEW AND DISCUSSION

1. Distinguish among federal, confederated, and unitary systems of government. What are the advantages and disadvantages of each?

2. Discuss the "states' rights" and "nationalist" perspectives on federalism.

3. What factors have contributed to the expansion of the power of the national government relative to that of the state governments?

4. Discuss the relative benefits and costs of federalism.

5. How does federalism affect your daily life? Give examples.

TERMS TO REMEMBER

coercive federalism	inherent powers
concurrent powers	necessary and proper clause
confederation	police powers
cooperative federalism	privileges and immunities clause
dual sovereignty	reserve clause
enumerated powers	reserved powers
federalism	states' rights
federal mandates	supremacy clause
general welfare clause	unitary system
implied powers	war powers

WEB SOURCES

Website of the National Governors Association (www.nga.org), which works with Congress and the executive branch on issues of concern to the states. The site includes links to state constitutions and laws.

A collaboration of organizations such as the National League of Cities and the National Association of Counties (www.localgov.org), this site contains extensive information on issues important to local governments.

This site, operated by National Association of State Resource Executives (www.nasirc.org), holds a huge library of information on and for state governments.

SUGGESTED READINGS

Samuel Beer, *To Make a Nation: The Rediscovery of American Federalism* (Cambridge, MA: Harvard University Press, 1993). Develops a "national theory" of federalism by examining key leaders and events in American history. In this theory of federalism, the American people look to the federal government to safeguard their basic rights and liberties and, ultimately, preserve the country as one nation. This development of a "national union" has been tested during the Civil War, economic depression, and racial conflict.

Thomas R. Dye, *American Federalism: Competition Among Governments* (Lexington, MA: Lexington Books, 1990). Develops a theory of "competitive federalism," in which competition among state and local governments encourages them to offer citizens/taxpayers the best possible combination of services at the lowest cost. Competitive federalism also helps to minimize the potential abuse of power by any one government, and ultimately best serves the interests of all Americans.

Paul Peterson, *The Price of Federalism* (Washington, D.C.: The Brookings Institution, 1995). Analyzes the allocation of major responsibilities among national and state governments. States are best positioned to support local economic development, whereas the national government has assumed responsibility for such broad social policies as welfare and social security. Problems persist in terms of the costs of programs such as welfare, disparities in state fiscal capacities, and the expense in providing services in urban areas.

David Walker, *The Rebirth of Federalism: Slouching Toward Washington* (Chatham, NJ: Chatham House Publishers, 1995). Assesses the current state of "permissive federalism," in which power is shared between the national and state governments even as the national government clearly has the upper hand. Walker emphasizes the constitutional division of authority, the role of the Supreme Court, the importance of state representation in the national government, and the role of political parties in shaping federalism.

NOTES

1. Mary English, *Siting Low-Level Radioactive Waste Disposal Facilities: The Public Policy Dilemma* (New York: Quorum Books, 1992).

2. "U.S. Nuclear Waste Disposal Programs Progressing, but Slowly," *Environmental Science & Technology*, vol. 31, no. 10 (1997), p. 458A.

3. "U.S. Nuclear Waste Disposal Programs Progressing, but Slowly," p. 458A.

4. Alexis de Tocqueville, *Democracy in America*, vol. 1 (New York: Schocken Books, 1967), p. 52.

5. William Clark, *Railroads and Rivers: The Story of Inland Transportation* (Boston: L.C. Page and Company, 1939), p. 25.

6. See Raoul Berger, *Federalism: The Founder's Design* (Norman, OK: University of Oklahoma Press, 1987).

7. H. G. Nicholas, *The Nature of American Politics*, 2d ed. (London: Oxford University Press, 1986), p. 17.

8. See Bert A. Rockman, *The Leadership Question: The Presidency and the American System* (New York: Praeger, 1984).

9. Jack W. Peltason, *Understanding the Constitution*, 14th ed. (New York: Holt, Rinehart, and Winston, 1997), p. 65.

10. *United States v Curtiss-Wright Export Corp.*, 299 US 304 (1936).

11. Peltason, *Understanding the Constitution*, p. 19.

12. Richard A. Epstein, *Takings, Private Property, and the Power of Eminent Domain* (Cambridge, MA: Harvard University Press, 1986).

13. Bill Richards, "Governors' Decisions in Extradition Cases Vary All over the Map," *Wall Street Journal*, May 27, 1984, p. 1.

14. Peltason, *Understanding the Constitution*, p. 145.

15. Michael C. Tolley and Bruce A. Wallin, "Coercive Federalism and the Search for Constitutional Limits," *Publius: The Journal of Federalism*, vol. 25, no. 4 (1995), pp. 73–90.

16. *New York v United States*, 488 US 1041 (1992).

17. David Osborne, *Laboratories of Democracy* (Boston: Harvard Business School Press, 1990).

18. *Brown v Board of Education of Topeka et al*, 347 US 483 (1954).

19. Daniel J. Elazar, *American Federalism: A View from the States* (New York: Crowell, 1966).

20. Nicholas, *The Nature of American Politics*, p. 17

21. U.S. Bureau of the Census, *1987 Census of Governments* (Washington, D.C.: U.S. Government Printing Office, 1987).

PRIMARY SOURCE READINGS

JAMES MADISON
Federalist No. 39, The Conformity of the Plan to Republican Principles

For the Independent Journal

To the People of the State of New York:

In order to ascertain the real character of the government, it may be considered in relation to the foundation on which it is to be established; to the sources from which its ordinary powers are to be drawn; to the operation of those powers; to the extent of them; and to the authority by which future changes in the government are to be introduced.

On examining the first relation, it appears, on one hand, that the Constitution is to be founded on the assent and ratification of the people of America, given by deputies elected for the special purpose; but, on the other, that this assent and ratification is to be given by the people, not as individuals composing one entire nation, but as composing the distinct and independent States to which they respectively belong. It is to be the assent and ratification of the several States, derived from the supreme authority in each State, the authority of the people themselves. The act, therefore, establishing the Constitution, will not be a NATIONAL, but a FEDERAL act.

That it will be a federal and not a national act, as these terms are understood by the objectors; the act of the people, as forming so many independent States, not as forming one aggregate nation, is obvious from this single consideration, that it is to result neither from the decision of a MAJORITY of the people of the Union, nor from that of a MAJORITY of the States. It must result from the UNANIMOUS assent of the several States that are parties to it, differing no otherwise from their ordinary assent than in its being expressed, not by the legislative authority, but by that of the people themselves. Were the people regarded in this transaction as forming one nation, the will of the majority of the whole people of the United States would bind the minority, in the same manner as the majority in each State must bind the minority; and the will of the majority must be determined either by a comparison of the individual votes, or by considering the will of the majority of the States as evidence of the will of a majority of the people of the United States. Neither of these rules have been adopted. Each State, in ratifying the Constitution, is considered as a sovereign body, independent of all others, and only to be bound by its own voluntary act. In this relation, then, the new Constitution will, if established, be a FEDERAL, and not a NATIONAL constitution. . . .

The difference between a federal and national government, as it relates to the OPERATION OF THE GOVERNMENT, is supposed to consist in this, that in the former the powers operate on the political bodies composing the Confederacy, in their political capacities; in the latter, on the individual citizens composing the nation, in their individual capacities. On trying the Constitution by this criterion, it falls under the NATIONAL, not the FEDERAL character; though perhaps not so completely as has been understood. In several cases, and particularly in the trial of controversies to which States may be parties, they must be viewed and proceeded against in their collective and political capacities only. So far the national countenance of the government on this side seems to be disfigured by a few federal features. But this blemish is perhaps unavoidable in any plan; and the operation of the government on the people, in their individual capacities, in its ordinary and most essential proceedings, may, on the whole, designate it, in this relation, a NATIONAL government.

But if the government be national with regard to the OPERATION of its powers, it changes its aspect again when we contemplate it in relation to the EXTENT of its powers. The idea of a national government involves in it, not only an authority over the individual citizens, but an indefinite supremacy over all persons and things, so far as they are objects of lawful government. Among a people consolidated into one nation, this supremacy is completely vested in the national legislature. Among communities united for particular purposes, it is vested partly in the general and partly in the municipal legislatures. In the former case, all local authorities are subordinate to the supreme; and may be controlled, directed, or abolished by it at pleasure. In the latter, the local or municipal authorities form distinct and independent portions of the supremacy, no more subject, within their respective spheres, to the general authority, than the general authority is subject to them, within its own sphere. In this relation, then, the proposed government cannot be deemed a NATIONAL one; since its jurisdiction extends to certain enumerated objects only, and leaves to the several States a residuary and inviolable sovereignty over all other objects. It is true that in controversies relating to the boundary between the two jurisdictions, the tribunal which is ultimately to decide, is to be established under the general government. But this does not change the principle of the case. The decision is to be impartially made, according to the rules of the Constitution; and all the usual and most effectual precautions are taken to secure this impartiality. Some such tribunal is clearly essential to prevent an appeal to the sword and a dissolution of the compact; and that it ought to be established under the general rather than under the local governments, or, to speak more properly, that it could be safely established under the first alone, is a position not likely to be combated.

If we try the Constitution by its last relation to the authority by which amendments are to be made, we find it neither wholly NATIONAL nor wholly FEDERAL. Were it wholly national, the supreme and ultimate authority would reside in the MAJORITY of the people of the Union; and this authority would be competent at all times, like that of a majority of every national society, to alter or abolish its established government. Were it wholly federal, on the other hand, the concurrence of each State in the Union would be essential to every alteration that would be binding on all. The mode provided by the plan of the convention is not founded on either of these principles. In requiring more than a majority, and principles. In requiring more than a majority, and particularly in computing the proportion by STATES, not by CITIZENS, it departs from the NATIONAL and advances towards the FEDERAL character; in rendering the concurrence of less than the whole number of States sufficient, it loses again the FEDERAL and partakes of the NATIONAL character.

The proposed Constitution, therefore, is, in strictness, neither a national nor a federal Constitution, but a composition of both. . . .

—PUBLIUS

GEORGE C. WALLACE
"The Civil Rights Movement: Fraud, Sham, and Hoax," July 4, 1964

George C. Wallace (1919–1997) served as governor of Alabama on and off for 16 years between 1963 and 1987. In his early years in office, Wallace became synonymous with opposition by southern states to federal government mandates on racial desegregation, most famously when he tried to physically bar the admission of black students to the University of Alabama. A hero to many who saw the federal government as intruding into the rights of the states, Wallace ran for president three times, largely on conservative populist issues. As the South changed, so did Wallace; in the 1980s he was supported by many black voters because of his efforts to improve the quality of life in Alabama. This excerpt is taken from a speech attacking the passage of the federal Civil Rights Act of 1964.

We come here today in deference to the memory of those stalwart patriots who on July 4, 1776, pledged their lives, their fortunes, and their sacred honor to establish and defend the proposition that governments are created by the people, empowered by the people, derive their just powers from the consent of the people, and must forever remain subservient to the will of the people. . . .

It is therefore a cruel irony that the President of the United States has only yesterday signed into law the most monstrous piece of legislation ever enacted by the United States Congress.

It is a fraud, a sham, and a hoax. . . .

Never before in the history of this nation have so many human and property rights been destroyed by a single enactment of the Congress. It is an act of tyranny. It is the assassin's knife stuck in the back of liberty. . . .

This bill is fraudulent in intent, in design, and in execution. It is misnamed. Each and every provision is mistitled. It was rammed through the Congress on the wave of ballyhoo, promotions, and publicity stunts reminiscent of P. T. Barnum. . . .

It threatens our freedom of speech, of assembly, or association, and makes the exercise of these Freedoms a federal crime under certain conditions.

It affects our political rights, our right to trial by jury, our right to the full use and enjoyment of our private property, the freedom from search and seizure of our private property and possessions, the freedom from harassment by Federal police and, in short, all the rights of individuals inherent in a society of free men.

Ministers, lawyers, teachers, newspapers, and every private citizen must guard his speech and watch his actions to avoid the deliberately imposed booby traps put into this bill. It is designed to make Federal crimes of our customs, beliefs, and traditions. Therefore, under the fantastic powers of the Federal judiciary to punish for contempt of court and under their fantastic powers to regulate our most intimate aspects of our lives by injunction, every American citizen is in jeopardy and must stand guard against these despots. . . .

I am not about to be a party to anything having to do with the law that is going to destroy individual freedom and liberty in this country.

I am having nothing to do with enforcing a law that will destroy our free enterprise system.

I am having nothing to do with enforcing a law that will destroy neighborhood schools.

I am having nothing to do with enforcing a law that will destroy the rights of private property.

I am having nothing to do with enforcing a law that destroys your right—and my right—to choose my neighbors—or to sell my house to whomever I choose.

I am having nothing to do with enforcing a law that destroys the labor seniority system.

I am having nothing to do with this so-called civil rights bill. The liberal left-wingers have passed it. Now let them employ some pinknik social engineers in Washington, D.C., to figure out what to do with it. . . .

A left-wing monster has risen up in this nation. It has invaded the government. It has invaded the news media. It has invaded the leadership of many of our churches. It has invaded every phase and aspect of the life of freedom-loving people.

It consists of many and various and powerful interests, but it has combined into one massive drive and is held together by the cohesive power of the emotion, setting forth civil rights as supreme to all.

But, in reality, it is a drive to destroy the rights of private property, to destroy the freedom and liberty of you and me.

And, my friends, where there are no property rights, there are no human rights. Red China and Soviet Russia are prime examples.

Politically evil men have combined and arranged themselves against us. The good people of this nation must now associate themselves together, else we will fall one by one, an unpitied sacrifice in a struggle which threatens to engulf the entire nation. . . .

We must destroy the power to dictate, to forbid, to require, to demand, to distribute, to edict, and to judge what is best and enforce that will of judgment upon free citizens.

CIVIL RIGHTS AND LIBERTIES

THE BILL OF RIGHTS
THE BILL OF RIGHTS AND DEMOCRACY
RIGHTS AND LIBERTIES DEFINED
CIVIL RIGHTS: SETTING A LARGER TABLE
THE RIGHT TO BE INCLUDED
RACIAL DISCRIMINATION
GENDER DISCRIMINATION
OTHER CIVIL RIGHTS ISSUES

CIVIL LIBERTIES:
KEEPING GOVERNMENT AT BAY
FIRST AMENDMENT FREEDOMS
RIGHTS OF THE ACCUSED
THE RIGHT TO PRIVACY
THE RIGHT TO BEAR ARMS
PRIVATE PROPERTY RIGHTS

OBJECTIVES

❑ To explain why Americans believe that an explicit Bill of Rights is necessary to preserve their basic rights and liberties

❑ To describe the civil rights guaranteed to Americans, particularly the right to equal protection under the law, and to assess the "nationalization" of rights throughout U.S. history

❑ To describe the civil liberties guaranteed to Americans, particularly freedoms of religion and expression, the rights of individuals accused of crimes, and the right to private property

❑ To show that neither rights nor liberties are absolute but instead involve balancing the needs of the individual against those of society

The typical student union, with the usual array of student groups seeking new members. Universities, which thrive on openess and diversity, are fertile breeding grounds for the clash of rights and liberties that often characterize American society.

In 1990 Ronald Rosenberger and other undergraduates at the University of Virginia (UVA) formed a Christian student group, Wide Awake Productions. The group applied to UVA's student activities fund to pay for a printing of its newsletter, *Wide Awake: A Christian Perspective*. The student activities fund at UVA, as at most universities, is financed through an activities fee assessed on all undergraduates and is used to support extracurricular activities and student groups.

Their request for funding was denied. The fund's administrators argued that because UVA is a state institution, and as Wide Awake Productions obviously was engaged in a religious activity, any direct university support for the group's newsletter would violate the principle of separation of church and state enshrined in the "establishment clause" of the First Amendment to the U.S. Constitution. In other words, student activities funds at a public university could not be used to "establish" or support a religious organization.

Rosenberger's group filed a lawsuit in federal district court, claiming that the university violated the group's First Amendment guarantee of free speech and the "free exercise of religion." They also argued that UVA violated the Fourteenth Amendment's guarantees of "equal protection" of the laws, because the student activities fund had financed publications by Jewish and Islamic groups. The university responded that, as a public institution, it could not directly fund activities that had a clear religious purpose.

The federal district court ruled in the university's favor. Rosenberger's group, financially supported by sympathetic religious organizations, appealed the decision. The U.S. Court of Appeals for the Fourth Circuit (which covers Virginia) agreed with the district court, ruling that UVA had a "compelling interest" in maintaining a strict separation between church and state. The student group appealed this decision to the United States Supreme Court, which agreed to hear the case during its 1994–1995 term.

The Supreme Court, by a 5–4 vote, reversed the lower federal court's decision and ruled in favor of the student group. Writing for the majority, Associate Justice Anthony Kennedy argued that discrimination against the expression of religious viewpoints violates the First Amendment's guarantee of free speech. Furthermore, he argued, the First Amendment's "establishment clause" did not prevent the university from funding the newsletter:

> It does not violate the Establishment Clause for a public university to give access to its facilities on a religious-neutral basis to a wide spectrum of student groups, including groups which use meeting rooms for sectarian activities, accompanied by some devotional exercise. . . . The University provides printing services to a broad spectrum of student newspapers. . . . Any benefit of religion is incidental to the government's provision of secular services for secular purposes on a religion-neutral basis.[1]

Four of the justices disagreed. They worried that allowing direct government support for a religious activity would breach the "high wall" of separation between church and state. In his dissenting opinion, Associate Justice David Souter wrote:

> Using public funds for the direct subsidization of preaching the Word is categorically forbidden under the Establishment Clause, and if the Clause was meant to accomplish nothing else, it was meant to bar this use of public money. . . . The principle against direct funding is patently violated by the contested use of today's student activity fee.

In *Rosenberger v. University of Virginia*, the Supreme Court had to reconcile conflicting rights. Did the university violate the students' rights to free speech and free exercise of religion? Or did it uphold the right of all students to be free from state-sponsored religion? Was it "establishing" religion by giving the Christian group money, or was it being hostile to religion by refusing to do so? The Court's decision in some ways was a compromise: The university could fund the newsletter without actually supporting the group's religious message. But the compromise was controversial, as are so many that involve conflicts over the rights of some individuals and the interests of the larger community.

THE BILL OF RIGHTS

In June 1776, a month before the colonies declared independence, the Virginia House of Burgesses enacted a formal Declaration of Rights that laid out the basic rights and liberties guaranteed to Virginians. Article I of the document, primarily drafted by George Mason, is of particular interest. It declared:

> That all men are born equally free and independent, and have certain inherent natural rights, of which, when they cannot, by any compact, deprive or divest their posterity; among which there are the enjoyment of life and liberty, with the means of acquiring and possessing property, and pursuing and obtaining happiness and safety.[2]

If this sounds familiar, it should. Thomas Jefferson, a Virginian, had this document on hand when he helped draft the Declaration of Independence. But Jefferson made a subtle change in wording that influenced how Americans view basic rights and liberties. In particular, he changed the Virginia Declaration's right to acquire and possess property into a broader right to "happiness." This alteration was important: It avoided claiming that people had an inherent right to own "unnatural" forms of property—that is, slaves—even while the topic of slavery itself was excluded from the Declaration to satisfy the demands of delegates from slave-holding colonies.[3]

Americans seem very concerned about rights and liberties.[4] Few political arguments get far before someone claims a basic right to do something or demands freedom from government restrictions on some kind of activity or lifestyle. Talking about rights is as natural to Americans as complaining about the weather. But debates over rights and liberties are not mere philosophical concerns. They pose key questions about the proper role of government: Should government actively promote and expand basic rights and liberties? Should it actively restrict them? Should it just stay out of the way? These sorts of questions stem from fundamental conflicts over what government may and may not do.

As we saw in chapter 2, the idea that a people should be explicit about basic rights and liberties shaped the development of the American system. The rationale was straightforward: Explicit guidelines regarding what government can and cannot do place clear restraints on government power. Nothing should be left to chance.

By 1787, the year in which the U.S. Constitution was drafted, each of the original 13 states had drafted its own state constitution, and each of these constitutions contained an explicit "bill of rights." Yet no bill of rights was originally included in the U.S. Constitution, whose supporters considered it unnecessary for three reasons: First, they argued that mechanisms such as separation of powers and checks and balances were adequate to restrain the national government and prevent abuses by the majority in power. Second, they argued that the national government could exercise only the powers delegated to it in the Constitution, and that it had no power to interfere in the jurisdictions of the states or in the rights and liberties of individual citizens. As Alexander Hamilton wrote in *Federalist* No. 84, "Why declare that things shall not be done which there is no power to do?"[5] Third, they argued that a bill of rights was unnecessary because such matters were concerns for the states and were already addressed in state bills of rights.

Antifederalists were not swayed by these arguments. They argued that the proposed constitution could undermine the individual liberties that they had fought so hard to preserve and that had later been guaranteed in their state bills of rights. They did not think that the Constitution, even in its final form, was explicit enough about the limits on national government power, which might usurp the powers of the states. For them, a national bill of rights would serve as insurance against a potentially tyrannical national government.

Anti-federalists had political leverage, and the Constitution was ratified largely because its supporters promised to add a bill of rights. Congress discussed more than 100 possible amendments to the Constitution during its first session (1789–1790). It approved 12 amendments, which were sent to the states for approval. Ten of the 12 amendments won the necessary support of three-quarters of the states and were added to the Constitution in 1791 (an eleventh, not ratified until 1992, became the Twenty-seventh Amendment). These first 10 amendments are known as the Bill of Rights.

THE BILL OF RIGHTS AND DEMOCRACY

The debates in Congress over framing the Bill of Rights suggest that these amendments were intended to provide the same protections against the power of the federal government that citizens had secured from their state governments. It did not appear to supersede the various state bills of rights. Rather, each had the effect of protecting fundamental rights and liberties within its respective sphere: The Bill of Rights applied to actions of the federal government; the state bills of rights to the actions of the states.

It was less clear whether the Bill of Rights pertained to the actions of the federal government with respect to individual citizens. This issue was a matter of intense debate as individual citizens challenged state actions as violations of their rights as American citizens under the Constitution. The conflict eventually found its way to the Supreme Court. In *Barron v. Baltimore* (1833), the Court declared that the provisions in the Bill of Rights did not protect against encroachments by state and local government but were limited to potential abuses of rights and liberties by the federal government.[6] Individual rights and liberties were largely state matters.

It was not until after the ratification of the Fourteenth Amendment in 1868 (discussed later) that the doctrine embodied in the *Barron* decision began to erode. In the early 20th century, the Supreme Court began to apply provisions of the Bill of Rights to the states, in effect overriding state laws with respect to the treatment of citizens' basic rights and liberties. This process of "nationalizing" the guarantees found in the Bill of Rights is known as **incorporation.** For example, as Table 4.1 shows, the First Amendment's guarantee of freedom of speech was incorporated and applied against state actions beginning in 1927.

Today most individual rights and liberties have been effectively nationalized. The Bill of Rights now affirms the basic rights and liberties of all citizens from *any* government—national, state, or local. More important, most Americans see rights and

TABLE 4.1.   THE NATIONALIZATION OF THE BILL OF RIGHTS

Year	Amendment	Provision	Case	Issue
1896-97	5	"Public use," "just compensation" and conditions in the taking of private property	*Missouri Pacific Railway Co. v. Neb.* and *Quincy Railway v. Chicago*	P
1927	1	Freedom of speech	*Fiske v. Kansas* and *Gitlow v. New York*	CL
1931	1	Freedom of the press	*Near v. Minnesota*	CL
1932	6	Right to fair trial and to counsel in capital cases	*Powell v. Alabama*	P
1937	1	Freedom of assembly	*De Jonge v. Oregon*	CL
1940	1	Free exercise of religious belief	*Cantwell v. Connecticut*	CL
1947	1	Protections against the establishment of religion	*Everson v. Board of Education*	CL
1948	6	Right to public trial	*In re Oliver*	CP
1949	4	Protection against unreasonable search and seizure	*Wolf v. Colorado*	CP
1958	1	Freedom of association	*NAACP v. Alabama*	CL
1961	4	Exclusionary rule—freedom from illegal search and seizure	*Mapp v. Ohio*	CP
1962	8	Freedom from cruel and unusual punishment	*Robinson v. California*	CP
1963	6	Right to counsel in felony cases	*Gideon v. Wainwright*	CP
1964	5	Freedom from self-incrimination	*Malloy v. Hogan*	CP
1965	6	Right to confront witnesses	*Pointer v. Texas*	CP
1965	1,3,4,5,9	Right to privacy	*Griswold v. Connecticut*	CL
1966	6	Right to impartial jury	*Parker v. Gladden*	CP
1967	6	Right to a speedy trial	*Klopfer v. North Carolina*	CP
1967	6	Right to obtain witnesses	*Washington v. Texas*	CP
1968	6	Right to a jury trial	*Duncan v. Louisiana*	CP
1969	5	Protection against double jeopardy	*Benton v. Maryland*	CP
1972	6	Right to counsel in cases with possible jail term	*Argersinger v. Hamlin*	CP

Amendment	Provisions not Incorporated Provisions
2	All
3	All
5	Right to grand jury indictment
7	All
8	Freedom from excessive bail or excessive fines

Key: P—Property rights; CL—Civil liberties; CP—Criminal law/procedural rights

Source: Richard C. Cortner, *The Supreme Court and the Second Bill of Rights: The Fourteenth Amendment and the Nationalization of Civil Liberties* (Madison: University of Wisconsin Press, 1981).

liberties in national terms, as common to all citizens. Moreover, the influence of the Bill of Rights extends beyond the United States. Its guarantees have been copied in some form in many of the constitutions drafted since World War II. It also is the basis for the contemporary notion of "human rights," rights that all people should have regardless of their national citizenship.

Finally, the guarantees contained in the Bill of Rights are the basic building blocks of democracy. Putting citizens' basic rights and liberties on paper makes them more permanent, something that in theory cannot be taken away. For this reason alone, the idea that a bill of rights might help ensure restrained and democratic government has become universal.

RIGHTS AND LIBERTIES DEFINED

The terms *rights* and *liberties* are often used interchangeably. Although there is some overlap between them, they are actually somewhat distinct, both conceptually and legally.

Civil rights refer to protections against arbitrary discrimination by government or by other people solely because of personal characteristics or beliefs. Civil rights protect a person's freedom to do something regardless of race, creed, gender, sexual orientation, age, or physical disability. This can include, among many things, the right to vote, the right to equal access to job opportunities, or the right to serve in the armed forces. Civil rights have to do with equality, about having equal opportunity to enjoy the full benefits of American citizenship.

Civil liberties encompass matters such as freedom of speech, freedom of worship, and the rights of individuals accused of crimes. Civil liberties are protections against unwarranted intrusion by government or others in how people live their private lives or how they act in public. For example, civil liberties keep government from abusing a person's freedom to speak out on political issues. Civil liberties have to do with protection from governmental tyranny, or the abuse of power by an antidemocratic majority.

We discuss civil rights first. In many ways the greatest conflict in American history has been over who shall be a citizen with equal rights under the law. This struggle to extend equal rights to previously excluded individuals, particularly black slaves, was shaped by broad societal contexts and intense conflicts. Sometimes these conflicts have produced compromises that slowly expanded basic rights. When compromise was not possible, as with slavery, the results were often tragic, in this case a bloody war.

Conflicts over civil liberties have also been difficult. Americans generally (but not always) err on the side of limiting government's ability to meddle in a citizen's rights to life, liberty, or property. But they often disagree over what those words really mean. Does the right to "life" extend to those not yet born? Does it prohibit the death penalty? Where does "liberty" end and "responsibility" begin? Does the right to own property mean that one can do whatever one pleases with it? The Constitution is silent on these matters, and the Bill of Rights is often vague. Each generation of Americans has had to decide these issues.

CIVIL RIGHTS: SETTING A LARGER TABLE

Conflicts over civil rights are not abstractions. They have real consequences for real people, as a recent example illustrates.

Derrick Bell, an African American, was a professor at the Harvard Law School. In 1992 he gave up his position to protest what he saw as the school's inadequate record in hiring and keeping minority faculty, particularly black women. Other faculty disagreed with Bell's charges. They felt that the school had tried to recruit "qualified" women and minorities but that there simply were too few black female law professors throughout the nation with high enough qualifications for Harvard. Nonsense, Bell retorted, arguing that the "old-boy network" at Harvard favored white males over blacks and women with similar records.[7]

This dispute involved powerful people at a prestigious university, but it was not unique. Similar conflicts are played out every day in less well-known places. They reflect a central struggle in American society: the struggle over who shall be treated as equals. Indeed, as Bell wrote in 1992, one way to understand the Constitution is to look at it through the eyes of those who did not enjoy equal rights from the start.[8] From their perspective, the ratification of the Constitution was just the beginning of a long struggle for equality that is far from over.

THE RIGHT TO BE INCLUDED

Efforts to prevent discrimination against individuals because of race, gender, sexual orientation, physical disability, or age are rooted in demands that the ideals of equality embodied in the Bill of Rights actually extend to *all* citizens. The common theme expressed by those seeking equal rights is a simple one: We want to sit at the main table with everyone else.

This sounds fair. Yet those already seated at the main table often fight against allowing newcomers to join them. Some resistance has been based on bigotry and intolerance; for example, opposition to equal rights sometimes stems from pseudoscientific notions of innate racial or ethnic superiority. Every society has its share of fear, even hatred, of "others."

Yet it isn't that simple. Resistance to demands for equal rights may reflect more than racism, xenophobia, or sexism. It often surfaces when those already at the main table feel threatened by potential competition for their jobs or political advantages, particularly if their own economic or social status is shaky. They may feel, correctly or not, that the claimants are seeking not equal rights but unequal *advantages.* Often opposition to policies seeking to redress racial or gender discrimination in college admissions or the workplace comes from those whose ethnic or racial group made its own gains only recently. At one time, for example, Irish immigrants faced ethnic and religious discrimination in obtaining jobs in big-city fire and police departments. Their sons and grandsons eventually dominated these professions, but they resisted efforts to give women and African Americans equal access to these jobs. Women and African Americans now worry about competition from citizens of Hispanic or Asian descent. The struggle to be included never ends.

The political scientist E. E. Schattschneider once wrote that all political conflict is about dominant and subordinate interests, the interests of those on the inside versus the desires of those looking in.[9] So it goes with conflicts over civil rights. Perhaps the most difficult conflict has been over racial equality, not only because of racism but also because it involves conflicts over social, economic, and political power. The key issues arising in conflicts over racial discrimination also appear in conflicts related to gender, sexual orientation, age, personal beliefs, or disability.

RACIAL DISCRIMINATION

"All men are created equal," states the Declaration of Independence, but this ideal did not match reality in the America of the late 1700s. Full citizenship and the right to vote were largely limited to white men. Women had few legal rights. Even white men who did not own property often could not vote. Only property owners had a sufficient "stake in society"; it was believed that those who lacked property might act out of jealousy or greed. Finally, the Constitution treated Indian tribes as sovereign nations and Native Americans as foreigners.[10]

Slavery and the Constitution   Black slavery was the most extreme contradiction of the ideals professed in the Declaration of Independence, the Constitution, and the Bill of Rights. As we saw in chapter 2, the "three-fifths compromise" on slavery made the Constitution possible. But, as Derrick Bell argues, the compromise "served to protect the property interests of slave-owners at the cost of freedom for blacks."[11] The compromises made in drafting the Constitution reflected what delegates thought was possible at the time, but they also made it more difficult to abolish slavery later. In fact, they made it difficult for any group seeking equal rights to overcome opposition by powerful economic and political interests. The fundamental clash was between political rights and property rights, a tension that is a constant theme throughout American history.

Early Conflicts   In 1808 Congress banned importation of slaves from Africa, but it left the matter of slavery itself up to each state. Many plantation owners saw great potential in the fertile lands in the West and moved their operations, slaves and all, to the new territories. They also wanted these territories to become states. Opponents of slavery fought against admitting new slave-holding states into the Union. This was a crucial issue: Any change in the balance of political power in Congress between "slave" and "free" states would affect the future of slavery itself.

For a while Congress maintained a balance by admitting new slave and free states in pairs. For example, Missouri, which allowed slavery, was not admitted into the Union until 1821, when it was paired with Maine, which banned slavery. This pairing occurred only after Congress came up with the Missouri Compromise (1820), which tried to settle the issue by extending a line westward from Missouri's southern border all the way to the Pacific Ocean and outlawing slavery everywhere north of that line. Thus, for the time being, Congress sidestepped the issue of westward expansion and new slave states.

BOX 4.1.
THE DRED SCOTT DECISION

In 1833, a slave named Dred Scott (1795–1858) was purchased by an army doctor from a family in Missouri, a slave state. His new owner took him to Illinois, a free state. After two years they moved to the free territory of what is now Minnesota, and they later returned to Missouri. Scott's owner died a few years after that, and the owner's widow left Scott in the hands of his previous owners. With their help, Scott sued for his freedom, declaring that residence in the free territory made him a free man. A lower court agreed, but the Missouri Supreme Court reversed the decision. Scott, the state court argued, was still property under Missouri law and therefore must remain a slave. With the legal assistance of antislavery lawyers and the cooperation of the former owners, Scott's case reached the U.S. Supreme Court.

The central question before the Court was whether a slave automatically became a free man by residing in a territory where slavery was illegal. Both sides in the increasingly volatile slavery issue eagerly awaited the decision, which many hoped would settle the issue and avoid the probability of secession by slave states. These hopes were dashed. The Court, led by Chief Justice Roger Taney, declared in a 7–2 decision that Scott was property, not a citizen, and hence had no right to sue in court in the first place. Taney noted that the framers of the Constitution had not seen fit to make slaves citizens in 1787, so 70 years later they "had no rights and privileges but such as those who held the power and the Government might choose to grant them." Missouri considered Scott to be property, and he had no inherent right to freedom or citizenship.

→

But the notion that slaves were property remained an explosive issue. Abolitionists increasingly helped runaway slaves reach freedom. Slave owners regarded this as theft of private property and persuaded their states to pass laws requiring the return of runaways. This conflict between civil rights and property interests was woven into the broader issue of state sovereignty. Could one state order citizens of another to return runaway slaves? Both issues were at the core of the *Dred Scott* decision (see Box 4.1), which failed to resolve these conflicts and probably hastened the onset of secession and the Civil War.

The Civil War Amendments   Slavery was abolished in 1865, when the states of the Union ratified the Thirteenth Amendment to the Constitution. The states of the former Confederacy could not prevent the end of slavery, but many sought to restrict the rights of freed blacks within their borders. Congress, dominated by the states of the victorious Union, reacted with the **Civil War Amendments,** which were in-

HISTORICAL PERSPECTIVE

But the Court did not end the matter there. It declared the Missouri Compromise of 1820 itself unconstitutional, only the second time the Court had struck down a law passed by Congress (the first was *Marbury v. Madison* in 1803, see chapter 11). Congress had no power to keep slavery out of new territories, Taney announced, because the Constitution gave the national government no power to interfere in the right to own property. Said the Court, "No word can be found in the Constitution which gives Congress a greater power over slave property, or which entitles property of that kind to less protection than property of any other description." Slaves were property, so Congress had acted unconstitutionally in 1820 by limiting the areas in which slavery could exist.

The *Dred Scott* decision, a judicial attempt to find a way out of a conflict, was a political disaster. The Court's staunch defense of property interests over the rights of human beings infuriated abolitionists and further divided the nation. It led to the election of Abraham Lincoln, the candidate of the new Republican party, which had made abolition of slavery a major goal. Lincoln's election in 1860 in turn led to the secession of the states of the Confederacy. The Civil War, not the Supreme Court, would decide the issue of slavery.

Sources: Dred Scott v Sandford, 60 US (19 How.) 393 (1857); Robert S. Peck, *The Bill of Rights and the Politics of Interpretation* (St. Paul, MN: West Publishing Company, 1992), pp. 141–143; Jay Shafritz, *The Harper Collins Dictionary of American Government and Politics*, concise edition (New York: Harper Collins, 1993), p. 155.

tended to guarantee full citizenship to freed slaves and equal rights to anyone born in the United States (except Native Americans, who were still considered foreigners).

The Fourteenth Amendment (1868) was designed to protect blacks from oppression by former slave owners. In fact, southern states were required to ratify the Fourteenth Amendment before they were readmitted to the Union.[12]

The Fourteenth Amendment is important in four ways: First, it granted automatic American citizenship to anyone born in the United States—which, of course, applied to most former slaves. Second, it mandated that "no state shall make or enforce any law which shall abridge the privileges and immunities of citizens of the United States." This **privileges and immunities clause** aimed to prevent states from interfering with the basic civil and political rights enjoyed by citizens. Third, it forbade any state from depriving "any person of life, liberty, or property, without due process of law." This clause was meant to prevent arbitrary actions by state governments. Fourth, the Fourteenth Amendment guaranteed the "equal protection of the laws" to all citizens. This **equal protection clause** meant that Americans are citizens of one nation, not of their respective states, and therefore are entitled to equal treatment regardless of place of residence.[13]

To emphasize its intentions, Congress also passed the Fifteenth Amendment, ratified in 1870, which explicitly prohibits any state from abridging the right to vote "on account of race, color, or previous condition of servitude." However, the voting rights of women of any race were not covered by this or any other amendment, and women did not gain the right to vote in federal elections until the ratification of the Nineteenth Amendment in 1920.

Enforcing the Civil War Amendments   The Civil War Amendments (the Thirteenth, Fourteenth, and Fifteenth amendments) granted full rights of citizenship to former slaves—but words on paper guaranteed very little. The slaves were free, but most were poor and without property. Many were forced to work as tenant farmers or laborers—often for their former owners.

The protections contained in the Civil War Amendments also depended on the national government's willingness to enforce them. In the years immediately after the Civil War, federal troops protected blacks' voting rights and several southern states had black governors and members of Congress. But federal enforcement ceased after the southern states were readmitted into the Union in the late 1870s, largely because presidential candidates seeking the southern vote promised to ease up on federal enforcement. Readmission of the southern states also meant that southern senators again were able to oppose federal interference in state affairs.

Without federal protection or economic and political power, blacks in the South soon found themselves prevented from exercising the rights that had been granted to them only a few years earlier. Southern whites were unwilling to give up economic and political advantages, especially if equal rights meant creating a politically powerful black majority. Most southern states soon passed laws designed to bypass the Fifteenth Amendment and effectively prevent blacks from voting. For example, many enacted **grandfather clauses** that restricted the right to vote to those individuals whose grandfathers had been qualified to vote before March 30, 1870, the date on which the Fifteenth Amendment went into force. Most blacks did not qualify under this restriction, so they were prevented from voting. Without black votes, black southerners soon disappeared from Congress and state governments. At about the same time, the Ku Klux Klan, a "fraternal order" of former Confederate officers, emerged to "defend the white race" and intimidate blacks. Blacks were no longer slaves, but they were not free.

Early Court Decisions   The South was not alone. Prevailing social attitudes about white racial superiority, even among many whites who had fought against slavery, fostered widespread discrimination. Such attitudes were augmented by the belief that the national government should not interfere in the rights of the states.

These views were given legal justification by Supreme Court decisions that undermined the spirit of the Civil War Amendments. In the *Slaughterhouse Cases* (1873) the Court held that an individual's most important rights, such as the right to vote,

White water, colored water: the old face of racial discrimination. Discrimination was once as blunt as segregated toilets and drinking fountains. Today, the issues of racial discrimination are more subtle and complex.

were not among the rights of U.S. citizenship protected by the privileges and immunities clause of the Fourteenth Amendment.[14] The decision was based on the premise that citizenship in a nation is distinct from citizenship in a state, and any rights and liberties enjoyed by citizens came from their state citizenship. The Court's narrow interpretation of the Fourteenth Amendment meant that individuals still had to depend on state constitutions and laws for protection of their basic rights and liberties, seemingly against the intentions of the framers of the Fourteenth Amendment.

In the *Civil Rights Cases* (1883), the Court struck down as unconstitutional the Civil Rights Act of 1875, which outlawed racial discrimination in public accommodations such as theaters or restaurants.[15] Here the Court ruled that the Fourteenth Amendment forbade discrimination only by states and "state actors." Private individuals were neither "agents" nor "instrumentalities" of the states, so private individuals could discriminate as much as they wished, free from government oversight or intervention.

Finally, in *Plessy v. Ferguson* (1896) the Court ruled that separate railroad cars for whites and blacks did not violate the equal protection clause of the Fourteenth Amendment so long as equal facilities were available for people of all races.[16] Southern states in particular used this **separate but equal** justification to segregate the races in virtually every aspect of life, from hospitals and schools to theaters and cemeteries. These **Jim Crow laws** (named after a white entertainer who performed in blackface) were common in the South until the 1960s.

Thus, by 1900 the federal government played almost no role in safeguarding the rights of blacks. This reluctance to enforce the Civil War Amendments must be understood in the context of the times. Resistance to equal rights was partly due to racial bias, but it was also ideological: Both Congress and the Supreme Court tended to support a minimal federal government role on most issues. They typically sided with property interests on issues that affected *all* individuals, for instance opposing child labor laws or the right to organize unions. In many ways discrimination against blacks was only the most blatant manifestation of the political atmosphere of the times.

Changing Societal Contexts   These social attitudes changed only gradually over the next few decades. Even so, the broader economic and political contexts surrounding discrimination against blacks began to change as the nation itself changed. For example, the strict defense of property that was common in the late 1800s slowly gave way to greater demand for federal intervention in the marketplace, including regulation of dangerous products or fraudulent business practices and protection of workers' health and safety. The depression of the 1930s ushered in Franklin Roosevelt's "New Deal," a set of policies that gave the national government an active role in economic affairs, including more extensive regulation of workplace conditions.

World War II contributed to this more active federal government role. Wartime demands for labor meant that blacks (and women) were offered jobs in factories and in the armed forces, where few opportunities had existed before. These experiences transformed American society. Tens of thousands of blacks migrated to northern states during the war, dramatically changing the composition of the workforce as well as the face of urban America. Equally important, tens of thousands of black Americans entered the armed forces. They were placed in segregated units and often treated badly by white superiors, but many died in combat. The contradiction between black soldiers' defense of liberty abroad and the discrimination they faced at home led President Harry Truman to order the racial integration of the armed forces in 1948. His action provoked controversy and prompted southern Democrats to run their own "Dixiecrat" candidate against Truman in the 1948 presidential election; nevertheless, the armed forces were eventually integrated.

Desegregation   The economic and social transformation of post–World War II America accelerated the breakdown of the legal and social barriers that African Americans had faced since the Civil War. Laws enforcing racial segregation were increasingly controversial. Black and white civil rights activists began to ask why blacks who served their country and paid their taxes were shunted into separate, usually inferior, public schools, health facilities, and even baseball leagues. What did it say about America when Jackie Robinson was finally allowed to play major league baseball but still could not stay in the same hotels as his white teammates? Such contradictions made segregation more difficult to defend, even for Americans who weren't particularly open minded about relations between the races.

Organizations such as the National Association for the Advancement of Colored People (NAACP) chipped away at segregation in the federal courts. In fact, during the 1940s and 1950s, the courts were the primary vehicles for change because segregationists still wielded political power in Congress and the state governments.[17] In the 1950s the NAACP embarked on a judicial strategy, invoking the equal protection clause of the Fourteenth Amendment in efforts to overturn the "separate but equal" doctrine. Finally, in a unanimous decision in *Brown v. Board of Education of Topeka, Kansas* (1954), the Supreme Court overturned "separate but equal." The Court's ruling was unambiguous: Racially segregated public schools were inherently unequal, violated the equal protection clause of the Fourteenth Amendment, and therefore were unconstitutional.[18]

The Civil Rights Era   In many ways the decision in *Brown* also ushered in what is generally referred to as the "Civil Rights era." Federal courts began striking down state laws mandating racial segregation in public accommodations. Federal enforcement of civil rights for African Americans became more rigorous, with a series of presidents sending the Federal Bureau of Investigation and federal troops to enforce compliance with federal court orders when state officials either could not or would not do so.

The tide against segregation grew stronger in the 1960s. President Lyndon Johnson, aided by the increasing numbers of antisegregation northern Democrats elected to Congress in the early 1960s, persuaded Congress to pass the Civil Rights Act of 1964 and the Voting Rights Act of 1965. The Civil Rights Act forbade discrimination in public accommodations because of race, religion, or national origin. It also outlawed discrimination in employment because of race, religion, national origin, or sex. This last provision was added by a southern member of Congress who thought that demanding prohibitions against sex discrimination might prevent the bill from being passed. It passed anyway, suggesting how much times had changed.

The Civil Rights era reached its peak with the passage of the Voting Rights Act. This law forbade any state from interfering with a person's right to vote because of race or national origin, and required federal oversight of any election law or process that might have the effect of restricting the right to vote because of race. The Voting Rights Act essentially reasserted and enforced the protections guaranteed by the Fifteenth Amendment a century earlier, but in a very different societal context.

Contemporary Issues   The kinds of legal discrimination that were typical before the 1960s are less common today. The federal government is unlikely to stop enforcing civil rights laws, as it did in the late 1800s. Nor do most people support segregation the way they did only a generation ago. National life is more integrated; the South in particular has seen the emergence of a politically powerful African American middle class; and racial minorities increasingly occupy positions of authority in all levels of government. Most important, few Americans today would accept the inequities that were once considered normal.

This said, numerous racial issues remain. It is one thing to take away blatant barriers to access that most people admit were unfair. It is a far different matter to agree about how to provide equal access to jobs or good schools, or to ensure "adequate" political representation for any racial minority. The philosophical line between "equal access" and "unfair advantage" lies at the heart of the issue of **affirmative action** in employment and college admissions (see Box 4.2). Few people agree about how much racial diversity in the public schools is "enough," whether a search for diversity for its own sake compromises quality, or how greater diversity can be achieved

BOX 4.2.
AFFIRMATIVE ACTION AND THE UNIVERSITY

Affirmative action began in the 1960s as a federal rule that required the employment of women and racial minorities on projects financed with federal funds. In subsequent years the idea expanded throughout the society to ensure a degree of racial and gender equity in employment opportunities and access to schools. In its narrowest sense, affirmative action seeks to ensure equal opportunity for those previously excluded by overt and less-conscious discrimination.

One of the sharpest debates over affirmative action focuses on university admissions. Most colleges and universities desire some degree of "diversity" in the student body, whether measured by gender, race, or specific talents such as athletic ability or musical aptitude, because they want the student body to at least partly reflect the external society. *How* to achieve this goal is the issue.

In particular, there is sharp debate over how much standard achievement exams such as the SAT should dictate admissions. Many white Americans believe that admissions decisions should be based solely on exam scores, because any other criteria are less precise. In their view, it is "reverse discrimination" to use criteria such as gender and race in admissions decisions, especially if "less-qualified" students get desired slots in a class. Admission should be based solely on "neutral" indicators such as test scores. Those with the highest scores gain admission.

Defenders of affirmative action dispute such arguments. First, they argue, nobody complains when superb athletes or the sons and daughters of wealthy alumni somehow manage to gain admission despite lower SAT scores. Second, SAT scores are not perfect indicators of academic potential. In particular, achievement test results reflect the relative quality of secondary schools, the affluence and cohesion of families, and, even, whether students were able to take exam preparation classes to boost their results. In short, the critics argue, test achievement scores themselves reflect societal problems, and affirmative action programs have given minorities a chance to succeed.

without placing undue burdens on children and families of any race. Such conflicts usually involve balancing the rights of racial minorities *and* majorities.

History shows that these conflicts are never really "solved." They usually come back in new forms. For example, today's racial issues don't involve just whites and blacks. They increasingly involve Americans from other racial and ethnic backgrounds, particularly those of Hispanic heritage, who now make up the nation's largest racial minority. In the competition for scarce resources or opportunities, how to ensure equal rights without creating new inequities or social tensions is an enduring dilemma.

A CLOSER LOOK

For over a century the University of California–Berkeley, had used a two-track admissions system, with one based on academic merit and the other waiving some rules for candidates whom the university wanted to admit for other reasons. Few complained about this system until diversity became synonymous with race, as opposed to income, personal experiences, or unique talents. In 1996 voters in California passed Proposition 209, a ballot initiative outlawing "preferential treatment" based on race, sex, color, ethnicity, or national origin in public employment and education. The law was challenged in federal court but ultimately went into effect in 1997.

The effects on admissions to Berkeley were immediate. The number of African American and Hispanic freshmen admitted for fall 1998 dropped by 52 percent from fall 1997: In a class of 3,660, only 98 were African American, down from 260 in 1997, while the number of Hispanic freshmen fell from 492 to 264. However, the number of Asian students admitted for fall 1997 outnumbered white students, by 1,527 to 1,083.

California's public universities, like others throughout the nation, now struggle to maintain diverse student bodies without openly considering race or ethnicity. Some want to discontinue using achievement scores entirely, although this might be hard to do if Berkeley has to screen some 20,000 applicants annually. Others argue that Berkeley should focus more on class rank, which would enable it to admit bright students from schools in African American and Hispanic communities regardless of achievement test scores. Whatever the strategy, balancing diversity and quality in the university will remain a controversial issue.

Source: Patrick Healy, "Berkeley Struggles to Stay Diverse in Post Affirmative Action Era," *The Chronicle of Higher Education*, May 29, 1998, p. A31.

GENDER DISCRIMINATION

Women also have faced discrimination in the voting booth, the workplace, and the legal arena. Like discrimination against African Americans, resistance to equal rights for women was based on social attitudes about innate differences between the sexes and about their respective roles. For example, in 1873 the Supreme Court ruled that barring women from the practice of law was constitutional because, as one justice wrote, "God designed the sexes to occupy different spheres of action, and that it belonged to men to make, apply, and execute the law."[19] Men also resisted equal rights out of fear that women would compete with them for jobs. Social and economic motives are intertwined whenever matters of inequality are involved.

Political Rights   The battle for equal rights for women and men began with demands for woman suffrage, the right to vote. Resistance to woman suffrage was so strong that women did not gain the right to vote even when the Fifteenth Amendment extended suffrage to freed slaves. Most men (and some women) felt that the "weaker sex" needed to be "protected" from the rough business of politics, or from any activity that might corrupt women's morals. A great deal of this opposition was also based on fears that women might vote to regulate business activities, provide social services for the poor, or ban liquor.[20]

Yet by the late 1800s women had at least partial voting rights in many states, notably in the West, where frontier life stripped away genteel notions about female fragility. Widespread woman suffrage also came about as more women became educated and an active woman suffrage movement agitated for equal rights. The movement for suffrage also grew out of the strategic needs of the political parties, which saw women as a possible source of votes. Even so, resistance to woman suffrage was so strong, especially in the South, that not until 1920 did the nation adopt the Nineteenth Amendment to the Constitution guaranteeing women the right to vote in all elections.

Equal Opportunity   Even with the right to vote, before the 1960s women typically faced a wide range of legal and social barriers to equal opportunity in the workplace and in the legal arena. Dominant societal values limited women's roles to those of mother and homemaker. With some notable exceptions, women who worked outside the home were confined to low-paying jobs that few men wanted, or were paid less than were men for identical work, as was the case in factories during World War II. Some even lost their jobs when—and because—they got married. These inequities were supported by the rationale that men were the breadwinners for their families. So pervasive were such views about the proper place of women that women were not called to serve on juries until the 1960s.

The transformation of American society during and after World War II had effects on women similar to its effects on African Americans. More women went to college and chose to work outside the home. More became lawyers, doctors, and university professors. Advances in contraceptive technology also gave women greater control over decisions about having children. But legal equality lagged behind social change, and by the late 1960s a forceful women's movement had emerged to fight for equal treatment under the law.

Equality of opportunity for women and men was first addressed in the Civil Rights Act of 1964, which prohibited sex discrimination in employment. Within a few years the federal government also banned sex discrimination in access to federally funded educational institutions, mandated affirmative action programs and equal pay provisions on all federal projects, and, by creating tax credits for child care expenses, made it easier for mothers to hold jobs. Federal court decisions attacked gender discrimination in numerous areas, including inheritance law and eligibility for credit. By the mid-1970s gender discrimination had little legal basis. The primary exception was in areas in which there were cogent arguments against gender equality, such as military combat duty.

The Equal Rights Amendment   Despite these advances, groups such as the National Organization for Women (NOW) argued that legislative advances for women could be reversed by Congress, which is dominated by men. They also noted that the equal protection clause of the Fourteenth Amendment did not apply explicitly to women, so any gains by women in the courts were left open to reinterpretation by unsympathetic federal judges. Only a constitutional amendment, they believed, could safeguard the advances that had been made toward gender equality.

In 1972 Congress approved the **Equal Rights Amendment** (ERA) and sent it to the states for ratification. On its face the ERA seemed straightforward: "Equality of rights under the law shall not be denied or abridged by the United States or by any state on account of sex." Of the 38 states (3/4 of the 50 states) needed for ratification, 35 approved the amendment within five years, but momentum slowed in the late 1970s. In 1979 Congress extended the original seven-year deadline for ratification for another three years, but on July 1, 1982, the ERA still needed the support of three more states, and therefore was not ratified.

The ERA failed for several reasons. Women themselves were divided on the need for and the implications of the amendment. Promoters of the ERA tended to be better-educated professional women, many of whom had avoided having children. They regarded the traditional notion that women needed "protection" against the cruelties of the world as an impediment to equal opportunity. Women who opposed the ERA tended to be less well-educated homemakers who worried that the amendment might undermine traditional protections such as rights to alimony in cases of divorce. Proponents of the ERA tended to favor abortion rights; opponents feared that it would endorse a constitutional right to abortion. Some of the more zealous supporters of the ERA claimed that, among other things, it would allow women to engage in military combat, an issue that troubled people of both sexes. In some ways the fight over the ERA was part of a broader cultural conflict about the proper role of women in society.

Above all, political scientist Jane Mansbridge argues, the amendment's supporters could not show that it would produce benefits for women beyond those already provided under federal law or court decisions.[21] However, those who opposed the ERA could claim that it might lead to any number of undesirable outcomes, many of them (such as unisex toilets) probably exaggerated. Although most Americans voiced at least mild, general support for the ERA, a determined minority was large, vocal, and organized enough to keep the required number of states from ratifying the amendment.

The demise of the ERA did not mean the reversal of the movement for equal rights. Indeed, today an even higher percentage of women work outside the home and hold elected or appointed government positions. Women pilots have flown combat missions in the Persian Gulf. Congress and the courts have provided more pro-

The crew chief and her fighter. The role of women in the military has expanded significantly to include duty in combat areas (if not in actual ground combat). Without mandatory military service for all men, the military relies heavily on women to fill its demand for qualified personnel.

tection in such areas as sexual harassment and equal pay. Men and women alike are more sensitive to gender issues, just as more whites are sensitive to issues of race. Even so, proponents of the ERA fear that these advances could be reversed or narrowed if social and economic support were to decline, and they argue that women should be given the same explicit guarantees that are already extended to racial minorities. In the future, such fears may renew the drive for an explicit equal rights amendment.

OTHER CIVIL RIGHTS ISSUES

Other Americans have sought similar explicit guarantees of equal protection, either through federal legislation or through reinterpretation of existing laws by the federal courts. As with race and gender, these areas of civil rights encompass a range of conflicting interests.

Age Discrimination solely on the basis of age occurs on two fronts. Americans under age 18 generally have fewer rights than do adults. No one under 18 can vote or serve on a jury. In fact, for Americans 18 to 21 years of age the right to vote was not ensured until the passage of the Twenty-sixth Amendment in 1971. As with suffrage for African Americans and women, passage of this amendment came in part because of the rationale that Americans who paid taxes and served their country in wartime certainly should have the right to vote.

Whether they should be able to drink liquor is another question. In fact, no one has a basic "right" to buy alcoholic beverages. Liquor has been a political issue throughout American history, and organized "temperance leagues" managed to convene a special constitutional convention to ratify the Eighteenth Amendment (1919) prohibiting the sale and use of alcohol anywhere in the nation. Prohibition proved wildly unpopular with the majority of Americans, who evaded it at every turn; furthermore, it directly led to an increase in organized crime and possibly produced the very "immoral" social behaviors its supporters had hoped to halt. This failed social experiment ended with the repeal of Prohibition by the Twenty-first Amendment (1933), but most states continued to ban sales of alcohol to anyone under 18.

In 1984, concerns about teenage drinking and driving led President Ronald Reagan and Congress to reduce federal highway aid to states that did not impose a minimum drinking age of 21. All of the states complied, though not without complaints about federal intrusion into an area that had traditionally been governed by state law. Some states sued the federal government over the constitutionality of the mandate, but the Supreme Court ruled that the federal government's "relatively mild encouragement" to the states to impose a higher minimum drinking age did not infringe on states' rights.[22] That Americans between the ages of 18 and 21 had the rights of full citizenship but could not buy a beer was a matter of social values, not inalienable civil rights.

For older Americans, the primary issue is whether age can be used as a factor in hiring, promotions, or firing. The Age Discrimination in Employment Act of 1967 forbids discrimination against workers aged 40 to 65. Employers cannot use age as a factor in hiring, nor can they lay off older workers in favor of younger ones if age is the primary factor in such decisions. The law was later amended to prohibit employers from instituting mandatory retirement. This has sparked controversy because the reluctance of many older workers to retire means that younger workers may be excluded from jobs or promotions. Again, the struggle over equal opportunity is often a conflict between competing social and economic interests.

Disabilities Laws that were initially passed to prevent discrimination because of race or gender have been extended to cover Americans with physical or mental disabilities. It was once common to confine the disabled to institutions, but today the challenge is to "mainstream" people with disabilities into society without placing "unreasonable" burdens on other citizens.

The Americans with Disabilities Act of 1991 marks a watershed in efforts to ensure equal protection for citizens with physical or mental disabilities. It guarantees equal access to employment, public accommodations, public transportation, and communications service, and requires that government and the private sector make it as easy as possible for the disabled to participate as equal citizens under the law. This may include redesigning physical layouts, installing new technology, or providing assistance (such as sign language interpreters for the hearing impaired) to accommodate disabled workers or customers. The law is controversial because of disagreements over which specific disabilities are covered, to what extent government and business must accommodate the disabled, and of course, who ultimately pays the possibly huge costs of compliance. Such issues will be fought out in Congress and the courts for years.

Sexual Orientation   Equal rights for gays and lesbians are controversial because many Americans hold strong religious views that regard homosexuality as immoral and because, unlike race or gender, sexual orientation is not obvious to the casual observer. Americans who may tolerate what consenting adults do in the privacy of their own homes may nonetheless disagree over whether sexual orientation itself should be covered under civil rights laws. For their part, gay and lesbian activists argue that nobody should be required to conceal their sexual orientation in order to be allowed to hold a job or rent an apartment.

Federal and state governments have focused on preventing obvious discrimination based on sexual orientation in such areas as employment, housing, and access to health insurance. The AIDS epidemic, of which most initial victims were gay men, greatly complicates these issues. Fears about contracting the deadly disease frequently collide with basic rights such as equal access to jobs and housing.

One controversy concerns the exclusion of homosexuals from the military. Homosexuals have always served in the military, but those who revealed their homosexuality were dishonorably discharged, regardless of their service record. Military leaders defend the ban, arguing that "open" homosexuality makes military units less cohesive and complicates situations in which privacy is nonexistent (for example, on submarines). Moreover, many people who serve in the military are strongly opposed to homosexuality in itself.

In 1993 newly elected President Bill Clinton tried to broker a compromise on the issue. The "don't ask, don't tell" rule would not allow military officials to ask about the sexual orientation of uniformed personnel and likewise not require personnel to disclose their sexual preferences. As before, sexual activity of any sort while on duty was banned.[23] The compromise hasn't entirely worked. Although "don't ask, don't tell" was supposed to discourage "witchhunts" for gays and lesbians in the military, the number of homosexuals who have been excluded from the military actually has increased since the policy went into effect.[24] For President Clinton, as for President Truman after he ordered the racial integration of the armed forces in 1948, making a rule is one thing but making it work is another matter. It is likely to take a long time before homosexuals are widely accepted in the military.

CIVIL LIBERTIES: KEEPING GOVERNMENT AT BAY

Struggles over civil liberties often center on desires by individuals to be treated fairly or to be simply left alone to live their lives as they see fit. More often than not, unpopular groups such as Jehovah's Witnesses, avowed communists, or homosexuals, find themselves relegated to society's margins. Americans who are content with the ways things are do not agitate for change; in fact, they are more likely to resist change as a threat to their way of life or position in society. Thus, as with the battles over civil rights, struggles over civil liberties involve a complex mixture of economic, social, and political interests.

FIRST AMENDMENT FREEDOMS

The First Amendment guarantees four essential civil liberties: freedom of religion, freedom of expression, freedom of assembly, and freedom to petition government. Taken together, these First Amendment freedoms are central to the health of an open and democratic society.

Freedom of Religion   The First Amendment states that "Congress shall make no law respecting an establishment of religion, or prohibiting the free exercise thereof." The relationship between government and religion thus has two dimensions. The first prohibits the government from *establishing* any religion. Fear of government-sponsored religion runs throughout American history: Like the Pilgrims, many early immigrants came to the New World to escape religious persecution. The drafters of the amendment wanted to prevent any one religion from enjoying government backing, to the possible detriment of others. They also feared the corruption of religion through government interference.

On its face, the **establishment clause** means simply that the government will not set up or support an official state religion or favor one religion over others. Yet the picture is more complicated in a society characterized by strong religious beliefs and great religious diversity. As we saw in the *Rosenberger* case, today the main argument is whether the First Amendment constructs a "wall" between church and state, whether it prohibits *any* government support for *any* religious activities or values. How high and thick is the wall between church and state? Should it be so high and impregnable as to bar any interaction? Or should some interactions be allowed so that government is not construed as hostile toward religion in general?

Perhaps the best answer is "high but not impregnable." The standards used now were first developed by the Supreme Court in the case of *Lemon v. Kurtzman* (1971).[25] Any law dealing with the relationship between church and state is constitutional *only* if (1) the law being challenged has a secular (or nonreligious) purpose; (2) its principal or primary effect is one that neither promotes nor hinders religion; and (3) it does not foster "excessive entanglement" by government in religion. But what exactly constitutes "secular purpose," "primary effect," or "excessive entanglement?" The ambiguities in this standard show the difficulty of balancing competing interests and values.

Issues of church and state are especially explosive when they involve public elementary or secondary schools, largely because children are especially susceptible to indoctrination of any sort. In *Engel v. Vitale* (1962) the Supreme Court banned state-sponsored prayer in public schools on the ground that mandatory Christian prayer violates the rights of religious minorities and children of nonbelievers.[26] Religion is not entirely excluded from the public schools, however. Reading of the Bible can be included in a secular course on religion or literature; students can hold prayer meetings on school property outside of class time; and students can pray silently to themselves—so long as such "moments of silence" are not mandated by government.[27] In general, since about 1960, the Court has been reluctant to let government bodies (such as public school

TABLE 4.2.   PUBLIC ASSISTANCE TO RELIGIOUS SCHOOLS:
              WHAT KINDS OF AID ARE ALLOWED?

In *Everson v. Board of Education* (1947), the U.S. Supreme Court upheld a New Jersey statute that reimbursed the parents of parochial school children for bus transportation expenses. Since then the Court has struggled with cases challenging state statutes that provide aid in some form or another to religious schools. Some kinds of public assistance have been allowed, whereas others have been struck down as a law respecting an establishment of religion.

Public Assistance Allowed	*Public Assistance Prohibited*
Everson v. Board of Education (1947), transportation costs	*Lemon v. Kurtzman* (1971), teachers salaries
Board of Education v. Allen (1968), textbooks	*Sloan v. Lemon* (1973), tuition reimbursement
Waltz v. Tax Commission (1970), tax exemptions	*Comm. for Public Educ. v. Nyquist* (1973), tax relief to parents not qualifying for tuition reimbursement
Tilton v. Richardson (1971), construction grants for colleges	*Meek v. Pittenger* (1975), counseling, testing, psychological services, speech and hearing therapy
Hunt v. McNair (1973), revenue bonds for private colleges	*Wolman v. Walter* (1977), instructional materials, field trip transportation
Meek v. Pittenger (1975), textbooks	*Aguilar v. Felton* (1985), teacher salaries and supplies for remedial instruction
Roemer v. Maryland Public Works (1976), state aid to colleges	*Grand Rapids School Dist. v. Ball* (1985), using public funds to students in parochial schools leased by the state
Wolman v. Walter (1977), testing and diagnostic services	*Board of Education of Kiryas Joel Village School District v. Grumet* (1994), public school district created to serve Satmar (Orthodox Jewish) children
Mueller v. Allen (1983), tax deductions for tuition, textbook, and transportation expenses	
Zobrest v. Catalina Foothills School District (1993), providing sign language interpreter to a deaf child in a religious high school	
Agostini v. Felton (1997), special education classes taught in parochial schools	

boards) sponsor or encourage religious activities. Public aid to church-supported schools is forbidden except when the aid serves distinctly secular purposes, such as paying for an interpreter for hearing-impaired students (see Table 4.2).

Beyond issues having to do with public schools, the establishment clause is currently interpreted as permitting greater accommodation of interactions between church and state when those interactions do not endorse specific religious beliefs. Thus, federal and state governments finance the construction of science buildings at religious colleges and routinely provide special-needs instructors and special-education classes for children in parochial schools.[28] U.S. currency can have "In God We Trust" printed on it if Congress so wishes, and both chambers of Congress begin each day with prayers by their official chaplains. Town governments can erect holiday displays that do not endorse any single religious view. Of course, some of these activities are controversial, and some people question why taxpayers should subsidize any activity with religious overtones. Conflicts over the establishment clause therefore are unlikely to subside.[29]

The First Amendment also contains the **free exercise clause** asserting Americans' right to worship whomever, whatever, and however they wish, with few restrictions. The question here is the degree to which government must protect free exercise of religion when it involves unpopular religious groups or beliefs. The Supreme Court has tended to uphold *beliefs* as sacred. Jehovah's Witnesses, for example, believe that it is sinful to worship "graven images," and they have won the right *not* to recite the Pledge of Allegiance in school. Other Americans may regard Jehovah's Witnesses as unpatriotic, but the courts have defended their right not to go along with the majority.

However, protection of religious *actions* is less rigorous. In *Reynolds v. United States* (1879) the Court refused to accept the proposition that the then-accepted Mormon practice of polygamy (having more than one wife) was protected by the free exercise clause.[30] The government, the Court ruled, could regulate religiously motivated actions so long as there is a "rational basis" for doing so. Citizens cannot claim religious beliefs as a reason for not paying income taxes, nor can they grow marijuana for religious purposes when the drug is illegal throughout the country. In general, actions that are defended on religious grounds are not necessarily protected when the government can present a compelling case for limits on those actions in the name of public health, safety, and morals. Still, the courts are rather careful in such disputes because they invariably involve conflicts over the right to worship.

Freedom of Expression   "Congress shall make no law . . . abridging the freedom of speech, or of the press." Freedom of expression involves more than spoken or written words, and it applies beyond the news media. It means that under most conditions government cannot stop a person from expressing controversial or unpopular ideas, that it cannot censor the press, and that it cannot interfere with freedom of expression in art, literature, movies, or plays.

Freedom of expression, as all civil liberties, is never absolute. The First Amendment's guarantees are often balanced against other values, such as social harmony, public order, or national security. Striking a balance is difficult at best in an open society that includes so many different sets of religious and cultural values. Language that is ordinary to one person may be profane to another. Or, as Justice John Harlan once stated, "One man's vulgarity is another's lyric."[31] One person may proclaim ideas that others find reprehensible or frightening. One person's art may be another's pornography; one person's erotic novel another's obscenity. The points of conflict are infinite, and they often end up in court.

Limits on Speech   Nobody can say anything they want, if only out of respect for the basic norms of civility. Beyond these norms, however, there are limits on free speech based on the "harm principle." Even "political speech" directed at a public figure or political issue is not entirely free from legal limits if it is used in a potentially harmful manner. For example, you have the right to express your opposition to a president's policies or character, but you cannot threaten the president's life. However, none of these limits are etched in stone. They, like American society, have changed over time.

The Supreme Court has tried to devise standards for dealing with issues involving constitutional limits on free expression. The **clear and present danger** standard formulated in *Schenck v. United States* (1919) is the oldest of these. The Court reasoned that just as freedom of speech does not protect a person who falsely shouts "fire!" in a crowded theater, anyone who expresses "inflammatory" views can be prosecuted for posing a danger to public order or safety. "The question in every case," explained Justice Oliver Wendell Holmes, "is whether the words used are used in such circumstances that they will bring about the substantive evils that Congress has a right to prevent."[32] This rather loose standard was applied in a slightly modified form as late as 1951 in *Dennis v. United States*, in which the Court affirmed the convictions of eleven communists who had advocated violent overthrow of the government.[33]

However, it soon became clear that the "clear and present danger" test did not protect basic speech. It had permitted punishment of individuals whose speech merely had a "tendency" to encourage or cause lawlessness, or speech by people who were part of a political movement, such as communism, that advocated possibly violent revolutionary change. In *Brandenburg v. Ohio* (1969), the Court fashioned a test that better protected speech by allowing government to punish advocacy of illegal activities only if "such advocacy is directed to inciting or producing imminent lawless action *and* is likely to incite or produce such action."[34] The **imminence test,** which is still in use, is a more rigorous standard that leans toward greater individual freedom of expression.

Other issues related to free political expression include symbolic actions, such as the right to burn the American flag discussed at the beginning of chapter 2, to put campaign signs on one's property despite a town ordinance against lawn signs, or to wear a jacket bearing the words "Fuck the Draft." The last example arose in the case of *Cohen v. California* (1971).[35] The defendant, Paul Cohen, wore a jacket bearing the statement and was arrested and convicted for violating a California law prohibiting any person from "disturbing the peace . . . by offensive conduct." The Supreme Court conceded that the statement was vulgar but nonetheless concluded that Cohen had the right to express opposition to the Vietnam War and the military draft in this manner—that the statement on his jacket was a form of speech that was protected by the First Amendment. The statement neither "incited" illegal action nor was obscene. Nor did the words used constitute "fighting words" aimed at a person in such a way as to invite retaliation. Just because California wanted to "clean up" public discourse was an insufficient reason to convict Cohen for wearing the jacket. Thus the Court sided with the individual, no matter how much the person's words or expressions might offend others—as long as the words do not actually incite social unrest. At its heart, free speech really means the right to express any political idea, no matter how annoying or insulting it may be to others.

Obscenity and Pornography   Another area of conflict over freedom of expression concerns materials that some people consider obscene or sexually pornographic. Laws outlawing obscenity and pornography go back to colonial days, and materials that are deemed obscene or pornographic are not fully protected by the First Amendment. However, exactly what constitutes obscenity or pornography is unclear, and views on this subject change. Books that were once judged obscene by prevailing societal standards, including works by such authors as James Joyce and D. H. Lawrence, today are widely regarded as literary monuments. The same ambiguity applies to films and works of art, among other materials. Not everyone everywhere in the society holds the same standards, and as a result conflicts are inevitable.

Again, over time the Supreme Court has tried to strike a balance among differing values. The test of obscenity in use today was created in the case of *Miller v. California* (1973). In that case the Court ruled that a work can be considered obscene or pornographic if (1) its predominant theme is "prurient" or appeals to "lustful interests" according to the sensibilities of an average person in the community; (2) it portrays sexual activity in a patently "offensive" manner; and (3) if, taken as a whole, it lacks "serious literary, artistic, political, or scientific value."[36] The potential for broad interpretation and hot disagreement in these standards is obvious: Even "reasonable people" in the same town can disagree about what is prurient or offensive or even serious.

The *Miller* test has worked fairly well in that courts have been able to distinguish hard-core pornography from mere nudity or pictures of nudity that are not obscene. As a result, artistic works that deal with sexuality are strongly protected, and magazines such as *Playboy* for the most part are immune from prosecution. However, some conservatives and feminist activists argue that the test is too permissive. Conservatives argue that it undermines their efforts to keep pornography out of their communities, while some feminist scholars believe that the *Miller* test upholds forms of pornography that perpetuate the subordination of women.[37]

Freedom of the Press   A free press is one of society's most potent tools for controlling government and making it accountable for its actions, but a free press has limits of its own. For example, freedom of the press does not mean freedom to write or speak falsely about a person. Private citizens have a relatively unlimited right to sue on claims of libel (false written statements) or slander (false oral statements).

Public officials, however, are held to a higher standard. In *New York Times v. Sullivan* (1964), the Supreme Court considered the extent to which the First Amendment limits libel actions brought by public officials against those who criticize their official conduct. Sullivan, an elected official in Montgomery, Alabama, sued four African American clergy and the *New York Times*, alleging that he had been libeled by statements appearing in an advertisement alleging civil rights violations in his city. The ad contained inaccurate statements, which Sullivan used as a basis to sue the defendants.

Your typical Web site: a coming civil liberties battleground. The openness of the Internet poses new challenges to anyone who worries about issues of free speech. These concerns range from the ability to spread false information to the ease with which children can view explicit images of sexual behavior or violence.

In a ruling that revolutionized libel laws, the Court said that public officials may not seek damages for defamatory statements related to their official conduct unless they can prove "actual malice." They must be able to prove that the statements were made with knowledge that they were false or with "reckless disregard" for the truth.[38] This standard is high enough to keep most public officials from suing. On the other hand, it does not preclude a lawsuit, so most people in the media still must be careful in deciding what to publish and about whom.

Issues of freedom of the press also center on whether and to what degree government can prevent disclosure of information. The federal courts are generally reluctant to grant government the power to "restrain" the media, and they tend to impose high standards of proof in such cases. The rule of "no prior restraint" was laid out in *Near v. Minnesota* (1931), in which the Court ruled that government censorship of the press is the kind of prior restraint that the First Amendment was designed to prevent. But, the Court added, censorship might be allowed in "exceptional cases" such as in times of actual war when specific information might be useful to the enemy.[39] In *New York Times v. United States* (1971), however, the Court prevented the government from stopping publication of a classified Department of Defense study (the so-called "Pentagon Papers") of how the United States became embroiled in the Vietnam War.[40] The Court's decision that publication of the study did not harm national security firmly established the vital role of the media in keeping the people informed about the actions of their government.

Other First Amendment Freedoms   The First Amendment also forbids Congress from making any law abridging "the right of the people peaceably to assemble, and to petition the Government for a redress of grievances." Citizens have the right to engage in most forms of protest, attend political meetings, organize demonstrations, and make demands on their government, so long as these activities are peaceful. The right to petition includes the right of a person or interest group to try to persuade (or "lobby") a member of Congress to vote a certain way on pending legislation. It also protects the right of individuals or groups to circulate petitions that might be used to put pressure on government officials to act in one way or another.

RIGHTS OF THE ACCUSED

Perhaps no area of civil liberties is more controversial than the rights of individuals accused or convicted of crimes. The accused get little sympathy, particularly when they are accused of brutal crimes. Yet the rights of the accused are important to all citizens. They concern what government can and cannot do in using its formidable powers against anyone suspected of criminal conduct or formally arrested and charged with a criminal offense. Any citizen, after all, might be "the accused" at one time or another.

Due Process   Underlying the rights of the accused is the notion of **due process,** a general standard of fairness when it comes to how accused individuals are treated throughout the criminal justice process. Under the Constitution citizens are presumed to be innocent until they are proven guilty by the government. This is a key distinction: Those who are accused do not have to prove their innocence. The burden is on the government to prove "beyond a reasonable doubt" that an accused person is guilty.

The list of protections related to due process is a long one. It is derived both from the Constitution and from provisions in the Bill of Rights. These protections have been applied to the states as well as to the federal government as a result of Supreme Court decisions incorporating key provisions contained in the Fourth, Fifth, Sixth, and Eighth Amendments (see Table 4.1, p. 138).

Due process begins with the right to know the reasons for an arrest. Article I of the Constitution includes the protection of *habeas corpus* (Latin for "you shall have the body"), which forbids imprisonment without an actual charge. A court can issue a *writ of habeas corpus*, which orders that a prisoner be produced and demands to know the reasons for holding that person.[41] If the evidence is deemed to be insufficient to justify further detention, the person must be set free, although the possibility of rearrest exists if new evidence comes to light.

Protection against Unreasonable Search and Seizure   Police are not free to do whatever they want in order to obtain such evidence. Under the Fourth Amendment citizens are guaranteed a degree of freedom from "unreasonable searches and seizures." They may not be arrested without "probable cause," and their homes may not be searched without a court warrant that specifies the place to be searched and the persons or things to be seized. This last protection is part of a general Fourth Amendment right to "privacy" that has evolved through Supreme Court decisions over the past few decades (discussed in the section "The Right to Privacy" later in this chapter).[42]

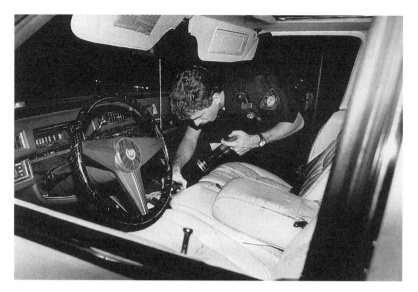

Probable cause. A police officer searches an automobile for additional evidence after the arrest of a suspect on an illegal drug charge. Under the "exclusionary rule" of the Fourth Amendment, evidence obtained without clear cause or a search warrant can be excluded from consideration in a trial.

Evidence seized in an illegal or improper manner can be "excluded" from a trial, even if it proves guilt. How this **exclusionary rule** is applied can lead to major controversies. Applying it too broadly can create situations in which solid evidence is excluded from a trial even when all that was wrong was a typing error on a search warrant. Police and victims understandably become upset when accused criminals "get off on a technicality," and in recent years the Supreme Court has allowed items that were obtained by police "in good faith" to be entered as evidence even if mistakes were made on the search warrant. On the other hand, applying the exclusionary rule too narrowly can be an invitation for police to use dubious means to obtain evidence.

Protection against Self-Incrimination   The second set of protections involves what happens to an accused person upon arrest. "Miranda warnings," named after the defendant in *Miranda v. Arizona* (1966), must be stated verbally to the person at the time of the arrest.[43] The accused has the right to remain silent and is notified that any statement he or she makes can be used as evidence during a trial. The accused also has the right to have a lawyer present while being questioned by police, and those who cannot afford a lawyer are provided with one. Critics argue that the Court's decision in *Miranda* tilted the balance too far in the favor of criminal suspects. Why should the Fifth Amendment's provision against self-incrimination be used to overturn convictions of individuals who are foolish enough to volunteer information while in police custody? Nevertheless, after more than 30 years of experience one thing is clear: The *Miranda* decision embodied a delicate balance that was designed to protect both the accused and society's interests.

Trial Procedures   The Sixth Amendment guarantees that people who are formally indicted of crimes shall have a "speedy" and "public" trial by an "impartial" jury, although the speed with which a trial actually occurs varies. During the trial the accused has the right to present favorable witnesses and to cross-examine witnesses presented by the prosecution. The Fifth Amendment's guarantee against self-incrimination means that no one who is accused of a crime can be compelled to testify or to make self-incriminating statements at any point in the judicial process. More important, silence is not to be construed as admission of guilt: The government still bears the burden of proving guilt in all criminal matters.

Punishment   The Eighth Amendment forbids "excessive fines" and prohibits "cruel and unusual punishments." What these terms mean has changed over time: Forms of punishment that were once acceptable, such as public whippings, are no longer condoned by most Americans.

Individuals who have been convicted of crimes do not automatically lose all the rights of citizens. Those who are imprisoned—even convicted murderers awaiting execution—cannot be tortured by the guards, denied medical care, or subjected to "inhumane" conditions. The punishment also must be roughly proportional to the crime—someone who has been convicted for speeding may not be given a life sentence. Except for issues surrounding the death penalty, however, the courts generally have allowed state legislatures and Congress, as representatives of the people, to decide the severity of punishment for various categories of crime (see Box 4.3).

The greatest debate over the rights of the convicted has to do with capital punishment. The United States is one of the few Western nations that still uses the death penalty, but how, and to whom, it is applied are subjects of controversy. In *Furman v. Georgia* (1972) the Supreme Court held that the death penalty as administered by the state of Georgia in cases of murder and rape was applied in so "arbitrary" a manner, especially against poor African Americans, as to be "cruel and unusual." This decision led to a national moratorium on capital punishment.[44] During this period states revised their laws to remove the arbitrary manner in which the death penalty was imposed. Four years later, in 1976, the Supreme Court upheld new, more rigorous state laws, and executions resumed. So long as due process concerns are met, and so long as a majority of the American people demand it, the death penalty is likely to be in place for the foreseeable future.

THE RIGHT TO PRIVACY

The Fourth Amendment states that individuals are protected against unreasonable searches and seizures in their persons, houses, papers, and effects. This and other amendments, taken together, suggest that citizens have a right to *privacy*, although the word itself does not appear anywhere in the Constitution or the Bill of Rights. Perhaps privacy issues were much simpler before the age of modern technology and social complexities. Whatever the reason, since the mid-1960s the Supreme Court has recognized the notion of a constitutionally protected "zone of privacy" around an individual into which government cannot intrude without cause. In a number of landmark decisions the Court has expanded this notion as protection against government invasion of one's home, papers, and personal effects to include the protection of personal choice in matters of a deeply personal nature, such as sexual behavior, the decision to terminate a pregnancy, or requesting medical assistance to end one's life.

BOX 4.3.
THREE STRIKES AND YOU'RE OUT

Nowhere is the constant struggle to balance individual rights with the needs of the community better illustrated than in instances concerning criminal justice.

During the 1990s citizens' fear of crime remained high. Yet at the same time rates for most crimes fell dramatically, in many cases to their lowest levels in over 30 years. The two phenomena may have been intertwined: High citizen concern about crime led to harsher punishments, thus taking more convicted felons off the streets for longer periods. Prison populations swelled as crime rates fell.

Citizens were especially angry about the degree to which many crimes were committed by repeat offenders, those who served a sentence for one crime, got out of prison, and then committed another crime. Indeed, statistical evidence shows that a large proportion of crimes are committed by repeat offenders. This reality led about 20 states to pass laws designed to severely punish repeat offenders, and in many cases these "three strikes" laws did put especially violent criminals behind bars for life. Whether these laws accounted for the steep drop in violent crime is less certain. Other factors, such as a healthy economy with low unemployment, more effective policing practices, and a drop in the sheer number of young men (who statistically commit the most crimes) in the population may also have had an effect.

Sexual Behavior   Among the most obvious issues involving privacy are those stemming from personal relationships, especially sexual ones. In *Griswold v. Connecticut* (1965) the Supreme Court struck down a state statute that made the use of birth control, even by married couples, a crime and forbade encouragement of contraception use (for example, through medical counseling).[45] The Court stated that guarantees in the Bill of Rights protect the right of married couples to use contraceptives and the right of medical professionals to offer advice about their use. More important, the Court argued that individuals have a "zone of privacy" that is implicit in other provisions in the Bill of Rights, particularly in the First, Third, Fourth, Fifth, and Ninth Amendments. As a result of the Court's decision in *Griswold*, the right to privacy now enjoys constitutional status.

It is less clear whether the right to privacy also protects the rights of individuals to engage in certain sexual acts. Most states have decriminalized homosexual activity, but laws against sodomy (anal and oral intercourse) between any consenting adults are still on the books in many states. In *Bowers v. Hardwick* (1986) the Supreme Court upheld one such law in Georgia, but only as it applied to homosexual activity.[46] The decision did not mean that states automatically began to prosecute gays and lesbians for what they did in their bedrooms. Since the 1970s state governments have in fact become far less intrusive in all matters of sexuality and

WHAT DO YOU THINK?

But all laws have unintended consequences. In 1994 California enacted a tough "three strikes and you're out" law that requires very long sentences for people convicted of a third felony. The aim of the law was to keep violent offenders off the streets. In March 1995 Jerry Dewayne Williams was convicted of his third felony and sentenced to 25 years to life in prison. His crime: stealing a piece of pizza from a group of children. Williams was not exactly a sympathetic figure, having previously been convicted of robbery, attempted robbery, drug possession, and "unauthorized use of a vehicle." Stealing the slice of pizza came under the classification of "felony petty theft" because it involved physical intimidation. It was his third "strike." Williams must serve 20 years of his life sentence before being eligible for parole.

Williams was not alone. In December 1998 Richard Montoya was convicted in Olympia, Washington, of robbing a man of $1. The robbery was categorized as a violent crime, and because it was Montoya's third "strike" under state law, he was sentenced to life in prison.

Cases such as these have prompted some prosecutors to "undercharge" defendants who face a life sentence under a "three strikes" law because they didn't think the potential life sentence fit the actual third crime. But state legislatures or governors are reluctant to make these laws more flexible: The voters want tough laws, even if they have some unintended consequences.

The nation's streets are safer, but more people are in prison for longer periods at taxpayer expense. Sometimes the punishment does not seem to fit the specific crime.

What do you think?

Sources: "25 Years for a Slice of Pizza," *New York Times*, March 5, 1995, p. A21; "Carnival Worker Will Get Life," *Seattle Times*, December 17, 1998, p. B2.

---

personal lifestyle. Perhaps more important, in *Romer v. Evans* (1996) the Supreme Court upheld the right of gays and lesbians to be free from discrimination in areas such as employment and housing. Sexual orientation, if not sexual activity, does enjoy some constitutional protection.[47]

Abortion Perhaps the most controversial privacy issue is reproductive rights, particularly abortion. By the 1960s public pressure to reform restrictive state abortion laws led several states to expand access to safe and legal abortion. However, disparities among state laws remained.

In *Roe v. Wade* (1973) the Supreme Court tried to settle the issue by devising a national "abortion code" based on the trimesters of pregnancy.[48] Building on its decision in *Griswold*, the Court held that a woman's right to privacy includes the right to choose to have an abortion, but that government has a valid interest in regulating abortion and protecting the "potential life" of the fetus. The result was a compromise: During the first three months of pregnancy, when the viability of the fetus is most in doubt, the woman has an unrestricted right to choose abortion. During the second trimester, a state may regulate, but not prohibit, abortions, in the interest of protecting the health of the mother. Only in the third trimester, when the fetus is understood to be viable (that is, capable of living outside of the womb) does a state's interest in protecting the life of the fetus warrant severe restrictions or outright bans on abortion. Even then, the Court ruled, a state must permit abortion to save the life of the mother.

The *Roe* decision pleased no one. Those supporting a woman's right to choose an abortion thought the Court had allowed for too much government control; those opposed to abortion complained that it had set no effective limits on abortion. Since then, opponents of abortion have succeeded in narrowing the scope of abortion rights. Congress and most states have prohibited the use of public funds to pay for abortions for poor women. More important, by the late 1980s several of the Supreme Court justices who supported the *Roe* decision had retired or died. Their replacements, appointed by Presidents Ronald Reagan and George Bush, were less supportive of abortion rights, and the Court eventually allowed more limits on the right to choose abortion.

However, in *Webster v. Reproductive Health Services* (1989) the Court was asked to decide the constitutionality of a Missouri law that declared that life begins at conception, denied the use of public facilities for abortions, and barred public employees from performing abortions except to save a woman's life.[49] In a 5–4 decision, the Court struck down these restrictions as an "undue burden" on a woman seeking an abortion. Abortion is still legal, but states can regulate it at any stage of pregnancy so long as the regulations do not exceed the "undue burden" standard.

Americans are ambivalent about abortion. Most don't like the idea, but most don't want to make it a criminal act. This ambivalence is reflected in the inability of antiabortion forces to gain passage of a constitutional amendment banning abortion or to convince the Supreme Court to overrule *Roe*. Even justices who are generally opposed to abortion have been content to modify the *Roe* standard rather than discard it, because they aren't sure that there is a better alternative.

Other Privacy Issues   Recent societal trends and technological innovations raise new and uncomfortable questions about privacy. Many of these concerns stem from the ability to detect drug and alcohol use, certain diseases, and even genetic patterns that may predispose people to get certain kinds of diseases or disorders. How such information should be used and who should use it are central issues. Other privacy concerns include mandated drug tests to qualify for employment and the ability to keep track of massive amounts of data about individuals, from credit or health records to the kinds of movie videos they rent or groceries they buy. Privacy once meant simply closing one's curtains, but that quaint notion is long out of date.

Finally, in an era when medical technology can keep people alive almost indefinitely, privacy issues extend to the "right to die," especially the question of who has

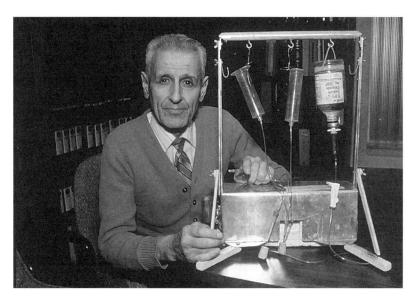

"Dr. Death." Dr. Jack Kevorkian displays the machine he designed to enable the terminally ill to end their own lives. Kevorkian's crusade to legalize "assisted suicide" earned him a jail sentence for second-degree murder. However, many believe that Kevorkian defended the individual's "right to die" as and when they wish.

the right to make end-of-life decisions. The first famous case in this regard arose in 1976 and concerned the fate of Karen Ann Quinlan, a woman who was in a coma and, according to her doctors, had no chance of recovery. Her family wished—and asserted the right—to disconnect the equipment that was keeping her body alive.[50] The family argued that she should be allowed to die in peace because she had been known to express views indicating that she would not want to be kept alive artificially. Her doctors had refused to disconnect the equipment. The New Jersey Supreme Court upheld the family's claim that this action was permitted as part of their right to privacy, and the U.S. Supreme Court refused to overturn the decision. Quinlan was disconnected from the equipment and allowed to die.

Within a few years most states adopted standards allowing family members to make decisions in such cases. However, in a case brought by the family of Nancy Cruzan, another comatose patient, the Missouri Supreme Court refused to allow the removal of feeding tubes because there was no "clear and convincing" evidence that Cruzan would have wanted to die under such conditions. The case was appealed to the U.S. Supreme Court, which upheld the Missouri court's decision.[51] Months later the Cruzan family introduced new testimony from Nancy's friends indicating that she would not have wanted to live in such a condition. The state court then allowed the feeding tubes to be removed, and she died. After *Cruzan* many Americans began arranging for "living wills" that explicitly state how they want to be treated if they should become comatose with no hope of recovery.

A related issue is doctor-assisted suicide for terminally ill patients. Does a person suffering from a fatal illness have a constitutional right to take his or her own life with the assistance of a physician? In 1997 the Supreme Court ruled that doctor-assisted suicide was not protected by any constitutional right to privacy or due process.

BOX 4.4.
HOW TO FIND THE TEXTS OF
SUPREME COURT DECISIONS

A CLOSER LOOK

You may want to read for yourself the full text of the Supreme Court opinions mentioned in this text. If so, you will need to know how to locate them.

Locating Supreme Court opinions is easy if you have access to a law library and have the case citation. A case citation has been provided in the footnotes for each case mentioned in the text.

Take, for example, *New York Times Co. v Sullivan*, 376 US 254 (1964). The citation means that this case appears in volume 376, page 254 of the *U.S. Reports*, the official record of Supreme Court opinions. The *U.S. Reports* will be housed in the "federal courts" section of your law library. If your school does not have a law library, there is a very good chance that the reference section of a library you can use will contain a full set of the *U.S. Reports*.

In addition to these printed volumes, the full text of landmark Supreme Court opinions can be obtained from a number of sites on the Web. The indexes of the following sites will direct you to those decisions:

The Legal Information Institute
http://www.law.cornell.edu/
The Villanova Center for Information Law and Policy
http://www.law.vill.edu/Fed-Ct/sct.html
Find Law
http://www.Findlaw.com/

However, the court's opinion acknowledged that the issue was far from settled: "Throughout the Nation, Americans are engaged in an earnest and profound debate about the morality, legality, and practicality of physician-assisted suicide. Our holding permits this debate to continue, as it should in a democratic society."[52] End-of-life issues and the decisions regarding care or termination of care are likely to become center-stage conflicts in the coming decades as the population ages and the technology of health care advances.

THE RIGHT TO BEAR ARMS

A good way to start an argument is to declare that the Second Amendment does *not* guarantee the right of a private citizen to own a gun. Another good way to start an argument is to declare that the Second Amendment *does* guarantee this right.

Scholars do not agree on whether gun ownership is a basic right of citizenship. On one hand, the Second Amendment does seem to guarantee a right to possess a gun as a way to keep government in check. However, the historical context surrounding ratification of the Second Amendment suggests that it was intended to keep Congress from abolishing "well-regulated" state militias, which at the time were the only trained armed forces in the fledgling nation. Today, with all armed forces, including state National Guard units, essentially under federal control, the issue is whether the Second Amendment guarantees the right of individuals to own guns.

Those who support restrictions on gun ownership express the "collective right" view that the Second Amendment's sole purpose was to provide for the common defense by state militias. The amendment did not cover private gun ownership. By contrast, those who oppose gun controls express an "individual right" view, claiming that the "right of the people to keep and bear arms" means the right—even the duty—of every free citizen to keep a gun to provide for the defense of individual liberty.

Over the course of the nation's history the Supreme Court has consistently supported the constitutionality of gun control laws.[53] Congress and the states can regulate private gun ownership, yet the debate continues. The nation's history and culture make it highly unlikely that private gun ownership will ever be outlawed, nor is there any constitutional reason to do so. Citizens do have a right to keep and bear arms, but this right is not without restrictions. The nature of those restrictions is a political issue, not a constitutional one.

PRIVATE PROPERTY RIGHTS

As we noted earlier, in drafting the Declaration of Independence Jefferson changed the right to acquire and possess property into a vaguer right to "happiness." However, the economic chaos afflicting the new nation in the 1780s led to great concerns about protecting private property from those who might use majority political power to confiscate it. Thus, the Fifth Amendment declares that no person shall be "deprived of life, liberty, or property, without due process of the law; nor shall private property be taken for public use, without just compensation."

Property rights defined the general role of government during the 19th century. The federal government left most matters involving property to the states, which through the 1800s imposed few, if any, regulations on businesses. However, around 1900 many states began enacting legislation to curb some of the negative effects of industrialization and corporate capitalism, such child labor and dangerous or shoddy products.

But regulations affect profits, so business interests fought against these regulatory efforts at every turn. They found support in the Supreme Court. In *Lochner v. New York* (1905) the Court struck down a state law that attempted to protect the health and safety of bakery employees by allowing them to work no more than 10 hours per day and 60 hours per week. Lochner, a bakery owner, challenged the law as an infringement on his right to run his bakery as he saw fit. The Court agreed, ruling that the law "interferes with the right of contract between the employer and employees," an economic liberty that is protected by the Fourteenth Amendment.[54]

As we saw in chapter 3, this "laissez-faire" era of minimal government regulation ended with President Franklin Roosevelt's efforts to pull the nation out of the Great Depression through direct government intervention in the free market system. More important, a newer generation of Supreme Court justices was more sympathetic toward government regulation of the economy. In *West Coast Hotel v. Parrish* (1937) the Court upheld Washington state's attempt to create a minimum wage for workers. In this case the Court argued that "the liberty safeguarded is liberty in a social organization which requires the protection of law against the evils which menace the health, safety, morals, and welfare of the people."[55] In other words, the right of workers to earn a decent wage sometimes outweighed the economic liberty of the business owner. After this case, and for the next 50 years, the Supreme Court took the general view that government regulation that touches economic rights was constitutional so long as there was a "rational basis" for it.

However, recently the Court has sought stronger justifications for restrictions on economic liberty. In *Nollan v. California Coastal Commission* (1987) it revived the "takings clause" of the Fifth Amendment. Its decision struck down a state agency's attempt to force a private property owner to limit the size of his beachfront house in order to ensure public access across his land to a public beach. California could provide public access to the beach, the Court ruled, but it must fairly compensate the owner for restrictions it places on the use of his property.[56]

The notion of an unregulated economy appeals to relatively few Americans, who look to government to act as a counterweight to the power of business and to alleviate some of the harsher effects of market competition. Congress and the states can regulate business practices in virtually any area, from product safety and workplace conditions to banking regulations and environmental laws, and "human" rights tend to receive greater protection than do property rights. Even so, private property is still a protected right, requiring frequent efforts to balance the rights of the individual property owner and broad community interests.

CONCLUSION

Rights and liberties are not absolutes. The language of the Bill of Rights places no explicit limits on citizens' rights and liberties, yet most people understand the need for some balance between individual rights and liberties and the need for social order and public safety. In fact, the bills of rights adopted by many other countries are much more explicit about the inherent limits on individual rights. For example, Section 1 of the Canadian Charter of Rights and Freedoms, adopted in 1982, "guarantees the rights and freedoms set out in it subject only to such reasonable limits prescribed by law as can be demonstrably justified in a free and democratic society." This standard is not precise, but it clearly states that rights and limits are balanced against other factors.

Americans seem to understand the need for balance. Most would agree that to yell "fire!" in a crowded theater when there was no fire, or to publicly threaten somebody with physical harm, are acts that lie outside the sphere of protected expression. For government to punish this misuse of speech is necessary in order to maintain a free and democratic society. Most also would agree that the right to own a gun comes with certain limits and responsibilities. But creating a "proper" balance for any right or liberty is always a matter of considerable conflict.

In this vein, each new generation of Americans must give concrete meaning to the rights and liberties embodied in the Bill of Rights. Eighteenth-century Americans certainly could not envision the issues of free speech that might arise with the advent of Web sites and Internet chat rooms. Nor could their views on the "right to bear arms" have foreseen the sheer firepower of modern weaponry. The "right to property" once supported the right to own slaves, an interpretation that few people would support today. In short, the way Americans understand and assert their basic rights and liberties parallels changes in U.S. society and in the world as a whole.

This continuous process of reinterpretation changed the nature of democracy itself as more Americans claimed equal rights and as their civil liberties were protected more vigorously. Furthermore, citizens were the primary agents of change, whether through legislation, court rulings, or the long, slow process of social change. None of this change came easily. Protections against arbitrary government actions and the possible tyranny of the majority are so central to American democracy that the battles over what they mean and to whom they extend have been difficult ones, fought in legislative chambers, in courtrooms, and sometimes in the streets.

In theory, today more Americans enjoy political equality than ever before. No longer can government or the private sector discriminate blatantly against a person on the basis of race, gender, age, disability, or sexual orientation. More subtle forms of discrimination still exist, and a society that is entirely free of it may be impossible to achieve. Even so, more Americans of more differing backgrounds and orientations have the right to vote, to participate in the political process, to compete for jobs.

The picture is less clear with respect to civil liberties. At no time has freedom of religion or expression been more fully protected, nor have the rights of the accused ever been taken more seriously. In many respects Americans are freer than ever from official or legal restrictions on how they live their lives. This greater freedom certainly makes it possible for more Americans to engage more vigorously in public debate, or simply to live their lives as they see fit.

On the other hand, at no time in history has the technological potential for government or business intrusion into citizens' private lives been so great or so troubling. The sheer amount of information about individuals kept by government and business is staggering, from health records and credit histories to career records and consumer tastes. In the wrong hands, such information could be put to devastating use. Thus, the struggle to protect citizens' civil liberties from potential tyranny on the part of government or other institutions will continue.

This last point is worth repeating. The rights and liberties guaranteed to citizens are listed in the Constitution, but their actual application is a political matter. Remember Derrick Bell's protest over the lack of minority women at Harvard Law School? In 1998 Harvard offered tenure to Lani Guinier, an African American woman who was a law professor at the University of Pennsylvania. In announcing the appointment, the dean of the law school described Professor Guinier as "a gifted and extraordinarily effective teacher" and "a first-rate scholar" whose presence "will further the mission of Harvard Law School to produce the best possible legal education and scholarship. I also expect her appointment will help the School to attract other top scholars of diverse backgrounds, including more women of color."[57]

Did Guinier get her position because she was qualified or because of affirmative action? The answer is a bit of both. Without Bell's protest, Harvard might not have tried so hard to hire someone like Guinier, but she still had to pass a minimum threshold of scholarly and teaching excellence to get the job. The conflict provoked by Bell's protest produced a happy outcome for both Harvard and Guinier.

Thus, politics in its broadest sense shapes who is included and to what degree government must stay out of our lives. No right is extended automatically, and no liberty remains guaranteed without constant vigilance. Finding an appropriate balance between the rights of the individual and the needs of the community was, is, and always will be a political struggle.

SUMMARY

▶ The basic civil rights and civil liberties of Americans are set forth in the Bill of Rights, the first 10 amendments to the Constitution. These rights and liberties are stated broadly. Thus, it has been necessary for each generation of Americans to make them fit into contemporary social, economic, technological, and political contexts. In some instances this process required a constitutional amendment, but more often it depended on new interpretations of the existing language found in the Constitution.

▶ Civil rights refers to the right to receive equal treatment under the law regardless of race, creed, gender, sexual orientation, age, or physical disability. Civil rights thus have to do with political equality—that is, equal opportunity to enjoy the full benefits of American citizenship, such as the right to vote. These rights did not apply to all Americans from the start, so the nation's history has been marked by conflicts over clearly extending equal rights to those previously excluded.

▶ Civil liberties are protections against unwarranted intrusions into citizens' private lives or how they act in public, whether by government or by other individuals. Civil liberties include guarantees of freedom of speech and religion, of the rights of the accused and the convicted, and of the right to privacy. Civil liberties thus have to do with freedom from arbitrary constraints on individual liberty.

▶ The Constitution guarantees Americans the right to own private property, with protections against the taking of that property without proper compensation. It also guarantees that Americans have some basic right to possess weapons, although this right does appear to have limits.

▶ Despite the language often used to discuss them, rights and liberties are not absolute, nor have they remained unchanged through history. The rights and liberties of the individual have always been balanced against other social needs, such as public safety or social peace. Throughout the nation's history the trend has been toward greater individual freedom, but there will always be limits.

QUESTIONS FOR REVIEW AND DISCUSSION

1. Distinguish between civil rights and civil liberties, and give examples of each.

2. Why has it been so hard to extend equal rights to groups that did not originally enjoy them? Which factor has proven most problematic in this regard—race, gender, or sexual orientation?

3. What rights are guaranteed to individuals accused of crimes? What do you believe is the proper balance between the rights of the accused and the rights of victims?

4. Are rights and liberties ever absolute? Are there times when we should *not* balance rights and liberties with other goals or needs? Give examples.

TERMS TO REMEMBER

affirmative action	establishment clause	imminence test
civil liberties	exclusionary rule	incorporation
civil rights	due process	Jim Crow laws
Civil War Amendments	free exercise clause	privileges and immunities
clear and present danger	grandfather clause	clause
equal protection clause	*habeas corpus*	separate but equal
Equal Rights Amendment		

WEB SOURCES

American Civil Liberties Union (www.aclu.org). Probably the best-known and most controversial organization dedicated to defending individual civil rights and liberties. The ACLU's lawsuits have led to a number of major Supreme Court decisions.

National Abortion and Reproductive Rights Action League (www.naral.org) and the National Right to Life Committee (www.nrlc.org). NARAL advocates for the right to a legal abortion; the NRLC spearheads the opposition to abortion.

U.S. Department of Justice, Civil Rights Division (www.usdoj.gov/crt). A good source for official U.S. government views on civil rights and liberties issues, as well as links to the texts of laws and Supreme Court decisions.

SUGGESTED READINGS

Taylor Branch, *Parting the Waters: America in The King Years, 1954–1963* (New York: Simon and Schuster, 1988). A penetrating account of the American Civil Rights movement during the critical years beginning with the Montgomery bus boycott and culminating with the march on Washington and Martin Luther King's "I Have a Dream" speech.

James MacGregor Burns and Stewart Burns, *A People's Charter: The Pursuit of Rights in America* (New York: Random House, 1991). An account of the making and remaking of the American Bill of Rights, in which the historians demonstrate that rights are not static concepts, but dynamic forces used by each generation to give concrete meaning to the ideals of freedom and justice.

Peter Irons, *The Courage of their Convictions: Sixteen Americans Who Fought Their Way to the Supreme Court* (New York: Penguin, 1990). This book, based on interviews with 16 ordinary Americans who initiated Bill of Rights cases that reached the U.S. Supreme Court between 1940 and 1986, is a unique look at the human stories that have given shape to civil rights and civil liberties in the United States.

Samuel Walker, *In Defense of American Liberties: A History of the ACLU* (New York: Oxford University Press, 1990). An in-depth look at the American Civil Liberties Union, an organization with an uncompromising view on the Bill of Rights and whose actions have shaped the principles of individual liberty that are the cornerstones of American law.

NOTES

1. *Rosenberger v Rector and Visitors of the University of Virginia, et al.*, 515 US 819 (1995).

2. See Pauline Maier, *American Scripture: Making the Declaration of Independence* (New York: Alfred A. Knopf, 1997), pp. 126–127.

3. Merrill D. Peterson, "The Idea of a Written Constitution in the Thought of the Founders: The Organization of Consent," in A. E. Dick Howard, ed., *The United States Constitution: Roots, Rights, and Responsibilities* (Washington, D.C.: Smithsonian Institution Press, 1992), p. 48.

4. Mary Ann Glendon, *Rights Talk: The Impoverishment of Political Discourse* (New York: The Free Press, 1993).

5. Alexander Hamilton, James Madison, and John Jay, *The Federalist Papers*, Clinton Rossiter, ed. (New York: New American Library, 1961), p. 513.

6. *Barron v Baltimore*, 32 US 243 (1833).

7. Efrain Hernandez, "Elitism at Harvard Hinders Changes in Hiring, Bell Asserts," *The Boston Globe*, August 22, 1992, p. B13.

8. Derrick Bell, "Victims as Heroes," in Howard, ed., *The United States Constitution: Roots, Rights, and Responsibilities*, pp. 163–182.

9. E. E. Schattschneider, *The Semi-Sovereign People: A Realist's View of Democracy in America* (Hinsdale, IL: The Dryden Press, 1960), p. 71.

10. Today Native Americans are American citizens, but Indian reservations are exempt from certain state and federal laws. Thus, gambling can be legal on a reservation but not in the rest of the state.

11. Bell, "Victims as Heroes," p. 167.

12. Jack W. Peltason, *Understanding the Constitution*, 12th ed. (New York: Holt, Rinehart, & Winston, 1992), p. 318.

13. Robert S. Peck, *The Bill of Rights and the Politics of Interpretation* (St. Paul, MN: West Publishing Company, 1992), p. 145.

14. *The Slaughterhouse Cases*, 83 US (16 Wall.) 36 (1873).

15. *Civil Rights Cases*, 109 US 3 (1883).

16. *Plessy v Ferguson*, 163 US 537 (1896).

17. Juan Williams, *Eyes on the Prize: America's Civil Rights Years* (New York: Viking, 1987).

18. *Brown v Board of Education of Topeka, et al.*, 347 US 483 (1954).

19. Justice Samuel F. Miller in *Bradwell v Illinois*, 83 US 130 (1873).

20. See Eileen L. McDonagh, "Gender Politics and Political Change," in Lawrence C. Dodd and Calvin Jillson, eds., *New Perspectives on American Politics* (Washington, D.C.: CQ Press, 1994), pp. 58–73.

21. Jane Mansbridge, *Why We Lost the ERA* (Chicago: University of Chicago Press, 1986).

22. *South Dakota v Dole*, 483 US 203 (1987).

23. Randy Shilts, *Conduct Unbecoming: Gays and Lesbians in the U.S. Military, Vietnam to the Persian Gulf* (New York: St. Martin's Press, 1993).

24. "Number of Gays Discharged from Military Rises," *Florida Today*, February 27, 1997, p. 5A.

25. *Lemon v Kurtzman*, 403 US 602 (1971).

26. *Engel v Vitale*, 370 US 421 (1962).

27. *Wallace v Jaffree*, 472 US 38 (1985).

28. *Zobrest v Catalina Foothills School District*, 509 US 1 (1993) and *Agostini v Felton*, 521 US 203 (1997).

29. Robert Cord, *Separation of Church and State: Historical Fact and Current Fiction*, 2d ed. (Grand Rapids, MI: Baker Books, 1986).

30. *Reynolds v United States*, 98 US 145 (1879).

31. *Cohen v California*, 403 US 15 (1971).

32. *Schenck v United States*, 249 US 47 (1919).

33. *Dennis v United States*, 341 US 494 (1951).

34. *Brandenburg v Ohio*, 395 US 444, at 447 (1969); emphasis added.

35. *Cohen v California*, 403 US 15 (1971).

36. *Miller v California*, 413 US 15 (1973), as altered by *Pope v Illinois*, 481 US 497 (1987).

37. Catherine MacKinnon, "Pornography, Civil Rights, and Speech," *Harvard Civil Rights-Civil Liberties Review*, vol. 20 (1985), pp. 1–70.

38. *New York Times v Sullivan*, 376 US 254 (1964).

39. *Near v Minnesota*, 283 US 697 (1931).

40. *New York Times v United States*, 403 US 713 (1971).

41. *Fay v Noia*, 372 US 391 (1963).

42. *Mapp v Ohio*, 367 US 643 (1961).

43. *Miranda v Arizona*, 384 US 486 (1966).

44. *Furman v Georgia*, 408 US 238 (1972), reversed by *Gregg v Georgia*, 248 US 153 (1976).

45. *Griswold v Connecticut*, 381 US 481 (1965).

46. *Bowers v Hardwick*, 478 US 186 (1986).

47. *Romer v Evans*, 571 US 620 (1996).

48. *Roe v Wade*, 110 US 413 (1973).

49. *Webster v Reproductive Health Services*, 492 US 490 (1989).

50. *In re Quinlan*, 70 NJ 10, 355 A2d 647 (1976), cert. denied.

51. *Cruzan v Director, Missouri Dept. of Health*, 497 US 261 (1990).

52. *Washington v Glucksberg*, 117 S Ct 2258, 138 L Ed 2d 772 (1997).

53. *United States v Miller*, 307 US 174 (1939).

54. *Lochner v New York*, 198 US 45 (1905).

55. *West Coast Hotel v Parrish*, 300 US 379 (1937).

56. *Nollan v California Coastal Commission*, 483 US 825 (1987).

57. Press Release, Harvard Law School, January 23, 1998.

PRIMARY SOURCE READINGS

MARTIN LUTHER KING JR.
Letter from the Birmingham Jail

Martin Luther King Jr. (1929–1968) advocated acts of nonviolent civil disobedience as a means to combat racial discrimination. These tactics, which included protest marches and sit-ins, drew criticisms from two sides: More "radical" black activists thought King was too willing to compromise with whites, whereas other blacks thought he was pushing too hard. In this excerpt, King writes an open letter to black clergy who worried that his actions were upsettng race relations in Birmingham.

April 16, 1963, Birmingham, Alabama

My Dear Fellow Clergyman:

While confined here in the Birmingham City Jail, I came across your recent statement calling our present activities "unwise and untimely." Seldom, if ever, do I pause to answer criticism of my work and ideas. If I sought to answer all the criticisms that cross my desk, my secretaries would be engaged in little else in the course of the day, and I would have no time for constructive work. But since I feel that you are men of genuine goodwill and your criticisms are sincerely set forth, I would like to answer your statement in what I hope will be patient and reasonable terms. . . .

You deplore the demonstrations that are presently taking place in Birmingham. But I am sorry that your statement did not express a similar concern for the conditions that brought the demonstrations into being. I am sure that each of you would want to go beyond the superficial social analyst who looks merely at effects, and does not grapple with underlying causes. I would not hesitate to say that it is unfortunate that so-called demonstrations are taking place in Birmingham at this time, but I would say in more emphatic terms that it is even more unfortunate that the white power structure of this city left the Negro community with no other alternative. . . .

You may well ask: "Why direct action? Why sit-ins, marches, etc.? Isn't negotiation a better path?" You are exactly right in your call for negotiation. Indeed, this is the purpose of direct action. Nonviolent direct action seeks to create such a crisis and establish such creative tension that a community that has constantly refused to negotiate is forced to confront the issue. It seeks so to dramatize the issue that it can no longer be ignored. I just referred to the creation of tension as a part of the work of the nonviolent resister. This may sound rather shocking. But I must confess that I am not afraid of the word tension. I have earnestly worked and preached against violent tension, but there is a type of constructive nonviolent tension that is necessary for growth. Just as Socrates felt that it was necessary to create a tension in the mind so that individuals could rise from the bondage of

myths and half-truths to the unfettered realm of creative analysis and objective appraisal, we must see the need of having nonviolent gadflies to create
the kind of tension in society that will help men to rise from the dark depths
of prejudice and racism to the majestic heights of understanding and broth-
erhood. So the purpose of the direct action is to create a situation so crisis-
packed that it will inevitably open the door to negotiation. . . .

We know through painful experience that freedom is never voluntarily
given by the oppressor; it must be demanded by the oppressed. Frankly, I
have never yet engaged in a direct action movement that was "well timed,"
according to the timetable of those who have not suffered unduly from the
disease of segregation. For years now I have heard the words [sic] "Wait!" It
rings in the ear of every Negro with a piercing familiarity. This "Wait" has
almost always meant "Never." We must come to see with the distinguished
jurist of yesterday that "justice too long delayed is justice denied."

We have waited for more than three hundred and forty years for our
constitutional and God-given rights. The nations of Asia and Africa are
moving with jet-like speed toward the goal of political independence, and
we still creep at horse and buggy pace toward the gaining of a cup of coffee
at a lunch counter. I guess it is easy for those who have never felt the sting-
ing darts of segregation to say, "Wait." But when you have seen vicious
mobs lynch your mothers and fathers at will and drown your sisters and
brothers at whim; when you have seen hate filled policemen curse, kick,
brutalize and even kill your black brothers and sisters with impunity; when
you see the vast majority of your twenty million Negro brothers smothering
in an airtight cage of poverty in the midst of an affluent society; when you
suddenly find your tongue twisted and your speech stammering as you seek
to explain to your six-year-old daughter why she can't go to the public
amusement park that has just been advertised on television, and see tears
welling up in her eyes when she is told that Funtown is closed to colored
children, and see the depressing clouds of inferiority begin to form in her
little mental sky, and see her begin to distort her little personality by unconsciously developing a bitterness toward white people; when you have to
concoct an answer for a five-year-old son asking in agonizing pathos:
"Daddy, why do white people treat colored people so mean?"; when you
take a cross-country drive and find it necessary to sleep night after night in
the uncomfortable corners of your automobile because no motel will accept
you; when you are humiliated day in and day out by nagging signs reading
"white" and "colored"; when your first name becomes "nigger," your middle name becomes "boy" (however old you are) and your last name becomes
"John," and your wife and mother are never given the respected title
"Mrs."; when you are harried by day and haunted by night by the fact that
you are a Negro, living constantly at tip-toe stance never quite knowing
what to expect next, and plagued with inner fears and outer resentments;
when you are forever fighting a degenerating sense of "nobodiness"; then
you will understand why we find it difficult to wait. There comes a time

when the cup of endurance runs over, and men are no longer willing to be plunged into an abyss of despair. I hope, sirs, you can understand our legitimate and unavoidable impatience.

DEBATING GUN CONTROL

On April 20, 1999, two teenage boys shot and killed twelve classmates and a teacher at Columbine High School in Littleton, Colorado, after which they killed themselves. Some of the guns they used were purchased for them at gun shows, markets that under then-current law were exempt from federally mandated waiting periods and background checks for purchasers of weapons. In the excerpts that follow, two members of the House of Representatives debate an amendment that would require a three-day waiting period and background checks on those seeking to purchase weapons at gun shows. Speaking in favor of her own amendment is Rep. Carolyn McCarthy (D.-NY), who ran for Congress in 1996 primarily on the issue of gun control after her husband and son were among more than a dozen people shot by a deranged gunman on a commuter train. Her husband died, and her son was left disabled. Speaking against the amendment is Rep. William McCullom (R.-FL). The amendment failed, 235–193, with six members absent.

> *Mrs. McCARTHY of New York.* Mr. Chairman, I thank all of my colleagues for their support. This is very hard for me tonight. It is hard for me because I have heard so many different things. I have been here just about three years and I am used to all the different spins. I do not understand them all the time, but that is what I do.
>
> What we were supposed to be doing tonight was trying to serve the American people. What we are doing tonight is saying and listening to the victims across this country. That is all we are trying to do. That is the only reason I came to Congress.
>
> Someday I would like to hopefully not have to meet a victim and say I know, because it is really hard. We have heard the arguments on both sides, and I wish we had more time to really say the truth about everything. My amendment closes the loophole. That is all I am trying to do.
>
> I am trying to stop the criminals from being able to get guns. That is all I am trying to do. This is not a game to me. This is not a game to the American people.
>
> All of my colleagues have to vote their conscience, and I know that. But I have to tell my colleagues, mothers, fathers, who have lost their children, wives that have lost their loved ones, this is important to them.
>
> We have an opportunity here in Washington to stop playing games. That is what I came to Washington for. I am sorry that this is very hard for me. I am Irish, and I am not supposed to cry in front of anyone. But I made a promise a long time ago. I made a promise to my son and to my husband. If there was anything that I could do to prevent one family from going

through what I have gone through and every other victim that I know have gone through, then I have done my job. Let me go home. Let me go home.

I love working with all of you people. I think all of my colleagues are great. But sometimes we lose sight of why we are all here. I am trying to remind my colleagues of that.

Three business days, an inconvenience to some people. It is not infringing on constitutional rights. It is not taking away anyone's right to own a gun. I do not think that is difficult for us to do. If we do not do it, shame on us, because I have to tell my colleagues, the American people will remember.

Mr. McCOLLUM. Mr. Chairman, all of us who are here tonight are here with poignance and concern and feel for the sincerity of the speech we just heard. I have three sons, my wife and I do, and I can only imagine the pain that those such as the gentlewoman from New York (Mrs. McCarthy) who have lost their children to violence must feel. That is why we are all here.

Fundamentally, one would think we had some huge disagreement tonight. Yet, in reality, I do not think there is a Member of this body who disagrees with the fundamental purpose that we are here tonight to do, and that is to try our darnedest to close the loophole in every way we possibly can in the existing laws that might allow some convicted felon to get ahold of a gun who could go out there and use that gun to kill one of our kids or grandkids.

That is what every one of us believes in who is here tonight. We may disagree over the product, over the nature or the style of it, but that is what we are here about, every one of the provisions. Each of us believes that his or her version is better for one reason or another. That is what we are here, all of us, are about.

Unfortunately, I think the amendment of the gentlewoman from New York goes too far. It is overly broad. It would turn gatherings of friends into gun shows. I do not think that is what she intends, but that is what I believe it would do.

It would turn neighborhood yard sales into gun shows, and I do not think that is what she intends, but I believe that is what it would do.

It would force gun promoters to really go out of business, I believe, because I do not think that they could comply with the kind of restrictions placed on them without becoming criminally liable. Therefore, I believe they would not continue to conduct gunshows.

So I want to close the loophole just as much as anyone elsehere does tonight. I have offered a bill that would do that, and an amendment has already been passed that I did not agree with that would modify that slightly, but the authors of that amendment want to close that loophole.

But I cannot agree with the amendment of the gentlewoman from New York tonight because I believe the McCarthy amendment would do more than close the loophole. It would close down gun shows. I believe it. So I urge a no vote on it. But I am with the gentlewoman, I am with everybody here to help our kids, and stop the killing that is going on in America, and close this loophole.

So, regretfully, I urge a no vote on the McCarthy amendment.

Congressional Record, 106th Congress, 1st Session, vol. 145, p. H4603, Thursday, June 17, 1999.

PUBLIC VALUES, PUBLIC OPINION, AND MASS MEDIA

OBJECTIVES

❑ To understand how shared public values shape the nature of political debate and public policy decisions

❑ To discuss the importance of ideology in political debate and action, and to examine the core traits of liberal and conservative ideologies that dominate American political discourse

❑ To assess the dimensions of public opinion, how it is shaped, and its effects on political debate and policymaking

❑ To examine the role of mass media in deciding which issues dominate the national agenda of debate and action

In 1996, after years of often bitter political conflict, the U.S. Congress ended over six decades of guaranteed federal support for poor people under the umbrella of the Aid to Families with Dependent Children program (AFDC). It replaced AFDC with lump-sum grants to the states, which would enjoy a great deal of freedom to decide who was eligible for aid, for how long, the kinds of benefits they would receive, and, in some cases, the jobs they would have to perform in order to retain benefits. Congress also cut over $5 billion in federal spending on welfare for the following five years.[1]

Conservatives, led by the Republicans who then controlled both chambers of Congress, for years had tried to limit federal welfare spending, reduce the federal budget, and return more authority over welfare policy to the states. They succeeded this time because they were joined by President Clinton, who in 1992, had run for office promising to "end welfare as we know it." Clinton, regarded as relatively liberal, knew that the system was unpopular and had to change. However, he demanded that reform include job training, child care, and health care programs, which together would enable low-income mothers to work while ensuring that their children received adequate care. Conservatives were skeptical about whether Clinton's plan would be any better than the old federal program.

This conflict over welfare reform reflected very different perceptions about human nature. Conservatives believed that giving poor people a check did nothing to help them develop their intellectual and moral capacity to work. The only way to help poor people escape the "cycle of dependency" was to get them into the workforce. Liberals attacked this view as simplistic, saying that it ignored the fact that welfare recipients frequently were single women with children who had limited job skills, education, or, even the self-esteem needed to compete in the marketplace. Liberals also attacked the reforms as harmful to children and the mentally ill, charges that conservatives rejected as false and unfair.

In the end, conservatives dominated the public debate over welfare reform because most Americans believed that the old system was broken. Many congressional

The public face of welfare. To most Americans, welfare was simply a handout to people who did not want to get a job. Such widespread images, especially when recipients were immigrants or racial minorities, created an environment conducive to major changes in the welfare system.

liberals, sensing that working Americans had grown weary of giving money to poor people, reluctantly went along. In an election year, few members of Congress wanted to be portrayed as defenders of a program most people disliked. President Clinton, who refused to support earlier welfare reform efforts that conflicted with his goals, also was eager to fulfill his promise to change welfare. In doing so, he would take away a campaign issue from his Republican opponent in the 1996 presidential election, Senator Robert Dole of Kansas.

What will happen as a result of welfare reform? Conservatives believe that most former welfare recipients will go out and work. Any job was better than being on public assistance. However, liberals believe that many former welfare recipients will do badly in a job market for which they have few skills, that the jobs they can get won't pay enough to make up for the benefits they lost, and that the new law will lead to increased poverty and homelessness. In truth, neither side really *knew* what would happen, but the common desire to get rid of welfare was so strong that Congress was willing to rip up the old program and start all over. The poor themselves had little to say about the whole matter.

THE POWER OF PUBLIC VALUES

The debate over welfare was affected profoundly by public images about those who depended on welfare. To many Americans "welfare" raises up images of "someone else"; that is, people of low work ethic and dubious morality who cheat the system.[2] Such images come from many sources: television and newspaper stories about welfare fraud; complaints on talk radio programs about welfare recipients who use food stamps to buy liquor and cigarettes; politicians who focus on "welfare queens" during election campaigns; parents' laments about their hard-earned tax money going to people who don't work; and, perhaps, an occasional personal experience with some-

BOX 5.1.
PUBLIC IMAGES OF WELFARE

In a December, 1995, telephone survey 1,000 adults were read the following statement: "I am going to read some statements about the welfare system which may or
may not be true. Please tell me if you think each is a serious problem or not." The
following data indicate what percentage of those surveyed thought each of the statements indicated a serious or somewhat serious problem. Responses were listed both
for everyone surveyed (*n* = 1,000) and for those who are in households in which
someone receives welfare benefits (*n* = 122, or about 12 percent of the total).

Remember: The statement itself *may or may not be true,* but what matters are the
perceptions that people hold about welfare and its effects.

	Percent indicating that this is a serious or somewhat serious problem	
Statement	*General public*	*Individuals in households receiving welfare*
"Welfare encourages teenagers to have kids out of wedlock."	60%	64%
"People cheat and commit fraud to get welfare benefits."	64%	67%
"People abuse the system by staying too long and not trying hard enough to get off."	73%	67%

Those surveyed then were asked to respond to the following: In general, do you think
the welfare system should be:

left alone	3%
eliminated altogether	4%
adjusted somewhat	34%
adjusted fundamentally	59%
don't know	1%

one on welfare. Although it was unclear whether most Americans knew about or
wanted the specific changes that were contained in the 1996 law, widespread beliefs
about the failures of the old system created an atmosphere for major policy change
(see Box 5.1).

WHAT DO YOU THINK?

There were some racial differences within these responses. Whites (*n* = 803) were more likely than blacks (*n* = 295) to want major changes, just as whites generally were likely to demand greater changes in the welfare system than were those in households receiving welfare (*n* = 122).

	Whites	*Blacks*	*Welfare*
Left alone	3%	6%	9%
Eliminated altogether	4%	3%	3%
Adjusted somewhat	32%	51%	46%
Adjusted fundamentally	61%	40%	42%
Don't know	1%	1%	0%

Notice that welfare recipients were as likely as everyone else to recognize that the system had problems, but far less likely to want major changes in that system.

From these data you might infer that most of those surveyed who were on welfare also were black. This may be the case, but you cannot support that inference from these data. You would need to show the racial breakdown of welfare recipients themselves to make this inference. Or you might infer from the data that close agreement on issues between blacks and welfare recipients (as compared to whites) indicates that blacks are more likely to know and sympathize with someone on welfare. However, again, you cannot prove this inference from the data. So be careful about how you interpret survey data.

Note: The breakdowns by race do not add up to 1,000.

Source: Adapted from *The Values We Live By: What Americans Want from Welfare Reform* (New York: The Public Agenda Foundation, 1996), http://ww.publicagenda.org/issues/nation_divide

As we saw in chapter 1, the shared values that are at the core of the American political culture set broad boundaries on what activities Americans believe should be allowed. Of course, such abstract public values do not automatically determine what happens. The outcome of any issue debate also hinges on economic and social conditions as well as the relative persuasiveness of competing politicians, media personalities, and even the occasional professor. Even so, as the welfare case illustrates, it is easier to achieve major change if it resonates with the core beliefs most Americans hold. If the American value system says that individual effort and hard work is the key to success, then there is little public sympathy for those who don't work.

The debate over national health care, which is discussed further in chapter 7, also illustrates how public values limit the options available to policymakers. Most major nations have some form of national health insurance. In some, such as Great Britain, the government directly operates the health care system. In others, such as Germany, citizens are guaranteed access to private health care insurance, with the government regulating standards and costs. In either case, citizens are guaranteed access to health care and government plays a major role in providing it.

However, the United States does not guarantee access to health care, nor does the national government directly regulate medical practices or costs. Although there are a number of state and federal health care programs such as Medicare, which serves the elderly, the nation's health care system is dominated by private health care providers and insurance companies. Nobody designed this system; it just evolved. Its structure reflects strong cultural beliefs about the sanctity of private property, the need for local control, and a desire for freedom of choice. Whatever complaints Americans have about health care, they do not want a "radical" idea such as a government-run system. Yet such a system does not seem too radical for Canadians, who accept a greater role for government than most Americans would consider legitimate.[3] Different cultural values can mean diverging answers to the same policy problems.

The point here is that no society considers every possible answer to a problem. Each society has its own biases, ideals, prevailing values, and popular opinions. Every society has topics that it will not discuss or ideas it considers radical. These values affect which problems are debated, how they are defined, and which proposed solutions are deemed acceptable.

In this chapter we explore how public values affect political debate and action by examining conservatism and liberalism, the two major, competing belief systems that shape American politics. We then go beyond these broad belief systems to look at public opinion and how it sets boundaries on public discussion. As in the case of health care, public opinion may not tell policymakers what to do, but it certainly tells them what they *cannot* do. On welfare, public opinion did not direct policymakers toward specific reforms; it just told them to change a system no one liked, period.

Finally, we examine the role of the mass media in contemporary politics, with a special focus on the roles various media play in how Americans look at the world and how they develop their beliefs about how it should work. As we shall see, mass media are part of that broad and often amorphous process by which Americans create the "pictures in their heads" that, as in the cases of welfare and health care, eventually affect the direction of public policy.

THE ROLE OF IDEOLOGY

Americans generally adhere to broad values embodied in the nation's political culture but they are far more divided over how these values should be applied to real problems. For example, two people can agree that "individual liberty" is a good thing. But, as we saw in chapter 4, they can disagree over *how much* liberty an individual should enjoy, whether the community's interests outweigh individual rights, and what role government should play in promoting liberty. One person may argue that there

Presidential candidates and their ideologies (clockwise, from top right)—Elizabeth Dole (2000), conservative; Steve Forbes (1996, 2000), libertarian; Jesse Jackson (1984, 1988), liberal; Patrick Buchanan (1992, 1996, 2000), conservative populist. By comparison, President Bill Clinton would be considered moderately liberal on most dimensions.

should be few limits on individual freedom and that government itself poses the greatest threat to liberty. The other may argue that individual liberty is a worthy value, but it must be balanced with the need for social stability and public order. One wants tight limits on government; the other might be willing to accept a more active government role.

These two individuals hold different belief systems about how the world should work. Indeed, when we call someone a "liberal" or a "conservative," a "radical" or a "moderate," we imply that he or she holds a particular **ideology.** For our purposes, this is defined as a *coherent* and *patterned* set of beliefs about how society and government are supposed to work, and particularly about the kinds of things government should and should not do. Compared to abstract ideals such as "freedom" or "equality," an ideology is a focused belief system about the proper role of government.[4]

IDEOLOGICAL CONSISTENCY

Notice the term "system." The beliefs and values that make up an ideology are not random. Instead, the notion of an ideology suggests coherence, consistency, and integration. A person who considers himself a strong liberal should hold consistently liberal values on matters of public policy ranging from abortion and gun control to public school funding and welfare; a person who considers herself a strong conservative should hold consistently conservative views on these same issues. Individuals who display little consistency in their values are not, and should not consider themselves, strongly ideological.

By this standard, most Americans are not strongly ideological. As we will see, whatever they may call themselves, Americans tend to hold liberal views on some issues and conservative views on others, often without realizing these inconsistencies.

How coherent, consistent, and integrated a person's ideological views are seems to stem most from that person's **socioeconomic status**—a term that reflects an individual's overall educational, income, and occupational profile. In general, people who are better educated and hold professional jobs such as doctors or lawyers tend to pay more attention to and are more active in politics than people with less education, lower incomes, and less-prestigious occupations. Those with higher socioeconomic status also tend to hold more consistent ideological views and to act on their views more predictably than do those whose views are less consistent or coherent. Simply having a college education tends to make a person more politically aware and ideologically coherent, if only because that person has been exposed to more information, has been asked to think analytically about issues, and probably has mixed more with different kinds of people.

This correlation in no way implies that a factory worker with a high school education is not able to pay close attention to and participate in politics, nor does it suggest that such a person cannot display high ideological consistency. Broad statistical indicators such as overall levels of education, income, or types of occupation say very little about any one individual's passions or political interests. However, looking at the population as a whole, there is a strong relationship between socioeconomic status and ideological consistency.[5]

Older people also tend to display more ideological consistency than do younger people. This is no surprise as one's views about the world tend to solidify and get more sophisticated as one experiences all that life has to offer, owns a home, raises children, and, perhaps, plays an active role in the larger community. Young people, particularly those under 25 years of age, are still developing their value systems and matching their beliefs against their experiences. We will discuss the processes by which we develop our values later in the chapter.

LIBERALS AND CONSERVATIVES

In talking about ideology, we inevitably run into the issue of whether we as individuals are **liberal** or **conservative**. What do these terms mean? To many Americans the first simply means "more government," the second, "less government." These characterizations contain kernels of truth, but they are simplistic. These different orientations are best understood as fundamentally distinct notions about how the world works, and about the proper role of government in that world.

The two ideologies also cannot be understood without reference to their philosophical and historical roots. The meanings of liberalism and conservatism today differ somewhat from what they meant 200 years ago, for important reasons that tell us a lot about how core values are shaped by broad economic, social, and political contexts. In this section, we take a closer look at how these ideologies evolved over the course of American history so that we can better understand what they mean today.

LIBERALISM

Thomas Jefferson is the best example of a late 18th-century liberal. Jefferson was a renowned inventor, scholar, plantation owner, architect, and gourmet, not to mention the primary drafter of the Declaration of Independence and third president of the United States. Next to Benjamin Franklin, Jefferson may have been the most talented individual in the new nation. Jefferson was a strong believer in rational thought, the inherent goodness of human nature, political equality, and the inalienable rights of the individual.[6] Above all, he believed in the right of the individual to be free from undue constraints. A "wise and frugal Government," he stated during his first inaugural address in 1801, "shall restrain men from injuring one another, shall leave them otherwise free to regulate their own pursuits of industry and improvement, and shall not take from the mouth of labor the bread it has earned."[7]

To Jefferson, government was the primary threat to individual liberty; it should be constrained so that individuals are able to enjoy their natural rights. Ideally, government should be close to the people so that there would be little difference between what the people wanted and what government did. The will of the majority, determined through votes on the issues, should prevail in all instances. Local government, where it was easiest to identify the majority, was best suited for ensuring government by the people. Indeed, as we saw in chapter 4, liberals such as Jefferson opposed the Constitution until it was agreed that a bill of rights would be added. Later conflicts over the powers of the national government led Jefferson and other liberals to create the Republican-Democratic Party, the predecessor of today's Democratic Party.

In sum, 18th-century liberals, as exemplified by Jefferson, defended the rights of the individual and the power of the states against the national government. They believed that government, especially the national government, was the primary threat to individual rights and liberties. For the Jeffersonian liberal, the government that governs least governs best.[8]

CONSERVATISM

Alexander Hamilton, New York lawyer and businessman, was a classic 18th-century conservative. He certainly believed in the importance of liberty, but he also stressed the importance of a stable society and strong nation.[9]

Above all, conservatives such as Hamilton feared economic and social disorder. Shays's Rebellion in 1786 had underscored the ills afflicting the new nation, and conservatives wanted to change the Articles of Confederation in order to strengthen the national government and forge a stronger and more unified nation. As we saw in chapters 2 and 3, they generally succeeded in getting their way. The primary emphasis of the Constitution is not on individual rights but on themes such as unity, justice, social order, common defense, and the general welfare. The Constitution was a conservative plan for effective government, whereas the Bill of Rights arose from the demands of liberals to place constraint on the power of that government.

Conservatives were skeptical about the inherent equality and rationality of the individual. In their view, individuals were not born equal. Some were smarter or more capable than others. Those endowed by nature or God with superior talents and wisdom should be given the authority to govern on behalf of the public good. As a result, conservatives doubted that a majority could govern wisely or well. It might be driven by short-term passions or irrational impulses that would interfere with the rights and liberties of those who disagreed or were in some minority. "Why has government been instituted at all?" asked Hamilton in *Federalist* No. 15. "Because," he answered, "the passions of men will not conform to the dictates of reason and justice, without constraint."[10] Those who governed thus needed to be insulated from the momentary passions of the public that could undermine the stabilizing effects of tradition and custom. Change, if it did occur, should be evolutionary, not revolutionary.

In general, Hamilton and other 18th-century conservatives stressed national power, economic stability, protection of private property, and the supremacy of the national government. Although they wanted to preserve individual rights, they were more concerned with social order, a stable economy, and, finally, the notion that only the most capable individuals should be eligible to lead.

THE GREAT TRANSFORMATION

This distinction between the liberal's belief in limited government and individual liberty and the conservative's belief in a strong government and social order lasted until the late 1800s. Liberals, generally Democrats, supported states' rights and the secession of the Southern states that led to the Civil War. Conservatives, generally Republicans, supported national supremacy and the preservation of the Union.

But this ideological division had developed at a time when most people farmed their own land or worked in small businesses. By the 1890s, however, more Americans were living in cities and working for the huge industrial corporations that produced the nation's manufactured goods. Others lived in "company towns" that depended on a single industry for their livelihoods, such as the coal towns of Appalachia, or in the farm towns of the Midwest that relied on the railroad to transport their produce or livestock to distant markets. Increasingly, most Americans' economic and personal lives were dominated by forces beyond their immediate control.

The greatest of these economic forces was the industrial corporation, an entity that did not exist a century earlier. By the late 1800s, the corporations that owned the railroads, mined the coal, pumped the oil, made the steel, and processed the nation's food were immensely powerful. In many cases one or a few of them monopolized entire sectors of the economy, dictating product supply and demand, setting wages and prices, and dominating the economic and social lives of entire cities. To average citizens, these corporations were more important than government itself.

Those who owned these corporations were known as **capitalists** because they provided capital—the money to buy machines, pay workers, and produce goods for sale. Men such as John D. Rockefeller (oil), Andrew Carnegie (steel), Mark Hanna (coal), Cornelius Vanderbilt (railroads), and, later, Henry Ford (automobiles) became fabulously wealthy—indeed, wealthier in real terms than Microsoft founder Bill Gates is today! With their wealth came unparalleled economic and political power. These "captains of industry" could dominate local and state governments eager for their business, order their employees to vote for particular candidates, or spend huge sums of money on political campaigns.[11] In short, the corporations of the late 1800s and early 1900s had a degree of economic and political power that the nation's founders could not have imagined in 1787, power equal to if not greater than anything possessed by government itself.

Effects on Liberalism For liberals the power of the corporation posed a serious threat to their ideals of limited government and local control. They began to see the corporation, not government, as the primary threat to individual freedom. For farmers, miners, and workers, the central economic, social, and political power in their personal lives was not government but a railroad, a coal company, or a steel plant. If this was so, government was the only institution strong enough to check the potentially tyrannical power of the corporation. Only government had the legal, financial, political, and police power to protect individuals against the corporation and its owners, so liberals began to turn to government to protect individual rights and liberties.

More important, liberals increasingly appealed to the *federal* government to restrain the power of the corporation.[12] Local governments often were controlled by a few powerful individuals and companies, whose money and influence over workers' votes also allowed them to dominate state governments. But the federal government was different. The size of the nation and the diversity of the constituencies represented in Congress, augmented by separation of powers and the system of checks and balances, in theory made the national government more difficult for any one company or group of companies to control. Faced with the power of the corporation, liberals saw the federal government as a means of protecting individual rights and liberties on a national basis.

Free Market Conservatives As with Hamilton before them, late 19th-century conservatives favored economic stability, national power, and social order. But this generation of conservatives saw the corporation, not government, as the primary promoter of economic health, social stability, and national power. The corporation, working within the market economy, generated wealth. Wealth in turn led to broader social stability and, ultimately, national power.

To conservatives, government's role in this equation was restricted to maintaining social order and defending the nation. Beyond these basic functions, government should not interfere with the workings of the market system. This doctrine, known as *laissez-faire* (French for "leave things alone"), had been made famous by the Scottish economist Adam Smith in *The Wealth of Nations* (1776). According to Smith, if left alone, the "invisible hand" of the market by itself would regulate the supply and demand of goods and services. By extension, the "invisible hand" would regulate prices, product quality, and working conditions. Consumers could decide not to buy products that were too expensive, inferior, or tainted, and workers who were dissatisfied with their wages or working conditions could quit and find a job elsewhere. To conservatives, the market ran itself, and very little government invervention was necessary.

Private Property   The power of the corporation complicated the classic liberal view of private property formed in an older world of self-sufficient farmers and small merchants. The growing dependence of citizens on large institutions for their jobs, housing, even food, and the dominance of the corporation over their economic and social lives, forced liberals to look increasingly to government to protect individual *civil* rights and liberties (see chapter 4). Thus, while conservatives looked to Standard Oil, U.S. Steel, or Armour Meats as generators of wealth and national power, liberals feared that these companies had too much control over the lives of individuals. For them, the company's property rights had to be balanced against the individual's right to earn a decent living, work under safe conditions, eat unadulterated food, and organize labor unions. For liberals, government was necessary to restrain free market capitalism's inequities in wealth and power, which they believed ultimately undermined civil rights and liberties.

For conservatives, government had no right to get involved in these matters; if it did so, it would be interfering with private property rights and the workings of free markets. The capitalists who took financial risks should be able to reap the benefits, so government had no right to confiscate private property, whether in the form of taxes or through regulations that affected a company's products or its ability to run its operations.

Social Darwinism   Capitalism dovetailed with conservatives' traditional skepticism about equality, and about the capacity of most individuals to govern wisely or well. For Hamilton such skepticism had been expressed in the idea that government is best left in the hands of the talented and virtuous few, the "natural aristocracy" that included people such as himself.

For many late 19th-century conservatives it also translated into a doctrine known as **social Darwinism,** a simplistic application of Charles Darwin's theory of evolution. In particular, Darwin's notion of the "survival of the fittest," the argument that animal and plant species that survived were those able to adapt to changing climates or physical conditions, was extended to an understanding of human societies. In this regard, individuals who adapted to and prospered in the new economy were the "fittest." They had worked the hardest, educated themselves, and succeeded—and they deserved it.[13]

As a political doctrine, social Darwinism put the burden for success squarely on the shoulders of the individual. For its part, government should not interfere with the "natural order" that determined individual success or failure. Conservatives did not advocate that the poor be left to starve, and capitalists set up extensive philanthropies such as Andrew Carnegie's endowment of numerous public libraries. Still, conservatives maintained that government should not involve itself in the private sphere any more than was necessary to maintain social peace. If people were to be free, they needed to be free to fail as well as to succeed. For their part, liberals regarded social Darwinism as a rationale for unchecked corporate power and the accumulation of massive wealth by "robber barons." To allow so much power and wealth to flow into the hands of the few, they warned, was dangerous to civil rights and liberties, and even to democracy itself.

Conservatives and liberals thus waged an ideological conflict during the late 1800s and early 1900s over the relationship between government and business. Conservatives largely won this battle, because belief in free markets and limited government more or less agreed with Americans' traditional views about individual freedom and responsibility. Yet liberals, aided by an equally widespread fear of unchecked corporate power, did manage to impose some restraints on the power of business through national laws that, for example, limited the power of companies to fix prices, use child labor, or refuse to reveal the ingredients that went into their products.

Liberals also tried to expand the political power of the masses to counteract the economic power of the corporation. For example, the passage of the Seventeenth Amendment (1913), which required direct election of senators, took the selection of senators out of the hands of state governments, which were often controlled by local corporate interests. As in the battle over adding the Bill of Rights to the Constitution, with the Seventeenth Amendment a majority of voters was able to impose a liberal check on the generally conservative thrust of the national government.

The New Deal   The transformation of liberal and conservative views on the role of government was complete in the 1930s. Many Americans believed that the depression had been caused by the excesses of the market system, particularly rampant speculation in the stock market. The president, Herbert Hoover, was a conservative Republican who argued that recovery would take place on its own, aided by the "invisible hand" of the market. But the nation's economic distress worsened, with almost a quarter of the labor force without work. Businesses, faced with low demand for their products, could not generate jobs. Without jobs, fewer people bought goods such as automobiles and refrigerators. And around it went. Nevertheless, Hoover was reluctant to intervene in the economy, and state governments had little money to address the crisis.

In 1932, voters turned against Hoover and to Democrat Franklin Roosevelt for help. Immediately after his inauguration in 1933, Roosevelt spurred on Congress to pass a dizzying array of economic and social programs known collectively as the **New Deal.** These sweeping programs restructured the failed national banking system, spent federal money on jobs programs and economic development, guaranteed rights of workers to organize unions, created Social Security for the elderly, and brought electricity to rural areas that were too remote and too sparsely settled for private companies to serve profitably.[14]

A Depression-era bread-line. The apparent inability of the market economy to solve the problem of widespread unemployment in the 1930s led to the election of liberal Democrat Franklin Roosevelt and the creation of "New Deal" government programs designed to "prime the pump" and get the economy moving again.

Through it all, Roosevelt stressed that government's role was to free individuals from the fear of economic insecurity. If the market failed, it was government's responsibility to get it going again. In a broader sense, Roosevelt applied Hamiltonian means to Jeffersonian ends. That is, a strong national government led by the enlightened few would help the average citizen to earn a decent living, own a home, enjoy fair economic competition, and, above all, be free from the unchecked power of other institutions, particularly big business. Individual freedom, in this sense, was enhanced by a strong and active national government.

Conservatives opposed what they saw as Roosevelt's interference in the market system. Although some admitted that government intervention was sometimes needed to promote economic stability or to correct market "failures," most regarded any government activity as an impediment to the efficient workings of the free market and a threat to economic rights such as private property. Conservatives were also uncomfortable with liberals' use of the federal government to protect and expand civil rights and liberties, actions that they felt threatened private property, undermined traditional community relationships, and led to social discord.[15]

CONTEMPORARY DEFINITIONS

These characterizations of liberalism and conservatism continue to this day. Despite their tendency to paint the other in extreme terms, liberals and conservatives agree on the basic principles embodied in American political culture. That is, in the abstract both support a free market economic system, limited government, individual liberty, and the importance of civil rights and liberties. They differ, however, over the

degree to which government should be involved in regulating the economy or promoting individual rights and liberties. The basic disagreement between liberals and
conservatives is about means, not ends.

Liberals stress active government involvement in protecting individual civil rights
and liberties. They believe that government should protect citizens against the less
desirable aspects of market competition, such as cost cutting through wage cuts or
failure to provide safe working conditions, and worry that sharp income inequalities
produced by an unrestrained market can be harmful for a democratic society.[16] On
the other hand, liberals are wary of government intrusion into individual rights and
liberties in the name of fighting crime or maintaining national security. Liberals are
aware of the need to ensure social stability and national defense, but they emphasize
the rights of the individual over the group.

Contemporary conservatives tend to advocate a minimal role for government.
They believe that individual liberty is tied to the right to obtain and hold private
property, so they tend to stress *property* rights more than civil rights. By extension,
conservatives see government as an obstacle to the effective operation of the market
and government regulation as destructive of private property rights. They are also
leery of an active government role in expanding individual rights and liberties, especially when such actions threaten property rights or, in the case of mandatory racial
integration, upset traditional social relationships.[17] Social change should evolve naturally rather than being forced by energetic and possibly ill-conceived government
initiatives.

Conservatives today, just as conservatives in 1787, believe that government must
ensure domestic peace and social order, and it must maintain national security.
Threats to any of these are threats to liberty itself. Conservatives thus are more likely
to support increased power for law enforcement authorities and higher defense
spending. Beyond those functions, conservatives are wary of using government, and
citizens' tax money, to try to achieve ends such as social equality.

POPULISTS AND LIBERTARIANS

This liberal-versus-conservative discourse about how the world works and the proper
role of government in it is complicated by variations on the two themes.[18] The most
important of these variations are provided by populists and libertarians.

Populists share conservatives' wariness about using government to expand civil
rights and liberties, but at the same time share liberals' belief in an active government
role in regulating the market system. Populists, for example, may be white, urban,
working-class Catholics who oppose abortion and dislike affirmative action programs
as "reverse discrimination" but who also fear big business and belong to labor unions.
Populists believe in an active government role in protecting their jobs and communities against the excesses of free markets and global trade, but oppose programs that
they perceive as giving others "unfair" advantages. They also support an active government role in moral causes such as banning abortion.

Libertarians, like liberals, support individual civil rights and liberties but, like
conservatives, oppose an active government role in the economy. Libertarians, in

fact, call for minimal government in all respects. They may support decriminaliza-
tion of drug use in the name of individual freedom and oppose government regulation of private property. Libertarians see conservatives as too willing to restrict individual civil rights and liberties while fighting crime or defending the nation, and they
see liberals as too willing to undermine property rights while regulating business.
Above all, libertarians believe in the rationality of the individual and the virtues of
minimal government. They see themselves as Jefferson's true heirs.

These variations point to the kinds of ideological coalitions that can emerge on
any given issue. Populists and liberals may agree on federal protection for the rights
to organize into labor unions and on spending for public education. Likewise, populists and conservatives may join to oppose using affirmative action to achieve racial
diversity in police departments or public colleges. Libertarians and conservatives may
oppose federal environmental regulations on business; libertarians and liberals may
fight governmental or corporate intrusions into citizens' private lives.

The coalitions that emerge in any one era depend on political contexts and the issues under debate. The depression, Roosevelt's New Deal, and World War II combined to unite liberals and populists into a powerful coalition based on an active role
for government in the economy and an assertive military role in defending democracy abroad. This coalition dominated American politics for about 30 years, until the
1960s, when it was split apart by issues such as civil rights and the Vietnam War.[19]

Beginning in the late 1970s, conservatives and libertarians united to dominate the
national debate in favor of shrinking the size and role of the federal government.
This coalition led to the election of Ronald Reagan, and its power was evident in the
case of welfare reform discussed earlier. In the late 1990s this "antigovernment"
coalition seemed to suffer from internal fractures over social issues such as abortion
and economic issues such as free trade with China, but it is likely to endure as the
dominant ideological coalition until new issues and social conditions reshape the ideological battlefield.

ARE AMERICANS LIBERAL OR CONSERVATIVE?

Broad ideological distinctions do not matter to most Americans. Indeed, when asked
to describe their own views, many more Americans are likely to call themselves "middle of the road" or "moderate." Among those who are willing to classify themselves
today, somewhat more people generally call themselves "conservative" than "liberal."
This tendency is not new. As Figure 5.1 shows, even during the 1960s, an era that
most Americans regard as a "liberal" decade, self-described conservatives outnumbered self-described liberals.

However, if we examine ideology in terms of public support for specific ideas or
programs, we find that since the 1970s Americans have become somewhat more liberal on a number of issues and more conservative on others. According to political
scientist William Mayer, Americans have become generally more liberal on issues
concerning civil rights and liberties, racial equality, sexual behavior, the role of
women, and environmental protection. On the other hand, he also points out that
Americans are also more conservative on economic matters, more wary about gov-

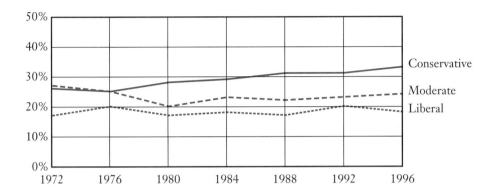

FIGURE 5.1. IDEOLOGY IN AMERICAN POLITICS, 1972–1996

The ideological predisposition of the American public has remained relatively stable over the past 30 years when measured according to self-identified ideological orientation. When asked, far more Americans consider themselves ideologically "middle of the road" or "conservative" than "liberal." However, their self-identification does not prevent them from supporting ideas or programs that can be considered more liberal.

Source: National Election Studies, May, 1998. The categories for conservative and liberal are aggregates of three subgroups within each category. The other respondents indicated either "don't know" or "haven't thought" about it.

ernment intervention in the economy and about the overall size and power of government in general.[20]

Mayer's observations underline the complexity of citizens' ideological views. Indeed, Americans can be described as *ideologically* conservative, but *programmatically* more liberal.[21] That is, they are philosophically opposed to "big government" and respond to the symbols of individual liberty and free markets, but they have often been willing to support a more active government when it comes to actual programs. This has been particularly true on issues relating to the protection of individual rights and liberties, on environmental problems that affect individual health and safety, or simply when people want the benefits of programs such as Social Security. Many populist conservatives, for example, are as afraid of big business as they are of government: They often join with liberals to demand that government keep business power in check.

IDEOLOGY AND PARTY

Ideological self-identification is closely associated with party loyalty. Today, people who call themselves conservatives tend to be Republicans, whereas those who call themselves liberals tend to be Democrats. Those who call themselves "strong Republicans" or "strong Democrats" almost always vote for candidates from their respective parties. As a result, the two main political parties really do profess distinct philosophies about the role of government (see chapter 6).

On the other hand, most self-described "independents" call themselves moderates or "middle of the road." These people, who account for about 30 percent of voters, typically lack the strong ideological stance of self-described liberals and conservatives.[22] They are more fickle in their support for candidates, often shifting from one political party to the other. Self-described "independents" generally hold either populist or libertarian views, and therefore are important—though temporary—allies for whichever party can persuade them to support it views.

POLITICAL SOCIALIZATION

Whether a person is liberal or conservative does not appear to depend on broad social characteristics. Except for age—people under 30 tend to be more liberal and those over 50 are more conservative—there are few significant ideological differences associated with gender, religion, education, income, or occupation. There are poor blacks who are conservative and affluent whites who are liberal—and vice versa.

What matters most to an individual's ideological predisposition is the process of **political socialization.** This is the process by which people learn their values and beliefs. Especially important in this regard are a person's family, church, and school. These early **agents of socialization** operate in two key areas. First, they are critical to developing an individual's *cognitive* element. This term basically refers to knowledge or thought. From a political perspective, it enables a person to identify a particular piece of cloth as the American flag and a specific person as the president, or, later, to grasp abstract concepts such as democracy. Through socialization in the cognitive domain, young people learn to attach a meaning to symbols or words.[23]

Early agents of socialization also are critical to developing the *affective* element, the feelings that an individual attaches to symbols, people, or words. Not only is a piece of cloth recognized as the American flag, but it should be treated with respect as the symbol of a great nation. A specific person is not only the president, but someone who protects the nation from its enemies. Not only does democracy mean government by the people, it also is a "good" form of government. Other forms, by extension, are "bad."

In the broadest sense, socialization is the process by which the core beliefs of a society's political culture are handed down from generation to generation. Every society engages in some process of socialization, whether by "indoctrination" (which is done only by "bad" governments) or in a typical American high school civics course. The resilience of any political system depends on the degree to which its people believe in its values and goals. People who believe in these core values are more likely to support that system even when the going gets rough.[24] Thus, Americans stood by their system during the depression, the world wars, and other crises.

Television, agent of socialization. At this age, a child's values are influenced most directly by parents, teachers, friends, and, yes, television. What image of socialization does this picture convey? What values are likely to be passed on to the child?

Small wonder, then, that Americans so often find themselves in conflicts over how to raise children or what kinds of lessons should be taught in school. It also is no surprise that issues such as school prayer or flag burning are so controversial, or that citizens become so concerned about the kinds of messages young people get from movies and television shows. Each of these controversies strikes at the heart of how a society socializes its next generation.

Even so, any adult's core ideological beliefs are not determined by parents, religious upbringing, or schools. Also of critical importance are one's friends, the mass media, and the experiences one has in college, on the job, in personal relationships, or as a parent. These experiences in particular sharpen the *evaluative* dimension of an individual's belief system—that is, assessing how "real life" compares with the ideals taught in earlier years. Ideals reinforced by experience are retained, and strengthened. Problems emerge when experiences do not reinforce the values instilled by parents, church, and school. For some people, the gap between ideals and experiences can lead to adjustment in or replacement of the ideals themselves. For others, however, the goal is to make the "real world" match their ideals. This leads them to advocate changes in public policy or even dramatic reforms in the way government works.

In general, then, the process of socialization has two stages. The earliest stages, dominated by parents, teachers, and religious leaders, shape an individual's core set of beliefs, particularly about right and wrong, good and bad (see Tables 5.1 and 5.2). Later stages, in which the individual evaluates core beliefs with other messages, such as those delivered in the mass media, and with personal experiences, help to fine-tune an individual's ideological beliefs on the proper balance between the individual and the society or on the proper role of government.

TABLE 5.1. THE CLASS OF 2002: SELF-IDENTIFIED IDEOLOGICAL CLASSIFICATION

In a survey of over 275,000 students in the class of 2002, respondents were asked to classify themselves according to their general ideological beliefs. Compare these data with the broader profile of Americans shown in Figure 5.1.

Far Left	2.7%
Liberal	20.8
Middle of the Road	56.5
Conservative	18.6
Far Right	1.5

Source: "The American Freshmen: National Norms for Fall 1998," The American Council on Education and the Education Research Institute, University of California at Los Angeles, as reported in *The Chronicle of Higher Education*, vol. 45, no. 21, January 29, 1999, p. A39; http://chronicle.com/weekly/v45/i21/ff4521activities.htm.

GENERATIONAL DIFFERENCES

The era in which a person emerges into adulthood can profoundly affect his or her belief system. For example, those who came of age during the 1930s and 1940s—that is, during the depression and World War II—hold different values than do those in the "Baby Boom" generation born between 1946 and 1964.[25] Members of the older generation tend to support a stronger government role in maintaining economic stability, and because of World War II, the "good" war, they are also likely to feel strong emotional attachments to the nation and its political system.

Their children's views are more complicated. Baby Boomers came of age in the 1950s and 1960s, a period of great national prosperity. They took affluence for granted, and to many of them the economic problems of the 1970s meant that the system itself had failed. Thus, they were less likely to assume that government could manage the economy effectively. Baby Boomers also grew up in a time when traditional social norms, such as in premarital sexual behavior, loosened considerably, so their social values varied from those of their parents. It was, after all, the age of "sex, drugs, and rock-n-roll." Finally, Baby Boomers came of age during the Vietnam War, an ultimately ambiguous conflict that divided Americans, followed sharply by the Watergate scandal (see chapter 9), causing Baby Boomers to be more critical of their nation's policies and its leaders. So great were these differences that many observers spoke of a "generation gap" between Baby Boomers and their parents.[26]

The children of the Baby Boomers have grown up during a time when the almost half-century-long rivalry between the United States and the Soviet Union has disintegrated into a more diffuse and fluid world where the nation's interests are less clear. Tremendous national and global changes have produced a great deal of uncertainty, even with broad economic prosperity in the 1990s, and as a result there is once again

TABLE 5.2.   THE POLITICAL VIEWS OF THE CLASS OF 2002

A survey of over 275,000 students in the class of 2002 drew out their opinions on a number of issues. Table 5.2 shows the percent of students who agreed with the statement.

Agree Strongly or Somewhat That:	*Total*	*Male*	*Female*
There is too much concern about the rights of criminals	72.8%	74.3%	71.5%
The death penalty should be abolished	22.8	19.5	25.6
Abortion should be legal	50.9	52.5	49.5
Marijuana should be legalized	32.4	38.6	27.2
Colleges should prohibit racist/sexist speech on campus	61.8	58.0	65.1
Employers should be allowed to require drug testing of employees or job applicants	78.5	74.6	81.8
It is important to have laws prohibiting homosexual relationships	33.3	43.4	24.8
Same-sex couples should have the right to legal marital status	49.4	41.1	56.4
The federal government should do more to control the sale of handguns	82.5	72.7	90.8
Racial discrimination is no longer a major problem in America	21.1	25.2	17.6
Wealthy people should pay a larger share of taxes than they do now	58.7	60.3	57.3
Material on the Internet should be regulated by the government	43.2	32.0	52.6
Realistically, an individual can do little to bring about changes in our society	31.9	36.6	27.9

Source: "The American Freshmen: National Norms for Fall 1998," The American Council on Education and the Education Research Institute, University of California at Los Angeles, as reported in *The Chronicle of Higher Education*, vol. 45, no. 21, January 29, 1999, p. A39; http://chronicle.com/weekly/v45/i21/ff4521activities.htm.

an intense debate over the role of government itself. This debate is being shaped by the differing experiences and outlooks of three generations of Americans, and it will profoundly affect the experiences of generations to come.

PUBLIC OPINION

Ideology is an abstraction in many ways. What matters more in everyday politics is **public opinion,** the views Americans express about specific issues, controversies, or political leaders. Public opinion is supposed to shape the outcomes of government action in a democracy, so "what the people think" is a matter of great importance to

BOX 5.2.
HOW POLLING WORKS

Public opinion polls operate according to established rules of statistical probability. As a result, reputable polling operations expend a lot effort to eliminate randomness or bias in their samples, polling techniques, and means of assessment.

In this regard, it is important to realize that the kinds of polls that require you to call into a 900 number or to click on a button on a Web site are not statistically valid. They are biased in favor of those who take the time to call the number (and who are willing to pay the toll call) or who happen to visit the Web site in question. This kind of poll is good for discussion, but little else.

In the ideal world, you would interview every individual who fits the category of person whose views interest you. For example, if you want to understand the views of all Asian Americans over the age of 30, you would interview everyone in this category. But this is impossible to do. You can never be sure that you will get to everyone in the category, and even if you could, it would be very expensive.

So pollsters live in the real world of *probability sampling*. That is, by correctly selecting a representative cross-sample of all registered voters, pollsters can obtain a valid assessment of the attitudes of all registered voters. The sample must reflect the broader population of registered voters with respect to breakdowns by gender, age, race, ethnicity, and so on, or at least as much as possible. For example, the sample would have to reflect the fact that voters over the age of 60 are more likely to be registered than are voters under the age of 25. Second, every registered voter in each of these categories must have an equal chance of being selected. If both conditions are met, then the survey sample should be a reasonable reflection of the views held by the larger population of registered voters.

How many respondents does it take to get a valid sample? Not as many as you might think. Most major polling organizations use a sample size of between 1,000 and 1,500 to assess the attitudes of adult Americans. Assuming that the survey is done correctly, this sample should give you a reasonably accurate picture of the overall adult population. Large sample sizes might improve accuracy a little, but not enough to be worth the cost.

policymakers and candidates for office, not to mention political polling organizations and, of course, political scientists.

In this regard, Americans are asked about everything, from their views on the president's budget and American policy toward China to the guilt or innocence of accused murderers. Rarely a day goes by without a newspaper or a television news program presenting data obtained through some kind of poll (see Box 5.2 on polling techniques). Yet, despite the prevalence of polls, most Americans spend little time thinking about the president's budget or the nation's foreign policy. Most spend far

A CLOSER LOOK

In this regard, any reputable survey will report the *margin of error* along with its results. The margin of error is the statistical probability that the views represented in the sample will be biased or wrong because of errors in selecting respondents or, even, because respondents lied. This sometimes happens, particularly on questions regarding controversial issues such as racial bigotry, on which respondents may not want to express their true feelings. In general, the greater the margin of error, the less reliable the results will be.

A national poll that surveys 1,000 or more adults should produce results with a margin of error of no more than plus or minus 3 percent. For example, a June, 1999, *Washington Post*/ABC News Poll asked 1,206 adults, "Do you approve or disapprove of the way Bill Clinton is handling his job as president?" Of those who expressed an opinion, 58 percent approved of Clinton's performance, and 38 percent disapproved. The poll had a margin of error of 3 percent. This meant that Clinton's approval rating actually lay somewhere between 61 and 55 percent. In this case the margin didn't matter—most voters approved of Clinton's performance—but it might matter in a poll gauging support for two candidates for office in which the gap between the two lies within the margin of error. In such a case the poll is essentially showing a tie.

Finally, interpreting poll data is a science. For example, the ways in which questions are worded can influence the results. Look again at the survey data in Box 5.1. In it, respondents were asked to agree or disagree with the statement, "People cheat and commit fraud to get welfare benefits." Obviously, this statement was designed to elicit a gut response, and any assessment of attitudes about welfare from these data will need to keep this wording in mind.

Public opinion polls can be useful snapshots of public opinion on particular issues or persons, but their results are only as good as the quality of the survey itself.

Sources: The Gallup Organization (www.gallup.com/poll); Richard Morin, "Americans Are Split on War Role," *Washington Post*, June 7, 1999, p. A16.

more time thinking about their jobs and families. Most people also have little knowledge about specific policies, particularly those that don't affect them directly. They may answer a pollster's questions about the president's budget or the nation's foreign policy, but frequently their answers are based on general impressions, not complete information.

Even so, what Americans think is important to policymakers and candidates for elected office alike. Average citizens may know little about a specific public policy, or even about politics, but they have strong overall beliefs about how the world should work.[27] In particular, as with options for reforming welfare or health care, they have strong opinions about what *should not* be done. Politicians who violate these core values sometimes arouse sudden and sharp reactions from a public that otherwise seems not to be paying much attention.

Permissive versus Directive Opinion

In this sense, public opinion on most issues can be described as relatively **permissive.** That is, most citizens neither pay close attention to nor have a deep understanding of most issues, so they tend to give policymakers leeway in shaping specific programs or policies. For example, most Americans have little expertise or interest in the technical aspects of regulations governing interstate trucking. Those who do care tend to be those who are directly affected by the issue in question—in this case, trucking companies, their competitors, and those whose businesses are affected by interstate commerce issues.

At any time, however, there are topics about which citizens express **directive** opinions that make clear demands on policymakers. Elected political leaders are reluctant to go against such demands. For example, as we discussed in chapter 4, most Americans favor long prison sentences for individuals convicted of crimes. Conversely, they express little support for "coddling criminals" through educational or counseling programs for prison inmates, even if experts argue that long prison terms by themselves do little to rehabilitate criminals. Faced with differences of opinion between experts and the mass public, elected officials usually go with the public's views, especially when the issue is highly visible and an election is just around the corner.

Sometimes there is a directive opinion that *something* must be done but exactly what should be done is in question. When this occurs, leaders must act, but they have a lot more leeway in doing so. This was true to some extent in welfare reform, about which the public wanted action but was less directive about the specifics. More dramatically, citizens confronted with a disaster such as a flood expect action, but they do not dictate the precise response. If Americans feel that the nation's defense capability is weak, they demand that it be made stronger, but they do not usually specify the types of weapons systems to be built. By the same token, Americans are quick to let their leaders know when the policy or action put forth is wrongheaded, too expensive, or impracticable.

Domestic Policy Issues   Public opinion is more directive on domestic policy issues. Citizens are likely to be more concerned and better informed about issues that affect them directly. What is more, nearly everyone has an opinion about controversial social issues such as abortion, affirmative action, welfare, health care, gay rights, or prayer in public schools.

However, even here, most people aren't rigid in their opinions. For example, on abortion most Americans can be characterized as mildly "pro-choice." That is, most don't like the idea of abortion, nor in most instances do they favor public funding for abortions, but they are unwilling to ban abortion entirely. These attitudes are in line with Americans' general fear of government intrusion into their personal lives.[28] Even so, policymakers are careful in dealing with these kinds of issues because a significant minority of Americans *do* hold intense views. For example, those who oppose abortion on moral or religious grounds are unlikely to make any compromises in their beliefs. They also are likely to turn out heavily to vote for candidates who agree with their views or against candidates with whom they disagree. As in the case of abortion, intense and active minorities have a disproportionate influence on policy making.[29]

The general public is a bit more permissive on economic and tax policies. The average citizen does not have strong opinions about what particular kind of tax is better or which type of economic policy is more effective—unless, of course, an individual perceives direct costs or benefits from a particular program. For example, senior citizens are far more sensitive about proposals to levy income taxes on their pension benefits than are college students for whom retirement is a long way off. Senior citizens thus are likely to express stronger and more focused opinions about the issue, views that policymakers will ignore at their peril.

In general, what most people know about the intricacies of any particular policy matters less than their opinions about whether the proposed policy is consistent with strongly held values or biases. For example, a proposed tax cut that seems to benefit only the affluent is unlikely to gain broad public support unless those making the proposal can convince the public that it will have wider social benefits, such as more jobs.

Foreign Policy Issues   Public opinion is essentially permissive on matters of foreign policy. As noted earlier, most Americans have little direct experience with foreign affairs and thus tend to give their leaders a great deal of leeway in making foreign policy decisions. Even here, however, policymakers are constrained by public values and biases. Americans tend to oppose sending aid to other countries, arguing that domestic problems should get priority. The fact that foreign aid makes up only about 1 percent of the overall federal budget—far less than most people realize—does not seem to matter.[30]

Americans are wary of getting involved in foreign military conflicts unless there is a clear threat to the nation's security. This can be a difficult standard to establish. For example, in the 1990s Americans expressed little desire to get involved in the civil war in the former Yugoslavia, even though many foreign policy experts believed that only the United States had the power to end a conflict that they thought threatened the stability of southeastern Europe. Mindful of public attitudes, neither George Bush nor Bill Clinton was eager to commit U.S. troops to the Balkans.

However, in early 1999 Americans expressed surprisingly strong support for a U.S.-led air attack on Serbia in order to halt that government's persecution of the Albanian majority in its province of Kosovo. In this case Americans seemed to agree that it was time to stop the ethnic bloodshed and bring some semblance of stability to the troubled region, but these attitudes did not form spontaneously. They were formed after years of news media coverage of the ongoing war as well as efforts by Clinton and other national leaders to show why it was important for the United States to take part in the effort to end the conflict. Whether Americans would have supported a possibly protracted ground war was another matter, as was underscored by the president's reluctance to commit ground troops to Kosovo except as part of an international peacekeeping force.[31]

Complicating this distinction between foreign policy and domestic policy issues is the fact that the two are becoming increasingly intertwined. For example, the relationship between the United States and China alone encompasses a wide array of issues ranging from human rights and the security of other Asian nations to allegations of pirating computer software and movie videos. Foreign policy issues extend to the nation's dependence on other countries for resources such as oil, which can create pressures to send American troops when instability erupts in those places; natural disasters, such as when Hurricane Mitch devastated much of Latin America in 1998, that can lead to illegal immigration problems in the United States; economic crises in Asia that affect jobs at home. Americans are increasingly aware of this linkage between the foreign and domestic policy realms. As they are, their interest in such issues also will increase, and perhaps become less permissive.[32]

MOST IMPORTANT ISSUES

Public opinion may not direct specific government action, but *public attention* to a particular issue has important influence on policymakers. Policymakers care about issues that the public cares about. As Table 5.3 shows, these "most important issues" tend to fall into four broad areas: economic, domestic policy, social policy, and foreign policy.

Economic Problems   As the data in Table 5.3 show, the economy is always the top issue of concern. In general, Americans worry less about the economy when they have jobs and, more important, a sense of economic security. When they feel economically insecure, however, the economy becomes a primary concern. Issues such as illegal immigration and affirmative action also rose closer to the top of the agenda of attention in the 1990s, reflecting many Americans fear that "others" are gaining an advantage in a time when many worry about their own economic security.

Domestic Policy Issues   Domestic policies usually deal with questions such as whether the government should spend more or less on education, health care, social security, and other programs. In such instances public attitudes are often reactions to government actions, not prescriptions about what should be done. During the 1980s, for example, many Americans expressed broad concern about environmental protection because the Reagan administration had cut federal spending on environmental programs.[33]

Social Policy Issues   Social issues such as civil rights, crime, and morality, usually gain a higher position on the list of public concerns in reaction to major events or highly publicized crises. For example, in April, 1999, two heavily armed teenagers walked into their suburban Littleton, Colorado, high school and fatally shot 12 other students and a teacher before killing themselves. The tragedy, which followed other incidents in which youths shot their peers on school grounds, shocked the nation and propelled crime to the top of the list of "most important issues" despite the fact that

TABLE 5.3.   MOST IMPORTANT ISSUES, 1990-1999

What kinds of issues do Americans think are most important at any one time? This table lists the percent of respondents who, when asked to name the most important issues facing the nation at that moment, cited one of these five broad issues. Note the saliency of economic issues during most of 1991–92: Bill Clinton defeated George Bush in the 1992 presidential election largely because of voters' concerns about the economy.

Date	Economic Issues*	Crime	Health Care	Federal Deficit	Drugs
1/99	6	13	7	2	6
9/98	4	10	6	2	9
4/98	11	20	6	5	12
12/97	16	16	7	5	12
8/97	18	20	6	5	15
1/97	21	23	7	8	17
7/96	20	25	8	12	8
5/96	25	25	10	15	10
1/96	25	18	10	28	9
7/95	21	25	7	11	10
1/95	25	27	12	14	6
8/94	23	52	29	3	9
7/94	26	30	21	5	7
1/94	34	49	31	8	8
9/93	46	16	28	15	6
1/93	57	9	18	13	6
8/92	64	7	12	9	6
5/92	50	8	7	5	10
3/92	67	5	12	8	8
11/91	55	6	6	4	10
7/91	24	4	3	6	13
7/90	10	—	1	21	18

* Includes references to "the economy," "jobs," and "unemployment."

Source: The Gallup Organization; www.gallup.com/poll/trends.

the nation's overall levels of violent crime were at their lowest in over 30 years. The general issue of moral values also got more attention as a result of the tragedy, leading various politicians to call for actions ranging from mandatory school uniforms to stricter gun control laws."[34] The urban riots and political assassinations of the 1960s, coupled with the war in Vietnam, led many Americans at that time to place "law and order" high on their list of important issues. Illegal drug use became a big issue in the

Grieving for comrades long dead at the Vietnam War Memorial. The Vietnam War (1955–1975) left more than 58,000 Americans dead. It also left lasting scars on the nation's politics. After Vietnam, Americans grew more cynical about government and wary about sending American troops into foreign conflicts.

1980s partly because policymakers and citizens, including First Lady Nancy Reagan, sought to make it a major issue.[35]

Foreign Policy Issues   Foreign policy issues usually do not rank high on the public's agenda except in periods of perceived national crisis or when Americans are involved in hostile actions. The Vietnam War obviously was an issue of major public concern, particularly as the war dragged on for more than a decade, and dominated both the 1968 and 1972 presidential elections. The seizure of the U.S. Embassy in Iran in 1979 and President Jimmy Carter's inability to free the Americans held hostage contributed to his defeat in the 1980 election. On the other hand, as we will see in chapter 9, President George Bush found that Americans' view on foreign policy issues is secondary to their focus on domestic economic ones. Bush led a resounding military victory against Iraq in the Persian Gulf War of 1991, but lost reelection in 1992 to Bill Clinton because more Americans believed that Clinton would be better able to respond to their economic concerns.

In the same vein, the public is likely to focus on foreign policy issues that have clear effects on domestic policy concerns. During the 1970s, for example, Americans became much more concerned about the nation's dependence on oil imports from the Middle East after Arab nations halted oil exports to the United States in retaliation for U.S. support of Israel during the 1973 Arab-Israeli War. The oil embargo quadrupled gasoline prices overnight, revealing the nation's growing dependency on imported oil, and drove home to Americans the connections between foreign and domestic policy.

SHAPING PUBLIC OPINION

Public opinion about such "most important issues" is shaped by **issue salience,** how visible and important the issues are to the average person. As we will discuss later, attitudes about major issues also reflect the extent of mass media coverage on them.[36] Except during a crisis, the issues that citizens worry about often are those that are being discussed by "policy elites" such as members of Congress or high-level bureaucrats or opinion leaders such as newspaper columnists, academics, business leaders, and talk radio hosts.

Most citizens don't pay close attention to most issues, but opinion leaders do. As with all activists, they want to influence public opinion in order to achieve desired goals, whether one that is relatively narrow (such as which type of jet fighter the Navy will purchase) or a fundamental redefinition of the purpose of government itself. The first step in any such effort is to get people to pay attention to the issue. In this regard, the role of mass media is critical.

MASS MEDIA AND THE PICTURES IN OUR HEADS

Social commentator Walter Lippmann wrote that "what each man does is based not on direct and certain knowledge, but on pictures made by himself or given to him."[37] This statement is simple and profound: Most Americans have not visited the countries they read about in newspapers or see on television, most have not fought in a war or been on welfare, and most have not directly experienced violent crimes. Americans form mental images about the countries, wars, crimes, and other objects or events that they hear about or see depicted in various mass media, and these "pictures" influence their actions and opinions. They also hold strong opinions about politicians, events, and issues—opinions that are shaped less by direct experience than by broad cultural values, their own upbringing, deeply held ideals, and personal biases.

In short, Americans hold opinions about what *should* be, mental "pictures" about good and evil, right and wrong, that have powerful impacts on what government can and cannot do. The power of public values and attitudes to shape government action starts with perceptions about the issues under debate. Take, for example, the case of welfare reform discussed at the beginning of the chapter. How did the public image of welfare reflect reality? Some welfare recipients no doubt fit the negative stereotype, but all of them? Most? Some? In truth, no one knew for certain, yet everyone acted as if the truth were obvious. In fact, whether our subjective notions about welfare are supported by objective evidence may not matter: If Americans *believe* that all welfare recipients are lazy cheats, it is no surprise they have little sympathy for people who depend on public support.

Imagine how the debate about welfare might have looked if poor people were instead seen as unlucky victims of economic or social forces beyond their control. Americans have no trouble viewing poor children this way ("It's not their fault they're poor") and hence are more likely to support programs that are designed to help children achieve a brighter future. Indeed, the most heated debates over welfare reform were directed at its effects on children, not their parents.

The debate over welfare reform underscores the point that the process by which society defines its problems is political. "Political conflict is not like an intercollegiate debate in which the opponents agree in advance on a definition of the issues," wrote political scientist E. E. Schattschneider. "As a matter of fact, the definition of the alternatives is the supreme instrument of power."[38] Whoever is able to define the nature of the problem has the advantage when it comes to deciding what to do about the problem. In this vein, conservatives successfully painted welfare as a failure, so any "reform" was going to proceed on their terms. Similarly, liberals have successfully defined a healthy environment as a basic "right" for all Americans. As a result, any changes in environmental programs are going to proceed from the premise that the federal government will play a major role in cleaning up and protecting the environment.

THE PUBLIC AGENDA

Just deciding whether something *is* a problem to worry about is also a political process that involves conflicts. No society can address all of its problems at any one time. There is not enough knowledge, energy, time, or money to do everything. This reality raises an important question: With all of the possible problems that a society *could* address, why does it deal with some problems and not others? Why do some problems get onto the **agenda** of government and become subjects of national discussion and debate, while others are missed or ignored?[39]

For one thing, not all problems are obvious to everyone. An objective or measurable condition that could be considered as "bad" can exist but not be widely perceived as a "problem." We have all heard the question: "If a tree falls in the forest but nobody is there to hear it, does it make a sound?" In the same way, if nobody perceives that a particular condition is "bad," is there a "problem" to be placed on the agenda of government?

Consider an example. Americans are generally willing to accept an unemployment rate of about 6 percent as "natural" or "normal." Why? One answer lies in self-interest: Most Americans have jobs, and they don't usually worry much about the relative few who are unemployed.[40] The second answer is more subtle: It might be impossible to ensure "full" employment, even if taxpayers were willing to spend a lot more money on programs to provide jobs. In this regard, the existence of a certain percentage of unemployed people may not be regarded as a "problem" at all.

Even if we do agree that some condition is a problem that needs to be addressed, there's no guarantee that we will do anything about it. To use another example, residents of a town in which the only industry is a steel mill may be willing to accept a certain level of air pollution if they believe that the only solution is to close the plant.[41] This "solution" is not very palatable to people who are concerned about their jobs. Thus, sometimes we choose not to address problems that we know exist because doing something about them might be too difficult, or because the solutions might threaten existing ways of life. For example, Americans complain about clogged highways, dirty air, and long commutes to work, but they also want to be able to drive their sports utility vehicles and build houses farther away from where they work.

Of course, some residents of the town will want to clean up the pollution. They might argue that the supposed trade-off between clean air and jobs is a false one, that both goals can be achieved. Whether their views are considered seriously will depend partly on the actions of those who prefer not to deal with the problem at all.[42] The mill owners may try to wield economic and political power to keep the issue of pollution off the agenda. They may also want to talk about other problems that they regard as more important, such as wages or productivity.

The point here is that except in times of crisis or when there is a natural disaster, politics determines which issues we shall discuss from the infinite variety of issues we could discuss. In other words, often we fight about which fights we are going to fight.

THE ROLE OF MASS MEDIA

The mass media sit at the center of these profound questions about how citizens confront problems about which they have little or no direct experience. Media—whether newspapers, radio, television, magazines, or the Internet—are the means by which we learn about issues and about what government is doing. Media also help connect citizens to those who govern. In this section we examine mass media and their influence in shaping the conflicts that dominate the agenda for debate.

Media have always been central to politics. Thomas Paine's pamphlets helped fuel colonial fervor against Britain, and the publication of the *Federalist* papers was part of a fierce newspaper war over ratification of the Constitution. So critical was freedom of the press to democratic politics that it is protected in the First Amendment. An active, openly political, free press has been a fixture of American politics ever since.

Newspapers were the first true mass medium and were particularly influential in the late 1800s. The advent of radio, however, transformed the way Americans received news and how news itself was presented. Above all, radio made it possible for a president such as Franklin D. Roosevelt to talk *directly* to the American people about the banking crisis of 1933 or the nation's entry into World War II. Roosevelt's ability to use radio contributed greatly to his popularity. Radio forces listeners to use their imagination, and Americans who listened to Roosevelt's authoritative voice forgot that the president could not walk (he was stricken by polio in his late 20s). Roosevelt easily won reelection three times despite the fact that most newspapers, owned by conservative men such as Robert McCormick of the *Chicago Tribune*, endorsed his Republican opponents.[43]

The arrival of television in the early 1950s again transformed the way people received news and looked at the world. Television helped the young, handsome John F. Kennedy win election in 1960 over the less-telegenic Richard Nixon. In the 1960s television news broadcasts beamed video images of assassinations, urban riots, and the Vietnam War directly into Americans' living rooms, undermining government's ability to control press coverage of those events. Television also made it easier for Americans to observe environmental problems, to put human faces on

TABLE 5.4.   SOURCES OF MOST NEWS, 1959-1994

Every year the National Association of Broadcasters takes a poll that asks people to list where they get most of their news about what is going on in the world. Multiple answers are allowed, so the results exceed 100%. Note the decline of newspapers and, especially, radio as primary news sources over this period.

Source	1959	1968	1978	1988	1994
Television	51	59	67	65	72
Newspapers	57	49	49	42	38
Radio	34	25	20	14	18
Magazines	8	7	5	4	8
Other people	4	5	5	5	n/a

Source: Harold W. Stanley and Richard G. Niemi, *Vital Statistics in American Politics,* 5th ed. (Washington, D.C.: CQ Press, 1999), p. 173.

previously anonymous citizens in other nations, and, to some extent, to watch their leaders in action.

Today most Americans get most of their news from television, while the percentage who read a daily newspaper decreases each year (see Table 5.4). More important, the current age is one of virtually instantaneous television coverage on a global scale. Today the average person can watch the Cable News Network (CNN) or any number of other all-news cable television channels on a 24-hour basis, and hear about major (and a lot of minor) news stories as soon as they occur. President Bush, like most Americans, watched live CNN coverage of U.S. planes attacking targets in Baghdad, Iraq, at the beginning of the Persian Gulf War in January 1991. The television age is an instantaneous one, with many events covered in real time. Of course, the choices available on cable also enable a person to avoid watching any news at all, something not possible in the "old days" when the three major television networks (ABC, CBS, and NBC) were the only options.

But the choices available with cable television pale in comparison to the newest medium of them all—the Internet. This new medium poses incredible opportunities and challenges to news presenters and consumers alike. With the Net an individual can essentially decide which information sources to examine and which ones to avoid, regardless of analytical quality, factual accuracy, or political bias. Once the term "broadcasting" applied to the capacity of any single television network to reach everyone, and it was almost guaranteed that virtually every American watched some of the same news or entertainment programs. But with the Internet, even more than with cable television, the term "narrowcasting" is more appropriate. We now have the unparalleled ability to pick and choose among our sources of news and opinion, with no guarantee that any two individuals are receiving the same information.

GOOD PICTURES, BAD PICTURES

How this fragmentation of media affects politics is not yet well understood, but it will have major impacts on citizens and policymakers alike. At minimum, technological changes in media have profound effects on how individuals look at their world. The way a visual medium such as television presents the world differs from the way print media or even radio portray events. A viewer of television news does not have to interact with the medium to get information. That viewer does not even have to know how to read—only to see.

Visual media technology creates an interesting problem both for those who present the news and for those who watch it. Television depends on compelling images to attract viewers, particularly as most people watch television news while engaged in other activities, such as eating dinner. "Good" pictures convey drama, conflict, or novelty. "Bad" pictures are boring, and may cause viewers to change channels—and today viewers have plenty of options.

This dependence on compelling visual images creates impressions of the world that may vary sharply from reality. For example, people who rely on television for all of their news tend to think that there is more random violent crime in the nation than is actually the case. The tendency of local news programs to lead newscasts with often horrifying crime stories, many of which have occurred elsewhere in the country, contributes to this perception.

THE MEDIA BUSINESS

The nature of the mass media as businesses also affects how they cover issues. Whatever members of the media may say about their craft, media in the United States are private businesses that seek to make profits. Only a small part of the electronic media receives public support, notably the nonprofit stations affiliated with National Public Radio and public television's Corporation for Public Broadcasting. No newspaper receives direct government subsidies.

Most media outlets are private businesses. Moreover, they are increasingly owned by large corporations. Today relatively few small-town daily or weekly newspapers are owned locally. Instead they are owned by large holding companies such as Gannett and Knight-Ridder. The same is true of many major regional newspapers: The *Boston Globe*, for example, is owned by the *New York Times*. Major television networks and most local television and radio stations are also owned by large media conglomerates, such as General Electric (NBC), Viacom (CBS), or Disney/Capitol Cities (ABC). The concentration of major media in fewer but larger companies has accelerated in the past two decades, with some conglomerates—for example, Time-Warner (CNN) and Paramount (UPN)—having stakes in print, radio, television, movies, and emerging computer-based media such as CD-ROMs and Web sites.

The point is that mass media are, above all, profit-making businesses that rely heavily on advertising income. More viewers or readers translate into higher fees charged to advertisers, which itself means more income and higher profits for the television network or newspaper in question. The effects of this competition over and dependency on advertising revenue on the nature of news coverage are often overlooked, but they should not be. Most obviously, they raise concerns about whether any particular newspaper or television station is truly free—or will hold back on covering stories that might alienate a major advertiser or, even, its parent company. For example, in 1998 ABC News was accused of killing a news story that criticized the treatment of workers at Walt Disney World, which, like ABC, is owned by Disney/Capitol Cities. Officials at the network denied that the parent company pressured them to withhold the story, which they argued was not well substantiated. They also pointed out that ABC had not shied away from new stories critical of Disney in the past.[44] Whatever the truth, it again raised the issue of how corporate ownership and the need to maintain profits might affect the ways in which information is gathered and presented.

This concern over profit and competition for ratings has three other major impacts: a bias toward "new news," a focus on scandal, and a tendency to miss big but less visual stories.

New News Is Good News   The rush to find new and dramatic stories grows as a result of the competitiveness of the media marketplace. In particular, cable television's dozens of news channels require a constant stream of new stories to attract and keep viewers. Otherwise, nobody might watch, and cable companies might drop the station. News operations that break new stories publicize their achievements, hoping to attract even more attention. It helps if the new stories include attractive or striking pictures. Old stories, even vitally important ones, are harder to "sell" to viewers or readers—who become bored with an issue after a while.

Scandal   Television news in particular depends on conflict and drama to appeal to viewers (and advertisers). Critics complain that reporters often take an adversarial stance when interviewing or reporting on public officials. In part this tendency grows out of the reluctance of reporters to be seen as "soft" on public officials, but it also stems from the desire to get the next big story. In the 1970s, the *Washington Post* was credited with exposing the Watergate affair that eventually led to the resignation of President Richard Nixon after it became clear he had badly abused the power of his office. The two reporters who broke the Watergate scandal became famous, a lesson absorbed by a generation of journalists. Today the mere hint of "scandal" is likely to set off a frenzy of media investigations, often creating an image of more extensive wrongdoing than may actually have occurred (see Box 5.3, p. 216). The effect, it is argued, is to create the impression among the news-consuming public that politics is uniformly corrupt and all politicians are liars and thieves.[45]

No Picture, No Story?   Despite all this, the mass media often miss huge stories. This happens because some of the biggest stories of any era develop slowly and are hard to figure out without spending a lot of time (and money) on research and investigation. Few media outlets in a highly competitive and fast-paced market are willing or able to devote the necessary resources to these issues. For example, in the 1980s few media outlets paid attention to the precarious condition of the nation's savings and loan system until the system literally went bankrupt, a disaster that eventually cost taxpayers an estimated one *trillion* dollars and ruined numerous individual lives.

The story itself was complex, difficult to portray in pictures, and for a long time did not have any identifiable "villains."[46]

However, despite this competitive frenzy, no major media outlet dares to stand out too much from its competitors, particularly on controversial matters. Doing so invites uncomfortable scrutiny from critics always on the lookout for media "bias." Indeed, despite the immense array of outlets, there is relatively little variety in American national news media. The major newspapers and television networks tend to pay attention to the same issues, and they tend to pursue those stories in pretty much the same manner. They are rivals, but rivals that stay together in a pack.[47]

MEDIA AND THE PUBLIC AGENDA

Except for natural catastrophes such as earthquakes or surprise events such as the 1990 Iraqi invasion of Kuwait, most issues don't just leap onto the agenda for national debate and action. Instead they are pushed onto it by competing political actors, by news outlets looking to boost their own ratings, and, even by crusading reporters seeking to right some wrong. Because any society can deal only with one or two big issues at a time, those that are not on the agenda, even if they are important, simply will not be addressed.

Because issues compete for attention, the choices made by the media as to what constitutes news are important both to policymakers and to the public. Whether the media can actually change public opinion is a matter of debate, but few would deny that media do affect what Americans pay attention to. How an issue is presented— both in words and in pictures—has a profound influence on whether and in what way the public responds.

Issue-Attention Cycles   As we noted earlier, most people pay little attention to most issues, even those that would seem to deserve attention. But sometimes the public becomes riveted on an issue. This level of attention, as political scientist Anthony Downs observed, runs in cycles.[48] The cycle usually begins with the "alarmed discovery" of some undesirable condition, frequently one that has existed for quite some time. For example, in the 1980s a dire famine in Ethiopia continued for several years before most Americans found out about it. Why? Largely because the famine did not make it onto the evening network news. To most American media, a famine in Africa was not "new news," and not until one television network's officials saw especially graphic scenes of starving children did anyone "break" the story. Strong public reaction to the story spurred even more coverage and led to a global effort to provide famine relief.[49]

The cycle also applies to domestic issues. For example, the environment emerged as a big issue in the late 1980s in the wake of highly publicized ecological disasters such as the fire at the Chernobyl nuclear power plant in the former Soviet Union and the massive oil spill from the *Exxon Valdez* tanker off the coast of Alaska. Public concern about the environment prompted policymakers to promise action. For example, a major revision of the Clean Air Act that had been stalled in Congress for several years was passed in 1990 largely because President Bush, respond-

BOX 5.3.
TAILWIND: A SAGA OF THE MEDIA BUSINESS

It was a great news story. At the height of the Vietnam War, a secret army of U.S. Army Special Forces personnel and native Laotian tribesmen engaged in a covert war against the Viet Cong in supposedly neutral Laos. The illegal use of deadly sarin nerve gas against the enemy and alleged American defectors working with them, in violation of international treaties banning the use of chemical weapons. And now, 30 years later, startling revelations of a massive and longtime government coverup that probably involved every American president since Nixon. Operation Tailwind had all of the elements of a major scandal.

There was only one problem. It might not have been true.

Tailwind first came to national attention on Sunday, June 7, 1998, during the premier of "Newstand: CNN and *Time*," a new Cable News Network (CNN) collaboration with *Time*, the national weekly newsmagazine. As narrated by Peter Arnett, CNN's star foreign correspondent, the story alleged that the military's "secret war" in Laos—which by 1998 was not new news—involved the illegal use of nerve gas to kill possible American traitors. The story relied heavily on the testimony of a few retired U.S. military personnel and their Laotian colleagues, supported with some grainy video footage of airplanes spraying a substance over the jungle. It was a sensational story, and it was backed up by the reputations of two of the nation's major news operations.

The broadcast provoked a political firestorm. Not surprisingly, U.S. military officials heatedly denied that the United States had ever used nerve gas in the Vietnam War. They also criticized CNN's producers for overlooking evidence that contradicted their own charges. More important, the charges also were attacked by other former military and government officials who were in a position to verify the truth or falsity of the story. Their criticism of the report was so devastating that within days CNN officials backtracked on the allegations and commissioned an independent investigation to look into the matter. Within a few weeks the panel reported that the charges on Operation Tailwind could not be supported. On July 2, 1998, CNN released a statement retracting its allegations. The network subsequently fired the story's top producers and reprimanded Arnett, who later left CNN for another network.

What had happened? Floyd Abrams, who led the independent investigation, criticized the news-gathering techniques used by the Tailwind producers and reporters. Although the journalists who investigated the story did not invent facts, Abrams said, he did think that they believed in their story so much that they discounted contrary information.

ing to public opinion, made environmental protection a major part of his 1988 election campaign.[50]

But intense issue saliency doesn't last very long, particularly as the difficulty and costs of addressing a problem become more apparent and as other issues reach the top of the national agenda. The cycle is also affected by the tendency of the media to

A CLOSER LOOK

The story's top producers still believe that the story was accurate, and they were disappointed by the lack of support from CNN. "We presented the facts that we gathered," said one. "Let the people judge. This was a report on America's secret army. There is no documentation."

But that was the problem, said the critics. With no proof, why make the allegations in the first place? The answer might have had more to do with the competitive pressures of the marketplace than with journalism.

It was easy to see why CNN used the Operation Tailwind story to inaugurate their new show. "Newstand" was meant to show off the strengths of the two media outlets: CNN would broadcast the story on Sunday night, which *Time* would then feature in that week's issue. This partnership made some sense. Together, the two could stand out in the increasingly crowded news marketplace. CNN gave its news magazine an edge in the tough competition with the other television networks, where ratings points translated into advertising revenues. Likewise, *Time* could distinguish itself and sell more copies in its competition with *Newsweek* and *U.S. News & World Report*, among other weekly magazines.

The partnership also made business sense insofar as both are owned by Time-Warner, a vast media conglomerate formed by the merger of Time and Warner Brothers, the movie production company. CNN, which Time-Warner purchased a couple of years earlier, also owns cable television stations TBS, TNT, and Turner Classic Movies. Its founder, Ted Turner, also owns the Atlanta Braves baseball team, whose games are shown on TBS. The partnership marked an effort to integrate the various parts of Time-Warner and make more profitable use of what are very expensive news operations.

So "Newstand" was a high-stakes gamble. Some observers regard the Tailwind episode as emblematic of the market pressures that force reporters and producers to seek the Big Story. However, others were far less sympathetic. They believed that Tailwind showed how much news operations will sacrifice for ratings.

Sources: Walter Goodman, "Going Astray on High-Profile Report," *New York Times*, July 7, 1998, p. B3; "CNN's Tailwind Latest in Series of Media Embarrassments," July 2, 1998, Cable News Network, www.cnn.com.

become bored with "old" news and look for new stories. By the early 1990s the environment was no longer a dominant public concern. People were more concerned about their jobs as the nation's economy slowed and massive corporate layoffs became nightly headlines. Advocates of strong environmental protection found it harder to get their voices heard as policymakers rushed to address economic issues.

The environment may have been just as important as it was only a year or two earlier, but it no longer commanded public or media attention. Other stories mattered more.

MEDIA BIAS

A perennial debate in American politics is whether members of the mass media, particularly reporters, display any systematic political bias (see Table 5.5). Conservatives particularly complain that mainstream media outlets have a liberal political and cultural bias, one that is hostile to conservative values and viewpoints. There is some truth to their complaints insofar as *some* parts of the mass media have *some* liberal bias. As a group, reporters tend to support strong government protection of civil rights and liberties. The average reporter also is more likely to be liberal on social issues such as abortion, partly because reporters are educated professionals who, as a group, generally share this outlook. In part, this bias also reflects the importance of the First Amendment freedoms of speech and the press when it comes to reporting events. For example, reporters generally oppose efforts by religious groups to censor or restrict what the groups consider obscene or pornographic material.[51]

On the other hand, influential national talk radio hosts such as Rush Limbaugh and G. Gordon Liddy tend to be conservatives. More important, liberals argue that the American mass media has a systematic bias in favor of conservative economic views. Most news media outlets are owned by major corporations, which tend to oppose labor unions, a higher minimum wage, or any criticism of the free market system.[52]

For their part, reporters for most major newspapers are reasonably well paid, and major television news personalities may have annual salaries of over a million dollars. Critics argue that such high incomes create a bias against ideas that might affect reporters' economic interests, such as proposals that might increase taxes on higher incomes. Thus, although reporters may well be social liberals, they may also be economic conservatives, a combination that puts them comfortably into the libertarian viewpoint discussed earlier in the chapter.

It is easy to find examples of bias if one looks hard enough. But the debate may not really matter much to the average viewer or reader. Most people are selective consumers of media anyway, choosing magazines, talk radio shows, or Webzines that share their ideological views. Those who want a "Christian" slant on the news can watch their own cable television channels and radio stations; those who hold liberal views can read their own journals and access their own Web sites. The two groups rarely rely on the same media sources any more than necessary. The Internet, with its virtually infinite number of possible sources of information, only magnifies this tendency toward selective media exposure.

Indeed, the issue of media bias seems increasingly irrelevant. It may have mattered more when Americans were limited to three television networks, but today media are fragmented into hundreds of more specialized choices. The cumulative effect may be a media with no single bias except an insatiable desire for new and ever more provocative news images. But this tendency is sobering enough to make anyone wonder about the quality of the information that makes its way into the public psyche.

TABLE 5.5. TRUSTWORTHINESS OF MEDIA SOURCES, 1959-1994

An annual National Association of Broadcasters poll asks people about their use of and views on the news media. One question asks, "If you got conflicting or different reports of the same news story from radio, television, the magazines, and the newspapers, which versions would you be most inclined to believe: the one on the radio or television or magazines or newspapers?"

Source	1959	1968	1978	1988	1994
Television	29	44	47	49	51
Newspapers	32	21	23	26	21
Radio	12	8	9	6	8
Magazines	10	11	9	7	5
Don't know/ No answer	17	16	12	12	15

Source: Harold W. Stanley and Richard G. Niemi, *Vital Statistics in American Politics,* 5th ed. (Washington, D.C.: CQ Press, 1999), p. 173.

CONCLUSION

Citizens in a democratic society bear a great burden. They must assess problems and act on them, or at least compel the government to do so. After all, in a democracy what government does is supposed to reflect the values and desires of the people. But public opinion is often diffuse and permissive, open to manipulation by opinion leaders and activists. When the public does focus its attention on a problem it can force government to act, but such attention is fleeting. New problems come along and old ones are forgotten, often without having been solved.

Above all, public opinion is reactive. It *responds* to images and choices presented to it. In this respect, the role of mass media is more critical than ever. The globalization of news gathering and dissemination is worth attention, especially as instantaneous global communication is redefining the relationship between governments and the media. These trends can have beneficial impacts. Media can "shrink" the distances between nations and their peoples, as appears to have happened with Americans and citizens of the former Soviet Union. Old enemies suddenly look a lot more normal when they dress like you, eat at McDonald's, and listen to the same music.

The increasing ease with which we bring the world into our homes can also make it more difficult for governments to conceal information. If nothing else, the media's incessant focus on scandal and general distrust of government keeps those in power on their toes. Just the ability to know what is going on in the world makes it less likely that governments can control their people. The demise of the communist governments of Eastern Europe, for example, was helped along by the ability of citizens in those countries to compare their living standards with those of people in Western European countries. How did they do so? By watching Western television programs.

On the other hand, technology does not necessarily eliminate old problems. Cable television does not change the desire to distort images or whip up old animosities any more than newspapers did. The Internet cannot solve the problems of racism or ethnic bigotry. Indeed, the technological capacity to manipulate images may be greater than ever, challenging the individual's capacity to discern truth from falsehood. The framers of the Constitution worried about demagogues stirring up the passions of the moment for their own political purposes. The power of contemporary mass media in our daily lives makes such possibilities an even greater concern.

The political implications of these trends are not entirely clear. Certainly governments have more difficulty maintaining control over their own agendas, particularly when issues cross national boundaries. The rapidity with which issues bounce around the world makes the task even more difficult. This phenomenon is not confined to the world stage, however, as any local official can attest when television crews converge on the town hall following allegations of wrongdoing by a police officer or a school teacher.

In short, new technology can make the world seem smaller and more familiar, but by itself it cannot ensure greater understanding, harmony, or wisdom. The task of the citizen in a democratic society—to be able to separate good from bad, and to ensure that government acts accordingly—is as challenging as ever.

SUMMARY

▶ No society considers every possible answer to every problem. Every society has its own biases, ideals, prevailing values, and popular opinions. Every society has topics that it will not discuss, or ideas it considers radical. These values affect which problems are debated, how they are defined, and which proposed solutions are deemed acceptable.

▶ Liberals and conservatives tend to agree on the values of a free market economic system, limited government, individual liberty, and the importance of civil rights and liberties. However, they strongly disagree over how to achieve these ends. In particular, they disagree about the proper role of government. Liberals tend to stress a more active government role in regulating the market as well as protecting individual civil rights and liberties. Conservatives tend to stress a minimal governmental role in the market and tend to emphasize property rights over civil rights.

▶ Americans tend to support conservative views on limited government and free markets, but often support liberal programs, such as workplace safety and health regulations, designed to protect the individual against the potentially harmful effects of market competition.

▶ Public opinion places constraints on what policymakers can do, particularly on salient issues, but is far more permissive on specific issues. Public opinion tends to be more permissive on issues that are not seen as directly relevant to Americans' lives, such as foreign policy issues. In general, public opinion does not always tell policymakers what to do, but public attention to issues defines the agenda of government.

▶ The mass media influence how we look at the world. Most Americans get most of their news from television, which raises important issues as to the potential technological, economic, and ideological baises within the news media. Moreover, the globalization and rapidity of modern telecommunications, in particular, the Internet, creates dilemmas for citizens and policymakers.

QUESTIONS FOR REVIEW AND DISCUSSION

1. Choose an issue and discuss how public values affect the political debate about that issue.

2. Discuss the differences between liberal and conservative ideologies. Which of these philosophies about the role of government best fits your views?

3. On what kinds of issues is public opinion permissive? On what kinds of issues is public opinion directive? Why?

4. How many different kinds of media can you identify? What kinds of "biases" does each type of media seem to have?

5. How will the Internet change the way we look at the world and how we interact with each other?

TERMS TO REMEMBER

agenda	issue salience	political socialization
agents of socialization	*laissez-faire*	populist
capitalists	liberal	public opinion
conservative	libertarian	social Darwinism
directive opinion	New Deal	socioeconomic status
ideology	permissive opinion	

WEB SOURCES

Accuracy in Media (www.aim.org) and Fairness & Accuracy in Reporting (www.fair.org). AIM and FAIR both are self-labeled "media watchdogs" that monitor the media for signs of overt ideological or issue bias. AIM targets what it believes are liberal media biases, whereas FAIR monitors the media for indications of corporate influence in reporting.

Americans for Democratic Action (www.adaction.org) and the American Conservative Union (www.conservative.org). The ADA is the oldest and probably best-known organization that promotes liberal perspectives; the ACU is the oldest and probably best-known organization that promotes conservative perspectives.

Gallup Poll (www.gallup.com/thepoll.htm). The official site for the Gallup Poll, one of the nation's oldest polling organization. A good source for polling data on all types of issues as well as an excellent guide to how polling works.

SUGGESTED READINGS

Timothy E. Cook, *Governing with the News: The News Media as a Political Institution* (Chicago: University of Chicago Press, 1998). An expert on mass media and politics explains how the news media act as political institutions in their own right and looks at the media strategies used by those in government to influence public opinion. Cook also examines how to maintain some degree of media accountability to the public.

E. J. Dionne, *Why Americans Hate Politics* (New York: Simon & Schuster, 1991). A well-written history on the post–World War II evolution of American liberalism and conservatism that helps to explain the contemporary meanings of those two belief systems. It also explains the current ideological divisions within the two major political parties and helps to make sense of the ideological and policy directions of the Clinton presidency.

Robert S. Erikson and Kent L. Tedin, *American Public Opinion: Its Origins, Content, and Impact*, 5th ed. (New York: Allyn & Bacon, 1995). A good standard textbook on the dimensions of public opinion, how it is measured, how individuals develop their beliefs, the roles played by opinion elites and mass media in shaping opinion, and the impacts of public opinion on elections and public policymaking.

Paul Light, *Baby Boomers* (New York: W. W. Norton and Company, 1988). A political scientist dissects the generation of Americans born between 1946 and 1964, a massive group born in relative affluence and sharing many of the same experiences but one also split along racial, religious, regional, and class lines. The size and influence of this generation, both in the past on cultural issues such as the "sexual revolution" and in the future on issues such as Social Security, makes it important to understand Boomers' needs and desires.

NOTES

1. Jeffrey L. Katz, "Welfare: After 60 Years, Most Control Is Passing to States," *Congressional Quarterly Weekly Report*, vol. 54, no. 31 (August 31, 1996), pp. 2190–2196.

2. Linda Gordon, *Pitied But Not Entitled: Single Mothers and the History of Welfare* (New York: Free Press, 1994).

3. See James Morone, *The Democratic Wish: The Limits of American Government* (New York: Basic Books, 1990).

4. See Robert E. Lane, *Political Ideology* (New York: Free Press, 1962).

5. See Norman H. Nie, Sidney Verba, and John R. Petrocik, *The Changing American Voter*, 2d ed. (Cambridge, MA: Harvard University Press, 1979).

6. Daniel J. Boorstin, *The Lost World of Thomas Jefferson* (New York: Henry Holt and Company, 1948).

7. J. D. Richardson, ed., *Messages and Papers of the Presidents, 1792–1897*, vol. 1 (Washington, D.C.: U.S. Government Printing Office, 1897), p. 313.

8. Scarlett Graham, "Government and the Economy," in George J. Graham and Scarlett G. Graham, eds., *Founding Principles of American Government: Two Hundred Years of Democracy on Trial*, 2d ed. (Chatham, NJ: Chatham House, 1984), pp. 280–304.

9. Noemie Emery, *Alexander Hamilton: An Intimate Portrait* (New York: Putnam, 1982).

10. Alexander Hamilton, James Madison, and John Jay, *The Federalist Papers*, Clinton Rossiter, ed. (New York: New American Library, 1961), p. 110.

11. Richard Hofstadter, *The Age of Reform: From Bryan to F.D.R.* (New York: Random House, 1955).

12. See E. E. Schattschneider, *The Semi-Sovereign People: A Realist's View of Democracy in America* (Hinsdale, IL: Dryden Press, 1960), ch. 7.

13. Hofstadter, *The Age of Reform*, pp. 148–149.

14. Arthur M. Schlesinger, Jr., *The Coming of the New Deal* (Boston: Houghton Mifflin, 1959).

15. E. J. Dionne, *Why Americans Hate Politics* (New York: Simon & Schuster, 1991).

16. See Robert N. Bellah, et al., *The Good Society* (New York: Alfred E. Knopf, 1991).

17. Russell Kirk, *The Conservative Mind: From Burke to Santayana* (Chicago: Henry Regnery Company, 1953).

18. William S. Maddox and Stuart A. Lilie, *Beyond Liberal and Conservative* (Washington, D.C.: The Cato Institute, 1984).

19. See Dionne, *Why Americans Hate Politics*, ch. 1.

20. William G. Mayer, *The Changing American Mind: How and Why American Public Opinion Changed between 1960 and 1988* (Ann Arbor, MI: University of Michigan Press, 1992).

21. See Kenneth Dolbeare, *American Ideologies Today* (New York: Random House, 1988).

22. See William J. Keefe, *Parties, Politics, and Public Policy in America*, 7th ed. (Washington, D.C.: CQ Press, 1994), pp. 208–209.

23. See M. Kent Jennings and Richard Niemi, *The Political Character of Adolescence* (Princeton, NJ: Princeton University Press, 1974).

24. An argument made by Samuel Huntington in *American Politics: The Promise of Disharmony* (Cambridge, MA: Harvard University Press, 1983).

25. See Katherine S. Newman, *Declining Fortunes: The Withering of the American Dream* (New York: Basic Books, 1993).

26. Todd Gitlin, *The Sixties: Years of Hope, Days of Rage* (New York: Bantam Books, 1981).

27. W. Russell Neumann, *The Paradox of Mass Politics: Knowledge and Opinion in the American Electorate* (Cambridge, MA: Harvard University Press, 1986).

28. Based on a *Washington Post*/ABC News poll, March 11–14, 1999.

29. Robert Dahl, *A Preface to Democratic Theory* (Chicago, IL: University of Chicago Press, 1956).

30. Barbara Crossette, "Foreign Aid Budget: Quick, How Much? Wrong," *New York Times*, February, 20, 1995, p. A6.

31. Richard Morin, "Americans Back Peacekeeping in Kosovo," *Washington Post*, June 16, 1999, p. A32.

32. See John Spanier and Stephen Hook, *American Foreign Policy Since World War II* (Washington, D.C.: CQ Press, 1997).

33. Riley E. Dunlap, "Public Opinion and the Environment," in Robert Paehkle, ed., *Conservation and Environmentalism: An Encyclopedia* (New York: Garland Publishing, 1995), p. 536.

34. "School Shooting Makes Crime Top Concern," *CBS News*, April 28, 1999; http://www.cbs.com.

35. Elaine Sharp, "Paradoxes of National Anti-Drug Policymaking," in David A. Rochefort and Roger W. Cobb, eds., *The Politics of Problem Definition* (Lawrence, KS: University Press of Kansas, 1994), pp. 98–116.

36. See Michael X. Delli Carpini and Scott Keeter, *Information and Empowerment: What Americans Know about Politics and Why It Matters* (New Haven, CT: Yale University Press, 1996).

37. Walter Lippmann, *Public Opinion* (New York: Free Press, 1965), p. 16.

38. Schattschneider, *The Semi-Sovereign People*, p. 68.

39. Charles O. Jones, *An Introduction to the Study of Public Policy*, 3d ed. (Monterey, CA: Brooks/Cole, 1983; reissued in 1997).

40. Kay Lehmann Schlozman and Sidney Verba, *Injury to Insult: Unemployment, Class, and Political Response* (Cambridge, MA: Harvard University Press, 1979).

41. Charles O. Jones, *Clean Air: The Policies and Politics of Pollution Control* (Pittsburgh, PA: University of Pittsburgh Press, 1975).

42. Roger Cobb and Marc Ross, eds., *Culture Strategies of Agenda Denial: Avoidance, Attack, and Redefinition* (Lawrence, KS: University Press of Kansas, 1997).

43. William Manchester, *The Glory and the Dream: A Narrative History of America, 1932–1972*, vol. 1 (Boston, MA: Little, Brown, 1973).

44. Howard Kurtz, "ABC Kills Story Critical of Owner Disney; Official Denies Corporate Link Influenced Decision," *Washington Post*, October 18, 1998, p. C1.

45. Kathleen Hall Jamieson, *Dirty Politics: Deception, Distraction, and Democracy* (New York: Oxford University Press, 1992); Thomas E. Patterson, *Out of Order* (New York: Vintage, 1994).

46. Kathleen Day, *S&L Hell: The People and Politics Behind the $1 Trillion Savings and Loan Scandal* (New York: Norton, 1993).

47. Doris A. Graber, *Mass Media and American Democracy*, 5th ed. (Washington, D.C.: CQ Press, 1996).

48. Anthony Downs, "Up and Down with Ecology—The 'Issue-Attention' Cycle," *The Public Interest*, vol. 28, no. 2 (1972), pp. 38–50.

49. Christopher J. Bosso, "Setting the Public Agenda: Mass Media and the Ethiopian Famine," in Michael Margolis and Gary Mauser, eds., *Manipulating Public Opinion: Essays on Public Opinion as a Dependent Variable* (Monterey, CA: Brooks/Cole, 1989), pp. 153–174.

50. Richard E. Cohen, *Washington at Work: Back Rooms and Clean Air* (New York: Macmillan, 1995).

51. S. Robert Lichter, Stanley Rothman, and L. S. Lichter, *The Media Elite* (Bethesda, MD: Adler and Adler, 1986).

52. Michael Parenti, *Inventing Reality: The Politics of the Mass Media*, 2d ed. (New York: St. Martin's Press, 1993).

PRIMARY SOURCE READINGS

RONALD REAGAN
First Inaugural Address

Ronald Wilson Reagan (1911–) served for two terms as president (1981–1989). A former "New Deal Democrat" who gradually grew disenchanted with his party and its ideology, Reagan became a Republican and served two terms as governor of California. In 1980, he defeated President Jimmy Carter, in large part due to voter frustration with the nation's economy. Reagan's views on the essential purpose of government are expressed in his January 20, 1981 inaugural address.

The business of our nation goes forward. These United States are confronted with an economic affliction of great proportions. We suffer from the longest and one of the worst sustained inflations in our national history. It distorts our economic decisions, penalizes thrift, and crushes the struggling young and the fixed-income elderly alike. It threatens to shatter the lives of millions of our people.

Idle industries have cast workers into unemployment, causing human misery and personal indignity. Those who do work are denied a fair return for their labor by a tax system which penalizes successful achievement and keeps us from maintaining full productivity.

But great as our tax burden is, it has not kept pace with public spending. For decades, we have piled deficit upon deficit, mortgaging our future and our children's future for the temporary convenience of the present. To continue this long trend is to guarantee tremendous social, cultural, political, and economic upheavals. . . .

In this present crisis, government is not the solution to our problem.

From time to time, we have been tempted to believe that society has become too complex to be managed by self-rule, that government by an elite group is superior to government for, by, and of the people. But if no one among us is capable of governing himself, then who among us has the capacity to govern someone else? All of us together, in and out of government, must bear the burden. The solutions we seek must be equitable, with no one group singled out to pay a higher price. . . .

So, as we begin, let us take inventory. We are a nation that has a government—not the other way around. And this makes us special among the nations of the Earth. Our Government has no power except that granted it by the people. It is time to check and reverse the growth of government which shows signs of having grown beyond the consent of the governed.

It is my intention to curb the size and influence of the Federal establishment and to demand recognition of the distinction between the powers granted to the Federal Government and those reserved to the States or to the people. All of us need to be reminded that the Federal Government did not create the States; the States created the Federal Government.

Now, so there will be no misunderstanding, it is not my intention to do away with government. It is, rather, to make it work—work with us, not over us; to stand by our side, not ride on our back. Government can and must provide opportunity, not smother it; foster productivity, not stifle it.

If we look to the answer as to why, for so many years, we achieved so much, prospered as no other people on Earth, it was because here, in this land, we unleashed the energy and individual genius of man to a greater extent than has ever been done before. Freedom and the dignity of the individual have been more available and assured here than in any other place on Earth. The price for this freedom at times has been high, but we have never been unwilling to pay that price.

It is no coincidence that our present troubles parallel and are proportionate to the intervention and intrusion in our lives that result from unnecessary and excessive growth of government. It is time for us to realize that we are too great a nation to limit ourselves to small dreams. We are not, as some would have us believe, doomed to an inevitable decline. I do not believe in a fate that will fall on us no matter what we do. I do believe in a fate that will fall on us if we do nothing. So, with all the creative energy at our command, let us begin an era of national renewal. Let us renew our determination, our courage, and our strength. And let us renew; our faith and our hope.

FRANKLIN D. ROOSEVELT
Second Inaugural Address

Franklin D. Roosevelt (1882–1945) served as president from 1933–1945, longer than any other individual. Roosevelt was first elected in 1932 to attack the Great Depression, which he did with a massive federal effort known as the "New Deal." In his second inaugural address, given on January 20, 1937, FDR reflects on the purpose of government.

When four years ago we met to inaugurate a President, the Republic, single-minded in anxiety, stood in spirit here. We dedicated ourselves to the fulfillment of a vision—to speed the time when there would be for all the people that security and peace essential to the pursuit of happiness. . . .

Our covenant with ourselves did not stop there. Instinctively we recognized a deeper need—the need to find through government the instrument of our united purpose to solve for the individual the ever-rising problems of a complex civilization. Repeated attempts at their solution without the aid of government had left us baffled and bewildered. For, without that aid, we had been unable to create those moral controls over the services of science which are necessary to make science a useful servant instead of a ruthless master of mankind. To do this we knew that we must find practical controls over blind economic forces and blindly selfish men.

We of the Republic sensed the truth that democratic government has innate capacity to protect its people against disasters once considered inevitable, to solve problems once considered unsolvable. We would not admit that we could not find a way to master economic epidemics just as, after centuries of fatalistic suffering, we had found a way to master epidemics of disease. We refused to leave the problems of our common welfare to be solved by the winds of chance and the hurricanes of disaster. . . .

Nearly all of us recognize that as intricacies of human relationships increase, so power to govern them also must increase—power to stop evil; power to do good. The essential democracy of our Nation and the safety of our people depend not upon the absence of power, but upon lodging it with those whom the people can change or continue at stated intervals through an honest and free system of elections. . . . In fact, in these last four years, we have made the exercise of all power more democratic; for we have begun to bring private autocratic powers into their proper subordination to the public's government. . . .

Our progress out of the depression is obvious. But that is not all that you and I mean by the new order of things. Our pledge was not merely to do a patchwork job with secondhand materials. By using the new materials of social justice we have undertaken to erect on the old foundations a more enduring structure for the better use of future generations. . . .

But here is the challenge to our democracy: In this nation I see tens of millions of its citizens—a substantial part of its whole population—who at this very moment are denied the greater part of what the very lowest standards of today call the necessities of life.

I see millions of families trying to live on incomes so meager that the pall of family disaster hangs over them day by day.

I see millions whose daily lives in city and on farm continue under conditions labeled indecent by a so-called polite society half a century ago.

I see millions denied education, recreation, and the opportunity to better their lot and the lot of their children.

I see millions lacking the means to buy the products of farm and factory and by their poverty denying work and productiveness to many other millions.

I see one-third of a nation ill-housed, ill-clad, ill-nourished.

It is not in despair that I paint you that picture. I paint it for you in hope—because the Nation, seeing and understanding the injustice in it, proposes to paint it out. We are determined to make every American citizen the subject of his country's interest and concern; and we will never regard any faithful law-abiding group within our borders as superfluous. The test of our progress is not whether we add more to the abundance of those who have much; it is whether we provide enough for those who have too little. . . .

Government is competent when all who compose it work as trustees for the whole people. It can make constant progress when it keeps abreast of all the facts. It can obtain justified support and legitimate criticism when the people receive true information of all that government does.

If I know aught of the will of our people, they will demand that these conditions of effective government shall be created and maintained. They will demand a nation uncorrupted by cancers of injustice and, therefore, strong among the nations in its example of the will to peace.

Today we reconsecrate our country to long-cherished ideals in a suddenly changed civilization. In every land there are always at work forces that drive men apart and forces that draw men together. In our personal ambitions we are individualists. But in our seeking for economic and political progress as a nation, we all go up, or else we all go down, as one people. . . .

POLITICAL PARTIES AND ELECTIONS

OBJECTIVES

❑ To discuss the purpose of elections and describe how the electoral system in the United States works

❑ To explain the general functions of political parties and assess how well American parties fulfill these functions

❑ To explore why the American system is dominated by two political parties and to understand how this system shapes the dynamics of pre-election coalition building

❑ To analyze the conditions under which elections effectively translate public opinion into government policy

Who says elections don't mean anything? In 1988 they meant a great deal in Indiana. For decades the 100-seat Indiana House of Representatives was controlled by the Republican party, reflecting the state's generally conservative Republican leanings. Despite their traditional minority status, Indiana Democrats never stopped competing. They recruited candidates to run against Republicans in state legislative districts; they tried to present credible alternatives to the voters; and finally, in 1988 they managed to win 50 seats. But so did Republicans. The result, when all 100 legislators showed up on the first day of the new session, was a state House of Representatives that was evenly split between the two parties.

The result was that the two parties were on an equal basis after decades during which the Republicans, as the majority party, elected the chamber's leaders, ran its committees, dominated the process of passing bills, and even decided who got the largest offices. But no more: Instead of one House Speaker presiding over the body, there were two, one Republican (on odd-numbered days) and one Democrat (on even-numbered days). This unusual division went all the way down the line, even to Republican and Democratic switchboard supervisors, each in place to ensure that their party's representatives received their phone calls. Democrats even measured Republicans' offices to make sure that they received equal treatment. To the voters this may have looked silly, but it came as no surprise that each party fought to get its fair share of the power and resources.

More surprising was how the 50–50 split forced the parties to work together. Without a clear party majority, and with party members unwilling to defect to the other side, nothing could be done unless the two parties compromised. The only alternative was continued partisan conflict and legislative deadlock. Neither party wanted to anger voters by blocking progress on important issues, so they cooperated. The result was the passage of many bills that had been blocked by previous Republican majorities. Some of these bills failed to gain passage in the Indiana Senate, where Republicans still held a majority, but a number of them were enacted into law.

Election Day. Voters in Texas line up at the polls to cast their ballots. As the signs suggest, on this day voters chose among candidates for governor, state representative, state agricultural commissioner, county commissioner, and county judge. There were probably others, indicating just how many offices are elected.

In subsequent elections the Democrats took over as the majority party in the state House of Representatives, reflecting broader changes in the state's political environment. The chamber reverted to a more conventional pattern of majority party control: one speaker, one switchboard supervisor, and so on. However, after 1989 fewer Indiana residents doubt that elections matter.[1]

THE IMPORTANCE OF ELECTIONS

The United States probably holds more elections for more positions at more levels of government than does any other country. Americans elect members of Congress, the president and vice president, state governors and legislators, state auditors and treasurers, district attorneys (who prosecute criminal cases), county sheriffs, mayors, town councilors, township supervisors, state insurance commissioners, some local and state judges, school boards, county clerks of courts, delegates to political party conventions, city medical examiners, town building inspectors, and even dog catchers. Many of these are administrative positions, but they are often filled through elections because voters want to maintain direct control over those in government.

So elections are woven into the nation's political fabric. Yet Americans seem skeptical about their value. Citizens frequently express the attitude that politicians are all alike, so choosing between them is a meaningless exercise with no practical effect on what government does. Simply stated, many Americans believe that elections do not matter. A popular bumper sticker sums up this attitude: "Don't Vote: It Only Encourages Them."

To some extent this pessimism is derived from the pervasive suspicion of government that lies at the heart of the American political culture. Americans are wary of

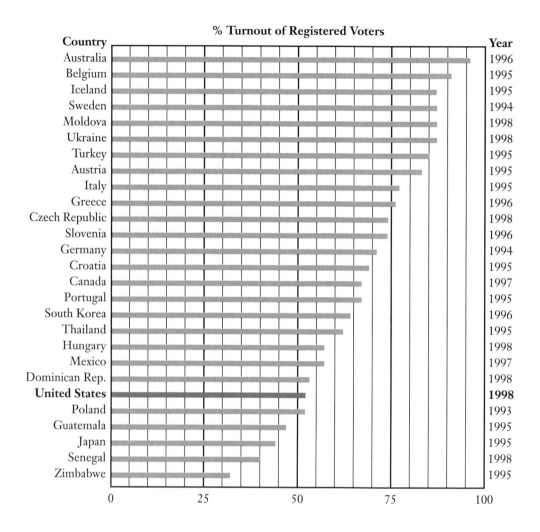

FIGURE 6.1. TURNOUT IN RECENT LEGISLATIVE ELECTIONS COMPARED

Source: The International Foundation for Election Systems (IFES) and various national election commissions, as presented by the Federal Elections Commission (www.fec.gov).

government, and they have never shown great reverence for politicians. But this skepticism has serious consequences.

One is low voter turnout. The United States has one of the lowest voter turnout rates of any democratic political system (see Figure 6.1). Representative government depends on elections, but many Americans do not vote, a fact that raises important questions about whether government actions reflect what most citizens want.

Faced with this evidence, many argue that the solution is *more* and *better* elections. We tinker with election laws to encourage more candidates to run, argue about how to "fix" the problem of the role of money in elections, and try to figure out ways to entice voters to the polls. Through these efforts advocates of reform seem to be saying, "Build better elections and you will get better candidates; better candidates make for more competitive races; more competitive races will attract more voters to the polls; higher voter turnout will translate into a stronger connection between what voters want and what government does." If all this comes to pass, the theory goes, a better democracy will result.

Supporting any reform efforts is the belief that elections are the lifeblood of democracy. However, such elections must be free and fair, an assumption that cannot be taken for granted. An election in which there is only one official candidate is neither free nor fair. Nor is one in which a government prevents people from voting because of their ethnicity, religion, or political views, or one that intimidates voters on election day.

In a free and fair election, there must be honest and open competition between opposing candidates, and the government must not impose unreasonable restrictions on who can run for office or who can vote. Most democracies, including the United States, do not meet all these standards perfectly. However, this does not mean that they are not democratic. No system is, or ever will be, perfect. The distinction between democratic and nondemocratic systems depends on whether such shortcomings are the exception or the norm.

PURPOSES OF ELECTIONS

Ideally, elections serve to connect people with their government. In doing so, they serve four important purposes: choosing those who govern, enforcing democratic accountability, influencing public policy, and providing legitimacy.

CHOOSING THOSE WHO GOVERN

In a democracy the main function of elections is to choose those who will occupy important positions of authority and power, and for how long. Equally important, officeholders peacefully hand power over to their successors when their terms expire or when they fail to win reelection. Skepticism aside, it is worth pondering how the successful development of democratic institutions in the United States has depended on the fact that no American president has refused to leave office when his term ended.

ENFORCING DEMOCRATIC ACCOUNTABILITY

In a democracy, those who govern must run for reelection. Elections thus are a routine means by which voters can hold officials accountable for their actions.[2] Requiring candidates for public office to compete for votes forces them to listen to voters' demands. More important, those who want to stay in office are forced to explain their past actions. An honest and open debate is a minimal requirement for democratic accountability.

INFLUENCING PUBLIC POLICY

Ideally, elections shape public policy. This connection is clearest when citizens vote directly on issues, such as when they vote on whether to increase property taxes to raise money for a new high school. In this case, the vote determines what government does: The school is built or it is not, depending on the vote totals. However, as we discussed in chapter 1, the United States is a *representative* democracy in which voters choose among competing candidates. Ideally, competing candidates offer distinctive ideas for addressing the issues; voters base their selections on these competing proposals; election results clearly reflect voters' preferences on the issues; and the winners do what they promised.[3] As we will see later in the chapter, these conditions are not easily met, so whether elections enable citizens to determine public policy is an important concern.

PROVIDING LEGITIMACY

Democratic government rests on the voluntary consent of the people. Free and fair elections are the means by which the people in a democracy grant their political leaders **legitimacy,** the legal authority to govern. If elections are free and fair, and if the losers accept the results, the process is said to validate the outcome. Winners gain the right to govern on behalf of the people, and the people agree to abide by their decisions, at least until the next election gives the people an opportunity to change their minds. After losing reelection in 1992, George Bush simply handed over control over the world's most powerful military to Bill Clinton, the man who defeated him. Bush never considered defying the outcome of the election, thus affirming the legitimacy of the system itself.

In chapter 4 we learned that civil rights and liberties make democracy possible. But elections make democracy *work*. They are means by which a free people keep their government responsive, responsible, and accountable. In the absence of competitive elections in which voters participate in great numbers, the health of a democracy would be in question.

We will address this fundamental concern throughout this chapter. In order to do so, we must begin by looking at the electoral system in the United States and how elections work.

THE ELECTION SYSTEM

Elections seem noisy and chaotic, but they are not free-for-alls. They are *structured* means of participation. The ways in which candidates campaign and citizens vote are dictated by specific rules and procedures. These "rules of the game" have important impacts on elections. They affect who runs for office, what kinds of resources candidates use during campaigns, and what level of voter support is necessary for a candidate to declare victory. Rules affect who can vote, when, and how, and they may also be the key to why so many Americans don't vote.

All rules or laws encourage some kinds of behavior and discourage others.[4] Electoral rules are no different. The biases in some of them are easy to see. For example, young children cannot vote, so issues of concern to them (such as education) may be overlooked during a campaign unless adults work on behalf of these issues. By contrast, the elderly can and do vote in very high numbers, so candidates pay attention to issues that are of concern to them, such as Social Security.

The effects of other rules are more subtle. In the United States, elections for president and members of Congress are held on the first Tuesday in November. This constitutional provision dates back to the 1700s, when almost everyone farmed and spent Sundays in church. By November the crops were harvested, so people had time to get involved in politics. They could worship on Sunday and then take a day or two to travel to town to hear the candidates, attend campaign rallies, and vote. For them, elections were as much social occasions as political ones. The traditional date endures, even though farmers now account for less than 2 percent of the population.

Why does this matter? For one thing, holding elections on Tuesday may reduce voter turnout. Unlike most democracies, in the United States election day is not an official holiday; it is a regular work day. For many people it is inconvenient to vote before or after work, especially if they have children to send to school or if they commute a fair distance to their jobs. Whether turnout might increase if Election Day were a national holiday is hotly debated, but such a change would have an impact. Whenever you change the rules, you affect the possible outcomes, which explains why we spend so much time arguing over the rules themselves.

MULTIPLE SYSTEMS

Voter turnout is also affected by the structure of the American electoral system, which is among the most complicated in the world. In fact, the term "system" is misleading. "Systems" may be more accurate, as elections occur at several levels and contexts in the United States.

The Constitution does not provide many rules for electing the president or members of Congress. The framers left these matters to the states, although they granted Congress the power to make laws affecting federal elections. Over time, Congress "nationalized" aspects of election law dealing with the right to vote (see chapter 4), but the basic mechanics of how candidates get onto the ballot, how people register to vote, whether polling places use voting machines or paper ballots, and the hours during which the polls remain open are governed primarily by state laws. For their part, the states give local governments some flexibility in how they manage local elections.

This variety of federal, state, and local election rules increases the burden on citizens to stay informed and active, especially when they move from one place to another. For example, if you live in a college dormitory you might not have the right to vote in the town where your college is located. You are not a resident, so you either must go home to vote or you must apply for an absentee ballot weeks before the election. In either case, you might find it too inconvenient to vote at all. For their part, candidates for office must wrestle with a wide array of state and national rules governing procedures for getting onto the ballot and raising campaign funds, especially in presidential elections.

Proposals to nationalize election rules are unlikely to gain much support in a nation whose traditions and culture strongly support state and local control. Nor is having a single set of rules necessarily desirable. What might work well in metropolitan Atlanta might not in rural Idaho, and vice versa. As with federalism generally, citizens and candidates must cope with a level of complexity that undoubtedly affects who votes, who runs, and who wins.

SEPARATE AND INDEPENDENT ELECTIONS

In a parliamentary system like that of Canada, the political party that wins a majority of seats in the legislature literally *becomes* the government until the next election. The majority party also selects the prime minister, who is the head of the government. The system is straightforward: The majority party governs the nation.

As we saw in chapter 2, the framers of the Constitution sought to avoid the kind of majority power found in parliamentary systems. The American system thus is characterized by separation of powers and separate elections. Congress does not elect the president; state legislatures do not pick governors. The president is not a member of Congress, nor are governors members of state legislatures. Members of Congress and state legislatures are elected separately from presidents and governors. Legislators and executives represent different constituencies and serve distinct terms of office. This pattern is repeated throughout the American political system to the local level, creating a system that many voters find daunting.

STRICT TERMS OF OFFICE

In most parliamentary systems the government has some discretion about the timing of elections. For example, in Great Britain the prime minister can call a new election any time within a five-year period. This might happen if the prime minister resigns, if the majority party loses support, or if the prime minister wants to solidify the majority's power after a political victory. For example, in the 1980s Prime Minister Margaret Thatcher twice called for elections before they were due: in 1983, when she rode a wave of patriotism after British forces defeated those of Argentina in a brief war over the disputed Falkland Islands, and in 1987, when she took advantage of healthy economic conditions to enlarge her party's parliamentary majority.

By contrast, in the United States elections occur every four years for president and every two for Congress as prescribed by the Constitution without fail, even during the Civil War. The president cannot call for new congressional elections, nor can Congress schedule new presidential elections. The situation is the same in the states. Except for an occasional special election to fill a legislative seat or mayoral position left vacant because of death or resignation, the American system runs by a rigid calendar. Elections occur when they are supposed to occur.

This rigidity has two major results: First, no president can call an election to take advantage of favorable political conditions. Unlike Thatcher, President Bush could not capitalize on his popularity after the Persian Gulf War in 1991, when a U.S.-led military coalition ousted Iraqi forces from Kuwait. He had to wait until the next election in November, 1992, by which time public support had plummeted because of voters' doubts about his leadership on economic issues. Bush lost the election. (We discuss this situation further in chapter 9.)

Second, the rigid calendar forces opponents to work together.[5] No new election can be called to break a partisan stalemate, nor can the party with the majority in Congress pick a new president. The same is true for the states. This condition has drawbacks in that a conflict over a major issue may not be resolved easily or quickly, but it also forces politicians of opposite parties or values to seek compromise. As the members of the Indiana House of Representatives discovered, they are stuck with one another whether they like it or not until the next election.

DETERMINING WINNERS

Elections in the United States generally operate according to a **winner-take-all** rule. With a few local exceptions, only one person can win a specific seat or position. The other candidates get nothing. There is no second place.

What difference does this make? As we will see later in the chapter, winner-take-all elections favor candidates from larger political parties, which are usually the only coalitions of voters large enough to win the seat. Candidates from small parties or who represent narrow constituencies normally have little chance of winning.

Some political systems utilize a form of **proportional representation,** in which a party wins a percentage of seats in the legislature that is roughly equal to the proportion of votes it received in the election (see Box 6.1). This system allows small political parties to survive by giving them formal representation in proportion to their overall electoral support. In the United States, however, parties with a narrow appeal usually cannot win enough votes to win a race, and winner-take-all rules provide no consolation prize. As we will see later in this chapter, these rules explain why American politics is dominated by two major political parties.

PLURALITY VERSUS MAJORITY-RULE ELECTIONS

Electoral outcomes in the United States are usually determined by a **plurality,** in which the candidate who receives the most votes wins. This plurality can be just one more vote than the total won by any other candidate. The Constitution says nothing about a plurality "rule," but over time it has become the normal way to determine winners in races for Congress, state governor, and most other state and local offices.

A few elections do operate according to a **majority** rule, in which the winner must receive at least one more than half of all the votes. A winner-take-all election that re-

BOX 6.1.
SHOULD THE UNITED STATES ADOPT PROPORTIONAL
REPRESENTATION?

American politics might look very different under a proportional representation sys-tem. To understand how, let's look at the Federal Republic of Germany.

The Bundestag, or lower house of the German legislature, at this writing has 663 seats. Election to the Bundestag is through a combination of winner-take-all and pro-portional representation, with voters casting one vote for a candidate and a second vote for a prefered party. However, the end result is a system whereby any party that wins at least 5 percent of the nationwide popular vote wins that proportion of seats in the Bundestag.

As a result, the German system usually produces a coalition government whereby one of the two major parties—either the more conservative Christian Democrats or the more liberal Social Democrats—pairs up with a minor party to obtain the major-ity of seats necessary to form a government and name a chancellor (or prime minis-ter). From 1982 to 1998, this coalition was made up of the Christian Democrats and the Free Democrats, a smaller party that expounds American-style libertarianism, with Helmut Kohl serving as chancellor during the entire period. However, the Sep-tember, 1998, elections produced the following results:

Social Democrats	41.0%
Christian Democrats	35.0%
Free Democrats	6.3%
Green Party	6.7%
Party of Democratic Socialism	5.1%
Other parties (together)	5.9%

The Social Democrats replaced the Christian Democrats as the majority party and agreed to a coalition with the Green party, which espouses a strong environmen-tal platform. Together, the parties had 345 seats, enough to form a coalition govern-ment headed by Social Democrat Gerhard Schroder. For their part, Green party leaders were given key positions in the new government.

quires a majority is an even greater obstacle for candidates from smaller political par-ties or who advocate relatively narrow agendas. To win a majority, a candidate needs a very large and very broad base of support.

Majority-rule elections are rare today. In the past, some southern states man-dated a runoff between the two top vote-getters when neither received a majority of the votes, but most of these rules were struck down by federal courts in the 1970s

WHAT DO YOU THINK?

Imagine that the United States used such a system, that a party's percentage of the popular vote translated into a percentage of seats in the House of Representatives. The following results measure the percentage of the presidential vote in 1992, when H. Ross Perot led a strong third-party challenge, and how that percentage would have translated into House seats:

1992 Election	Popular Vote	Seats in House (theoretical)	Seats in House (actual)*
Democrats (Clinton)	43%	187	259
Republican (Bush)	37%	161	176
Reform Party (Perot)	19%	87	0

Under this scenario, the Reform party becomes very influential. It could form a coalition government with the Republicans with 248 (or 57 percent) of 435 House seats. If we went one step further and connected the House election to the election of the president, George Bush would stay on as president, while H. Ross Perot would receive an important position in the new government. However, under the U.S. electoral system of winner-take-all, Democrats obtained a percentage of House seats in excess of their proportion, and the Reform Party won no seats.

Of course, the U.S. electoral system does not connect presidential elections with the election of House members, nor is there a strict relationship between the proportion of party's popular vote and its proportion of House seats.

But should there be? What do you think?

* The Democrats actually had 258 seats, but Independent Bernie Sanders of Vermont usually voted with Democrats and was included in their caucus.

Sources: Roger Cohen, "The German Election: An Overview," *New York Times,* September 28, 1998, p. A1; Mark Kesselman, et al., *European Politics in Transition,* 3d ed. (Boston, MA: Houghton Mifflin, 1997), pp. 305–309.

because they were deemed to discriminate against racial minorities. For example, assume that 55 percent of a House district's residents are white and 45 percent are African American. If history is any guide, assume that most residents will vote only for candidates of the same race.[6] Finally, assume that an election involves three candidates, two white and one African American, and the African American candidate receives 45 percent of the overall vote, one white candidate receives 35 percent, and the other white candidate receives 20 percent.

In a plurality election, the African American candidate wins. Yet because the election required a majority, the African American candidate has to face the second-place finisher in a runoff, which the remaining white candidate is likely to win. In a plurality election with two candidates, a white might win anyway, but the requirement that the winner receive a majority raised the barrier against an African American candidate even higher. It is because of this use of majority-rule elections to discriminate against racial minorities that few elections today can require that the winner receive a majority of the votes.

ELECTING THE PRESIDENT

One election that continues to require a majority is the presidential election. Americans cast votes for presidential candidates on election day, but the president is selected by the **electoral college,** not by the popular (or direct) vote. This "college" of electors represents the states, not the people, and was intended by the framers to be made up of individuals who would use their independent judgment to select the president (see chapter 2).

The arithmetic of the electoral college is simple. To win the presidency, a candidate must win an absolute majority of the electoral college votes. Today there are 538 electoral votes, equal to the 435 seats in the House of Representatives, the 100 seats in the Senate, and the three electoral votes allotted to Washington, D.C., by the Twenty-third Amendment (1961). Thus, to win the presidency a candidate must win at least 270 electoral votes, or one more than half of 538.

Each state is allotted a number of electors equal to its total number of House members and senators. As with House seats, electoral votes are apportioned on the basis of state population, so shifts in population throughout the nation affect the distribution of electoral votes. The electoral college thus skews presidential campaigns toward the concerns of highly populated states such as California, New York, Florida, and Texas. Figure 6.2 shows the distribution of electoral votes for the presidential election in the year 2000.

Electoral and Popular Votes   Today the outcome of the electoral vote is linked to the outcome of the popular vote. Slates of electors are nominated by presidential candidates, not by state legislatures or governors. On election day a plurality of the popular vote in each state determines which of these competing slates of electors is chosen. For example, in 1996 Bill Clinton won a plurality (47 percent) of the popular vote in Ohio. Clinton's slate of electors was selected. The popular vote determined the electoral vote.

However, in all but two states electoral college votes are subject to the **unit rule.** That is, a candidate who wins a plurality of a state's popular vote gets *all* of its electoral votes. (In Maine and Nebraska, electoral votes are based on the popular vote in individual House districts.) The unit rule explains why candidates can end up with different electoral and popular vote percentages. Going back to Ohio in 1996, Clin-

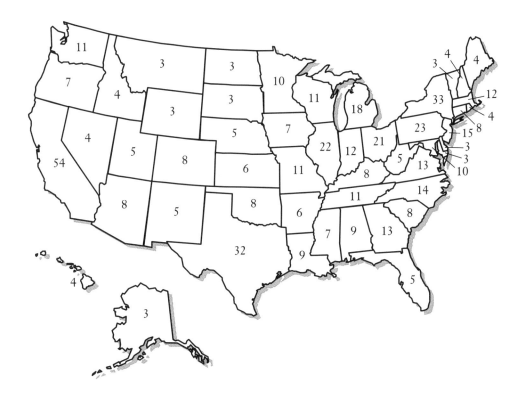

FIGURE 6.2. DISTRIBUTION OF ELECTORAL VOTES, 2000

ton won 100 percent of the state's 21 electoral votes despite winning only 47 percent of its popular vote.

On a national scale, the unit rule exaggerates the electoral-vote percentages for the winner and shrinks them for the losers. In 1992 Clinton won just over 43 percent of the national popular vote against then-President Bush and Texas businessman H. Ross Perot, but he won almost 69 percent of the electoral vote. Bush won 38 percent of the popular vote, but only 31 percent of the electoral votes. He lost the popular vote in several states by narrow margins, but in doing so he lost all of those states' electoral votes. Perot won 19 percent of the popular vote, but no electoral votes because he did not win the popular vote in any state. National popularity aside, the electoral college forces candidates to win *states*.

Is it possible for an elector selected by one candidate to vote for another? Yes, but it is rare. For one thing, electors are party loyalists who are dedicated to the candidates who selected them for the ballot. Most states also require that electors obey the popular vote. However, a few states allow electors to vote for any eligible candidate. In 1988 Michael Dukakis won the popular vote in West Virginia, but one elector there cast her ballot for Dukakis's vice presidential running mate, Lloyd Bentsen. It didn't matter: The electoral college totals were 426 for Bush, 111 for Dukakis, and 1 for Bentsen. Despite the possibility of "faithless electors" voting contrary to the popular vote, in no presidential election has the outcome been affected by such a vote.

Can a candidate win the electoral vote but not the popular vote? Theoretically, yes, but such an outcome is improbable. It was more probable in the 19th century, when state legislatures or party conventions still determined the electoral vote regardless of the popular vote. Thus both Rutherford B. Hayes (1876) and Benjamin Harrison (1888) won the presidency despite losing the popular vote. In 1824, when many states did not hold a popular vote for president, no candidate won a majority of the electoral votes, so the election had to go to the House of Representatives according to the process prescribed by the Constitution (Article II, Section 1, as modified by the Twelfth Amendment). In it, the group (or *delegation*) of House members from each state casts a single vote, and John Quincy Adams was elected over the more popular Andrew Jackson.

Because the popular vote determines the electoral vote, some scholars argue that the electoral vote should be abandoned. But few Americans seem to support such a drastic change. In part, they hold the view that "if it ain't broke, don't fix it." Others believe in keeping the system for the same reasons that the founders created the electoral vote: It forces candidates to mount national campaigns; it discourages purely regional candidates or those representing minor parties; and it requires that the winner build support among a broad spectrum of voters in many states.

COSTS AND BENEFITS OF THE SYSTEM

In sum, the electoral system forces candidates and their parties to build broad coalitions of voters before the election. The winner-take-all rule makes it difficult for candidates from smaller parties to win elections, and therefore it theoretically robs some voters of the opportunity to see their candidates in office. It also accounts for two phenomena: the two-party system, discussed later in the chapter, and, as we will discuss in chapter 7, the proliferation of narrow interest groups that seek representation though nonelectoral methods because their voices get lost in the broad coalition of voters required to win the election.

On the other hand, this system forces candidates to appeal to the broadest possible range of voters, so candidates who express what might be considered antidemocratic views rarely win. For example, in Louisiana avowed white supremacist David Duke, who once led the Ku Klux Klan, managed to win 44 percent of the vote in the race for U.S. Senate in 1990 and 39 percent of the vote in the race for governor in 1991. However, in neither race did he appeal to enough white voters to overcome the almost unanimous opposition of the state's African American voters.[7] This does not mean that Duke could not win a local election or one for the state legislature, because in each case the constituency would be smaller and more homogeneous. But he cannot win statewide or national office unless he moderates his views and appeals to a broader range of voters.

The electoral system also reinforces political stability. Proportional representation systems may better represent the full breadth of voters' views. However, the need to build a multiparty coalition government after the election can produce a high degree of political instability if too many small parties have to included in a coalition government. By contrast, the American system errs on the side of stability by forcing groups of voters to build broad coalitions *before* the election. These coalitions are the two major political parties.

Winner-take-all elections may seem less democratic because smaller parties tend not to be represented in Congress or the state legislatures. Those who support these parties therefore are less likely to vote. However, the framers favored the greater stability generated by a system that required coalition building and compromise before the election, not after. Given the general political stability that has prevailed in the United States throughout the nation's history, few Americans are likely to want to make major changes in that system.

TYPES OF ELECTIONS

Not all elections are alike. Presidential elections are especially visible contests that generate high levels of voter interest and turnout. Other elections, such as those for the local school board, may be important to what government does, but they generate lower levels of interest and turnout. In this section we discuss different types of elections and how voters respond to them.

Direct Elections Direct elections do not involve candidates. Instead, citizens vote directly on a proposed law or constitutional amendment. Almost half of the states allow for some form of direct election. An **initiative** occurs when a group of citizens uses a petition (which requires a specified number of valid signatures) to bypass the state legislature and put an issue directly on the ballot. In a **referendum,** the state legislature places the issue on the ballot for the voters' consideration. Many states require a referendum to amend their constitutions.

If it is approved by the voters, an initiative or referendum becomes law automatically. In 1998, for example, voters in California approved Proposition 168, an initiative that abolished bilingual education in the public schools. The federal courts decided that the new law was constitutional, so it forced major changes in the state's educational system.

The U.S. Constitution makes no provision for a national initiative or referendum. In part, this is because the framers assumed that the states, not the federal government, would be the focus of most electoral action. But another reason was the framers' belief in the stabilizing effects of representative government and their skepticism about direct or popular democracy. They feared the "passions" of the public, particularly with respect to unpopular groups or ideas, and thought that policy should be made by "reason" through the people's representatives.

Critics of initiatives and referenda argue that voters often don't have enough information on or a clear idea about the issues on which they are asked to decide. They also argue that a process intended to provide for direct citizen control over government has been corrupted by powerful interest groups that have the money to organize initiative petitions and subsidize expensive media campaigns (see chapter 7). However, supporters argue that direct elections still enable the people to express their demands clearly. There are plenty of cases to illustrate either view, and the increased use of initiatives and referenda since the 1960s indicates that many are eager to bypass state legislatures and impose greater direct control over lawmaking.[8]

Electing Officeholders   Referenda aside, most elections in the United States are held to select individuals who will hold a public office for a specific period. This process usually involves two separate phases: primary elections and general elections.

The **primary election** chooses a party's nominee for the general election. It enables a party's membership to select its nominee rather than leave that power in the hands of party leaders. In this sense, the primary was meant to be a democratic way to pick nominees, because local or state parties may be controlled by a few powerful people who do not reflect the views of the average party member. Today, primary elections are used to pick virtually every party nominee for federal, state, or local office.

There are two kinds of primary elections. A **closed primary** is restricted to registered voters who previously declared their affiliation with the party in question. Those who did not are not allowed to vote in that primary. However, today most states use some variation on the **open primary,** in which voters can show up and vote in whichever party primary they wish. In these states voters can switch their party affiliation from one election to the next.

Technically, a primary is the "private" activity of a political party, because it only picks that party's nominee for the general election. However, primary elections are subject to federal laws prohibiting discrimination against prospective voters, especially because of race. Before the 1940s, Democrats in many southern states held **white primaries** to pick party nominees. Because the Democratic party was so dominant in the region at the time, the primary was essentially the "real" election. Keeping blacks out of these "private" nominating activities thus prevented them from having any impact on the outcome. White primaries were declared unconstitutional in 1944.[9]

Primary elections do not generate high voter turnout compared to the general election. However, those who vote in primaries tend to be more informed about and active in politics, they are more likely to affiliate openly with a political party, and they tend to hold strong ideological views. For these voters, the primary election is an important event: It allows them to choose their party's nominee, a choice with major significance for *all* voters.

A **general election** officially decides who takes office, so it is considered more important than the primary election. Exceptions, as noted earlier, occur in areas where a political party is so dominant that there is little competition. This said, general elections usually do involve competition between candidates from opposing parties. Presidential elections or statewide races for governor or senator are especially visible and generate relatively high voter turnout. Compared to those who turn for both primary and general elections, voters who turn out *only* for general elections are not usually as politically informed or active.[10] They tend to be more moderate in ideological views, less partisan, and likelier to make decisions based on considerations such as a candidate's personal character traits or perceived leadership ability rather than ideological purity or loyalty to a party.

We will examine various aspects of voting later in the chapter. For now, it is important to keep in mind that the choices voters make are part of a much broader process that includes nominating candidates, holding campaigns, and getting voters to the polls. These other phases determine whose names are on the ballot on election day and who actually votes. In many ways, the general election is but the final, and not always the most important, act of an intricate process.

WHO CAN VOTE

Not everyone is allowed to vote. Every political system excludes some people from voting, usually because they are not deemed competent to make informed decisions. Thus, no political system allows young children to vote. Patients in mental institutions sometimes are regarded as not sufficiently rational for such an important civic activity. Others, such as people who have been convicted of serious crimes, may forfeit their right to vote.

The Constitution was not specific about who may vote. The framers generally believed that **suffrage**—the legal right to vote—should be limited to property holders with a material stake in the community, but they largely left such issues up to the states.[11] However, in Article I, Section 4, Congress is granted the express power to set rules on elections for federal offices, thus leaving open the possibility of bringing many aspects of election law under federal control.

At first the states had a wide range of rules on suffrage. In 1788, the first election held under the Constitution, some states allowed any adult taxpayer to vote whereas others based eligibility on the possession of property (which could include cash). A few free black men in some northern states met these requirements and hence were able to vote. Most states limited voting to males, but in New Jersey some women voted in the first presidential election.[12] However, during the early decades of the nation's history most states effectively limited suffrage to white males over 21 years of age who owned property.

EXPANDING SUFFRAGE

A key factor in the development of American democracy has been the expansion of the right to vote. By the 1840s most states, starting with new states such as Tennessee, extended suffrage to all white males, not just property holders, and in many northern states the right to vote was granted to all free African American men as well.

As we saw in chapter 4, African American males were given the right to vote (or "enfranchised") by the Fifteenth Amendment (1870). However, during the 20th century many southern states found ways to keep the former slaves and their offspring from voting. Some levied a **poll tax,** allegedly to pay the administrative costs of the election, but the practical effect was to discourage poor voters, black and white. Others required voters to pass difficult **literacy tests,** or relied on the aforementioned white primaries to keep out blacks. Another ingenious device was the **grandfather clause,** which stipulated that a person could not vote unless his ancestors had voted prior to 1867. Most southern blacks were descended from slaves, so the grandfather clause effectively prevented them or their descendants from voting.

These various obstacles to black suffrage were slowly removed over time. The Supreme Court declared the grandfather clause unconstitutional in 1915.[13] As noted earlier, it ruled the white primary unconstitutional in 1944. The Twenty-fourth Amendment (1964) prohibited the use of poll taxes in federal elections, and the Voting Rights Act of 1965 banned the use of literacy tests and similar devices to determine eligibility to vote. The act affected mainly southern states, where voting rates among African Americans rose dramatically within a few years of the law's passage.[14]

Women slowly obtained suffrage in state elections by the end of the 1800s, starting in sparsely populated western states, but not until the ratification of the Nineteenth Amendment in 1920 did women win the right to vote in national elections. The pool of potential voters doubled overnight. The Twenty-third Amendment (1961) gave residents of Washington, D.C.—the federal District of Columbia—the right to vote in presidential elections, although Washingtonians still are not represented formally in the House or Senate. Finally, the Twenty-sixth Amendment (1971) extended suffrage to 18 to 20 year olds. However, as we will discuss later in the chapter, turnout among young people has never met expectations.

THE POLITICS OF SUFFRAGE

The forces promoting the expansion of suffrage came from many directions. In some cases, the arguments were based on moral grounds: If 18 year olds pay taxes and fight and die to defend the nation, they must be allowed to vote for representatives and officials who would levy the taxes and declare the wars. In some cases, the arguments *against* suffrage were also based on moral grounds. Although it is hard to imagine today, opponents of suffrage for women once argued that politics was a rough business in which women should play no part.

However, conflicts over suffrage are usually political. Those who expect support from the new voters usually favor suffrage, whereas those who fear the influence of the newly enfranchised tend to oppose it. Suffrage for women was opposed by makers of beer and liquor, who feared that women would vote in favor of prohibition.[15] In fact, some did and some didn't; women turned out to be no more uniform in their voting patterns on this issue than men. Similarly, Democrats expected heavy support from newly enfranchised 18 to 20 year olds, but many voted for Republican candidates; the "youth vote" turned out to be just as varied in its outlook and values as any other age group.

REGISTERING TO VOTE

A key factor in voting is whether people are registered to vote in the first place. Those who are not registered cannot vote, even if they decide at the last minute that they want to do so. In fact, people who take the time to register are more likely to

Votes for women. For over half a century, women sought the right to vote, only to be opposed by most men—and many women—who felt that politics was too rough for the "weaker sex." Women won the right to vote with the ratification of the Nineteenth Amendment in 1920.

take an interest in the campaign and to go to the polls on election day. This apparent connection between registration and voting raises the question: Why are so many Americans not registered?

Voter registration is not an issue in other Western democracies. In most, the government automatically registers all citizens of voting age. Voters simply show up on election day, which may help explain why these nations have higher rates of voter turnout. In the United States, with very few exceptions, the responsibility of registration is placed on the individual.

As with other facets of election law, registration requirements differ somewhat from one state to another. In most states, residents must register to vote at least a month before an election, and voters' names are taken off registration lists if they do not vote or reregister within a specified length of time. Only in North Dakota can residents register to vote on election day.

The Politics of Registration   The debate over registration is complicated by political self-interest and idealism. Registration requirements can be manipulated to keep out some kinds of voters. For example, requiring people to travel to the town hall on weekdays between 10:00 a.m. and 2:00 p.m. would hinder those who lack adequate transportation or cannot take time off from work. These are likely to be poorer and working-class voters, and in many places they might also be racial minorities. Similarly, many college towns once required potential voters to live in the area for a full year without going to school. This residency restriction was intended to prevent college students from dominating local elections. In sum, groups that want to maintain an electoral advantage are unlikely to make it easier for other kinds of people to register.

On the other hand, stringent registration requirements can be viewed as a way to keep elections honest. Elections once were rather corrupt affairs by today's standards. In the late 1800s political party bosses literally stuffed ballot boxes by allowing non-residents—even newly arrived immigrants—to vote or by shuttling party loyalists around the city to vote at several different polling places.[16] Although stringent registration rules can reduce turnout among less-educated or less-organized voters, they also were meant to make elections more fair and honest.

Finally, the American tradition of stringent registration requirements also stems from the view that voting is a responsibility of citizenship. From this perspective, making voting too easy devalues it, and only those who are serious about it should be allowed to vote.

Making Registration Easier   Over time, federal law and court decisions have struck down the most discriminatory or burdensome registration laws. States can no longer demand residency requirements longer than 30 days, and they must allow registration during hours that fit normal work schedules. Almost half of the states now permit registration by mail, and as noted earlier, North Dakota allows registration on election day.

A major national effort to simplify registration came in 1993 when Congress passed the "Motor-Voter" law. Under this law, states are required to allow people to register to vote when they apply for a driver's license or for some forms of public assistance (such as disability or welfare). Democrats, led by President Clinton, supported the law because they believed that it would improve registration rates among poorer and minority citizens—who are also more likely to vote for Democrats. Most Republicans opposed the law for the same reason, and because they saw it as intruding on state prerogatives. Although the Motor-Voter law did boost registration rates among many groups of potential voters, it did not increase overall voter turnout in 1996 or 1998, nor did it necessarily help Democrats.[17] Getting people registered is one thing; getting them to show up on election day and vote for you is another.

Even so, failure to register is a major factor in the failure to vote. For example, in 1998 turnout among eligible voters—that is, adults who are 18 years of age or older—was only 36 percent (see Figure 6.3, p. 251), but turnout among *registered* voters was 52 percent (see Figure 6.1, p. 232). The apparent relationship between registration and turnout explains much of the impetus behind the Motor-Voter law, regardless of its actual impact.

WHO VOTES, WHO DOESN'T

Most adult citizens have the right to vote, yet barely half of all eligible voters do so, even in presidential elections. **Voter turnout** in congressional or statewide elections is lower yet, whereas local races often attract less than a third of eligible voters. Several factors that combine to produce low turnout are discussed in this section.

SOCIOECONOMIC FACTORS

The leading factors affecting voter turnout are socioeconomic ones. People who vote do not reflect a true cross-section of the eligible electorate (see Table 6.1). Voters are typically older, better educated, and have higher incomes than average. Turnout rates are lowest among young people (ages 18–24) and highest among those over 60, regardless of gender or race. Better-educated, more-affluent citizens, regardless of gender or race, vote in high percentages, whereas poorer and less-educated citizens vote the least. In fact, getting a college degree will increase a person's probability of voting, regardless of income.

Many young people do not vote because they are transient and have yet to establish roots in a community. They may also feel that their votes have little practical impact on public policy or that public policy has little practical impact on their lives. In fact, turnout does increase with age, to the point that people over age 60 register and vote at levels above any other age group. Older people often have more time to take part in politics, and they tend to be better informed about issues that affect them personally, such as Social Security. Indeed, for them the connection between voting and what government does is clearer.

There may also be generational factors at work. Those who first voted in the 1930s, the so-called New Deal generation, continue to vote in high proportions compared to those who first voted in subsequent decades, regardless of income or education.[18] For this generation, voting seemed to matter a lot. Perhaps the issues and characters of the decade—the depression, Franklin Roosevelt, the coming of World War II—were sufficiently compelling to cause them to develop a lifelong attachment to voting that has not been repeated in later generations. Whatever the cause, the passing of the New Deal generation is likely to produce a lasting decline in overall turnout.

ELECTION-RELATED FACTORS

Turnout is affected by the election at hand. Presidential elections get great media coverage, generate a lot of excitement, and produce the highest turnout rates. By contrast, local elections for school board or town council often attract little attention, despite the importance of those institutions to the everyday lives of residents.

A long-standing pattern in voter turnout is called **surge and decline** (portrayed in Figure 6.3, p. 251).[19] Presidential elections generate a surge of "casual" voters who, compared to those who turn out regularly in state and local elections, are less informed about or interested in politics, and are generally less partisan. This surge usually helps congressional candidates from the party of the winning presidential candidate. Similar surges occur in some highly visible races for governor or the U.S. Senate.

The decline comes two years later, in nonpresidential, or *midterm* election years. Casual voters are less likely to turn out, and those who vote tend to be more active and partisan. Candidates who were helped by the surge two years earlier may now ex-

TABLE 6.1.   SELF-REPORTED TURNOUT, SELECTED
CHARACTERISTICS, 1986-1996*

	1986	1988	1990	1992	1994	1996
Gender						
Male	46	56	47	60	44	53
Female	46	58	45	62	45	56
Race						
White	47	59	47	64	47	56
Black	43	52	39	54	37	51
Hispanic	24	29	21	29	19	27
Age						
18–20 yrs	19	33	18	39	16	31
21–24 yrs	24	38	22	46	22	33
25–34 yrs	35	48	34	53	32	43
35–44 yrs	49	61	48	64	46	55
45–64 yrs	59	68	56	70	56	na
65+ yrs	61	69	60	70	61	na
Education						
No high school	33	37	28	35	23	28
1–3 yrs. high school	34	41	31	41	27	34
High school grad	44	55	42	58	40	49
College grad	62	78	62	81	63	73

*Note: Reflects percentage of voting-age population.

Source: Statistical Abstract of the United States, 1998 (Washington, D.C.: Government Printing Office, 1998), p. 296.

perience a decline in support. Over the 20th century this pattern usually caused the president's party to lose some of the seats in Congress that it had picked up in the previous election.[20] However, this tendency is not absolute: In 1998 Democrats picked up five House seats, the first time since 1934 that the president's party didn't lose seats in the midterm election. Whatever its impact, the surge-and-decline cycle shows that different elections attract differing levels of voter turnout.

ELECTION RULES AND TURNOUT

The electoral system may also reduce voter turnout. To many voters, the system's complexity, registration requirements, and election times may act as obstacles to participation. These complications may be increased by the winner-take-all rule. Sup-

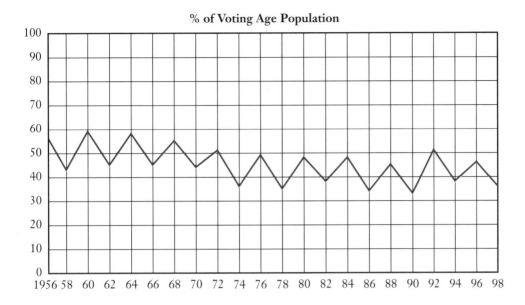

% of Voting Age Population

FIGURE 6.3. SURGE AND DECLINE, 1956–1998

High visibility presidential elections draw more voters, whereas turnout declines during non-presidential election years. The peaks all indicate presidential election years.

Does turnout have any impact on election outcomes? Maybe. In 1994, the Republicans took control of the U.S. House of Representatives and the U.S. Senate for the first time in 40 years. In the 13 closest House races combined, a total of 19,500 votes—or 1,500 votes per race—spelled the difference between Republican and Democratic control of the House. Each House district contains approximately 600,000 people, so the relatively low turnout in nonpresidential election years may have made a difference in 1994.

Sources: Statistical Abstract of the United States, 1998 (Washington, D.C.: Government Printing Office, 1998), p. 297; Federal Election Commission, www.fec.gov.

pose that a conservative Republican and a liberal Democrat compete for a U.S. House seat in a district in which conservatives outnumber liberals by 60 to 40 percent. The Republican is likely to win, and nearly half of the voters will feel left out. If this happens repeatedly, many may stop voting. Indeed, voter turnout typically is lowest in places where one group of voters has a consistent lock on the outcome of elections, whether because of party, ideology, race, class, or ethnicity. Voter turnout is highest in contests in which there is real competition.

Separation of powers also may dampen voting because winners may be frustrated in doing everything they promise. A presidential candidate can promise anything, but a president must build support in Congress in order to fulfill those promises. The same dynamics operate at the state level. Without compromise little gets done, even when the same party controls both the executive and legislative branches, and voters might react by not bothering to vote next time around.

Finally, turnout may be lower in the United States because Americans believe that there are better ways to transmit their demands or concerns to government. Many have turned to more direct forms of action: forming interest groups, marching in demonstrations, using media to publicize their causes, organizing letter-writing campaigns, meeting with legislators, and so on.[21] In this regard, American democracy may be healthier than low voter turnout rates would indicate. We will look at some of these other kinds of participation in chapter 7.

POLITICAL PARTIES

You may have noticed references to political parties throughout the preceding discussion. This is no accident: We cannot talk about elections without talking about parties. In fact, political scientist John Aldrich argues that "democracy is *unworkable* save in terms of parties."[22]

This controversial assertion has some validity. "Factions" such as parties and interest groups are natural by-products of political activity in a free society. They are inevitable when people are free to express complaints and promote shared values or issues. "The latent causes of faction," James Madison noted in *Federalist* No. 10, "are thus sown in the nature of man."[23] In other words, when left to their own devices people will divide up into factions.

Factions were active in American politics before the ink was dry on the new Constitution. As we saw in chapter 2, the ratification debate split Americans into opposing factions—Federalists and Antifederalists—that became the predecessors of today's major political parties (see Figure 6.4). The Democratic party, the world's oldest continuously operating political party, traces its lineage to the Antifederalists. The Republican party emerged in 1854 from antislavery elements of the Democratic and Whig parties, the latter of which grew from remnants of the original Federalist party. Thus, parties have been fixtures of American politics from the very beginning.

PARTIES AS INSTRUMENTS OF POLITICAL ACTION

A **political party** is a unique kind of faction. After all, a faction also can be an interest group, a labor union, a religious organization, or any other kind of identifiable collection of people who share certain characteristics, values, or interests. Why a political party forms, and why it figures so prominently in a democracy, stems from what it is designed to do: win votes.[24] Whether the contest is to elect the president or to pass a bill in Congress, the goal is the same. No other type of faction tries to do this consistently. As a result, we need to look closely at the general functions of parties and at how well American parties perform them.

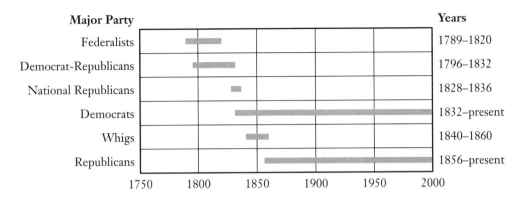

FIGURE 6.4. THE EVOLUTION OF THE TWO-PARTY SYSTEM

Promote Shared Interests   A party is created when a group of people seek to maximize their political influence in situations in which winning votes matters. Historically parties emerged in legislatures, when legislators with similar interests decided to work together by sharing information and by voting together on legislation.[25] They also worked to get more people who shared their views elected to the legislature in order to control it, and thereby increase their ability to pass the laws they favored. Those who were not part of this group were compelled to form their own parties rather than risk losing consistently to the one that was already organized. These parties then competed to get their candidates elected to other offices, including the presidency. The desire to win votes produced political parties.

Overcome Structural and Geographic Barriers   Parties are not mentioned in the Constitution. Yet, from the beginning members of Congress and presidents struggled to work together within a constitutional system that split them apart. They eventually built organizations designed to span the constitutional separation of powers. They built parties.

In a broader sense, the parties evolved as ways to unite like-minded people who were separated by geography, institutional boundaries (House versus Senate), or both. Party organizations united legislators from across the nation and helped close the constitutional gap between the president and members of Congress. In essence, the party provided some of the "glue" necessary to make the system work more effectively and efficiently.[26]

Develop Leaders   In some societies, leaders are groomed within military organizations; in others, they are developed in religious institutions or trained in elite schools. Some come into leadership positions because of their wealth, ancestry, or control of corporations, or because they are charismatic media personalities.

However, the talents and values that are useful for advancement in the military, a corporation, or a religious organization may not be the skills and attitudes needed to maintain a representative democracy. In this regard, parties are democratic instruments for recruiting and developing political talent. Politics is like any other endeavor: Doing it well takes time and practice. Party organizations traditionally were used to identify promising individuals and groom them for leadership through a succession of increasingly important positions. The individuals with the best political skills—including the ability to get elected—rose through the ranks of local and state offices to Congress and, in a few cases, the presidency.

Historically, party organizations also provided avenues for advancement for immigrants and racial minorities to whom opportunities in business and the professions were limited. Parties recruited supporters and eventual leaders from these groups, and these individuals moved up the political ladder into public office. The parties did not do this out of charity, but to win votes. In the process, however, they were agents of social change. The saga of the Irish in Boston and New York, or of African Americans in cities such as Atlanta, suggests that the parties were valuable routes to social and political mobility.[27] While this is less true today, party organizations still try to reach out to the newest Americans in recognition that the earliest partisan attachments tend to endure.

Unite and Mobilize Voters   To win elections, a party must unite a diverse array of people under a common set of issues and get them to vote. In doing so, parties ideally work to bring together voters and connect them to government. And, because a candidate must build a large base of support to win an election, the major parties are reluctant to "throw away" potential voters.

American parties are broad coalitions of interests, but this does not mean that they lack core values. As we discussed in chapter 5, Republicans tend to be conservative, Democrats more liberal. In most instances, a staunch conservative is unlikely to vote for Democrats. In the same vein, labor unions are traditionally aligned with the Democratic party, whereas business groups gravitate toward the Republican party because of its ideological support for free markets and private property rights. On the other hand, Democrats cannot ignore business, and Republicans cannot ignore labor. Neither party wishes alienate possible sources of political support.

Simplify Voters' Choices   Parties make voting easier by giving citizens a "label" to use in making decisions. Someone who supports the values promoted by the Republican party naturally tends to vote for Republicans under the reasonable assumption that they generally share his or her beliefs. A voter who disagrees with the philosophy of the Republican party can just as easily use the party label to vote against Republican candidates. Either way, party labels simplify the voter's task, particularly for races in which little information is available.

Until relatively recently in many places a person could vote a **straight ticket** (or *party-line)* **ballot.** One could vote for a party's candidates for all offices, from president to local town clerk, by pulling one lever or marking one spot. This option had the virtue of simplicity, especially for voters who could not read or who lacked the time to inform themselves about all the candidates. Such ballots are rare today because many activists and scholars feared that they made it easier for political party "machines" to amass the votes of less-educated, poorer, and relatively new citizens, and because they believed that voters *should* make an effort to inform themselves. Many states enacted laws forbidding party-line ballots or instituted "nonpartisan" ballots that do not list party affiliation beside candidates' names. Even so, voters rely on party labels to simplify their choices. Without them, the burden on the voter might be even greater.[28]

Organize Elections   Parties have a vested interest in how elections work. They want to win, so they compete to enact election rules that are favorable to their candidates and voters. For example, a party whose supporters are better educated and more affluent may not want to make it too easy to register or vote, whereas a party whose supporters are less educated and poorer may want to make registration and voting more convenient. Despite this obvious self-interest, the competition between parties keeps the electoral system more honest than it might be otherwise. Parties check on each other during the campaign, thereby reducing the opportunity for fraud.

Develop Policy Options   Parties compete to win elections, and in their competition will continuously develop programs and ideas that will attract votes. Ideas that no longer are popular are modified or discarded. The party that succeeds in assembling a winning coalition of ideas wins election. This competition over ideas is of critical importance in a democratic society. Without it, voters have no real choice, which in turn undermines the validity of elections as the foundation of democratic government.

Make Government Work   Contrary to what one might think, parties can make government work more effectively and efficiently. As we noted earlier, American parties can be understood as "extra-constitutional" organizations that are created to help bridge the gaps created by separation of powers. A president finds it easier to work with members of Congress of the same party, and shared partisan values can make Congress work more efficiently. Without parties, those who govern must work harder to construct the majorities necessary to pass laws and settle disputes. To some extent parties simplify the process of governing.

Make Democracy Workable   These general functions of political parties lead us back to Aldrich's argument that democracy is unworkable without parties. That is, without parties future leaders would have to be developed through some other institution or route to power. Without parties, voters would have to spend more time and effort making choices among candidates for the many elections that characterize the American system. Without parties, some other mechanism would be needed to keep elections honest, or to develop the policy options available to voters, or simply to make government work. Without parties, elected officials would have to find other ways to overcome the separation of powers in the American system.

Without parties democratic government would be different but not necessarily better. No other organization—the military, churches, mass media, interest groups, corporations, or government bureaucracies—tries so hard to bring together as many different kinds of people or to get them to vote. No other organization seeks to develop leaders who are expert at the art of political compromise, and no other entity is created expressly to make elections work, or even to govern. In short, parties may be essential to the working of democratic politics.

AMERICAN PARTIES TODAY

Political parties in the United States fulfill some of these general functions well, but they perform others badly or not at all. How they perform is shaped by the constitutional system as well as by contemporary factors such as "candidate-centered" campaigns dominated by mass media. We will consider these factors in order.

The Constitutional System and Parties   In the United States separation of powers and separate elections complicate the ability of parties to unite officials who serve in these separate institutions. Separation of powers may encourage the creation of parties as a way to span the constitutional gap between the branches, but it also makes it difficult for a party to speak and act in a unified manner.

Also, in the American system one party may control the presidency while another controls at least one house of Congress. The same possibility exists in states, as we saw with the Indiana House of Representatives. In these situations, nothing gets accomplished without strenuous efforts at compromise. But separation of powers requires such efforts even when both branches are controlled by the same party. The views of members of the House of Representatives can differ from those of senators, and the perspectives of members of Congress often conflict with those of the president even when they are from the same party (see chapter 8). This is as the framers intended.

Federalism is another factor to be considered. Just as it decentralizes political power, federalism decentralizes political parties. Indeed, the major parties really are loose confederations of state and local party organizations that seek to elect candidates who run under their labels.[29] The parties differ from one another in ideology and issues, but state-by-state variations within each party can be just as pronounced. For example, Democrats in Minnesota are likely to be more liberal than Democrats in Alabama, a reflection of distinct regional political cultures.

The party system thus reflects the constitutional system. Parties help bridge the separation of powers, just as they help bridge geographic and social gaps within American society, but they can never fuse these elements together very well or for very long. The forces of separation that are built into the system eventually prove far more resilient. Thus, the relative weakness of political parties in the United States is traced directly to the Constitution.

Candidate-centered Elections   In many ways the 19th-century political party was the only truly national organization. It functioned to recruit leaders, bring together diverse societal interests, and mobilize voters. State and local parties often had their own newspapers, and they often were as much social organizations as political ones. The parties also provided services: Local party leaders helped supporters find jobs or housing. They did so in return for votes, of course, but for many Americans the party organization was a major part of their lives.[30]

Today the parties are more confined to electoral functions. Government programs such as Social Security and unemployment insurance have negated the party's role as a service provider. Civil service laws, which fill government jobs through competitive examinations, took away most of the ability of party leaders to give jobs to supporters (see chapter 10). Most important, the convergence of open primary elections and modern mass media creates "candidate-centered" campaigns that enable individuals to run for office independent of party organizations. With enough money, candidates can nominate themselves, win the primary, and, using television, communicate with voters. In fact, candidates often don't bother to seek the endorsement of party leaders. Most still rely on party *labels* to simplify voters' choices on election day, but few need or rely on parties themselves. American parties thus are left as little more than support organizations for self-selected and independently financed candidates.

Even so, despite Americans' wariness about them, parties won't go away anytime soon.[31] For one thing, parties are important sources of policy ideas, campaign expertise, and funding for candidates. For another, there still is no other organization that exists solely to mobilize voters to elect like-minded people and translate their views into public policy. As we will see in chapter 7, interest groups do not fulfill these crucial roles because they do not compete in elections. Only parties do. As long as this function is fulfilled by political parties, people will continue to create and use them.

THE ENDURING TWO-PARTY SYSTEM

Although the two-party system is a characteristic feature of American government, there is no provision for such a system in the Constitution. In fact, the Constitution says nothing at all about parties. And, despite appearances, many parties compete for attention and votes. For example, 98 percent of the popular vote in the 1996 presidential election went to three candidates: Democrat Bill Clinton (49 percent), Republican Bob Dole (41 percent), and Reform Party nominee H. Ross Perot (8 percent). The remaining 2 percent of the vote was split among nearly 20 other "minor-party" candidates, including Ralph Nader (Green Party), Harry Browne (Libertarian Party), and John Hagelin (Natural Law Party). Profiles of some of these parties appear in Box 6.2.

To be precise, the United States does not have a "two-party" system; rather, it has a "two-party dominant" one. With so many parties supporting candidates, why do only those from the Democratic and Republican parties usually have any chance of winning?

The electoral system creates the two-party system. Winner-take-all rules hurt candidates from smaller parties, who can rarely win even a plurality of the overall vote. Votes cast for minor-party candidates are, in a sense, "wasted" on people who cannot win, so few voters will support "third-party" candidates unless neither major party candidate represents their views. For the same reason, candidates usually are

Reform Party candidate H. Ross Perot. In 1992, Perot won 19 percent of the national popular vote, the best showing for a "minor" party candidate since George Wallace in 1968. Perot ran again in 1996, with less success, but the party he founded is still a force in American politics.

Democratic Socialists (www.dsausa.org/dsa.html) "The Democratic Socialists of America (DSA) is the largest socialist organization in the United States, and the principal U.S. affiliate of the Socialist International. At the root of our socialism is a profound commitment to democracy, as means and end. We are activists committed not only to extending political democracy but to demanding democratic empowerment in the economy, in gender relations, and in culture. Democracy is not simply one of our political values but our means of restructuring society. Our vision is of a society in which people have a real voice in the choices and relationships that affect the entirety of our lives. We call this vision democratic socialism—a vision of a more free, democratic and humane society."

→

not inclined to run as minor-party nominees. Under the electoral system their practical options are limited to the two parties that are able win a plurality.

Minor-party candidates fare worse in presidential elections. In 1992, for example, H. Ross Perot won 19 percent of the national popular vote, but no electoral votes. In fact, only three times in 60 years has a third-party candidate won any appreciable

A CLOSER LOOK

Green Party (www.greens.org) "The Green Party's philosophy is that all things are connected in the web of life. Awareness of the interdependence between the world and its creatures is part of the Green philosophy. We are a part of nature—not above it—and the future of our society depends on our learning to live wisely in our fragile home. The Ten Key Values of the Greens: Social Justice, Community-Based Economics, Nonviolence, Decentralisation, Future Focus/Sustainability, Feminism, Personal and Global Responsibility, Respect for Diversity, Grassroots Democracy, and Ecological Wisdom."

Libertarian Party (www.lp.org) "Libertarians respect the right of every individual to make his or her own choices in every aspect of life. Who knows better how to run your life: you, or the government? Libertarians also recognize that with choice comes responsibility—the responsibility to respect the rights of others, and the responsibility to deal with the consequences of your choices. The government shouldn't force you to pay for other people's choices—but you shouldn't expect government to force your neighbors to pay for your choices, either. And Libertarians recognize that people won't always make the right choices. Libertarians don't take their stand for choice because they necessarily support the choices that some people might make, but because letting individuals make their own choices and take responsibility for those choices is the only way to respect their rights."

Natural Law Party (www.natural-law.org) The Natural Law Party was founded in 1992 to "bring the light of science into politics." The party is affiliated with the Transcendental Meditation movement, which espouses the value of meditation to promoting world peace. The Natural Law Party advocates government "in accord with natural law. Solve problems at their basis by bringing individual life, and our national policies, into greater harmony with natural law through proven educational programs; natural, preventive health care; renewable energy; sustainable agriculture; and other forward-looking, prevention-oriented programs."

The Reform Party (www.reformparty.org) "We shall seek to reform our electoral, lobbying and campaign practices to ensure that our elected government officials and our candidates owe their allegiance and remain accountable to the people whom they are elected to serve rather than other influence-seeking agencies."

number of electoral votes. In each case—Strom Thurmond of South Carolina in 1948, Harry Byrd of Virginia in 1960, and George Wallace of Alabama in 1968—the candidate was a southern Democrat who split with the party over civil rights issues. In each case the electoral votes came entirely from southern states, suggesting that a successful third party needs a strong regional base.[32]

FACTORS WORKING AGAINST MINOR PARTIES

Four other factors reinforce this bias toward a two-party system: election laws, campaign donations, the ideological flexibility of the major parties, and tradition.

Election Laws   Election laws are made by those in power—members of the two major parties—who have every incentive to make it more difficult for minor-party candidates to draw votes away from them. For example, state requirements that candidates file petitions containing the signatures of thousands of registered voters to get onto the ballot tends to discourage minor parties. Likewise, rules that presidential candidates must get a minimum percentage of the popular vote to qualify for federal campaign funding have a similar effect at the national level.

Bias in Campaign Donations   As we will discuss in chapters 7 and 8, few individuals or organizations are willing to contribute money to candidates who have little chance of winning. Because candidates from the two major parties have a built-in advantage, they also tend to get most of the campaign donations. This creates a vicious cycle—of no funding, less chance of winning, resulting in no funding—for minor-party candidates, at least for those who are not as wealthy as H. Ross Perot, the nominee of the Reform Party, who used his personal fortune to get onto the ballot and compete nationally in two presidential elections.

Ideological Flexibility   Oddly enough, minor parties are also hindered by the flexibility of the major parties. Any minor party that takes a popular position on an important issue is likely to find its issue "stolen" by major-party candidates. In 1992, for example, many voters embraced Perot's call for a balanced federal budget. But this cause was picked up by Bill Clinton, who then worked with congressional Republicans to produce a budget surplus by 1998. How much Perot's candidacy advanced the cause of a balanced budget is hard to say, but the fact that Clinton embraced the issue in order to win in 1992 illustrates how major-party candidates will adopt issues that they sense will garner votes.

Tradition   For many Americans the two-party system makes sense. Proposals to institute some form of proportional representation never get far. For all their criticisms of the parties and the party system, few Americans seem to prefer the greater political stability that a two-party system tends to produce over the better representation of smaller interests offered by proportional representation.

THE DYNAMICS OF COALITION BUILDING

The electoral system thus creates incentives for large parties. This invariably results in two broad coalitions of distinct interests, each of which is constructed before the election in order to be able to win it. Building such a coalition assumes that the partners can cooperate. This is not always possible: In the 1850s, for example, the issue of slavery split both the Democratic and Whig parties into southern and northern wings; elements of the latter became the Republican party.

Yet, throughout history unlikely partners have managed to stick together to win elections and maintain power. In the 1930s Franklin Roosevelt built a Democratic party coalition consisting of northern liberals, southern conservatives, urban ethnic Catholics, African Americans, and Jews. This New Deal coalition dominated American politics until the 1960s, when issues such as civil rights and the Vietnam War split it apart.[33] The Republican party took advantage of these splits within the Democratic coalition by emphasizing issues of concern to certain groups of voters: southerners upset about civil rights and Vietnam, middle-class voters concerned about crime and the economy, and working-class Catholics who were concerned about social issues such as abortion.

By the 1990s the Republican party had come to dominate American electoral politics. Democrats thus were forced to rethink some of their positions, particularly on issues that appealed to middle-class voters who had moved to the Republican party. Welfare reform, discussed in chapter 5, was one such issue. In turn, Bill Clinton's ability to construct winning coalitions in both 1992 and 1996 (see Table 6.2) sparked debates among Republicans about whether their positions on issues such as gun control and Social Security were out of step with the majority of voters. And so the competition for votes goes on.

ELECTIONS, PUBLIC OPINION, AND PUBLIC POLICY

This analysis of the electoral and party systems inevitably leads to the most important question: How well do elections ensure that the people control what government does? In a system of representative democracy in which voters select other people to represent their views, four general conditions must hold for elections to effectively translate opinion into public policy: Competing candidates must offer clear alternatives; voters must care about the issues; the outcome of the election must be easy to interpret; and winners must do what they promise.[34]

COMPETING CANDIDATES, CLEAR ALTERNATIVES

Americans complain that the two major parties are mirror images of each other and that major-party candidates never offer clear alternatives on the issues. This perception has some validity in that the two parties tend to gravitate toward the center of the ideological spectrum in order to attract the most voters. No major-party candidate wants to be seen as out of touch with mainstream opinion, so a great deal of effort is spent trying to figure out where the average voter stands on controversial issues such as welfare or the death penalty. Nor is he or she likely to advocate the abolition of the free-market economic system, support legalization of marijuana, or suggest that Americans give up their right to own guns. A candidate who is seen as "extremist" on the issues of the day is going to lose.

Having said this, whether a voter perceives that candidates offer clear alternatives on any issue can depend on that voter's own ideological sophistication and knowledge of the issues. Despite their relative centrism, the major parties do promote distinctive ideological and policy agendas. Republicans profess more conservative views, whereas Democrats tend toward more liberal ones. Whether these differences are apparent may depend more on the voter than on the candidate.

TABLE 6.2. HOW CLINTON WON IN 1992

In 1992, the Democratic challenger, Governor Bill Clinton of Arkansas, defeated a sitting president, Republican George Bush. A third major candidate, Texas businessman H. Ross Perot, also competed strongly in the election. This table shows how different kinds of Americans voted.

Did Perot help defeat Bush? It's hard to say. Public opinion polling data suggest that Perot's presence didn't hurt Bush: in a hypothetical head-to-head matchup, Clinton still defeats Bush by 53.5% to 46.5%. So in one sense Perot actually hurt Clinton more by taking away a clear majority mandate for the challenger.

	% of Voters	Clinton	Bush	Perot
All voters	100	44%	37%	19%
Men	46	41	37	21
Women	54	47	36	17
Whites	87	40	39	21
African Americans	8	83	11	7
Hispanics	3	62	24	14
Age 18–24	11	47	31	22
Age 25–29	11	41	35	24
Age 30–39	25	42	38	21
Age 40–49	24	44	37	19
Age 50–59	13	42	39	19
60 and up	16	50	37	12
Less than High School	6	56	27	18
High School grad	25	44	36	21
Some College	29	43	36	21
College grad	24	41	39	20
Postgrad	16	50	35	15
Family income				
Less than $15,000	14	59	22	19
$15,000–$29,999	24	46	34	20
$30,000–$49,999	30	42	37	21
$50,000–$74,999	20	41	41	18
$75,000 and higher	13	38	46	16
Protestant	56	34	45	21
Catholic	27	42	37	21
Jewish	4	78	10	11
Democrats	39	78	10	13
Republicans	34	11	72	18
Independents	28	39	31	30
Liberals	22	69	13	18
Moderates	50	49	30	21
Conservatives	29	18	64	17

Source: "Voter Research and Survey Exit Polls," *National Journal*, November 7, 1992, p. 2543.

Second, even if major-party candidates do not differ widely on consensual issues such as the free market, for most voters there are enough policy or ideological differences between them to make a clear choice. For example, for decades every Democratic party nominee for president has supported a woman's basic right to have a legal abortion, and every Republican nominee has opposed it. On abortion at least, voters have had clear choices. However, as we will see, for some voters, the candidates' views on abortion may matter little; to them, other issues are more important.

Retrospective Voting   Even if voters are not always aware of candidates' positions on the issues, they do make judgments about the past performance of the office holder or the party in power.[35] This is truest in presidential elections, which tend to be based on broad and highly symbolic appeals. Going back to 1992, voters had a clear choice: Stay with Republican George Bush, the incumbent, or vote for change by siding with Democrat Bill Clinton or Reform party candidate H. Ross Perot. Given this choice, 62 percent voted for change. However, in 1996 voters stuck with Bill Clinton over Perot and Republican Senator Robert Dole because they generally approved of the way Clinton was doing his job. To be sure, individual voters may not have liked something Clinton did or didn't do in his first term, but when given the chance they decided that his overall performance merited another term.

VOTERS AND THE ISSUES

Even when they are offered clear alternatives, voters are often uninformed about the details of issues, especially complex ones. As a result, they frequently cast their vote based on rather amorphous calculations, such as whether one candidate seems to fit their conception of the office or the direction in which the nation should go. For example, in 1984 public opinion polls showed that many people who agreed with challenger Walter Mondale on specific issues still voted for the incumbent president, Ronald Reagan. They did so partly because they were satisfied with the way things were going, but also because they regarded Reagan as more "presidential," as the kind of leader they desired.[36] To critics, the 1984 election results supported their contention that image had triumphed over substance and that voters were uninformed and irrational.

This perception may not be totally true or fair. In many ways issues are largely perceived through assessments of the candidates. In 1984 voters liked and trusted Reagan as president, so their continued support for him seemed rational. In 1988 they voted for George Bush, the sitting vice president, over Governor Michael Dukakis of Massachusetts largely because Bush was more familiar and pledged to continue Reagan's policies. On the other hand, in 1992 voters decided that the nation needed to go in a different direction on a range of policy questions, so they turned against Bush in favor an another relatively unknown southern governor, Bill Clinton of Arkansas. In this instance the voters were delivering a simple verdict: It was time for a change.

In general, voters don't elect issues; they elect people. A candidate whom voters do not trust is unlikely to get their support, even if they dislike the other candidates, unless the issue differences between the candidates are so great that personal characteristics are irrelevant. But this is rare. With the tendency of major-party candidates to seek out the middle ground on issues, a candidate's personal traits and private be-havior can make the difference in a close election.

What conclusions can we draw? In some elections, a voter's choice may be aided by clear differences among candidates on major issues. For example, in an election for town council the candidates may disagree over whether the town needs to build a new firehouse. In this case the issue is clear and relatively simple, and the choice of candidates may decide the issue. At the other extreme, a presidential election usually involves bundles of issues, some of which, such as "national defense" or "the direc-tion of the nation," are rather abstract. In such instances voters base their decisions on a personalized mix of specific positions on key issues and broad assessments of candidates' personal characteristics. These decisions, in turn, often hinge on whether voters are content with the direction of the nation or have faith in a candidate's abil-ity to govern.

INTERPRETING THE OUTCOME

In a referendum, such as when voters decide whether to raise a state sales tax in order to finance a new football stadium, the result is easy to interpret: Either taxes will be raised or they won't. In elections involving candidates for office, however, the "mes-sage" often is less clear.

First of all, the winner may not receive a majority of the vote. The winner may take office with a plurality, but he or she may be perceived as lacking a clear "man-date" from the public. In such cases the winner may find it harder to achieve major accomplishments, particularly if others regard the newcomer as lacking significant public support. Clinton, for example, won only 43 percent of the popular vote in 1992. As a result, few Republicans in Congress felt compelled to support the new president's initiatives, which made it much more difficult for Clinton to gain passage of new programs. By contrast, Reagan's overwhelming victory over incumbent presi-dent Jimmy Carter in 1980 was seen by almost everyone as a mandate for change. As a result, Democrats avoided open confrontation with Reagan early in his first term.

Second, individual voters might support the same candidate for different reasons. For example, someone who supports the right to a legal abortion might vote for a "pro-choice" candidate even if he or she dislikes the candidate's views on free trade with Canada and Mexico. For that voter, women's rights take precedence, whereas another voter might not approve of the pro-choice position but feels strongly about free trade. The electoral system forces voters to make these trade-offs, and winners usually are supported by coalitions of voters who nevertheless disagree with one an-other. For example, Reagan's coalition included a contradictory mix of social conser-vatives who opposed abortion but supported federal spending on a wide range of pro-grams and libertarians who opposed federal spending but supported abortion rights. Under such conditions winners often find themselves trying to keep the peace within their own camps.

Finally, low voter turnout can muddy the waters, raising questions about whether those who voted had different priorities or values from those who didn't, or whether higher turnout would have made any difference in the outcome. In elections in which the winner had broad support, the views of those who voted probably did not differ much from those who stayed home. But in other elections the differences may matter, especially if they run along class or racial lines. For example, racial minorities may not bother to vote if they don't see much of a difference between two white major-party candidates for mayor. The question here is whether the eventual winner will end up overlooking or ignoring issues that are important to members of that minority because their votes weren't part of the winning candidate's coalition of support.[37]

At best, the message of any election is a broad one: An incumbent officeholder is retained or rejected. But in making this choice, the voters may be signaling strong discontent with the direction of their government or their society. Clinton may have received only 43 percent of the vote in the 1992 presidential election, but Bush received only 38 percent. Voters may not have rushed to champion Clinton, but they certainly revealed a lack of support for a second term for the incumbent president.

KEEPING CAMPAIGN PROMISES

Despite public cynicism, winners do try to do what they promised. In 1980 Ronald Reagan pledged to cut taxes, raise defense spending, and balance the federal budget. He carried out the first two promises but not the third. George Bush promised to never raise taxes, but eventually he agreed to a compromise with Congress that paired a tax increase with budget cuts in order to achieve a balanced budget. Bill Clinton promised to remove prohibitions against homosexuals serving in the armed forces. He tried to fulfill this promise during his first days in office, but the ensuing controversy threatened to derail progress on what he felt were more important issues, such as the federal budget deficit and health care reform, so he was forced to compromise on the issue.

As these examples suggest, candidates sometimes make conflicting promises or find that they cannot deliver on them. Reagan's pledge to cut taxes and raise defense spending generated massive deficits that undercut his promise to balance the federal budget. Bush's resistance to a tax increase led to a stalemate with Congress over the budget that threatened programs he supported, so he reluctantly went back on his promise. Clinton's attempt to end the ban on gays in the military met with stiff opposition in Congress and the armed forces, and in the end Clinton managed to get only a modest change in the policy. In these cases the structure of the American system of government hindered the winners' ability to fulfill their promises. They tried, but only Congress makes the law, regardless of what presidential candidates promise.

CONCLUSION

Elections are organized forms of political conflict. They are designed to allow voters to assess competing candidates and select those who will represent them in government. In the process, elections ensure that the people will control what government does.

However, as we have seen, this is a tall order. Voters aren't always presented with clear choices, nor do they necessarily know much about the substance of the issues under debate. Many people do not even bother to vote, especially in low-profile state and local elections, thus making the message of any election less clear. And of course, those who win cannot always do what they promised.

At a minimum, elections give the people opportunities to express themselves on the past conduct of incumbents, the broad directions of government, and limits on the actions of elected officials. If anything, voters tell elected officials what they *cannot* do. In any form of government, this is no small achievement.

Despite their limitations, elections will always matter because they are the means by which the people choose those who govern. They are imperfect mechanisms for democratic control, but they may be the best ones available. The challenge is to make them work better, and to convince the people that they are still relevant to their lives.

SUMMARY

▶ The electoral system in the United States is characterized by winner-take-all plurality or majority elections. The structure of the electoral system forces candidates and their political parties to build broad coalitions of support and to move toward the center of the ideological spectrum in order to attract enough votes to win. The result is an electoral system that favors stability over the more accurate representation of political perspectives found in proportional representation systems.

▶ Political parties are organizations designed specifically to win elections. They function to unite and mobilize voters, recruit leaders, and develop public policies. In parliamentary systems such as Great Britain the majority party also runs the government. However, in the United States parties have no formal role in governing. Thus, the parties are relatively weak when compared to parties in other nations. Even so, American political parties are the only organizations dedicated to building large coalitions of voters in order to win elections.

▶ The winner-take-all electoral system produces a party system dominated by the two major political parties. The electoral college system for selecting the president raises a particularly high barrier to candidates from smaller parties. These candidates may influence how issues are defined or get onto the agenda for discussion, but they can win elections rarely. Voters therefore are often confronted by relatively mainstream major-party candidates who may differ little on major issues.

▶ The conditions whereby elections effectively translate public opinion into public policy are rarely met. Voters may not care about the issues, or may not discern differences between the candidates; the message of the election may be unclear; winners may not be able to do what they promised. However, if elections are imperfect mechanisms for translating voters' opinions into public policy, they nevertheless serve important purposes. Above all, elections are the means by which the people select those who will govern on their behalf.

QUESTIONS FOR REVIEW AND DISCUSSION

1. What specific functions do elections fulfill? Which of these functions is the most important?

2. What factors best explain whether an individual is likely to vote? Knowing this, what can be done to increase overall voter turnout?

3. Discuss the various functions performed by political parties and the degree to which American parties fulfill each function.

4. What are the four general conditions that must hold for elections to accurately translate public opinion into public policy? To what extent are these conditions met, and why?

TERMS TO REMEMBER

closed primary	open primary	straight ticket ballot
electoral college	political party	suffrage
general election	poll tax	surge and decline
grandfather clause	plurality	unit rule
initiative	primary election	voter turnout
legitimacy	proportional	white primary
literacy test	representation	winner-take-all
majority	referendum	

WEB SOURCES

Democratic Party (www.democrats.org) and Republican Party (www.rnc org). The official Web sites of the Republican and Democratic parties, respectively.

League of Women Voters (www.lwv.org). The League is one of the nation's oldest nonpartisan organizations dedicated to helping citizens learn more about and take part in elections.

Project Vote Smart (www.vote-smart.org). Project Vote Smart is a nonpartisan citizens' information service staffed by college students and other volunteers. An excellent resource on virtually every aspect of campaigns and elections, as well as politics generally.

SUGGESTED READINGS

Walter Dean Burnham, *Critical Elections and the Mainsprings of American Politics* (New York: Norton, 1970). A classic study that examines key election periods in American history to understand the shifts in partisan dominance and how these "realignments" shaped the broad directions of public policy. For example, the election of 1932 marked the emergence of the New Deal coalition that would dominate American politics for over three decades.

William G. Mayer, *The Divided Democrats: Ideological Unity, Party Reform, and Presidential Elections* (Boulder, CO: Westview Press, 1996). A politicial scientist argues that of the two major parties, the Democratic party has a more difficult time maintaining party unity because it is more ideologically fragmented and internally diverse. The task is for Democrats to develop a new vision of what binds them together as a party.

Warren E. Miller and J. Merrill Shanks, *The New American Voter* (Cambridge, MA: Harvard University Press, 1996). In the classic study, *The American Voter* (University of Chicago Press, 1960) Miller and colleagues found that voters were not always as informed and active as believers in democracy thought they should be. In this more recent study, Miller and Shanks assess the decline in rates of voter turnout and changes in party identification since 1960, and how voters make their choices at the polls.

Gerald M. Pomper, ed., *The Election of 1996: Reports and Interpretations* (Chatham, NJ: Chatham House, 1997). In this sixth in a series of studies on presidential elections, seven other political scientists join Pomper in assessing the 1996 presidential and congressional elections from a variety of angles: the nominating process, use of mass media, campaign finance, and the connections between public opinion and voting behavior.

NOTES

1. Isabel Wilkerson, "Indiana Lawmaking Is Fit to Be Tied," *New York Times*, National Edition, March 20, 1989, p. A12.

2. Theodore J. Lowi and Benjamin Ginsberg, *American Government: Freedom and Power*, 2d ed. (New York: Norton, 1993), p. 461.

3. Taken from Gerald Pomper, *Elections in America* (New York: Dodd, Mead, 1968).

4. E. E. Schattschneider, *The Semi-Sovereign People: A Realist's View of Democracy in America* (Hinsdale, IL: Dryden Press, 1960).

5. James A. Sundquist, *Constitutional Reform and Effective Government* (Washington, D.C.: The Brookings Institution, 1986).

6. Carol Swain, *Black Faces, Black Interests: The Representation of African Americans in Congress* (Baton Rouge, LA: Louisiana State University Press, 1993).

7. Michael Barone and Grant Ujifusa, *Almanac of American Politics, 1998* (Washington, D.C.: The National Journal, Inc., 1998), p. 620.

8. Thomas Cronin, *Direct Democracy: The Politics of Initiative, Referendum, and Recall* (Cambridge, MA: Harvard University Press, 1989).

9. *Smith v Allwright*, 321 US 649 (1944).

10. Nelson W. Polsby, *Consequences of Party Reform* (New York: Oxford University Press, 1983).

11. Jack W. Peltason, *Understanding the Constitution*, 12th ed. (New York: Holt, Rinehart, & Winston, 1992), p. 40.

12. Neil Spitzer, "The First Election," *The Atlantic Monthly*, November 1988, p. 18.

13. *Guinn v United States*, 238 US 347 (1915).

14. Gerald M. Pomper, *Elections in America: Control and Influence in Democratic Politics*, 2d ed. (New York: Longman, 1980), pp. 194–195.

15. Richard Hofstadter, *The Age of Reform* (New York: Random House, 1955).

16. William L. Riordon, *Plunkett of Tammany Hall* (New York: E. P. Dutton, 1963).

17. B. Drummond Ayers, Jr., "Easier Voter Registration Doesn't Raise Participation," *New York Times*, December 3, 1995, p. A22.

18. Warren E. Miller and J. Merrill Shanks, *The New American Voter* (Cambridge, MA: Harvard University Press, 1996), pp. 56–58.

19. Angus Campbell, "Surge and Decline: A Study of Electoral Change," in Angus Campbell, Philip E. Converse, Warren E. Miller, and Donald E. Stokes, eds., *Elections and Political Order* (New York: John Wiley & Sons, 1966).

20. M. Margaret Conway, "Political Participation in Mid-Term Congressional Elections," *American Politics Quarterly* 9 (April 1981), pp. 221–244.

21. Richard A. Brody, "The Puzzle of Political Participation in America," in Anthony King, ed., *The New American Political System* (Washington, D.C.: The American Enterprise Institute, 1979), pp. 287–324.

22. John H. Aldrich, *Why Parties? The Origin and Transformation of Party Politics in America* (Chicago, IL: University of Chicago Press, 1995), p. 3; emphasis in original.

23. Alexander Hamilton, James Madison, and John Jay, *The Federalist Papers*, Clinton Rossiter, ed. (New York: New American Library, 1961), p. 79.

24. Schattschneider, *The Semi-Sovereign People*, p. 59; Aldrich, *Why Parties?*, p. 35.

25. Gianfranco Poggi, *The Development of the Modern State: A Sociological Introduction* (Palo Alto, CA: Stanford University Press, 1978).

26. H. G. Nicholas, *The Nature of American Politics*, 2d ed. (New York: Oxford University Press, 1986), p. 42.

27. Everett Carll Ladd and Charles D. Hadley, *Transformations of the American Party System: Political Coalitions from the New Deal to the 1970s*, 2d ed. (New York: Norton, 1978).

28. Norman Nie, Sidney Verba, and Robert Petrocik, *The Changing American Voter* (Cambridge, MA: Harvard University Press, 1976), ch. 16.

29. Nicholas, *The Nature of American Politics*, pp. 42–57.

30. William N. Chambers and Walter Dean Burnham, eds., *The American Party Systems: Stages of Political Development* (New York: Oxford University Press, 1976).

31. See L. Sandy Maisel, ed., *The Parties Respond: Changes in American Parties and Campaigns*, 3d ed. (Boulder, CO: Westview Press, 1998).

32. James L. Sundquist, *Dynamics of the Party System: Alignment and Realignment of Political Parties in the United States* (Washington, D.C.: The Brookings Institution, 1983).

33. E. J. Dionne, *Why Americans Hate Politics* (New York: Simon & Schuster, 1991).

34. Thomas R. Dye and Harmon Zeigler, *The Irony of American Democracy: An Uncommon Introduction to American Politics*, 10th ed. (Belmont, CA: Wadsworth, 1996), pp. 190–192.

35. Morris P. Fiorina, *Retrospective Voting in American National Elections* (New Haven, CT: Yale University Press, 1981).

36. Samuel Kernell, "Campaigning, Governing, and the Contemporary Presidency," in John E. Chubb and Paul E. Peterson, eds., *The New Direction in American Politics* (Washington, D.C.: The Brookings Institution, 1985), pp. 117–142.

37. Kenny J. Whitby and Frank D. Gilliam Jr., "Representatives in Congress: Line Drawing and Minorities," in Herbert F. Weisberg and Samuel C. Patterson, eds., *Great Theatre: The American Congress in the 1900s* (New York: Cambridge University Press, 1998), pp. 33–51.

PRIMARY SOURCE READINGS

1996 DEMOCRATIC NATIONAL PLATFORM
August 27, 1996

Today's Democratic Party is determined to renew America's most basic bargain: Opportunity to every American, and responsibility from every American. And today's Democratic Party is determined to reawaken the great sense of American community.

OPPORTUNITY

For 220 years, America has been defined by a single ideal: Opportunity for all who take the responsibility to seize it. . . .

Today's Democratic Party knows that the private sector is the engine of economic growth, and we fought to put America's economic house in order so private business could prosper. We worked to tap the full potential of a new global economy through open and fair trade. We fought to invest in the American people so they would have the capacity to meet the demands of the new economy. And we have invested in the roads, bridges, and highways that are the lifelines of American commerce.

Education. Today's Democratic Party knows that education is the key to opportunity. In the new global economy, it is more important than ever before. Today, education is the fault line that separates those who will prosper from those who cannot.

Economic security for American families in the 21st century. In the old economy, most workers could count on one job for life. They knew that hard work was rewarded with raises and steady jobs; they were confident the company would take care of them, their families, their health, and their retirement. . . . In the new economy, the rules have changed. We need to find new ways to help working families find economic security: better training to help workers learn skills to get new and better jobs; the security of good health care and safe pensions so they can take care of themselves and their families.

RESPONSIBILITY

Government's job should be to give people the tools they need to make the most of their own lives. Americans must take the responsibility to use them, to build good lives for themselves and their families. Personal responsibility is the most powerful force we have to meet our challenges and shape the future we want for ourselves, for our children, and for America.

Fighting crime. Today's Democratic Party believes the first responsibility of government is law and order.

Immigration. Democrats remember that we are a nation of immigrants. We recognize the extraordinary contribution of immigrants to America throughout our history. We welcome legal immigrants to America. We support a legal immigration policy that is pro-family, pro-work, pro-responsibility, and pro-citizenship, and we deplore those who blame immigrants for economic and social problems.

Welfare reform. Today's Democratic Party knows there is no greater gap between mainstream American values and modern American government than our failed welfare system. When Bill Clinton became President, the welfare system undermined the very values—work, family, and personal responsibility—that it should promote. The welfare system should reflect those values: we want to help people who want to help themselves and their children.

Choice. The Democratic Party stands behind the right of every woman to choose, consistent with *Roe v. Wade*, and regardless of ability to pay. . . . We believe it is a fundamental constitutional liberty that individual Americans—not government—can best take responsibility for making the most difficult and intensely personal decisions regarding reproduction.

Reinventing government. The mission of today's Democratic Party is to expand opportunity, not bureaucracy. We have worked hard over the last four years to rein in big government, slash burdensome regulations, eliminate wasteful programs, and shift problem-solving out of Washington and back to people and communities who understand their situations best.

SECURITY, FREEDOM, AND PEACE

The firm, sustained use of American might and diplomacy helped win the greatest victory for freedom in this half of the century—the end of the Cold War. But to meet the challenges of this new era of promise and peril, America needed leadership that was able to see the contours of the new world—and willing to act with steadiness, strength, and flexibility in the face of change to make the most of it. . . .

Strengthening our security. The highest imperative for our security is the protection of our people, our territory, and our key interests abroad. While both parties share a commitment to strong security, there is a real difference. The Republican desire to spend more money on defense than the Pentagon requests cannot obscure their inability to recognize the challenges of a new era and build the balanced defenses we need to meet them.

Promoting peace and democracy. Today's Democratic Party knows that peace and democracy are products of decisive strength and active diplomacy. That diplomacy must protect our interests while also projecting our values. The Republican Party too often has neglected diplomatic opportunities, slashed the budgets necessary for diplomatic successes, and overlooked the importance to our own security of democracy and human rights abroad. At its core, the Republican Party is locked in a Cold War mentality, and lacks a coherent strategy to nurture and strengthen the global progress toward peace and democracy.

COMMUNITY

Across America, in far too many places, the bonds of community that tie us together and remind us that we rise or fall together, have too often frayed.

Today's Democratic Party believes we must reawaken the strong sense of community that has helped America to prosper for 220 years. America is uniquely suited to lead the world into the 21st century because of our great diversity and our shared values. We must never let our differences divide us from each other; instead we must come together on a new common ground, based on the enduring values we share. . . .

Putting families first. The first and most sacred responsibility of every parent is to cherish our children and strengthen our families. The family is the foundation of American life. We support the fundamental themes of the Families First Agenda—promoting paycheck, health care, retirement, and personal security; creating greater educational and economic opportunity; and requiring greater responsibility from individuals, businesses, and government.

Protecting our environment. Today's Democratic Party wants all Americans to be able to enjoy America's magnificent natural heritage—and we want our people to know that the air they breathe is pure, the water they drink is clean, and the land they live on is safe from hazard. We understand we have a sacred obligation to protect God's earth and preserve our quality of life for our children and our children's children.

The American community. Today's Democratic Party knows that when America is divided we will likely fail, but when America is united we will always prevail. Americans will always have differences, and when we reach across those differences, we are stronger for it. And we share an abiding set of values that define us as Americans. Our task is to draw strength from both—from our great diversity and our constant values—to fashion the future we want for our children.

Fighting discrimination and protecting civil rights. Today's Democratic Party knows we must renew our efforts to stamp out discrimination and hatred of every kind, wherever and whenever we see it.

Religious freedom. Today's Democratic Party understands that all Americans have a right to express their faith. The Constitution prohibits the state establishment of religion, and it protects the free exercise of religion.

Responsibility to our community and our country. Today's Democratic Party believes every American has a duty and a responsibility to give something back to their community and their country.

We applaud the American spirit of voluntarism and charity. As we balance the budget, we must work even harder in our own lives to live up to the duties we owe one another. We must shrink the government, but we cannot shrink from our challenges. We believe every school and college in America should make service a part of its basic ethic, and we want to expand national service by helping communities give scholarships to high school students for community service. We challenge Americans in all walks of life to make a new commitment to taking responsibility for themselves, their families, their communities, and their country.

If we do our job, we will make the next American century as great as each one that has come before it. We will enter the 21st century with the American Dream alive for all, with America still the world's strongest force for peace and freedom, and with the American community coming together, enriched by our diversity and stronger than ever.

America's best days lie ahead, as we renew our historic pledge to uphold and advance the promise of America—One nation, under God, indivisible, with liberty and justice for all.

1996 REPUBLICAN PLATFORM
Adopted August 12, 1996

This is what we want for America: real prosperity that reaches beyond the stock market to every family, small business and worker. An economy expanding as fast as American enterprise and creativity will carry it, free from unnecessary taxes, regulation and litigation.

This is what we want for America: the restoration of self-government by breaking Washington's monopoly on power. The American people want their country back. We will help them to regain it.

This too we want for America: moral clarity in our culture and ethical leadership in the White House. We offer America, not a harsh moralism, but our sincere conviction that the values we hold in our hearts determine the success of our lives and the shape of our society. It matters greatly that our leaders reflect and communicate those values, not undermine or mock them.

The diversity of our nation is reflected in this platform. We ask for the support and participation of all who substantially share our agenda. In one way or another, every Republican is a dissenter. At the same time, we are not morally indifferent. In this, as in many things, Lincoln is our model. At a time of great crisis, he spoke both words of healing and words of conviction. We do likewise, not for the peace of a political party, but because we citizens are bound together in a great enterprise for our children's future. . . .

None of the extraordinary things about our country are gifts of government. They are the accomplishments of free people in a free society. They are achievements, not entitlements—and are sweeter for that fact. They result when men and women live in obedience to their conscience, not to the state. All our efforts as Republicans are guided by the fixed star of this single principle: that freedom always exceeds our highest expectations.

PRINCIPLES OF THE 1996 REPUBLICAN PLATFORM
Because the American Dream fulfills the promise of liberty, we believe it should be attainable by all through more and secure jobs, home ownership, personal security, and education that meets the challenges of the century ahead.

Because a dynamic and growing economy is the best way to create more and better paying jobs, with greater security in the work place, we believe in lower taxes within a simpler tax system, in tandem with fair and open trade and a balanced federal budget.

Because wasteful government spending and over-regulation, fueled by higher taxes, are the greatest obstacles to job creation and economic growth, we believe in a Balanced Budget Amendment to the Constitution and a common-sense approach to government rules and red tape.

Because we recognize our obligation to foster hope and opportunity for those unable to care for themselves, we believe in welfare reform that eliminates waste, fraud and abuse; requires work from those who are capable; limits time on public assistance; discourages illegitimacy; and reduces the burden on the taxpayers.

Because all Americans have the right to be safe in their homes, on their streets, and in their communities, we believe in tough law enforcement, especially against juvenile crime and the drug traffic, with stiff penalties, no loopholes, and judges who respect the rights of law-abiding Americans.

Because institutions like the family are the backbone of a healthy society, we believe government must support the rights of the family; and recognizing within our own ranks different approaches toward our common goal, we reaffirm respect for the sanctity of human life.

Because our children need and are entitled to the best education in the world, we believe in parental involvement and family choice in schooling, teacher authority and accountability, more control to local school boards, and emphasis upon the basics of learning in safe classrooms.

Because older Americans have built our past and direct us, in wisdom and experience, toward the future, we believe we must meet our nation's commitments to them by preserving and protecting Medicare and Social Security.

Because a good society rests on an ethical foundation, we believe families, communities, and religious institutions can best teach the American values of honesty, responsibility, hard work, compassion, and mutual respect.

Because our country's greatest strength is its people, not its government, we believe today's government is too large and intrusive and does too many things the people could do better for themselves.

Because we trust our fellow Americans, rather than centralized government, we believe the people, acting through their State and local elected officials, should have control over programs like education and welfare—thereby pushing power away from official Washington and returning it to the people in their communities and states.

Because we view the careful development of our country's natural resources as stewardship of creation, we believe property rights must be honored in our efforts to restore, protect, and enhance the environment for the generations to come.

Because we are all one America, we oppose discrimination. We believe in the equality of all people before the law and that individuals should be judged by their ability rather than their race, creed, or disability.

Because this is a difficult and dangerous world, we believe that peace can be assured only through strength, that a strong national defense is necessary to protect America at home and secure its interests abroad, and that we must restore leadership and character to the presidency as the best way to restore America's leadership and credibility throughout the world. . . .

The sole source of equal opportunity for all is equality before the law. Therefore, we oppose discrimination based on sex, race, age, creed, or national origin and will vigorously enforce anti-discrimination statutes. We reject the distortion of those laws to cover sexual preference, and we endorse the Defense of Marriage Act to prevent states from being forced to recognize same-sex unions. Because we believe rights inhere in individuals, not in groups, we will attain our nation's goal of equal rights without quotas or other forms of preferential treatment. . . .

The unborn child has a fundamental individual right to life which cannot be infringed. We support a human life amendment to the Constitution and we endorse legislation to make clear that the Fourteenth Amendment's protections apply to unborn children. Our purpose is to have legislative and judicial protection of that right against those who perform abortions. We oppose using public revenues for abortion and will not fund organizations which advocate it. We support the appointment of judges who respect traditional family values and the sanctity of innocent human life. . . .

We defend the constitutional right to keep and bear arms. We will promote training in the safe usage of firearms, especially in programs for women and the elderly. . . .

As a nation of immigrants, we welcome those who follow our laws and come to our land to seek a better life. New Americans strengthen our economy, enrich our culture, and defend the nation in war and in peace. At the same time, we are determined to reform the system by which we welcome them to the American family. We must set immigration at manageable levels, balance the competing goals of uniting families of our citizens and admitting specially talented persons, and end asylum abuses through expedited exclusion of false claimants. . . .

America's ethnic diversity within a shared national culture is one of our country's greatest strengths. While we benefit from our differences, we must also strengthen the ties that bind us to one another. Foremost among those is the flag. Its deliberate desecration is not "free speech," but an assault against our history and our hopes. We support a constitutional amendment that will restore to the people, through their elected representatives, their right to safeguard Old Glory.

English, our common language, provides a shared foundation which has allowed people from every corner of the world to come together to build the American nation. The use of English is indispensable to all who wish to participate fully in our society and realize the American dream.

THE GOAL IS FREEDOM

The bravery, skill, and sacrifice of America's fighting forces; the dedication, industry, and ingenuity of the American people; the superiority of U.S. technology; and the abundance of America's wealth and resources are sufficient to overcome any foreign threat or challenge. But these gifts are cause for gratitude and humility, not complacency. And these national treasures can be used to safeguard the nation effectively in a time of volatile change only if genuine leadership, wisdom, discernment, courage, and honor are present in the Commander-in-Chief and in the officials he or she appoints to critical national security posts. With such a president at the helm, America will know a new birth of freedom, security, and prosperity. And this nation, and the benefits it has bestowed upon mankind throughout our history, shall not perish from the earth.

INTEREST GROUPS, CONFLICT, AND POWER

OBJECTIVES

❑ To understand why the United States has so many interest groups and so many different kinds of interest groups

❑ To understand the roles interest groups play and the factors that motivate people to form groups

❑ To examine the ways by which interest groups seek to influence policymaking and what these methods reveal about the workings of the American political system

❑ To address the practical and philosophical questions posed by the power of interest groups in American democracy

During the 1992 presidential campaign, voters responded enthusiastically to Bill Clinton's promise to overhaul the nation's health care system. The United States, unlike other economically advanced nations, does not guarantee its citizens access to health care, and in 1992 approximately 37 million Americans, most of them working people, lacked health insurance. Many who had insurance worried that the added expense of covering a major illness could bankrupt them financially.[1]

For over 50 years American presidents had tried unsuccessfully to ensure universal access to health care, but with Clinton's election the goal seemed on the verge of reality. In 1993 the Democratic party controlled both the presidency and Congress, and congressional Democrats were eager to support the new president. For his part, Clinton stressed the importance of health care reform by appointing his wife, Hillary Rodham Clinton, to head a special task force that would devise legislation to present to Congress later that year.[2]

Public opinion polls showed strong general support for Clinton's proposal to guarantee access to private health care when he proposed the outlines of his plan in a televised speech to Congress and the nation on September 22, 1993. Moreover, corporate executives and labor union leaders saw health care reform as a way to cut costs and still provide affordable health insurance to their workers. For state and local government officials, the plan promised affordable care for the elderly, poor, and disabled. Reforming health care was going to be a big, complex, and difficult achievement, but the political conditions for major change seemed right.[3]

A year later, in a stunning political turnabout, Clinton's health care reform effort was dead. One reason for this outcome was that conservatives, most of them Republicans, were opposed to *any* governmental role in the private health care system, so they opposed Clinton's proposal from the beginning. Many Republicans, including some who hoped to win the presidency in 1996, also did not want to give Clinton a

Winning hearts and minds on health care. In 1993–94, interest groups opposed to President Clinton's health care reform plan mounted a media campaign to convince Americans that the plan would impose government control over health care, limit their choice of doctors, and raise their costs. The campaign worked.

victory on health care reform.[4] Their opposition posed tremendous problems for Democrats, who did not have a big enough majority in either house of Congress to withstand defections among party members if the reform effort got bogged down.

In this regard, health care reform failed because Clinton could not maintain the high levels of public support necessary to overcome the determined opposition of some of the nation's most powerful organized interest groups. Many of the nation's doctors, represented by the American Medical Association (AMA), feared that Clinton's plan would undermine their independence and reduce their incomes. Older Americans, led by the 30-million-member American Association of Retired Persons (AARP), initially supported Clinton's plan, but their enthusiasm softened as many worried that the plan might disrupt their ability to choose their own doctors or would force them to pay more for health insurance.

Most important, Clinton ran up against stiff resistance from elements of the business community that resisted any requirement that they provide health insurance for their employees. Two organized groups were especially influential. One was the National Federation of Independent Businesses (NFIB), which represented some 600,000 small businesses. Small business owners, ranging from restaurateurs to software designers, are usually staunch opponents of government regulation of any kind. In this instance they were joined by the nation's big insurance companies, represented by the Health Insurance Association of America (HIAA), which saw Clinton's plan as a threat to the private health insurance industry. Although the two groups often disagree over issues such as the costs of insurance to small businesses, they nevertheless joined forces in opposing Clinton's plan. Together, they launched an expensive national media campaign that attacked the plan as a "government takeover" of the health care system that would reduce the quality of care and take away citizens' freedom to choose their own doctors.

These attacks were a bit misleading insofar as Clinton's plan called for guaranteed access to *private* health insurance, not for a government-owned health care system. Moreover, most people who already had private insurance did not have an unlimited choice of doctors to begin with. But the anti-reform campaign sowed seeds of doubt among Americans who were already confused by the complexity of a health care reform proposal that ran to over 1,300 pages.[5] Clinton's reform effort lost momentum through 1994 as growing public uncertainty unsettled Democrats facing tough campaigns in the 1994 congressional elections.[6] It finally died after the November elections, in which Republicans gained control of both chambers of Congress for the first time in 40 years—a result that was partly due to public anger over the failure of Congress to pass health care reform!

For many, the lesson from this case is that organized and well-funded interest groups can stop even a proposal that is promoted by the president and supported, at least in general, by the people. If politics is a process of trying to turn conflict into compromise, these groups made it especially hard for Clinton to put together a workable coalition of support. Like every president, Clinton found it almost impossible to make major policy changes when enough people begin to think the flawed present is preferable to some unknown future.

TWO VIEWS OF INTEREST GROUPS

First, a definition. For our purposes an **interest group** is defined as a collection of people who (1) share some kind of goal or trait, be it financial, occupational, social, or otherwise; and (2) organize themselves to make some specific claim on society or government to fulfill this goal. In short, it is an organized group that uses the political process for some purpose.[7]

Using this logic we can distinguish between an interest group and one that has a purely social, cultural, or athletic purpose. By itself, a group of in-line skaters is not an interest group. However, if the skaters organize themselves to seek city funds to build a new skating area, we consider the organization an interest group.

Thus, any group that organizes to make claims through or upon the institutions of government becomes an interest group, also referred to as a *pressure group*, *special interest*, or *lobby*. The latter term is a variation on **lobbyist**, an interest group representative who seeks to influence (or "lobby") legislators in the halls of Congress or state capitols.

No one who studies American politics disputes the fact it involves interest groups. What is in dispute is whether such groups are essential for or a danger to democracy.

THE OPTIMISTIC VIEW

As the case of health care reform suggests, the role of interest groups in American politics poses a dilemma. According to one view, the ability of citizens to organize themselves to promote shared values or goals is proof that the political system allows yet another way for Americans to shape public policy. In theory, interest groups provide for effective representation of diverse societal views, especially those that are not represented by the major political parties in the process of coalition building that precedes elections (see chapter 6). Strong and watchful interest groups also keep government on its toes, thus helping to prevent abuses of government power. In doing so, interest groups help to maintain democratic accountability.

The optimistic view was best stated by the French aristocrat Alexis de Tocqueville, who visited the young nation in the 1830s and observed, "As soon as several inhabitants of the United States have taken up an opinion or a feeling which they wish to promote in the world, they look for mutual assistance; and . . . they combine."[8] Tocqueville saw this tendency to "combine" as a healthy sign that Americans were not content to be passive subjects of a king; instead, they were active participants in a democracy.

To political scientist Robert Dahl, American politics is best characterized by constant bargaining and compromise among many organized groups, each representing different parts of the society. Dahl and others who take this position, known as **pluralism,** argue that competition and conflict among groups is not only natural in a democracy but it is good for it. Such conflict ensures that many views will be heard and, more important, that no one group will be able to hold total power.[9] In the pluralist view, health care reform failed because groups that were intensely opposed to Clinton's plan won the debate. In the pluralist view, this is the way that democracy works.

THE PESSIMISTIC VIEW

The contrary view is that there is something troubling about the ability of well-organized and well-funded groups to stop important legislation that is supported both by elected officials and by the public. Health care reform promised to help millions of working Americans who either had no health insurance or who feared losing what benefits they already had. Their views seemed to be drowned out by the capacity of organizations such as the NFIB to mobilize their more affluent members, buy expensive television ads, and donate campaign funds to key members of Congress. From the pessimistic viewpoint, interest groups undermine democracy.

As we saw in chapter 6, James Madison admitted that "faction" was inevitable in a free society. Like Tocqueville, he knew that people would naturally "combine" to form competing factions. Conflict between factions also is normal. However, Madison feared that the tendency toward factions might undermine representative government. Each faction, be it of farmers, bankers, Protestants, war veterans, or foes of alcohol, would try to win at the expense of the others. Any "common good" would be swamped by a flood of competing private demands, the most powerful of which would dominate the political system.

What could be done to prevent this from happening? As Madison knew, it was impossible to prevent the creation of factions without also destroying citizens' civil rights and liberties. Citizens had the rights to speak their minds, to organize themselves, and to petition government for the redress of their grievances. So as we saw in chapter 2, the framers created a republican form of government that they hoped would make it harder for any faction or group of factions to control government. In one of Madison's more memorable phrases, the system was designed to "cure" the "mischiefs of faction."[10]

Those sharing Madison's concerns about "faction" might look at the demise of Clinton's health care plan and conclude that interest groups are too powerful. As two journalists who observed the health care battle lamented, groups such as the National Federation of Independent Businesses "have become crypto-political parties of their own—unelected and unaccountable."[11] In other words, interest groups can achieve their goals without going before the voters for judgment. This absence of democratic accountability raises profound questions about who has power in America. After all, who elected the NFIB or the AMA? What gives these "intense minorities" the right to decide what is good for all Americans?

In chapter 6 we asked whether democracy can be understood without political parties. Here we ask, are interest groups good for democracy? As with parties (those other "factions"), there is nothing in the Constitution about interest groups. Yet, as with parties, American democracy cannot be understood without them. The issue that is still unclear is the degree to which our politics *should* be influenced by groups and their demands.

INTEREST GROUPS IN AMERICAN SOCIETY

How many interest groups are there? It is impossible to say. For example, roughly 4,000 *political action committees*, groups designated solely to contribute funds to political campaigns (discussed later), are officially registered with the Federal Elections Commission, but this category is a small part of the overall picture.[12] According to another estimate, in the early 1990s there were more than 69,000 people in Washington, D.C., alone employed as lobbyists or by firms that engaged in lobbying.[13] But even this figure understates the actual number of organized groups that focus in some way on some part of the federal government, as many groups do not employ Washington lobbyists. What is more, beyond the nation's capital, thousands of other groups exist primarily to influence politics at the state and local levels.

So overall there are probably tens of thousands of organized groups, differing in size, membership, levels of organization, resources, and activity (see Table 7.1). Some are small and represent relatively minor interests—maybe only a single business—whereas others are massive national organizations with huge staffs, hundreds of thousands of members, and million-dollar budgets. Name any issue, and there is certainly at least one group that is organized to focus on it.

WHY ARE THERE SO MANY GROUPS?

The United States stands out for the sheer number of interest groups and their roles in making public policy. Why are there so many groups? Some reasons lie in

TABLE 7.1. ASSORTED INTEREST GROUPS

Group	Year Founded	Membership	Annual Budget
American Civil Liberties Union	1920	275,000	$14,000,000
American Physical Therapy Association	1921	72,000	25,000,000
American Turkish Council	1992	200	700,000
Association of Medical Illustrators	1945	1,000	400,000
Christian Coalition	1989	2,000,000	20,000,000
Fellowship of Christian Peace Officers	1971	4,100	225,000
Fund for Animals	1967	200,000	2,400,000
League of Women Voters	1920	110,000	3,500,000
Mothers against Drunk Driving	1980	3,200,000	53,000,000
National Federation of Independent Businesses	1943	600,000	65,000,000
National Organization for the Reform of Marijuana Laws	1970	80,000	400,000
National Rifle Association	1871	2,800,000	66,000,000
National Associate for Black Veterans	1970	25,000	350,000
National Audubon Society	1905	575,000	47,000,000
Common Cause	1970	250,000	10,000,000
Veterans of Foreign Wars	1899	2,100,000	24,000,000

Sources: *Public Interest Profiles, 1998–99* (Washington, D.C.: Foundation for Public Affairs, CQ Press, 1998); *Encyclopedia of Associations*, 33d ed. (Detroit, MI: Gayle Publishing, 1998).

human nature, whereas others are linked to the unique structure of the American political system.

The Group Basis of Society   Humans are social animals. As individuals, we seek out others who share our traits, values, needs, or interests. Farmers socialize with other farmers; college students with a passion for games such as "Dungeons and Dragons" or "Risk" spend huge amounts of time with one another; Jehovah's Witnesses or Hassidic Jews build their lives around a shared community of faith; new immigrants form "social clubs" with other emigres from their homeland. Given the freedom to form such groups, most people will do so.

An Active Political Culture   Humans may naturally form groups, but they don't necessarily do so to the same extent or in the same way in every society. Political scientists note that although Americans are less likely to vote than are citizens in other political systems (see chapter 6), they are more likely to join groups and engage in forms of direct political activity such as calling up legislators or going to court.[14] These traits are not absolutes, but nevertheless there is evidence that Americans are reluctant to limit their political role to voting and obeying the law.

Societal Complexity   A major reason for the proliferation of groups in American politics is the size and complexity of American society. The smaller and more homogeneous a society, the fewer the differences that divide people into distinct groups. A society in which everybody works on the farm, shares the same ethnic background, speaks the same language, and practices the same religion has fewer lines of conflict. Even the United States was much less complex in the 1830s, when Tocqueville made his observations, than it is today. Today, by contrast, it is immensely diverse, with 270 million people representing innumerable ethnicities, races, religions, occupations, and cultural values. A large, complex, and pluralistic society breeds a large, complex, and pluralistic set of interests.

Economic Change   Societies become more complex over time. The transformation of the United States from a farm economy to an industrial one in the late 19th century brought with it new conflicts between factory owners and workers, suppliers and consumers, and the expanding urban society and the waning rural one. Economic change also created new interests: labor, finance, natural resources, and so on. Today's global economy expands that complexity even more, providing endless potential bases for interest group formation and conflict.

Each change in the structure of the nation's economy also reshuffles the array of interest groups. In the 1870s, for example, the National Grange was a farmers' organization with tens of thousands of members and great political influence in Congress and the states. But farm groups such as the Grange no longer wield the same clout because few Americans work on farms. Today's economy is dominated by computer hardware and software industries, education, manufacturing, and health care, and groups representing various aspects of those economic sectors proliferate. As groups such as the Grange lapse into obscurity, new ones such as the Association of On-Line Professionals emerge.

Effects of Technological Change   New technologies create new interests. Think about the impact of the automobile. Besides leading to the emergence of huge automobile companies and labor unions, the automobile also led to the creation of the American Automobile Association, representing the interests of auto travelers, and trade associations representing highway builders, service stations, car washes, hotels, fast food restaurants, and, before the advent of the multiplex, drive-in theaters. The personal computer has transformed our lives and spawned numerous groups dedicated to virtually every aspect of computing, such as hardware and software, use of computers in schools, and government support for research on new products. The impact of the Internet is potentially huge. An entire world of Internet-based interest groups on virtually any subject or issue already exists, with as-yet-unknown effects on the nation's—and the world's—social and political fabric.

Global Dynamics   The increasingly global scale of trade, travel, culture, and communications, not to mention problems such as ozone depletion, has led to the formation of more globally focused groups, for instance Greenpeace, an environmental organization based in The Netherlands with chapters throughout the world. In fact, a growing development in world politics involves not just relations between nations but relations between national governments and international "nongovern-mental organizations" such as Greenpeace, Amnesty International, FIFA (the inter-national soccer federation), and even the International Dairy Foods Association.[15]

THE ROLE OF THE POLITICAL SYSTEM

Societal complexity by itself does not translate into organized interest groups. It could result in a system of government that represses political freedom. But in the United States, several features of the political system nurture the creation of active interest groups. They include constitutional guarantees, federalism, separation of powers, weak parties, and lower costs of organizing.

Constitutional Guarantees   In theory, First Amendment rights such as freedom of speech and assembly create an implied right to freedom of association that thereby removes most of the legal roadblocks to group formation and participation. Yet throughout American history some groups have been discouraged from forming or banned from a role in politics. For example, at times during the 20th century, avowed communists were forbidden to hold meetings because they were seen as a threat to the nation. Other groups face prosecution because their goals run contrary to law, such as when advocates of legalized marijuana break state and federal laws against use of the drug. However, in general the civil rights embodied in the Bill of Rights put the burden on government to explain why a group should not have the right to exist, organize, and participate in the political system.

Federalism   The structure of government influences how groups emerge, orga-nize, and operate. In this regard, federalism in the United States provides many points of access to government. State governments have authority over vast areas of public policy—for example, education—so citizens do not need to form a big na-tional group when a smaller, more state-focused group will suffice. Many groups are formed solely to deal with local concerns such as preserving a town library or pro-moting local economic development.

Moreover, groups that don't succeed at one level of government may at another. For example, environmentalists seeking tougher antipollution laws have had more success with Congress than with state legislatures, which are often dominated by local economic interests.[16] On the other hand, as we saw in chapter 4, groups op-posed to abortion have had more success in states such as Missouri than at the federal level. In each case the federal system offered groups several points of access.

Separation of Powers   Separation of powers also multiplies points of access. For example, before the 1960s the National Association for the Advancement of Colored People (NAACP) based its strategy on getting the federal courts to overturn state laws promoting racial segregation because the group's leaders knew that state legisla-tures, and even Congress, were unwilling to take on such controversial issues. By contrast, groups that are dissatisfied with a judicial decision may lobby for new legis-lation to overturn it. In 1996 conservative religious groups were able to get Congress to ban federal recognition of marriages between two people of the same sex after the

Going to court. Thurgood Marshall devised the National Association for the Advancement of Colored People's strategy for using lawsuits to break down the barriers of racial segregation. Marshall was later appointed to the Supreme Court by President Lyndon Johnson, and served on the Court until his death in 1993.

Supreme Court of Hawaii had recognized the legality of such unions. The same pattern exists at the state and local levels: The system creates multiple avenues for access, providing more opportunities for more groups to influence public policy.[17]

Weak Parties   Interest groups are more numerous, stronger, and more independent in the United States also because of the relative weakness of its political parties. Unlike in parliamentary systems, American parties do not govern. It thus is irrational for citizens to rely entirely on the parties to promote their views, particularly if they are controversial minorities such as atheists or gays. Moreover, groups try to avoid being linked to a particular party for fear that leaders of the other party will ignore their views. For example, conservative Christian groups may have more in common with Republicans, but they are unlikely to turn their backs entirely on the Democrats. Nor are environmental groups, which tend to support Democrats, eager to alienate Republicans. Separation of powers makes it likelier that neither party will control the government, so citizens hedge their bets by forming groups that operate independent of the party system.

Lower Costs of Organizing   These structural factors lower the "costs" of organizing in the United States. The constitutional system frustrates party control, but it also makes it easier for small groups of citizens to organize and gain access to government. For example, in the late 1970s a band of activists in Niagara Falls, New York, led by a self-described housewife who was worried about the health of her children, effectively used the media and state courts to force state government officials and a major chemical corporation to clean up toxic wastes in their Love Canal neighborhood. In the process, they focused the entire nation's attention on the effects of toxic chemicals on human health. One does not always need a major national organization to bring about change. Sometimes a small but intense group can be very effective.[18]

GOVERNMENTAL ACTION

Interest groups are also created because of the government's actions or policies. Sometimes these effects are inadvertent: Veterans' groups such as the American Legion or the Veterans of Foreign Wars did not exist before the nation was involved in wars on foreign soil. Sometimes the effects are more direct. For example, the local farm organizations that make up the American Farm Bureau Federation were created by the U.S. Department of Agriculture as part of the Smith-Lever Act of 1914, which set up federal agricultural assistance stations throughout the nation.[19] In this case the government itself organized a group of people in order to serve them more effectively.

Such direct intervention is rare. More generally, each time government creates a new program (such as student loans), passes a new law (such as a crime bill), or offers a new benefit (such as Social Security), someone affected by the action will organize to fight for—or against—the continued existence of the program, law, or benefit in question.

For example, the federal government spent billions of dollars over several decades building dams and reservoirs throughout the nation to control floods, provide water for irrigation, and produce electricity. But these waters also turned out to be good habitats for largemouth bass, and bass fishing became a major recreation activity. The Bass Anglers Sportsman Society (or BASS) was eventually formed to promote the sport and to get involved in issues such as maintaining water quality and ensuring federal support for fish hatcheries. It even endorsed George Bush, a BASS member, for president. Today BASS has more than 1 million members.[20] BASS is not the norm in terms of size or influence, but the factors that led to its creation are repeated for all types of issues at all levels of government.

COUNTERMOBILIZATION

Finally, groups beget other groups. That is, when one group mobilizes around an issue, some other group will probably form and mobilize in opposition to the first group. For example, environmental groups that emerged in the early 1970s were opposed by business groups formed in the late 1970s.[21] The National Rifle Association is opposed by Handgun Control, Inc., and the National Right to Life Committee is opposed by the National Abortion Rights Action League. The same condition occurs in almost every policy area: Rarely does a group go unchallenged. In this sense at least, the pluralist view of interest group competition has some validity.

WHAT INTEREST GROUPS DO

What interest groups do is often misunderstood. In fact, they fulfill many of the same functions as do parties (see chapter 6). However, for many citizens an interest group is a more effective way to directly express their views to policymakers. This can best be understood by looking at the general functions groups perform. They include representing citizens, enhancing political participation, monitoring government and other groups, educating citizens, publicizing issues, and influencing public policy.

REPRESENTING CITIZENS

Interest groups are "transmission belts" between citizens and government. However, unlike the major political parties, most groups represent relatively narrow concerns. The American Bankers Association represents only the views of the banking industry. The National Rifle Association was formed in 1871 to fight for what it sees as citizens' inalienable right to bear arms. The National Abortion Rights Action League defends the right to choose to have a legal abortion. The American Bar Association (1878) represents lawyers.

By contrast, political parties exist to win elections. To do so they must reach out to as many voters as possible. But within the parties are a great many constituencies, ranging from wheat growers and veterans to insurance agents and environmentalists, all of whom worry that their needs will get overlooked in the crush of demands competing within a major party. It thus may be better to organize an interest group than to depend on a political party.

In theory, groups also enhance the representation of the previously underrepresented. The NAACP was organized in 1909 to promote the rights of African Americans because neither major party addressed their needs and because so many African Americans were denied their legal right to vote. The Children's Defense Fund, created in 1973, seeks to represent the interests of children, especially poor children, whereas the National Right to Life Committee defends what it sees as the rights of the unborn fetus. In short, the political landscape is full of groups whose purpose is to express the views of those who may not be adequately represented within the party system.

ENHANCING POLITICAL PARTICIPATION

In this respect, as political scientist Jack Walker noted, groups are avenues "outside the conventional political parties and elections through which individual citizens can be mobilized for political action."[22] Groups enable citizens to participate in the political system in more direct and focused ways than is possible through electoral politics. People who despair that their votes won't make a difference, or who do not understand how politics works, nevertheless may join a group that is dedicated to their views.

For example, the AARP reaches out to millions of older Americans on issues such as Social Security and Medicare; in the process, it encourages its members to write to or call their members of Congress and go to the polls on election day. In fact, the AARP's political clout stems from its ability to mobilize millions of elderly voters, a voting bloc that no elected official can ignore. At the other end of the age spectrum are organizations such as Rock the Vote, which tries to mobilize people under age 25—the age group that is least likely to vote. In this regard, it may not be a surprise that interest group membership has grown while voting turnout has declined (see chapter 6). Fewer Americans want to rely exclusively on elections to get their views heard.[23]

MONITORING GOVERNMENT

Interest groups keep an eye on government and publicize its failings and errors. Sometimes it seems as if there is a group monitoring every part of government. For example, the American Taxpayers Union is a conservative group that criticizes what it considers wasteful federal spending. Its liberal counterpart, Common Cause, does the same thing, although the two groups may disagree over how to define "waste." Environmental groups such as the Sierra Club and industry groups such as the American Mining Congress monitor the Bureau of Land Management, which regulates mining on federal lands. Consumer groups such as Public Citizen and industry groups such as the Tobacco Institute monitor the Food and Drug Administration. Likewise, organizations such as the conservative American Family Council and the liberal People for the American Way monitor Congress and the courts on issues such as prayer in the public schools. Ideally, such groups act as the busy citizen's eyes and ears and thereby help keep government honest.

MONITORING OTHER GROUPS

These groups also keep an eye on one another, trying to make sure the others don't get an advantage or become so powerful that no other views are heard. Public health groups keep an eye on the tobacco industry; conservative public interest law groups monitor environmental groups; gun-control advocacy groups such as Handgun Control keep watch on the National Rifle Association, which opposes restrictions on gun ownership. To pluralists, this competition among active and interested groups helps to maintain democracy.

EDUCATING CITIZENS

Groups can perform an educational function. For example, the League of Women Voters provides nonpartisan information about candidates so that citizens can make more informed decisions at the polls. However, most groups are far less neutral, and the information they give out isn't unbiased, or even accurate. Chemical producers

Seeking attention. In 1979, the American Agricultural Movement tried to focus the nation's attention on the financial distress of its farmers by organizing a "tractorcade" to Washington, D.C. The protest was only partially successful, and in the 1980s AAM shifted to more conventional lobbying tactics.

claim that pesticides, when used properly, will not harm wildlife. Environmentalists argue otherwise. Each side produces scientific data to support its view. Smoking cigarettes causes lung cancer, argue public health groups. Not necessarily, argue tobacco companies. And so on. Every issue attracts competing groups that serve up conflicting information to suit their own narrow purposes, usually leaving citizens a bit confused. Even so, in theory everyone benefits from hearing competing views on the issues.

PUBLICIZING ISSUES

Regardless of the quality of their information, groups are useful for getting issues before the public and onto the agenda of government. When the United Mine Workers publicizes a problem of mine safety or an industry group airs its views on the costs of regulation, these groups add to the public discourse.

On some issues the effects are dramatic. In 1989, the Natural Resources Defense Council (NRDC), an environmental organization, used the CBS news program *60 Minutes* to claim that baby food made from apples treated with the pesticide Alar was unsafe to eat. Apple growers complained that NRDC's claims were overblown and simplistic, but the impact was immediate: Sales of baby food containing apples dropped dramatically, and the chemical was soon taken off of the market.[24] In 1996, conservative religious groups rallied at the national level to prohibit reluctant state governments from having to recognize "same-sex" marriages made lawful in other states. Few Americans knew about this issue, and few such marriages had been performed. Even so, the fear that these religious groups could mobilize tens of thousands of voters spurred Congress and President Clinton to approve a law that allowed states to avoid granting legal recognition to the practice.[25]

INFLUENCING PUBLIC POLICY

For interest groups, the purpose of the functions discussed earlier is to influence the direction and content of public policy. As in the example of the religious groups, they may try to publicize an issue until it is addressed by policymakers. As in the case of the opponents of health care reform discussed at the beginning of this chapter, they may work to define an issue in such a way to discourage the enactment of policies. Groups may organize their members to vote for certain candidates, contribute money to election campaigns, create advertising designed to arouse the public, send members to demonstrate at the state capital, sue government agencies in court, or directly lobby legislators on important bills. All these activities seek to shape public policy, and all the other functions of interest groups stem from this single goal.

On the surface, then, interest groups resemble political parties. But they are not the same. Parties seek to win elections, a goal that puts their candidates before the voters and forces the parties to build the largest possible coalition in order to win. Interest groups never come before the voters for judgment. Therein lies the dilemma of interest groups in democratic government.

RECRUITING AND MOBILIZING MEMBERS

There are many good reasons for organizing interest groups, and in the American system there are few barriers to doing so. *Why* any single group actually forms is less clear—why it is successful in attracting members, how it gets its members to participate in political action, or why it has any influence over public policy. Some people never seem to organize or to get their views heard. Others do, to a degree that exceeds their overall proportion of the population. Why some people are organized and others are not tells us a lot about the political system in general.

DISTURBANCES

Groups often emerge as a result of some "disturbance," some crisis or event that affects people adversely.[26] Sometimes the disturbance is sudden, such as when a ghastly murder mobilizes residents to pressure the state legislature to enact the death penalty. At other times the disturbance builds more gradually, eventually causing concerned citizens to form a group to deal with the problem. A good example of how this works was the emergence of ACT-UP, a group of gay activists fighting for more research into a cure for AIDS. This group was not formed until some years after the disease had begun to cut a deadly swath through American society in the mid-1980s.[27]

BOX 7.1.
A LEADER WHO MADE A DIFFERENCE

We Americans are ambivalent about farm workers. On one hand, we need people who are willing to do hours of back-breaking work in the hot sun. On the other hand, we don't want to pay more for farm labor if that means higher prices for our fruits and vegetables. Moreover, most Americans farm workers usually are out of sight and out of mind. Sometimes a media expose—for example, the famous 1960 CBS documentary, *Harvest of Shame*—will expose the conditions under which they work and live, but such attention is usually shortlived.

Farm workers are hard to organize. Most are legal or illegal immigrants who move from region to region with the harvest, picking crops on a price-per-bushel basis. They are generally poor and have little education. Most are noncitizens who speak little if any English. Few are willing to make a fuss about wages or working conditions for fear of losing their jobs. Thus, farm workers have had to rely on charismatic leaders such as Cesar Chavez to promote their cause.

Cesar Chavez was born in Arizona in 1927, the son of poor Mexican immigrants. His family worked as migrant farm workers in the fields throughout California, during which time he attended 37 different public schools. As a young adult he was influenced by the teachings of Catholic priests on social justice and nonviolent protest, and began to read the teachings of St. Francis of Assisi and Mahatma Ghandi. During the 1950s he worked to register farm workers to vote. In 1962, he founded the United Farm Workers in order to organize farm workers so that they could get better wages and working conditions.

This was not an easy task; few farm workers were willing to join a union for fear that they would lose their opportunity to make a living or, worse, get kicked out of the country if they tried to organize. These fears were real inasmuch as growers were strongly anti-union, wielded tremendous political clout at the local and state levels, and fequently resorted to intimidation and outright violence to scare farm workers away from joining a union.

To counter the power of the growers, Chavez and other UFW leaders used nonviolent protest techniques to attract national media attention to the plight of the farm workers. For example, in 1966 Chavez led UFW members on a 340-mile protest march through the California agricultural region to rally farm workers and lobby for state laws to improve working conditions, permit farm workers to organize, and enable them to negotiate binding agreements with growers over improved wages and working conditions.

Chavez also built coalitions with organized labor, religious groups, civil rights organizations, and college student groups to help impose national boycotts on specific crops until the growers agreed to work with the union. The most famous of these actions was the grape boycott of the early 1970s, which eventually led major grape growers to accept union contracts.

→

HISTORICAL PERSPECTIVE

Finally, at moments when he suspected that Americans had grown tired of hearing about farm workers and their needs, Chavez would resort to personal protest by living on nothing but water for weeks at a time. In 1968, he fasted for 25 days; in 1972, for 24 days; in 1988, for 36 days—a fast that almost destroyed his health.

These tactics yielded some successes. Federal and state laws improved farm workers' wages and working conditions to some degree, and at one point in the 1970s the UFW claimed 50,000 dues-paying members. However, success has been hard to maintain in the face of continued opposition by growers as well as the inherent difficulty of keeping Americans focussed on farm workers when so many other issues and groups compete for attention.

Cesar Chavez died on April 23, 1993, just hours after testifying in court against a giant lettuce and vegetable producer that had sued the UFW for millions of dollars in damages over a boycott of its lettuce (the company eventually lost the suit and signed a UFW contract). More than 50,000 people from throughout the world attended his funeral. According to the UFW, he never earned more than $5,000 a year during his lifetime.

A year later, Cesar Chavez was honored posthumously with the Medal of Freedom, the nation's highest civilian honor, which President Bill Clinton presented to his widow in his name.

Source: The United Farm Workers; www.ufw.org.

THE ROLE OF LEADERS

But a disturbance is not a necessary and sufficient condition for a group to exist. As political scientist Robert Salisbury points out, whether any concerned people actually form an organized interest group depends on leaders.[28] History is laden with examples of situations in which energetic and charismatic leaders made a major difference: Cesar Chavez and the United Farm Workers in the 1960s, Marian Wright Edelman and the Children's Defense Fund in the 1970s, and Ralph Reed and the Christian Coalition in the 1990s (see Box 7.1)

The degree to which individual leaders matter to a group's success varies according to the nature of the members and the group's goals. It isn't very difficult to organize bankers, lawyers, and insurance agents, professionals with sufficient resources who are accustomed to working in groups and whose goals rarely threaten dominant social or political values. However, it is a lot more difficult to organize and represent the interests of people such as the homeless, immigrants, and the mentally ill. In these cases individual leaders matter a great deal.

Leaders make a difference. Cesar Chavez organized and led the United Farm Workers for over 30 years, using such tactics as nonviolent civil disobedience, boycotts, and hunger strikes to focus Americans' attention on the wages and working conditions faced by those who pick the crops.

WHY DO PEOPLE JOIN?

Most American adults belong to at least one **voluntary association,** such as a softball league or a church, but a relatively small percentage belongs to groups organized specifically for political purposes, such as the League of Women Voters, the National Federation of Independent Businesses, or the American Conservative Union. Salisbury argues that people join interest groups in exchange for three general types of benefits: material, solidary, and purposive.

Material Benefits   Farmers who join the American Farm Bureau Federation and political scientists who pay dues to the American Political Science Association become members of their respective organizations partly because they receive a **material benefit** from membership. Members of the AFBF enjoy group rates on farm equipment or health insurance, and members of the APSA receive professional journals and discounts on hotel accommodations at conferences. For farmers, the benefits of membership may be substantial, whereas for political scientists they are relatively small, but in both cases membership grants tangible rewards. In general, groups that offer such benefits have an easier time attracting members.

Solidary Benefits   Some groups attract members primarily because of a social or **solidary benefit,** that is, because they offer a sense of belonging or inclusion. People usually join fraternal orders such as the Sons of Italy, the International Order of the Elks, or the Knights of Columbus because they want to be with people like themselves, not because they expect material benefits. Someone who joins the Rotary Club or Kiwanis might also see membership as a good way to make business contacts, but the primary motivation is more social, a desire to belong.

The importance of solidary benefits should not be overlooked. According to political scientist Robert Putnam, belonging to such groups, even if they do not promote openly political goals, helps individuals develop a sense of connection to others, the kind of "civic engagement" that students of politics believe is essential to the maintenance of a healthy democracy.[29] We will return to this theme in chapter 12.

Purposive Benefits   Some groups attract members because of a **purposive benefit,** a cause that members consider worthwhile. Groups that protect the environment, fight for or against legal abortion, seek or oppose equal rights for gays and lesbians, or demand reforms in the political system attract people who join because they believe in the cause, not because they will receive a calendar or totebag if they join.

Most groups offer a mix of benefits. People join the Sierra Club because they want to protect the environment, but the organization finds that it doesn't hurt to give members a magazine and discounts on special field trips. After all, there are many environmental groups competing for members. Senior citizens join the AARP because it defends programs such as Social Security and Medicare, but they also enjoy the the AARP discounts on prescription drugs and life insurance. However, the emphasis isn't always on a material benefit. Groups that pursue a cause, such as People for the Ethical Treatment of Animals, offer members a sense of fellowship, of being part of a community of people who share an ideal.

THE FREE-RIDER PROBLEM

Groups try to enhance their attractiveness to potential members because of what economist Mancur Olson calls the **free-rider problem.** That is, potential members of large groups, such as senior citizens, or groups that pursue goals that benefit the entire society, such as environmental groups, know that they can enjoy any benefits the group might obtain without paying membership dues, investing time or money, or even paying attention.[30] For example, all older Americans, not just members of the AARP, gain if Congress increases Social Security benefits. Everyone enjoys cleaner air, not just members of the Environmental Defense Fund. Even professional groups such as the American Medical Association face this problem. Only about one-half of the nation's doctors are AMA members even though any new law that benefits doctors helps all doctors, not just AMA members, so even groups that represent relatively affluent constituencies must find ways to counteract the normal tendency to seek a free ride.[31]

THE CLASS BIAS IN MOBILIZATION

As you might have gathered by now, people with more education and higher incomes tend to join groups in numbers that are significantly larger than their proportion of the overall population, just as they tend to have higher rates of general participation in politics. By contrast, less-educated and less-affluent people have low overall rates of participation. This connection between socioeconomic status and group membership is not absolute: There are factory workers who belong to labor unions, parent-teacher associations, fraternal organizations, and community improvement associations, just as there are college professors who never join a single group. However, in general, socioeconomic status is a good predictor of rates of group membership.

This imbalance also shows up in the kinds of groups that dominate politics. Groups that represent business interests, professions such as law and medicine, and middle-class economic and social issues outnumber groups that represent the less educated and less affluent. Moreover, these groups have more resources at their disposal, and therefore tend to have an easier time gaining access to and influencing policymakers. The interest group community has a distinct class bias, thus raising questions about how well interest groups reflect the society as a whole.[32]

PUBLIC VERSUS PRIVATE INTEREST GROUPS

Whom do groups represent? Do they represent the broad public, as every group claims, or do they represent only narrow or "special" interests? It is important that we distinguish between **private interest** groups and **public interest** groups.

One way to distinguish between the two types of group is to ask whether membership in or access to a group is restricted in some way—for example, by income, occupation, or some other trait. For instance, one must be a doctor to be a voting member of the American Medical Association. However, one does not need to own a gun to join the National Rifle Association; nor does one have to be a woman to belong to the National Organization for Women. By this line of reasoning, then, the AMA is a private interest and the NRA and NOW are public interests.

However, this distinction is imprecise. Most groups seek as many members as possible. Larger memberships translate into more resources and more clout with policymakers. Even the AARP does not require its members to be retired or even close to retirement age. So it is more useful to look instead at the primary benefits or goals that a group seeks.

PRIVATE INTERESTS

Private interest groups largely seek *exclusive* benefits. That is, the primary benefit goes to members of the group or to the sector of society that the group represents. For example, a trade association representing builders advocates tax breaks for buyers of second homes. It claims that the tax break will benefit the nation's economy by spurring more home building, thus producing jobs for builders, as well as making it easier for people to buy vacation homes. However, the greatest direct benefit goes to the builders. They will make more money. As a result, we consider this trade association a private interest group.[33]

The American Bar Association fits the private interest profile. In most states one must pass a "bar exam" to be permitted to practice law. This exam is administered by the state bar association, which is made up of lawyers. The ABA also decides on standards for law schools. In effect, lawyers regulate the market for lawyers. The ABA insists that bar exams ensure that only qualified people practice law. This may be true, but having the power to regulate the influx of new lawyers also ensures that the legal "market" isn't flooded with too many competitors, which might push down the price of legal assistance and cut into lawyers' incomes. By this standard, the ABA is a private interest. So is a cooperative of wheat growers seeking federal subsidies, a bankers' association seeking regulations to allow banks to charge customers for using automatic transaction machines (ATMs), or an industry group demanding fewer restrictions on the use of jet skis.

PUBLIC INTERESTS

By contrast, public interest groups seek *inclusive* benefits—benefits that can be enjoyed by everyone regardless of income, gender, race, age, or any other characteristic. For example, the National Audubon Society is considered a public interest group because its primary goal, a healthier environment, is inclusive. Whereas only some people can afford a vacation house, even the poor can enjoy the benefits of cleaner air and water. In fact, either everyone benefits from cleaner air—not just members of the Audubon Society—or no one does.

By this standard, the National Rifle Association is a public interest group. Its overriding goal, defending what it views as the constitutional right of Americans to possess firearms, is not divisible. That is, either everyone has the theoretical right to bear arms or nobody does. The National Organization for Women seeks goals that benefit all women, not just its members, and men as well. For example, in 1993 NOW helped gain passage of the federal Family and Medical Leave Act, which requires employers to allow workers of either gender to take unpaid leave to care for a newborn child or a sick parent or spouse without fear of losing their jobs.

Many public interest groups promote liberal causes, largely because conservative voices tend to be well represented by business organizations and by a political culture that favors free markets and a minimal role for government. There are nonetheless a great many well-organized and well-financed public interests groups that promote conservative views and goals.[34] The NRA is an example. "Pro-life" groups are also considered public interest groups because theoretically the whole society is affected if abortion is restricted or banned. The same is true for groups promoting term limits for members of Congress, prayer in the public schools, tax cuts, or a balanced federal budget. Regardless of ideology, as long as the primary benefits they seek go to the whole society, these groups are considered public interests.

We are the NRA. National Rifle Association members examining possible purchases at a gun show. The size and breadth of the NRA's membership, along with deep-seated beliefs in the individual's right to bear arms, enables the group to withstand most efforts to enact tougher gun control laws.

MAJOR TYPES OF PRIVATE INTEREST GROUPS

Tens of thousands of private interest groups dot the landscape of American politics at the local, state, and national levels. Most of these groups are organized around economic goals.

Business Groups   Anything government does affects business, so businesses have always been heavily involved in politics. From early debates over taxes on imported goods (also known as *tariffs*) to more current conflicts over issues such as health care or family leave, the business sector has played an active role in shaping national policy. Organized business interests are strongly represented in Washington and the state capitals—more fully represented, in fact, than any other economic or social interest.

Large corporations such as General Motors usually employ their own lobbyists to work with members of Congress or officials in the executive branch. However, it is common for a business to join a **trade association** that represents an entire sector of the economy, such as the American Bankers Association, the Tobacco Institute, or the National Association of Real Estate Brokers. Several thousand trade associations maintain offices in Washington, D.C., to monitor the activities of Congress, federal agencies, and the courts.[35] Trade associations are also active at the state level.

Businesses are united by beliefs in limited government, free markets, and low taxes, but they often are divided over specific issues.[36] For example, U.S. textile makers support higher tariffs on inexpensive imported clothing to protect their factories and markets; clothing importers and big discount chain stores such as Wal-Mart oppose these tariffs. As noted at the beginning of the chapter, big corporations supported Clinton's health care plan because they saw it as a way to control the costs of the health insurance they provide to employees. However, small businesses opposed health care reform because it would require them to provide health insurance. A policy that helps the trucking industry is likely to meet resistance from the railroads, a direct competitor for the shipping business. Many similar examples could be given.

Even so, businesses set aside their differences when facing a common foe, whether organized labor, new taxes, or government regulations. On such issues American business usually speaks with a unified voice; and when it does, it often gets its way.

Organized Labor   The major labor interest group, the American Federation of Labor-Congress of Industrial Organizations (AFL-CIO), encompasses some 100 separate unions, including auto workers, miners, truck drivers, musicians, steelworkers, teachers, and a variety of local, state, and federal government employees. Like their business counterparts, members of organized labor don't always agree on everything, and competition among unions for members can be fierce. However, also like business, unions band together when facing a common foe.

A little over 16 million men and women currently are members of labor unions, a figure that represents only about 14 percent of the total adult workforce. In 1965, in contrast, union workers made up nearly 25 percent of the workforce.[37] Since then, major economic changes have affected the ability of unions to attract and keep members. Once dominant industries such as automobile manufacturing, mining, or trucking depended on huge labor forces. Bonds of solidarity among workers, the sense of being part of a common purpose, were easier to maintain when all were faced with dangerous conditions and often abusive bosses. Today these industries are not so dominant, and it is more difficult to organize unions of college teachers, doctors, and software designers, occupations that by nature are far more individualistic and in which people tend to see themselves as professionals, not workers.

The rate of unionization is comparatively low in the United States also because of the staunch opposition of businesses and most conservatives, which is reflected in state and federal laws that make it easier for companies to keep out unions. Another important factor is a cultural belief that individuals should be able to control their own economic fate, including having the right *not* to belong to a union. As a result, in major parts of the nation—particularly in the South— it is difficult for unions to organize workers.

Even so, throughout the history of industrial economies, organized labor has played a major role in winning better wages, benefits, and working conditions for a wide range of workers, not just union members. Unions pushed to outlaw child labor and improve workplace safety, and actively supported legislation creating the minimum wage, Social Security, and Medicare. Organized labor usually finds Democrats more responsive on these kinds of issues. On the other hand, union members often are populists (see chapter 5) who are conservative on social issues such as abortion, and will vote for Republicans when those types of issues dominate the debate.

Professional Organizations   Americans today are less likely to be auto workers and more likely to be restaurant managers, teachers, or computer programmers. As a result, some of the greatest growth in interest groups has occurred among professional organizations.

Professional associations, like other private groups, usually confine their activities to issues that directly concern their members. Teachers' associations focus on issues such as teacher accreditation, whereas groups representing accountants worry about issues such as standards and licensing. However, these groups also participate in policy issues that affect their members more broadly. Teachers' associations lobby for more money for education; the American Medical Association tries to protect doctors' incomes by fighting against government-regulated health care; and most professional associations get involved on broad issues such as taxes.

Professional associations are not labor unions. They do not organize workers in order to seek higher wages and better working conditions, nor in most cases do they control access to a profession. Unlike unionized machinists, members of the American Bar Association do not go out on strike. In addition, professionals such as doctors or software designers are usually well paid and accustomed to being independent.

However, in 1999 the AMA decided to create a union in order to address concerns about the ways in which health maintenance organizations limit their doctors' salaries and independence. As more doctors work for large HMOs instead of their own practices, they are subject to the same tensions with management that led other workers to organize into unions. The AMA's support for a union struck some observers as ironic given its staunch opposition to health reform.[38]

Producer Groups   Today little more than 1 percent of all Americans works on farms, yet the almost mythic place of the family farm in American culture gives farmers a special place in the nation's political psyche.[39] Farmers are also important constituents for many members of Congress, so agriculture will always have a voice in government.

Farm groups tend to differ in ideology and economic needs. The largest, the American Farm Bureau Federation, is conservative, has strong relations with Republicans and the business community, and tends to represent large-scale farms and agriculture-related businesses such as farm equipment makers. The smaller National Farmers' Union often sides with Democrats on economic issues and favors a stronger government role in agriculture, particularly with policies that support small "family farms."

There are also numerous groups devoted to commodities such as peanuts, corn, wheat, soybeans, cotton, or pigs. As with other business groups, these specialized producer groups often compete with one another over government policies such as import tariffs. Some, such as chicken producers and corn growers, worry that higher tariffs on imported products will create a backlash from other nations and hurt their own exports. Others, such as those that run "fish farms," may demand that the government protect their markets by raising tariffs on less-expensive imports.

Government Lobbies   Governments also try to influence each other. States, cities, and counties have offices in Washington, D.C., where their representatives work to get federal support for local projects, such as a tax break for a new baseball stadium, to persuade federal agencies to enact regulations favorable to their interests, and to address common issues, such as the problem of unfunded federal mandates discussed in chapter 3. Other groups act as "associations" for various governments; they include the United States Conference of Mayors, the National Governors' Conference, and the National Association of Counties.

Foreign governments also hire professionals to represent them in Washington. For example, the government of Japan has long employed American lawyers and policy experts to advise it on U.S. policies such as air pollution regulations on new automobiles, and it uses public relations firms to promote positive images of Japan among U.S. policymakers and the public. These activities indicate the importance the Japanese place on political and, especially, economic relations with the United States. China has recently followed Japan's lead, reflecting that nation's more assertive efforts to influence American policymaking. Other nations are content to hire a single part-time lobbyist whose job is to watch out for legislation or regulations that might affect that nation.[40] Whatever their form, such efforts by foreign nations and corporations to influence American politics are especially controversial.

TYPES OF PUBLIC INTEREST GROUPS

Public interest groups span a range of issues: consumer protection, government reform, the environment, civil rights and liberties, health care, abortion, and the rights of children, to name just a few examples. As noted earlier, what makes these groups "public interests" are the causes they promote, which, at least in theory, directly benefit the entire society, not just a particular subgroup.

Consumer Protection   Many groups claim to speak on behalf of the vast and unorganized mass of consumers on issues such as product safety and food purity. These groups tend to have a liberal orientation, largely because their agendas by nature bring them into confrontation with business and, to some extent, government regulators.

One of the more famous of these groups is Public Citizen, founded by activist Ralph Nader, whose career began in the 1960s, when he accused General Motors of marketing the Chevrolet Corvair even though it knew the car had serious safety flaws.[41] Today Nader's group works on an array of product safety and health issues. Other groups include the Consumer Federation of America, which focuses on the rights of consumers in areas such as product warranties and business ethics, and the Center for Science in the Public Interest, which criticizes certain food industry practices, such as selling snack foods containing the "fake fat," Olestra.[42]

Government Reform   Many public interest groups focus on broad issues related to government reform. As noted earlier, the League of Women Voters focuses on improving the election system and encouraging people to vote. Other groups are more ideological. Common Cause is a liberal group that works on policy areas such as a "fairer" tax system, and on issues such as public financing of political campaigns and ensuring open meetings in federal agencies. The National Taxpayers Union is a conservative group that promotes tax cuts and less regulation. However, at times its demands, such as requiring Congress to open its committee meetings to the public, may agree with those promoted by Common Cause.

Rights and Liberties   Groups fighting to defend civil rights and liberties have a long history in American politics. The most famous such group is the American Civil Liberties Union, which believes that there are few good reasons for government to interfere with citizens' rights and liberties. The ACLU fights against efforts to make it easier for police to search citizens' homes and cars or, more recently, efforts to restrict the kinds of information available on the Internet. Although it is seen as a liberal organization, the ACLU has defended the right of the Ku Klux Klan, a white supremacist group, to march in the predominantly Jewish town of Skokie, Illinois. On the conservative side is the American Center for Law and Justice, an organization affiliated with Christian evangelical groups that focuses on issues such as abortion, prayer in public schools, and the right of parents to educate their children at home.

Other organizations focus on the rights and liberties of specific groups of people, based on characteristics such as gender, race, sexual orientation, or disability. The NAACP fights to protect the rights and liberties of African Americans; the National Organization for Women has promoted equal rights for women; La Raza represents Latino and Hispanic Americans; the National Alliance of the Mentally Ill defends people whose illnesses often leave them open to discrimination in the workplace. Although such groups may focus primarily on the rights and liberties of their respective constituencies, they can be considered public interest groups insofar as *any* expansion or defense of basic rights and liberties affects all Americans (see chapter 4).

The Environment   In the United States there are thousands of environmental groups, which vary in size, issues, and ideological orientation. Some, such as Mothers of East Los Angeles, are small, have modest resources, and focus on local issues such as pollution in their neighborhoods. By contrast, large national groups such as the Sierra Club, the National Audubon Society, and the National Wildlife Federation, have hundreds of thousands of members, budgets that run into the tens of millions of dollars, and a major presence in national and, increasingly, international politics (see Figure 7.1).

Although there is some ideological diversity among the major environmental groups, their shared concern about the environment makes their differences relatively minor, especially when they are united against adversaries in business and government. Most major national environmental groups also try to avoid being seen as overly partisan, although in recent years they and their members have tended to side with the Democratic party.

Single-Issue Groups   A **single-issue group** focuses exclusively on a single controversial issue. Groups that seek to ban (or defend) abortions, mandate (or oppose) prayer in public schools, and toughen (or weaken) gun control laws usually see their goals in moral terms. For such groups there is only "right" versus "wrong" on these issues, and compromise is far more difficult to achieve. Politicians who take the "wrong" stance on the issue are threatened with dire consequences on election day.

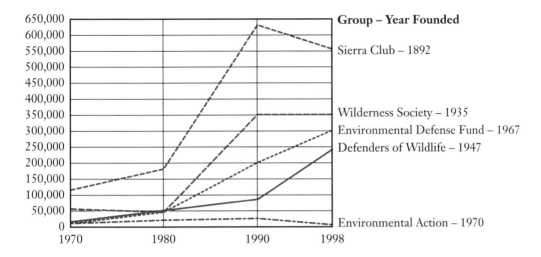

FIGURE 7.1. MEMBERSHIP TRENDS FOR FIVE SELECTED ENVIRONMENTAL GROUPS, 1970–1998

Source: Adapted from Christopher J. Bosso, "Environmental Groups and the New Political Landscape," in Norman J. Vig and Michael E. Kraft, *Environmental Policy in the 1990s*, 4th ed. (Washington, D.C.: CQ Press, 1999), p. 64.

The list of single-issue groups seems endless: For years Term Limits USA sought to limit the terms of office of elected officials; US English wants a constitutional amendment making English the nation's official language; the National Rifle Association stoutly defends gun owners' rights, whereas Handgun Control wants tougher gun laws; the National Abortion Rights Action League wants to preserve a woman's right to obtain a legal abortion, and Operation Rescue uses an array of confrontational tactics to try to shut down abortion clinics.

Single-issue groups often have a disproportionate influence on policymaking because the other side is not as well organized or intense. Operation Rescue may not represent the majority view of the American people on abortion, but its actions have succeeded in forcing clinics to close and doctors to stop performing abortions. Such groups demonstrate that an active and intense minority can hold its own against an unfocussed and unorganized majority.

INTEREST GROUPS AND POLICYMAKING

In the United States it seems that no piece of legislation, bureaucratic regulation, or judicial decision occurs without some input by or pressure from interest groups. Maybe it is no surprise that political scientist Jeffrey Berry calls the United States "the interest group society."[43]

In this regard, groups use a range of tactics to gain access to and influence policy-makers. Most of these tactics are obvious, even mundane, but some are subtle and surprising. In this section we look at interest group tactics and the factors that can affect their success or failure.

FACTORS IN INTEREST GROUP INFLUENCE

The ability to affect public policy is not spread equally among groups. Among the factors that affect interest group influence are membership, resources, leadership, and goals.

Membership   Whom a group's members are, how many belong, and where they live all affect a group's influence. For example, the American Association of Retired Persons is large (more than 30 million members); its members are intense about the group's goals (protecting Social Security and Medicare); and they are spread through so many states and congressional districts that few members of Congress can afford to ignore them.

The same can be said for the National Rifle Association, which is renowned for its ability to get its more than 2 million members to vote against candidates who favor gun control.[44] In 1994 the NRA claimed credit for helping to defeat several Democratic members of Congress who supported the 1993 Brady Law, which imposed a waiting period and background checks for gun purchasers in order to keep guns out of the hands of convicted felons and the mentally ill. These defeats enabled Republicans to take control of both houses of Congress for the first time since 1954. How much credit the NRA should get for the 1994 election results is a matter of debate, but the election's outcome reinforced the message that the organization cannot be ignored.

But even the NRA loses battles. In 1993 it could not counteract President Clinton's ability to rally public support for enacting the Brady Law in the first place. In 1999, it barely evaded tougher restrictions on sales at gun shows in the wake of the shootings at Columbine High School in Littleton, Colorado, in which two teenagers killed twelve classmates and a teacher with weapons that had been purchased for them, by another teenager, at a gun show. The Senate passed the restrictions only after several Senate Republicans who opposed the measure changed their minds, apparently because of public anger over the Littleton shootings. The NRA was able to mobilize its members and weaken the restrictions in the House; however, Representative Tom Tancredo, a Republican from Littleton who was elected in 1998 with the support of the NRA, voted for tougher restrictions.[45]

In contrast to senior citizens and gun owners, poor people rarely organize. When they do, they don't necessarily have the same commonality of interests that unite senior citizens or gun owners. Poor people often are divided by such factors as race, ethnicity, and religion. They are either clustered in urban areas in which they are represented by relatively few members of Congress, or so dispersed throughout rural areas that they almost disappear from view.

College students also have little political influence. They rarely speak with one voice, and like the poor, they are divided by a great many other factors. Students also are transient, tend not to vote, and generally have many demands on their time and energy. Unlike the elderly, students rarely connect government action with their own livelihoods. It comes as no surprise that politicians who would not dare touch Medicare have far less difficulty cutting student aid.

Resources   Putting aside the money given to campaigns (discussed later), groups that can afford professional lobbyists, technical experts, and public relations firms, not to mention television and newspaper advertisements, enjoy greater access to policymakers and the public than do groups with fewer resources. For example, the tobacco industry has few members but usually outspends its public interest group opponents. However, as the tobacco industry knows, money alone does not buy respect or success. Its past efforts to deny any link between smoking and cancer, along with the decline in cigarette smoking among Americans, has weakened (but not eliminated) the industry's political influence.[46]

Leadership   Effective leaders matter, regardless of the type of group. Good leaders understand the needs and values of members, have a vision of where the group should go, and can communicate effectively with policymakers. Leadership is particularly important for groups whose members are attracted to a cause. In the 1970s, for example, conservative activist Phyllis Schlafly organized the forces that eventually prevented ratification of the Equal Rights Amendment to the Constitution.[47] Sarah Brady, whose husband James was left disabled after a 1981 assassination attempt on President Ronald Reagan, was instrumental in the passage of the 1993 Brady Law, discussed earlier. Individual leaders are critical to a group's success or failure.

Goals   Groups whose goals resonate within American political culture have a far easier time than those whose goals conflict with core societal values. For example, groups espousing communist ideals have rarely connected among Americans because of strong cultural beliefs in free markets and private property (see chapter 5). Yet social values are not unchangeable: In the 1920s, tens of thousands of average Americans belonged to the Ku Klux Klan. Today the Klan is a rather small group that exists on the fringe of mainstream public values. Gays and lesbians, by contrast, enjoy far greater general social acceptance than they did in the 1960s, though not among all Americans and not in all parts of the country.

TECHNIQUES OF INFLUENCE

The classic image of interest group influence is a high-priced lawyer chasing a hapless legislator in the hallways (or "lobby") of the capitol. So plentiful were such lobbyists during the battle over the Tax Reform Act of 1986 that people on Capitol Hill took to calling the hallway outside a key committee room "Gucci Gulch," after the expensive Italian-made shoes worn by many lobbyists.[48] But lobbying takes on many forms, some of which are much less direct than pursuing lawmakers in the halls of Congress.

Direct Lobbying   Our image of lobbying is usually confined to personal encounters between professional lobbyists and legislators. The term also applies when professors give expert testimony before a congressional committee, when members of a group talk with legislative staff, or when a group's lawyers meet with bureaucrats to devise a new regulation. Lobbyists can be former legislators, who are valued because they have expertise on the issues and tend to have access to their former colleagues. Today, however, they are more likely to be professionals with expertise in the technical specifications of issues such as pollution control technologies or weapons systems, or lawyers versed in the legal aspects of, say, federal regulations on cable television.

Image aside, a good lobbyist is not someone who only slaps backs and plays golf. An effective lobbyist knows the issues, understands policymakers' needs and views, and is able to compromise when necessary. Good lobbyists also don't just ask for favors; they help sympathetic legislators obtain useful information, work with friendly staff on strategies for getting legislation passed (or defeated), build coalitions with other groups, and even help draft legislation. In the best case, an effective lobbyist helps policymakers do their jobs.

Less Direct Methods   Relatively little lobbying involves personal meetings between paid lobbyists and policymakers. Journalist William Greider looks at the activities of one major corporation—General Electric—to come up with a vastly more complex and interesting picture of effective lobbying in his book *Who Will Tell the People? The Betrayal of American Democracy*.[49]

General Electric naturally employs a large number of "Washington representatives" (lobbyists), and its affiliated political action committee (discussed later) gave over $500,000 to candidates for Congress in 1998 alone.[50] But GE influences policymaking in less obvious ways. Its tax exempt foundations give money to colleges and secondary schools for "educational" programs that stress values such as free markets and private property; it supports friendly and influential "think tanks" such as the American Enterprise Institute; it sponsors the "McLaughlin Group," a weekly television "debate" among well-known journalists; it belongs to many business associations and forms temporary coalitions with other companies on important issues; and it engages in "image advertising"—more than $25 million a year during the 1980s—for products such as jet engines, which no consumer can buy. These ads are aimed at decision makers.[51]

GE also has tens of thousands of employees and enters into contracts with firms that employ thousands more. It has major manufacturing facilities spread throughout the nation, whole towns depend on its economic health, and their residents are likely to vote for the candidates it supports. GE also owns NBC, a major television network, and therefore can have some influence on the mass media. Thus, General Electric can rely on the support of thousands—perhaps even millions—of people whose lives in some ways depend on its getting new government contracts or making sure that public policies do not hurt the company.

Grassroots Lobbying   An increasingly important kind of indirect lobbying involves getting citizens to contact decision makers themselves. As in the case of GE, all interest groups try to "educate" the public through advertising, mass mailings, press releases, or, especially if money is a problem, public relations stunts designed to attract media attention to an issue or cause.[52] For example, the environmental group

Greenpeace is known for its widely publicized nonviolent protests, such as sailing its boats into restricted waters to stop French nuclear weapons tests or draping banners on smokestacks to protest air pollution.[53] Such actions can affect public opinion, generate new members and financial support, and, as a result, influence public policymakers.

Lawsuits   Groups frequently bring lawsuits in federal and state courts. Often the courts are avenues of last resort, the place to go when a group cannot gain access to or influence other policymakers, especially Congress. Although many such actions pertain to relatively narrow interests—such as when two trade associations go to court over a copyright issue—at other times they have major national impact. As we discussed in chapter 4, one of the most famous examples was the suit brought by the NAACP against the school board of Topeka, Kansas, over the issue of racially segregated schools, which led to the landmark Supreme Court decision in *Brown v. Board of Education* (1954).

Working with Regulators   It is common to find close ties between administrative agencies and their interest group "clients," as they often have similar needs and interests. In such instances the relationships among regulators, interest group representatives, and key members of Congress is said to form an **iron triangle.**[54] For example, the airline industry, the Federal Aviation Administration, and congressional committees that oversee aviation often collaborate to ensure that air travel is safe; farm groups, the Department of Agriculture, and members of Congress from farming areas all want a healthy farm economy; labor unions have strong ties to the Department of Labor as well as to members of Congress from regions with large labor union memberships. In Box 7.2 we look more closely at what we might call the tobacco iron triangle.

Such cozy relationships are not universally the case. Timber industry groups, for example, often fight with the Bureau of Land Management over allowing more logging in national forests, and there usually is little love lost between environmental groups and the Department of Energy, which historically has promoted nuclear power. However, these groups have good working relationships with policymakers in other parts of the federal government.

Influencing Elections   Groups try to affect the outcomes of elections. Federal law allows only political action committees (discussed in the next section) to make direct contributions to campaigns, but any group can provide voters with "educational materials" that compare the records of opposing candidates and mobilize its own members to get to the polls. In 1994, for example, the Christian Coalition distributed 33 million "voter guides" through some 60,000 affiliated evangelical churches throughout the nation. Coalition leaders credited the guides, which rated local candidates for Congress on controversial issues such as abortion and prayer in public schools, with helping to elect dozens of new conservative (mostly Republican) members of Congress.[55] As was discussed earlier, that lesson was not lost on Congress and President Clinton when the Coalition pressed to prohibit federal recognition of same-sex marriages.

BOX 7.2.
INTEREST GROUPS AND THE TOBACCO IRON TRIANGLE

The common image of lobbying is of interest groups putting pressure on policy-makers. However, the relationship between interest groups, members of Congress, and officials in executive branch agencies is often far more cooperative, with those involved sharing a concern about a specific policy or problem. These partners also try to keep others who may not share their views from participating in decision-making.

Political scientists have used the term *iron triangle* to portray such a three-sided relationship among interest groups, members of Congress, and federal bureaucrats. The "iron" refers to the strength of that relationship—and to its rigidity when confronted by external threats.

A good example is tobacco, a crop that has been such an important part of the nation's economy that sculpted tobacco leaves adorn the columns of the U.S. Capitol. In 1998, America's smokers purchased 470 *billion* cigarettes. Although this level of consumption was down from a high of 640 billion cigarettes in 1981, the industry still enjoyed over $50 billion in sales, much of it in exports to other countries. Sales taxes on cigarettes also produce revenue for the federal and state governments; in 1997, cigarette smokers paid $5.6 billion in federal sales taxes alone.

For much of the 20th-century members of the congressional committees on agriculture (see chapter 8) and officials in the U.S. Department of Agriculture (USDA; see chapter 10) worked with representatives of the tobacco industry to improve tobacco crops and to support the production and sale of tobacco products. This relationship began in the 1930s, when the federal government established programs to support struggling farmers and promote sales of their crops. Thereafter, growers and tobacco companies worked with members of Congress from tobacco-growing states to maintain these programs, and with the USDA to promote tobacco as a crop.

INTEREST GROUPS AND MONEY

An especially troubling issue is whether interest group money has a corrosive effect on democratic processes and outcomes. As is obvious by now, money buys television ads, endows university programs, mobilizes high-visibility reactions to proposed laws, pays for lobbyists, and of course, helps finance election campaigns. Groups without money have a more difficult time doing any of these things. Whether money guarantees success is a more complicated matter. Often it does not, as the tobacco in-

A CLOSER LOOK

All involved shared a need for a healthy tobacco industry. Tobacco is a legal product that employs thousands of people throughout the nation. Members of Congress from tobacco states represent constituents whose livelihoods depend on the crop, so they are already sympathetic to the industry. Of course, tobacco companies and growers help to seal this relationship with political support for and campaign donations to their friends (to be discussed further in Box 8.2, p. 354). For its part, the job of the USDA is to promote American agriculture; tobacco is just another crop.

Yet, use of tobacco poses serious health risks. This fact increasingly threatened the once-cozy world of tobacco, and by the 1950s the industry began to better organize itself in order to respond to the growing public debate. The tobacco companies created the Tobacco Institute, which became the industry's lobbyist and public relations arm, and the Tobacco Industry Research Committee to support research that would dispel concerns of a link between cigarette smoking and lung cancer. This research cost the industry more than $60 million over the next 30 years.

Today, the promoters of tobacco no longer control the debate over smoking. Now they compete with groups, such as the American Cancer Society, American Heart Association, and American Lung Association, organized around health concerns as well as newer activist groups such as Stop Teenage Abuse of Tobacco (STAT) and Groups Against Smoking Pollution (GASP). These organizations work with members of Congress who are less sympathetic to the tobacco industry and with parts of the federal bureaucracy, such as the Food and Drug Administration, that are responsible for promoting consumer health, not the sale of a product.

However, if the tobacco iron triangle no longer reigns supreme, it still wields considerable influence in state governments and in Congress, as we will discuss in Box 8.2.

Sources: Richard McGowan, *Business, Politics, and Cigarettes: Multiple Levels, Multiple Agendas* (Westport, CT: Quorum Books, 1995); A. Lee Fritschler and James M. Hoefler, *Smoking and Politics: Policy Making and the Federal Bureaucracy*, 5th ed. (Upper Saddle River, NJ: Prentice Hall, 1996).

dustry knows. Still, for interest groups, just as for college students, having money is generally better than the alternative.

CAMPAIGN DONATIONS: WHO GIVES, WHO GETS

Direct contributions by interest groups to political campaigns are especially controversial, largely because candidates depend on donations to help them keep up with the skyrocketing costs of running for office.

Early Money Is Like Yeast. Former journalist Linda Ellerbee addresses attendees at a fund-raising event for EMILY's List, a political action committee that provides female candidates (mostly Democrats) with early financial support. Such donations make it easier for candidates to raise other funds, which makes them more competitive.

Political Action Committees   An interest group that contributes funds to election campaigns must do so through an affiliated **political action committee** (or PAC), a legal entity set up by the group for the purpose of making campaign contributions. Most of the thousands of PACs in existence are created by industries such as tobacco or automobiles, or by professionals such as lawyers, doctors, or real estate brokers. However, PACs are also used by labor unions, single-issue groups, and even some public interest groups. For example, the Sierra Club uses its own PAC to contribute money to "pro-environmental" candidates. The Sierra Club PAC is legally separate from the Sierra Club, which as a nonprofit group is prohibited by federal law from contributing money directly to campaigns.

Federal law currently allows a political action committee to donate up to $5,000 for each primary and general election for any particular candidate for Congress or the presidency, although the average donation is more like $250. Still, the total amount of PAC money that flows directly into campaigns is impressive: PACs contributed $220 million to candidates for Congress in 1998 alone, or roughly 26 percent of total contributions.[56] Table 7.2 shows the top 20 PACs in terms of overall spending on the 1998 congressional elections.

Who Receives the Money?   As we will see in chapter 8, most PAC money goes to incumbent members of Congress. PACs, like individuals, also support candidates who already favor the group's views. Labor union PACs tend to support Democrats, who usually support organized labor, whereas the National Rifle Association's PAC is likely to support conservatives, mostly Republicans, who oppose gun control. Not surprisingly, the more ideological a PAC is, the more it exclusively supports "true believers."[57]

By comparison, businesses such as GE and professional groups such as the American Medical Association are more pragmatic in their decisions and play it safe by

TABLE 7.2.   TOP 25 POLITICAL ACTION COMMITTEES IN OVERALL
             SPENDING, 1997-1998*

Name	Amount (in millions)
EMILY'S List—*supports women candidates, mostly Democrats*	$13.8
Teamsters Union PAC—*labor, supports Democrats*	8.1
National Rifle Association—*supports mostly Republicans*	8.0
Campaign America, Inc.—*affiliated with 2000 Republican presidential candidate Dan Quayle*	6.7
Campaign for Working Families—*affiliated with 2000 Republican presidential candidate Gary Bauer*	6.6
Association of Trial Lawyers of America—*professional association, supports Democrats*	6.0
New Republican Majority Fund—*affiliated with Senate Republican Leader Trent Lott (R.-LA)*	5.9
National Education Association—*professional association, mostly supports Democrats*	5.2
American Medical Association—*professional association, mostly supports Republicans*	4.9
International Brotherhood of Electrical Workers—*labor, mostly supports Democrats*	4.4
Campaign for a New American Century—*affiliated with 2000 Republican presidential candidate Lamar Alexander*	4.2
Leadership '98—*affiliated with 2000 Democratic candidate Albert Gore, Jr.; supports Democrats*	3.9
Machinists Union—*labor, mostly supports Democrats*	3.7
United Auto Workers—*labor, mostly supports Democrats*	3.5
American Federation of Teachers, AFL-CIO—*teachers union, mostly supports Democrats*	3.4
Black America's PAC—*affiliated with Rep. J.C. Watts (R.-OK), donates to Republican candidates*	3.3
GOPAC—*donates largely to Republican candidates*	3.3
National Automobile Dealers Association—*business association, mostly supports Republicans*	3.1
American Federation of State, County, and Municipal Employees—*labor, mostly supports Democrats*	3.0
National Association of Realtors—*business association, supports candidates from both parties*	2.8
United Transportation Union—*labor, mostly supports Democrats*	2.8
Spirit of America—*supports Republican candidates*	2.7
United Food and Commercial Workers—*labor, mostly supports Democrats*	2.7
United Parcel Service—*corporate, supports candidates from both parties*	2.6

* Where appropriate, the name indicates the organization, union, or company with which the PAC is affliated. They are legally separate entities. Spending includes direct contributions to candidates as well as independent expenditures such as issue-related advertising, get-out-the-vote efforts, and other issue education purposes. Figures are rounded, and are for January 1, 1997 through December 30, 1998.

Source: Federal Election Commission; http://www.fec.gov/press/pacdistp.htm. See also FEC Info, Inc.; www.tray.com/fecinfo.

giving to candidates of both parties. However, these groups tend to give more money to incumbents, preferring to stick with someone they already know and can work with rather than to give money to untested challengers. On the other hand, business PACs are not sentimental: If the incumbent loses, the PAC will often turn around and give money to the winner.

What Does the Money Buy?   The less-sinister view is that a PAC donation only gives a group access to a busy politician. The amount that any one PAC can give directly to any one candidate is limited by federal law, and individual PAC donations often account for a small part of a candidate's overall campaign spending. Candidates who accept PAC money may feel obligated to listen to the group that donated the money, but there is no guarantee that the candidate will support the group's goals. Even in this view, however, using donations to buy "access" implies that the door is more open to some than to others.

A less-charitable view is that interest group money corrupts the electoral process and undermines representative government. According to this view, politicians become beholden to interest groups that donate to their campaigns. Although each PAC donation may be rather small, they do add up. As Table 7.3 shows, large amounts of money were donated to congressional campaigns by groups opposed to President Clinton's health care plan, lending some credibility to the view that PAC money "buys" politicians. However, although most members of Congress who received these campaign donations opposed Clinton's plan, it is difficult to prove that this money actually shaped their decisions. Most probably already opposed Clinton's plan or had strong doubts about it.

PAC money also probably doesn't "buy" influence when the issues affect a legislator's constituents. For example, it is no surprise that tobacco companies give most of their campaign funds to members of Congress in whose districts or states tobacco is a major crop. These legislators have constituents whose livelihood depends on the crop, so they already support the industry. PAC money generally goes to friends.[58]

In general, interest group money seems to have less direct impact on major issues about which constituents express strong opinions. For example, campaign donations will not matter in the debate over abortion or the death penalty. On issues in which a legislator or the legislator's constituency has little direct interest, however, PAC money may induce the legislator not to oppose a particular program or law.[59]

What PAC money "buys" thus is a matter of debate. At a minimum, it obligates the recipient to listen when so many voices want to be heard.[60] Money buys access. At worst, the sheer volume of money spent during campaigns, and the importance of interest group money in elections, undermines the legitimacy of representative government.

CONCLUSION

The question we stated at the beginning of the chapter remains: Are interest groups healthy for American democracy or a danger to it? For pluralists, American democracy involves extensive conflict and compromise among interest groups, in the process enabling everyone involved to gain at least something. Pluralists are not so

TABLE 7.3.   EXPENDITURES BY SELECTED HEALTH CARE AND
              INSURANCE COMPANY PACS, 1993-1994*

PAC	Amount
American Medical Association	$3,924,000
National Committee to Preserve Social Security and Medicare	2,209,000
National Association of Life Underwriters	1,891,000
Texas Medical Association	1,567,000
American Academy of Opthalmology	1,404,000
American Dental Association	1,397,000
American Hospital Association	1,354,000
American Chiropractic Association	1,270,000
American Optometric Association	948,000
Florida Medical Association	832,000
Ohio Medical Association	722,000
California Medical Association	711,000
American Council of Life Insurance	694,000
Independent Insurance Agents of America	680,000
American Health Care Association	671,000
Illinois State Medical Society	653,000
Pennsylvania Medical Association	638,000
American Society of Anesthesiologists	627,000
Glaxo Pharmaceuticals PAC	609,000
Podiatry Political Action Committee	554,000
American College of Emergency Physicians	537,000

* Figures rounded.

Source: Federal Election Commission, as tabulated by FEC Info, Inc.; www.tray.com/fecinfo.

naive as to believe that all groups enjoy equal access or influence. Yet they assert that over time there is a good chance that any group that organized would at least get heard.

Nonsense, retort critics such as political scientist Michael Parenti, who argues that the political arena is dominated by the rich and powerful, particularly business groups.[61] Unlike the pluralist view of competing groups, in this view the public has little influence over policy decisions. Looking back at the capacity of powerful groups to stop Clinton's health care plan, it does seem that the activities of interest groups opposed to reform lend credence to Parenti's concerns.

However, the picture is probably more complicated. Interest groups may dream about "owning" Congress or a regulatory agency, but the relationship between them and policymakers is more of a two-way street than the common image suggests. Legislators work with groups to write legislation and mobilize support for its passage. So do presidents. Most groups also lack the resources to get what they want without making compromises with other groups. When compromises cannot be reached, the result can be a stalemate that Congress or the president is unable to break, as was the case with the failure of Clinton's health care plan.

Moreover, even powerful groups lose battles, especially when confronted by an activated majority. Even the NRA struggles when a determined president is able to generate public support for new gun control laws. Regardless of its money, the tobacco lobby can no longer control the debate over smoking. Groups may be able to defend their narrow interests for a long time because the political system tends to give intense minorities an advantage over apathetic majorities, but they cannot necessarily keep a determined majority from achieving its goals.

If groups have too much influence, the challenge for the system is to make it more possible for diffuse majority opinion to translate more directly into public policy. Groups are not to blame for their influence. After all, they are only playing by the rules of the game. Moreover, interest groups were never meant to act on behalf of the entire society or even to seek workable consensus on major political issues. Those roles are played by the institutions of government, particularly Congress.

Remember health care reform? In August, 1996, President Clinton signed into law a bill that put into place a few of the more widely accepted provisions of his failed health care reform plan. The law, a compromise supported by both Republicans and Democrats over the opposition of insurance and business groups, helps people keep their health insurance if they change jobs, and makes it more difficult for insurers to deny coverage because of an existing illness. The law did little for the millions of Americans who still lack health insurance, but as the president acknowledged, it was a step in the right direction.[62]

SUMMARY

▶ Thousands of interest groups dot the landscape of American politics. The number and diversity of these groups reflect the size and complexity of American society and its political system. Other factors contributing to the proliferation of groups include elements of the American political culture, economic change, the design of the political system, the comparative weakness of American political parties, and actions by government.

▶ Interest groups play a variety of roles. Groups represent the views of a set of citizens, organize people to take political action, keep an eye on the actions of government and other groups, educate citizens and policymakers on important issues, provide resources (such as campaign donations) to policymakers, and work to publicize the issues on which they seek action.

▶ Groups do not represent all sectors of society equally. In general, there are far more groups representing the interests of the more educated and affluent than the less educated and less affluent. In this sense, there is a class bias in interest group representation.

▶ It is useful to distinguish between private and public interests. Private interests, which include business groups, labor unions, and professional associations, seek exclusive benefits. Public interests tend to pursue inclusive goals such as consumer protection, government reform, defense of rights and liberties, and environmental protection.

▶ Interest groups use a variety of methods to influence policymaking, ranging from discussions with legislators and mobilizing supporters to write to the president to making campaign contributions and bringing lawsuits in court. How well these methods work depends on a number of factors, including the size and nature of the group's membership, its resources, the quality of its leadership, and, finally, the kinds of goals it seeks.

▶ Interest groups have a controversial role in American politics. On one hand, they are a vibrant part of the bargaining and compromise that characterize the policymaking process. On the other hand, not all groups are represented equally, and some wield power that is far disproportionate to their overall size or the degree to which they represent the average citizen.

QUESTIONS FOR REVIEW AND DISCUSSION

1. What factors distinguish an interest group from groups that have a more purely social, cultural, or recreational focus? Give examples.

2. Why are there so many interest groups in the United States? Discuss the factors that give rise to interest groups.

3. Distinguish between private and public interest groups. Give examples of each kind, and identify the features that define each type.

4. Are interest groups a benefit or a danger to American democracy? Give examples to support your view.

TERMS TO REMEMBER

free-rider problem	political action	purposive benefit
interest group	committee	single-issue group
iron triangle	private interest	solidary benefit
lobbyist	professional association	trade association
material benefit	public interest	voluntary association
pluralism		

WEB SOURCES

Center for Responsive Politics (www.opensecrets.org). A nonpartisan, nonprofit research group that tracks money in politics, and its effect on elections and public policy. A good place for data and analysis on PAC donations.

Federal Election Commission (www.fec.gov). The official source for data on campaign contributions by interest groups, although the information often is in relatively raw form. The site contains data that can be downloaded and covers all federal elections from 1992 onward.

Environmental Web Directory (www.webdirectory.com). An excellent site for finding information on and links to environmental organizations. For a different perspective on environmental issues, see the Alliance for America (www.allianceforamerica.org/mutual.htm), a conservative group that defends property rights.

SUGGESTED READINGS

Jeffrey M. Berry, *The Interest Group Society*, 3d ed. (New York: Longman, 1997); Allan J. Cigler and Burdett A. Loomis, eds., *Interest Group Politics*, 5th ed. (Washington, D.C.: CQ Press, 1998). Two very good sources for understanding the nature of interest group politics in the United States.

Jeffrey H. Birnbaum, *The Lobbyists: How Influence Peddlers Work Their Way in Washington* (New York: Random House, 1992). A journalist looks at the world of the professional Washington lobbyist by following a number of interest group representatives as they try to influence Congress, executive branch officials, and successive presidents on major and minor issues. Birnbaum shows the human side of lobbying, as well as the "revolving door" between government and lobbying as former government employees (members of Congress, bureaucrats, White House staff) become lobbyists—and vice versa.

Jane Mansbridge, *Why We Lost the ERA* (Chicago, IL: University of Chicago Press, 1986). A political scientist examines the failed effort to achieve ratification of the Equal Rights Amendment during the 1970s. Mansbridge shows that although Americans expressed diffuse support for the amendment, its opponents were better organized, able to raise doubts about the amendment's impact on women, and more adept at using the structure of the American constitutional system to their advantage. An excellent case study in how groups organize and engage in politics.

Darrrell M. West and Burdett A. Loomis, *The Sound of Money: How Political Interests Get What They Want* (New York: W. W. Norton, 1998). Two political scientists examine four recent efforts to make major changes in federal policy—Clinton's 1994 health care plan, the Republican effort to change the direction of federal regulation in 1995, telecommunications policy, and Medicare—and look at the roles of interest groups in each of these instances. They find that well-funded interest groups wield tremendous influence, and raise concerns about the viability of representative democracy.

NOTES

1. Haynes Johnson and David Broder, *The System: The American Way of Politics at the Breaking Point* (Boston, MA: Little, Brown, 1996), pp. 61–62.

2. Bob Woodward, *The Agenda: Inside the Clinton White House* (New York: Simon & Schuster, 1994), p. 104.

3. See Theda Skocpol, *Boomerang: Heath Care Reform and the Turn Against Government* (New York: Norton, 1996), pp. 1–8.

4. Johnson and Broder, *The System*, pp. 460–475.

5. *Ibid.*, p. 171.

6. Ken Kollman, *Outside Lobbying: Public Opinion and Interest Group Strategies* (Princeton, NJ: Princeton University Press, 1998), pp. 72–73.

7. Jeffrey M. Berry, *The Interest Group Society*, 3d ed. (New York: Longman, 1997), pp. 4–9.

8. Alexis de Tocqueville, *Democracy in America* (New York: Schocken Books, 1961), p. 216.

9. Robert A. Dahl, *A Preface to Democratic Theory* (Chicago, IL: University of Chicago Press, 1956), p. 145.

10. Alexander Hamilton, James Madison, and John Jay, *The Federalist Papers*, Clinton Rossiter, ed. (New York: New American Library, 1961), p. 77.

11. Johnson and Broder, *The System*, p. 630.

12. Norman J. Ornstein, Thomas E. Mann, and Michael J. Malbin, *Vital Statistics on Congress, 1997–1998* (Washington, D.C.: American Enterprise Institute/CQ Press, 1998), p. 108.

13. Kevin Phillips, *Arrogant Capital: Washington, Wall Street, and the Frustration of American Politics* (Boston, MA: Little, Brown, 1994), p. 34.

14. Gabriel Almond and Sidney Verba, *The Civic Culture: Political Attitudes and Democracy in Five Nations* (Princeton, NJ: Princeton University Press, 1963).

15. James Rosenau, *Turbulence in World Politics: A Theory of Change and Continuity* (Princeton, NJ: Princeton University Press, 1990).

16. James Lester, "A New Federalism? Environmental Policy in the States," in Norman J. Vig and Michael E. Kraft, eds., *Environmental Policy in the 1990s*, 2d ed. (Washington, D.C.: CQ Press, 1994), pp. 51–68.

17. See Frank R. Baumgartner and Bryan D. Jones, *Agendas and Instability in American Politics* (Chicago, IL: University of Chicago Press, 1993).

18. Adeline G. Levine, *Love Canal: Science, Politics, and People* (Lexington, MA: Lexington Books, 1982).

19. Christiana Campbell, *The Farm Bureau and the New Deal* (Urbana, IL: University of Illinois Press, 1962), p. 5.

20. Burdett A. Loomis and Allan J. Cigler, "The Changing Nature of Interest Group Politics," in Allan J. Cigler and Burdett A. Loomis, eds., *Interest Group Politics*, 5th ed. (Washington, D.C.: CQ Press, 1998), pp. 14–17.

21. David A. Vogel, *Fluctuating Fortunes: The Political Power of Business in America* (New York: Basic Books, 1989).

22. Jack L. Walker Jr., *Mobilizing Interest Groups in America: Patrons, Professions, and Social Movements* (Ann Arbor, MI: University of Michigan Press, 1991), p. vii.

23. Richard Brody, "The Puzzle of Participation in America," in Anthony King, ed., *The New American Political System* (Washington, D.C.: The American Enterprise Institute, 1979), p. 316.

24. Keith Schneider, "Fears of Pesticides Threaten American Way of Farming," *New York Times*, May 1, 1989, p. A14.

25. *Congressional Quarterly Weekly Report*, vol. 54, no. 28 (July 16, 1996), p. 1976.

26. David B. Truman, *The Governmental Process: Political Interests and Public Opinion* (New York: Knopf, 1951).

27. Randy Shilts, *And the Band Played On: Politics, People, and the AIDS Epidemic* (New York: St. Martin's Press, 1987).

28. Robert Salisbury, "An Exchange Theory of Interest Groups," *Midwest Journal of Political Science*, vol. 13 (February 1969), pp. 1–32.

29. Robert D. Putnam, "Bowling Alone: America's Declining Social Capital," *Journal of Democracy*, vol. 6, no. 1 (January 1996).

30. Mancur Olson, *The Logic of Collective Action: Public Goods and the Theory of Groups* (Cambridge, MA: Harvard University Press, 1965).

31. Steven Greenhouse, "AMA's Delegates Decide to Create Union of Doctors," *New York Times*, June 24, 1999, p. A1.

32. E. E. Schattschneider, *The Semi-Sovereign People: A Realist's View of Democracy in America* (Hinsdale, IL: Dryden Press, 1960), p. 20.

33. Schattschneider, *The Semi-Sovereign People*, pp. 22–26.

34. Kay Lehman Schlozman and John T. Tierney, *Organized Interests and American Democracy* (New York: Harper & Row, 1986), pp. 28–29.

35. *The Encyclopedia of Associations* (Detroit, MI: Gayle Research, Inc., 1998).

36. Raymond A. Bauer, Ithiel de Sola Pool, and Lewis Anthony Dexter, *American Business and Public Policy* (New York: Atherton, 1968).

37. *Statistical Abstract of the United States* (Washington, D.C.: General Printing Office, 1998), p. 444; *Vital Statistics on American Politics* (Washington, D.C.: CQ Press, 1994), p. 176.

38. Greenhouse, "AMA's Delegates Decide to Create Union of Doctors," p. A1.

39. Ann Schneider and Helen Ingram, "The Social Construction of Target Populations: Implications for Politics and Policy," *American Political Science Review*, vol. 87, no. 2 (June 1993), pp. 334–347.

40. Ronald J. Hrebenar and Clive S. Thomas, "The Japanese Lobby in Washington: How Different Is It?" in Allan J. Cigler and Burdett A. Loomis, eds., *Interest Group Politics*, 4th ed. (Washington, D.C.: CQ Press, 1995), pp. 349–368.

41. Ralph Nader, *Unsafe at Any Speed* (New York: Bantam Books, 1965).

42. Marian Burros, "Food Heroes or Zealots?" *New York Times*, May 29, 1996, p. C1.

43. Jeffrey Berry, *The Interest Group Society*, p. xi.

44. *Public Interest Profiles, 1992–1993* (Washington, D.C.: CQ Press, 1994), p. 174.

45. Frank Bruni, "Reversing Stance, Republicans Urge a Gun-Sale Curb," *New York Times*, May 14, 1999, p. A1; James Brooke, "Congressman from Littleton Explains Vote for Gun Control," *New York Times*, June 21, 1999, p. A10.

46. See A. Lee Fritschler and James M. Hoefler, *Smoking and Politics: Policy Making and the Federal Bureaucracy*, 5th ed. (Upper Saddle River, NJ: Prentice Hall, 1996).

47. Jane Mansbridge, *Why We Lost the ERA* (Chicago, IL: University of Chicago Press, 1986).

48. Jeffrey Birnbaum and Alan Murray, *Showdown at Gucci Gulch: Lawmakers, Lobbyists, and the Unlikely Triumph of Tax Reform* (New York: Random House, 1987).

49. Willliam B. Greider, *Who Will Tell the People? The Betrayal of American Democracy* (New York: Simon & Schuster, 1992), p. 338–340.

50. Press Release, "FED Releases 18-Month Summary on Political Action Committees," U.S. Federal Election Commission, September 24, 1998; http://www.fec.gov/press/pac1898.htm.

51. Greider, *Who Will Tell the People?* p. 338–340.

52. See Kollman, *Outside Lobbying*.

53. Christopher Manes, *Green Rage: Radical Environmentalism and the Unmaking of Civilization* (Boston, MA: Little, Brown, 1990).

54. See Randall B. Ripley and Grace A. Franklin, *Congress, the Bureaucracy, and Public Policy*, 4th ed. (Chicago, IL: Dorsey Press, 1987).

55. Christopher J. Farley, "Prodding Voters to the Right," *Time*, vol. 144, no. 23 (November 21, 1994), p. 62.

56. Press Release, "FEC Reports on Congressional Fundraising for 1997–98," U.S. Federal Election Commission, April 28, 1999, http://www.fec.gov/press/canye98.htm

57. M. Margaret Conway, "PACs in the Political Process," in Allan Cigler and Burdett Loomis, eds., *Interest Group Politics*, 3d ed. (Washington, D.C.: CQ Press, 1991), pp. 199–216.

58. A. Lee Frischler and James M. Hoefler, *Smoking and Politics: Policy Making and the Federal Bureaucracy*, 5th ed. (Upper Saddle River, NJ: Prentice Hall, 1996), pp. 95–97.

59. Diana M. Evans, "PAC Contributions and Roll-Call Voting: Conditional Power," in Allan Cigler and Burdett Loomis, eds., *Interest Group Politics*, 2d ed. (Washington, D.C.: CQ Press, 1986), pp. 114–132.

60. Dan Clawson, Alan Neustadtl, and Denise Scott, *Money Talks: Corporate PACs and Political Influence* (New York: Basic Books, 1992), pp. 53–87.

61. Michael Parenti, *Democracy for the Few*, 6th ed. (New York: Prentice Hall, 1995).

62. Todd S. Purdum, "Clinton Signs Bill to Give Portability in Insurance," *New York Times*, August 22, 1996, p. B12.

PRIMARY SOURCE READINGS

DWIGHT D. EISENHOWER
"Farewell Address," January 17, 1961

Dwight D. Eisenhower (1890–1969) was the Supreme Commander of Allied forces in Europe during World War II and served two terms as president (1953–1961). In his last televised address as president, "Ike" sounded an uncharacteristically somber warning to Americans about what he termed the "military-industrial complex." Coming as it did from a former general, this warning has resonated among Americans ever since.

My fellow Americans: This evening I come to you with a message of leave-taking and farewell, and to share a few final thoughts with you, my countrymen. . . .

We now stand ten years past the midpoint of a century that has witnessed four major wars among great nations. Three of these involved our own country. Despite these holocausts, America is today the strongest, the most influential, and most productive nation in the world. Understandably proud of this prominence, we yet realize that America's leadership depends, not merely upon our unmatched material progress, riches and military strength, but on how we use our power in the interests of world peace and human betterment. . . .

A vital element in keeping the peace is our military establishment. Our arms must be mighty, ready for instant action, so that no potential aggressor may be tempted to risk his own destruction.

Our military organization today bears little relation to that known by any of my predecessors in peacetime, or indeed by the fighting men of World War II or Korea.

Until the latest of our world conflicts, the United States had no armaments industry. American makers of plowshares could, with time and as required, make swords as well. But now we can no longer risk emergency improvisation of national defense; we have been compelled to create a permanent armaments industry of vast proportions. Added to this, three and a half million men and women are directly engaged in the defense establishment. We annually spend on military security more than the net income of all United States corporations.

This conjunction of an immense military establishment and a large arms industry is new in the American experience. The total influence—economic, political, even spiritual—is felt in every city, every Statehouse, every office of the Federal Government. We recognize the imperative need for this development. Yet we must fail to comprehend its grave implications. Our toil, resources and livelihood are all involved: so is the very structure of our society.

In the councils of government, we must guard against the acquisition of unwarranted influence, whether sought or unsought, by the military-industrial complex. The potential for the disastrous rise of displaced power exists and will persist.

We must never let the weight of this combination endanger our liberties or democratic processes. We should take nothing for granted. Only an alert and knowledgeable citizenry can compel the proper meshing of a huge industrial and military machinery of defense with our peaceful methods and goals, so that security and liberty may prosper together.

Akin to, and largely responsible for, the sweeping changes in our industrial-military posture has been the technological revolution during recent decades.

In this revolution, research has become central, it also becomes more formalized, complex, and costly. A steadily increasing share is conducted for, by or at the direction of the Federal Government.

Today, the solitary inventor, tinkering in his shop, has been overshadowed by task forces of scientists in laboratories and testing fields. In the same fashion, the free university, historically the fountainhead of free ideas and scientific discovery, has experienced a revolution in the conduct of research. Partly because of the huge costs involved, a government contract becomes virtually a substitute for intellectual curiosity. For every old blackboard there are now hundreds of electronic computers.

The prospect of domination of the nation's scholars by Federal employment, project allocations, and the power of money is ever present—and is gravely to be regarded.

Yet, in holding scientific research and discovery in respect as we should, we must also be alert to the equal and opposite danger that public policy could itself become the captive of a scientific-technological elite. . . .

Another factor in maintaining balance involves the element of time. As we peer into society's future, we—you and I, and our government—must avoid the impulse to live only for today, plundering, for our own ease and convenience, the precious resources of tomorrow. We cannot mortgage the material assets of our grandchildren without asking the loss also of their political and spiritual heritage. We want democracy to survive for all generations to come, not to become the insolvent phantom of tomorrow. . . .

You and I—my fellow citizens—need to be strong in our faith that all nations, under God, will reach the goal of peace with justice. May we be ever unswerving in devotion to principle, confident but humble with power, diligent in pursuit of the nation's great goals.

JAMES MADISON
Federalist No. 10, The Union as a Safeguard against Domestic Faction and Insurrection
From the New York Packet, *Friday, November 23, 1787*

To the People of the State of New York:

AMONG the numerous advantages promised by a well-constructed Union, none deserves to be more accurately developed than its tendency to break and control the violence of faction. The friend of popular governments never finds himself so much alarmed for their character and fate, as when he contemplates their propensity to this dangerous vice. He will not fail, therefore, to set a due value on any plan which, without violating the principles to which he is attached, provides a proper cure for it. . . .

By a faction, I understand a number of citizens, whether amounting to a majority or a minority of the whole, who are united and actuated by some common impulse of passion, or of interest, adversed to the rights of other citizens, or to the permanent and aggregate interests of the community.

There are two methods of curing the mischiefs of faction: the one, by removing its causes; the other, by controlling its effects. . . .

It could never be more truly said than of the first remedy, that it was worse than the disease. Liberty is to faction what air is to fire, an aliment without which it instantly expires. But it could not be less folly to abolish liberty, which is essential to political life, because it nourishes faction, than it would be to wish the annihilation of air, which is essential to animal life, because it imparts to fire its destructive agency. . . .

The latent causes of faction are thus sown in the nature of man; and we see them everywhere brought into different degrees of activity, according to the different circumstances of civil society. A zeal for different opinions concerning religion, concerning government, and many other points, as well of speculation as of practice; an attachment to different leaders ambitiously contending for pre-eminence and power; or to persons of other descriptions whose fortunes have been interesting to the human passions, have, in turn, divided mankind into parties, inflamed them with mutual animosity, and rendered them much more disposed to vex and oppress each other than to co-operate for their common good. . . . But the most common and durable source of factions has been the various and unequal distribution of property. Those who hold and those who are without property have ever formed distinct interests in society. . . . The regulation of these various and interfering interests forms the principal task of modern legislation, and involves the spirit of party and faction in the necessary and ordinary operations of the government. . . .

The inference to which we are brought is, that the CAUSES of faction cannot be removed, and that relief is only to be sought in the means of controlling its EFFECTS.

If a faction consists of less than a majority, relief is supplied by the republican principle, which enables the majority to defeat its sinister views by regular vote. It may clog the administration, it may convulse the society; but it will be unable to execute and mask its violence under the forms of the Constitution. . . .

The two great points of difference between a democracy and a republic are: first, the delegation of the government, in the latter, to a small number of citizens elected by the rest; secondly, the greater number of citizens, and greater sphere of country, over which the latter may be extended.

The effect of the first difference is, on the one hand, to refine and enlarge the public views, by passing them through the medium of a chosen body of citizens, whose wisdom may best discern the true interest of their country, and whose patriotism and love of justice will be least likely to sacrifice it to temporary or partial considerations. . . . [H]owever small the republic may be, the representatives must be raised to a certain number, in order to guard against the cabals of a few; and that, however large it may be, they must be limited to a certain number, in order to guard against the confusion of a multitude. . . .

The smaller the society, the fewer probably will be the distinct parties and interests composing it; the fewer the distinct parties and interests, the more frequently will a majority be found of the same party; and the smaller the number of individuals composing a majority, and the smaller the compass within which they are placed, the more easily will they concert and execute their plans of oppression. Extend the sphere, and you take in a greater variety of parties and interests; you make it less probable that a majority of the whole will have a common motive to invade the rights of other citizens; or if such a common motive exists, it will be more difficult for all who feel it to discover their own strength, and to act in unison with each other. . . .

The influence of factious leaders may kindle a flame within their particular States, but will be unable to spread a general conflagration through the other States. A religious sect may degenerate into a political faction in a part of the Confederacy; but the variety of sects dispersed over the entire face of it must secure the national councils against any danger from that source. A rage for paper money, for an abolition of debts, for an equal division of property, or for any other improper or wicked project, will be less apt to pervade the whole body of the Union than a particular member of it; in the same proportion as such a malady is more likely to taint a particular county or district, than an entire State.

In the extent and proper structure of the Union, therefore, we behold a republican remedy for the diseases most incident to republican government. . . .

—PUBLIUS

CONGRESS

OBJECTIVES

❑ To understand how conflicting views about the core functions of Congress affect perceptions of its role in American government

❑ To assess the process by which members of Congress are elected and how it shapes the way Congress works

❑ To follow the legislative process from the time a bill is introduced until the time it is—or is not—signed into law by the president

❑ To understand the often rocky relationship between Americans and Congress

President Clinton swears in AmeriCorps members in a White House ceremony. Clinton's plan for a massive national program tying public service to financial support for a college education was pared down by Congress to a more modest program, but for supporters of AmeriCorps it was better than nothing.

During the 1992 presidential election campaign, younger voters were attracted to Bill Clinton's proposal to allow college students to pay off their student loans through some kind of community service. The program, which came to be called AmeriCorps, would also allow students who took meaningful but lower-paying jobs such as social worker or teacher to pay back their loans over time as a percentage of their income.

The idea seemed both practical and noble. It would help ease the burden of college loans, and it would make available a pool of enthusiastic talent to a range of public purposes, such as tutoring poor children. In the process, it might foster a stronger sense of community and citizenship in a time of growing concern about Americans' cynicism toward government. Liberals liked helping students get financial support; some conservatives liked the idea of connecting a benefit (student aid) to some kind of responsibility (service). Colleges liked the idea of allowing students to pay back loans over a longer period. Clinton also made the plan a major priority, ensuring that it would get attention. Luckily for him, in 1993 both houses of Congress were controlled by Democrats eager to help the new president fulfill a popular campaign promise.

So the signs for passage looked good. Yet, AmeriCorps almost didn't happen.[1]

For one thing, a national service program would cost money. With the federal budget deficit at the time running to over $200 billion, many members of Congress were skeptical of any new program. Under a 1990 law designed to reduce the deficit, any proposal that called for new spending required an equal amount in cuts elsewhere in the budget, and making cuts is never pleasant.

Naturally, many interest groups voiced concerns. Veterans' groups complained that the plan gave AmeriCorps volunteers more educational aid than veterans received. Teachers' organizations and labor unions that generally supported Clinton worried that some states and cities might use AmeriCorps workers as cheap labor. Some colleges opposed major changes in the student aid system because it would force them to revise their own procedures. Some critics saw Clinton's call for national service as a campaign gimmick; some regarded it as an unnecessary government intrusion into the student loan marketplace; and many did not want to allow Clinton to score a success in his first year as president.

Clinton got his national service program and the new student loan repayment program, but only after a very close contest on Capitol Hill, and only after a lot of compromises. He had to scale back the scope of the program to make it more acceptable to members of Congress who were concerned about the deficit. He also had to placate veterans' groups, student loan organizations, colleges, and unions. Some compromises designed to get support from individual members of Congress seemed like outright vote buying: One senator even demanded, and received, federal aid for municipal sewer projects in his state as the price for supporting the bill.

AmeriCorps was born on September 21, 1993. It was a smaller program, but it would still cost more than a billion dollars over a five-year period. It would still enable thousands of students to earn money toward college through community service, and allow thousands more to pay back their loans as a percentage of their income. For supporters of AmeriCorps, it was a start.

THE MANY ROLES OF CONGRESS

The birth of AmeriCorps is but one account of how a bill became a law in Congress. Few bills have the same level of presidential attention, but most are complex and require hard choices. Any tale of how a bill becomes a law has its heroes and villains, its moments of generosity as well as selfishness, and of course, occasional moments of silliness. Some members of Congress end up looking noble and public-spirited. Others look petty and small-minded, seeming to care more about their own political needs than about what might be good for the nation. In every such tale, members of Congress end up sounding like regular people.

Because its members are elected directly by the voters, Congress is—in theory—the most important institution in the system of representative government. It is the national government's most open and democratic institution. However, Congress is also our most heavily criticized, ridiculed, and even reviled institution. Its members are often portrayed as dolts, if not thieves and liars, and the institution itself is criticized as slow, fickle, cowardly, and narrowminded, if not corrupt or dangerous to democracy itself. So how can the nation's most open, most democratic, and most representative institution also be its least admired?

This fundamental contradiction in people's views of Congress is no coincidence. Congress is an institution that must pursue several goals at the same time. Any one of these goals is likely to conflict with others. For example, Congress is both a legislative and a representative body. It alone has the authority to make the law, the most important function of any institution of government. Its members also seek to repre-

The U.S. Capitol. To the left, the chamber of the House of Representatives. To the far right, the Senate. At the center, under the great dome sits the Rotunda, the symbolic center of Congress—and of American democracy. Atop the dome is a statue symbolizing Freedom.

sent the people.[2] But to do both Congress must balance competing public demands with the broader interests of the nation. It also must keep an eye on the president, oversee the federal bureaucracy, appropriate funds for national programs, declare war, preserve the nation, and defend the Constitution.

Americans endlessly debate whether Congress is "doing its job," although there doesn't seem to be much agreement about what exactly the "job" entails or how to determine whether Congress is successful at doing it. This disagreement grows out of distinct and inherently incompatible visions about the proper role of the legislature in a democratic political system.[3]

THE CLASSICAL VIEW

The framers of the Constitution believed that Congress should be the most important branch of government. Other branches, particularly the executive branch, were given the means to prevent Congress from becoming too powerful, but they were not meant to be its equal. Congress alone has the constitutional authority to make the law. In a representative government it is important for the legislature to debate the big issues and forge the nation's policies. Allowing presidents or unelected bureaucrats and judges to dominate the process would ignore the status of Congress as the nation's representative body, the voice of the people.

This view is based on the argument that, as the representative body, Congress has a unique link to the ultimate source of democratic authority—the people. Members of Congress represent specific geographic areas—districts for House members and states for senators—and are elected by relatively small local constituencies. In theory, the members of Congress come to Washington from all over the nation knowing which ideas and programs their constituents support and, equally important, which ones they oppose.

Thus, Congress is the arena in which the representatives of the people can argue out their differences on the issues in a peaceful manner and begin to work toward a compromise on which most can agree. In this view, neither speed nor the passage of a large number of laws is important. Congress has the right and duty *not* to pass laws that would provoke disharmony. It is more important to establish a strong and lasting consensus, which in turn will enhance the legitimacy of the system in the eyes of the people.

In this view, the president is a secondary player. The president can recommend legislation, but Congress alone should initiate action. It alone makes the laws. Nor can a president claim to represent the will of the people. The president's constituency is too national, too diffuse, too vast. Only Congress reflects the many different sectors of the society.

The classical view of Congress dominated American politics for more than half of the nation's history. With a few exceptions, 19th-century presidents were secondary figures. Given their fear of monarchy, the framers probably intended this. But presidential activism and power grew immeasurably during the 20th century, parallelling the growth in the size and scope of the federal government and the emergence of the nation as a world power (see chapter 9). This worries those who believe that a strong and effective Congress is essential to democracy.

THE PRESIDENTIAL LEADERSHIP VIEW

To others, Congress is the problem. It is too big. Its members are seen as more concerned about local needs than about those the nation as a whole. Congress, its critics argue, is disorganized, inefficient, and unable to lead a complex nation whose citizens demand effective and responsive government. It may have functioned well in simpler times, but today's world of weapons of mass destruction, a tightly integrated global economy, and rapid change demands strong and stable executive leadership. Only the president is able to lead the nation in carrying out its global responsibilities.

The presidential leadership view holds that the president should have wide latitude in decisionmaking and substantial insulation from legislative "obstruction." In this view, the president *should* take the lead in shaping the nation's priorities and *should* initiate legislation. On foreign policy, the president should be even freer from congressional restraint. An age of constant military preparedness demands strong executive leadership.

The presidential leadership view rests on a concept of representation that sees the president as the steward of the people, the caretaker of the nation's health and future. Only the president is elected by all Americans. Only the president speaks for the general will of the people, not just the local and state interests represented in Congress.[4]

In the presidential leadership view, Congress should play a reactive role; it should be the "consenting power." As with AmeriCorps, Congress should criticize, remake, and even refuse to approve presidential initiatives, but it should not initiate important policies because it is too big, fragmented, and slow to act decisively on major issues. Congress should delegate to the president a great deal of flexibility in administering laws and programs, and should avoid overly scrutinizing executive branch actions. In this view, the nation cannot afford the luxury of government by deliberative assembly. Congress should step aside and let the president lead.

THE PARTY GOVERNMENT VIEW

Still other observers believe that neither the classical nor the presidential leadership view addresses the real problems of contemporary American government. To these critics the constitutional system itself is the problem in the sense that separation of powers, the election system, and checks and balances combine to fragment the will of the people into a large number of separate interests.[5] This system often produces a Congress dominated by one party and a presidency dominated by another, becoming deadlocked in their opposing ideological and partisan views (see Table 8.1). As a result, nothing seems to get done quickly, or at all.

To these critics the constitutional system cannot meet the needs of today's complex world. Ineffective government, in this view, is just as bad as unrepresentative government. Neither Congress nor the president is at fault. The problem lies in the system itself.

Promoters of the party government view believe in the ideal of majority rule. They want Congress to reflect the majority of the people, not narrow constituency interests. They support a "responsible" party system in which the party that wins a majority in Congress actually governs. Under such a system the voters will know who is in charge, and they will know whom to blame if government does not work as the voters intended. Such a government would be responsive to the majority of the people and accountable for its actions.

The party government view calls for a parliamentary system such as can be found in most other representative democracies (see chapter 6). In such a system, true power would reside in the majority party, not in any single institution. The executive branch would be tied directly to Congress, and both would be judged together by the voters. Of course, barring a complete collapse of the current constitutional system, it is unlikely that Americans would support a major change in their form of government.

THE CENTRAL DILEMMA OF CONGRESS

Thus, there are three different conceptions of the role of Congress as an institution. One view makes Congress the most important institution, the second has the president as the leader and primary lawmaker, and the third advocates majority party rule. These are dramatically distinct notions about the distribution of political power and about the purpose of a legislature in a system of representative government.

Regardless of the ideal view one accepts, Congress will always be characterized by multiple responsibilities. Two of the legislature's primary functions—representing local constituencies and making laws for the entire nation—seem to be in constant conflict. This tension between representing and legislating affect the making of public policy; perhaps more important, it defines everything about Congress and influences public perceptions of it.

TABLE 8.1. PARTISAN DIVISION OF THE BRANCHES, 1945-2000

Period	President	Congress
1945–1946	**Democrat**	**Democrat**
1947–1948	Democrat	Republican
1949–1950	**Democrat**	**Democrat**
1951–1952	**Democrat**	**Democrat**
1953–1954	*Republican*	*Republican*
1955–1956	Republican	Democrat
1957–1958	Republican	Democrat
1959–1960	Republican	Democrat
1961–1962	**Democrat**	**Democrat**
1963–1964	**Democrat**	**Democrat**
1965–1966	**Democrat**	**Democrat**
1967–1968	**Democrat**	**Democrat**
1969–1970	Republican	Democrat
1971–1972	Republican	Democrat
1973–1974	Republican	Democrat
1975–1976	Republican	Democrat
1977–1978	**Democrat**	**Democrat**
1979–1980	**Democrat**	**Democrat**
1981–1982	Republican	*Split* (D-House; R-Senate)
1983–1984	Republican	*Split* (D-House; R-Senate)
1985–1986	Republican	*Split* (D-House; R-Senate)
1987–1988	Republican	Democrat
1989–1990	Republican	Democrat
1991–1992	Republican	Democrat
1993–1994	**Democrat**	**Democrat**
1995–1996	Democrat	Republican
1997–1998	Democrat	Republican
1999–2000	Democrat	Republican

REPRESENTATION: BECOMING A MEMBER

Even its defenders admit that Congress is often unable to make quick decisions. Speed, however, is not always the important point. As a representative body, Congress is primarily a deliberative assembly, a forum in which the people's representatives can debate the major issues. As such, who these representatives are, and how they get to Congress, matters a great deal.

THE REPRESENTATIVE SYSTEM

The United States has roughly 270 million people, yet only 535 men and women serve as full members of Congress. At present there are 435 members of the House of Representatives, as well as nonvoting delegates from Guam, Puerto Rico, American Samoa, the District of Columbia (Washington, D.C.), and the American Virgin Islands. There are only 100 senators, two from each state. So opportunities to be a member of Congress are few, and the process of getting elected is rigorous enough to screen out all but the most exceptional (not to mention lucky) candidates.

Congress is a **bicameral,** or two-chamber, **legislature.** As we noted in chapter 2, members of the House of Representatives (the "lower" chamber) serve for two years, and all 435 must seek reelection every second year. House members represent districts whose shape and composition is determined by state legislatures, and the number of districts per state varies according its to overall population (each state is guaranteed at least one House seat). House members have always been elected by popular, or direct, vote, as provided by Article I, Section 2 of the Constitution.

Every state, regardless of its population, has two senators. Senators serve for six years, with the terms staggered so that only one-third of the "upper" chamber comes up for reelection every other year. Until the 20th century, senators were generally chosen by their respective state legislatures, which was meant to guarantee that the interests of the states would be defended against the more populist passions generally found in the House. Since the passage of the Seventeenth Amendment to the Constitution in 1913, senators have been elected by direct vote.

House Districts   Why the House has 435 members is a matter of happenstance. The Constitution originally called for one House member for every 30,000 persons; the size of the House would grow as the nation grew. But the framers never reckoned with the explosive growth of the nation's population in the late 1800s, much of it due to immigration. The size of the House swelled as a result, reaching its current size by 1911. But the House chamber in the U.S. Capitol had become crowded, so the House placed a cap on its size. Without this limit, the House would today have 9,000 members!

Because the size of the House no longer grows as the nation's population increases, it goes through a process every 10 years called **reapportionment** in which it redistributes its 435 seats so that its membership accurately reflects where Americans live (see Figure 8.1). That is, if the center of the nation's population shifts from the Northeast and Midwest to the South and West, as it has since the 1940s, the composition of the House should reflect those changes.

Reapportionment begins with the **census,** which the Constitution requires every 10 years. The Census Bureau, located in the Department of Commerce, counts every single person in the nation. The census thus determines the official size of the nation's population as well as the population of each state. The national population figure determined by the census is then divided by 435—the number of House seats—to calculate the number of people to be represented by each House district. After the 1990 census, this figure was close to 600,000 people per district, a figure that will grow to more than 620,000 people per seat after the 2000 census. The population of

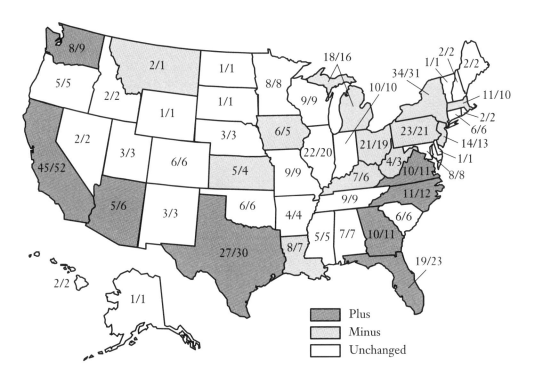

FIGURE 8.1. DISTRIBUTION OF HOUSE SEATS BEFORE AND AFTER THE 1990 CENSUS

each state is divided by this number. The result is the number of House seats allotted to each state. For example, Massachusetts had a population of 6 million after the 1990 census. Dividing this figure by 600,000 gave Massachusetts 10 House seats.

This process of reapportionment is simple enough, but its implications are huge. States that lose population or do not grow much lose House seats—and political power—to states with growing populations. Massachusetts, to return to our example, had 11 House seats after the 1980 census but lost one of those seats after the 1990 census because states such as Texas and California had far greater population growth (see Figure 8.1). Texas and California thus get more House seats at the expense of states such as Massachusetts, New York, and Pennsylvania.

Citizens in states that lose House seats often argue that the census undercounts poorer and less-educated people, the homeless, and recent immigrants, classes of people who never receive a census form, cannot fill it out, or are afraid to respond when census takers come to their doors. By contrast, citizens in states that expect new House seats because of major population growth may not want to make any changes in the process. Republicans representing southern and southwestern states that have gained seats oppose changing the system; Democrats who represent older urban areas where undercounting is more prevalent want to find new ways to ensure an accurate count. Even the seemingly straightforward act of counting people is a political issue.

Redistricting   Once each state has been allotted its number of House seats, it goes through **redistricting.** This process requires the state to redraw existing district lines to match the new number of seats. Redistricting is done by the state legislature, often in conjunction with the governor, although some states appoint special commissions for this purpose.

Because House districts must be equal in population size, even a state that keeps the same number of representatives may have to redraw district lines to match changes in population patterns within the state. This numerical equality among districts was not always so carefully protected. In fact, **malapportionment,** or the deliberate creation of House districts of unequal population sizes, was once common. Until the 1960s, House districts in urban areas often contained far more residents than did districts in rural areas. This occurred because state legislatures were frequently dominated by rural legislators, who often packed urban residents into fewer House districts than the population size merited. As a result, rural interests, particularly those of farmers, had far more political power in the House than they deserved.

Such inequalities in the size of House districts are no longer permitted. In *Wesberry v. Sanders* (1964), the U.S. Supreme Court ruled that such inequalities in district population size undermined the "one person, one vote" doctrine on which the House is based.[6] That is, the framers intended House members to represent equal numbers of people (originally 30,000 per representative); allowing unequal districts violated their intent. After the *Wesberry* decision, over 250 House districts were reapportioned, with more representation and political power going to previously underrepresented urban and suburban areas.[7]

Drawing District Lines   However, politics still determines a particular district's shape. This may seem trivial, but it isn't. Which specific areas lie within a district determines what kinds of voters reside in the district, which in turn affects the types of candidates who can hope to win that seat. For example, a state legislature that is dominated by Republicans will want to draw a district's lines so as to include more conservative middle-class suburban Republican voters, thus making it easier for a Republican to win that seat. The party that controls state government thus can shape the voting composition of House districts.

To accomplish this partisan goal it is sometimes necessary to draw district lines in bizarre ways. Some district lines even split streets down the middle, with neighbors represented by different House members. This enduring and often controversial practice is known as **gerrymandering,** named after Elbridge Gerry, an early governor of Massachusetts, who drew one district's lines in such a way as to resemble a salamander, a small lizard. Legend has it that one wit looked at the district's map and commented, "It's a gerrymander!" The term stuck.

The likelihood of gerrymandering increases the more the majority party in a state seeks to protect its own House incumbents, punish current House members whom it dislikes, or improve its prospects of winning additional House seats. To some, gerrymandering is raw politics at its worst, but the Supreme Court generally considers the practice a political issue, and therefore constitutional, as long as it does not crudely discriminate by race (see Box 8.1) or consistently devalue a particular group's votes. This is a fuzzy line, however, and gerrymandering is likely to remain controversial.

Constituency Biases As the discussion of redistricting suggests, any constituency has a bias in terms of the types of candidates who have a chance of succeeding. The more homogeneous it is, the more likely its voters are to favor candidates like themselves. This equation is clearest with House districts. A district in Nebraska in which everybody is white, Republican, and works on a farm is an unlikely place for a non-white Democrat who moved into the district from New York City. At the same time, a House district located in Harlem, where most voters are African American or Latino Democrats, is not a fertile ground for a white Republican from Nebraska. Utah, in which the majority of the residents are Mormons, is likely to have senators and representatives who are also Mormons.

In short, voters support candidates who are like themselves, or at least are able to speak to the needs of those who live in the district or state. Non-Hispanics (or "Anglos") running for Congress in southern California are advised to learn Spanish, just as an earlier generation of House members in such cities as New York or Philadelphia learned Italian, Greek, or Portuguese.[8] This equation is not absolute, as voters sometimes support candidates despite racial, ethnic, or ideological differences; but the greater the gap, the harder it is for a candidate to win.

So not everybody who *could* run for Congress will do so. Some will not bother to run in the first place, figuring that they have little chance to win in a particular district or state simply because they do not fit the profile of the average voter in that place.

CONGRESSIONAL ELECTIONS

Those who decide to run for a seat in the House or Senate normally must be nominated by their party in a primary election before they can move on to the general election. In states or districts in which one party dominates (producing "safe seats"), the primary election in effect becomes the real contest, and the greatest competition is among candidates from the same party.

The competitiveness of a congressional election, whether primary or general, depends most on whether there is an **incumbent,** or currently sitting member of Congress, seeking reelection. As Table 8.2 (see p. 338) shows, most incumbents who seek reelection win. Even fewer lose in the party primary. Indeed, in many places incumbents have traditionally been safe from challenges from within their own parties. Party members hoping to serve in Congress are expected to wait until the incumbent steps aside. For candidates from the other party, the competitiveness of the primary depends on whether the incumbent is seen as vulnerable to defeat in the general election.[9]

The most competitive primary races are for **open seats,** in which no incumbent is up for reelection. The same patterns hold true in general elections. The majority of

BOX 8.1. GERRYMANDERING AND RACE

The House of Representatives is supposed to represent the people. Yet its members remain disproportionately white and male (see Table 8.3, p. 344). Some scholars believe that the House should be embody the principle of "descriptive representation," that it should reflect the characteristics of the population at large. If we use the current breakdown of the U.S. population (see Table 1.2, p. 19), the House today would look very different. First of all, it would be 51% female, instead of the current 13%. In terms of race, the changes would be just as profound, as a glance at this table suggests:

	Actual House Seats	*Under Descriptive Representation*
White	372 (86%)	326 (75%)
African American	39 (9%)	65 (15%)
Hispanic	19 (4%)	44 (11%)
Asian	5 (1%)	17 (4%)

Hispanics can also be classified as either white or black, so the totals aren't quite accurate, but you get the idea: An electoral system that considers race more accurately would change the composition of the House.

In 1982, Congress amended the Voting Rights Act to allow states to create "majority-minority" districts in which the percentage of minority residents would be maximized in order to ensure the election to the House of more racial minorities. However, creating such districts often required outright gerrymandering, with district lines wending their way over a long distance in order to connect enough minority-dominated residential areas to constitute a majority of the district's population. In such instances, African Americans or Hispanics were concentrated in rather odd-looking districts (see maps, next page). Moreover, neighboring districts often saw big increases in the percentage of white residents. Even so, the cumulative effect of these efforts was an approximately 50 percent increase in the number of African Americans and Hispanics elected to the House during the early 1990s.

However, to critics this process violated U.S. Supreme Court standards that districts should be reasonably compact and should incorporate entire communities as much as possible. The Court sided with the critics. In *Shaw v. Reno* (1993), the Court ruled that the 12th District in North Carolina constituted "political apartheid" by splitting communities into separate, racially defined districts. In *Miller v. Johnson* (1995), the Court went further by ruling that states could not use race as the "predominant factor" in creating districts. Thus, although gerrymandering can be used to improve one party's electoral prospects, it cannot be used explicitly to enhance the prospects of racial minorities. Most of these districts had to be redrawn (see maps, next page).

There are two ironies here. First, most of the African American or Hispanic House members first elected in these districts were able to gain reelection in their new ones, even with lower percentages of minority voters. It appears that their status as incumbents and, particularly, the resources that come with incumbency (discussed

→

WHAT DO YOU THINK?

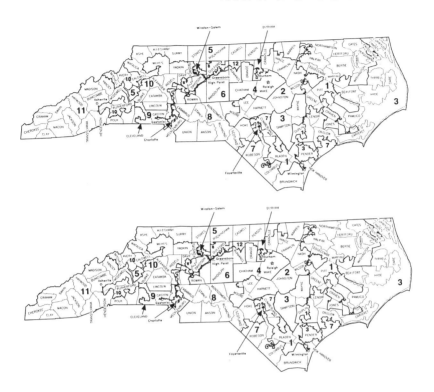

in the next section) enabled them to overcome whatever resistance white voters might have had to them had they run as first-time candidates.

Second, to create many of these "majority-minority" districts, the states had to concentrate whites in other ones. In many cases not only were these districts whiter; they also were more conservative and Republican. The cumulative effect may have cost Democrats as many as 10 House seats, thereby contributing to the Republican takeover of the House in 1994. And, because almost all African Americans in Congress are Democrats, that switch in party control led to three African American committee chairs and thirteen African American subcommittee chairs losing their positions.

All of this still begs the question: Are minorities better served by being concentrated into districts that guarantee the election of a racial minority, or will minorities have more influence if they make up sizeable parts of many more districts and thereby force all candidates, regardless of race, to take their interests into account? What do you think?

Sources: Shaw v Reno, 509 US 630 (1993); *Miller v Johnson*, 515 US 900 (1995); Kenny J. Whitby and Frank D. Gilliam, "Representatives in Congress: Line Drawing and Minorities," in Herbert F. Weisberg and Samuel C. Patterson, eds., *Great Theatre: The American Congress in the 1990s* (New York: Cambridge University Press, 1998), pp. 33–51.

TABLE 8.2.   REELECTION RATES FOR HOUSE AND SENATE
             INCUMBENTS, 1968-1998*

| | House | | Senate | |
Year	Total Seeking Reelection	Percent Reelected	Total Seeking Reelection	Percent Reelected
1968	409	96.8	28	71.4
1970	401	94.5	31	77.4
1972	390	93.6	27	74.1
1974	391	87.7	27	85.2
1976	384	95.8	25	64.0
1978	382	93.7	25	60.0
1980	398	90.7	29	55.2
1982	393	90.1	39	93.3
1984	409	95.4	29	89.6
1986	393	98.0	28	75.0
1988	408	98.3	27	85.2
1990	406	96.0	32	96.9
1992	368	88.3	28	82.1
1994	387	90.2	26	92.3
1996	384	94.0	21	90.5
1998	401	98.2	29	91.2

* Reelection rates for incumbents who run for reelection. Note the number of incumbents who do not run, or run for other offices (such as Senate). As a reference point, remember that every two years, all 435 House seats and 1/3 of the 100 Senate seats are up for election.

Source: Norman J. Ornstein, et al., *Vital Statistics on Congress, 1997–1998* (Washington, D.C.: CQ Press, 1998), pp. 61–62; *Congressional Quarterly Weekly Report*, November 7, 1998, p. 2980.

House seats are safely in the hands of one party or another, and rarely do incumbents win reelection with less than 55 percent of the vote. Even in contests for open seats, the advantage usually goes to the party that dominates the constituency: Republican districts usually elect Republican representatives; Democratic districts usually elect Democratic ones. One reason is redistricting. As far as party dominance is concerned, there are relatively few competitive House districts.

Senate elections are usually more competitive. For one thing, states are larger and have more diverse constituencies, increasing the probability of a challenge. Moreover, being a senator is seen as more prestigious than being a member of the House, and many see election to the Senate as a step toward possibly running for president.

In fact, at least one senator has run for president in every presidential election to date. Senate races thus draw more numerous and experienced candidates. Even so, incumbent senators still have the advantage.

Advantages of Incumbency   Incumbency notwithstanding, the membership of Congress changes constantly, and in some years it changes a great deal. Members retire, die, seek other offices, or move on to other careers. Some even fail to win reelection. Indeed, despite the popular image of "lifers" in the Congress, most members serve for less than 12 years.[10]

However, as Table 8.2 showed, few incumbents actually lose if they run for reelection. Incumbency by itself is a major reason for this high success rate. Being a member of Congress gives a candidate advantages that other candidates do not usually enjoy. For instance, he or she enjoys a certain prestige and name recognition among voters. For incumbents, as for all candidates, positive name recognition is the key to electoral success. In this regard, according to political scientist David Mayhew, members of Congress engage in three kinds of activities that strengthen their name recognition with the voters. Because these activities are part and parcel of being a representative, being a "good" representative may be the best way to keep winning reelection to Congress.[11]

The first of these activities is what Mayhew calls "advertising." Members of Congress get a lot of free public exposure just by doing their jobs. For example, as we will discuss later, members try to be assigned to committees with jurisdiction over issues that affect voters back home. Urban legislators gravitate toward committees with authority over issues such as mass transit or housing; members from Rocky Mountain mining regions want seats on committees that deal with natural resources; those from farm areas want seats on the agriculture committees. Having seats on committees that are relevant to constituency interests not only makes it easier to influence policymaking but also enables members to "advertise" their work to the people back home.

Members also get positive recognition when they help constituents with problems such as finding lost Social Security checks, or when they help local officials obtain federal funding for a new sewer project. Some members gain more exposure through speeches on the House or Senate floor: These are carried live on C-SPAN, the privately funded cable network that televises congressional floor sessions and committee hearings. And of course, members can advertise directly to constituents through newsletters sent under their **franking privilege,** which allows them to send subsidized mailings to constituents. Being a good representative obviously means keeping in contact with constituents about what is happening in Congress, but doing a "good" job in this respect has undeniable electoral benefits.

Second, members of Congress engage in what Mayhew calls "position-taking." They know that any vote they take on legislation has political ramifications, so they look at it as a way to take a position on an issue. Sometimes bills that have no chance of passing are proposed simply to allow legislators to express a position that may be important only to a relatively narrow constituency. An example might be a bill to expel the United Nations headquarters from U.S. soil. Members may propose such a

Representative Christopher Shays, a Republican from Connecticut, in front of a "town meeting" of his constituents. In this case, the issue was whether Shays should vote in favor of articles of impeachment against President Bill Clinton. Constituents' views were split: Shays eventually supported some, but not all, of the articles.

bill for serious personal or ideological reasons, but their efforts are also symbolic statements that they hope will gain the approval of voters back home.

Above all, members want to be able to explain their votes to the people back home. Bills that may entail costs to constituents are unpopular, and members of Congress know that any vote in favor of a new tax is potentially deadly to their political careers, even if the tax is necessary to reduce the budget deficit or pay for popular programs.[12]

Third, members of Congress engage in what Mayhew calls "credit-claiming." As the saying goes, "Success has many fathers, while failure is an orphan." Members of Congress, like all smart politicians, take credit for popular programs even if they did relatively little to ensure their passage. They are also quick to deny responsibility for unpopular laws or actions. Avoiding blame is as important as taking credit. This is human nature at work.

Incumbents also have other resources that few challengers enjoy. They are important people back home, and the local media seek their comments on national issues as well as local concerns. This is true especially for senators, who rarely have trouble getting on local television news if they want to do so. Members of Congress also take frequent subsidized trips home to see their constituents, and they have substantial staff support to help them work on legislation and handle constituents' mail or problems. Members take such **casework** seriously: No letter goes unanswered, even if only with a form letter, and no constituent problem goes ignored. A satisfied constituent becomes a vote in the next election.

These resources can be defended as part of the job of being an accountable and effective representative, and few voters would want their elected officials to be out of touch. Nevertheless, these resources also enhance an incumbent's ability to win reelection. The line between being a good representative and running for reelection is a thin one indeed.

FINANCING CAMPAIGNS

Incumbents also enjoy a clear advantage in raising campaign funds. Winning a seat in Congress requires a lot of money, and the cost is increasing steadily. Raising adequate funds is a serious problem, especially for candidates challenging an incumbent member, and candidates spend considerable time and effort just raising enough money to wage a credible campaign.

Overall spending on congressional campaigns has skyrocketed since the mid-1970s. In 1998 winning candidates for the House spent an average of nearly $670,000 on their election campaigns—almost double the average for 1986—and their Senate counterparts spent an average of $4.7 million on their statewide races.[13] Even incumbents without serious challengers spent large sums to maintain name recognition and prepare for future campaigns.

Why Campaigns Are Expensive   Campaigns are expensive for two main reasons. First, candidates increasingly rely on television advertising and sophisticated campaign tools such as opinion polls. Both require a lot of money, especially in metropolitan areas in which television advertising is expensive. Senate races are particularly costly because candidates use television to reach out to voters throughout their states. For example, anyone running for senator in California must run advertising in major television markets such as San Diego, Los Angeles, Sacramento, and San Francisco. In 1998, incumbent Senator Barbara Boxer spent nearly $14 million to defeat her Republican challenger, state treasurer Matthew Fong, who spent another $11 million.[14]

Second, candidates feel compelled to spend all the funds they can get their hands on, unwilling to take a chance that not spending a few more dollars might spell the difference between victory and defeat. It is better to spend it all and win than to have money left over and lose. And as one candidate spends so do the others, resulting in a monetary "arms race." In short, there are few reasons for candidates not to raise and spend as much money as they can. Winning the election is the goal. There is no second place. Even candidates without major opposition will spend hundreds of thousands of dollars to ensure victory and, perhaps equally important, keep their names before the voters. It never hurts to reinforce positive name recognition; there is always another election around the corner.

Where Does the Money Come From?   Relatively small donations by private individuals are still the single largest source of funds for congressional candidates. However, reliance on donations by political action committees (see chapter 7) has grown, partly because of increasing costs and because, unlike presidential races, congressional campaigns receive no public financing. Interest group money therefore becomes critical, especially for House candidates, who represent smaller constituencies in which it is hard to raise large amounts of money. For example, in 1998 nearly 40 percent of the funds spent by House candidates came from political action committees, compared to less than 20 percent for Senate races.[15] Direct contributions by the national party organizations run a distant third, but both major parties supply services, such as public opinion polling and phoning voters, to remind them to go to the polls.

At present there is no limit on the amount a person can spend on his or her own campaign, so the phenomenon of wealthy individuals spending tens of thousands, even millions, of dollars on their own campaigns has become more common. In 1998, for example, candidates for Congress "loaned" their campaigns over $52 million. This amounted to less than 10 percent of all money spent on congressional elections in 1998, but in some instances these personal funds made a difference. In Illinois, for example, challenger Peter Fitzgerald spent over $11 million of his own money to beat incumbent Senator Carol Moseley Braun.[16] Fitzgerald probably will pay back his loan to his own campaign by holding fundraisers, which will be attended by representatives of interest groups seeking to establish cordial ties with the new senator.

Of course, personal wealth does not guarantee victory. In 1992, Michael Huffington spent $5.2 million of his own money to win a House seat in California, but two years later lost a race for the Senate despite spending more than $25 million of his own money.[17] Still, the idea that wealthy individuals might be able to "buy" their way into Congress troubles many observers of American politics. It also feeds the money "arms race," because candidates who lack personal wealth must raise as much campaign money as possible to compete with those who have money of their own.

Who Gets What?   Incumbents find it easier to raise campaign funds than do challengers. Indeed, in 1998 House incumbents raised three times as much money as did their challengers. Campaign donors, whether individuals or interest groups, tend to hedge their bets by donating to someone who is already in Congress rather than risk supporting someone who probably cannot win because of the advantages incumbents enjoy. They would rather stick with a known quantity than risk alienating someone whose help they might need in the future.

Spending is highest in campaigns for open seats in which there is no incumbent running for reelection. In such races most candidates are relatively unknown, so money helps to buy the television and radio advertising needed to raise name recognition. In races against incumbents, challengers improve their chances of winning by outspending the incumbent.[18] However, as discussed earlier, incumbents usually can raise and spend more money.

What Does the Money Buy?   Their heavy reliance on campaign money gives rise to concerns that legislators are "selling out" to their campaign donors. Such a perception is fed by the explosive growth in the amounts of money given by industries and other economic interests. On paper, there are strict legal limits on the amount an individual or group may donate to any one candidate, but industries such as real estate or insurance often "bundle" together large numbers of small donations to friendly candidates. This process can increase the cumulative amount given to any one candidate to tens of thousands of dollars, money that no candidate can afford to ignore.

The key issue, of course, is whether in the process the group "buys" a member of Congress—that is, whether campaign money influences the member's future behavior on actual legislation. As we discussed in chapter 7, it is difficult to prove that donations by specific donors actually determined how a member voted on specific pieces of legislation. However, the sheer amounts of money involved, particularly funds that are bundled together and delivered as a package by interest groups, probably make representatives and senators cautious about how they treat bills that affect important sources of campaign money.[19]

At a minimum, campaign donors gain access. A member of Congress will at least sit down and listen to a person or group who donates money; after all, nobody wants to appear ungrateful. For example, in October 1998 the American Medical Association bundled together more than $286,000 in donations to Representative Ernest Fletcher, a Republican from Kentucky who won an open seat. The AMA's total contributions equaled nearly one-quarter of Fletcher's total spending in that campaign.[20] If nothing else, Fletcher will listen when representatives of the AMA come by discuss legislation. To critics of the campaign finance system, this is bad enough.

At worst, campaign money distorts, perhaps corrupts, the legislative process in favor of those whose money buys access and possibly influence. As we will see later in this chapter, few members of Congress would dream of favoring campaign donors on issues that affect constituents directly. The real concern is how members make decisions on issues with little or no direct impact on their constituents or, as we discussed in chapter 7, on issues about which the public lacks strong opinions. Campaign money buys influence. How much is not clear, but it is a troubling issue nonetheless.

THE MEMBERS OF CONGRESS

The electoral system shapes the composition of Congress. For one thing, as Table 8.3 shows, members of Congress as a group are not a cross-section of the American people. Even today they are disproportionately white, male, and Protestant. Women and minorities have made gains during the past 30 years, but, particularly in the Senate, neither group represents their proportion of the general population. The religious backgrounds of members, on the other hand, more accurately reflect those of the society as a whole.

Members of Congress are more highly educated than is the average American; many have advanced degrees and work in professions such as law, medicine, and education. Congress naturally has its share of lawyers—though far less so today than in previous generations—whereas business, banking, and academic backgrounds are also common. Few, if any, members come directly to Congress from working-class occupations.

A key question is how much this gap between the composition of Congress and that of society matters. The answer is not clear, although on some kinds of issues (such as affirmative action or tax credits for child care) minorities and women tend to hold perspectives that differ from those of many white males.[21] It is also safe to say that middle-class economic and social concerns tend to receive greater attention from the majority of members, who are middle-class professionals themselves.

Even so, one should not automatically infer that members' views and actions stem only from their own backgrounds. For example, some of the greatest advocates of

TABLE 8.3. WHO MEMBERS ARE, 1969 AND 1999

	House		Senate	
	1969	*1999*	*1969*	*1999*
Political Party				
Democrats	248	211	64	45
Republicans	187	222*	36	55
Independents	0	1	0	0
Gender				
Men	425	377	99	91
Women	10	58	1	9
Average age (years)	52.2	52.6	56.6	58.3
Race				
White	424	372	95	96
Black	5	39	1	0
Hispanic	3	19	1	0
Asian	3	5	3	2
Native American	0	0	0	1
Religion				
Protestant**	202	183	59	40
Roman Catholic	96	126	13	25
Jewish	17	23	2	11
Other	100	103	26	24
*Prior Profession***				
Actor/entertainer	0	1	0	2
Agriculture	34	22	16	6
Business/banking	159	159	25	24
Clergy	2	1	0	3
Education	59	84	14	13
Engineering	6	9	2	0
Journalism	39	9	8	0
Labor leader	3	1	0	0
Law	242	163	68	55
Law enforcement	2	10	0	--
Medicine	5	15	0	21
Military	0	1	0	1
Professional sports	0	2	0	1
Public service/politics	n/a	106	n/a	18
Real estate	n/a	20	n/a	4
Military veteran	320	136	69	43

n/a = not asked

* In 1999, there was a vacancy due to a death midyear.

** Designation limited to Baptists, Episcopalians, Methodists, and Presbyterians.

*** Members sometimes cited two or more prior professions, such as both lawyer and politician.

Sources: Norman Ornstein, et al., *Vital Statistics on Congress, 1997–98* (Washington, D.C.: CQ Press, 1998), pp. 22–40; Charles Pope, "New Congress Is Older, More Politically Seasoned," *Congressional Quarterly Weekly Report*, vol. 57, no. 2 (January 9, 1999), pp. 60–63.

federal programs for the poor, women, and minorities have been affluent white men such as Senator Edward Kennedy, a Democrat from Massachusetts, and Senator David Rockefeller, a Democrat from West Virginia. On the other hand, some of the toughest opponents of government programs such as welfare have been "self-made" individuals from modest beginnings, such as former Kansas Senator and 1996 presidential nominee Robert Dole.

In general, the outlooks of members of Congress reflect a mixture of factors—personal experience, political ideology, party affiliation, and constituents' needs—and usually do not simply reflect race or social status. Of course, whether Congress *should* constitute a cross-section of American society remains an important question with implications for effective representation and democratic legitimacy. Whether, or how, a Congress that is more female and more racially diverse would act differently is also an intriguing question.

VOTERS' ATTITUDES TOWARD CONGRESS

Americans have ambivalent feelings about Congress. On one hand, the public has very harsh attitudes about the institution as a whole. For example, a June 1999 *Washington Post*/ABC News poll found that only 48 percent of those polled "approve of the job Congress is doing."[22] If that sounds low, it shouldn't: From a historical perspective, that level of approval was on the high end. Yet, as we saw in Table 8.2 (p. 338), voters continue to reelect their own representatives and senators at a very high rate. More intriguing, in the poll just cited, 70 percent of those polled approved of the way *their own* representatives were handling their jobs. Voters like their own members of Congress—why don't they like the institution itself?

Voters are harsh on Congress partly because they judge its performance on criteria such as efficiency and effectiveness, standards that a deliberative body often fails to meet.[23] Congress is always seen as slow; its members are regarded as foolish, wrong, and too cut off from the views of the public; and Congress too often gets in the president's way. Lawmaking takes a lot of time and effort, especially when the issues involved are controversial, but for the public the message is that Congress cannot get its act together. Congress also tends to look bad on television: The arguments that occur in floor debate give the impression that members would rather squabble than work together. Such impressions lower the public's faith in the legislature.

But voters rarely extend these harsh assessments to their own representatives or senators. Attitudes about their own members of Congress seem to hinge less on the effectiveness or speed of the institution and more on individual performance. Here, voters apply standards such as how well members provide services to constituents, their success in obtaining federal funds for local projects, and their personal trustworthiness. Such standards are far easier for incumbents to meet. As individuals, they may not be able to eliminate crime or improve education nationally, but they can help their elderly constituents iron out problems with Social Security or obtain funding for a science building at the local college. Those many small favors make a difference on election day.

That voters reelect incumbents to Congress even as they criticize the institution is an enduring contradiction of American politics, and it is not likely to change. The problem, after all, is not our own representative or senator. They are like us, and we trust them to do what is right. The problem is all the other members of Congress, who were elected by other voters.

ORGANIZING CONGRESS

Once they have been elected to Congress, the 435 representatives and 100 senators *become* Congress, an institution that is accused of being slow, noisy, and ineffective. Critics wonder why Congress can't work more quickly and efficiently, more as a business would. This is a good question, but the answer is not simple.

Imagine a business in which each employee, regardless of title or seniority, has an equal vote in deciding what kinds of products the company makes, how the products are marketed, and how any profits are to be divided. In addition, imagine that no employee can hire or fire any other employee, no one can give orders to anyone else, and all decisions are arrived at through a long and painstaking process of seeking compromise until enough employees' views and needs have been taken into account.

Congress is this kind of place. Its members ("employees") are in fact "independent contractors" who are "hired" and "fired" by their various "bosses," the voters to whom they owe their primary loyalty. Members of Congress are also equal. That is, each member has exactly one vote, regardless of official position, seniority in office, intellect, charisma, or good looks.[24]

A body made up of equals poses serious practical problems for the institution itself. First, how do its members organize themselves to do work? Who, if anyone, is in charge, what powers do they have, and how are they selected? What procedures do members use to make decisions, and who has the authority to enforce those decisions? Without some kind of formal organization, with rules and procedures, Congress would be in a state of constant turmoil. Nothing would ever get done. But whatever organizational structure is developed also must meet the needs of members, especially the need to represent their diverse constituencies.

The internal organization of Congress can be described as a *limited hierarchy*, with members imposing on themselves only enough structure and rules to enable them to pursue their dual goals of representation and legislation. No member of Congress will surrender authority to any other member without a very good reason, and then only under clearly defined conditions. As we will discuss later, even congressional leaders know that their power is derived from the members' willingness to go along.

Congress is also decentralized. Each of the 435 House members and 100 senators heads a separate legislative "enterprise" with its own office and staff. Each of these 535 "enterprises" functions independently, and each is designed to focus on the needs of the individual member. Added to this mix is a complex array of committees and subcommittees, interest groups, party leaders and organizations, other government officials, the media, and a great many constituency groups. Perhaps the best image of Congress is that of an ancient marketplace, with hundreds of people engaged in constant debate and bargaining. No one, and everyone, is in charge.

Complexity and decentralization are natural to Congress, regardless of whatever changes its members make in its structures or rules. As is any legislature, Congress is shaped by the way members are elected to it. And because its members are elected separately by different constituencies, Congress cannot avoid being decentralized.

CONGRESSIONAL PARTIES

The political party is the only institution that tries to counteract this natural tendency toward fragmentation and decentralization in Congress. In fact, American political parties evolved in Congress as ways for like-minded members to band together, build a majority, and enact laws they wanted. But as we saw in chapter 6, political parties in the United States are not parliamentary parties; they have no constitutional role in governing as they do in Great Britain, for example.

Nevertheless, political parties play a central role in Congress. At present all members of Congress are either Democrats or Republicans except one: Representative Bernie Sanders of Vermont, a self-professed Socialist who tends to vote with Democrats on most issues. The majority party in each chamber is the chief agent for centralization of power. It organizes the committee system, makes the rules (especially in the larger and more formal House), and takes the lead in setting the legislative agenda.

Partisan activities in each chamber revolve around the Democratic or Republican **party caucus** or conference. In the caucus, the members of the party select party leaders, who then take on formal leadership duties if the party has the majority in that chamber. The caucus adopts rules dictating how members of the party should behave, and it tries to forge an official party position on pieces of legislation. This last function always proves difficult, because within each party caucus there is a range of ideological opinions on every issue, and members worry more about their constituents than about party unity anyway. Constituents, not the parties, elect members of Congress. Having said this, the party caucus is the most important force for bringing members of Congress together.

Party Leaders   No single individual or group really controls Congress, but party leaders try to induce party members to "go along" in the name of party unity. The majority party "controls" each chamber in the sense that the Speaker of the House, the House majority leader, and the Senate majority leader usually are the institution's most influential members.

The **Speaker of the House** of Representatives is the most visible and powerful member of Congress and the only congressional officer mentioned specifically in the Constitution (the vice president is nominally the president of the Senate but rarely assumes this role). The Speaker is also third in line for succession to the presidency, after the vice president. However, no Speaker has become president in such a manner.

The Speaker occupies a position with two distinct roles. On one hand, the Speaker presides over the entire House and therefore must make an attempt to treat members of either party with respect and fairness. As presiding officer of the House, the Speaker has an array of formal and informal powers and resources that are useful in influencing members and shaping legislation.

On the other hand, the Speaker is a partisan figure elected by the members of the majority party. As leader of the majority party caucus, the Speaker has a great deal of influence over committee assignments and can use this influence to reward loyalty and, on occasion, punish disloyalty. The Speaker, through tight control over the Rules Committee, can also shape the rules for House floor debates and decide when bills will come up for a vote. In short, the Speaker is in a position to help the majority party enact its legislative priorities. That role becomes even more important when the president is from the other party. In such instances the Speaker is often seen as the leader of the president's opposition, although no Speaker has been able to use the position to win election to the presidency. Indeed, history shows that House members must first win election to a statewide office (that is, senator or governor) to have any credible chance of seeking the nation's highest office.

Even with the powers that come with the position, the Speaker's overall effectiveness depends more on intangible factors such as personality and political skill, as well as the degree to which the Speaker can promote the goals of the majority party. "Strong" speakers have been willing and able to use their resources to mold cohesive party majorities.[25] Party loyalty is difficult to cultivate even in the best of times because unity may not serve members' individual electoral needs. Speakers also must avoid being too partisan; the votes of members from the other party might be necessary to pass important legislation, and the rights of all House members must be respected if Congress is to work as a democratic institution.

Newt Gingrich, a Republican from Georgia who served as Speaker from 1995 to 1999, illustrates these points. Gingrich enjoyed strong support from fellow Republicans during his first two years in office because he was credited with helping them win control of the House for the first time in 40 years. In fact, many Republicans then saw Gingrich as a legitimate contender for president in 2000. However, Republicans suffered a series of political defeats at the hands of President Clinton, culminating in unexpected losses in the 1998 midterm election that seriously reduced the party's majority in the House. Gingrich was blamed for these defeats and, sensing that he had lost the support of his fellow Republicans, resigned from both the position of Speaker and his House seat.

In the Senate there is no position equivalent to that of Speaker of the House. The **president pro tempore** is the nominal head of the Senate, but the position is largely honorary and is given to the most senior member from the majority party. The Constitution states that the vice president shall act as president of the Senate, but vice presidents undertake this role only rarely, and vote only when it is necessary to break a tie.

Each of the parties elects **majority and minority leaders,** who work to build support for their party's positions on particular bills. The House majority leader typically works with the Speaker to lead the majority party, whereas the minority leader is seen as a potential Speaker should the minority party take control after the next

Former House Speaker Newt Gingrich, Republican from Georgia. In 1994, Gingrich helped his party to gain control of the House for the first time in 40 years. He was elected Speaker, a post he held until he resigned in December, 1998, after Republicans fared badly in that year's congressional elections.

election. This is what happened to Gingrich, who was minority leader in the 103rd Congress (1993–94) but became Speaker in the 104th Congress (1995–96), after the Republicans took over the House following the 1994 elections.

At other times the minority leader's primary task is to maintain party cohesion and take advantage of divisions within the majority in order to push the minority's agenda. The degree to which this can happen depends on the size of the majority party's advantage. If it is large, the minority party can do little but try to draw public attention to its issues; if the majority advantage is small, the minority party can have an influential role in legislation. In 1999, House Republicans had only a six-seat majority, thus affording Minority Leader Richard Gephardt, a Democrat from Missouri, an opportunity to promote his party's goals when they meshed with those of enough Republicans to forge a bipartisan majority.

The Senate majority leader is the most visible member in a chamber that is far more loosely organized than is the House. More than the Speaker, who has a range of formal powers over committee assignments, the House schedule, and the rules for floor debate, the Senate majority leader depends almost entirely on personal skills to get colleagues to go along. As a result of the Senate's long tradition of treating all senators as equals on all matters, the Senate majority leader cannot order other senators to do anything.

The majority and minority leaders in each chamber employ **party whips** to round up members' support for votes. Each party in each chamber has a chief whip and several assistant whips, who transmit the wishes of party leaders to the members and the members' views to the leadership. Ideally, the whips help maintain party cohesion, but given the relative independence of members of Congress, particularly in the Senate, this is never an easy task.

THE COMMITTEE SYSTEM

After the party, the most important institution in Congress is the committee system, the primary means by which Congress organizes itself to do its work. Unlike the party system, however, the committee system can fragment Congress into separate "little legislatures," each focusing on a particular part of public policy.[26]

The legislative process flows through committees and subcommittees. They screen the bills that are introduced into Congress; bring specialized expertise to bear on complex policy questions; and allow members to develop a thorough understanding of particular issues. They also give members opportunities to influence policies that are of interest to them and their constituents. In all, committees serve as preliminary arenas for conflict and compromise over important legislative matters. President (and political scientist) Woodrow Wilson once wrote that "Congress in its committee-rooms is Congress at work."[27]

Standing Committees The most important of these working groups are the **standing committees,** which are organized according to important subject areas—for example, agriculture or education. These permanent committees enable Congress to process the thousands of bills proposed each year in a more specialized and efficient manner. Any bill that is proposed must go to a standing committee for consideration. Bills pertaining to farming go to the committees on agriculture; problems in the banking industry are examined by the committees on banking; and so on. In each of these committees, members with expertise in these areas judge the desirability of the legislation. Because bills that are not approved by the relevant standing committee rarely go beyond this stage, standing committees are important players in lawmaking. During the 106th Congress (1999–2000) the House had 19 standing committees and the Senate had 17 (see Table 8.4).

Each standing committee has a number of **subcommittees** that deal with even more specialized aspects of legislation. The number of these subcommittees and the power they wield are controversial issues within Congress, because breaking legislation down into smaller and more specialized pieces makes the process of consensus-building even more difficult. Yet given the complexity of modern policy questions, such specialization is almost inevitable.

Select Committees From time to time Congress creates **select committees,** temporary committees for specific purposes such as investigating the problems of the elderly. Although these committees do not normally authorize legislation, they can recommend it to the standing committees. Some select committees, such as the Permanent Joint Select Committee on Intelligence, remain in existence for years, but most last for only one term of Congress.

Joint Committees **Joint committees** span the chambers, with members from the House and Senate meeting to coordinate activities (such as running the Library

TABLE 8.4. STANDING COMMITTEES IN THE 106TH CONGRESS, 1999-2000

House of Representatives	*Senate*
Agriculture	Agriculture, Nutrition, and Forestry
Appropriations	Appropriations
Armed Services	Armed Services
Banking and Financial Services	Banking, Housing, and Urban Affairs
Budget	Budget
Commerce	Commerce, Science, and Transportation
Education and the Workforce	Energy and Natural Resources
Government Reform	Environment and Public Works
House Administration	Finance
International Relations	Foreign Relations
Judiciary	Governmental Affairs
Resources	Judiciary
Rules	Health, Education, Labor, and Pensions
Science	Indian Affairs
Small Business	Rules and Administration
Standards of Official Conduct	Small Business
Transportation and Infrastructure	Veterans Affairs
Veterans Affairs	
Ways and Means	

of Congress) or, as with the Joint Committee on Taxation, hold joint House-Senate hearings on specialized issues. A special type of joint committee is the **conference committee,** a temporary work group created to enable members of both chambers to negotiate compromises between contrasting House and Senate versions of a bill. Such negotiations are critical: no bill can become law unless it is passed in identical form by both houses of Congress.

Committee Assignments   Members of Congress care deeply about their committee assignments. A seat on a "good" committee helps to promote a member's goals, constituents' interests, and of course, reelection. Committees such as Senate Finance and House Ways and Means are seen as prestigious because they deal with important national issues such as economic policy and taxes. As a result, seats on either committee give members a great deal of policymaking influence and high media visibility, and open the way to more campaign contributions by industries or interests affected by the committee's actions. For these reasons, members also covet seats on the House and Senate Appropriations committees, which allocate the funds for programs authorized in legislation, and the Budget committees, which manage the congressional budget process.

Other committees are less prestigious. For example, no member seeks a seat on the Committee on House Oversight: It deals with minor internal matters such as the House food service and computer system, has almost no media visibility, and generally offers few immediate benefits to members. No senator volunteers to sit on the Senate Ethics Committee and thereby be forced to make judgments about the ethical behavior of colleagues. Indeed, having a seat on one of these committees might be regarded as punishment for disloyalty to party leaders. However, more frequently it is the price a member has to pay to get a seat on a prestigious committee. In this regard, most members end up serving on at least one "good" committee and one "bad" one.

The value of a particular committee assignment depends primarily on the member's own goals. As political scientist Richard Fenno argues, members who seek *reelection* above all else usually desire seats on committees with direct relevance to their constituents.[28] For example, a member of Congress from North Dakota who is concerned about reelection might want a seat on a committee dealing with natural resources or agriculture. Especially coveted are seats on the important appropriations committees, which decide how much money is spent on each program authorized by the other committees. Having a seat on the appropriations committee is a good way to help make sure federal funds are directed toward the member's home district or state.

By contrast, members who seek *influence within Congress* often desire less visible but very influential positions such as a seat on the House Rules Committee, which clears all bills for floor debate and vote, or on the Senate Judiciary Committee, which approves all presidential nominees for the federal courts. These committees have less direct relevance to most constituents, but they are important to the workings of Congress itself.

Finally, members for whom *public policy* is the primary goal may seek out committees such as Senate Foreign Relations or House Judiciary, both of which deal with controversial issues but are not especially good places for members who are worried about reelection. For example, the House Judiciary Committee deals with highly controversial issues such as affirmative action and gun control. Only members with safe seats usually want to be on that committee.

Party leaders are careful in assigning members to committees. They take into consideration factors such as a member's seniority in office, political needs, policy interests and expertise, ideology, party loyalty, and overall reputation, as well as regional and state balance. As noted earlier, "good" committee assignments can also be used as rewards for loyalty and "bad" ones as punishment for disloyalty. Seniority is still important, particularly when several members are competing for the same committee assignment, but it does not determine committee assignments.

For these reasons, committee memberships are often criticized for being "stacked" with certain kinds of members. The House Judiciary Committee tends to be split between Republicans who are strong conservatives and Democrats who are strong liberals, with few moderates in between, because the committee deals with ideologically charged issues that many members would rather avoid. Similarly, Senators from oil-producing states tend to gravitate toward the Senate Committee on Energy and Resources, "stacking" that committee with members who support policies that are favorable to the domestic oil industry.

For their part, party leaders try to accommodate members' requests. They also recognize that members have more interest in and knowledge about the problems of the areas they represent. After all, what does a House member representing the central part of Los Angeles know about the problems of pig farming? However, as we see from the case of the House Agriculture Committee, discussed in Box 8.2, such close ties to local needs or specific industries contribute to the tendency of members of Congress to serve narrow constituency interests over broader national interests.

Committee Leaders Those who chair congressional committees traditionally have a great deal of influence over committee agendas, schedules, and overall operations. Indeed, a bill opposed by the committee chair is unlikely to get out of committee without major changes, if at all. Historically, committee chairs attained their positions by virtue of their seniority on their respective committees. Strict reliance on the seniority system rewarded long service but it also made it harder for party leaders to maintain party cohesion or control over the legislative process.

However, beginning in the 1970s, in the House the majority party caucus occasionally overrode seniority to install as chair a less senior member of the committee in order to enforce party loyalty or because the more senior representative was not regarded as an effective leader. As a result, House committee chairs today work closely with the Speaker and the majority party caucus on major pieces of legislation, but still have leeway on most issues that come before their committees. By contrast, in the Senate seniority is rarely violated, and Senate committee chairs tend to be very independent of party leadership.

STAFF AND SUPPORT AGENCIES

Congress is an independent legislative body, not just an outgrowth of a political party majority as in a parliamentary system. Therefore, Congress has its own support staff, a congressional bureaucracy of about 28,000 people that ranges from policy experts, lawyers, economists, and accountants to secretaries, janitors, and even barbers. Roughly one-third of the people who work for Congress are personal and committee staffs, aides with specialized expertise and information who work closely with the members.

House members may employ up to 18 full-time staff members. Senate staffs vary according to state populations—the range is 13 to 71—but average around 35 people.[29] About 60 percent of personal staff members work with representatives and senators on Capitol Hill, where they assist members with legislative duties such as research on specific bills or meeting with lobbyists on issues of concern. They spend even more time processing the many constituent problems and requests that flow into their offices, both in Washington and in the home district or state. As we noted earlier, no member takes casework lightly. The other personal staff members operate out of offices in the respective districts or states. Their primary role is to meet with

BOX 8.2.
CONGRESS AND THE TOBACCO IRON TRIANGLE

In Box 7.2 we examined the interest group side of the tobacco "iron triangle," in which public policymaking is seen to be shaped by close working relationships among representatives from the tobacco industry, members of Congress, and officials within the federal bureaucracy. In this box we examine the congressional side of the relationship.

Not surprisingly, tobacco is particularly important to members of Congress from a number of southern states where it is a major agricultural crop. Declared Senator Jesse Helms (R.-NC), "In North Carolina, tobacco isn't a commodity, it's a religion." Throughout most of the 20th century the House and Senate committees on agriculture have been chaired by legislators sympathetic to the tobacco industry, and often from tobacco-producing states. Members on these committees steered tobacco legislation through the Congress and protected the industry from legislators and regulators whose views were less friendly to tobacco. They also worked closely with officials in the U.S. Department of Agriculture to improve crop yields, support crop prices, and expand tobacco sales to other nations.

The heyday of the tobacco iron triangle came in the decades immediately following World War II, during which time members of Congress from tobacco states were in powerful positions on key committees and in the House and Senate leadership. In the 1960s, for example, nearly one-fourth of all Senate committees were chaired by senators from the six leading tobacco-producing states. These senators, and their counterparts in the House, assisted by their industry allies, protected tobacco support programs, supported USDA budgets, and killed any legislation that would be detrimental to the industry.

Members friendly to the tobacco industry also benefited from financial contributions to their congressional campaigns. Between 1987 and 1996 alone, the tobacco industry gave nearly $25 million to members of Congress in both parties. However, the greatest share went to members who are *not* from tobacco states: The industry made sure to spread out its support beyond its natural base. Tobacco industry PACs also contribute extensively to party leaders such as former House Speaker Newt Gingrich (R.-GA) and House minority leader Richard Gephardt (D.-MO), who play a key role in setting the congressional agenda.

→

constituents, perform casework, and make sure that the representative or senator is kept aware of the issues and problems back home.

About 2,500 more staff members are assigned to the various committees and subcommittees. They help members work out the details of bills, arrange and conduct committee business, meet with interest group representatives and executive branch officials, write reports, and investigate whether government agencies are doing their

A CLOSER LOOK

Even so, defenders of tobacco must increasingly deal with critics whose focus is on health concerns, not the financial condition of tobacco growers or cigarette makers. Although they still have influence, members of Congress from tobacco states no longer hold tight reins over policies that affect the crop. Indeed, members from tobacco states have been outnumbered by urban and suburban legislators when Congress passed laws restricting of the industry, such as requiring health warning labels on cigarette packages, banning tobacco advertising on television and radio, and doubling the federal excise tax.

However, if the tobacco iron triangle is certainly weaker than it once was, legislators from the tobacco states still wield influence. In June, 1998, for example, tobacco-state senators killed an attempt to resolve the longstanding legal battle with the tobacco industry by enacting a $516 billion federal initiative that would have settled all outstanding liability lawsuits and instituted extensive anti-smoking programs. The bill had passed the House, where defenders of tobacco are now outnumbered, but it died in the Senate because a few senators were able to stop it in its tracks.

In November, 1998, after Congress failed to enact a compromise over tobacco liability suits, most of the state attorneys general entered into a $206 billion settlement with the tobacco industry that resolved outstanding lawsuits brought by states against tobacco companies and, in return, included payments to states, a ban on billboard advertising, and support for the development of smoking prevention programs. Critics charged that the tobacco industry got off too lightly because most of the money in the settlement would come out of higher taxes on cigarettes, but state governments decided to move on their own and not wait for Congress.

Sources: Common Cause, "Tobacco Giving Hits Record $9.9 million for '96 Elections," Tuesday, May 13, 1997; http://www.commoncause.org/publications/051397_sdyapx2.htm; Silvia Nasar, "Smokescreen: The Ifs and Buts of the Tobacco Settlement," *New York Times*, November 29, 1998, Section 4, p. 1.

jobs. Some committee staff members are known throughout Washington for their expertise on complex policy issues.[30]

Congressional staffs expanded beginning in the 1970s because of a growing need for specialized information and expertise on increasingly complex policy issues such as energy, the environment, and technology. Staff also expanded because Congress was reluctant to rely on the president, the executive branch bureaucracy, or lobbyists for information or advice. As a result, members of Congress depend on and value their staffs, although many observers worry that their aides are too influential in shaping public policy. As we will see in chapter 10, this kind of criticism is aimed at any bureaucratic organization. Anyone who knows important facts or who is a policy expert ultimately can influence the details of legislation.[31]

The congressional bureaucracy also includes three nonpartisan research agencies that provide services to all members of Congress. The Congressional Research Service (CRS) is part of the Library of Congress. It provides information upon request for members of Congress, most of it pertaining to pending legislation. For example, senators who want to make changes in existing air pollution laws can consult CRS experts on what Congress intended to achieve when it passed a specific provision in that law years or even decades ago. Knowing this imay help these senators avoid "reinventing the wheel."

The Congressional Budget Office (CBO) employs economists and budget experts who monitor federal spending, help the congressional budget committees prepare the annual budget, and advise Congress on the budgetary impacts of proposed programs, new spending, or tax cuts. As we will see in chapter 10, in the executive branch the Office of Management and Budget (OMB) performs many of these same tasks for the president, and the two budget agencies sometimes disagree with each other over whose assessments are more accurate.

Finally, the General Accounting Office (GAO) acts as the legislature's auditing arm, reporting to Congress on the effectiveness of government programs. Members of Congress often rely on GAO reports to provide the impetus for making changes in existing policies.

CONGRESS AS AN ORGANIZATION

As should be evident by now, Congress is an immense organization with its own distinct structures, rules, and traditions. The organizational aspects of Congress have evolved mainly to help its members meet their responsibilities as representatives and legislators. But they also allow members to be policy experts and monitors of the executive branch.

To some observers, Congress is too large and complex, with members sometimes less concerned with constituents than with their own power and privileges. These criticisms have some merit, and Congress periodically attempts to address them through reforms in its structures and ways of operating.[32] However, despite the desire for a "simpler" Congress, the real question is whether a large and complex nation can have anything but a large and complex legislature.

CONGRESS AND LAWMAKING

Those who enjoy sausages and laws, the old saying goes, should never watch either being made. The process of lawmaking is certainly messy. Sometimes good ideas are never embodied in law; sometimes bad ones are. As we saw in the case of AmeriCorps, sometimes lawmakers exhibit noble leadership; sometimes they show little but self-interest, even greed. But as we have emphasized in this chapter, Congress as

TABLE 8.5. HOUSE AND SENATE COMPARED

House	*Senate*
435 members*	100 members
More structured	Less structured
More rule-driven	Less rule-driven
Committees dominate process	Committees less dominant
Limited floor debate	Unlimited floor debate
Strict rules for amending bills	Few rules on amending bills
Majority party-dominated	More individualistic
Operates more quickly	Operates more slowly

* Number does not include nonvoting delegates from Guam, American Samoa, the American Virgin Islands, Puerto Rico, and Washington, D.C.

an institution reflects all that is good and bad about human nature in general, and this is especially true of the lawmaking process.

HOUSE VERSUS SENATE

Before going further, it will be useful to point out a few distinctions between the House and the Senate as institutions (see Table 8.5). These differences affect lawmaking in that each chamber must pass the same bill in exactly the same language before it can be sent to the president for consideration (discussed later).[33]

In general, the House works more quickly than does the Senate. This may seem counterintuitive, but the House's large size, and the cohesion generated by the majority party caucus, makes it a more formal body. Bills supported by the majority party move quickly through the process, because the minority has little chance of stopping the majority. More work gets done in committee, with very few amendments on the House floor, and debate on the House floor tends to operate according to strict rules and time limits.

By contrast, the Senate is more informal, and tends to give individual senators far more freedom. Senate leaders do not have the same formal powers over the legislative process that their House counterparts enjoy. They must spend more time negotiating with colleagues in both parties on every matter, including the amount of time allotted to floor debate. Senate committees also have less control over the shape of a bill, because senators have a great deal of freedom to make changes in bills on the Senate floor. In contrast to the House, the Senate's tradition of unlimited debate grants all senators the right to speak as long as they wish, even to the point of blocking a vote on a bill. This right forces senators to take into account the views of all of their colleagues, regardless of party. The Senate thus operates by the principle of "unanimous consent." If all senators agree to go along, the Senate can work quickly.

If not, it moves very slowly, and sometimes not at all. For them, speed is less important than consensus.

We should not overstate the importance of these distinctions. At times the House moves very slowly, and the Senate can move with great speed. Senators also are just as likely as House members to care about enacting legislation and serving constituents. But the different sizes of the two bodies, the different sizes of their constituencies, and the different lengths of their terms of office do affect the lawmaking process.

THE STAGES OF LAWMAKING

It is useful to picture lawmaking as a linear process involving a series of distinct stages (see Figure 8.2). Keep in mind, however, that in real life lawmaking is a lot messier and less predictable than a linear depiction of the process suggests. Still, thinking about legislating as a series of stages helps us to make sense of the often bewildering process of turning ideas into laws.

Each stage of the legislative process involves a struggle between those who want to pass a bill and those who oppose it. Those in favor must work a lot harder, because they must assemble enough support to push the bill to the next stage of the process. And they must do this repeatedly. Those opposed to the bill, by contrast, only have to fight to keep the bill from moving to another stage. Those who oppose change, therefore, have the advantage.

Ideas   Any bill begins with an idea. Although average citizens sometimes propose new legislation, most proposals come from the executive branch, interest groups, public policy institutes, political parties, or individual members of Congress. Many pieces of legislation arise out of ideas that have been floating around in Congress for years, surfacing when the "windows of opportunity" for passage seem to be open.[34] For example, the idea of a national service corps had been circulating for years, but it made little headway until Bill Clinton made community service a focus of his 1992 campaign and a major initiative of his new administration. On the other hand, as we saw in chapter 7, the "window of opportunity" for comprehensive health care reform opened and closed rather quickly.

Consideration by Committees   Whatever its origins, a bill must be formally proposed by a member of either chamber, after which it is assigned to a standing committee and, from there, usually to a subcommittee for consideration. Identical bills are often introduced simultaneously in both chambers in hopes of speeding up the process.

For most bills, subcommittee **hearings** are convened to allow interested individuals and organizations to testify for and against the proposal. After the hearings the subcommittee has a **mark-up** session in which members go over the bill line by line, approving or revising parts of it, often after considerable debate and negotiation. If it

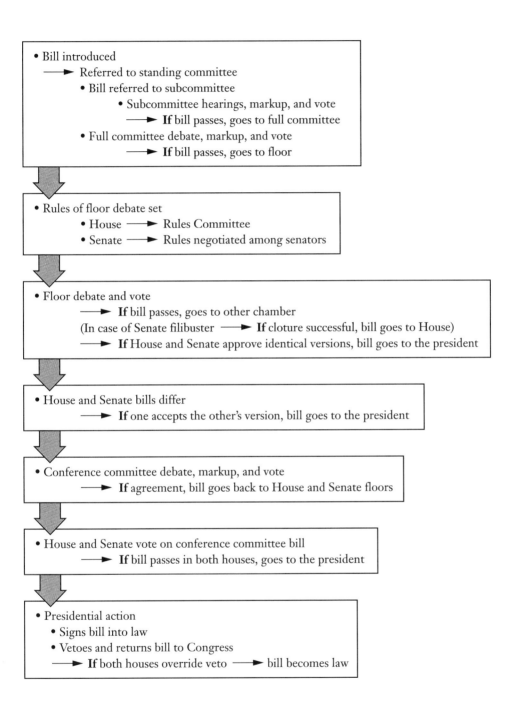

FIGURE 8.2. THE LAWMAKING PROCESS

is approved by the subcommittee, the bill is reported to the full committee for further consideration. The full committee may hold its own hearings, especially on major pieces of legislation. The committee then votes on whether to send the bill to the floor for debate. Most bills do not get past this stage.

Floor Action   Bills that are approved by a committee go to the floor of the chamber for debate and action. In the House, the Rules Committee must first determine the length and timing of floor debate, as well as whether amendments will be allowed. To be brought to the floor, most bills must obtain a *rule* from this committee. The Rules Committee (and, therefore, the majority party leadership) thus acts as a "gatekeeper" and has a good deal of leverage over which bills can proceed further. The Senate is more informal in this respect: The rules of debate are negotiated by the majority and minority party leaders and are always subject to the unanimous consent of the senators.

Floor action consists of debate, consideration of amendments, and a final vote on the bill. House debate runs according to a tight schedule, with few members allowed more than a minute or two to speak. Senate debate traditionally continues until all senators who wish to speak have done so. The Senate's tradition of free debate can lead to a **filibuster,** in which one or more senators try to "talk a bill to death," sometimes holding up action until the bill's sponsors give up or agree to a compromise. The only way to defeat a filibuster is through a vote on a motion of **cloture,** which must be approved by a three-fifths majority of the senators present. Some complain that the filibuster gives too much power to one or a few senators, but senators are reluctant to abolish a tool for influencing lawmaking that they might want to use themselves someday.[35]

A bill that is passed in one chamber must also win approval in the other, normally by the same process as before. Both chambers must pass the bill in identical form and language for it to become law, so as discussed earlier, differences between the House and Senate versions are often ironed out by a conference committee. If the conference committee reaches a compromise, the new version must be approved with no changes by both chambers before it can be sent to the president. Sometimes one chamber simply accepts the version passed by the other, so no conference committee is needed. If the two chambers cannot agree, the bill "dies," and its supporters must decide whether and when to try again.

PRESIDENTIAL ACTION

Having received a bill that has been passed by both chambers, the president has three options. The president can sign the bill, which then becomes law. Or the president can **veto** the bill and return it to Congress. For a vetoed bill to become law it must be passed again by both houses of Congress, but this time it must be approved by a two-thirds majority of those present in each chamber. Bills that do not meet this standard die. (The president's veto power is discussed more fully in chapter 9.)

Finally, the president can do nothing, in which case the bill becomes law automatically after 10 legislative days. However, when Congress passes a bill fewer than 10 days before it is scheduled to adjourn and the president does not sign the bill, it automatically dies at the end of the congressional session. Such a condition is called a **pocket veto** because the president has, in effect, "pocketed" the bill. Pocket vetoes cannot be overridden, because Congress has adjourned.

MAKING DECISIONS

What factors shape how members of Congress make decisions on individual bills? For one, members of Congress differ considerably in their perceptions of how they do their jobs: These differences are based on their backgrounds, values, and political circumstances. Members also behave differently depending on the type of issue before them. A key factor here is whether their constituents know or care about an issue.

There are three basic models of representation based on how members see themselves and their roles. Each affects how a member of Congress behaves. In the **delegate model,** legislators vote according to their constituents' opinions on issues about which they clearly hold strong feelings, such as abortion. Members thus act as "delegates" of their constituencies, faithfully mirroring voters' views in Congress.[36] For example, almost all of the House Republicans who voted for the two articles of impeachment against President Clinton in December,1998, represented districts in which the voters did not support Clinton in either the 1992 or the 1996 presidential elections. These House members saw themselves as delegates of their constituents, and voted accordingly.

But, as we saw in chapter 5, public opinion is often divided on issues such as welfare or affirmative action. In such cases members are likely to vote according to their party's ideological stance. Democrats will vote along party lines because they hold similar values on such issues, at least when compared to Republicans. This fits into the **party responsibility model** of representation, in which the ideological differences between the parties more accurately predict members' voting behavior.[37]

On some issues constituents have no strong views and the party takes no stand. In such instances members are free to vote according to their own beliefs about what is good public policy. Such cases fit the **trusteeship model** of representation, in which members of Congress are said to act as "trustees" of the public good. Foreign policy issues tend to fit this model, except when the policy affects specific ethnic constituencies (such as policy toward Cuba or Israel) or when members face the prospect of sending American troops into armed conflict (such as when U.S. forces were sent to Kuwait, Somalia, and parts of the former Yugoslavia).

Voting Cues   Beyond these rough models of representation, figuring out why members vote the way they do is not easy. Many factors are subtle, hidden, or interwoven. Political scientists such as John Kingdon argue that members are influenced most by their constituents, followed by their colleagues.[38] That is, on issues with no direct impact on or clear message from constituents, a member of Congress will often look to colleagues who hold similar values for "cues" to how to vote when the member has little direct knowledge of or interest in the issue. Banding together with

Voting on the floor. In the House, members usually vote electronically, using encoded plastic cards that they slide through a reader and then punch in their vote. In the Senate, most votes are by roll call, during which senators call out their votes when the clerk calls out their names.

colleagues also makes it is easier to cast a vote on controversial issues. Also, as we noted earlier in discussing the party responsibility model of representation, members usually vote with their party on issues where there are clear differences between the parties. For example, most Democrats supported Clinton's AmeriCorps proposal, whereas most Republicans opposed it. Some of this division was partisan, but much of it was ideological.

As we saw in chapter 7, interest groups also influence voting behavior, particularly when their needs coincide with those of constituents. Groups with little influence over or connection to the people back home carry far less weight in influencing a member's vote. Interest group money by itself might influence behavior if the issue does not affect constituents, but most groups donate to members who already support their views.

Except under extraordinary conditions, the president has only a modest impact on voting behavior, even for members of the president's party. Presidents are most influential when they are popular among a member's own constituents; by contrast, representatives or senators rarely go against constituents' views, even to support a generally popular president.[39] For example, no president can influence a member's vote on abortion if doing so goes against constituents' views or the member's own values. Even on far less controversial issues, presidential capacity to influence congressional voting behavior hinges on the degree to which the issue has public support. Presidents know this, so they spend a great deal of time trying to generate public approval for their proposals. As we will see in more detail in chapter 9, a president's ability to persuade the public is a key factor in winning the approval of Congress.

FACTORS IN LEGISLATIVE SUCCESS AND FAILURE

Only a very small percentage of the bills that are proposed become law, so it is important to understand the factors that determine legislative success or failure.

First, the committee stage is crucial—and usually fatal. Most bills do not make it past this stage because their supporters were unable to put together a large enough coalition of committee members to win approval. A majority of the members in the House or Senate can vote to "discharge" a bill from a recalcitrant committee, but this rarely occurs. Few members will interfere with the decisions of other committees.

Second, legislating is a slow, drawn-out process. This creates an environment that encourages consensus building and fosters fairness. All sides are supposed get a chance to express their views. This makes Congress look inefficient but also helps members avoid hasty deliberations. And, as the framers of the Constitution noted, sometimes it is better not to pass a bill if the alternative is a bad one.

Third, under normal conditions the lawmaking process reflects the decentralization of Congress. Power is spread out among members and committees, and no one wants to be left out. If everyone is included, it is difficult for any individual or group to dominate. However, there is a tension between the centralizing force of the party system and the decentralizing force of the committee system.[40] Party leaders have tremendous influence, especially in the House, but the committee system's ties to members' particular needs allows it to dominate the legislative process despite the more national focus of party leaders. When in doubt, members of Congress stick with their constituents.

Fourth, the legislative process offers many points of access to those who seek to affect a bill's future. Congress is a remarkably open institution, which makes members highly vulnerable to outside pressures, and its structure provides many avenues through which constituents, lobbyists, members of the media, and others can gain access to legislators. All of this adds to the institution's decentralization and slowness.

Finally, it is important to keep in mind that success depends on the willingness of members to compromise, thereby creating the necessary majorities of support at each stage of the process. It is far easier to block a bill than to pass one, a reality that reflects the system's bias in favor of forcing consensus, especially on controversial issues.

CONCLUSION

Look at a dollar bill. It says, in Latin, *e pluribus unum*, or "out of many, one." Out of many people, many states, many diverse interests, is built one nation. That, in short, is the primary task of the constitutional system in general and of Congress in particular.

Lawmaking is a slow, deliberative process. Failures are common. Those who created the system intended it to be this way. Yet to many Americans the process of bargaining and consensus building necessary to build winning majorities looks ungainly.

A public that demands fast action on major problems such as health care or crime is likely to become frustrated with this process, so it is no surprise that so many people look to the president for leadership. This is inevitable: Congress was designed to represent, to deliberate, to build consensus. It was not designed to lead.

Even so, Congress is the most open and democratic institution in the American political system. Its flaws are similar to those found in any institution in which people from all over the country come together to debate the issues, argue about their differences, and try to find common ground. No matter how it is organized, Congress is destined to be loud, messy, frustrating, and slow. But so is democratic government generally. Demands for efficiency and speed inevitably collide with the desires to be heard and to make a difference. Congress is where these competing impulses come together. It is the nation's grand arena for conflict and compromise.

In 1998 House Republicans tried once again to get rid of AmeriCorps, the national service program that many conservatives did not support. As before, President Clinton threatened to veto any appropriations bill that eliminated the program. Republicans gave in on AmeriCorps, but they won some concessions on other spending items. The conflict over AmeriCorps continues where it should: in Congress.

SUMMARY

▶ Congress has several core functions, some of which conflict with others. It alone has the authority to make the law, but its members also seek to represent the people. It must keep an eye on the president, oversee the federal bureaucracy, appropriate funds for national programs, declare war, preserve the nation, and defend the Constitution. Differing views about the proper role of Congress shape public perceptions of the institution's role in government.

▶ Members of the House are elected from districts, senators from states. Congressional elections tend to be influenced more by local factors than by national ones, and incumbents have an advantage under most conditions. These advantages include greater name recognition, easier access to media, an array of resources that go along with being a member of Congress, and, finally, a greater ability to raise campaign funds from individuals and organized interest groups.

▶ The inherent decentralization of Congress as an institution reflects the relative independence of its members. In this regard, both the power of party leaders and the workings of the committee system reflect the degree to which members are willing to impose on themselves the structure and rules necessary to pursue their dual goals of representation and legislation.

▶ The lawmaking process contains many roadblocks, and only a relative few of the thousands of bills introduced each year make it to the president's desk for approval. The key to passage of a bill is compromise and the creation of majorities of support at every stage of the process. In general, it is far easier to stop legislation than to get it enacted.

❯ Congress may be the most important institution in representative government, yet it is the one that is most likely to generate public ridicule or hostility. This is a normal, if regrettable, result of an open institution that reflects the vagaries of human nature.

QUESTIONS FOR REVIEW AND DISCUSSION

1. Why do people dislike Congress as an institution even when they hold positive views about their own members of Congress? What is the practical impact of this phenomenon?

2. How would you encourage greater diversity in terms of gender, race, occupation, and affluence among the members of Congress? Would this have any impact on how Congress acts on particular issues?

3. Compare the organizational structure of a university faculty, a corporation, and Congress. In what ways are these three hierarchies similar? How are they different? What are the effects of these similarities and differences?

4. What factors influence success or failure in legislating? What does this tell you about the nature of lawmaking in the American political system?

TERMS TO REMEMBER

bicameral legislature	incumbent	party whips
casework	joint committee	pocket veto
census	majority and minority	president pro tempore
cloture	leaders	reapportionment
conference committee	malapportionment	redistricting
delegate model	mark-up	select committee
filibuster	open seats	Speaker of the House
franking privilege	party caucus	standing committee
gerrymandering	party responsibility	subcommittee
hearings	model	trusteeship model
		veto

WEB SOURCES

Congressional Budget Office (www.cbo.gov) and the General Accounting Office (www.gao.gov). Sites operated by two of the three major congressional support agencies (the third is the Library of Congress, at www.loc.gov). The CBO advises Congress on the federal budget, whereas the GAO assesses federal programs.

How to Lobby Congress (www.iaff.org/iaff/GovAff/index.html). A site operated by the International Association of Firefighters that offers a primer on how to be an effective advocate on Capitol Hill. Another interesting site is offered by a lobbying firm, Marlowe & Company (www.netlobby.com/pgic.html).

Thomas (http://thomas.loc.gov/). A Library of Congress site that allows the user to follow the progress of any piece of legislation as it goes through the process. An excellent place to start any research on Congress and its members. The official sites of the U.S. House of Representatives (www.house.gov) and U.S. Senate (www.senate.gov) are good for links to individual members' Web pages and for seeing how each house operates.

SUGGESTED READINGS

There are many good treatments of "how a bill becomes a law," but two of the best are: Jeffrey Birnbaum and Alan Murray, *Showdown at Gucci Gulch: Lawmakers, Lobbyists, and the Unlikely Triumph of Tax Reform* (New York: Random House, 1987), in which the authors trace the often unpredictable path of a major 1986 tax reform legislation; and Steven Waldman, *The Bill: How the Adventures of Clinton's National Service Bill Reveal What Is Corrupt, Comic, Cynical—and Noble—about Washington* (New York: Viking, 1995), which relates to the creation of AmeriCorps. Both books are well written, lively, and convey a sense of how Congress really works.

Thomas P. O'Neill Jr. with William Novak, *Man of the House* (New York: St. Martin's Press, 1987). The autobiography of "Tip" O'Neill, Speaker of the House (1977–1986) that conveys both the "old" Congress of smoke-filled rooms and the "new" Congress dominated by mass media. O'Neill, a product of the "old" Congress, was able to make the transition to the "new" Congress and, in the process, redefined the office he occupied. One of the best, and most enjoyable, books of its kind.

David R. Mayhew, *Congress: The Electoral Connection* (New Haven, CT: Yale University Press, 1974). A classic look at the ways in which members of Congress do their jobs, and in the process make it easier for them to gain reelection. Among Mayhew's contributions are the three advantages of incumbency—advertising, position taking, and credit claiming—discussed in this chapter.

NOTES

1. Steven Waldman, *The Bill: How the Adventures of Clinton's National Service Bill Reveal What Is Corrupt, Comic, Cynical—and Noble—about Washington* (New York: Viking, 1995).

2. Roger Davidson and Walter Olezsek, *Congress and Its Members*, 6th ed. (Washington, D.C.: Congressional Quarterly Press, 1998), pp. 4–5.

3. Leroy N. Rieselbach, *Congressional Reform* (Washington, D.C.: Congressional Quarterly Press, 1986), pp. 6–9.

4. James McGregor Burns, *Presidential Government* (Boston: Houghton Mifflin, 1966).

5. James Sundquist, *Constitutional Reform and Effective Government* (Washington, D.C.: Brookings Institution, 1986).

6. *Wesberry v Sanders*, 376 US 1 (1964).

7. Bruce Cain, *The Reapportionment Puzzle* (Los Angeles: University of California Press, 1984).

8. Richard Fenno, *Home Style: House Members in Their Districts* (Boston: Little, Brown, 1978).

9. Gary C. Jacobsen, *The Politics of Congressional Elections*, 4th ed. (New York: Harper Collins, 1997).

10. Gerald Benjamin and Michael J. Malbin, eds., *Limiting Legislative Terms* (Washington, D.C.: Congressional Quarterly Press, 1992).

11. David Mayhew, *Congress: The Electoral Connection* (New Haven: Yale University Press, 1974).

12. R. Douglas Arnold, *The Logic of Congressional Action* (New Haven: Yale University Press, 1990).

13. Federal Election Commission, "FEC Reports on Congressional Fundraising for 1997–98," April 28, 1999; www.fec.gov/press/canye98.htm.

14. Ibid.

15. Ibid., as calculated from FEC data; www.fec.gov/press/canye98.htm.

16. Federal Elections Commission; http://www.fec.gov/press/s30gself.htm.

17. Leroy N. Rieselbach, *Congressional Politics: The Evolving Legislative System*, 2d ed. (Boulder: Westview Press, 1995), p. 74, n. 15.

18. Gary C. Jacobson, "The Misallocation of Resources in House Campaigns," in Lawrence C. Dodd and Bruce I. Oppenheimer, eds., *Congress Reconsidered*, 5th ed. (Washington, D.C.: Congressional Quarterly Press, 1993), pp. 115–140.

19. See Diana M. Evans, "PAC Contributions and Roll-Call Voting: Conditional Power," in Allan J. Cigler and Burdett A. Loomis, ed., *Interest Group Politics*, 2d ed. (Washington, D.C.: Congressional Quarterly Press, 1986), pp. 114–132.

20. FEC, "Independent Expenditures Aggregating $1,000 or More Made after October 14, 1998," Report, November 6, 1998; http://www.fec.gov/1996/24cannm.htm.

21. Rieselbach, *Congressional Politics*, pp. 64–70.

22. *Washington Post*/ABC News Poll, June 6, 1999; www.washingtonpost.com/wp-srv/politics/polls/vault/vault.htm.

23. Roger H. Davidson and Walter J. Oleszek, *Congress against Itself* (Bloomington: Indiana University Press, 1977).

24. Joseph Cooper and David Brady, "Institutional Context and Leadership Style: The House from Cannon to Rayburn," *American Political Science Review*, vol. 75, no. 2 (June 1981), pp. 411–425.

25. Ronald M. Peters Jr., *The American Speakership: The Office in Historical Perspective* (Baltimore, MD: Johns Hopkins University Press, 1990); Richard A. Baker and Roger H. Davidson, eds., *First Among Equals: Outstanding Senate Leaders of the Twentieth Century* (Washington, D.C.: Congressional Quarterly Press, 1991).

26. Steven Smith and Christopher Deering, *Committees in Congress*, 2d ed. (Washington, D.C.: Congressional Quarterly Press, 1990).

27. Woodrow Wilson, *Congressional Government* (New York: Meridian Books, 1956; originally published 1885), p. 69.

28. Richard Fenno, *Congressmen in Committees* (Boston: Little, Brown, 1973).

29. Davidson and Oleszek, *Congress and Its Members*, pp. 144–146.

30. Ibid., pp. 212–214.

31. Harrison W. Fox Jr. and Susan W. Hammond, *Congressional Staffs: The Invisible Force in American Lawmaking* (New York: Free Press, 1977).

32. Roger H. Davidson, ed., *The Post-Reform Congress* (New York: St. Martin's Press, 1992).

33. See Ross K. Baker, *House and Senate*, 2d ed. (New York: Norton, 1995).

34. John W. Kingdon, *Agendas, Alternatives, and Public Policy* (Boston: Little, Brown, 1984).

35. See Fred R. Harris, *Deadlock or Decision: The U.S. Senate and the Rise of National Politics* (New York: Oxford University Press, 1993).

36. John C. Wahlke, Heinz Eulau, William Buchanan, and Leroy C. Ferguson, *The Legislative System* (New York: Wiley, 1962).

37. Warren E. Miller and Donald E. Stokes, "Constituency Influence in Congress," *American Political Science Review*, vol. 57, no. 1 (March 1963), pp. 45–57.

38. John W. Kingdon, *Congressmens' Voting Decisions*, 2d ed. (New York: Harper & Row, 1981); see also Aage R. Clausen, *How Congressmen Decide: A Policy Focus* (New York: St. Martin's Press, 1973).

39. See George C. Edwards III, *At the Margins: Presidential Leadership in Congress* (New Haven: Yale University Press, 1989).

40. See William J. Keefe, *Congress and the American People*, 3d ed. (Upper Saddle River, NJ: Prentice Hall, 1988).

PRIMARY SOURCE READINGS

THE CASE FOR TERM LIMITS

During the 1990s many Americans supported efforts to enact limits on the number terms of office that could be served by members of Congress. Knowing the difficulty of passing an amendment to the U.S. Constitution, pro-term-limits activists turned instead to getting voters to amend state constitutions to limit terms of office of members of Congress from those states. This strategy was later ruled unconstitutional by the U.S. Supreme Court. This excerpt is from a legal brief filed by one pro-term-limits group in support of a Washington State term limits law.

Some believe that those who have served for long in elective public office tend to derive accumulated wisdom about the problems they face, gather knowledge of the branch of government for which they are responsible, acquire skill at making the machinery of government work and develop both a perceptive discernment of their constituents' needs and wishes and a keen skepticism for lobbyists' blandishments. Others are convinced that a long period in office tends to create arrogant, cynical careerists, resistant to reform, out of touch with the electorate, skilled at—and caring for—little but how to get reelected. . . .

Term limits reduce pressure on voters to express parochialism in their votes. This is the attitude expressed by so many candidates, and accepted by so many voters, that a legislator's role is to act as an ambassador or lobbyist, seeking to advance the interests of his own constituency rather than a committee member seeking the welfare of the whole population for whom the laws are made. . . .

Term limits reduce the practice of pork. 'Pork' may be defined as public spending that benefits some in the particular place where the cost for the total jurisdiction is exceeded by its value; for example, an unnecessary dam or highway or a tax break to a local manufacturer. Long service, seniority, enables pork to be dispensed in the senior legislator's district due to his clout. Many voters would like to reduce pork, as being against the public interest, and know that they can do so by replacing a pork-dispensing senior with a junior. They are unwilling to do this, however, where they must pay the price of losing their share of pork, yet knowing that the total quantity of pork dispensed remains unabated. . . .

By ousting all legislators over a certain seniority level and reducing the penalty for replacing incumbents below that level, term limits can both decrease ideological slack and lessen overall pork. The result is not to fetter democratic references but to further them. With term limits, each district gets both ideological representation closer to its views and a lower overall amount of pork it prefers. . . .

Term limits may be compared to an arms control agreement. Such a treaty gets rid of an arms race that puts a burden on all, while leaving the parties with no change in their relative power. It avoids what most will not consider: unilateral disarmament—or its counterpart, ousting a powerful senior incumbent. . . .

Two of the main purposes of term limits are: (1) to break the alliance between entrenched incumbents and special interest groups and their lobbyists who make contributions in support for reelection campaigns, . . . and (2) to reduce the parochialism of supporting actions which help a legislator's district, but less than it harms (generally costs) the total jurisdiction.

Term limits cannot fix special interest politics, but they do ease the problem. First, the expected returns are drastically reduced for special interest lobbyists investing time in personal relationships and contributing to campaigns for a short term as compared to that of a lifelong incumbent. . . . Second, lobbyists cannot trade on long term personal relationships, and campaign contributions, but must marshal facts and evidence to support their clients' positions. . . . Third, term limits make politicians more beholden to their party for support in elections, and the party has to consider all voters of the state, not just the special interest of the district. . . . Fourth, if legislators must return to ordinary civil society and live under the laws and pay the taxes which they pass, their incentives change; they become more aligned with the public. . . .

Term limits offer voters a choice of a better quality of candidates by reducing entry barriers. The longer the service, the greater the advantage given an incumbent over a challenger. . . . The prospective burden of overcoming a long-established incumbent's advantage tends to deter prospective candidates from entering a race. The deterrent tends to be stronger upon those of high quality because they have other appealing opportunities. This leaves the field to second raters who run because their limited vocational opportunities make them willing to bet on themselves as long shots.

Term limits encourage successful and effective politicians to compete with each other for another office, rather than holding a seat that long incumbency has made safe. Not only does seniority "clout" enable legislators to marshal special interests to defeat challengers, but other advantages of office make it difficult for challengers: name recognition, case work for constituents, press conferences, appearing on radio and television programs, opportunities to speak at civic clubs and preside over public ceremonies all give incumbents enormous "brand name" advantages. . . .

While it is intuitively obvious that term limits reduce the political barriers to entry and brandname advantages, less obvious is that term limits not only bring in new citizen politicians, but also press those interested in a political career to challenge incumbents more often. Term limits thus cause structural change which should be seen as beneficial even for those who continue to believe in the professionalization of politics. Under a term limits regime, a politician can have a career only on an "up or out" basis. . . .

Term limits advance the following important state interests: (1) provide rotation in office; (2) counter incumbents' indifference to conditions and concerns of the people; (3) reduce incumbents' advantages in elections; (4) prevent discouragement of qualified citizens who want to run for office; (5) reduce the influence of special interests.

THE CASE AGAINST TERM LIMITS

Testimony before the U.S. House of Representatives, Subcommittee on the Constitution. Becky Cain, President, League of Women Voters of the United States, February 3, 1995

Mr. Chairman, our political system is failing the American people. Citizens are disgusted—and they have every reason to be—with the role of special interests and "big money" in the political process, with the emptiness of modern political campaigns and with our government's seeming inability to deal in a meaningful way with national problems such as health care, crime and the economy. And just as the American people have a number of complaints about the ways in which government responds—or fails to respond—to their needs and concerns, so too are there a number of things we can do to fix the American political system. But, term limits for members of Congress are not one of them.

Rather, term limits are a smoke screen, a simplistic answer to hard questions about our government, questions that demand equally hard choices. It is easy, as it always has been, to holler, "Throw the bums out!" It is a more complicated, thoughtful process, however, to throw out the pieces of the system that are corrupting or that don't work and to keep and strengthen what's good and productive about our government. Term limits are a "meat axe" approach that does not distinguish between legislators whose careers deserve to be cut short and those who deserve reelection. . . .

The truth is, we already have term limits. They're called elections. If we don't like the job that our elected representatives in Washington are doing, we can support other candidates and vote incumbents out. The [1994] election provides the clearest demonstration of the power of the ballot box. Not only were the Speaker of the House, the Chair of the House Ways and Means Committee and the Chair of the Senate Budget Committee defeated, but control of both houses turned over, bringing to power new chairs for every committee and subcommittee in Congress, including this one. . . .

In addition to arbitrarily limiting voter choice, here's what else is wrong with term limits:

1. Term limits would weaken the legislative branch of government—and strengthen an already powerful Presidency, upsetting the constitutional balance of powers. . . . A Congress of amateurs . . . would by its very nature be more pliable and deferential—and the institution would be robbed of its historic role of restraining the power of the Executive, who controls the entire federal bureaucracy. As a result, the branch of government closest to the people would become a less-effective advocate for its constituents.

2. Term limits would result in increased reliance on congressional staff, lobbyists and other unelected "insiders." Novice legislators would depend much more on staff to sort out complicated issues and to keep things running—at a time when many argue that congressional staff is already too influential. Inexperienced representatives would also be forced to turn to Washington lobbyists and other "insiders" for advice on issues. . . .

3. Term limits ignore the need for experience in management of public policy. There is nothing wrong with entrusting decisions about complex and crucial issues that can affect our lives and the world we live in to people with professional experience. We recognize the importance of experience in other walks of life. . . . Surely experience counts. Term limits would require legislators to exit the system just as they are developing a working knowledge of how it does and doesn't work—and just as their developing understanding of the system would place them in a position to offer meaningful proposals for making it work better.

4. Term limits would put our elected officials in a position of always thinking about their "next job," giving them an excuse not to be responsive to the people who elect them. Elected representatives with a built-in cutoff date are less likely to be swayed by their constituents' interests and more likely to respond to the special interests who might provide them with a job—or at least a hand in finding one—after their term is over. . . .

5. Term limits would limit the field of potential candidates for public office. Running for and holding public office is too expensive, too life-dis-

rupting, too privacy-invading and too time-consuming to become a popular "sabbatical" choice for dedicated and serious citizens who are pursuing other careers. Candidates running for term-limited offices will tend to be the rich or the retired.

6. Term limits would encourage legislators to consider the short-term over the long-term. Term-limited legislators would know for certain that they wouldn't be around to deal with the long-term consequences of many of their decisions. Their limited time in office would encourage them to focus on "quick fixes," gimmicks and programs that might be wildly popular at the moment but that might result in severe repercussions down the road.

We in the League of Women Voters believe that there are many effective ways to deal with the public's disillusionment and anger, and to reform the American political process. Comprehensive campaign finance reform would be a good start. The public understands the role of special interests and "big money" in politics, and the public understands that reform is needed. We also need to reform the ways that campaigns are run. We need to build civic activism. We need to encourage informed voting.

What we don't need is a constitutional amendment to set term limits for members of Congress. The voters don't need to be regulated.

THE PRESIDENCY

OBJECTIVES

- ❑ To understand the symbolic role of the presidency in American society
- ❑ To make the distinction between presidential authority and presidential power
- ❑ To compare the formal bases of presidential authority to public expectations about what presidents can achieve
- ❑ To explore the contextual bases of presidential leadership, particularly the president's relationship with Congress
- ❑ To assess the connection between the president and the public in a democratic system

The Hero of Kuwait, February, 1991. President George Bush meets with U.S. troops aboard an aircraft carrier in the Persian Gulf after the expulsion of Iraqi troops from Kuwait. Bush's role in leading the victory over Iraq did not prevent his defeat in the 1992 presidential election.

In August, 1990, Iraq invaded and occupied the neighboring nation of Kuwait on the assertion that it was reclaiming a former province. U.S. President George Bush was outraged that one nation would so brazenly invade another and feared that Iraq's actions might further destabilize the politically volatile Persian Gulf region. He dispatched tens of thousands of American troops to Saudi Arabia, which borders both Iraq and Kuwait, and ordered other American naval and air force units into the region. The deployment of U.S. troops was meant to warn Iraq against further aggression and assure to American allies in the Middle East that the United States would take an active role in forcing Iraq to withdraw from Kuwait.

President Bush also began building several coalitions. The first was a coalition of nations, organized as both a symbolic and a military response to the invasion. Sensitive to potential charges that the United States was throwing its weight around, Bush and U.S. military leaders assembled a multinational military force, including units from nations such as Great Britain, Germany, Canada, Australia, and Italy, as well as Arab nations Egypt and Saudi Arabia, to assist American forces in ousting Iraq from Kuwait. On the diplomatic front, Bush built a coalition in the United Nations to support a formal authorization of the use of force against Iraq should such an action become necessary. Although the United States alone had the military power to force Iraq out of Kuwait, Bush knew that the legitimacy of any action depended on gaining the support of the world community.

Bush also had to build coalitions at home. He had sent American troops to the Middle East without formal congressional approval, using existing treaties with Kuwait and Saudi Arabia as justification for his actions. Because of these treaties, and with United Nations support, the president probably had the legal authority to carry out military actions against Iraq without formal action by Congress. But because armed conflict was likely to result in American casualties, Bush and American military leaders understood the symbolic importance of gaining broad domestic support for any military action in the Persian Gulf. These concerns were widespread in the wake of the nation's bitter experience in Vietnam, where 58,000 Americans died in a long war that was never formally declared by Congress.

The Bush administration thereupon set out to convince the American public and Congress that Iraq's actions could not go unanswered. Although many Americans were not convinced that the United States should be fighting a war in the Middle East, they nonetheless expressed support for the American military forces in the Gulf. In January, 1991, after often heated debate, Bush won the bipartisan support of Congress. A few days later the military coalition commenced a massive air campaign against Iraq, followed two weeks later by a short ground assault that expelled the Iraqi forces from Kuwait. George Bush was hailed as a hero, and according to public opinion polls, nearly 91 percent of Americans approved of the job he was doing as president.[1]

Twenty months later George Bush was out of a job. In November, 1992, Bush, the liberator of Kuwait, was defeated for reelection to a second term by Governor Bill Clinton of Arkansas. The issues driving the 1992 election were the economy, health care, and the federal budget deficit—not Kuwait, or foreign policy generally—and on these issues a majority of the voters wanted a change in leadership. Bush, who had been able to command the world's most powerful military and build coalitions among the nations of the world, lost the presidency because he could no longer convince Americans that he was the right person to lead them for another four years. In this regard, he found out in an especially blunt way what all presidents discover: the intangibility and fleeting nature of presidential popularity and power.

THE SYMBOLIC PRESIDENCY

The presidency occupies a special place in the American political system, in part because of the unique structure of the office itself. Article II of the Constitution makes the president both head of government and head of state. As head of government, the president seeks to shape public policy and is in charge of the daily workings of a vast federal bureaucracy (see chapter 10). As a result, the president invariably becomes embroiled in intense, often partisan struggles with other political actors, especially members of Congress.

As head of state, however, the president is expected to rise above "petty politics" and act as a symbol of the nation as a whole, as Bush did with regard to Kuwait. President Ronald Reagan, who as head of government regularly engaged in partisan politics, acted as head of state in 1986, when he represented the nation at memorial services for the astronauts killed in the explosion of the space shuttle *Challenger*. So did President Bill Clinton, another noted political fighter, when in 1993 he presided over the signing of a new Middle East peace agreement on the White House lawn.

The American presidency thus combines two often contradictory roles. By contrast, in Great Britain the two roles are performed by different individuals; the prime minister, a political figure, is the head of government while the monarch, the symbol of the nation, acts as the nonpolitical head of state. The same pattern holds in most other democratic nations.

The symbolic presidency. President Bill Clinton deplanes from *Air Force One*, to be greeted in full ceremony. Such images convey the impression that the American president is the contemporary version of the Roman Emperor, the most powerful person in the world. Whether reality fits the image is another matter.

Much of the distinctiveness of the American presidency also stems from the sheer size, wealth, and global power of the United States. The nation's status gives the president a level of automatic prestige and visibility that is shared by few political figures anywhere. Indeed, the *office* of the presidency commands greater public recognition and respect than any *person* who occupies it.[2] So great is the prestige of the office that the vice president (see Box 9.1, p. 378) is automatically considered a serious contender to succeed the incumbent.

The modern presidency is also a constant focus of global media attention. For the sitting president this is mixed blessing. On one hand, the president can get media coverage for almost any pronouncement or activity, and a major speech is guaranteed national and international television coverage. On the other hand, presidents find themselves in a media fishbowl, their every action or comment a juicy topic for public speculation by virtually every newspaper, magazine, talk radio commentator, Internet chat room, and television network. By extension, presidential spouses and children, even presidential pets, come under intense and often unflattering public scrutiny. The media frenzy surrounding Bill Clinton's sexual imbroglios is a spectacular example of this reality, but it is not unique.

Finally, public perceptions about the grandeur and power of the presidency are shaped by the almost imperial trappings of the office, which are largely designed to protect the president from harm. Presidents fly exclusively in *Air Force One*, a modified Boeing 747 jumbo jet equipped with an office, advanced communications gear, and sleeping facilities. On the ground, presidents travel in convoys of armored limousines, accompanied by legions of personal assistants, reporters, and, of course, heavily armed Secret Service agents. Presidents work and live behind tight security in the richly decorated (if surprisingly small and crowded) White House, where they also entertain visiting dignitaries at elegant state dinners and from which they can fly by helicopter to relax in the protected privacy of the Maryland woods at Camp David. They rub elbows with movie stars, sports figures, artists, and corporate leaders, who in turn are eager to meet them. Presidents always complain that the trappings of the office isolate them from average citizens, but none willingly give up the job.

LIMITS ON THE PRESIDENCY

So an American president seems like a modern version of a Roman emperor, a demigod who occupies the center of the world. Yet this image masks real limitations. Despite the appearance of total power, presidents quickly discover that they usually cannot order Congress around or expect favorable rulings by the Supreme Court, cannot guarantee that state governments will follow federal policies, cannot single-handedly fix the economy or ensure world peace. In short, presidents cannot do a lot of the things Americans expect of them, nor can they assume that the average citizen will follow or even respect them. George Bush, the liberator of Kuwait, couldn't get Americans to elect him to another term of office. For all his popularity, Bill Clinton did not escape impeachment by the House and a trial in the Senate on charges of obstruction of justice relating to his relationship with Monica Lewinsky, charges of which he was ultimately acquitted.

As we will see, presidential success or failure is affected by broad, sometimes global, social and economic factors, by legal limits imposed by the Constitution, and, of course, by partisan politics. Some of these factors lie outside the ability of any president to control them. What we find in the end is that presidential power is based less on formal or legal authority than on intangible factors such as social and political contexts, personality, and even luck. As political scientist Richard Neustadt put it, presidential power is based to a large extent on the *power to persuade* others—be they members of Congress, other nations, or average Americans.[3]

This chapter looks at the formal authority granted to the presidency, the contextual bases of presidential power, and how presidents try to get things done. The president is our only nationally elected official and, for many Americans, the symbolic center of the political system. Americans expect their president to lead the nation in times of crisis, to solve problems, and, especially, to act as a national consensus builder. But there is a gap between what Americans expect and what presidents can

BOX 9.1.
THE VICE PRESIDENT

After being elected as the first vice president, John Adams lamented, "My country has in its wisdom contrived for me the most insignificant office that ever the invention of man contrived or his imagination conceived." Adams may have been pessimistic, as some vice presidents became important figures—as president. As vice president, they were virtually invisible.

The vice presidency is an odd position. On paper, it doesn't have much to do. The vice president is technically president of the Senate but rarely acts in that capacity and, except to break a tie, has no vote. The vice president's other constitutional role is to succeed the sitting president in cases of death, illness, removal, or resignation. This is hardly comforting to the president.

The problem of the vice presidency stems from the conditions of its creation. In essence, it was created as an afterthought. The framers originally designed an electoral college process that had electors choose *two* persons, at least one of whom is not from the elector's state (Article II, Section 1). This was to keep big states such as New York from dominating presidential elections. Whoever received the most electoral votes became president—but what to do with the second place finisher? In this regard, the framers decided to create the vice presidency as a way of ensuring that the smaller states had some advocate in the executive branch.

But electors had no way to designate first and second choices, even for two candidates of the same party, and the election of 1800 produced a tie, which was broken only after a vote in the House of Representatives. In the subsequent change in the process by the Twelfth Amendment (1803), electors cast one vote for president, one for vice president. That eased the problem of potential ties between candidates from the same party, but left the office of vice presidency even more of an afterthought. Not soon thereafter the vice presidency became what it was known for throughout much of the nation's history: an office with nothing to do inhabited by political mediocrities.

Today, however, the power of the presidency and the nation's role in the world makes the choice of vice president a major issue. This was brought home dramatically in 1945, when Harry Truman became president after Franklin Roosevelt's death from a cerebral hemorrhage. Truman immediately had to lead the war effort, and made the fateful decision to drop the atomic bomb on Hiroshima despite not even having known about the weapon's existence until he became president. In 1963, Lyndon Johnson became president after John Kennedy's assassination; in 1974, Gerald Ford took over after Richard Nixon resigned from office.

As a result of these events, today a lot of attention is paid to a presidential nominee's selection of a vice presidential running mate. Even so, choosing a vice president is not an open process. It is a more ambiguous and private one, dictated by the personal needs and biases of the presidential nominee.

→

A CLOSER LOOK

Vice presidents are chosen for a variety of reasons. They may help to balance the presidential ticket during the election in some way. In some cases, as with Massachusetts Senator John Kennedy's choice of Texas Senator Lyndon Johnson in 1960, the balance was both regional and to build party unity. In other cases, as with George Bush's selection of the much younger Indiana Senator Dan Quayle, it was more generational. In some cases the choice is based on compatibility. In 1992, Arkansas Governor Bill Clinton chose Tennessee Senator Al Gore—two men similar in ages, region, educational backgrounds, and ideology.

This said, a vice presidential nominee cannot win a presidential election. Walter Mondale's choice of Geraldine Ferraro in 1984 made history because of Ferraro's gender, but picking her could not help Mondale beat the popular Ronald Reagan. However, a nominee can hurt: Many voters regarded Quayle as unprepared for the office. Fair or not, this assessment hurt Bush at the polls, although not enough to lose the election to Michael Dukakis.

Once in office, the vice president does essentially whatever tasks the president assigns. Once this was nothing at all, and vice presidents were rarely seen or heard. But as presidents got busier, they needed more help. Today, the vice president is likely to work regularly with the president on important policy initiatives, act as the president's representative to important domestic political constituencies, preside over task forces such as Clinton's "reinventing government" initiative (see chapter 10), and act as the president's emissary to other countries. Vice presidents are kept busy.

Moreover, being vice president has become an important political asset. The office gives the person visibility and a base from which to build a strong campaign once the sitting president no longer can run for reelection. Indeed, political scientist William Mayer argues that an office once regarded as a political dead-end has become "the single-best steppingstone to the White House. . . . Today, a sitting vice president almost automatically becomes a prime contender—usually, in fact, the frontrunner—in his party's next open presidential nominating contest" (pp. 2–3).

In the end, however, the vice president's main job is to be prepared in case something happens to the president. For the president, and for the nation, the political costs of a poorly prepared successor are clear, so the choice of vice president is no small matter.

Sources: John Adams, Letter of December 19, 1793, quoted in Charles Francis Adams, ed., *The Works of John Adams, Second President of the United States: With a Life of the Author,* vol. I (Boston: Little, Brown, 1856), p. 460; William G. Mayer, "A Brief History of Vice Presidential Selection," in William G. Mayer, ed., *In Pursuit of the White House: How We Choose Our Presidential Nominees* (Chatham, NJ: Chatham House, 1999), pp. 313–374.

deliver. This gap can produce public disillusionment with the person in office. But there is always a chance to start anew after the next presidential election.

Individual presidents have had major, even historic, impacts on national events. Some presidents, such as Abraham Lincoln or Franklin Roosevelt, changed the direction of world history. Yet presidential "success" or "failure" is more a political matter than a constitutional one. It usually depends on the degree to which the person in the office takes advantage of the possibilities of the moment. In this sense it is often surprising, despite the imperial imagery of the office, just how little control presidents have over their own fates. Ask George Bush.

THE NATURE OF PRESIDENTIAL AUTHORITY

The Constitution is ambiguous about the presidency. Unlike the list of enumerated powers granted to Congress in Article I, the list of presidential powers in Article II is short and vaguely defined. Some of these powers also are shared with Congress, which the framers saw as the dominant institution of the national government. They were uncertain about how much power one person should have, and in many ways they left it up to George Washington, whom they knew would be the first president, to work out the details with Congress as he went along. Every president since Washington has faced a similar task of interpreting these vague powers and applying them to real events.[4]

AUTHORITY VERSUS POWER

The terms "authority" and "power" are used throughout this chapter. They seem to mean the same thing, but it is important not to confuse them. **Authority** is a narrow legal concept that pertains to what *legally* can or cannot be done. For example, presidents have the legal authority to pardon, or forgive, individuals convicted of most federal crimes. In reality, this authority is rarely used because pardons are politically unpopular. Indeed, President Gerald Ford's pardon of Richard Nixon for any crimes he may have committed in connection to the Watergate scandal (discussed later in the chapter) may have contributed to Ford's loss to Jimmy Carter in 1976.

Power is a broader concept. To echo Neustadt's definition, we can think of power as the ability to get others (either individuals or institutions) to do what is desired—even when they don't want to do so. Sometimes power is based on legal authority, as when a president stops legislation through use of the veto (discussed in the next section). Sometimes it is based on intimidation, as when a president threatens to deploy U.S. troops in order to dissuade another nation from taking hostile actions. But power can also be based on charm, charisma, cunning, or whatever else might help a president convince members of Congress and the public to support a program or some other action. Power, then, is something that is *perceived* to exist, and presidents work hard to convince others that they have it.

Any discussion of presidential authority and power is framed by the relationship between the president and Congress. This relationship is fluid, ambiguous, and often frustrating. Much of what presidents desire, particularly in domestic policy areas, requires the cooperation of Congress. Presidents need Congress to enact new laws, appropriate funds, and, in the case of the Senate, approve Supreme Court nominees and treaties with other nations. In short, the president needs Congress, and the relationship between the two branches at any given time defines the tone and substance of American national politics.

THE VETO

Any discussion of the relationship between Congress and the president begins with an examination of the **veto** (Latin for "I forbid"), the president's primary formal authority for shaping legislation. We discuss the veto first because all other ways of influencing lawmaking, be they as public as giving a televised speech to the nation or as personal as doing favors for members of Congress, are rooted in the president's legal authority to stop a bill from becoming a law. Without the veto, a president would have little actual leverage with Congress.

The veto gives the president a degree of independence from Congress. As Alexander Hamilton wrote in *Federalist* No. 73, "The primary inducement to conferring this power in question upon the executive is to enable him to defend himself; the second one is to increase the chances in favor of the community against the passing of bad laws, through haste, inadvertence, or design."[5] Allowing the president to threaten a veto might induce Congress to modify a bill to the president's liking, thus making actual use of the veto unnecessary. Opponents argued that the veto undermines democracy by allowing a single individual to thwart majority rule. Hamilton disagreed. An unrestrained Congress was more dangerous to liberty, he wrote, and "the injury which might possibly be done by defeating a few good laws will be amply compensated by the advantage of preventing a number of bad ones."[6]

The Veto in the Constitution   As noted in chapter 8, the Constitution gives the president three choices upon being presented with a bill passed by Congress. The president can, and usually does, sign the bill into law. As we will see, the ability of a president to veto a bill means that it usually doesn't get out of Congress unless it has been modified to meet the president's demands. Or, if Congress passes a bill against a president's wishes, the president can veto the bill and return it to the chamber where it originated within 10 legislative days after passage, Sundays excluded. Or, finally, the president can do nothing.

If the president does nothing, the bill becomes law automatically after 10 legislative days. This constitutional provision prevents presidents from subverting the will of Congress through simple inaction. The exception occurs when Congress passes a bill and then adjourns before ten legislative days have elapsed. A bill that has not been signed by the president when Congress adjourns automatically dies after adjournment. This condition is called a **pocket veto** because the president has "pocketed" the bill, although the president does not actually return the bill to Congress. Pocket vetoes are rare, but they offer the president a convenient way to keep Congress from passing "bad" legislation during the last few days before adjourning, when members are eager to go home.[7]

A "real" veto occurs when the president declares opposition to a bill and returns it to Congress, accompanied by a message stating reasons for disapproval. Sometimes the president cites constitutional concerns, at other times policy disagreements. In either case, a veto message is also a political statement directed at Congress and the public; hence it is another resource available to the president in attempting to influence public policy.

The president also cannot veto part of a bill. It is all or nothing. In 1998, the Supreme Court ruled invalid a law passed by Congress that gave the president a so-called *line-item veto*, that is, the authority to veto parts of a spending bill. We will discuss the line-item veto later in the chapter.

Several things can happen now. If Congress fails to act, the bill dies upon adjournment. Those who supported it will have to try again when Congress reconvenes. If two-thirds of the members present in each chamber pass the bill once again, it becomes law automatically over the president's opposition. Such "super-majorities" in each chamber combine to produce a veto **override.** Overrides are rare, as Table 9.1 shows, because to sustain a veto the president needs only one-third plus one of the votes of the members present in only one chamber. So even if the House overrides a veto by a huge margin, the veto stands if the Senate vote is 66 to 34, because supporters of the override needed 67 out of 100 votes. Failing an override, Congress can rewrite the bill to meet the president's demands, or it can give up.

Use of the Veto   James Bryce, a late 19th-century English observer of American politics, argued that the veto "conveys the impression of firmness."[8] This is true to some extent, as the president is saying "no" to Congress. Yet, beyond saying "no," the veto is a clumsy tool for influencing lawmaking. In fact, presidential scholar George Edwards III argues that the veto is a negative instrument; that is, it is good for stopping legislation, but its actual use shows that the president had failed to convince Congress not to pass a bill in the first place.[9] By extension, a veto override emphasizes a president's political weakness, particularly if Congress is controlled by the president's own party.

Two observations can be made about the political dimensions of the veto. First, presidents who face a Congress controlled by the other party use the veto more frequently than do presidents whose own party controls Congress. Since 1960, Democratic presidents Kennedy, Johnson, Carter, and Clinton have had the luxury of working with a Democratic Congress at some time during their presidencies. On average, they issued vetoes less frequently than did Republican presidents Nixon, Ford, Reagan, and Bush, none of whom worked with a Republican Congress. Clinton's first term alone shows the effect of partisan control over Congress. He issued no vetoes at all in 1993–94, when Democrats controlled Congress. In 1995–96, however, he had to use the veto repeatedly after Republicans gained control over Congress in the 1994 elections.

Second, presidents never assume that they will receive automatic support from fellow party members in Congress. Members of Congress don't like being seen by their constituents as rubber stamps for the president's wishes. This is especially true

TABLE 9.1.   VETOES AND VETO OVERRIDES, 1961-1998*

President	Years in Office	Vetoes	Veto Overrides
Kennedy	3	21	0
Johnson	5	30	0
Nixon	6	43	7
Ford	2	66	12
Carter	4	31	2
Reagan	8	78	9
Bush	4	44	1
Clinton[a]	6	25	1

*Does not include so-called "pocket vetoes," which are not sent back to Congress and thus cannot be overriden.

[a]Through December, 1998.

Sources: Norman Ornstein, et al., Vital Statistics on Congress, 1997–98 (Washington, D.C.: CQ Press, 1998), p. 169; U.S. Congress at thomas.loc.gov/home.

when a bill benefits members' districts or states. In 1992, for example, Congress easily overrode George Bush's veto of a bill that aimed to reduce cable television rates. Bush vetoed the bill because he saw it as government intrusion into the marketplace, but regulating cable television rates was so popular with voters that congressional Republicans failed to support Bush on this issue.

If, as Edwards argues, use of the veto is viewed as an admission that the president failed to convince Congress to go along, presidents who can get Congress to not enact a bill, or who can convince it to change the bill by threatening a veto, are viewed as showing strength. Indeed, a veto threat is a useful bargaining tool in the hands of a popular president, as long as the president carries out the threat once in a while. Franklin Roosevelt was known to beg aides to "find something I can veto" to remind Congress of his power.[10] Likewise, on several occasions Ronald Reagan's popularity enabled him to use a veto threat to get Congress to rework legislation to his liking.

However, whether a veto shows strength or weakness isn't a cut-and-dried matter. In his first two years in office, Bill Clinton avoided vetoes by working with congressional Democrats, yet he was unable to fulfill several major campaign promises because his party's majorities in Congress were not large or unified enough to overcome unified Republican opposition. Especially telling was the fate of health care reform, one of the few bills that Clinton actually threatened to veto if it did not contain key elements of his own plan. Clinton's threat had no effect; few believed that he would veto a health care reform bill passed by his own party. Democrats lost control over Congress in the 1994 elections, and Congress adjourned without passing health care legislation of any sort (see chapter 7). Not surprisingly, public opinion polls conducted after the failure of health care reform showed low public approval of the way Clinton was doing his job. "[11]

Clinton's second two years were a different story. In 1995 the new Republican majority in Congress quickly forced Clinton onto the defensive by passing a flood of bills that sought vast changes in the scope and direction of the federal government. Clinton fought back, using vetoes and threatened vetoes to block, delay, or alter a number of bills. Especially important were vetoes of budgets passed by Congress over his objections, which twice forced the federal government to shut down "nonessential" functions such as the national parks. The public blamed the debacle on Congress, and Clinton's political standing improved dramatically. Clinton's easy reelection in 1996, which few had foreseen two years earlier, could be traced to his use of the veto in 1995.

In sum, the veto can stop legislation when all other means fail, but it is less effective as a tool for shaping legislation. Its usefulness is determined by the president's popularity and political skills, as well as the political contexts within which conflicts with Congress take place. The veto is a blunt and unpredictable instrument, but sometimes it is all the president has.

MAKING RECOMMENDATIONS

The president has the authority to "from time to time give to the Congress information of the state of the Union, and recommend to their consideration such measures he shall judge necessary and expedient" (Article II, Section 3). This "power to recommend" seems trivial, but in fact it is an important means by which presidents shape the agenda of government. As we discussed in chapter 5, the ability to decide what is or is not a priority influences what government will or will not do.[12] A president's efforts to influence the national agenda are especially important because the office itself has few formal tools to make policy.

Presidents would love to dictate the agenda of government, especially at the outset of their administration, but at times their priorities are overwhelmed by unforeseen crises such as natural disasters, war, or sudden shifts in the economy. When that happens, presidential "success" or "strength" is judged by how well the president reacts to the crisis. Franklin Roosevelt's response to the collapse of the nation's banking system just as he took office in 1933 is often cited as an example of effective leadership. Within days of taking office Roosevelt persuaded Congress to reorganize the federal banking system. More important, he gave his famous "fireside chat" on national radio to persuade Americans to return their savings to the banks, instilling renewed faith in the financial system and setting the nation on the road to economic recovery.[13] Ronald Reagan, by contrast, was criticized for making a supposedly weak response to a steep plunge in the stock market in October, 1987, a downturn that analysts believed to be due to investor unease over the deadlock between the president and Congress over resolving a major federal budget deficit. It is hard to say whether the deadlock over the budget caused the market crash or whether Reagan's response was inadequate, yet the perception that he failed to deal forcefully with the situation eroded confidence in his leadership.

Crises aside, the president has a unique capacity to shape the nation's agenda of debate and action. According to political scientist Bruce Miroff, the president commands the "public space" in U.S. politics, largely forcing others to respond to issues as the president defines them.[14] No other political figure receives so much public attention, regardless of the issue, and no other person can subject Congress to so much public pressure in so organized a manner. This is true even in an era in which countless media sources compete for public attention.

This reality affects a president's success or failure on policy initiatives, particularly on issues with which Americans have little direct experience. For example, in the 1980s Reagan portrayed anti-Communist rebels fighting the Nicaraguan government as "freedom fighters," a picture that was so compelling to many Americans that the president's critics were forced to refute his definition before they could attack his policy. In some ways Reagan carried the rebels along through the sheer power of his office to dominate the agenda of discussion.[15] On the other hand, Bill Clinton's inability to shape the debate over national health care reform in 1993–94 was due to Americans' fears about making major changes in their health insurance coverage. Such public uncertainty about change played into the hands of those who opposed Clinton's plan. A president who cannot shape the definition of the issue under debate is going to be hard-pressed to convince Congress or the people to go along.

The State of the Union   The annual "State of the Union" address before a joint session of Congress has become a basic tool with which presidents seek to influence the national agenda. The "State of the Union" was once a rather dry annual report on the federal government's activities, and no 19th-century president bothered to appear before Congress to give it. But, beginning with Woodrow Wilson in 1913, the "State of the Union" has been transformed into a major national event. The reason is simple: modern mass media. Wilson used the young medium of radio to speak directly to the nation. The address was delivered before Congress, but its intended audience was listening at home.

Television magnified the importance of the "State of the Union." Indeed, it made the annual address (delivered in January) a moment of high ceremony, a public pageant attended by members of Congress, department secretaries, the heads of the nation's armed forces, Supreme Court justices, foreign dignitaries, and invited guests. Television cameras pan the House chamber as the president speaks, recording the reactions of members of Congress to specific presidential statements or proposals. Media commentators and other political experts judge the president's "performance" immediately after the speech, and the issues raised by the president receive serious consideration in the press.

The importance of the "State of the Union" in shaping public opinion and spurring Congress to action should not be underestimated. The nation discusses whatever presidents discuss, if only for a while. John Kennedy used the address to launch the nation's effort to land Americans on the moon in the 1960s; Lyndon Johnson used it to promote his civil rights and "Great Society" social programs; Richard

A "fireside chat" with Franklin D. Roosevelt. Using radio, Roosevelt could convey an image of optimism and strength to a people seeking both in tough times. Moreover, through this medium, Americans were not reminded about Roosevelt's inability to walk due to paralysis from polio. With radio, such visual images were not an issue.

Nixon used it to propose sweeping reorganization of the federal bureaucracy (see chapter 10) and to defend U.S. actions in Vietnam; Ronald Reagan used the address to spark national debate on tax reform; George Bush used it to support his decision to send troops to oust Iraq from Kuwait; Bill Clinton used it to announce his health care reform effort. As presidential scholar Charles O. Jones argues, the "State of the Union" address is an important part of the constant "conversation" between presidents and Congress.[16] Accordingly, since the early 1980s, the opposition party has requested television time to respond to the president's speech soon after it ends, though rarely with much impact.

The "State of the Union" has also taken on an important symbolic role. As an annual event, it emphasizes the continuity of the system itself despite new presidents or changes in party control over Congress. Nowhere was this more evident than in 1999, when Clinton used the address to propose an array of new policy ideas even as he was on trial in the Senate on impeachment charges of perjury and obstruction of justice. In the audience were the House members who had passed the articles of impeachment and the senators who were holding the trial, all of whom attended because of the important symbolic message of the occasion: The nation's government still functioned. A month later Clinton was acquitted by the Senate, and the proposals announced in the "State of the Union" formed the core of his policy agenda for the rest of the year.

The "State of the Union" message is required by the Constitution, but Congress has passed laws requiring other reports as well. The Budget Act of 1921 requires the president to submit an annual budget message, and the Employment Act of 1946 mandates an annual report on the economy. Hundreds of other reports, messages,

The State of the Union as theatre. Ronald Reagan uses props to argue for the need to eliminate government paperwork. Reagan also uses a TelePrompter, from which he can read his speech without looking at notes. Reagan was a master at using television to speak directly to the American people.

and legislative proposals are submitted to Congress each year, all expressing the president's views on important policy matters. Each has the potential to influence the nation's agenda, which is just part of successful presidential leadership.

THE PRESIDENT AS COMMANDER-IN-CHIEF

The Constitution authorizes the president to act as **commander-in-chief** of the armed forces. This authority was intended to place the responsibility for directing military efforts during wartime in the hands of one person, a civilian, after Congress had first declared war. Yet this clause is vague and open to various interpretations. As a result, the president's role as commander-in-chief may have been the most important constitutional basis for the expansion of presidential power as the United States grew as a military and economic power.

War Powers Whereas Congress alone has the constitutional power to declare war, the president as commander-in-chief has a vaguely defined responsibility to defend the nation. Throughout the nation's history assertive presidents, aided by cooperative Congresses, have expanded the scope of the role of commander-in-chief so that today it is the basis of broad and, some fear, almost unchecked presidential authority in foreign policymaking and the use of American armed forces abroad.

During the Civil War, Abraham Lincoln laid claim to inherent **war powers** growing out of the president's commander-in-chief role and the mandate to preserve the Union. For example, Lincoln claimed the authority to suspend civil liberties for suspected Confederate sympathizers and to spend money for military purposes without prior congressional approval. The Supreme Court later ruled that Lincoln had gone too far in claiming these extraordinary powers, but by that time the war was over.[17]

This was not the last time this pattern occurred: As history shows, neither Congress nor the Supreme Court challenge a president during a national crisis.

During World War II, Franklin Roosevelt claimed the power to "take measures necessary to avert disaster which would interfere with the winning of the war."[18] Even before the United States formally entered the war, and despite congressional declarations of neutrality, Roosevelt used the U.S. Navy to guard merchant ships delivering critical supplies to the British. After Congress formally declared war against Germany, Japan, and Italy, Roosevelt interpreted his war powers as including a wide range of actions, including the forced internment of Japanese-Americans in "relocation camps" without due process of law. Again, neither Congress nor the Supreme Court objected while the nation was at war.[19] However, 40 years later, Congress formally apologized to those who had been interned.

Cold war tensions between the United States and the Soviet Union created an especially favorable environment for assertive presidential action. Both nations possessed intercontinental ballistic missiles tipped with nuclear warheads, making actual war between the nations potentially catastrophic and requiring Congress to delegate to the president the authority to act unilaterally in case of a sudden Soviet missile attack. If the Soviet ICBMs were launched, there would be no time for a floor debate in Congress over the advisability of declaring war in return. During this time, successive presidents sent American troops to places such as Korea, Lebanon, the Dominican Republic, and Vietnam without prior congressional approval, pursuing a policy of "containing" or limiting the influence of Soviet and Chinese communism. This rationale was used also to expand the role of the nation's intelligence services overseas and, sometimes, at home. During this era the nation also entered into mutual-defense treaties such as the North Atlantic Treaty Organization (NATO), under which an attack on one member nation was legally regarded as an attack on all of them. Lyndon Johnson used one such treaty with South Vietnam as partial legal justification for the massive commitment of American troops to the nation in 1965.

The long war in Vietnam led to bitter conflicts over the scope of presidential war powers, particularly as President Nixon continued the war despite congressional efforts to bring U.S. involvement to an end. The result of this conflict between Congress and the president was the War Powers Resolution, which was passed in 1973 over Nixon's veto. The resolution was an attempt to align the constitutional power of Congress to declare war with the fact that modern warfare depends on swift action. It gave presidents the power to commit U.S. troops to potentially hostile situations without prior congressional approval, but it also required that Congress decide within 90 days whether to continue the commitment for a longer period.

Every president since Richard Nixon has considered the War Powers Resolution unconstitutional. Despite several attempts by members of Congress to test the act in federal court, the courts have been reluctant to interpret it as a restraint on presidential power. President Bush used treaty obligations as the initial rationale for committing American troops to oust Iraqi forces from Kuwait, and eventually won congressional support for the action, but he made it clear that he was prepared to move ahead without that support if necessary. President Clinton likewise sent troops as part of multinational peacekeeping forces in parts of the former Yugoslavia (Bosnia in

The president as world leader. President Richard Nixon greets Chinese leader Mao Zedong during Nixon's famous opening of diplomatic relations with what was then known as "Red China." Nixon's reputation as a staunch anticommunist made his 1972 trip to Beijing all the more dramatic.

1995 and Kosovo in 1999), and to Haiti to oust a military dictatorship there. None of these actions had formal congressional approval, but neither did Congress formally disapprove of them.

The ambivalence of Congress on the use of military force was best revealed in April, 1999, after Clinton had committed the U.S. forces to lead a NATO air campaign against the government of Yugoslavia to force it to cease alleged "ethnic cleansing" in the province of Kosovo. When given the opportunity to formally endorse the effort, the House of Representatives narrowly voted against it. However, the very next day the House voted to appropriate twice the amount of funds requested by the administration to carry out the air campaign.[20] Why the contradiction? The first vote reflected a general partisan opposition to the president among House Republicans, whereas the second reflected House members' unwillingness to be seen as obstructionist or, even, unpatriotic when a majority of Americans supported the president's Kosovo policy. Thus, as congressional scholar Barbara Hinckley observed, the War Powers Resolution may be irrelevant as long as presidents build public support for their actions.[21]

More telling, the Kosovo episode reflected a renewed debate over the extent of presidential war powers after the end of the cold war with the former Soviet Union. Many citizens believe that it is still too easy for presidents to send Americans into military conflicts. However, to others a complex and often dangerous world requires that the president be given flexibility in foreign affairs, especially in the use of the armed forces. If history is any guide, in the future the president's role as commander-in-chief will be shaped by the needs of the time, not by laws passed by Congress. However, future presidents may not have as much flexibility as their cold war predecessors. National security issues are more complicated now than they were then, and

Americans may be less willing to allow the nation to act as a global "police officer" in the absence of a Soviet threat. Even so, future presidents will have some institutional capacity as well as historical precedents to carry out foreign policy initiatives and military actions without prior congressional approval. This comes in part from being a superpower, with all the responsibilities such a role entails, but it also comes from the vague provisions in Article II dealing with executive war power.

EXECUTING THE LAW

In Article II the Constitution assigns to the president the "executive power," one of the document's least-specific but potentially farthest-reaching grants of power. The framers could not agree on the specific scope of executive power, but they also did not want to give that authority to Congress. So they left executive power relatively undefined and open ended. This lack of specificity had important consequences. When paired with the provision requiring presidents to "take care that the laws be faithfully executed," the executive power clause provides for a range of *implied* powers whose potential is beyond anything the nation's founders could have foreseen.[22]

On its face, the **take-care clause** directs the president to administer the statutes enacted by Congress. This sounds pretty simple: Congress makes the laws, which the president then executes. Indeed, as the framers may have intended, the Constitution gives the impression that Congress is dominant on most matters. In reality, however, presidents have a great deal of discretion in deciding precisely how laws are to be carried out.

The roots of presidential discretion are found in the nature of lawmaking. Congress cannot always spell out the means to achieve a law's goals, and it often authorizes the executive branch to figure out the details. Yet these details can have major effects. For example, Congress may order the president, through the Environmental Protection Agency, to ensure cleaner air by a certain year. At the presidents' direction, the EPA could ban the burning of high-sulfur coal, but this might cost thousands of coal mining jobs. The EPA could reduce the number of cars on the roads by limiting new highway construction, but this might anger local officials and highway construction firms and their workers. It could make rules to cut down on pollution by thousands of small firms, but this might impose heavy costs on small businesses. In short, any action will have social, economic, and political impacts, and the executive branch will be caught in a major controversy even though it is carrying out the will of Congress.[23]

The degree to which Congress delegates this kind of authority to the president also depends on the complexity of the issue. On some issues Congress can be very specific. For example, in 1996 it passed the Defense of Marriage Act, which allowed state governments to avoid recognizing the legality of marriages between two people of the same sex, even if those unions were allowed by another state. Although its constitutionality is still in question, the law was clear and to the point; in this case the president has little flexibility. On the other hand, in the Americans with Disabilities Act of 1990 Congress mandated that public and private institutions must ensure that people with physical disabilities can gain access to their facilities. But Congress did not specify how this was to be done. It gave the president, as head of the executive branch, the authority to set standards for wheelchair ramps, Braille signs, and the treatment of disabled workers.

Congress also cannot plan for every possible problem that might arise in carrying out a law, so it grants the president discretion in the name of flexibility, effectiveness, or efficiency. The Smoot-Hawley Tariff Act of 1930 is remembered in history largely because Congress tried to list on 170 pages of law virtually every known type of tariff and trade matter. It was a nightmare to administer. By contrast, the Reciprocal Trade Agreements Act of 1934 was only two pages long. Congress, having decided that the executive branch was in a better position to act flexibly on issues with broad domestic and international effects, simply authorized the president to do whatever was necessary to achieve the law's intent.[24]

Given such broad authority in carrying out the intent of Congress, it comes as no surprise that presidents vary in how they implement the letter and spirit of the law. The same law can have different impacts, depending on whether the president carries out the intent of Congress narrowly or broadly. The extent to which this happens is affected by the president's ideology, partisan affiliation, and overall perspective on the law in question. For example, presidents differ in how they implement environmental laws, partly because Congress gives the executive branch leeway in deciding how to achieve the goals set out in the law. To cite one case, the Bush administration had a relatively narrow definition of what constituted a "wetland," one that tended to err on the side of allowing more commercial development if it deemed the area in question to have marginal environmental importance. By contrast, the Clinton administration was more reluctant to allow development in these areas. These kinds of variations are found in many policy areas.[25]

Laws do not administer themselves. They are implemented by presidents and executive branch officials who have their own ideological beliefs and policy goals. These officials are not completely free in how they administer a law—Congress and the courts are ready to keep them from going too far—but they have a surprising amount of discretion.

THE APPOINTMENT POWER

Presidents have the important but often overlooked authority to appoint people to key government posts. All such appointees, including federal judges, ambassadors, secretaries of the executive branch departments, and other high-level executive branch personnel, must be approved by the Senate. As we will discuss in chapter 10, this power is important to the manner in which presidents implement the law, carry out federal programs, and run the federal bureaucracy. The authority to appoint judges is critical because those who sit on the federal courts serve for life or "good behavior." As we will see in chapter 11, the impact of the federal judiciary can outlast a president's term in office, with the president's appointees influencing public policy for years to come.

Most presidential appointees are confirmed by the Senate without controversy because presidents are careful not to make nominations that will generate major opposition. If a nomination runs into trouble, the nominee may be withdrawn from consideration before a vote takes place. This is especially true for appointments to important and sensitive positions. Bill Clinton's first two nominees for Attorney General (who heads the Justice Department) faced controversies over their personal finances, particularly the failure to pay Social Security taxes when they employed nannies to care for their children. These infractions seemed minor to some, but to others the nation's highest law enforcement official cannot afford the slightest hint of illegal behavior, and in each case Clinton withdrew the nomination. Most presidents will do likewise in order to avoid a fight with the Senate, which they usually cannot win.

However, presidents feel that they should have a great deal of leeway in appointing the people who serve under them, and sometimes they will not back down when problems with a nominee emerge. In these instances a nomination can degenerate into a bitter battle. A memorable example came in 1989, when President Bush nominated former Senator John Tower of Texas to be Secretary of Defense. Tower, long a staunch supporter of the military, was rejected by his former Senate colleagues because of allegations of reckless personal behavior and because some senators worried that he would not be able to run the Pentagon effectively.

Presidents also carefully screen potential judges to ensure that they are acceptable to most senators. Outright rejection of a nominee usually stems from partisan or ideological conflict with the president. The most recent case was in 1987, when a Senate dominated by Democrats rejected Reagan's nomination of Robert Bork, a conservative Republican judge known for his controversial views. However, the fight over Bork was not a simple matter of partisan politics; the Senate later voted for Antonin Scalia, whose views were equally conservative, but his style less confrontational.[26] Instead, the Bork nomination reflected an ideological struggle between the president and Senate Democrats over how the Court should interpret the Constitution (see chapter 11). In this case Reagan challenged the Senate to accept a controversial nominee and lost. Most presidents avoid such battles.

OTHER SOURCES OF LEGAL AUTHORITY

Not only is the Constitution vague about many aspects of presidential authority, but presidents and Congress are constantly confronted by real problems that the framers could not have imagined or planned for. For example, as Box 9.2 (p. 394) illustrates, it was silent on what would happen when a president is unable to fulfill the duties of the office because of illness. As a result, presidential authority is frequently augmented or reshaped by statutes (laws) passed by Congress. These clarify the president's authority to do things that are not explicitly covered in the Constitution.

Some statutes are designed to expand presidential authority. For example, the Constitution allows presidents to veto entire bills, not parts of them. This often leads to situations in which members of Congress will load a bill that the president supports with items that the president doesn't necessarily want, hoping that the president will accept the whole package. To some critics, this tendency was a reason for the federal budget deficits of the 1980s and 1990s. To try to remedy this situation, in 1996 Congress tried to give the president the limited authority to use an **line-item veto** to cancel some spending items in new legislation while approving other parts of the same bill. The bill's proponents argued that a line-item veto would enable the president to cut the "fat" out of federal spending. However, the City of New York filed a lawsuit in the federal courts to challenge this new authority after President Clinton used it to eliminate spending that benefited the state. City authorities claimed that the line-item veto was an unconstitutional transfer of power over the federal budget from Congress to the president. In 1998 the Supreme Court agreed.[27] Any effort to give the president a line-item veto will require a constitutional amendment, support for which declined in 1998, after the federal budget showed a surplus for the first time in 30 years.[28]

Other statutes limit presidential discretion, sometimes actually pulling back or placing new constraints on powers granted earlier. For example, the National Security Act of 1947 created the Central Intelligence Agency and authorized the president to carry out covert activities without prior congressional approval. However, in the 1970s Congress acted to limit what many felt had become an "imperial" presidency by passing a series of laws that clarified the boundaries of presidential discretion in areas such as spending, declaring states of emergency, and use of the nation's intelligence agencies without congressional oversight. Thus, what Congress gives it can take back, though usually not entirely: Presidents still have substantial authority to use covert actions.[29]

Court Decisions   The federal courts also can add to or limit presidential power. Indeed, given the Constitution's ambiguities and its silence on some topics, the role of the Supreme Court in fleshing out the boundaries of presidential authority is vital. For example, in a landmark decision, *U.S. v. Curtiss-Wright Export Corporation* (1936), the Court interpreted the Constitution as allowing presidential leadership in making foreign policy on matters about which the Constitution was silent. In this case, the president could ban exports of weapons by U.S. companies to two countries engaged in hostilities with each other.[30] On the other hand, the Court's decision in *Youngstown Sheet and Tube Company v. Sawyer* (1952) imposed limits on the president's powers. In this case the Court ruled that President Truman did not have an inherent right to impose federal control on steel mills facing labor strikes during the Korean War. Although the Court noted that in another context another president might have such authority, in this case Truman had not proved that such an action was required in the name of national defense.[31]

Precedent   Sometimes the way something was done in the past, even if that action has fuzzy legal justification, becomes important to later presidential claims of authority. Actions by past presidents can be used to justify the actions of a present president, and the practice of referring to a previous example, or **precedent,** has gradually expanded the scope of presidential power. This tendency is most noticeable in foreign

BOX 9.2.
DEALING WITH PRESIDENTIAL DISABILITY

The physical, emotional, and psychological rigors of the office of the presidency place great stresses on its occupant. Those stresses, combined with the average age of presidents and the hazards of contemporary life (such as the possibility of assassination), create distinct possibilities that a president may become physically or mentally disabled for some period during the term.

As originally drafted, the Constitution clearly passed presidential power on to the vice president should the president die, resign, or be removed from office, but it said nothing about what happens should the president be unable to fulfill the functions of the office, either temporarily or permanently. This constitutional silence became all the more notable after the nation's experience with two presidents, both of whom were far more incapacitated than their doctors or advisors admitted publicly at the time.

Franklin Roosevelt's (1933–1945) inability to walk due to the effects of polio was well known, but not regarded as relevant to his capacity to lead. However, few Americans realized the degree to which Roosevelt also suffered from heart problems, high blood pressure, and a variety of other illnesses (including cancer) throughout his last years in office, even during his last reelection campaign in 1944. The wear of wartime leadership worsened Roosevelt's health problems, and he died in office of a cerebral hemorrhage on April 12, 1945. His death shocked the nation, but not necessarily his doctors or closest aides. Their secrecy about Roosevelt's health may have been understandable given the symbolic importance of his wartime leadership, but scholars have debated whether the president's poor health affected his ability to negotiate with Soviet leader Josef Stalin about the shape of postwar Europe.

The health problems afflicting Dwight Eisenhower (1953–1961) and their possible effects on his capacity to make important decisions also raised profound questions about how to deal with presidential disability. Political scientist Robert E. Gilbert found that Eisenhower, who at 62 was one of the nation's oldest presidents when first elected, experienced more disabling heart attacks and painful digestive system illnesses throughout his presidency than anyone admitted. Moreover, Eisenhower went through both heart and colon surgery throughout his two terms in office, and was essentially unable to function fully as president for months at a time. As a result, Eisenhower delegated extensive decisionmaking authority to other members of his administration. But this raised profound questions: For example, if Eisenhower were unable to function, who would be able to authorize a nuclear attack? →

policymaking, particularly in the president's use of the armed forces without prior congressional approval. In this case actions by early presidents, such Thomas Jefferson's use of the navy to attack the home ports of Barbary pirates who had been raiding American merchant ships along the coast of North Africa, made it easier for later presidents to claim similar power.

HISTORICAL PERSPECTIVE

In 1958 Eisenhower drafted a letter to his vice president, Richard Nixon, granting Nixon temporary presidential authority should Eisenhower become too incapacitated to fulfill his duties as president. But this was only a temporary fix. Eisenhower's experiences eventually led to the enactment of the Twenty-fifth Amendment (1967), under which the vice president is constitutionally and statutorily authorized to take control should the president become disabled and unable to fulfill the functions of the office. Such a period may be temporary, in which case there are procedures for "returning" power to the president once he or she is capable of resuming duties; or the disability may be permanent, in which case the vice president fully assumes the office for the remainder of the term.

The Twenty-fifth Amendment deals specifically with the question of presidential disability, but no vice president has assumed the presidency even during several apparent instances in which the president might have been unable carry out the duties of the office. For example, Ronald Reagan—who was nearly 70 when first inaugurated in 1981—never relinquished control over the office in the months following the March, 1981, attempt on his life, in which he was more severely wounded than was openly admitted. This episode led to severe criticism of Reagan's aides for not invoking the Twenty-fifth Amendment and probably led to the only time in which it was put in force. In July, 1985, Reagan underwent colon surgery, for which he needed anesthesia. During the eight-hour period covering the surgery, Reagan officially handed over temporary authority to his vice president, George Bush, but immediately "took back" power upon coming out of surgery even though he probably was in no shape to fulfill his duties for a number of days thereafter.

Presidents are naturally reluctant to be seen as weak, and it comes as no surprise that none are willing to hand over power to their vice presidents, even on a temporary basis. Moreover, presidential aides and, especially, the vice president, are wary of being seen as wanting to "grab" power even if the president clearly is unable to function. There is only one president. The Twenty-fifth Amendment may set up a legal process for dealing with presidential disability, but political realities suggest that its provisions will be invoked only under the direst of circumstances.

Source: Robert E. Gilbert, *The Mortal Presidency: Illness and Anguish in the White House*, 2d ed. (New York: Fordham University Press, 1998).

Presidents are not legally bound by the actions of their predecessors. However, it is far easier for a president to follow accepted practice than to break with tradition. A president who seeks to make a lot of major changes in the absence of a perceived crisis faces many obstacles, not least of which is the reluctance of Congress to break with the past—especially if doing so grants the president new powers.

PRESIDENTIAL LEADERSHIP

This review of the president's formal authority makes it clear that presidential power and success depend far less on the wording of the Constitution than on a president's capacity to take advantage of opportunities to persuade others—Congress, the people, other nations—to go along. The capacity to do this consistently is referred to as *leadership.*

Leadership, like power, is an amorphous concept. It can mean one thing in times of crisis, when "strength" and "vision" may be critical, but it can mean something entirely different when qualities such as "sensitivity" or a "capacity for compromise" are needed. Different contexts can require different qualities, and a president who is considered successful in one context may fare far differently under other circumstances. For example, it is an interesting intellectual game to wonder whether Abraham Lincoln or Franklin Roosevelt would have been "great" presidents without the respective crises they faced.

Leadership also is not a one-way street. It does not depend entirely on the vigor, personal skills, or charm of the person in office—although these traits don't hurt. After all, in a democracy, leaders must appeal to the people for support. Leaders need followers, and the president's capacity to lead, particularly with respect to Congress, is affected by the degree to which the president maintains a strong link with the public. In this regard, presidents cannot assume that they have the public's support, nor can they force Americans to follow them.

PRESIDENTIAL CHARACTER

Most analyses of presidential leadership usually begin with the person in the office. After all, there is only one president, and the personal background, psychological makeup, and general values held by the person in the Oval Office all matter. How *much* they matter is the issue.

Studies of presidential character ask: What personal traits make for successful presidents? Which traits pose problems for presidents? Perhaps the best-known, and most controversial, study of presidential personality is political scientist James David Barber's *The Presidential Character: Predicting Performance in the White House* (first published in 1972).[32] Barber's focus is on a president's upbringing, emotional and intellectual development, attachments to other people, and personal outlook. This makes sense: Presidents, like all adults, are shaped by their childhood development as well as their experiences as young adults. Barber categorized previous presidents into four broad types based on two dimensions: the individual's "affect," or attitude toward the presidency as a job, and energy directed toward the job.

This typology of presidential character is presented in Figure 9.1. "Active-positive" presidents such as Franklin Roosevelt both enjoyed the job and put a lot of energy into it; "passive-positive" presidents such as Ronald Reagan enjoyed the job but didn't expend a great deal of energy in pursuing achievements. "Active-negative" presidents such as Richard Nixon were compulsive in the energy they put into the

Attitude toward Office

	Positive	Negative
Active **Energy Directed toward Job**	• High level of activity • High job enjoyment • Adaptable and flexible • High self-esteem Franklin Roosevelt Harry Truman John Kennedy Jimmy Carter George Bush Bill Clinton	• High level of activity • Low job enjoyment • Negatively aggressive • Low self-esteem John Adams Abraham Lincoln Woodrow Wilson Herbert Hoover Lyndon Johnson Richard Nixon
Passive	• Low level of activity • High job enjoyment • Compliant and cooperative • Low self-esteem James Madison Warren Harding Ronald Reagan	• Low level of activity • Does job out of sense of duty • Anxious and negative • Low self-esteem George Washington Calvin Coolidge Dwight Eisenhower

FIGURE 9.1. BARBER'S TYPOLOGY OF PRESIDENTIAL CHARACTER, AS APPLIED TO SELECTED PRESIDENTS

Sources: Adapted from James David Barber, *The Presidential Character: Predicting Performance in the White House*, 4th ed. (Upper Saddle River, NJ: Prentice Hall, 1992); Michael Nelson, "The Psychological Presidency," in Michael Nelson, ed., *The Presidency and the Political System*, 2d ed. (Washington, D.C.: CQ Press, 1988), pp. 185–206 (especially p. 194).

job but derived very little enjoyment in the process; "passive-negative" presidents such as Dwight Eisenhower neither enjoyed the job nor put a lot of effort into it. Instead, they did the job out of a sense of duty.

Which personality type best suits the presidency? This is hard to say. Given a choice, Barber says, voters should pick an "active-positive" personality—an optimist, a go-getter, someone who could inspire others. Few, given a choice, would pick an "active-negative" personality for fear that the person's dark side might breed disaster. However, this isn't guaranteed. As we will discuss later, voters want different things from a president at different times. A "passive-negative" president such as Eisenhower, a former general, may have suited voters who were worried about the cold war with the Soviet Union. Nixon, for all of his apparent faults, was elected to the office twice because the context of the times—the Vietnam War and civil unrest at home—prompted voters to seek a "tough" leader.

It is difficult enough to take these personality profiles and apply them to past presidents. For example, few would deny that Franklin Roosevelt wasn't a complete optimist who put a lot of work into the presidency, but how much did his personality make him what most scholars regard as a great president? Presidential scholar Jeffrey Tulis applied Barber's scheme to Abraham Lincoln, regarded by most Americans as a great president, and found that he fit the profile of an "active-negative," the kind of personality that should have produced problems. Yet Lincoln saved the Union.[33] Maybe his personality fit the needs of the times, and maybe other traits—such as political skill—mattered more.

Assessing the role of personality is also complicated by the fact that scholarly assessments of presidential "success" tend to change over time. For example, attitudes about Eisenhower have changed dramatically in recent years, producing a picture of "Ike" as more an active-positive leader than Barber believed him to be.[34] Except in clear cases such as those of FDR and Nixon, assessments of presidential character are often influenced by the perspective of the analyst and by the passage of time. Harry Truman was widely regarded as a failure when he left office in 1952, but 50 years later he is seen in a far more favorable light because of his tenacity and sense of purpose. Truman didn't change, but history's assessment of him did.

The real controversy began when Barber tried to predict whether new presidents would succeed or fail. His first test case was Richard Nixon, whom Barber labeled an "active-negative." Sure enough, Nixon's apparent paranoia eventually led to the Watergate scandal, named after the building where operatives loyal to Nixon broke into Democratic party headquarters. These actions, and Nixon's attempt to cover them up, eventually led to his resignation.

Barber's assessment of Nixon was on target, but predicting the success of presidents who succeeded Nixon proved far more difficult. Jimmy Carter was initially seen as an "active-positive" president, yet his presidency ended after one term with a widespread perception of weak leadership, the humiliation of American hostages in Iran, and his defeat by Ronald Reagan. In subsequent writing, Barber explained Carter's problems as the result of a mismatch between Carter's "active-positive" personality and the *public mood* at the time, which Barber characterized as "passive-negative."[35] That is, after Vietnam, Watergate, Nixon's resignation, and the economic crises of the 1970s, in 1980 the American people wanted a "father figure" who could reassure them about the nation and its future.

In truth, as Barber implies, the success or failure of any presidency is due to a mixture of personal and contextual factors, not to mention the tendency of later historians to rethink their judgments. Barber's typology has limitations, but it is useful as a starting point for thinking about the role of personality in leadership. For example, Bill Clinton's sexual excesses affected his performance in office, and no doubt will affect the way historians assess his presidency. Yet as we will discuss later, through most of his two terms Clinton maintained remarkably high levels of public support for the job he was doing as president. Why? Maybe other dimensions of his personality compensated for his flaws, or maybe the fact that the nation was enjoying a period of peace and prosperity, with a balanced federal budget, mattered more to voters than did the president's personal failings. Whatever the case, in assessing Clinton's presidency historians will have a lot to chew over.

CONTEXTUAL FACTORS OF PRESIDENTIAL LEADERSHIP

As just suggested, the context in which a president operates at any given time is essential to analyzing that president's ability to set an agenda and persuade others to follow. For example, in 1999 Congress was not likely to take up Bill Clinton's proposals until the issue of impeachment had been resolved. Clinton's task was all the more challenging because he had to work with a Congress dominated by the other party. Taken together, these political conditions created major obstacles for Clinton's proposals, regardless of his personal characteristics or political skills.

What kinds of contexts make it easier for presidents to lead? According to presidential scholar Louis Koenig, Congress and the public are most likely to follow presidential leadership in three situations.[36] The first is during a perceived *national crisis*, when Congress and the public turn to the president for leadership regardless of political party or ideological differences. A frequently cited example is Franklin Roosevelt's First Hundred Days, the period in 1933 when Congress passed almost every proposal offered by the new president to deal with the Great Depression. Roosevelt's massive New Deal agenda was possible only under such "crisis" conditions, when normal conflicts are put aside for some larger public purpose. By contast, neither George Bush nor Bill Clinton entered office under crisis conditions, and both found it difficult to get Congress to go along with major proposals.

Second, Congress and the public generally are more likely to follow presidential leadership on matters of *national security*. This was particularly true during the cold war, when politicians and citizens supported the view that "politics ended at the water's edge." Presidents therefore had great flexibility in matters of foreign policy, and they often defined domestic programs in national security terms in order to gain public support for them. In the 1950s, Dwight Eisenhower defended the building of the interstate highway system as a way to allow for more rapid deployment of defense forces in case of invasion by the Soviet Union. He also argued that increased federal spending on higher education would help the nation close the "science gap" with the Soviets, just as John Kennedy would later promote the space program as a way to win the "space race." Today, with the superpower confrontation between the United States and Soviet Union a memory, the president cannot easily rely on national security arguments to promote new policies.

Third, presidents benefit from occasional *windows of opportunity*.[37] For example, any new president usually enjoys a postelection "honeymoon" with Congress and the American people. During this relatively short period the president can propose new policies in an atmosphere of greater-than-normal cooperation. Indeed, presidents usually enjoy their greatest successes with Congress in the first six months following their first election victory. Other "windows" include the period after a major military or foreign policy success, such as after the defeat of Iraq in the Persian Gulf War of 1990–91, or even after a president has had a close shave with death, as in 1981, when Ronald Reagan was wounded in an assassination attempt. In each case the public and Congress may be willing to give the president a bit more support than usual.

But such "windows" close quickly, and the normal tendencies of the political system soon reassert themselves, regardless of the president's skills or charisma. Members of Congress begin to worry about their constituents or reelection, while citizens may lose interest in the issue under debate—especially if new and possibly more important issues surface. And of course, there's always a good chance that unexpected events will push the president's agenda to the side, as happened to Clinton's agenda for 1998 in the wake of the Monica Lewinsky scandal and the events that led to his impeachment and trial.[38] Clinton's eventual acquittal did nothing to make up for the fact that, for him, 1998 was a year of lost opportunities.

So leadership is contextual. It cannot be predicted by assessing an individual's physical attributes, personal history, or psychological traits. Nixon's tendency to see opponents as enemies certainly led to the illegal activities of the Watergate scandal, whereas Reagan's optimism and apparent lack of meanness made it difficult for even his opponents to dislike him. However, it is not clear how or under which conditions personal characteristics are significant. In Nixon's case, the social unrest of the late 1960s and the bitter national divisions over the Vietnam War may have created an environment in which all people were more likely to see their opponents as enemies, if not as traitors. This does not mean that Nixon should be excused for his actions, only that it is important to understand the context of the times in assessing a presidency.[39]

Not all contexts for leadership are equally influential. Some, such as the state of the economy, relations with other nations, technology, or public opinion, do change, sometimes quickly, and new conditions often require new kinds of ideas or tactics. Some contexts do not change much, if at all. The Constitution's system of checks and balances limits presidential power regardless of the political skills or charm of the individual in the White House.[40] Congress still has the sole constitutional power to pass laws and authorize spending. Presidents who forget these realities are likely to find themselves frustrated on many occasions.

THE ELECTORAL CONTEXT

The shape of any presidency begins with the president's election. Presidents who are elected by huge margins are usually said to have a "mandate" from the voters and hence are assumed to have the public's permission to carry out major new initiatives. In 1980, for example, former governor Ronald Reagan won a surprisingly large victory over President Jimmy Carter and in the process helped fellow Republicans win many seats in the House and even take over the Senate. Reagan thus was widely perceived as having a "mandate" to make major changes in the shape and direction of the federal government, which in fact he did.

By contrast, presidents who win by relatively small margins are said to lack a mandate. They must work harder after the election to earn the public's support, which they can then use to influence Congress to go along. In 1992 Governor Bill Clinton beat President George Bush and Texas businessman H. Ross Perot, but he only won 43 percent of the popular vote. Clinton, not surprisingly, had a more difficult time convincing Congress—even one controlled by his own party—that he had a clear mandate to make major changes in policy directions.

What do elections really tell the new president, or us? In reality, election results give few indications of what the winner is expected to do. As we saw in chapter 6, many people do not even vote, and those who do vote often base their choices less on specific issues than on their broad satisfaction or dissatisfaction with the previous administration. In 1996, for example, many voters supported Clinton's reelection not so much because they approved of him as a person but because they could not think of any compelling reason to replace him with either Bob Dole or Ross Perot at a time when the nation was experiencing peace and general economic prosperity. This was true even among people who agreed with Dole or Perot on some issues. Indeed, in most elections voters make general statements about what—and whom—they do *not* want, not about what they do want in terms of specific programs or policies.[41]

Even so, newly elected presidents try to act as if they have received clear signals of support for new programs or policy directions. The degree to which they are able to translate their election victory into major policy changes depends, however, on whether they can convince Congress and the people to go along.

THE PUBLIC CONTEXT

One reason that electoral "mandates" are so elusive is the nature of public opinion itself. A president can enjoy relatively high levels of general public support but may obtain little concrete support for specific programs.[42] Of course, general popularity cannot hurt (see Figure 9.2). As Clinton found during his impeachment trial, high levels of public satisfaction can protect a president against political defeats; in Clinton's case, strong public support played a major role in his acquittal on charges of perjury and obstruction of justice by the Republican-controlled Senate. Clinton's predecessor, George Bush, discovered just the opposite: Low popularity undermines a president's ability to succeed, regardless of the nature of the proposed program.

Building public support for specific programs or actions is easiest when large segments of the public already support the president's broad policy directions, when the public perceives the need for change, and when a great many citizens foresee no immediate and adverse impacts on their own lives. For these reasons, President Clinton and a Republican-controlled Congress were able to make sweeping changes in the nation's welfare laws in 1996 (see chapter 5), whereas in 1994 Clinton and a Democratic-controlled Congress could not reform the nation's health care system (see chapter 7). Most Americans, regardless of party or ideology wanted to eliminate a welfare system that served a relatively small population of poor people. That is, they wanted to reform a system that affected "other people." By contrast, most voters did

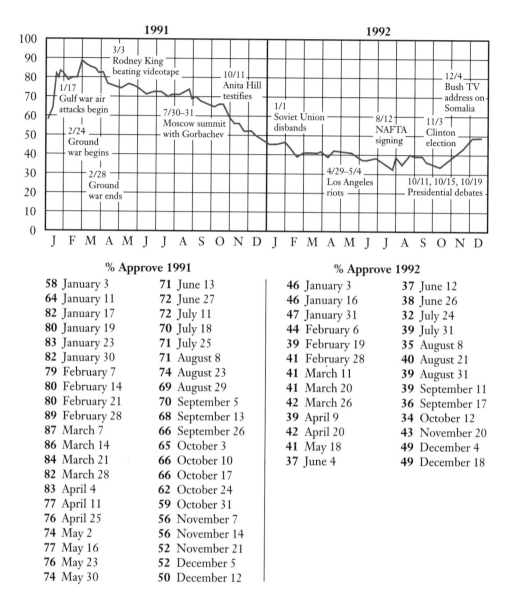

% Approve 1991

58 January 3	71 June 13		
64 January 11	72 June 27		
82 January 17	72 July 11		
80 January 19	70 July 18		
83 January 23	71 July 25		
82 January 30	71 August 8		
79 February 7	74 August 23		
80 February 14	69 August 29		
80 February 21	70 September 5		
89 February 28	68 September 13		
87 March 7	66 September 26		
86 March 14	65 October 3		
84 March 21	66 October 10		
82 March 28	66 October 17		
83 April 4	62 October 24		
77 April 11	59 October 31		
76 April 25	56 November 7		
74 May 2	56 November 14		
77 May 16	52 November 21		
76 May 23	52 December 5		
74 May 30	50 December 12		

% Approve 1992

46 January 3	37 June 12
46 January 16	38 June 26
47 January 31	32 July 24
44 February 6	39 July 31
39 February 19	35 August 8
41 February 28	40 August 21
41 March 11	39 August 31
41 March 20	39 September 11
42 March 26	36 September 17
39 April 9	34 October 12
42 April 20	43 November 20
41 May 18	49 December 4
37 June 4	49 December 18

FIGURE 9.2. APPROVAL RATINGS, BUSH 1991–1992; CLINTON, 1998–1999

Percentages are based on positive responses to the question: "Do you approve or disapprove of the way (president's name here) is handling his job as president?"

Source: The Gallup Poll, Data for 1991–1995 are taken from Michael Nelson, ed., *Guide to the Presidency*, 2d ed. (Washington, D.C.: Congressional Quarterly, Inc., 1996), p. 1703. Data for 1996–1999 tabulated by the authors from www.gallup.com/poll.

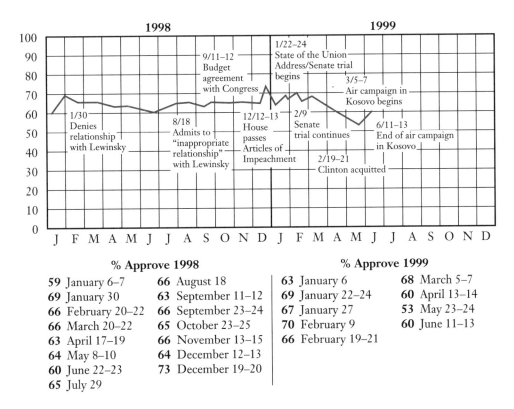

% Approve 1998

59 January 6–7	**66** August 18
69 January 30	**63** September 11–12
66 February 20–22	**66** September 23–24
66 March 20–22	**65** October 23–25
63 April 17–19	**66** November 13–15
64 May 8–10	**64** December 12–13
60 June 22–23	**73** December 19–20
65 July 29	

% Approve 1999

63 January 6	**68** March 5–7
69 January 22–24	**60** April 13–14
67 January 27	**53** May 23–24
70 February 9	**60** June 11–13
66 February 19–21	

FIGURE 9.2 CONTINUED

not want major, possibly unpredictable, changes in their own health care, and any proposal to make such changes generated intense opposition.

Thus, the capacity of any president to build support for a specific proposal varies greatly. Failure to do so on one issue can affect the ability to do so on other issues, because any "failure" can be interpreted as a sign of weak public support for the president. Indeed, the failure of national health care reform in 1994 was seen as an indicator of Clinton's overall political problems in his first term and played a role in the Republican takeover of Congress after the 1994 elections.

To be fair, not all problems are easily solved, campaign promises notwithstanding. Ronald Reagan promised to cut taxes, increase defense spending, and balance the federal budget. He did the first two but not the third, and federal budget deficits ballooned during his administration. It was easier and more politically acceptable to cut taxes and raise defense spending than to make the spending cuts necessary to balance the budget.[43] In 1992, candidate Bill Clinton promised a tax cut for middle-class Americans, but as president he discarded that goal in order to reduce the federal budget deficit, a goal that voters supported even more strongly. During the 1996 election, despite the best efforts of his opponents, the voters did not hold Clinton's failure to cut taxes against him. Why? Because the federal deficit had gone down, and in

1998 the federal budget showed a surplus for the first time in 30 years. There is an irony here: In 1992 many voters had turned against George Bush because he reneged on his 1988 promise never to raise taxes in order to bring the federal deficit under control.[44] Bush's action may have contributed to the eventual budget surplus, but too late to help him politically.

Some factors enhance the president's ability to create change. As we noted earlier, citizens and members of Congress generally are more willing to support the president when the nation is at war, in a severe economic crisis, or facing a disaster of some sort. A notable example was the April, 1995, terrorist bombing of the federal office building in Oklahoma City, which claimed 168 lives (see Box 10.1, p. 424). In the wake of this disaster President Clinton won support for a crime bill that had been stuck in Congress because it contained controversial antiterrorist measures. Members of Congress who had opposed the bill dropped their opposition for fear of being seen as insensitive to the Oklahoma City tragedy.[45] Crises thus can create opportunities for presidential action as well as opportunities to expand presidential power.

Finally, when all is said and done, many Americans care little about day-to-day politics. Their indifference can make it easier for presidents to make changes, particularly on foreign policy issues, which for most Americans seem remote from daily life. Indeed, political scientist Aaron Wildavsky used this point to propose what he calls the "Two Presidencies" thesis. In his view, the president has far greater leverage in gaining congressional support for foreign policy initiatives than in gaining support for policies dealing with domestic problems, in which there tends to be greater public and congressional involvement.[46] As a result, the foreign policy presidency is less constrained, and perhaps more powerful, than the domestic policy presidency. George Bush, the liberator of Kuwait, found this out the hard way.

However, public indifference can also make it more difficult for presidents to overcome intense opposition from Congress, organized interest groups, and even executive agencies. It thus is no surprise that presidents try to generate strong public support in their fights with Congress. Public support is their greatest asset.

THE CONGRESSIONAL CONTEXT

Newly elected presidents usually have a short "honeymoon" with Congress (see Figure 9.3). Yet success with Congress often depends on whether the president's own party controls the legislative branch. Even Ronald Reagan did not enjoy an unusually high level of success with Congress after his first year in office, partly because his own party did not control both the House and the Senate. By contrast, Bill Clinton's success in gaining congressional enactment of his budget plan, AmeriCorps (see chapter 8) and the 1994 Brady Handgun Control Act (see chapter 7), all depended on his party's control of both houses of Congress. However, as he discovered in connection with health care reform, even party control of Congress is no guarantee that the president's program will be passed.

So there is a good reason for discussing presidential success or failure in terms of relations with Congress. Having said this, it is impossible to discuss this relationship

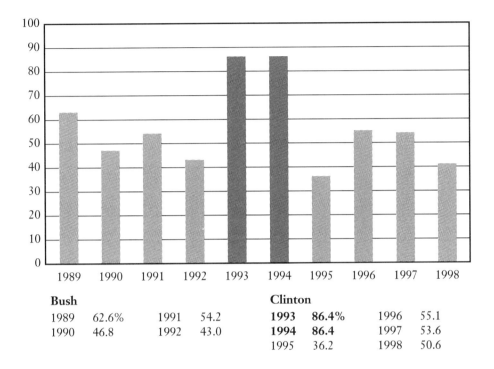

Bush					Clinton			
1989	62.6%		1991	54.2	**1993**	**86.4%**	1996	55.1
1990	46.8		1992	43.0	**1994**	**86.4**	1997	53.6
					1995	36.2	1998	50.6

FIGURE 9.3.   PRESIDENTIAL SUPPORT IN CONGRESS, 1989–1998

Note: Percentages reflect the percentage of contested votes (bills, amendments to bills, etc.) on which the president has prevailed. The usefulness of this indicator is limited by the fact that by the time legislation is voted on, it usually reflects compromises between the president and members of Congress that make it possible to gain passage. Note also that except for 1993–94, when the Democratic party dominated both houses of Congress, the presidency and Congress have been dominated by different parties (see Table 8.1, p. 331).

Source: Congressional Quarterly Weekly Report, vol. 57, no. 2 (January 9, 1999), p. 86.

without recognizing the basic differences between the two branches. In fact, it is no exaggeration to suggest that members of Congress and the president live in entirely different worlds. These differences help to explain why presidents succeed or fail in achieving their legislative goals.

Different Selection Processes   Presidents and members of Congress gain office through separate and distinct paths. The president and vice president are the only political figures who are elected in a nationwide election. That process, combined with the national responsibilities of the office, inevitably gives the president a broad perspective on most issues. Members of Congress come to government from more localized constituencies; they think first about how issues will affect the people back home. For members of Congress, as the late Speaker of the House Thomas P. ("Tip")

O'Neill was fond of saying, "All politics is local."[47] Members of Congress do think broadly on policy questions, of course, but their constitutional role as representatives requires that they tend to the needs of their constituents first.

Different Time Horizons Presidents and members of Congress also serve for different terms of office. The president serves for four years, but members of the House serve for only two years. This short term is intended to keep them sensitive to the current needs and opinions of the people they represent. House members thus focus on short-term concerns, which can conflict with the president's agenda when the short-term costs of new programs are perceived to outweigh the longer-term benefits. On Social Security, for example, members of Congress are more likely to respond to the short-term demands of senior citizens than to the longer-term needs of those who will not reach retirement age for several decades. Even senators, whose six-year terms theoretically insulate them from the momentary passions of the electorate, are careful not to anger senior citizens, who are organized and vote.

The election calendar influences the rhythms of lawmaking and the ability of presidents to get things done. All House members, and one-third of all senators, are up for reelection in the second year of the president's term, and midterm elections are often viewed as public judgments of presidential performance. As we discussed in chapter 6, the president's party almost always loses seats in Congress in midterm elections, a tendency that is viewed as a sign of voter disenchantment with the president. Members of Congress from the president's party are aware that their leader's problems can become their own. They may feel that they need to distance themselves from the president in order to win reelection. The opposition party, for its part, tries to use midterm elections to its advantage.

A dramatic example of this tendency occurred in 1994, when Republicans gained control of both chambers of Congress for the first time in 40 years. Whereas in 1993–94, Bill Clinton could at least count on Democratic control of both chambers of Congress to help him pass much of his legislative program, in 1995–96 Republican control over Congress altered the political situation. Clinton found himself on the defensive, and for a while control of the legislative agenda shifted from the White House to a new and assertive congressional majority led by Speaker Newt Gingrich. By contrast, Republicans lost five House seats in the 1998 midterm elections despite the sex scandal that led to Clinton's impeachment. Remarkably, it was the first time since 1934 that the president's party won seats in a midterm elections. Voters seemed to disapprove of Republican efforts to impeach Clinton, and Gingrich resigned from his position (and from Congress) shortly thereafter rather than face ouster by his own party members. In either case, the midterm election had significant political consequences.

The problem faced by the president in dealing with the Senate is a bit different. Senators serve for six years; only one-third of them are up for reelection every second year. Most are not directly affected by a presidential election and therefore have greater freedom to oppose presidential initiatives. The Senate also has leverage with the president through its power to approve presidential nominees and treaties with other nations. These realities guarantee problems for the president, even with senators of the same party, partly because ideological divisions *within* a party can matter more than does loyalty to the president. Despite his party's dominance in the Senate, Jimmy Carter failed to win Senate approval for the 1978 Strategic Arms Limitation Treaty with the Soviet Union because of opposition by conservative Democrats; similarly, the stiffest opposition to the 1987 Intermediate Force Missile Treaty came from Ronald Reagan's fellow Republicans.

Two Cultures The two branches also have distinct decisionmaking cultures. The president sits atop an executive hierarchy that speaks with a single official voice on policy matters. There may be vigorous debate within the executive branch, but final decisions are made by the Oval Office and are usually based on the president's policy views, ideology, and political agenda. Presidential appointees who do not toe the line after a decision is final can find their influence with the president severely limited. Resignation, even firings, may follow.[48]

Congress, by contrast, speaks with many voices, and as an institution it rarely displays a coherent sense of direction. Members of Congress both represent their constituents and make national policy. As we saw in chapter 8, these roles often conflict. What is good for a member's constituents, such as spending for new projects, may not necessarily be good for the nation as a whole. Each member has one vote regardless of seniority or party position, and no member can be expelled from the legislature because of his or her voting behavior or opinions. Congress as an institution thus operates according to a less hierarchical decisionmaking process. Decisions on new legislation are reached only by building coalitions that are large enough to win a succession of committee and floor votes. Consensus is a norm of congressional behavior: Legislative success depends on knitting together enough diverse interests and demands to overcome opposition, using whatever tactics seem reasonable or necessary.

This clash of cultures shapes how the executive and legislative branches interact. Presidents want to move quickly to make the most of their limited opportunities, often through dramatic policy initiatives. Yet Congress usually prefers more caution. Presidents also accuse Congress of waste, arguing that the local and state interests represented in Congress often outweigh the national good. For example, in 1977 Carter attacked "wasteful" spending for public works projects such as dams and irrigation canals, only to discover that these projects are "sacred cows" to legislators who are eager to serve their constituents.[49] A decade later Reagan vetoed a popular reauthorization of the Clean Water Act because he felt that its $20 billion appropriation for water and sewage treatment projects was wasteful. Congress overrode his veto by huge bipartisan margins, just as it overrode Bush's veto of a bill that regulated cable television rates. Clinton's effort to overhaul the nation's health care system ultimately fell prey to local concerns, with members of his own party unable or unwilling to push the president's plan past determined Republican opposition.

This often rocky relationship between the president and Congress is shaped by the Constitution.[50] The framers were far more concerned with preventing potential abuses of power than with speedy or easy lawmaking. They *wanted* Congress and the president to be at odds, and they therefore gave Congress the ability to withstand presidential pressure. Even when it is dominated by the president's party, Congress insists on playing its independent constitutional role according to its own needs and internal dynamics.

THE PRESIDENT AND THE PUBLIC

As is clear by now, any president's success ultimately depends on maintaining strong public support. Americans expect presidents to be accessible, and in this era of mass media it is possible for the president to communicate directly with the people. No longer must presidents depend on others—party leaders, members of Congress, or reporters—to speak for them. Nor, in this age of talk radio, the Internet, and public opinion polls, do presidents have any trouble knowing the public's views on almost any topic.

Even so, the relationship between the president and the people is not a simple one. As head of state, the president is supposed to speak for all Americans, yet because of the size and diversity of the nation, it is rare for Americans to speak with one voice. As head of government, the president must build popular support for new initiatives, yet so many citizens are uninformed or indifferent to so many issues that the president often hears only from organized interests.

Hence the dilemma: For whom does the president speak? The president is expected to be party head *and* nonpartisan leader of the nation, representative of the majority *and* protector of the rights of the minority, symbol of the nation *and* its most effective official. These conflicting responsibilities pose tremendous dilemmas for any president, especially because most contemporary issues don't have easy solutions.

For example, it is easy to say that the federal government should do everything possible to reduce cigarette smoking. Yet tobacco is an important part of the economies of several states; it is the source of jobs for many Americans; and it is defended as a legal business by members of Congress from tobacco states. So it comes as no surprise that presidents both support antismoking initiatives and continue to promote tobacco exports to other countries. These policies seem contradictory, but they illustrate the awkward compromises that often characterize the American political system.[51]

Perhaps the greatest dilemma of the presidency is how to walk the fine line between responding to the needs of the public and falling prey to the passing fancies of public opinion. After all, there are times when presidents are supposed to be effective leaders. They are supposed to make sure that the business of government is carried out efficiently and effectively, that important national needs are addressed, that the federal budget is kept under control, and that the nation is defended against possible harm. In doing all these things, presidents may have to take strong stands, even at the risk of stirring opposition.

For example, much of history's assessment of Lyndon Johnson will hinge on his escalation of the nation's involvement in Vietnam. Yet Johnson's legacy also included his willingness to take huge political risks and persuade Congress to enact the Civil Rights Act of 1964, which dismantled much of the apparatus of racial segregation. Johnson and the Democratic party ultimately paid a massive political price for their civil rights policies, especially in the South, but at some point Johnson decided that the rights of all Americans transcended political expediency.[52] Those moments of leadership, not any momentary popularity as measured by opinion polls, are what shape a president's legacy.

Seeking to persuade. President Clinton promotes health care reform during a Rhode Island "town meeting" in 1993. Clinton was generally able to persuade Americans to support his policies throughout his two terms in office, but he was unable to allay public fears about the effects of his reform plan.

CONCLUSION

The American presidency, like the political system in general, is going through a period of redefinition spurred by the end of the cold war. Members of Congress and citizens, accustomed to granting considerable discretion to the president in the interest of national defense are now debating how much power presidents should have. As they do so, they are also debating what kind of president they want.

This is nothing new. The nature of the presidency seems to change with each era of the nation's history. It has been shaped by the broad contexts that shape American politics generally. The nation's founders had a concept of leadership that did not depend on popularity but reflected the social context of the time. For them, the president should be selected from what Thomas Jefferson called the "natural aristocracy"—that is, people endowed with superior intellect, ingenuity, energy, and virtue. Such an approach would not be possible today. For one thing, Jefferson's "aristocracy" left out women, a omission that no one makes today. For another, few presidents, even some of the most effective, would fit that description to begin with, and since Jefferson's time the selection of presidents has been made more democratic (see chapter 6). So the real questions are, How do we define leadership, and what do we look for in potential presidents?

Whatever Americans feel about government, they still have a special place in their hearts for the presidency. In some ways Americans, despite their skepticism about politicians, still view new presidents as knights on horseback who will lead the nation to ever-greater power and stature. Each new election is a chance to start over, to clean the slate. Yet at the same time the president will occupy a position whose power is limited by the Constitution as well as by the people's unwillingness, as time goes on, to follow.

Thus, how Americans define presidential leadership is critical. As we saw with Barber's study of presidential character, there is no guarantee that an "ideal" person will be an effective president. The institutions of government, education, business, religion, media, and so on are not easily led. Presidents cannot make Americans support their proposals any more than they can make Americans love one another or stop them from spending their own money foolishly. Indeed, as we have seen, the president cannot force Americans to do things they don't want to do. Except in moments of crisis, the president must persuade them to go along.

As we saw in chapter 8, Congress is the institution that represents the people and makes the laws. But for many people, both here and abroad, the presidency is the public face and psychological center of the American political system. As such, the presidency is a force for cohesion in a system that otherwise tends toward fragmentation, and a force for initiative in a system that tends toward policy stalemate. Even "weak" presidents make significant contributions, and even "strong" presidents find that the system will not allow them to govern unchecked. The presidency as an office is a force for consensus building, but no president can make it happen with a wave of a hand. Americans must be persuaded to go along.

SUMMARY

▶ The public image of the American presidency is of an office of almost absolute power and majesty. However, despite the symbolic trappings of power, the presidency is more constrained than most people realize.

▶ The president relies on an array of formal powers granted by the Consitution. The veto enables the president to block, and thereby influence the shape of legislation. The president also has the authority to make recommendations to Congress, to implement the law, and, with Senate approval, appoint executive branch officials and federal judges. Moreover, as commander-in-chief the president wields authority over the nation's military, a role that has been the source of the greatest expansion in presidential power during the 20th century.

▶ However, the Constitution is vague about the shape of much of presidential authority, so presidential power has been defined largely through the actions of individual presidents as they have applied their formal authority to real events and conditions.

▶ Presidential leadership is shaped by broad structural, societal, and political dynamics. The personal traits of the president are relevant, but they do not determine presidential success. Contextual factors such as the relationship with Congress, the nature of public support, and the types of problems a president confronts matter just as much, if not more, to an individual president's record in office.

▶ The presidency after the cold war era will probably differ a great deal from the presidency that marked much of the late 20th century. For one thing, Americans are far less united about the purpose of government or the nation's role in the world, much less the power that should be granted to one person. In this regard, the presidency is shaped by what Americans require of it at any given time.

QUESTIONS FOR DISCUSSION

1. What factors expand presidential power? What factors limit it? What do these factors tell you about the nature of presidential power?

2. To what degree is the success or failure of any particular presidency due to the personal characteristics of the president versus other factors?

3. What factors explain presidential success or failure with Congress?

4. How does the nature of the presidency today differ from the nature of the office during the cold war period?

TERMS TO REMEMBER

authority	power
commander-in-chief	precedent
line-item veto	take-care clause
override	veto
pocket veto	war powers

WEB SOURCES

The White House (www.whitehouse.gov). The official site operated by the White House. Contains biographical information on the president and vice president and their spouses, texts of recent speeches and press releases, pictures of the White House, and a wide variety of links to other federal government Web sites.

Presidential libraries (www.nara.gov/nara/president/address.html). The site maintained by the National Archives and Records Administration contains links to presidential libraries that have Web sites. The presidential libraries (which are not operated by the federal government) are excellent sources of information on the respective presidents, their achievements (and even failures), and the times in which they occupied the White House.

Center for the Study of the Presidency (www.cspresidency.org). A nonprofit center dedicated to the scholarly study of the American presidency. Each spring the Center sponsors an annual student symposium in Washington, D.C., which typically includes talks by senior governmental officials. The Center also sponsors an annual student essay contest and the scholarly journal, *Presidential Studies Quarterly.*

SUGGESTED READINGS

Elizabeth Drew, *Showdown: The Struggle between the Gingrich Congress and the Clinton White House.* (New York: Simon and Schuster, 1996). Journalist Elizabeth Drew offers an excellent example of a "behind the scenes" perspective of the struggle between a president and Congress. She interviews all of the relevant political figures involved in the political conflicts of 1995, when a Congress newly dominated by Republicans challenged the leadership of a sitting Democratic president, and shows how these competitors tried to position themselves to attract public support for their priorities.

Charles O. Jones, *The Presidency in a Separated System* (Washington, D.C.: The Brookings Institution, 1994). A political scientist examines the post–World War II presidency by looking at the relationship between presidents and Congress. Despite images of the "imperial presidency," Jones shows how presidents are constrained by the impacts of divided government, the constitutional powers granted to Congress, partisan politics, and, finally, media scrutiny.

David Maraniss, *First in His Class: The Biography of Bill Clinton.* (New York: Touchstone Books, 1996). A balanced and thoroughly researched examination of Bill Clinton's upbringing, talents, personal character flaws, and political career prior to his election as president. Maraniss shows Bill Clinton, warts and all, and offers insight into why few Americans hold neutral feelings about him. A very good example of a biographical treatment of a sitting president.

NOTES

1. Ross K. Baker, "Sorting Out and Suiting Up: The Presidential Nominations," in Gerald M. Pomper, ed., *The Election of 1992* (Chatham, NJ: Chatham House, 1993), pp. 39–73.

2. Richard Rose, *The Postmodern President: George Bush Meets the World* (Chatham, NJ: Chatham House, 1991), pp. 287–304.

3. Richard Neustadt, *Presidential Power: The Politics of Leadership*, 3d ed. (New York: Wiley, 1980; originally published 1960).

4. James Sundquist, *Constitutional Reform and Effective Government* (Washington, D.C.: The Brookings Institution, 1986), ch. 1.

5. Alexander Hamilton, James Madison, and John Jay, *The Federalist Papers*, Clinton Rossiter, ed. (New York: New American Library, 1961), p. 443.

6. Ibid., p. 332.

7. See discussion in Christopher J. Bosso, "The President as Chief Legislator," in Michael Nelson, ed., *The Guide to the Presidency*, 2d ed. (Washington, D.C.: CQ Press, 1996), pp. 558–559.

8. James Bryce, *The American Commonwealth*, vol. 1 (New York: MacMillan, 1911), p. 64.

9. George C. Edwards III, *Presidential Influence in Congress* (San Francisco, CA: Freeman, 1980), p. 24.

10. Arthur M. Schlesinger Jr., *The Imperial Presidency* (New York: Popular Library, 1974), p. 237.

11. "October Vote Poll Results, 1998," *Washington Post*, October, 12, 1998; http://www.washingtonpost.com/wp-srv/politics/polls/vault/stories/data101298.htm.

12. David A. Rochefort and Roger W. Cobb, eds., *The Politics of Problem Definition: Shaping the Policy Agenda* (Lawrence, KS: University Press of Kansas, 1994).

13. Arthur M. Schlesinger Jr., *The Age of Roosevelt: The Coming of the New Deal* (Boston: Houghton Mifflin, 1959).

14. Bruce Miroff, "Monopolizing the Public Space: The President as a Problem for Democratic Space," in Thomas E. Cronin, ed., *Rethinking the Presidency* (Boston: Little, Brown, 1982), pp. 218–252.

15. Lance Bennett, "Marginalizing the Majority: Conditioning Public Opinion to Accept Managerial Democracy," in Michael Margolis and Gary Mauser, eds., *Manipulating Public Opinion: Essays on Public Opinion and a Dependent Variable* (Pacific Grove, CA: Brooks/Cole, 1989), pp. 321–362.

16. Charles O. Jones, "Presidential Negotiation with Congress," in Anthony King, ed., *Both Ends of the Avenue: The Presidency, the Executive Branch, and Congress in the 1980s* (Washington, D.C.: American Enterprise Institute, 1983), p. 99.

17. *Ex Parte Milligan*, 71 US 2 (1886).

18. Neustadt, *Presidential Power*, p. 63.

19. *Korematsu v United States*, 323 US 214 (1944).

20. Pat Towell, "Congress to Provide Money, but No Guidance, for Kosovo Mission," *Congressional Quarterly Weekly Report*, vol. 57, no. 18 (May 1, 1999), pp. 1036–1040.

21. Barbara Hinckley, *Less Than Meets the Eye: Foreign Policy Making and the Myth of the Assertive Congress* (Chicago, IL: University of Chicago Press, 1994), pp. 99–100.

22. Edward S. Corwin, *The President: Office and Powers*, 4th ed. (New York: New York University Press, 1957).

23. Richard E. Cohen, *Washington at Work: Back Rooms and Clean Air*, 2d ed. (Boston: Allyn & Bacon, 1995).

24. Allen Schick, "Politics through Law: Congressional Limitations on Executive Discretion," in Anthony King, ed., *Both Ends of the Avenue: The Presidency, the Executive Branch, and Congress in the 1980s* (Washington, D.C.: American Enterprise Institute, 1983), p. 162.

25. Norman J. Vig, "Presidential Leadership and the Environment: From Reagan to Clinton," in Norman J. Vig and Michael E. Kraft, eds., *Environmental Policy in the 1990s*, 2d. ed. (Washington, D.C.: CQ Press, 1997), pp. 95–118.

26. Christopher J. Deering, "Congress, the President, and War Powers: The Perennial Debate," in James A. Thurber, ed., *Divided Democracy: Cooperation and Conflict between the President and Congress* (Washington, D.C.: Congressional Quarterly Press, 1991), pp. 171–99.

27. *Clinton v City of New York*, 524 US 417 (1998).

28. Andrew Taylor, "Few in Congress Grieve as Justices Give Line-Item Veto the Ax," *Congressional Quarterly Weekly Report*, vol. 56, no. 26 (June 27, 1998), pp. 1747–1749.

29. Schlesinger, *The Imperial Presidency*.

30. *US v Curtiss-Wright Export Corporation*, 299 US 304 (1936).

31. *Youngstown Sheet and Tube Company v Sawyer*, 343 US 579 (1952); see Jack W. Peltason, *Understanding the Constitution*, 12th ed. (New York: Holt, Rinehart, & Winston, 1992), pp. 105–106.

32. James David Barber, *The Presidential Character: Predicting Performance in the White House*, 4th ed. (Upper Saddle River, NJ: Prentice Hall, 1992).

33. Jeffrey Tulis, "On Presidential Character," in Jeffrey Tulis and Joseph Bessette, eds., *The Presidency and the Constitutional Order* (Baton Rouge, LA: Louisiana State University Press, 1981), p. 287.

34. See Fred Greenstein, *The Hidden-Hand Presidency* (New York: Basic Books, 1982).

35. James David Barber, *The Pulse of Politics: Electing Presidents in the Media Age* (New York: Norton, 1980).

36. Louis Koenig, *The Chief Executive*, 5th ed. (New York: Harcourt Brace Jovanovich, 1986), pp. 145–146.

37. John Kingdon, *Agendas, Alternatives, and Public Policy* (Boston: Little, Brown, 1984).

38. David M. Shribman, "The Presidency Unshielded," *Boston Globe*, April 7, 1998, p. A3.

39. Barber, *The Presidential Character.*

40. Bert A. Rockman, *The Leadership Question: The Presidency and the American System* (New York: Praeger, 1984).

41. Lance Morrow, "The Triumph of Hope over Experience," *Time*, vol. 148, no. 23 (November 18, 1996), pp. 74–75.

42. Robert E. Erickson, Norman Luttbeg, and Kent L. Tedin, *American Public Opinion: Its Origins, Content, and Impact*, 2d ed. (New York: Wiley, 1980).

43. William Greider, "The Education of David Stockman," *The Atlantic Monthly*, vol. 248 (December 1981), pp. 39–54.

44. Bob Woodward, *The Agenda: Inside the Clinton Presidency* (New York: Simon & Schuster, 1994).

45. See Elizabeth Drew, *Showdown: The Struggle between the Gingrich Congress and the Clinton White House* (New York: Simon & Schuster, 1996), pp. 195–202.

46. Aaron Wildavsky, *The Presidency* (Boston: Little, Brown, 1969).

47. Thomas P. O'Neill Jr. with William Novak, *Man of the House: The Life and Political Memoirs of Speaker Tip O'Neill* (New York: Random House, 1987).

48. Hugh Heclo, *A Government of Strangers: Executive Politics in Washington* (Washington, D.C.: The Brookings Institution, 1977).

49. Jimmy Carter, *Keeping Faith: The Memoirs of a President* (New York: Bantam Books, 1982), pp. 78–79.

50. See Louis Fisher, *Constitutional Conflicts between Congress and the President*, 4th ed. (Lawrence, KS: University Press of Kansas, 1997).

51. A. Lee Fritschler and James M. Hoefler, *Smoking and Politics: Policy Making and the Federal Bureaucracy*, 5th ed. (Upper Saddle River, NJ: Prentice Hall, 1996).

52. Juan Williams, *Eyes on the Prize: America's Civil Rights Years, 1954–1965* (New York: Viking, 1987).

PRIMARY SOURCE READINGS

JAMES BRYCE (1888)
Why Great Men Are Not Chosen Presidents

James Bryce (1838-1922) was a British diplomat and historian who served as his nation's ambassador to the United States (1907-13). He is best known to Americans for his massive study, The American Commonwealth *(1888), from which this excerpt is taken. Bryce admired the country he wrote about, but he was struck by its peculiarities. How do his observations about the qualities of presidents (and presidential candidates) stand the test of time over a century later?*

Europeans often ask, and Americans do not always explain, how it happens that this great office . . . is not more frequently filled by great and striking men? In America, which is beyond all other countries the country of a "career open to talents," a country, moreover, in which political life is unusually keen and political ambition widely diffused, it might be expected that the highest place would always be won by a man of brilliant gifts. But since the heroes of the Revolution died out . . . no President except Abraham Lincoln has displayed rare or striking qualities in the chair. Who now knows or cares to know anything about the personality of James K. Polk or Franklin Pierce? The only remarkable about them is that being so commonplace they should have climbed so far.

Several reasons may be suggested for the fact, which Americans are themselves the first to admit.

One is that the proportion of first-rate ability drawn into politics is smaller in America than in most European countries . . . [where] the total quantity of talent devoted to parliamentary or administrative work is far larger, relatively to the population, than in America, where much of the best ability, both for thought and for action, for planning and for executing, rushes into . . . the business of developing the material resources of the country.

Another is that the methods and habits of Congress, and indeed of political life generally, seem to give fewer opportunities for personal distinction, fewer modes in which a man may commend himself to his countrymen by eminent capacity in thought, in speech, or in administration, than is the case in the free countries of Europe. . . .

A third reason is that eminent men make more enemies, and give those enemies more assailable points, than obscure men do. There are therefore in so far less desirable candidates. . . . Other things being equal, the famous man is preferable. But other things never are equal. The famous man has probably attacked some leaders in his own party, has supplanted others, . . . has perhaps committed errors which are capable of being magnified into offences. No man stands long before the public and bears a part in great affairs without giving openings to censorious criticism. Fiercer far than the light which beats upon a throne is the light which beats upon a presidential candidate, searching out all of the recesses of his past life. Hence, when the choice lies between a brilliant man and a safe man, the safe man is preferred. . . .

The safe candidate may not draw in quite so many votes from the moderate men of the other side as the brilliant one would, but he will not lose nearly so many from his own ranks. Even those who admit his mediocrity will vote straight when the moment for voting comes. Besides, the ordinary American voter does not object to mediocrity. He has a lower conception of the qualities requisite to make a statesman than those who direct public opinion in Europe have. He likes his candidates to be sensible, vigorous, and, above all, what he calls "magnetic," and does not value, because he sees no need for, originality or profundity, a fine culture or a wide knowledge. . . .

It also must be remembered that the merits of a President are one thing and those of a candidate another thing. An eminent American is reported to have said to friends who wished to put him forward, "Gentlemen, let there be no mistake. I should make a good President, but a very bad candidate." Now to a party it is more important that its nominee should be a good candidate than a good President. . . .

So far we have been considering personal merits. But in the selection of a candidate many considerations may have to be regarded besides personal merits, whether they be the merits of a candidate, or of a possible President. The chief of these considerations is the amount of support which can be secured from different States or from different regions, or, as the Americans say, "sections," of the Union. State feeling and sectional feeling are powerful factors in a presidential election. . . .

Other minor disqualifying circumstances require less explanation. A Roman Catholic, or an avowed disbeliever in Christianity, would be an undesirable candidate. Since the close of the Civil War, any one who fought, especially if he fought with distinction, in the Northern army, has enjoyed great advantages. . . .

These secondary considerations do not always prevail. Intellectual ability and force of character must influence the choice of a candidate, and their influence is sometimes decisive. They count for more when times are so critical that the need for a strong man is felt. Reformers declare that their weight will go on increasing as the disgust of good citizens with the methods of professional politicians increases. But for many generations past it is not the greatest men in the Roman Church that have been chosen Popes, nor the most brilliant men in the Anglican Church that have been appointed Archibishops of Canterbury. . . .

We may now answer the question from which we started. Great men are not chosen Presidents, firstly, because great men are rare in politics; secondly, because the method of choice does not bring them to the top; thirdly, because they are not, in quiet times, absolutely needed. . . . It would seem that the natural selection of the English parliamentary system, even as modified by the aristocratic habits of that country, has more tendency to bring the highest gifts to the highest place than the more artificial selection of America.

Sources: The American Commonwealth, 2d ed., vol. I (London: MacMillan and Co., 1891), pp. 73-80.

CLINTON V. JONES, 117 S. CT. 163 (1997).
Argued January 13, 1997—Decided May 27, 1997

Should the president be immune from civil lawsuits unrelated to the office of the presidency while serving in office? In this case, the Supreme Court ruled that Paula Jones could proceed with her sexual harassment lawsuit against President Bill Clinton. In her suit, Jones charged that then-governor Clinton had propositioned her in a hotel room and, after she rebuffed his advances, used the power of his office to hurt her career.

The president's pre-trial deposition in the Jones case in January 1998 led to accusations that he obstructed justice by trying to keep secret his sexual relationship with Monica Lewinsky. This led to his subsequent impeachment by the House of Representatives and trial in the Senate, in which he was acquitted on all counts. During this time Jones's sexual harassment lawsuit was dismissed by the federal trial judge, who ruled that Jones could show no evidence that Clinton had harassed her or used his power as governor to affect her career. To preclude an appeal, Clinton thereafter agreed to an out-of-court settlement with Jones, which did not include any admission of guilt on his part.

Respondent [Paula Corbin Jones] sued . . . to recover damages from petitioner, the current President of the United States, alleging, *inter alia*, that while he was Governor of Arkansas, petitioner made "abhorrent" sexual advances to her, and that her rejection of those advances led to punishment by her supervisors in the state job she held at the time. Petitioner promptly advised the Federal District Court that he would file a motion to dismiss on Presidential immunity grounds, and requested that all other pleadings and motions be deferred until the immunity issue was resolved. . . . The District Judge denied dismissal on immunity grounds and ruled that discovery could go forward, but ordered any trial stayed until petitioner's Presidency ended. The Eighth Circuit affirmed the dismissal denial, but reversed the trial postponement as the "functional equivalent" of a grant of temporary immunity to which petitioner was not constitutionally entitled. The court explained that the President, like other officials, is subject to the same laws that apply to all citizens, that no case had been found in which an official was granted immunity from suit for his unofficial acts, and that the rationale for official immunity is inapposite where only personal, private conduct by a President is at issue. The court also rejected the argument that, unless immunity is available, the threat of judicial interference with the Executive Branch would violate separation of powers.

Held:

. . . Deferral of this litigation until petitioner's Presidency ends is not constitutionally required.

(a) Petitioner's principal submission—that in all but the most exceptional cases, the Constitution affords the President temporary immunity from civil damages litigation arising out of events that occurred before he took office—cannot be sustained on the basis of precedent. The principal rationale for affording Presidents immunity from damages actions based on their official acts—i.e., to enable them to perform their designated functions effectively without fear that a particular decision may give rise to personal liability . . . provides no support for an immunity for unofficial conduct. Moreover, immunities for acts clearly within official capacity are grounded in the nature of the function performed, not the identity of the actor who performed it. . . . The Court is also unpersuaded by petitioner's historical evidence, which sheds little light on the question at issue, and is largely canceled by conflicting evidence that is itself consistent with both the doctrine of presidential immunity . . . and rejection of the immunity claim in this case.

(b) The separation of powers doctrine does not require federal courts to stay all private actions against the President until he leaves office. Even accepting the unique importance of the Presidency in the constitutional scheme, it does not follow that that doctrine would be violated by allowing this action to proceed. The doctrine provides a self-executing safeguard against the encroachment or aggrandizement of one of the three coequal branches of Government at the expense of another. But in this case there is no suggestion that the Federal Judiciary is being asked to perform any function that might in some way be described as "executive." Respondent is merely asking the courts to exercise their core Article III jurisdiction to decide cases and controversies, and, whatever the outcome, there is no possibility that the decision here will curtail the scope of the Executive Branch's official powers. The Court rejects petitioner's contention that this case—as well as the potential additional litigation that an affirmance of the Eighth Circuit's judgment might spawn—may place unacceptable burdens on the President that will hamper the performance of his official duties. That assertion finds little support either in history, as evidenced by the paucity of suits against sitting Presidents for their private actions, or in the relatively narrow compass of the issues raised in this particular case. Of greater significance, it is settled that the Judiciary may severely burden the Executive Branch by reviewing the legality of the President's official conduct . . . and may direct appropriate process to the President himself. . . . It must follow that the federal courts have power to determine the legality of the President's unofficial conduct. The reasons for rejecting a categorical rule requiring federal courts to stay private actions during the President's term apply as well to a rule that would, in petitioner's words, require a stay "in all but the most exceptional cases."

(c) . . . Moreover, the potential burdens on the President posed by this litigation are appropriate matters for that court to evaluate in its management of the case, and the high respect owed the Presidency is a matter that should inform the conduct of the entire proceeding. Nevertheless, the District Court's stay decision was an abuse of discretion because it took no account of the importance of respondent's interest in bringing the case to trial, and because it was premature in that there was nothing in the record to enable a judge to assess whether postponement of trial after the completion of discovery would be warranted.

(d) The Court is not persuaded of the seriousness of the alleged risks that this decision will generate a large volume of politically motivated harassing and frivolous litigation and that national security concerns might prevent the President from explaining a legitimate need for a continuance, and has confidence in the ability of federal judges to deal with both concerns. If Congress deems it appropriate to afford the President stronger protection, it may respond with legislation.

Justice Stevens delivered the opinion of the Court, in which Chief Justice Rehnquist and Justices O'Connor, Scalia, Kennedy, Souter, Thomas, and Ginsburg joined. Justice Breyer filed an opinion concurring in the judgment.

THE FEDERAL BUREAUCRACY

OBJECTIVES

❑   To discuss the importance of bureaucracy to the basic operations of government

❑   To describe the major units of the federal bureaucracy, their core functions, and how they are organized to fulfill those functions

❑   To examine the different ways in which career civil servants and political appointees are selected for their jobs, and how those differences shape the workings of the federal bureaucracy

❑   To explain the interactions among the federal bureaucracy, the president, Congress, and the groups representing various sectors of society

❑   To assess efforts to reshape the federal bureaucracy to help it meet new demands while also maintaining democratic accountability

For nearly a century the federal Food and Drug Administration has been responsible for regulating the purity of the nation's food and the safety of its medicines. The agency was created under the auspices of the 1906 Pure Food and Drug Act, which was enacted following widespread public outrage at unhealthy practices within the food industry as well as concerns about the safety and effectiveness of the many patent medicines being sold at the time.

During the agency's lifetime, its scientists, health experts, and lawyers have struggled to reconcile two often contradictory demands put upon them by Congress and the American people. On one hand, Americans want the government to ensure that their food is pure and their medicines are safe to use. They also want some guarantee that the health remedies they buy will do what they claim. For their part, the businesses that sell food or drugs want some level of government regulation to keep out unscrupulous competitors and to assure the public that their products are safe to buy. In effect, consumers and businesses both depend on the FDA to put its "seal of approval" on a wide range of food and drug products.

However, Americans also want to be able to buy whatever foods they wish, to be able to experiment with new health remedies, and to get access to potentially life-saving medical treatments as quickly and cheaply as possible. They may want products to be safe and effective but, in line with their general suspicion about government authority, they are also reluctant to entirely depend on government experts to tell them what is good for them or to keep them from getting the products they want. These concerns are old ones; time and again the FDA is embroiled in conflicts over whether it is keeping some potential "miracle cure" from getting to market quickly enough.

The most recent such conflict is over "dietary supplements," a broad classification that includes a wide array of vitamins and herbal remedies such as St. John's Wort, which is purported to enhance a person's emotional stability, and echinacea, which is supposed to suppress the effects of the common cold. The market for dietary supplements, which once was largely confined to health food stores, boomed during the 1990s as Americans became increasingly more health conscious and more willing to

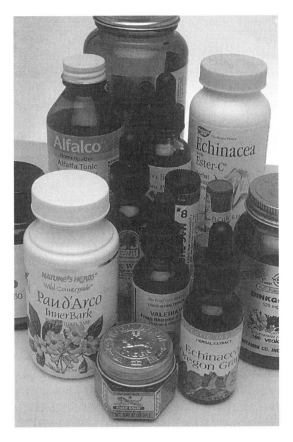

A profusion of dietary supplements. The consumer is confronted with a bewildering array of alternative medicines, vitamins, and other products that promise to improve one's health and happiness. However, despite popular impressions, the federal government has limited legal power to regulate nonprescription drugs and dietary supplements.

experiment with new kinds of products that promised to make them healthier and happier. Supplements were a $4 billion industry by the mid-1990s, and would reach nearly $12 billion by the end of the decade.[1]

However, the FDA was concerned about dietary supplements. Although the general health benefits of vitamins were well known, there was far less scientific support for some of the more specific claims about their effects on cancer, for example. Herbal remedies posed the same dilemma inasmuch as many were being sold with little or no scientific substantiation about their health claims. The FDA had the legal authority to regulate prescription drugs, thereby requiring manufacturers to undertake extensive tests on the safety and effectiveness of their products before taking them to market. In the early 1990s, the FDA proposed to extend this scrutiny to dietary supplements.

The FDA's proposal produced a political firestorm. The dietary supplements industry, which included many of the nation's largest food and pharmaceutical companies, opposed more stringent federal regulation over this increasingly profitable market. It began a massive lobbying campaign to convince Congress to stop the FDA. This campaign was supported by advocates of "alternative medicine" who believed that the FDA unfairly kept their remedies off of the market, and by members of Congress who were eager to reduce the role of the federal government in regulating consumer products. The industry's lobbying campaign included an extensive media effort aimed at convincing consumers that the FDA's efforts would rob them of "freedom of choice" of vitamins and other dietary supplements.[2]

The FDA, supported by medical associations and health advocacy groups, protested that the industry lobbying effort was misleading consumers into believing that the government was going to take away their vitamins when the FDA's real intent was to keep manufacturers from claiming benefits that lacked scientific proof. As FDA commissioner David Kessler said, "If someone wants to put sawdust in a bottle and sell it for $14, it is okay with me as long as they don't put a claim that it is useful to treat or prevent cancer, heart disease, diabetes or arthritis."[3]

However, Congress was in no mood to support stricter government regulation at a time when consumers wanted greater access to more products. In 1994, Congress passed the Dietary Supplement Health and Education Act, which was signed into law by President Clinton. Under the new law, dietary supplements are classified as a subcategory of food, not drugs, and thus were put outside the safety and efficacy standards that apply to prescription drugs. Manufacturers would not need FDA approval for the safety or health claims made for their products before they went on the market. The FDA would have to prove that the product was unsafe before it could pull it off the market.

Supporters of the law argued that it would remove unnecessary regulatory roadblocks and thereby give consumers readier access to new supplements, herbal treatments, and alternative medicines. The law's detractors argued that it would only open up the floodgates to all kinds of untested and potentially dangerous products. Whatever the truth of the matter, the FDA found itself squarely in the middle of a political conflict of its own making.

THE BUREAUCRACY IN AMERICAN POLITICS

Ask most Americans what they think of "bureaucracy" and the usual response includes terms such as "red tape," "inept," "inefficient," "too big," or "unresponsive," if not worse. For their part, presidents and members of Congress rarely miss a chance to attack the bureaucracy, especially during election campaigns. Jimmy Carter, Ronald Reagan, and Bill Clinton all campaigned as "Washington outsiders" determined to change the way government operates. Reagan was fond of saying, "I believe that government is the problem, not the answer."[4]

There are plenty of horror stories to support such dismal views. To critics of the FDA, the agency was deaf to consumers' desires for easier access to dietary supplements. Other bureaucratic units are seen as incredibly inefficient, particularly when compared to businesses in the private sectors. One classic example was the Air Force supply system that required 243 entries by 22 people on 13 forms just to get one spare part for an F-15 jet![5] Looking at such examples, many Americans conclude that the growth in federal spending over the past four decades can be mostly attributed to a bureaucracy that is out of control. This may not be true, because elected officials,

The bureaucrat—or, at least, the standard image of one. To Americans, the bureaucrat is synonymous with endless paperwork, arcane rules, and confusing processes. This image isn't necessarily inaccurate, but it is incomplete.

not bureaucrats, make the laws and authorize spending. Even so, according to public opinion polls, the average American believes that the federal government wastes almost half of every tax dollar, and only 20 percent of Americans trust the federal government to do the right thing most of the time.[6]

Yet the bureaucracy does work, often very well, as the response to the Oklahoma City tragedy illustrates (see Box 10.1). Emergency situations aside, many of the basic services provided by bureaucrats are essential to daily life in a modern society. Bureaucrats keep the nation's military prepared for war; they ensure the safety of the nation's food supplies; they implement laws that protect both individuals and communities; they provide food, shelter, and other social services to people in need; and they ensure a sound banking and financial system to support the economy. The accomplishments of the bureaucracy are as big as sending a man to the moon and as small as making sure product labels list ingredients as required by law. Indeed, the federal bureaucracy touches many aspects of modern life in ways that most Americans consider normal and desirable.

What, then, does the bureaucracy do? Basically, *it translates intent into action.* The federal bureaucracy organizes thousands of government employees into departments and agencies to carry out the goals, intentions, and decisions of the president, Congress, and the federal judiciary. The nation's agriculture policy, for example, may be formulated by the president and Congress, but it must be implemented by employees in the U.S. Department of Agriculture (USDA) and other federal agencies. This policy includes a number of specific programs that provide crop forecasts, financial and technical assistance to farmers, and other services that are critical to keeping the nation's people fed. Within the USDA are economists, financial experts, policy analysts, and other people with expertise in different aspects of farm policy.

BOX 10.1.
THE FEDERAL BUREAUCRACY AND
THE OKLAHOMA CITY BOMBING

At 9:02 A.M. on April 19, 1995, a rental truck stuffed with a mixture of fertilizer, fuel oil, and dynamite was left in front of the Alfred P. Murrah Federal Building in downtown Oklahoma City. When the truck bomb detonated, the blast tore off the front of the concrete-and-glass building, killing 168 federal government employees and citizens who had business in the building. It was the worst episode of domestic terrorism in modern American history.

The tragedy quickly became an example of how the federal bureaucracy can respond to crisis. Within 30 minutes of the blast, James Lee Witt, director of the Federal Emergency Management Agency (FEMA), was on the telephone in his Washington, D.C., office, assembling an expert response team from FEMA offices throughout the Midwest. The team was in Oklahoma City within hours, working with the Army Corp of Engineers and an array of local and state officials on rescue operations. Military airplanes flew in rescue teams from throughout the nation, while military police quickly moved in to establish security around the bomb site. That night Witt joined them as the highest-ranking federal official on the scene under a presidential order that gave him responsibility to coordinate rescue and relief efforts.

Just as quickly, the U.S. Department of Justice deployed the Federal Bureau of Investigation and other federal and state law enforcement agencies on a nationwide hunt to seek out and apprehend the individuals who had planned and executed the bombing. Thousands of local, state, and federal law enforcement agents took part in the search, which within days led to the arrest of Timothy McVeigh and James Nichols, members of a so-called antigovernment "militia," who apparently sought retribution for the deaths of alleged cult members in a gun battle with federal agents in Waco, Texas, two years to the day earlier. Both McVeigh and Nichols were eventually convicted, with McVeigh receiving the death penalty.

Crisis-response teams from other federal offices also moved into action. Agents from the Office of Personnel Management, which oversees the employment of all federal employees, along with the Labor Department's Office of Workers Compensation went to Oklahoma City to help affected employees and their families handle medical bills and process workers' compensation benefits. Professional counsellors were sent in to administer to the emotional needs of survivors and rescue team members alike. Federal funds were quickly allocated to help local businesses and residents repair or rebuild their buildings. More basic governmental functions also received immediate attention. For example, the Department of Housing and Urban Development, the Department of Veterans Affairs, and other federal agencies sent in teams of employees to recover and reconstruct as many records as possible so that basic services such as mortgage applications and veterans benefits could move forward with as little delay as possible.

→

A CLOSER LOOK

Bureaucrats in action. Local, state, and federal emergency personnel searched for survivors following the terrorist bombing of the Murrah Federal Building in Oklahoma City, Oklahoma, on April 19, 1995. Two men were later captured, tried, and convicted for their roles in the bombing, which killed 168 people.

The General Services Administration, which manages government property, helped federal agencies located in the Murrah Building find alternative sites for their operations. This was no small matter inasmuch as the Murrah building housed 500 government employees in the Departments of Defense, Health and Human Services, Housing and Urban Development, Agriculture, Labor, and Veterans Affairs; the Drug Enforcement Administration; the Bureau of Alcohol, Tobacco and Firearms; the Customs Service; Social Security; and the Generals Services Adminstration.

The Social Security Administration switched operations to its Dallas regional office, preventing major disruptions in service to people who depended on federal pension and disability benefits. The Federal Highway Administration moved into the offices of the Federal Aviation Administration, located elsewhere in the city, and the Department of Labor issued apprenticeship certifications from an employee's home.

The circumstances surrounding the Oklahoma City bombing were tragic, but the response to the crisis was an example of successful crisis response by the federal bureaucracy.

Sources: Stephen Barr, "Agencies Scramble to Resume Services," *Washington Post*, April 25, 1995, p. A17; Megan Garvey, "Bombed Agencies Begin to Reopen Offices," *Washington Post*, April 28, 1995, p. A25; Mike Causey, "Rising to the Occasion," *Washington Post*, April 28, 1995, p. B2.

Many people consider bureaucracy a boring topic. They shouldn't. The bureaucracy is vital to the operation of government. If it fails, government programs fail, and people who depend on those programs suffer, regardless of the good intentions of those who created or funded the programs. In this chapter, therefore, we take a close look at the federal bureaucracy, which is often referred to as the "fourth branch of government."

BUREAUCRACY IN CONTEXT

Sometimes it may not seem obvious, but the federal bureaucracy is characterized by as much conflict as Congress, the president, or the courts. Elected officials rely on bureaucrats for information and expertise when they seek to solve the nation's problems, and they rely on bureaucrats to carry out the policies they create. These roles often drag bureaucrats into political battles.

We saw an example of this in the case of dietary supplements that began this chapter. To use another example, as we saw in chapter 5, in 1996, President Clinton and the Republican-led Congress hammered out a controversial overhaul of the nation's welfare system. The issue of welfare reform pitted liberals against conservatives, but it also created divisions within both the Republican and Democratic parties. All sides in the conflict relied on career bureaucrats in the federal Department of Health and Human Services for expertise in revising the law, calculating the impacts of proposed policy changes, and figuring out how to make the new law work. The bureaucrats, for their part, had to respond to these conflicting views and demands.

The bureaucracy itself sometimes creates conflict. As we discussed in chapter 8, most laws are bundles of compromises put together to get the necessary majority vote in Congress. Sometimes these legislative compromises are left vague, since members of Congress may find it harder to pin down every last detail. This reality of lawmaking forces bureaucrats to figure out what Congress intended when it comes time to implement a new law. But this process itself is controversial, because other government officials and citizens might disagree about what the law means, or how it should be implemented. These disagreements demand new compromises. The 1996 welfare law, for example, includes work requirements and limits on benefits that affect state and local governments as well as welfare recipients themselves. As Box 10.2 (p. 440) shows, these provisions become sources of conflict between federal bureaucrats and their counterparts at the state level as both try to figure out how to implement the law effectively. Thus, despite its image of neutral professionalism, the bureaucracy is continually involved in political conflict.

DEFINING BUREAUCRACY

The term **bureaucracy** is derived from the French *bureau*, which refers to the cloth that once was used to cover a writing desk; more generally, it simply means "office." Today the term is applied to a particular way of bringing individuals together, with operating rules and procedures used to achieve the goals of an organization. Although this term is usually applied to government agencies, businesses and organizations in the private sector also exhibit features—such as clear lines of authority, rules, and personnel policies—that are characteristic of any bureaucracy.

THE CLASSICAL VIEW OF BUREAUCRACY

The classical definition of bureaucracy comes from Max Weber, a German sociologist (1864–1920). According to Weber, a bureaucracy is characterized by six major features: fixed jurisdictional areas, a hierarchy of authority, written documents, expertise, full-time workers, and general rules.[7] These characteristics are briefly outlined in this section, using the U.S. Department of Agriculture (USDA) as an example (see Figure 10.1, next page).

Fixed Jurisdictional Areas   Bureaucracies are characterized by a relatively stable and constant distribution of assignments and responsibilities among employees within the organization. That is, bureaucrats carry out specific duties in an organizational structure that remains stable over time. In the Department of Agriculture, for example, the division of functions and responsibilities of the various assistant secretaries is constant. Reorganizations of these functions do happen, but they are infrequent.

Fixed jurisdictional areas promote the development of professionalism and expertise, which in turn promote greater effectiveness. In the Agricultural Marketing Service, for example, economists and other federal employees specialize in helping farmers market their products. This area of responsibility and specialization does not often change. As a result, bureaucrats in this unit develop extensive knowledge and skills related to the marketing of agricultural goods. They become very good at their jobs, and those whom they serve come to depend on their expertise and assistance. Each unit in the Department of Agriculture has its own area of responsibility.

A Hierarchy of Authority   A bureaucracy operates on the basis of a formal **hierarchy.** That is, any bureaucratic unit is divided into distinct levels of authority in which the employees in lower offices work under the direct supervision of those in higher offices. In the USDA, employees in the Agricultural Marketing Service report to the director of that unit, who in turn reports to the Assistant Secretary for Marketing and Regulatory Programs, who reports to the Deputy Secretary, who reports to the Secretary, who reports to the president.

This hierarchy of authority clarifies the chain of command and establishes accountability for the organization's actions. At each level of the hierarchy, individuals supervise those below them while reporting to those above them. In this manner, responsibility for actions is clearer and communication within the organization is faster. Moreover, the hierarchy does not change when a new employee assumes a position in the chain of command. Accountability and authority are established by the position one holds in the hierarchy, not by personal relationships among individuals within the organization. At least in theory, the existence of hierarchy makes it easier for citizens to know who is responsible for any decision or action.

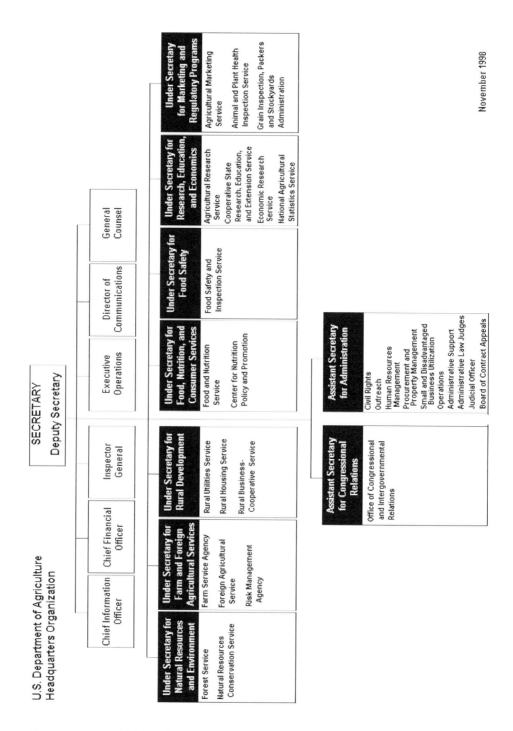

FIGURE 10.1. U.S. DEPARTMENT OF AGRICULTURE,
HEADQUARTERS ORGANIZATION

Written Documents and General Rules   Bureaucracies operate in an environment of written documents and general rules, which further strengthens communication within the organization and enhances accountability. The use of written documents such as memoranda and reports is in contrast to the typical practice of organizations such as small family-owned businesses, which rely primarily on verbal communications. As with hierarchy, dependence on written documents is supposed to ensure clearer communication within the organization. What is more, a thorough documentary record is supposed to enhance accountability to supervisors, to the president and Congress, and ultimately to the people. For example, if you go to the USDA's Web site (http://www.usda.gov), you will find dozens of reports documenting its programs and activities, as well as directions on how you can file requests for even more detailed information under the federal Freedom of Information Act. Having a written record that is available to the public is one way to prevent arbitrary government action.

Rules also help reduce arbitrariness. Rules such as requiring public records and clear standards for promoting employees to higher positions in the hierarchy are basic operating procedures for the organization. Rules are stable, known to both employees and the public, and attempt to cover all possible situations. They clarify lines of authority and establish basic procedures that guide the agency's operations, with respect to its own employees as well as in its relations with other agencies, elected officials, lobbyists, and the public.

Full-Time Expertise   Employment in a bureaucracy usually is a career, not a temporary assignment, and employees are trained for the specific duties and responsibilities of the position they hold. Such expertise helps the bureaucracy carry out its duties. An employee of the U.S. Forest Service, for example, typically is a full-time professional, with college training in forestry or environmental science, whose expertise and skills are essential to the protection and preservation of the nation's public forests and lands. By contrast, an employee in the USDA's Economic Research Service is likely to hold an economics degree and specialize in agricultural economics. Sometimes these government workers are leading experts in their fields.

NONBUREAUCRATIC ORGANIZATIONS

Not all organizations share these characteristics of a bureaucracy. In some private businesses, for example, lines of authority may change at the whim of the owner, and family members may work for the business regardless of their expertise. Also, there may be few written documents or general rules. These businesses operate in a different environment, one that is far less structured by procedures, practices, and rules. Then again, the family business is not open to constant media scrutiny, nor is it accountable to elected officials or the public.

Governments are not necessarily bureaucratic. In some countries government workers serve at the pleasure of a political leader who can appoint individuals to any level of an agency, regardless of their skills or expertise, and the leader can shift the hierarchy of authority and responsibilities of the agency without explanation. Indeed,

The most powerful man in America? Federal Reserve Chairman Alan Greenspan testifies before Congress. Greenspan, as head of the Federal Reserve Board, has tremendous influence over the setting of interest rates, changes in which can affect everything from home mortgages to the value of the dollar overseas.

in the early history of the United States, the federal government did not always demonstrate the characteristics of a modern bureaucracy. Nineteenth-century American presidents, for example, could appoint friends and supporters to government offices without much concern for expertise or accountability. Political loyalty often mattered more than competence. Today presidents can appoint individuals of their choosing to lead the various units of the bureaucracy, but as we will discuss later in the chapter, most federal bureaucrats are career employees who get their jobs because of their abilites or expertise, not because of their political affiliations or personal connections.

THE BUREAUCRACY TODAY

The federal bureaucracy has changed dramatically in the course of the nation's history. In 1816, 27 years after the ratification of the Constitution, the bureaucracy consisted of only 4,800 civilian employees, 70 percent of whom worked in the Post Office.[8] This was sufficient for a country with only 4 million people and a limited national government. By contrast, today the United States is a complex society with a population of 270 million. Providing government services to this vast population are nearly 2.9 million civilian employees (not counting military personnel) who work in the executive, legislative, and judicial branches of the federal government (see Figure 10.2).[9] Most of these employees work in the executive branch, and they include engineers, scientists, lawyers, doctors, nurses, accountants, custodians, diplomats, secretaries, and individuals working in a host of other occupations.

The federal bureaucracy is not the only one. In fact, there are more government workers in state and local governments (all combined) than in the federal government (see Table 10.1, p. 432). Collectively, these individuals provide the many services—from health care to education to national defense—that Americans expect from their government at all levels.

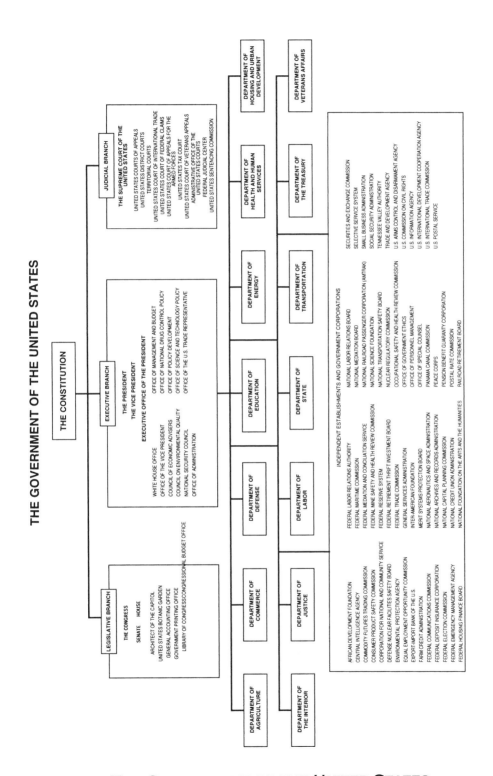

FIGURE 10.2. THE GOVERNMENT OF THE UNITED STATES

TABLE 10.1.   GOVERNMENT EMPLOYEES IN THE FEDERAL SYSTEM

The size of the federal government as measured by number of civilian employees has increased more slowly than has employment in state and local governments, and is actually *declining* as a percentage of all government workers.

Civilian Government Employment

	Federal	State and Local	Federal Government as Percent of Total
1964	2,500,000	7,236,000	26%
1974	2,893,000	11,713,000	20%
1984	2,910,000	13,504,000	18%
1994	2,973,000	16,171,000	16%

A majority of state and local government employees work in public schools and universities. On the other hand, defense-related and postal workers are the largest groups of federal employees.

Government Employment by Function, 1995
(by percentage)

	Federal Government	State and Local Government
National defense	32.3	0
Postal service	25.4	0
Education	.5	52.4
Highways	.1	3.6
Health and hospitals	10.2	9.8
Police and fire protection	2.9	8.1
Parks and recreation	.9	2.0
Natural resources	7.6	1.3
Financial administration	4.5	2.3
Judicial and legal	1.7	2.1
Other	13.6	16.4
	100%	100%

Source: Statistical Abstract of the United States, 1998 (Washington, D.C.: Government Printing Office, 1998), p. 331.

MAJOR UNITS OF THE FEDERAL BUREAUCRACY

As we saw in Figure 10.2, the executive branch is composed of units that differ in a number of ways, including size, purpose, and structure. One important way in which they differ is their relationship to the president. Some agencies of the bureaucracy are directly accountable to the president, whereas others are more removed from direct presidential authority. This distinction has important implications for how agencies operate and are held accountable.

CABINET DEPARTMENTS

Most federal employees work in one of the 14 departments. A **department** is the largest organizational designation in the federal bureaucracy. As we will see later, departments, such as the Department of Defense and the Department of Agriculture, include many specialized subunits that perform the work of the organization. For example, in the Department of Agriculture the General Counsel provides legal advice to other USDA officials and represents the department in federal courts whenever it is involved in a lawsuit (see Figure 10.1, p. 428).

Each department is headed by a **secretary,** such as the secretary of agriculture, who is appointed by the president and approved by the Senate. The secretaries of the federal departments, along with other top federal bureaucratic officials (such as the administrator of the Environmental Protection Agency), make up what is known as the president's **cabinet.** A new president chooses cabinet secretaries carefully, usually relying on people with similar political philosophies and goals. Whether they can manage a large government department is not necessarily an important criterion in their selection. In addition to heading their departments, cabinet secretaries advise the president on policy matters. They ultimately serve at the pleasure of the president, who may dismiss a secretary who is seen as ineffective or disloyal or, as sometimes happens, becomes a political liability because of scandal or public disagreement with the president.

INDEPENDENT COMMISSIONS

A second type of federal government organization is the **independent commission** or independent establishment. These units are less subject to direct presidential influence and control than departments. An important example of such an establishment is the Federal Reserve or "Fed," which is responsible for regulating the money supply and overseeing banking policy. The Fed consists of a seven-member board of governors, each of whom is chosen by the president and approved by the Senate. Each governor heads a regional Federal Reserve bank and is appointed to a 14-year term. A president who serves for four years thus may appoint only a few members to the board, and these appointees may serve longer than the president. Members can be removed from the Fed only for serious neglect of duty or specific illegal actions, not because they opposed the president's policies. These provisions are designed to minimize the role of partisan politics in the appointment of people whose decisions have huge impacts on the nation's economy. The Fed can oversee monetary and banking policy without being subjected to direct presidential and congressional pressure.

GOVERNMENT CORPORATIONS

A third type of federal government organization is the **government corporation.** Examples include the United States Postal Service, Amtrak (the passenger rail system), and the Corporation for Public Broadcasting (public television). Government corporations are designed to operate like private businesses, with a strong focus on cost-effective and efficient service. They are also designed to be as free from partisan political influences as possible. Some, such as Amtrak, are government owned and largely supported by public funds. Others, such as the Corporation for Public Broadcasting, operate with a mix of government and self-generated funds. The Postal Service, by contrast, runs entirely on revenue from stamps and other services that it provides to customers. In general, government corporations were established with the hope that they would become self-supporting and no longer require federal funds.

FUNCTIONS OF THE BUREAUCRACY

Another way to categorize the many units of the federal bureaucracy is by the type of service each unit provides. These categories—basic services, clientele services, and regulation—help us focus on the essential functions of the federal bureaucracy. They also highlight the changing nature of the services citizens expect of their government.

PROVIDING BASIC SERVICES

Foreign Policy   Relations with other countries are among the most important concerns of the bureaucracy. The Departments of State and Defense are the two major agencies responsible for the government's foreign policy. The Department of State, with over 25,000 employees, oversees 200 embassies and consulates around the world and provides foreign policy advice to the president. The Department of Defense is the largest single unit in the federal bureaucracy. It employs over 3 million men and women: 1.1 million as active duty military personnel, 1.5 million in reserve and National Guard units, and 750,000 civilian employees.[10] The department organizes and maintains the nation's military forces and also provides military advice to the president. Each of the major armed services operates under civilian control as a separate unit within the Department of Defense.

Financial Policy   Another major service provided by the federal bureaucracy is financial policy. The Department of the Treasury is responsible for a wide range of financial activities, including international finance, tax policy, and managing the government debt. The Federal Reserve Board also is involved in financial policy. Through its control over interest rates and banking policies, it determines the amount of money available in the economy.

Law Enforcement   The federal government has played an increasingly important role in law enforcement in recent decades. The attorney general, who heads the Department of Justice, is the chief legal counsel for the government and is responsible for enforcing the nation's laws. The Department of Justice employs many attorneys, who represent the United States as prosecutors in criminal cases and other legal actions throughout the country. The Federal Bureau of Investigation (FBI) is part of the Justice Department, but its director is given some independence to enable the bureau to investigate crimes committed within the federal government itself.

U.S. Forest Service employees evaluating timber. The Forest Service manages timber and other resources located in the nation's national forests. As a result, Forest Service personnel often are in the middle of conflicts between those who wish to preserve forests and those who make their livelihoods from timber products.

Mail Delivery   Perhaps one of the most important early functions of the federal bureaucracy was to maintain communication across a vast country before the advent of telephones and the Internet. The Postal Service operates a national mail system that handles more mail than any other in the world. Its 817,000 employees handle about 191 *billion* pieces of mail annually.[11] The Postal Service was a cabinet department until 1970, when it was reorganized as a government corporation that is required to support itself through revenues from services to customers.

The four departments just described, plus the Postal Service, were the beginnings of the American bureaucracy. All of these agencies focused on basic public services needed in a growing country. Since that time the federal bureaucracy has become involved in a number of other important services, each reflecting changes in the nation itself.

Natural Resources   Protecting and managing the use of the nation's natural resources is the primary responsibility of the Department of the Interior. First created in 1849 to coordinate federal lands in the West, today the department is responsible for preserving and protecting land and water resources throughout the country. Included in this department are the U.S. Park Service, which operates the national park system, and the Bureau of Indian Affairs, which is responsible for federal policy regarding Native Americans living on reservations.

The Department of Energy is a newer cabinet department; it was created in 1977 in response to the energy crisis that arose during that decade. Many Americans were concerned that the nation's increasing reliance on imported oil made it vulnerable to the demands of foreign leaders. The department plans and coordinates the nation's energy policy with the goals of achieving greater self-sufficiency, developing new energy technologies, and promoting wiser use of the nation's energy resources.

General Welfare   The general health and welfare of the nation's citizens is the focus of the Department of Health and Human Services. Established in 1953 as the Department of Health, Education, and Welfare, this department brought into a single agency many of the health and social service programs created in previous years. In 1980 educational policy was moved to another department. Major programs operated or funded by the Department of Health and Human Services include Medicaid, Medicare, Social Security, and Temporary Assistance for Needy Families (formerly known as Aid to Families with Dependent Children), which provides financial support for low-income families.

Housing   After World War II the hundreds of thousands of returning soldiers created a large demand for safe and affordable housing. The federal government responded with programs to increase the amount of available housing. In 1965 it brought these programs together with those focusing on the problems of cities, creating the Department of Housing and Urban Development. This department provides mortgage insurance and direct financial support for the construction and rehabilitation of single-family and multifamily housing, supports state and local government programs to foster housing development, and promotes and enforces fair housing and equal housing opportunity laws.

Transportation   Fostering an efficient and coordinated transportation system is another vital public service. The Department of Transportation, created in 1966 by the consolidation of several independent agencies, coordinates transportation policy. The department supports the development of aviation, railroads, highways, mass transit, and maritime travel. The U.S. Coast Guard, Federal Highway Administration, and Federal Aviation Administration are among the units contained within the Department of Transportation.

Education   In recent decades the federal government has become more involved in education policy, although public education is still dominated by state and local governments. The Department of Education was created in 1980 at the urging of educational professionals. The department supports research on effective educational practices and sponsors programs to promote excellence in education. In 1981 President Reagan vowed to eliminate the department, arguing that education was a state responsibility and that the department only served to represent the interests of teachers and other education professionals. However, the department's supporters in Congress were able to keep it from being eliminated.

Space Exploration   The National Aeronautics and Space Administration (NASA) was established in 1958 to coordinate the nation's civilian space program. NASA has over 23,000 employees, who conduct numerous space-related research projects and operate the agency's manned and unmanned space programs. The ability of NASA to land astronauts on the moon in 1969 was widely heralded as an example of how a bureaucracy could plan and achieve an ambitious goal. In contrast, the fatal 1986 explosion of the space shuttle *Challenger* raised troubling concerns about the agency's management and decisionmaking procedures.

SERVING SPECIFIC CLIENTS

Some bureaucratic units, even if performing broad public functions, also serve particular groups (or clients) within society; and some units were created specifically to protect and promote the interests of particular groups. Four of the fourteen cabinet departments serve the interests of major groups in American society: farmers, business, labor, and veterans. Not surprisingly, during budget and policy debates these departments receive much of their support from interest groups representing their clients. As we saw in chapter 7, these groups have considerable influence in Congress, leading some observers to argue that they have "captured" the congressional committees and executive branch departments that are concerned with their affairs.

Farmers   Created in 1862, when three-fourths of Americans lived in rural areas, the Department of Agriculture's primary mission is to promote farming. For example, it works to improve and maintain farmers' income by supporting the sale of agricultural products in the United States and overseas. To do so it may set prices for some agricultural products, such as pork, or buy others, such as wheat, to use in foreign aid programs. It also sponsors rural development programs, provides financial assistance to farmers, sponsors agricultural research, and protects the quality of agricultural products through inspection services. The USDA stamp on many foods is an example of the work done by this department.

Business and Labor   The Departments of Commerce and Labor serve the interests of businesses and workers, respectively. These two groups were served by a single department beginning in 1903, but 10 years later that department was divided to create the two departments that exist today. The Department of Commerce engages in a wide range of activities designed to encourage the growth of businesses. Financial programs, marketing assistance, and economic research are among its major activities. The Department of Labor, by contrast, fosters and promotes the welfare of workers. It coordinates job training programs, sponsors research on labor issues, and operates a number of programs dealing with wages, hours, and working conditions. Not surprisingly, those who work in the Department of Commerce may not agree with those in the Department of Labor about government regulation of business practices, particularly the rights of workers. They serve very different clienteles.

Veterans   The Department of Veterans Affairs provides services to the nation's hundreds of thousands of military veterans. Established as the Veterans Administration in 1930 to respond to the needs of World War I veterans, it became a department in 1989 after veterans' groups lobbied Congress to elevate its status and, they hoped, thereby increase the visibility of veterans' issues within the federal government.[12] The department operates programs that benefit veterans and their families, including disability assistance, home mortgage loans, education, and medical care.

REGULATION

Regulation is the third major type of activity carried out by the federal bureaucracy, and probably the most controversial. Rather than provide a general public service or serve a specific clientele, regulatory agencies monitor and regulate the activities of businesses and, sometimes, citizens. Regulatory agencies were created primarily in response to citizen demands. One purpose of these agencies is to protect the health and safety of citizens. Agencies such as the Food and Drug Administration, the Environmental Protection Agency, and the National Transportation Safety Board inspect the food we eat, monitor the water we drink, oversee our working conditions, check many of the products we buy, and inspect the cars, planes, and trains we use for transportation.

Regulatory agencies also operate to ensure fairness and competitiveness in business dealings. The Federal Trade Commission watches for unfair or sleazy sales practices, and the Securities and Exchange Commission monitors the nation's stock brokerages to prevent potentially harmful speculation. In some ways these agencies help maintain consumer confidence in the free market system. For example, a recent federal lawsuit against the Microsoft Corporation, one of the nation's largest companies, was intended to maintain competitiveness in the computer software industry and thereby keep prices as low as possible.

Economic and Financial Regulation As we saw in chapter 1, Americans believe in free markets and private property. However, they also approve of the use of government to intervene in the market or support important economic activities. In the 19th century, the federal government sold land to businesses and helped finance the construction of canals. It also engaged in regulatory activities, primarily in response to market "failures." A market failure occurred when an entire industry, such as railroads or oil, was dominated by one or a few producers. With no competition, consumers had few choices and faced high prices. For example, John D. Rockefeller's Standard Oil Company controlled the nation's entire oil industry by the 1880s, creating a monopoly that allowed him to dictate oil prices and supplies. In 1890 Congress responded to this and other monopolies by passing the Sherman Antitrust Act, which gave the federal government the authority to break up monopolies and ensure competition within specific industries. The same issue came up with Microsoft, the world's dominant maker of computer software. The appropriateness of economic regulation today is discussed later in the chapter.

Market failures also sparked the establishment of several important federal agencies. The first of these was the Interstate Commerce Commission (ICC), created in 1887. The ICC was responsible for regulating surface transportation—trains, trucks, and buses—to ensure fair and reasonable rates and safe service. Another major regulatory agency is the Federal Communications Commission, created in 1934 to regulate interstate and foreign communications by radio, television, wire, satellite, and cable. The National Labor Relations Board was created in 1935 to regulate labor markets by ruling on unfair labor practices and protecting the rights of workers and employers in the collective bargaining process. The nation's financial system is regulated by agencies such as the Federal Reserve System, created in 1913, and the Fed-

Scientists at the Centers for Disease Control in Atlanta, Georgia. The CDC acts as the federal government's first line of defense against the outbreak of infectious diseases. Once notified, CDC experts rush to the scene, analyze the health risk, and take actions to contain the potential spread of the disease.

eral Deposit Insurance Corporation (FDIC), created in 1933. All currency is distributed by the "Fed," as it is called, and most banks are regulated by the FDIC. Both agencies play an important role in ensuring the stability of the financial system.

Environmental and Safety Regulations Regulations also play a central role in how government addresses environmental and safety problems. The Environmental Protection Agency, created in 1970, has broad responsibilities for preventing air and water pollution, controlling the use and disposal of chemicals, and regulating solid wastes. Because these problems frequently require difficult economic and social decisions, the EPA often finds itself squarely in the middle of some of the nation's most visible public debates.

For example, the EPA is required to regulate the use of chemical pesticides in agriculture.[13] This assignment forces the agency to balance competing demands: Consumers want pest-free and inexpensive food, but they also worry about the effects of chemicals on human health and the environment; farmers want inexpensive, safe chemicals to keep pests from eating their crops; members of Congress want to help farmers, but they also want to protect consumers; chemical companies want to sell their products; environmental groups worry about the effects of pesticides on bird and animal populations. And the problem of pesticides is but one issue the EPA deals with.

BOX 10.2.
THE BUREAUCRACY AND   **A CLOSER LOOK**
CHILD SAFETY SEATS

Despite the image of confrontation that often characterizes relations between business and federal regulators, the reality is more complex. What follows is just one example of how federal bureaucrats work closely with industry representatives, state safety officials, and others to develop regulations that will satisfy their respective needs and still ensure a safe product for consumers.

Each year, about 600 children under the age of 5 are killed in motor vehicle crashes. Child safety seats have helped reduce this death rate. However the *improper* use of child safety seats has created an unforeseen hazard. By one estimate, 40 percent of children under 5 years of age are improperly restrained in child safety seats, and as many as 90 percent of seats are not installed correctly.

Enter the federal bureaucracy. The National Highway Traffic Safety Administration (NHTSA), part of the U.S. Department of Transportation, is charged by Congress with protecting public safety in a variety of transportation-related areas, including child safety seats. For more than 20 years, employees of NHTSA have developed regulations for the use of child restraint devices in motor vehicles. Federal engineers, scientists, economists, and others have studied different seat designs and how seats can be adapted to motor vehicles. During this process, hearings are held to collect information, experiments are conducted with different kinds of seats, and studies are made of restraint systems in other countries.

As a result, the *Code of Federal Regulations*, the official compendium of all federal regulations, contains 32 pages that regulate the development and sale of child safety seats. These regulations include mandatory seat performance standards and testing procedures, language that manufacturers must include in the instructions on seat installation that must accompany new seats, and warning labels regarding proper installation and use of seats. To improve safety further, in 1997 the NHTSA added regulations that require automobile and child seat manufacturers to develop vehicles and seats that can be secured independent of the traditional seat safety belt. These regulations offered manufacturers several options to achieve this new and more secure system.

Source: John Elliott Leighton, "Are Children Caught in the Seat of Disaster?" *Trial,* March 1998, pp. 54–64.

Safety regulations are designed to protect consumers and workers. For example, the Federal Trade Commission (FTC) regulates aspects of packaging and requires that product labels include information about the content of the product. The National Transportation Safety Board (NTSB) continues to play a major role in developing child safety seats (see Box 10.2). The Occupational Safety and Health Administration (OSHA) regulates employment and safety conditions for workers. For example, OSHA will inspect a chicken processing plant to ensure that the company is providing its workers with safe equipment and clean facilities, including sufficient toilets. This role often makes OSHA unpopular with businesses.

COMBINING FUNCTIONS

The three types of functions outlined here—providing basic services, serving specific clienteles, and regulation—differ in significant ways, but in the real world they are often mixed together. For example, the Department of Labor supports workers and the interests of labor. Yet it includes the Occupational Safety and Health Administration, whose functions are regulatory. Likewise, the Department of Transportation provides basic transportation services, but within it the Federal Aviation Administration (FAA) is responsible for enforcing airline safety regulations.

This mixture of roles within a department forces top officials to balance competing pressures. Thus, for example, the Secretary of Transportation promotes airline travel that is both inexpensive and safe. This can create tensions within the department. Whereas one unit of the department is encouraging airline companies to reduce costs as much as possible in order to maintain low airfares, another unit is enforcing air safety requirements, which can raise costs for airlines. Any bureaucratic unit must constantly deal with these internal conflicts and tensions.

WORKING IN THE BUREAUCRACY

Federal employees perform a broad range of tasks in order to deliver these services. What is more, the demands placed on the federal bureaucracy require a broad range of talents and types of expertise. Federal bureaucrats therefore include professionals such as lawyers, doctors, scientists, policy analysts, economists, librarians, and computer specialists, as well as secretaries, janitors, electricians, and many other kinds of support staff.

Each type of employee has specific tasks and areas of responsibility, all designed to help the organization fulfill its duties. For example, a lawyer employed by the Labor Department is there to help the department interpret and apply federal labor laws, draft new regulations, and represent the department in court when it brings lawsuits against those who violate federal law. A secretary in that department might perform support duties for the lawyer, including organizing legal materials and preparing legal briefs for trial. This kind of division of labor and expertise is typical of any large organization, whether it is the Department of Labor, General Motors, or the U.S. Army.

Most of the civilian employees in the federal bureaucracy attain their positions through the **civil service** system, in which employment is based on examinations and on the expertise of individual applicants. However, a small percentage of federal employees are **political appointees.** They obtain their jobs on the basis of political criteria, such as their political party affiliation or having worked in the president's election campaign. In general, political appointees occupy the top positions in any administration, working closely with the president and overseeing the activities of the career civil servants. Political appointees also are the president's eyes and ears in the bureaucracy; they enable the president to know how civil servants feel about new initiatives or how well programs are working.

The relationship between career civil service employees and temporary political appointees has changed over the years, but it remains controversial. Until the late 19th century nearly all federal employees were political appointees. The **spoils system,** as it was known, was based on the principle that "to the victor belong the spoils." New presidents were free to choose who would serve in their administrations, whereas most employees—from cabinet secretaries to office messengers and even postal workers—were subject to dismissal when a new president took office. Supporters of this system argued not only that the president should be free to choose the people who worked in the executive branch, but also that "rotation in office" allowed the bureaucracy to reflect the diversity and views of the population.

THE CIVIL SERVICE SYSTEM

Throughout the 19th century, many Americans grumbled about the potential for corruption in the spoils system. Dissatisfaction turned to action only after 1881, when President James A. Garfield was assassinated by a disgruntled campaign worker who had not received a government job. In 1883 Congress passed the **Pendleton Act,** which established a civil service system in which federal job appointments would be based on merit. The merit system relies on competitive examinations that are open to all job seekers, regardless of political affiliation. These examinations measure ability, not political loyalty, and different exams are given for different jobs. An office secretary, for example, is tested in typing, writing, and organizational skills, whereas a policy analyst must demonstrate analytical skills and knowledge of a particular policy area, such as transportation policy.

Once they have been hired through merit selection, individuals receive **tenure** in office after completing a probationary period. With tenure, a federal worker can be dismissed only for gross negligence, serious misconduct, or conviction on a criminal charge. In short, a new president could not dismiss all federal employees hired under the previous administration, even if those employees were opposed to the new president's policies.

Today over 90 percent of federal civilian employees are covered by civil service rules.[14] To further ensure the political neutrality of federal employees, the Hatch Act of 1949 prohibited federal employees from participating in political campaigns. However, more recent versions of the law allow federal workers greater flexibility to participate in political campaigns, although they still cannot run for elective political office or solicit campaign contributions from the public. These changes were made in the recognition that federal bureaucrats were also citizens who had First Amendment rights of free speech and freedom of assembly.

EMPLOYMENT OUTSIDE THE CIVIL SERVICE

The civil service system does not cover all federal workers. Two other groups of employees—presidential appointees and the Senior Executive Service—play a critical role in the federal bureaucracy.

Presidential Appointees   Approximately 5,800 of almost 3 million federal civilian employees are appointed by the president. Most of these officials occupy top policy-making and management positions, such as cabinet secretaries and deputy secretaries, or are ambassadors, members of the White House staff, or special assistants to high-level federal officials. About one-third of these appointments must be approved by the Senate.[15]

Political appointees work outside civil service rules because their primary responsibility is to carry out the president's policies. If they had tenure in the civil service, they would be insulated from presidential direction and could derail a new president's agenda. The president appoints these individuals because they share the administration's policy goals and are willing to direct the bureaucracy to meet those goals. Almost all of these individuals are replaced when a new president comes into office. Because they hold their positions for an average of only 22 months, presidential appointees are, as one political scientist noted, "birds of passage" on the political scene.[16] Compared to career civil servants, high-level political employees are temporary workers who sometimes find it difficult to get career civil servants to follow them. Still, they play a critical role in formulating and implementing the president's policy agenda.

The Senior Executive Service   The temporary nature of political appointments created a need for professional managers who are sensitive to the policy goals of the president but also experienced in guiding and managing bureaucratic units. The Civil Service Reform Act of 1978 created the Senior Executive Service (SES) to provide a level of professional managers below presidential appointees but above the general civil service. Composed of approximately 8,000 individuals, the SES consists of scientists, engineers, policy experts, and professional administrators who are skilled and experienced in managing government agencies.[17]

Like presidential appointees, bureaucrats in the SES can be moved around at the president's discretion to take advantage of their particular expertise or skills. For example, a new cabinet secretary might recruit an experienced member of the SES employed in another agency to take on an important administrative role in the department. However, like civil servants, that member of the SES is protected from arbitrary dismissal from federal employment. If a new president or cabinet secretary no longer wants that person's service in the SES, he or she returns to a regular position in the federal bureaucracy. Some members of the SES have served in important positions under successive presidents of either party. The SES, then, combines the flexibility of presidential appointment with the expertise and "neutral competence" of career civil service.

THE BUREAUCRATIC ENVIRONMENT

The life of a federal bureaucrat, then, depends very much on his or her position within the system. For those in the general civil service, written rules and procedures define appointment, advancement, and the nature of one's job. At the other end of the system, political appointees operate in a much more volatile world that depends entirely on the president's needs and demands. These are very different environments. As we will see, disagreements and conflicts between individuals at these different levels are quite common.

WORKING WITH OTHER BRANCHES OF GOVERNMENT

The federal bureaucracy is sometimes referred to as a "fourth branch" of government. Formally it is part of the executive branch and therefore under the general direction of the president, but like so much else in politics, the reality is far more complicated.

For example, bureaucrats at all levels sometimes deviate from positions advocated by the president. The bureaucracy implements policies and programs that continue for many years, beyond any single presidential administration. What is more, bureaucrats are responsible for implementing laws and programs that have been funded by Congress, which often has different goals than the president's goals. Some bureaucrats, such as the members of the Federal Reserve Board, are part of an agency that operates almost entirely independently. Moreover, over time programs seem to develop lives of their own, sometimes managing to survive despite efforts by a new president and members of Congress to eliminate them. At the same time, the bureaucracy must work closely with the president and Congress, the elected representatives of the people.

Some political scientists use what is called a **principal-agent model** to describe the relationships among bureaucrats, the president, and Congress. In this model, the president and Congress, as elected officials, are seen as "principals" who establish policies. These policies guide the activities of the "agents," the bureaucrats who are supposed to implement the laws and programs enacted by elected officials.[18] Simple enough. However, the relationship between principals and agents is more complex, subtle, and fluid than an organizational chart might suggest. For example, in the case of welfare reform (portrayed in Box 10.3, see pp. 446 and 447), elected officials and federal bureaucrats may disagree over how to implement the law, but bureaucrats often are in a position to influence the actual outcomes because of their greater expertise and longer experience with welfare programs. Sometimes their knowledge gives bureaucrats the advantage over elected officials. On the other hand, the president and Congress have a number of means by which to get bureaucrats to follow their directions.

THE BUREAUCRACY AND THE PRESIDENT

Conflicts between the president and the bureaucracy are inevitable. On paper, the president is head of the executive branch and its many units, yet every president ends up frustrated and dismayed by the difficulty of controlling or changing the bureaucracy. President Dwight Eisenhower, for example, was a former general who was accustomed to having his orders followed without question. President Harry Truman, Eisenhower's predecessor in the Oval Office, said of Eisenhower, "He'll sit here and he'll say, 'Do this! Do that!' *And nothing will happen*. Poor Ike—it won't be a bit like the Army. He'll find it very frustrating."[19] President Clinton also was frustrated when he took office in 1993 and found that a bureaucracy that had been shaped by Republican presidents for 20 of the preceding 24 years was not inclined to change its ways to suit his agenda.

Different Perspectives   This frustration is due in part to a clash of perspectives. The president and the bureaucracy operate in separate worlds, with different time frames and, often, different goals. A president's world is highly charged, partisan, and built around a four-year term that can end at the next election. This is a relatively short span of time in which to accomplish goals espoused during the campaign. Presidents find it hard to get interested in new initiatives that take four or more years to develop. Moreover, presidents focus on government actions and programs that appeal to the voting public. If the activities of the bureaucracy have little meaning to citizens, presidents are unlikely to pay much attention.

Bureaucrats, on the other hand, have time horizons that often extend for a decade or more. They are full-time professionals who see employment in the bureaucracy as a career. As part of that career, they develop expertise in their particular skill or assignment. Their goal typically is to perpetuate and perhaps expand the scope of their work. They are more loyal to their specific issue or program than to any president. If their work coincides with the president's goals, the bureaucracy and the president can proceed along a path of mutual support.

If the president does not approve of the work of a particular agency, however, a clash is almost inevitable. President Reagan, for example, encountered considerable resistance from within the federal bureaucracy when he tried to sharply reduce the scope of the social services sponsored by the federal government. Their opposition was not simply a matter of liberal Democrats opposing a conservative Republican. Rather, the bureaucrats who developed and ran the programs truly believed that what they did was important. Members of Congress who had helped create the programs also supported their continuation.[20]

Having said this, presidents do have some tools with which to influence the bureaucracy. Some of these tools are more direct than others, and none of them foolproof. They include the appointment power, the Executive Office of the President, the budget, and reorganization.

The Appointment Power   The president's power to appoint top officials is one major source of influence. The president appoints the secretaries of the major cabinet departments as well as many of the top officials farther down in a department's organizational structure. Presidents use considerable time and resources in making these choices, particularly for top officials.

When a new president is elected, a transition team collects and reviews applications for appointed positions. The president often personally reviews applicants for top positions to assess their compatibility with the new administration's goals, as well as their ability to lead a large department. In 1993 President Clinton chose Richard Riley as secretary of the Department of Education and Madeline Kunin as his deputy secretary of Education. Both were former governors (Riley of South Carolina, Kunin of Vermont) whom Clinton had known when he was governor of Arkansas. Both had

BOX 10.3.
THE BUREAUCRACY AND THE TOBACCO IRON TRIANGLE

In Boxes 7.2 (p. 308) and 8.2 (p. 354) we focused on the interest group and congressional sides of the tobacco iron triangle. Elements of the federal bureaucracy make up the third side of this close working relationship. In particular, employees within the U.S. Department of Agriculture (USDA) traditionally have strong ties with members of Congress from tobacco regions as well as representatives from the tobacco industry itself.

The USDA is responsible for nurturing and promoting all aspects of American agriculture, and tobacco is no different. USDA staff are experts in the needs and challenges faced by the tobacco industry. They work with growers to enhance the yield and quality of tobacco crops as well as oversee USDA standards on grades of tobacco used in cigarettes, cigars, and other products. Since the 1930s, the department has administered a tobacco price support program that restricts the production of tobacco and thereby helps ensure profitability for growers, many of whom run small family operations. The USDA also works with the Department of Commerce to expand the export of American cigarettes to other countries. To the USDA, tobacco is but another crop: In one instance, it even produced and distributed overseas a film that highlighted positive aspects of smoking.

However, federal agencies that do not have the mission of promoting tobacco have led the fight against cigarette smoking. For instance, the debate over cigarettes intensified in 1964, when the surgeon general of the United States, the nation's top health officer, released a report linking cigarette smoking to heart and lung disease. The surgeon general is located within the Department of Health and Human Services, and the primary mission of the office is to improve the health of all Americans. Despite efforts by the tobacco industry and its congressional allies to restrict the reach of the office, subsequent surgeons general have taken strong public stands opposed to tobacco and instigated the requirement that cigarette packs bear labels warning of the dangers of smoking.

→

developed skills and knowledge as leaders in state education reform efforts, and as former governors were skilled in executive management.

Making the "right" appointments does not guarantee that the president's wishes will automatically be translated into results.[21] President Reagan vowed to eliminate the Departments of Education and Energy and appointed top officials to both departments with instructions to abolish their own agencies, but strong opposition from members of Congress, organized interest groups, and officials within the departments themselves prevailed over the president's campaign pledge. Even his own appointees, having become immersed in the goals and culture of their respective departments, changed their minds. In Washington parlance, this is known as "going native."

A CLOSER LOOK

A few years later the Federal Communications Comission (FCC) banned cigarette advertising on television and radio, thereby putting cigarettes on the same status as hard liquor and guns. The FCC also required all print and billboard advertising, as well as any other items related to cigarettes (such as T-shirts) to bear the surgeon general's health warnings.

In the 1980s state and local governments entered the battle with restrictions on smoking in public areas, new taxes on cigarettes, and other policies to reduce smoking. In many respects, the states were responding to rising health care and disability costs related to smoking. In 1998 the 50 state attorneys general bypassed congressional defenders of tobacco and entered into a $226 billion agreement with the tobacco industry, whereby it would avoid further litigation by reimbursing the states for some of these health costs. For their part, private citizens have filed lawsuits against the industry, alleging that it covered up its knowledge of the addictive nature of cigarettes as well as the link between smoking and cancer.

Potentially most important, in 1997 the Food and Drug Administration (FDA) labeled tobacco a drug and asserted authority to regulate its sale and use. The tobacco industry has always resisted FDA oversight of tobacco and thus challenged the agency's decision in federal court. The lawsuit has made its way through the federal judicial system to the U.S. Supreme Court, which has agreed to hear the case in 2000.

Thus, just as the Tobacco Institute competes with antismoking groups, and tobacco-region members of Congress compete with antismoking members on other committees, the Department of Agriculture competes with other federal agencies that have quite different concerns about the tobacco industry. In this regard, the tobacco iron triangle no longer wields its old influence within the federal bureaucracy.

Sources: A. Lee Fritschler and James M. Hoefler, *Smoking and Politics: Policy Making and the Federal Bureaucracy*, 5th ed. (Upper Saddle River, NJ: Prentice Hall, 1996); Barry Meier, "Tide

The Executive Office of the President A second major source of influence and coordination is the Executive Office of the President (EOP). Created in 1939, the EOP was a response to a government commission's finding that President Roosevelt needed help to oversee the vast federal bureaucracy created during the New Deal period of the 1930s. Today the EOP has grown to over 1,600 employees in at least 10 offices. The primary role of the EOP is to advise the president, help the president oversee executive branch activities, and communicate presidential initiatives to the bureaucracy and Congress.

The EOP includes the White House Office, whose members specialize in particular policy areas, such as economic policy, or other areas of importance, such as relations with Congress. The chief of staff, who often is one of the president's closest advisors, directs the White House Office. The White House Office staff usually comprises individuals who have worked closely with the president over the years, people who are loyal to the president and strong advocates of the administration's policies.

Several other offices in the EOP assist the president in overseeing the bureaucracy. The National Security Council has more than 60 staff members, who oversee the administration's foreign policy and coordinate intelligence-gathering activities. The Council of Economic Advisors includes 40 staff members, who monitor the national economy and work with executive branch agencies that implement economic policies. Other major offices include the Office of Policy Development, the Office of Science and Technology Policy, and the Office of the United States Trade Representative.

The Budget   The federal budget is the third major source of presidential influence over the bureaucracy. The **Office of Management and Budget** (OMB), the largest office in the EOP, is responsible for the president's budget. Since the passage of the Budget and Accounting Act of 1921, presidents must submit budgets to Congress that include funding requests for all federal agencies. Previously, departments sent their budget requests directly to Congress, leaving no room for presidential coordination of federal government activities and spending. Today, however, the president works with each agency to determine the level of funding to be sought from Congress. This process of **central clearance** occurs over several months, during which the president and the departments discuss major policy and program initiatives.[22]

The OMB, which oversees this process, has extensive power to coordinate executive branch actions and spending. Any requests for funding, or new policy changes that require congressional action, must be approved by the OMB before the agency can seek support from Congress. In some instances the OMB even has discretion to adjust agency budgets to meet changing economic conditions without having to go to Congress for approval beforehand.

Reorganization   A fourth source of presidential influence on the bureaucracy is **reorganization** of the executive branch. Presidents periodically sponsor major studies of the executive branch to analyze ways to improve bureaucratic effectiveness and efficiency. These studies usually lead to recommendations for restructuring. Indeed, seven of the last eleven presidents have attempted to restructure the bureaucracy to enhance presidential control. Several presidents have proposed complete reorganizations. President Nixon, for example, proposed a drastic reorganization that would abolish four cabinet departments and substantially reorganize all but four of the remaining departments. Other reorganization efforts have been more selective. In response to the energy crisis of the 1970s, President Carter created the Department of Energy and reorganized the procedures for developing energy policy.

However, such efforts are not always successful. Reorganizations redraw the lines of power and hence are political in nature. Attempts to reorganize the bureaucracy generally meet with resistance from members of Congress, employees of the bureaucratic agency, and powerful interest groups for whom any change threatens existing political relationships—the "iron triangle" described in chapters 7 and 8. For example, no president is likely to have an easy time overcoming the longstanding political relationships among bureaucrats in the Department of Agriculture, members of the congressional agriculture committees and their staffs, and representatives of important agriculture interest groups.

For one thing, major reorganization efforts require the approval of Congress because they may affect how laws are carried out. Congress, for its part, tends to resist drastic changes that might affect constituents or disrupt relationships between congressional committees and executive agencies. Even minor reorganizations might disrupt longstanding relationships, so presidents usually move with caution. After all, members of Congress, bureaucrats, and interest group representatives may have known one another long before a particular president came to town; they can delay reorganization, knowing that they are likely to still be around after that president is gone.

Not surprisingly, congressional opposition prevented President Nixon from carrying out his massive reorganization proposal.[23] President Carter was successful in creating the Department of Energy, but other energy policy reforms were not approved by Congress. And as noted earlier, President Reagan's effort to eliminate two cabinet departments did not succeed. In sum, as a source of presidential influence, reorganization typically falls short of expectations.

THE BUREAUCRACY AND CONGRESS

The bureaucracy also works closely with Congress. In fact, there is a significant degree of interdependence between the bureaucracy and members of Congress. Congress touches nearly all aspects of an agency's operations. It controls the federal budget and has significant control over organizational structure, staff levels, work rules, wage rates, and many other aspects of the bureaucratic world. An agency that falls out of favor with Congress could find its budget severely cut or even eliminated. Congress also can save an agency that the president tries to cut or eliminate. President Reagan submitted budgets to Congress that either eliminated or substantially cut funding for the Legal Services Corporation, an agency that provides legal advice to the poor. Congress rejected the president's proposal.

Interdependence works both ways. Congress relies heavily on the bureaucracy, particularly for expertise on policy issues. Experts within the bureaucracy are major sources of knowledge and advice for members of Congress. Whether the issue is economic policy, welfare, foreign affairs, or any other concern of government, bureaucratic agencies typically possess considerable knowledge and expertise that is a valuable resource for members of Congress as they discuss and deliberate federal legislation.

In addition, the bureaucracy provides important services, ranging from mailing Social Security checks to providing agricultural marketing advice. Voters may not like "the bureaucracy" in the abstract, but they do like specific programs that provide benefits or services to them, and members of Congress depend on the bureaucracy to provide these services in a timely and effective manner. This connection to the home constituency is important for Congress. If the bureaucracy fails to provide these services, members of Congress stand to lose votes.

Committee Oversight   The congressional committee structure, described in chapter 8, allows Congress to keep an eye on the bureaucracy, a process known as **oversight.** Oversight typically takes place through hearings and investigations. *Hearings* are held by congressional committees as part of the process of considering agency budget requests and as part of the debate over particular pieces of legislation. Committees require agency representatives to provide testimony, answer questions, defend requests for funds, or explain how a program will be implemented. An *investigation* is similar to a hearing, but the focus is on alleged wrongdoing by the agency. Congressional staff members provide background information and the committee then conducts an inquiry, during which it can require agency employees to testify.

These investigations sometimes attract a great deal of public attention. In 1974, for example, the Senate Judiciary Committee's investigations of improper use of federal agencies by the Nixon administration were among the factors contributing to President Nixon's decision to resign. In 1989, the government's bailout of the failed savings and loan industry was preceded by congressional investigations of the Department of Treasury and other federal agencies responsible for oversight of this industry. In another example, the deadly shootout between federal law enforcement agents and the Branch Davidian "cult" in Waco, Texas, in 1993 also led to congressional investigations. The Senate Judiciary Committee heard testimony from many witnesses and federal employees on the conduct of federal agencies, such as the FBI, involved in the Waco incident.

Congressional Support Agencies   Congressional oversight also benefits from expertise provided by several support agencies of Congress. In many respects, these agencies comprise the legislature's own bureaucracy, one designed to help Congress oversee the executive branch bureaucracy (see chapter 8). The General Accounting Office conducts audits and evaluations of executive branch agencies; a recent GAO evaluation cited the Federal Aviation Administration for poor planning and lack of innovative management in the wake of two major airline crashes.[24] The Congressional Research Service performs research and presents policy papers on issues raised by members of Congress, whereas the Congressional Budget Office tracks agency budgets and expenditures and assesses the likely costs of policy proposals being considered by Congress. These congressional agencies provide an independent, nonpartisan source of expertise that can help members of Congress perform their oversight role.

Whistleblowers   Congressional oversight of the bureaucracy is achieved in several other ways as well. "Whistleblowers" can be a valuable source of information regarding activities within the bureaucracy. A **whistleblower** is an agency employee who goes to Congress or the public to expose (or "blow the whistle" on) wrongdoing by the agency. Such information often leads to congressional inquiries, including hearings and investigations. One of the most famous whistleblowers was Daniel Ellsberg, a former employee of the Department of Defense. In 1971 Ellsberg gave the news media copies of government documents that outlined official decisions leading to U.S. involvement in the Vietnam War. The Nixon administration attempted to stop Ellsberg but, as discussed in chapter 4, the U.S. Supreme Court granted approval for publication of what became known as the *Pentagon Papers*. Other famous whistle-blowers have exposed cost overruns on defense projects, safety problems at nuclear power plants, and irregularities in spending on housing programs.

Potential whistleblowers are sometimes reluctant to provide information to Congress or the media because they may face ostracism by coworkers or reprisal from their supervisors. Past whistleblowers have found themselves denied promotions, reassigned to dead-end jobs or to offices in remote places, or fired outright. To prevent such retaliation, in 1989 Congress passed the Whistleblower Protection Act, which strengthened protections for federal employees who bring to light wrongdoing within their agencies.

Casework Responding to constituents' complaints and concerns gives Congress another means of oversight, because issues raised by constituents often involve the bureaucracy. A senior citizen, for example, might complain about a missing Social Security check; a taxpayer might claim to have been mistreated by the Internal Revenue Service; a mayor might call to inquire about the status of a grant application sent to the Department of Justice. Members of Congress respond to these requests by contacting officials in the appropriate agency. In doing so, they learn about the strengths and weaknesses of various agencies and about problems that might warrant a hearing or even an investigation.

RESPONSIVENESS AND ACCOUNTABILITY

The federal bureaucracy is supposed to be responsive and accountable to the president and Congress. This goal is not always easy to achieve. The policies and programs implemented through the bureaucracy can become self-perpetuating. The longer time frame and expertise of the bureaucracy can prompt federal bureaucrats to place their own agendas ahead of those of elected officials. In terms of the principal-agent model described earlier, the bureaucrats (agents) may stray from the wishes of the elected officials (principals), often with little real risk.

However, as we also saw, the president and Congress have ways to monitor and direct the bureaucracy. The White House Office, budget process, and congressional hearings and investigations are among the more prominent oversight tools. Using these tools, the president and Congress try to keep the bureaucracy responsive and accountable to elected officials as well as to the general public.

THE CHANGING BUREAUCRACY

The federal bureaucracy is changing constantly. Congress and the president frequently look for new ways to restructure the bureaucracy to make it more flexible, responsive, and accountable. In recent years these efforts have taken three main forms: deregulation, privatization, and "reinvention."

DEREGULATION

Deregulation refers to eliminating government regulations that affect a particular industry or activity. The current trend toward deregulation began in the late 1970s as Congress responded to complaints that rigid government regulations hampered market competition. Markets, technology, and societal needs were changing, and regulations formulated in previous decades were no longer effective. Deregulation of the airline industry and certain areas of environmental policy offer two examples in which major policy changes also have reshaped the work of federal bureaucrats.

The airline industry was deregulated in 1978. Before then the Civil Aeronautics Board regulated the entry of new companies into the airline business, as well as air fares and the allocation of routes. Such regulations, many of which dated from the 1930s, allowed the fledgling commercial airline industry to develop under rules that sought to prevent unfair and potentially unsafe competition. By the 1970s, however, these rules were seen as obstacles to lower air fares. The Civil Aeronautics Board was dismantled, and airline schedules and air fares became subject to the competitive decisions of airline companies. The Federal Aviation Administration, an agency of the Department of Transportation, continues to regulate the safety of air travel, but the airlines' economic decisions are no longer under federal regulation.

In matters involving environmental protection, a different type of deregulation is underway. Historically the Environmental Protection Agency enforced "command and control" regulations that placed limits on the amount of pollution permitted by businesses, utility companies, and other enterprises; and it also specified remedies in cases of excess pollution. This approach reflected the view that polluters would not obey environmental laws unless the federal government stepped in to enforce them. As with airline regulation, this system may have made some sense in earlier decades, because in some industries there was tremendous resistance to reducing pollution. By the late 1980s, however, there was a widespread view that this often-inflexible system needed to change.

Today the government is moving toward "market" regulations in which pollution "rights" can be bought and sold. In this market-based regulatory system, each business is allocated the right to produce a certain level of pollution. If it develops a technology to reduce pollution below its permitted level, it can sell its "excess" pollution rights to another company that may be unable to reduce its pollution levels. In a sense, a company "pays to pollute," and eventually it may decide that reducing pollution makes economic sense. For its part, the EPA no longer specifies how companies will reduce their pollution, focusing instead on outcomes.[25]

PRIVATIZATION

The term **privatization** refers to a wide range of activities. It can include private-sector contracts for activities that were previously performed by government, or it can involve selling government agencies or functions to firms in the private sector. The characteristic that all these activities share is a greater reliance on the private sector to perform services and activities that were previously performed directly by govern-

Sorting the mail. The U.S. Postal Service handles tens of billions of pieces of mail annually, more than any other postal service in the world. Few Americans comprehend the scale and sophistication of the Postal Service's operations, nor do most care so long as their mail arrives promptly and intact.

ment. Advocates of privatization argue that businesses in the private sector can perform many tasks more efficiently and effectively because they are subject to market competition.

Contracting is one of the most common forms of privatization. In this arrangement government officials determine what product or service is needed, but the product or service is provided by a private organization. Examples of contracting range from the production of military weapons by a private company to the provision of custodial services by a private contractor. Military procurement is a major example of government privatization. Approximately two-thirds of the Pentagon's budget is spent on goods and services purchased from private suppliers.[26]

Another example of privatization is government corporations such as the U.S. Postal Service, discussed earlier, which are largely independent from the budget, personnel, and purchasing systems that apply to other government agencies. Postal workers are still employees of the federal government, but they operate under different rules than do regular federal civil servants. For its part, the Postal Service must compete with other carriers, such as United Parcel Service and Federal Express, which forces the Postal Service to make its operations more efficient and less dependent on taxpayer support.[27]

REINVENTING GOVERNMENT

Deregulation and privatization are part of a broad movement toward the **reinvention** of government. The origins of this effort can be traced to a book by David Osborne and Ted Gaebler, titled *Reinventing Government: How the Entrepreneurial Spirit is Transforming the Public Sector*. The book's theme is the need to change the way government operates. As the authors state, "The *people* who work in government are not the problem, the *systems* in which they work are the problem."[28] Critics such as Osborne and Gaebler argue that reinventing government is critical to the future effectiveness and relevance of the federal bureaucracy: Civil service rules are inflexible, hierarchies of authority stifle innovation, and work specialization is excessively rigid. Most important, they say, the bureaucracy focuses more on process than on results. Government agencies therefore are not prepared to respond to a changing environment. Reinvention calls for an "entrepreneurial" bureaucracy that is flexible enough to meet rapidly changing demands. Government should focus on results; it should anticipate problems before they arise; its functions should be decentralized; and most important, it must consider citizens as "customers." This requires a fundamental restructuring of the government workplace.

President Clinton and Vice President Gore joined the reinvention movement when they sponsored the National Performance Review (NPR) of the federal bureaucracy. Launched in 1993, NPR is an ongoing effort to "create a government that works better and costs less." Its first report outlined more than 380 recommendations that would cut a total of $108 billion in federal spending. Echoing Osborne and Gaebler, the report states, "The federal government is filled with good people trapped in bad systems: budget systems, personnel systems, procurement systems, financial management systems, information systems."[29] To change these "bad systems," the NPR seeks to cut government back to the basics, eliminate unnecessary rules and regulations, give employees more flexibility to innovate, and focus more clearly on serving customers.

Has the federal government been reinvented? There are signs of change. "Reinvention teams" exist in most federal agencies, and reinvention projects are under way. At the Department of Agriculture, for example, a major reorganization took place, and more than a dozen reinvention "laboratories" were created in response to 8,000 written survey responses from employees.[30] The Department of Labor established an Office of Reinvention to streamline decisionmaking systems, reduce regulations, and create new union-management partnerships. And as noted earlier, the Environmental Protection Agency is experimenting with market-based regulatory strategies. Overall, some 16,000 out of 86,000 pages of federal regulations have been eliminated as obsolete, and the review process continues. In addition, cuts in the federal bureaucracy reduced the number of federal employees by 10 percent, or 200,000 people.[31]

The National Performance Review has generated major changes, but many career civil servants believe that political leaders are using "reinvention" as a way to cut federal programs and agencies in order to meet political goals, not as a way to transform how the government works. In addition, the reinvention effort has limited support in Congress. The NPR was launched by President Clinton, not Congress, yet many of its proposals require congressional approval. Such support is not automatic. Many members of Congress resist changes that have limited positive effects on their constituents. Building a bridge between the president and Congress is essential if long-term change in the bureaucracy is to become a reality.

CONCLUSION

The movements for privatization, deregulation, and reinvention highlight once again the contexts within which the bureaucracy operates, as well as its capacity to adapt to new demands and expectations. Nobody agrees about the proper size, extent, or role of the federal bureaucracy, nor is there consensus on how to keep bureaucrats accountable to Congress, the president, and the American people. Few people deny the need for the bureaucracy, but there are plenty who emphasize its shortcomings. And despite the successful response to the Oklahoma City bombing cited at the beginning of the chapter, there are many stories of inefficiency or wrongdoing that spur efforts to reform the bureaucracy. Indeed, conflict over the goals and actions of the bureaucracy often generate compromises designed to allow the bureaucracy to continue to do its work.

Conflict and compromise are apparent both within the bureaucracy and between it and Congress and the president. Those who work within the bureaucracy frequently have differing goals and perspectives. Political appointees represent the president's goals, whereas career civil servants seek to protect existing programs. Career civil servants in one department can disagree over policy directions even as they all seek to faithfully serve the president. In this sense, the internal workings of the bureaucracy are as conflictual, as openly "political," as anything to be found in Congress. And, just as in Congress, those involved in conflict often seek to resolve their differences through some mutually beneficial compromise.

Externally, the bureaucracy is always under pressure from Congress, the president, and the public. Members of Congress place demands on bureaucrats to meet their constituents' needs, demands that may force bureaucrats to make decisions contrary to longstanding rules and procedures. The president looks to the bureaucracy to implement the administration's new policies and programs, even if those policies challenge existing relationships among bureaucratic units or disrupt connections between bureaucrats and external clienteles. And the public expects efficient and effective service delivery, even as it also demands that bureaucrats remain sensitive to their fears of rigid rules or heartless decisions. Public demands for efficiency conflict with such fears of bureaucratic facelessness, forcing numerous compromises between these competing needs.

In sum, the bureaucracy is no different from the more openly political parts of government. Like Congress and the president, it lives within a world of conflict, and it must seek compromises that help it do its job within a democratic political system. Efforts to reform bureaucracy can never solve its core problem—its image. The bureaucracy is a necessary but unloved part of government. Few Americans hold positive views about the bureaucracy in general, even though they support the agencies responsible for carrying out programs that they like. In short, the debate about the role of the bureaucracy reflects broader ideological views about the role of government, and in this respect the debate is likely to last as long as there is a government to complain about.

SUMMARY

▶ A bureaucracy is a type of organization characterized by fixed jurisdictional areas, hierarchy of authority, written documents, general rules, career employees, and expertise.

▶ Major types of units in the federal bureaucracy include cabinet departments, independent commssions, and government corporations. These units provide basic services, support particular groups in society, and implement regulations.

▶ Most federal employees are civil servants and are appointed on the basis of merit and expertise. Political appointees serve at the pleasure of the president, and are appointed to oversee the activities of career civil servants. Members of the Senior Executive Service combine the expertise of civil servants with the flexibility of political appointees.

▶ The president influences the bureaucracy through control over political appointments, the Executive Office of the President, the budget process, and reorganization. Congressional oversight of the bureaucracy occurs through committee hearings and investigations, congressional support agencies, whistleblowers, and constituent casework.

▶ Recent efforts to change and reform the bureaucracy include deregulation, privatization, and reinvention. These efforts are designed to make the bureaucracy adapt to changing needs and external contexts, and to keep it accountable to the people.

QUESTIONS FOR REVIEW AND DISCUSSION

1. If you worked in the federal bureaucracy, which department or agency would you work in? Why? What skills or types of experience would you need in order to do this job?

2. Should employment in the federal bureaucracy be controlled more by civil service rules or by political appointment? Describe the benefits and costs of each type of employment. Is the Senior Executive Service an effective middle ground?

3. Is the bureaucracy accountable? To whom? What are the most important ways of achieving such accountability?

4. Has the traditional notion of bureaucracy, with fixed jurisdictional areas, hierarchy of authority, and division of labor, outlived its usefulness? What new ways can you propose to fulfill the functions of government while still ensuring democratic accountability?

TERMS TO REMEMBER

bureaucracy
cabinet
central clearance
civil service
department
deregulation
government
   corporation

hierarchy
independent commission
Office of Management
   and Budget
oversight
Pendleton Act
political appointees
principal-agent model

privatization
reinvention
reorganization
secretary
spoils system
tenure
whistleblower

WEB SOURCES

American Society for Public Administration (www.aspanet.org). The nation's largest
   professional association dedicated to the profession of public administration. A
   good site for gaining a better understanding of what the profession is about and
   what public adminstrators do.

Brookings Institution (www.brookings.org). One of the nation's oldest nonpartisan,
   nonprofit research organizations, or "think tanks." Brookings focuses on improving the effectiveness of public institutions and public policy. It has the reputation
   of being on the liberal side of the ideological spectrum. The American Enterprise
   Institute (www.aei.org) is regarded as the somewhat more conservative counterpart to Brookings.

National Performance Review (www.npr.gov). Site operated by the Clinton administration's project to reform the way that the federal government works, in line with
   the "reinventing government" effort highlighted by David Osborne and Ted Gaebler in their book, *Reinventing Government: How the Entrepreneurial Spirit is Transforming the Public Sector.*

SUGGESTED READINGS

James Fesler and Donald Kettl, *The Politics of the Administrative Process* (Chatham,
   N.J.: Chatham House Publishers, 1996). Provides a comprehensive examination
   of the federal bureaucracy. Topics include theoretical approaches to bureaucracy
   as well as focussed discussion of topics such as civil service and other personnel
   systems, bureaucratic decisionmaking, budgeting, regulation, policy implementa-
   tion, and legislative control of the bureaucracy. The authors conclude with discussions of the ethical challenges facing the bureaucracy and the dilemma of maintaining democratic accountability.

Charles Goodsell, *The Case for Bureaucracy*, 2d ed. (Chatham, NJ: Chatham House
   Publishers, 1994). Seeks to dispel the prevailing notion that bureaucracy is inherently bad and that all bureaucratic actions fail. Assesses the major writings critical
   of bureaucracy in the United States, and agues that the negative perceptions and

stereotypes of the bureaucracy are not based in fact, and only serve to diminish the contributions made by government employees.

Richard Stillman II, *The American Bureaucracy: The Core of Modern Government* (Chicago: Nelson-Hall Publishers, 1996). Uses a "systems approach" to the study of bureaucracy in which attention is given to the impacts of broad external socioeconomic contexts on bureaucratic behavior and performance. That is, the way in which the bureaucracy in the United States operates cannot be separated from the broad context that shape American politics generally. Also shows how bureaucratic peformance is affected by internal dynamics of organizations.

NOTES

1. Marlys J. Mason, "Drugs or Dietary Supplements: FDA's Enforcement of DSHEA," *Journal of Public Policy and Marketing*, vol. 17, no. 2 (Fall 1998), p. 296.

2. Dante A. Ramos, "Vitamin Makers Try a Dose of Lobbying," *The National Journal*, vol. 25, no. 30 (July 24, 1993), p. 1879.

3. Beth Baker, "Political Kryptonite," *Common Cause Magazine*, vol. 20 (Spring 1994), pp. 5–6.

4. Hobart Rowen, "Reagan's Economic Ideas," *Washington Post*, April 20, 1976, p. A5.

5. *National Performance Review, Creating a Government That Works Better and Costs Less* (New York: Times Books, 1993), p. 5.

6. Ibid., p. 1.

7. H. H. Gerth and C. Wright Mills, *From Max Weber: Essays in Sociology* (New York: Oxford University Press, 1946).

8. *Historical Statistics of the United States, Colonial Times to 1970* (Washington, D.C.: Bureau of the Census, Department of Commerce, 1975).

9. *Statistical Abstract of the United States: 1998* (Washington, D.C.: Government Printing Office, 1998), p. 354.

10. Ibid., p. 360.

11. Ibid., pp. 353, 584.

12. See Paul Light, *Forging Legislation* (New York: Norton, 1992).

13. See Christopher J. Bosso, *Pesticides and Politics: The Life Cycle of a Public Issue* (Pittsburgh, PA: University of Pittsburgh Press, 1987).

14. Richard Stillman II, *The American Bureaucracy*, 2d ed. (Chicago: Nelson-Hall Publishers, 1996), p. 176.

15. Stillman, *The American Bureaucracy*, p. 145.

16. Hugh Heclo, *A Government of Strangers* (Washington, D.C.: The Brookings Institution, 1975), p. 103.

17. Ibid., p. 153.

18. Dan Wood and Richard Waterman, *Bureaucratic Dynamics: The Role of Bureaucracy in a Democracy* (Boulder, CO: Westview Press, 1994).

19. Richard Neustadt, *Presidential Power: The Politics of Leadership*, 3d ed. (New York: Wiley, 1980), p. 31.

20. Joel D. Aberbach and Bert A. Rockman, "Clashing Beliefs within the Executive Branch: The Nixon Administration Bureaucracy," *American Political Science Review*, vol. 70, no. 2 (June 1975), pp. 456–468.

21. See Heclo, *A Government of Strangers*, p. 111.

22. See Louis Fisher, *Presidential Spending Power* (Princeton, NJ: Princeton University Press, 1975), p. 31.

23. Richard P. Nathan, *The Plot That Failed: Nixon and Administrative Presidency* (New York: Wiley, 1975).

24. *U.S. General Accounting Office, Aviation Acquisition: A Comprehensive Strategy Is Needed for Cultural Change at FAA* (Washington, D.C.: U.S. General Accounting Office, 1996).

25. See Michael S. Greve and Fred L. Smith Jr., eds., *Environmental Politics: Public Costs, Private Rewards* (Westport, CT: Praeger, 1992).

26. John Donahue, *The Privatization Decision* (New York: Basic Books, 1989), p. 101.

27. *Office of Management and Budget, Budget of the United States Government, Fiscal Year 1998, Appendix* (Washington, D.C.: U.S. Government Printing Office, 1997), p. 1103.

28. David Osborne and Ted Gaebler, *Reinventing Government: How the Entrepreneurial Spirit Is Transforming the Public Sector* (Reading, MA: Addison-Wesley, 1992), p. xviii.

29. *National Performance Review, Creating a Government That Works Better and Costs Less*, p. 2.

30. Beryl Radin, "Varieties of Reinvention: Six NPR 'Success' Stories," in Donald Kettl and John DiIulio Jr., eds., *Inside the Reinvention Machine: Appraising Governmental Reform* (Washington, D.C.: Brookings Institution, 1995).

31. *Office of Management and Budget, 1997 Fiscal Year Budget: Supplement* (Washington, D.C.: U.S. Government Printing Office, 1996), p. 123.

PRIMARY SOURCE READINGS

UPTON SINCLAIR
The Jungle

The writer Upton Sinclair (1878–1968) expressed strong views on the dangers of free market capitalism. His most famous work, The Jungle *(1906), was meant to rally the working classes in favor of socialism. In this regard,* The Jungle *was a failure, although it did lead to demands that the federal and state government ensure better working conditions and fairer wages. More important, Sinclair's stark depiction of the horrific working conditions in the Chicago slaughterhouses and of the shoddy nature of consumer goods led to a public outcry that spurred on the passage the federal Pure Food and Drug Act of 1906, one of the first major consumer protection laws.*

Chapter Seven

There were many such dangers, in which the odds were all against them. Their children were not as well as they had been at home; but how could they know that there was no sewer to their house, and that the drainage of fifteen years was in a cesspool under it? How could they know that the pale-blue milk that they bought around the corner was watered, and doctored with formaldehyde besides? When the children were not well . . . she was obliged to go to the drugstore and buy extracts—and how was she to know that they were all adulterated? How could they find out that their tea and coffee, their sugar and flour, had been doctored; that their canned peas had been colored with copper salts, and their fruit jams with aniline dyes? And even if they had known it, what good would it have done them, since there was no place within miles of them where any other sort was to be had? . . .

Then there was old Antanas. The winter came, and the place where he worked was a dark, unheated cellar, where you could see your breath all day, and where your fingers sometimes tried to freeze. So the old man's cough grew every day worse, until there came a time when it hardly ever stopped. . . . Then, too, a still more dreadful thing happened to him; he worked in a place where his feet were soaked in chemicals, and it was not long before they had eaten through his new boots. Then sores began to break out on his feet, and grow worse and worse. . . . The sores would never heal—in the end his toes would drop off, if he did not quit. Yet old Antanas would not quit; he saw the suffering of his family, and he remembered what it had cost him to get a job. So he tied up his feet, and went on limping about and coughing, until at last he fell to pieces, all at once and in a heap. . . .

There was no heat upon the killing beds [of the slaughtering house]. . . . On the killing beds you were apt to be covered with blood, and it would freeze solid; if you leaned against a pillar, you would freeze to that, and if you put your hand upon the blade of your knife, you would run a chance of leaving your skin on it. The men would tie up their feet in newspapers and old sacks, and these would be soaked in blood and frozen, and then soaked again, and so on, until by nighttime a man would be walking on great lumps the size of the feet of an elephant. Now and then, when the bosses were not looking, you would see them plunging their feet and ankles into the steaming hot carcass of the steer, or darting across the room to the hot-water jets. The cruelest thing of all was that nearly all of them—all of those who used knives—were unable to wear gloves, and their arms would be white with frost and their hands would grow numb, and then of course there would be accidents. . . .

Chapter Eight

[H]er canning factory shut down! . . . And they had not given her any explanation, they had not even given her a day's warning; they had simply posted a notice one Saturday that all hands would be paid off that afternoon, and would not resume work for at least a month! And that was all that there was to it—her job was gone! . . .

The men upon the killing beds felt also the effects of the slump. . . . The big packers did not turn their hands off and close down, like the canning factories; but they began to run for shorter and shorter hours. They had always required the men to be on the killing beds and ready for work at seven o'clock, although there was almost never any work to be done till the buyers out in the yards had gotten to work, and some cattle had come over the chutes. That would often be ten or eleven o'clock, which was bad enough, in all conscience; but now, in the slack season, they would perhaps not have a thing for their men to do till late in the afternoon. And so they would have to loaf around, in a place where the thermometer might be twenty degrees below zero! At first one would see them running about, or skylarking with each other, trying to keep warm; but before the day was over they would become quite chilled through and exhausted, and, when the cattle finally came, so near frozen that to move was an agony. And then suddenly the place would spring into activity, and the merciless "speeding-up" would begin! . . .

All this was bad; and yet it was not the worst. For after all the hard work a man did, he was paid for only part of it. . . . One of the rules on the killing beds was that a man who was one minute late was docked an hour; and this was economical, for he was made to work the balance of the hour—he was not allowed to stand round and wait. And on the other hand if he came ahead of time he got no pay for that—though often the bosses would start up the gang ten or fifteen minutes before the whistle. And this same custom they carried over to the end of the day; they did not pay for any fraction of an hour—for "broken time." A man might work full fifty minutes, but if there was no work to fill out the hour, there was no pay for him.

There was another interesting set of statistics that a person might have gathered in Packingtown—those of the various afflications of the workers. . . . There were the men in the pickle rooms, for instance, where old Antanas had gotten his death; scarce a one of these that had not some spot of horror on his person. Let a man so much as scrape his finger pushing a truck in the pickle rooms, and he might have a sore that would put him out of the world; all the joints in his fingers might be eaten by the acid, one by one. Of the butchers and floorsmen, the beef-boners and trimmers, and all those who used knives, you could scarcely find a person who had the use of his thumb; time and time again the base of it had been slashed, till it was a mere lump of flesh against which the man pressed the knife to hold it. The hands of these men would be criss-crossed with cuts, until you could no longer pretend to count them or to trace them. They would have no nails—they had worn them off pulling hides; their knuckles were swollen so that their fingers spread out like a fan. There were men who worked in the cooking rooms, in the midst of steam and sickening odors, by artificial light; in these rooms the germs of tuberculosis might live for two years, but the supply was renewed every hour. There were the beef-luggers, who carried two-hundred-pound quarters into the refrigerator-cars; a fearful kind of work, that began at four o'clock in the morning, and that wore out the most powerful men in a few years. There were those who worked in the chilling rooms, and whose special disease was rheumatism; the time limit that a man could work in the chilling rooms was said to be five years. There were the wool-pluckers, whose hands went to pieces even sooner than the hands of the pickle men; for the pelts of the sheep had to be painted with acid to loosen the wool, and then the pluckers had to pull out this wool with their bare hands, till the acid had eaten their fingers off. There were those who made the tins for the canned meat; and their hands too were a maze of cuts, and each cut represented a chance for blood poisoning. Some worked at the stamping machines, and it was very seldom that one could work long there at the pace that was set, and not give out and forget himself and have a part of his hand chopped off. There were the "hoisters," as they were called, whose task it was to press the lever which lifted the dead cattle off the floor. They ran along upon a rafter, peering down through the damp and the steam; and as old Durham's architects had not built the killing room for the convenience of the hoisters, at every few feet they would have to stoop under a beam, say four feet above the one they ran on; which got them into the habit of stooping, so that in a few years they would be walking like chimpanzees. Worst of any, however, were the fertilizer men, and those who served in the cooking rooms. These people could not be shown to the visitor—for the odor of a fertilizer man would scare any ordinary visitor at a hundred yards, and as for the other men, who worked in the tank rooms full of steam, and in some of which there were open vats near the level of the floor, their peculiar trouble was that they fell into the vats; and when they were fished out, there was never enough of them left to be worth exhibiting—sometimes they would be overlooked for days, till all but the bones of them had gone out of the world as Durham's Pure Leaf Lard!

RALPH NADER
The Unelected Power of Alan Greenspan

In 1996 President Clinton nominated Alan Greenspan to a third term as Chairman of the Federal Reserve System. While this action was received with widespread enthusiam among Wall Street stock brokers, bond traders, bankers, and most economists, it didn't generate the same level of support from consumer advocates and other critics of Greenspan and the Federal Reserve Board. Consumer advocate Ralph Nader made these comments during a hearing of the Senate Comittee on Banking, Housing, and Urban Affairs. Greenspan's nomination was later approved by the Senate.

March 26, 1996

I'm struck by the time that the Senate gives to analyzing the record and performance of nominees to the Supreme Court compared to the time given to analyzing the record and views of members of the Board of Governors of the Federal Reserve. True, they do have different functions, but they both have very important functions, and I thank you, Mr. Chairman, for at least, shall we say, breaking precedent and allowing a bit of testimony from a different perspective. . . .

Now, the president's decision to keep monetary policy reins in the hands of Alan Greenspan, I think, is a decision to continue the present status quo policies, and while disagreeing, I have no illusions about the ultimate outcome of this nomination. For eight long years, the Congress has seemed willing to accept most, if not all, of Alan Greenspan's bland assurances when he visits Capitol Hill twice each year to report on monetary policy. But I would like to focus on the issue that . . . long-time congressional critics have brought to bear to the Federal Reserve. . . .

The independence of the Federal Reserve has become an article of faith to be intoned rather than a proposition to be examined. First of all, it has different functions—monetary function, consumer protection function, research function—and the rather hidden world of the way it operates without any paper trail to deal with such issues as the bailout of the Mexican government. . . . [T]hey're not reduced to observable or accessible to the Congress documentation, and unfortunately, the chairman of the Federal Reserve rarely gets asked questions about that. . . .

And of course, the claim of independence is a bit thin because the claim is directed toward the Congress, toward the president, toward the American people. No one really can make a strong case that the Federal Reserve is independent of the banks and other large business establishments. And so it's important to raise the issue that is presented when the Fed always defends what it does and repulses official inquiries, not to mention civic inquiries, by saying that it has to maintain its independence. The word independent does not appear in the Federal Reserve Act, but the Federal Reserve has assumed it and given the word a new and powerful definition. Proposals to change the Federal Reserve Act, board operating procedures and other policies are always greeted with sounds of alarm from the Federal Reserve and its apologists, claiming again a threat to the independence of the agency. Any call for accountability, openness, nee, even simply rationale—giving the rationale for their open market committee deliberations is interpreted as a threat to its independence as an attempt to exert political influence over its decisions.

Let's face it, the Federal Reserve is an autocracy that remains so as long as it doesn't particularly upset the established powers, but it is an autocracy unique in American government, covering all its functions, unfortunately, that keeps it from accountability to the legislative branch, not to mention the executive branch in important and prudently selected areas.

. . . In the final analysis, the Fed's independence is a shield against accountability, it shields the Fed from analysis of bad policy, outrageous mistakes, mismanagement and other problems. This so-called independence was never challenged, even in the era when the Federal Reserve was presiding over an extremely deteriorating banking industry only a few years ago, which required such ample congressional bailouts.

The second aspect of the Federal Reserve is secrecy. . . . [T]he transcripts of the open market—Fed open market committee . . . are now withheld for five years so that there is no way to judge the present governors of the Federal Reserve, including the chairman, on these decisions until 1998–99 for the decisions to increase interest rates that were occurring in 1993–94 or '94, part of '95. And even the transcripts, in the words of the Federal Reserve, are lightly edited. The full, unedited transcripts are locked away for 30 years.

I don't believe that this committee would accept the same secrecy from other agencies and departments under its jurisdiction, and it would not tolerate hidden agendas and only vague sketches of policy decisions from the Department of Housing and Urban Development or the Securities Exchange Commission. To tolerate it for the Federal Reserve would require the Federal Reserve to uphold a much greater burden of proof as to why business should continue as usual than has been tendered at hearings before the Senate Banking Committee. . . .

Secrecy, as we all know in government, is a kind of power, and it should be seriously challenged and not simply accepted because that's the way things have always been with the Federal Reserve.

. . . When the contest over consumer regulations is between consumers in the banking industry, the Fed can find some creative ways to support the industry. . . . As mergers sweep across the nation, neighborhoods and communities are facing the loss of banking facilities while borrowers in low- and moderate-income minority neighborhoods already starved for credit are seeing lending decisions move through distant lines of management in these merged—new merged giants. Eight hundred community organizations turned out on the West Coast recently to oppose the Wells Fargo/First Interstate merger on the grounds that the closure of 345 branches would severely wound local communities. The Fed heard the arguments and received the documentation, but in the end, the wishes of Wells Fargo were granted, and the 345 branches will be closed. . . .

It is important . . . for this committee to insist on changes at the Federal Reserve as a condition for confirmation, particularly changes that would remove some of the thick walls of secrecy that separate the agency from the people and the Congress. And if Alan Greenspan is confirmed, as he probably will be, overwhelmingly, he will control the Federal Reserve into the year 2000, and about all that can be said about that is it will give the Congress a few more years to develop more specific frames of reference to evaluate the Federal Reserve, to demand more specific disclosures of rationale, and above all, to expand the definition of market indicators to reflect the empirical reality that they now do not reflect, and that is what characterizes their lack of humanity, their lack of sensitivity to what millions of workers in this country know is going on, and that is the downsizing of the middle class.

THE JUDICIARY

OBJECTIVES

❏ To discuss how courts seek to resolve conflicts, and how court decisions often provoke more controversy

❏ To describe the basic structures and processes of the federal and state court systems

❏ To examine how the U.S. Supreme Court makes decisions

❏ To assess the methods used to select judges in the federal and state systems

❏ To discuss the origins of judicial review and the nature of constitutional interpretation

❏ To ponder the implications of courts as policymakers in the American system of government

Grand Central Station. The destruction of Penn Station in the 1960s sparked a legal and political movement to restrict the ability of private developers to raze architecturally or historically significant buildings without extensive review. As a result, many buildings once considered worthless have been rehabilitated for future generations.

Grand Central Station has long occupied a mythic place in American history and popular culture. The building's stately grandeur epitomized the golden age of passenger rail service, and its classic architecture spoke of a time when train stations were among the most important buildings in the nation. It is no surprise, then, that Grand Central Terminal was designated a landmark under New York City's Landmark Preservation Law. The law was enacted in the late 1960s after a number of historic buildings, notably the architecturally famous Penn Station, had fallen to the wrecking ball. The law requires the owner of a designated landmark to keep the building's exterior "in good repair" and to obtain approval from a special commission before making major alterations.

The owner of Grand Central Station, the Penn Central Transportation Company, wanted to increase its profitability by building an office tower on top of the terminal. Doing so would involve demolishing the existing building, leaving only the underground portion for the train station. Many New Yorkers, horrified at the prospect of losing another important piece of the city's architectural heritage, organized and fought hard against the plan. Responding to their arguments, the Landmarks Commission denied the company's request to build the office tower. The company sued the city, claiming that the application of the Landmark Preservation Law constituted an unconstitutional "taking" of its private property in violation of the Fifth Amendment. The case, *Penn Central Transportation Co. v. New York City* (1978), eventually came before the United States Supreme Court, the nation's highest court.[1]

In a 6-to-3 decision, the Supreme Court rejected Penn Central's claim. Justice William Brennan, writing for the majority of the justices, explained that a city may "place restrictions on the development of individual historical landmarks [without] effecting a 'taking.'" The city, in essence, had the power to regulate how private individuals or companies use their own property. But this power was not absolute. In addressing the dispute between the owner of Grand Central Station and the citizens of New York City, the Court was careful to balance the private property rights of individuals and the general welfare of the community. "The restrictions imposed," Justice Brennan reasoned, "are substantially related to the promotion of the general welfare and not only permit reasonable beneficial use of the landmark site but afford [the owner] opportunities further to enhance not only the Terminal site proper but also other properties." The compromise that emerged from the Court's decision meant that the residents of New York City would continue to enjoy the architectural splendor of Grand Central Station, and the building's owner would find a way to profit from the site that lay within the guidelines of the building's landmark status.

THE FUNCTIONS OF A JUDICIAL SYSTEM

Courts provide a forum for resolving disputes through the application of legal rules. This makes courts and the judicial branch of government different from the legislative and executive branches. Unlike the legislative branch, courts employ law, precedent, and evidence to reach their decisions and do not overtly function to transform conflict into compromise. Sometimes, as the Grand Central Station case points out, courts make decisions that strike a balance and try to reach a compromise. But in a constitutional system that values *judicial independence*, or the idea that courts and judges must be immune from outside pressures, courts can reject the open balancing of competing interests when principles of justice and fairness dictate a particular decision.

This search for justice is especially evident in the area of civil rights and liberties (see chapter 4). In interpreting and applying the law, courts often make decisions that are unpopular with the public. When courts uphold the rights of individuals to express views that the majority finds offensive, or when courts overturn the conviction of a person accused of a serious crime because the evidence was obtained improperly, the public is quick to charge the courts with being out of touch with the needs of society.

The key to understanding the functions of the **judiciary,** or judicial branch, in the U.S. system is to acknowledge that courts are both legal and political institutions. They are legal institutions in that they provide a forum for the resolution of disputes through the application of preexisting legal rules according to notions of justice, fairness, and equality. And they are political institutions in the sense that their deliberations do not take place in a vacuum. Because courts are part of the larger social, political, and economic environment, their efforts to resolve conflicts often provoke more controversy in American society.

GENERAL FUNCTIONS OF THE JUDICIARY

The legal scholar Lawrence Friedman describes four general functions of any judicial system: social control, dispute settlement, social engineering, and regime maintenance.

Social Control Courts are concerned with controlling behavior. That is, they are charged with determining whether wrongdoing has occurred and, if so, arriving at an appropriate punishment for those found guilty. In doing so, courts enforce the rules that society considers essential to the maintenance of order and stability. The trial of criminal cases and the entire criminal justice system, including prisons, are the most obvious examples of this function. But the trial of civil cases, such as those dealing with disputes over liability for damage to property or the validity of contracts, also help to maintain social order.

Dispute Settlement Courts also function to resolve disputes. However, their unique procedures set them apart from other institutions that handle conflicts in society. Courts are the forums in which conflicts between individuals, corporations, and government may be resolved on an equal basis. This ideal is expressed on the ornamental frieze the runs along the top of the U.S. Supreme Court building: "Equal Justice Under Law." The judiciary is the part of government that is responsible for settling disputes according to law regardless of the beliefs or resources of the parties involved.

Social Engineering In thinking about the judiciary, it is important not to overlook the ways in which courts force society to change. Probably the best example is the change in race relations ushered in by the U.S. Supreme Court's decision in *Brown v. Board of Education* (1954), which condemned racial segregation and the doctrine of "separate but equal" (see chapter 4). In this case the Supreme Court forced the society to confront the fact that it was treating citizens unequally solely on the basis of skin color. Other examples of court decisions that have engineered change in society abound, and they are often the target of the criticism that courts are playing too great a role in American government.

Regime Maintenance Despite occasional rulings like the *Brown* decision, courts generally are not revolutionary institutions. In fact, they are responsible for helping to maintain the political system. For example, when courts rule that evidence seized without a proper search warrant cannot be included in a criminal prosecution, they are reaffirming the political system's commitment to privacy and the individual's Fourth Amendment right to be free from "unreasonable searches and seizures." Such judicial independence gives citizens another safeguard against unwarranted government power and, in the process, reinforces the legitimacy of the political system. Systems that lack legitimacy in the eyes of their citizens do not long survive.

SEEKING COMPROMISE

In performing all these functions, courts sometimes balance the rights of individuals with the broader society's need for social peace and stability. Such balancing often re-

A Civil Action. In this popular image of the legal system, the attorney (here played by John Travolta) argues a client's case before a jury. In reality, many cases never actually get to trial. Instead, they are settled out of court by mutual agreement of the parties involved—a compromise.

sults in a relative loss of liberty for some individual or group. As we saw in the *Penn Central Transportation* case, the Supreme Court struck a balance between the private property rights of the owner and the general welfare of the community. In this case, the company lost some of its freedom in how it used its property.

In criminal law, plea bargaining between the prosecution and the defendant results in compromises. For example, the prosecution might accept a guilty plea to a lesser charge in a criminal case because it thinks it might have a hard time obtaining a conviction on the more serious charge. Likewise, the defendant might accept a shorter jail sentence because it is a safer bet than going to trial and risking conviction on the more serious charge. Each side gets part of what it wanted—the prosecution gets the guilty plea and the defendant avoids a harsher penalty.

Similar kinds of compromises occur in other areas of law. Formal agreements, called **consent decrees,** often are made by both parties to a dispute. These spell out in detail the actions the parties will take in the future. Consent decrees are frequently used in civil litigation over violations of environmental laws. In such cases agreement is reached by the defendant (the polluter) to cease activities that the government asserts are illegal. If the agreement is approved by the court, the government's action against the defendant is dropped.

THE STRUCTURE OF THE JUDICIARY

Court systems reflect the degree of centralization of the governments of which they are a part. As discussed in chapter 3, the United States has a federal system of government, so the dual system of federal and state courts is a distinguishing feature of the American judiciary.

Today there are 51 separate judicial systems: the federal, or national, judicial system and the 50 state systems. Each state has its own court system, which operates separately and independent of the national government's court system as well as those of other states. As a result, legal rules set by state courts are likely to vary from one state to another. Sometimes the differences are trivial, but sometimes they are quite dramatic. For example, some state courts have recognized the "right to die" by allowing the use of "living wills," but others have not.[2] However, as a result of the "full faith and credit" clause of Article IV of the Constitution (discussed in chapter 3), the decisions made by a court in one state must be respected by the courts in other states. The reason is simple: to prevent the relitigation of issues already settled in one state. For example, a divorce settlement reached in court in one state cannot be challenged or reopened in court in another state. But this principle does not mean that the development of a law or legal doctrine in one state is automatically binding on all others. As we will discuss later, state laws or state court decisions can be appealed to the U.S. Supreme Court if they potentially violate a provision in the U.S. Constitution.

State and federal judicial systems may be separate and independent, but they have several points of contact, and through the years they have established informal traditions of interaction. The federal and state court systems are connected at the top and bottom of the judicial hierarchies. The links at the top result from the power of the U.S. Supreme Court, the highest federal court, to review decisions of the highest state courts that involve the U.S. Constitution or acts of Congress. The links at the bottom are governed by federal statutes, particularly the Habeas Corpus Act of 1867, as amended in 1996.[3] This statute protects prisoners who believe that they were wrongfully convicted in the state trial courts by allowing them to ask a federal judge in one of the U.S. District Courts to review the lawfulness of their detention.

THE FEDERAL COURT SYSTEM

The delegates to the Constitutional Convention of 1787 were unanimous about the need for a Supreme Court. Article III, Section 1 of the U.S. Constitution states that "the judicial Power of the United States, shall be vested in one supreme Court." A Supreme Court was needed to decide cases that would arise out of conflicts between the "Laws of the United States" and the "Laws of any State." The provision in Article VI of the Constitution, declaring the supremacy of "this Constitution and the Laws of the United States," presupposed the need for a Supreme Court. Also, because the new Congress had legislative powers that would apply directly to the people, the Supreme Court was needed to maintain the uniformity of federal law across the country.

However, the framers disagreed as to whether the Constitution should establish lower federal courts. They compromised by giving Congress the power to create "inferior courts," the term used in Article III to refer to courts below the Supreme Court. Thus, as one of its first items of business the First Congress passed the Judiciary Act of 1789, which "ordained and established" a system of trial and circuit courts below the U.S. Supreme Court (Box 11.1, p. 472). Through the years, the fed-

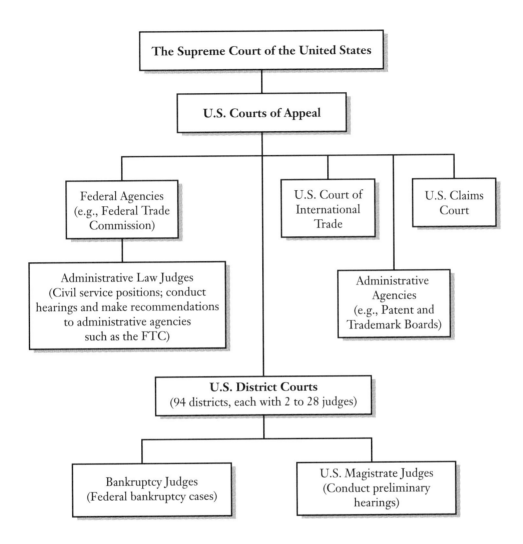

FIGURE 11.1. THE FEDERAL COURT SYSTEM

Source: Adapted from Frank M. Coffin, *On Appeal* (New York: Norton, 1994), p. 48.

eral judicial system has been modified and expanded by Congress to meet the needs of a growing nation.

The federal court system resembles a pyramid (see Figure 11.1). At the top is the nine-member Supreme Court. Below it are 12 federal courts of appeals, one in each of the 11 regional circuits and one in the District of Columbia (Washington, D.C.) circuit. At the bottom are 94 district courts, divided among the states according to population size and caseload, with each state assigned at least one court. There are also specialized federal courts, including the Court of Federal Claims, the Tax

BOX 11.1.
THE EARLY HISTORY OF THE FEDERAL JUDICIARY

Given the brevity of debates about the new federal court system at the Constitutional Convention, one gets the impression that the framers had a clear idea of what they wanted in the system. Maybe they did. During the 1780s there was one court, the Federal Appellate Prize Court, that had jurisdiction beyond the boundaries of the respective states. Most of the delegates assembled in Philadelphia in 1787 were lawyers, so certainly they knew about this court. In fact, some of the delegates, including George Washington, even had direct experience with it.

The Federal Appellate Prize Court was established by the Continental Congress in 1775 at Washington's direction in order to determine appeals in cases of capture of enemy vessels during the Revolutionary War. Historically, in times of war there has been a need for a judicial body of some kind to determine the legal ownership of vessels seized on the high seas. These bodies, known as admiralty courts, have for centuries applied the international law of "prize." That is, if the vessel seized is flying the flag of a hostile nation, then the seizure is adjudged a "lawful prize" of war and the captor is entitled to the vessel and all of its cargo. To seize a vessel under any other circumstances is piracy, a criminal offense punishable by death.

Thus, the nation's "first federal court" was an admiralty court, and its performance convinced the framers that the new national government needed one supreme court with the power to determine and apply federal law over the states.

On the other hand, the issue of creating lower federal courts was a controversial one that raised the sensitive issue of states' rights and federalism (see chapter 2). For example, would lower federal courts interfere with state courts? But the framers, exhausted after debating the nature of representation in Congress and unwilling to deal with another controversial issue, decided to pass the matter on to the first Congress. The result was the provision in Article III, Section 1: "The judicial Power of the United States, shall be vested in one supreme Court, and in such inferior Courts as the Congress may from time to time ordain and establish."

The first Congress took up the debate. In April, 1789, it created a committee "to bring in a bill for organizing the Judiciary of the United States." The bill, whose principal architect was Senator Oliver Ellsworth of Connecticut, reflected a number of important compromises. In particular, the committee avoided the issue of states' rights by seeking a minimal federal judicial system rather than one that enjoyed the full scope of federal power contained in Article III.

→

Court, the Court of Military Appeals, the Court of Veteran Appeals, the Court of International Trade, and the U.S. Court of Appeals for the Federal Circuit, which hears cases involving patents, copyrights, trademarks, and claims against the U.S. government.

HISTORICAL PERSPECTIVE

The Judiciary Act of 1789 created a Supreme Court with six members and alloted one federal district court with one judge in each state. The district court's jurisdiction was limited to admiralty cases (that is, cases arising from disputes over ships and maritime commerce) and a few criminal offenses. The act also created circuit courts that would hear cases in the three circuits into which the country was to be divided. A Circuit Court would consist of two Supreme Court justices, who literally would "ride circuit," and the district judge of the district in which they were sitting. Such a three-judge panel would have original jurisdiction over all federal crimes, over cases between foreign parties and citizens, or between citizens of different states. It also would have appellate jurisdiction over the district courts. Since appeals to the Supreme Court could be granted only on legal issues, the Circuit Courts became the court of last resort for most cases brought in the federal system. And, since the Circuit Court had two Supreme Court judges sitting on it, it could be thought of as a traveling mini–Supreme Court.

Today's federal court structure is roughly the same as it was in 1789, but the scope of federal judicial power is very different. During the nation's first century the federal courts were limited to admiralty cases and diversity jurisdiction (involving citizens from two or more states). The structure and jurisdiction of the federal court system began to take its present form with the Judiciary Act of 1875, which gave the federal courts broad "federal question jurisdiction;" the Circuit Court of Appeals Act of 1891, which transformed the old "circuit courts" into the intermediate courts of appeals we see today; and the Judiciary Act of 1925, which gave the Supreme Court discretionary control of its docket.

Sources: David R. Owen and Michael C. Tolley, *Courts of Admiralty in Colonial America* (Durham, NC: Carolina Academic Press, 1995); Henry J. Bourguignon, *The First Federal Court: The Federal Appellate Prize Court of the American Revolution, 1775–1787* (1977); Wilfred J. Ritz, *Rewriting the History of the Judiciary Act of 1789* (1990).

Cases are first heard by one of the federal district courts, the trial courts in the federal judicial system. The trial ordinarily takes place before a single judge and a jury. In some special cases, such as those dealing with the important subject of voting rights, the trial takes place before a three-judge panel. The losing party may make an appeal to one of the country's 12 federal courts of appeals. An **appeal** is a legal challenge to a decision by a lower court. In deciding appeals, the federal courts of appeals use rotating three-judge panels. On rare occasions, all the judges on the particular federal court of appeals may sit together in what is called an *en banc* hearing to re-hear a case that was already decided by a three-judge panel.

The federal courts of appeals may be second in importance only to the U.S. Supreme Court, but since most of the cases brought in the federal court system end there, they have the last word in many areas of law on which Supreme Court has yet to rule. The result is that the highest legal authority on many important questions of civil rights, antitrust, and federal criminal law, such as the Racketeer Influenced and Corrupt Organizations Act (RICO), is often traced to decisions by the courts of appeals and not the Supreme Court.

Each court of appeals has its own unique character and expertise, reflecting the ideological makeup of that court and the nature of the cases that arise most frequently in that area of the country. For example, because many cases involving the national government originate in the nation's capital, the court of appeals for the District of Columbia has become an authority on government regulation and administrative law. Similarly, the "old" court of appeals for the Fifth Circuit, which a generation ago covered Texas, Louisiana, Mississippi, Alabama, Georgia, and Florida, was important because so many cases decided there involved civil rights and voting rights issues.[4] Today there is considerable discussion in Congress about dividing the Ninth Circuit, which currently includes California, Nevada, Oregon, Washington, Idaho, and Montana, into two circuits: one for California, which by itself generates a huge caseload, and another for the remaining five states in the Ninth Circuit (see Figure 11.2).

Decisions by the federal courts of appeals are final, except that they are subject to discretionary review in the Supreme Court. As will be explained later, the Supreme Court has the power to decide which cases it is going to hear. If the Supreme Court chooses not to hear the case, the case ends and the judgment of the court of appeals remains undisturbed.

STATE COURT SYSTEMS

The distinguishing feature of the American judiciary is its dual system of state and federal courts. Each state has its own judicial system, and although no two are exactly the same, most share some of the same characteristics.[5] The typical state court system is a four-tiered structure, in contrast with the three-tiered structure of the federal judicial system. Apart from that distinction, the organization of the state judiciaries and the channel of appeals from lower trial courts all the way to the state supreme court follow the federal model.

At the top of the state judicial system is a court of last resort, generally called a *supreme court*. The next tier below is a court of appeals, often called an *intermediate court of appeals*, which hears appeals from the state trial courts. Today roughly three-fourths of the states have an intermediate court of appeals. Like the federal courts of appeals, these courts reduce the mounting caseload pressures on the states' highest courts by deciding the more routine appeals from the trial courts. In this way they allow states' highest courts to devote more time to the cases deemed to be most important to the development of state law.[6]

FIGURE 11.2. THE FEDERAL JUDICIAL CIRCUITS

At the base of the state judicial system are two levels of trial courts. Specialized trial courts, often referred to as *courts of limited jurisdiction*, include probate court (which deals with the estates of the deceased), juvenile court, traffic court, small claims court, and housing court. The trial courts, often called *courts of general jurisdiction*, are responsible for the trials of most major criminal offenses and civil cases involving personal injury claims, domestic relations, contract disputes and the like.

THE U.S. SUPREME COURT AS A LEGAL AND POLITICAL INSTITUTION

The federal and state court systems just described are the workhorses of the American judicial system. They handle the civil and criminal cases that we read about in the newspapers or sometimes see on television. But the U.S. Supreme Court, which sits atop this judicial pyramid, rarely tries a case and is never on television. Yet it is the most important of all the nation's courts because it is the court of last resort, the court whose decisions are meant to settle disputes that involve the fundamental meaning of the law and, particularly, the Constitution.

As a result, the Supreme Court has become an essential part of American political life. Its nine members—a chief justice and eight associate justices—are expected to deal with some of the most difficult problems facing American society. The Court's challenge is to maintain the stability and predictability needed in the legal system while also ensuring enough flexibility so that the Constitution and the political system can keep up with an ever-changing society.

JURISDICTION

Article III of the U.S. Constitution establishes the judicial branch of the federal government. The power exercised by this branch is called *judicial power* and is an integral part of the system of checks and balances. It includes the power to hear "cases and controversies" that arise under the Constitution, laws passed by Congress, and actions of the executive branch.

Article III is far shorter and less explicit than the articles establishing the legislative and executive branches of government. Article III, Section 1 vests the "judicial Power" in "one supreme Court, and in such inferior Courts as the Congress may from time to time ordain and establish." Section 2 lists the categories of cases that fall within the jurisdiction of the federal courts. The last, Section 3, defines treason, the only crime mentioned in the Constitution, and the requirements for securing a conviction for this offense.

The Constitution specifies nine kinds of "cases and controversies" that fall within the judicial power of the federal judiciary. A useful way to think of these cases is to group them into two categories: according to the nature of the parties and according to the nature of the dispute.

The Nature of the Parties   The first category is based on the nature of the parties involved in the dispute. Cases in this category include: (1) controversies in which the United States itself is a party, that is, in which it is being sued or is suing someone else; (2) in which the contending parties are different states, such over boundary issues; and (3) in which the parties are citizens of different states.

The Nature of the Dispute   The second category is based on the subject matter of the dispute. These include cases under so-called "federal question jurisdiction," that is, cases arising under the Constitution, such as the challenge to New York City's regulation of private property brought under the "takings clause" in the *Penn Central Transportation* case discussed earlier. This category also includes cases that fall under federal statutes, such as the Civil Rights Act of 1964 or the Antiterrorism Act of 1996, and those arising under admiralty and maritime law, such as suits stemming from the collision of vessels in navigable waters or the salvage of sunken wrecks.

ORIGINAL AND APPELLATE JURISDICTION

Most of the work of the Supreme Court comes under its **appellate jurisdiction,** that is, the power to review cases on appeal from the lower federal courts and the state supreme courts. The *Penn Central Transportation* case discussed at the beginning of the chapter arrived on appeal from the U.S. Court of Appeals for the Second Circuit. The Supreme Court may also try a few types of cases that arrive under the Court's **original jurisdiction.** These cases, such as those involving disputes between states

BOX 11.2.   **A CLOSER LOOK**
ORIGINAL JURISDICTION AND
THE STACK ISLAND CONTROVERSY (1995)

In its bill of complaint in this original action, the state of Louisiana asked the U.S. Supreme Court to define the boundary between that state and Mississippi along a seven-mile stretch of the Mississippi River. The disputed area involved an island, known as Stack Island, that had been within Mississippi's boundary before the river's main navigational channel shifted to the east of the island. In an opinion for a unanimous Court, Justice Anthony Kennedy applied what is known as the "island exception" to the rule of the *thalweg*, thereby confirming Mississippi's sovereignty over the disputed island:

> [T]he rule is that the river boundary between States lies along the main downstream navigational channel, or thalweg, and moves as the channel changes with the gradual processes of erosion and accretion. There exists an island exception to the general rule, which provides that if there is a divided river flow around an island, a boundary once established on one side of the island remains there, even though the main downstream navigational channel shifts to the island's other side.

Source: Louisiana v Mississippi, 516 US 22, at 25 (1995).

and those affecting ambassadors from other countries, make up only a small fraction of the Court's annual workload. The dispute between New York and New Jersey over who owns Ellis Island located in New York Harbor and the dispute between Louisiana and Mississippi over which state owns Stack Island are two recent examples of cases that have been part of the Supreme Court's original jurisdiction (see Box 11.2).

As noted earlier, the Supreme Court is not required to hear every case that comes to it. In the Judiciary Act of 1925, Congress gave the Supreme Court the right to control its caseload so that the Court would not get swamped by the growing numbers of cases being appealed to it. This law in effect gave the Court the power to choose cases that raise significant issues of law and policy. In doing so, Congress transformed the Court into a national policymaking institution.

When the losing party in a federal court of appeals or a state supreme court requests that the Supreme Court review the case, a petition for a **writ of *certiorari*** is filed with the Court. The request for *certiorari* (also known as "cert") is like an appeal, except that the Court is not required to accept it for decision. If the Supreme Court grants "cert," the lower court is ordered to prepare the record of the case and send it to the Court for review.

A temple to justice: the Supreme Court building. Constructed in the 1930s, the Supreme Court building sits directly opposite the Capitol Building in Washington, D.C. Prior to its construction, the justices of the Court heard cases in a chamber located near the Rotunda of the Capitol itself.

The Supreme Court's discretionary powers help to narrow down the number of cases reaching it (see Box 11.3). Each year the justices typically choose to hear only about 100 of the 5,000 or so cases appealed to the Court. They do so using the so-called **rule of four.** That is, for a case to be heard, four of the nine justices must agree to consider it. In cases in which a petition for *certiorari* is denied, the decision of the last court stands. Because such a small number of cases is heard annually by the nation's highest court, the Court's decisions on which appeals to hear are often as important as its decisions in the cases it accepts.[7] When the Court decides not to decide a case, the reason may be that at least six justices believe that the case does not raise a substantial enough federal question or that the issue raised in the case is not quite ready for judicial resolution.

Scholars have developed a general theory of the Supreme Court's case selection, called "cue theory," to explain how the Supreme Court selects cases. This theory hypothesizes that the justices accept cases that present one or more "cues" or indicators of the case's importance. Those cues include

▶ the involvement of the federal government as a party in the case,

▶ the presence of an issue that has been decided differently in two or more federal courts of appeals,

---

BOX 11.3.
RULE 10 OF THE *RULES OF*
THE SUPREME COURT

A CLOSER LOOK

Review on a writ of *certiorari* is a matter not of right, but of judicial discretion. A petition for a writ of *certiorari* will be granted only for compelling reasons. The following, although neither controlling nor fully measuring the Court's discretion, indicate the nature of the reasons the Court considers:

(a) A United States court of appeals has entered a decision in conflict with the decision of another United States court of appeals on the same important matter; has decided an important federal question in a way that conflicts with a decision of a state court of last resort; or has so far departed from the accepted and usual course of judicial proceedings, or sanctioned such a departure by a lower court, as to call for an exercise of this Court's supervisory power.

(b) A state court of last resort has decided an important federal question in a way that conflicts with the decision of another state court of last resort or of a United States court of appeals.

(c) A state court or a United States court of appeals has decided an important question of federal law that has not been, but should be, settled by the Supreme Court, or has decided an important federal question in a way that conflicts with relevant decisions of the Supreme Court.

(d) A petition for a writ of certiorari is rarely granted when the asserted error consists of erroneous factual findings or the misapplication of a properly stated rule of law.

Source: Rules of the Supreme Court.

▶ the degree of interest in the case, as measured by the number of *amicus curiae* or "friend of the court" briefs filed (discussed later), and

▶ the presence of a controversial issue, such as abortion, federalism, or First Amendment issues of separation of church and state, that may be reassessed by a new majority on the Court.

This said, it is sometimes difficult to predict which cases the justices will want to hear.

GAINING ACCESS TO THE SUPREME COURT

The rule of four is not the only barrier to getting a case heard by the Supreme Court. Often overlooked is the fact that bringing a case all the way to the nation's highest court is a costly and time-consuming endeavor. Sometimes those involved decide that these costs are too high no matter how strongly they believe in their cause.

A school prayer case from New Jersey is a good example. Highland High School's three-year judicial odyssey began as a local dispute over graduation prayers and ended by showing how the Supreme Court can be out of reach for many Americans. The dispute began in 1993 when Highland seniors voted to include prayers in their graduation ceremony. But one student objected, arguing that the majority was infringing on his right not to engage in public prayer. The local branch of the American Civil Liberties Union, acting on behalf of the student, successfully sued to block the prayers, citing the fundamental principle of separation of church and state (see chapter 4). The local school board, which supported the students, appealed the trial court's decision to the U.S. Court of Appeals for the Third Circuit in Philadelphia, which affirmed the lower court's decision. By this time three years had elapsed, and with the costs of litigation nearing $75,000 and likely to rise further, the school board had to decide whether an appeal to the Supreme Court was worth it. Even though board members felt that the school prayer issue as framed in this case seemed to present an ideal constitutional test, the board eventually decided that the potential price tag for an appeal to the Supreme Court was too high and chose not to appeal.[8]

So only a fraction of the cases that have merit ever reach the Court. Those that do reach the Court often have the financial backing of interest groups who stand to gain or lose by a Supreme Court decision in the case. Even in cases in which interest groups are not directly involved in the litigation, they may still try to influence the development of the law useful to their cause by filing *amicus curiae* or "friend of the court" briefs. In these briefs (legal arguments), the interest groups set forth the larger social, political, economic, and/or moral implications of the case and suggest legal strategies that the Court might follow in justifying its decision. These briefs provide the Court with information about the likely impact of a decision, and this information seems to be important to the Supreme Court's decisionmaking processes.

THE SUPREME COURT IN ACTION

The Court meets in the Supreme Court Building, a stately classical building located directly opposite the United States Capitol. Its term begins on the first Monday in October and ends in late June or early July, depending on the Court's caseload. Only rarely does the Court convene in the summer to hear and decide a case. One notable instance was *Cooper v. Aaron* (1958), which challenged the Court's school desegregation order in *Brown v. Board of Education* (1955). Given the seriousness of the issue and the need to settle it before the beginning of the school year, the case was argued on August 28 and again on September 11, 1958, and decided on September 12. But this was a rare exception to the Court's usual schedule.[9]

After the Court accepts a case for review, it asks the parties involved to submit written **briefs** setting forth their best legal arguments and to prepare for oral argument on a date set by the Court (see Figure 11.3). The justices decide a case after they have considered written briefs and oral arguments from the parties. Oral arguments generally are limited to one hour, with each side given 30 minutes. The lawyers come prepared with arguments that they want to present, but rarely do they get very far along before they are peppered with questions from the justices.

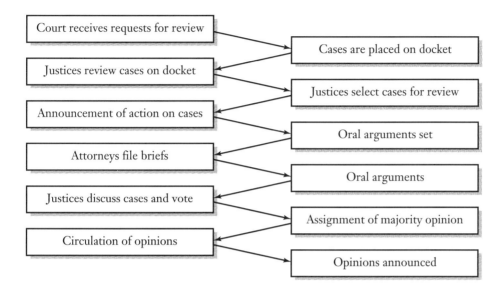

FIGURE 11.3. PROCESSING OF CASES IN THE SUPREME COURT

Source: Adapted from Lee Epstein, et al., *The Supreme Court Compendium: Data, Decisions, and Developments*, 3d ed. (Washington, D.C.: Congressional Quarterly, 1996), Figure 1.1.

The oral argument stage is the only part of the Supreme Court decisionmaking process that is open to the public. For important cases it is not unusual to see interested spectators lining up on the steps of the Supreme Court Building, waiting to be ushered into the few seats reserved for that purpose in the Great Hall, as the actual courtroom is called. Edward Lazarus, a former legal clerk who wrote a behind-the-scenes account of the Court, described the setting:

> There is something exquisite about the room's proportions, intimate but not cramped, magisterial but not overwhelming. From the pews of the courtroom, the panorama of lush marble, rich drapery, and gleaming appointments inspires an awe heightened by the dignity and ceremony of the proceedings themselves.[10]

After hearing oral arguments, the justices meet privately "in conference." They discuss the cases they have recently heard, take a tentative vote and assign the writing of opinions. The chief justice begins the discussion; then, in descending order of seniority, the associate justices present their views on the case. After all nine justices have spoken, the chief justice determines the number of justices favoring each side. If the chief justice is in the majority, he or she writes the Court's **majority opinion** (or "opinion of the Court") justifying the decision, or selects another justice in the majority to do so. If the chief justice is in the minority, the senior justice among those in the majority writes the majority opinion or assigns that duty to another justice in the majority.

The justices of the U.S. Supreme Court, 1999. Standing: Ruth Bader Ginsburg, David Souter, Clarence Thomas, and Stephen Breyer. Seated: Antonin Scalia, John Paul Stevens, Chief Justice William Rehnquist, Sandra Day O'Connor, and Anthony Kennedy.

It is at this point that the real work begins. The justice assigned to prepare the majority opinion drafts wording that reflects the views shared by the five or more justices in the majority. At the same time, the justices in the minority begin work on one or more **dissenting opinions,** which argue against both the vote and the legal reasoning behind the majority's decision.

Decisions of the Supreme Court are by majority vote. Written opinions, which have the force of law, announce the Court's decision and explain in detail the legal reasons for deciding the case the way it did. Drafts of the majority and dissenting opinions are circulated among the justices. It is still possible for a justice who had voted one way in conference to change his or her position on the strength of the arguments that emerge during the opinion-writing stage.

Given the difficulty of the issues before the Court and the ideological differences among the justices, it is not uncommon for a justice assigned to write the majority opinion to discover later that the majority has dissolved. In an effort to hold on to that majority, the opinion writer may have to make some concessions to the other members of the majority. But it is important to draw a distinction between the concessions the justices sometimes have to make to accommodate the views of others and the concessions legislators often make. In Congress legislators may say, "I'll vote for your bill, if you vote for mine," but in the Supreme Court the justices do not compromise by trading votes in individual cases.

In nearly every case, a majority opinion will emerge. In a few cases each term, the Court achieves only a plurality opinion, that is, an opinion in which only four justices have reached agreement on the reasoning. A justice may agree with the result of the majority decision, but not necessarily with the reasoning of the other justices. He or she may then write a **concurring opinion.** There are also likely to be one or more dissenting opinions. Dissenting opinions are not uncommon. For example, during the Court's 1997 term, there were 93 opinions of the Court, 52 concurring opinions, and 64 dissents.[11]

Once opinions have been drafted and the positions of the justices finalized, the decisions are announced to the public. In some high-profile cases the justices may read aloud excerpts from their opinions. Once the decisions have been announced, the opinions are made available to the public in several ways: published in the *United States Reports* and other law reports, and posted on the Internet at a number of official Web sites.

THE SELECTION OF JUDGES

The Constitution sets no qualifications for federal judges, but in Article II, Section 2, it provides that they shall be nominated by the president "by and with the Advice and Consent of the Senate." The phrase "advice and consent" implies more than a mere vote of approval or disapproval. In fact, it implies that the president should consult with the Senate before making a nomination. Although this consultative function never became an established practice, presidents usually ask important members of the Senate for their opinions about potential nominees.

Over time, the president and the Senate have developed their own criteria for selecting and evaluating nominees. Merit—that is, exceptional legal qualifications—figures prominently in the selection process. Every justice of the Supreme Court has had some legal training, although not all studied at law school, and many have had some prior judicial experience. However, a debate has raged over what factors, in addition to merit, should count. Some observers argue that judicial nominations are based more on politics than on merit. Here the term *"politics"* is being used broadly to refer to a number of considerations, including the desire to appoint justices who share the president's political and ideological views; who represent certain racial, ethnic, or religious groups; who are from a certain state or region; and who are of a certain gender. Although these considerations are clearly important in the process of judicial selection, nearly all agree that professional qualifications should matter most.

THE POLITICS OF ADVICE AND CONSENT

At each level of the federal judicial system, federal judges take their seat on the bench after their nomination by the president has been confirmed by the Senate. Following a hearing before and favorable vote by the Senate Judiciary Committee, the full Senate votes. A simple majority is all that is needed to confirm the nomination. Once the president's nominees for federal judges have been confirmed by the Senate, they may remain in office for life, or "during good Behavior," and Congress may not reduce their salaries (Article III, Section 1). Although the framers understood the need for judicial independence and tried to implement it with these provisions, they could not have imagined an institution without any political checks. This explains why they gave Congress the power to remove federal judges through the formal impeachment process (Article II, Section 4), why Congress has the authority to control and adjust the appellate jurisdiction of the federal courts (Article III, Section 2), and finally, why the Senate has the authority to approve the president's judicial nominations.

The Senate usually confirms a president's judicial nominations with few dissenting votes. In 1981, when President Reagan nominated Sandra Day O'Connor, the first woman named to the Supreme Court, the vote in the Senate was 99 to 0. The implicit understanding is that the judicial branch of government would be adversely affected by judgeships left open as a result of conflict between the other two branches. Nevertheless, there are times when a nomination is controversial and the Senate refuses to confirm, or just narrowly confirms, the president's nominee. In 1987, the Senate rejected President Reagan's nomination of Robert Bork by a vote of 42 to 58; in 1991, President Bush's nomination of Clarence Thomas squeaked by with a vote of 52 to 48.

Since the confirmation process began in 1789, 20 percent (30 out of 145) of all Supreme Court nominations have failed to win confirmation because they were rejected by the Senate, were withdrawn by the president, or did not get past the Senate Judiciary Committee. Because six of these failed nominations have occurred since 1968, some critics suggest that the confirmation process is more political today than at any other time in the nation's history.[12] However, this may not be true. Although history shows that the Senate usually defers to a president's choice of nominees, no president is assured that a nomination will be confirmed routinely. The fate of each nomination is uncertain because political considerations, in addition to the legal or judicial ability of the nominee, are important factors in the confirmation process. In dividing the responsibility for appointing federal judges between the Senate and the president, the framers expected conflict. It was another part of the elaborate system of checks and balances built into the new framework of government. How presidents go about selecting nominees and building consensus is crucial in the short run, with respect to relations between Congress and the president, and in the long run with respect to the quality and independence of the judiciary.

President Clinton's nominations to the Supreme Court illustrate the care a president takes in dealing with the Senate. Clinton's nominees—Ruth Bader Ginsburg and Stephen Breyer—lacked the controversy that accompanied President Reagan's unsuccessful nomination of Robert Bork and President Bush's successful, though controversial, nomination of Clarence Thomas. Ginsburg and Breyer were regarded as political moderates, and Clinton's choice of Breyer in particular was designed to avoid a major conflict with conservative Senate Republicans, just as President Bush's nomination of David Souter was designed to avoid battles with liberal Senate Democrats.[13] In each case the president's party was in the minority in the Senate, so it was essential to avoid a confirmation battle. The strategy worked, as both nominees won confirmation easily: Souter by a vote of 90 to 9, Breyer by a vote of 87 to 9.

However, even Breyer's confirmation hearing raised questions about the politics of advice and consent. For example, should characteristics other than a nominee's integrity, professional competence, and experience be considered by the Senate? Should a nominee be required to state his or her personal views on specific issues, such as abortion, and what weight should these views be given? Should senatorial concern about presidents' efforts to appoint justices who share their political views be relevant? Must the Senate defer to the president, allowing a certain amount of lee-way in the appointment of justices with similar views on the most pressing social, po-litical, and economic issues of the day? These questions take on special meaning in an era of divided government, when the party in control of the Senate is not the presi-dent's party.

THE RISE OF JUDICIAL REVIEW

The power of the Supreme Court and the other federal courts rests on the doctrine of **judicial review,** the power of courts to determine the constitutionality of state and federal legislation or executive actions. Yet it is striking that Article III does not pro-vide explicitly for judicial review. This omission is difficult to explain, because it is clear that the framers understood the need for such a power. In *Federalist* No. 78, Alexander Hamilton provides the following justification for judicial review:

> A constitution is, in fact, and must be regarded by the judges as fundamental law. It therefore belongs to them to ascertain its meaning, as well as the meaning of any particular act proceeding from the legislative body. If there should happen to be an irreconcilable variance between the two, . . . the Constitution ought to be preferred to the statute, the intention of the people to the intention of their agents.[14]

Hamilton's reflections were in response to Antifederalist complaints that the con-stitutional provisions for a national judiciary made the power of this branch of gov-ernment superior to that of the Congress. Hamilton disagreed, stressing that the ju-diciary was inherently weak. "The judiciary," he wrote, "has no influence over either the sword or purse; . . . It may truly be said to have neither FORCE nor WILL but merely judgment."[15]

MARBURY V. MADISON

The story of how the seemingly weak power of judgment was transformed into the more substantial power of judicial review begins with the landmark case of *Marbury v. Madison* (1803).[16] In it John Marshall, the fourth chief justice of the U.S. Supreme Court (1801–1835), established the authority of the federal courts to engage in judi-cial review.

Ironically, Marshall was the cause of the suit brought by one of the parties in this case. Shortly before his appointment to the Court in 1801, Marshall was secretary of state under President John Adams. In that role he had failed to deliver an official commission to William Marbury, who had been appointed justice of the peace in the District of Columbia. Marbury and several other Federalists had been appointed at the last minute to fill the judgeships created in the last days of the Adams administra-tion. The so-called Midnight Judges Act was an attempt by the Federalists, who had defeated by the Jeffersonian Republicans in the elections of 1800, to retain control of the federal judiciary. So great was the scramble to name and commission as many

Chief Justice John Marshall (1755–1835), author of the Court's opinion in *Marbury v. Madison* (1803), stands as one of the greatest Chief Justices in American history. Under his leadership the Court established itself as an independent constitutional check on the power of the two elected branches, especially Congress.

new judges before the new administration took office that Marbury's commission was not delivered.

Marbury naturally requested that James Madison, the new secretary of state under President Thomas Jefferson, deliver his commission. But Madison, acting on behalf of the president, refused to do so, largely because of anger over Adams's last-minute judicial appointments. Marbury went directly to the Supreme Court, claiming that under the Judiciary Act of 1789 the Court had original jurisdiction to issue writs of *mandamus*. A **writ of** *mandamus* is an order by a high court to a government officer or lower court directing it to carry out a duty prescribed by law. In this case, Marbury wanted the Supreme Court to order Madison to deliver his commission.

The *Marbury* case put Chief Justice Marshall in a bind. The Court had to do something. Doing nothing would allow the president to evade his legal duty to deliver a rightful appointment and would probably diminish the authority of the judiciary in the process. But what should be done? If the Court ordered the commission delivered and Madison refused, the result would be a major blow to the independent authority of the judiciary at a time when the powers of that branch were still being worked out. If the Court did not order the commission delivered, it would look weak in the face of presidential power. Either action would cause problems for the authority of the judiciary relative to the other branches.

Chief Justice Marshall took a different route. He held that Marbury was entitled to his commission and that Madison had withheld it from him wrongfully. In theory, the writ of *mandamus* was appropriate. The question, however, was whether in this specific case the Supreme Court actually had the power of *mandamus* under Article III's grant of original jurisdiction.

Marshall then answered his own question and thereby applied the doctrine of judicial review. Marbury was entitled to his commission, Marshall reasoned, but the Supreme Court lacked the ability to compel its delivery by *mandamus*. The chief justice arrived at this conclusion through a close reading of the Judiciary Act of 1789 and Article III of the Constitution. In the Judiciary Act, Congress had given the Court the power of *mandamus*, which in effect expanded the Court's power. To Marshall, this was not appropriate: Congress could not add to the Court's original jurisdiction, as part of the Judiciary Act attempted to do, because this was already established under Article III of the Constitution. The only way to change the Court's original jurisdiction was through a constitutional amendment. Congress, therefore, had acted unconstitutionally. As a result, the Supreme Court did not have the power of *mandamus* in this case, and it could not order Madison to deliver Marbury's commission.

Marshall's argument for judicial review rests on what is called "the theory of a written constitution." That is, the Constitution is the embodiment of the will of the people, the supreme law of the land. If an ordinary act of Congress, such as the Judiciary Act, could alter the Constitution by simple majority vote, the supremacy of the Constitution itself would be undermined. The only way to alter the Constitution was through a constitutional amendment. Because Congress had not followed the procedure for amending the Constitution, its action was declared "null and void."

JUDICIAL REVIEW AND DEMOCRACY

When federal courts strike down laws or policies that enjoy widespread support and are the result of the legislative process provided for in the Constitution, they are often criticized for exercising an undemocratic power. On the other hand, when courts strike down laws that interfere with the rights of individuals or rule in favor of groups that have been shut out of the political process by the majority, they are often lauded for promoting democracy. Therein lies the paradox of judicial power: Judicial power is both undemocratic and democratic. What better way is there to describe a small, elite group of judges who are largely unrepresentative of the general population yet make decisions that promote liberty and the other values essential to democracy?

The U.S. Supreme Court's decision in *Romer v. Evans* (1996) is a good example of how the power of judicial review may be used to advance democracy. This case arose when three Colorado cities passed ordinances banning discrimination against homosexuals in housing, education, public accommodations, and health and welfare services. These ordinances upset conservative Coloradans, particularly in rural areas, who mobilized in opposition. They gathered thousands of signatures on a petition to put the issue to a referendum or statewide vote (see chapter 5). The referendum battle ended with voters adopting an amendment to the state constitution, called Amendment 2, that forbade any governmental action designed to protect the status of individuals on the basis of their sexual orientation. Gay Coloradans brought suit in state court against the governor, Roy Romer, in an effort to have Amendment 2 declared invalid. A state trial court granted a preliminary **injunction,** a court order preventing the enforcement of the law.

On appeal, the Colorado Supreme Court sustained the injunction, holding that Amendment 2 infringed upon the fundamental rights of gays and lesbians to participate in the political process. The state appealed the decision to the U.S. Supreme Court. In a 6-to-3 decision, the Supreme Court upheld the rights of homosexuals against the majority of Colorado citizens who had voted for Amendment 2. The Court stated that a "law declaring that in general it shall be more difficult for one group of citizens than for all others to seek aid from the government is itself a denial of equal protection of the law in the most literal sense."[17]

In getting the Colorado Supreme Court and then the U.S. Supreme Court to strike down Amendment 2 on "equal protection" grounds, the plaintiffs in this case showed that courts are more than arbitrators of conflict. More important, the lawsuit revealed how courts can be used in the political debate over homosexuality. By choosing the judicial forum, those involved in this case applied a major lesson learned from other minority groups: that courts can be used to bring about change in American society.

JUDICIAL REVIEW: THE GUN BEHIND THE DOOR

The doctrine of judicial review has endured as an essential feature of American government. Since 1803 the Supreme Court has invalidated nearly 150 congressional statutes and over 1,000 laws passed by state and local governments.[18] Yet these numbers are small when one considers the tens of thousands of federal, state, and local legislative acts passed in the nearly 200 years of U.S. history since *Marbury v. Madison*.

Thus, the power of judicial review is not invoked as often as one would think. In fact, the real effect of judicial review is akin to the proverbial "gun behind the door." It keeps the other branches of government and the states honest with the threat that the courts could judge their actions unconstitutional. In deterring the "political" branches from acting unconstitutionally, judicial review has helped preserve American democracy.

JUDGING LAW VERSUS MAKING LAW

In *Democracy in America* (1835), the French aristocrat Alexis de Tocqueville observed that "scarcely any political question arises in the United States that is not resolved, sooner or later, into a judicial question."[19] Americans' tendency to invoke judicial power in matters of politics is even clearer today than it was in Tocqueville's time.

The "judicialization" of politics, in which national debates over highly charged political issues such as abortion, homosexuality, the right to die, or welfare are converted into legal issues and channeled through the judiciary, is a characteristic feature of American government.

JUDICIAL POLICYMAKING

Sometimes the judiciary is as openly involved in the process of transforming conflict into compromise as is any other institution. Throughout American history state and federal courts have made possible changes and reforms that were either stalled in the legislature or mired in political controversy. In doing so, the courts have acted as another outlet for individuals and groups seeking change. When courts effect change through their decisions, they are said to be engaged in judicial policymaking.

Courts make policy when they apply the law to novel situations or interpret it in creative ways. However, except in some state court systems, judges are not elected. The policymaking role of unelected (and, hence, unaccountable) judges must somehow be reconciled with the principle of representative government. In this regard, Felix Frankfurter, an associate justice of the Supreme Court (1939–1962), once observed that it is "not so much a question whether judges make law, but how and how much."[20] The debate on this issue has centered on a number of questions: To what extent do judges make new law? What values do they bring to bear on this process? Is this active exercise of judicial creativity to be applauded or deplored? And finally, how can an unelected judiciary be made accountable for its policy choices? With the extension of the concept of judicial review throughout the world, these questions are being raised elsewhere (see Box 11.4).[21]

The Supreme Court is so interesting and so important precisely because it blends traditional policymaking functions with its legal functions. To fully understand the nature and function of the Supreme Court, one must remember that it is as much a political institution as it is a court of law. This reality is exemplified by the history of the Court under Chief Justice Earl Warren (1953–1969), during which time it revolutionized several areas of law and ushered in new doctrines regarding civil rights and liberties (see chapter 4). In the words of legal historian Morton Horwitz, the Warren Court was "a time when American idealism showed its most generous and hopeful face."[22] In doing so, however, it unleashed a stormy debate over the proper role of courts in a system of representative government.

Even for those who like the results of the Warren Court's activism, two major criticisms need to be answered. The first is that the Supreme Court was basing its decisions on its own set of values and not on precedent and "neutral principles of law." In essence, the critics argued, the Court was "making law" through the judicial process. The second argument is that because the justices were appointed for life and did not go before the voters at election time, the Court posed a serious threat to democracy. These critics argued that the Court should be less concerned with the rights of minorities and defer more to the wishes of the majority as expressed through elected legislators and executives.

BOX 11.4.
JUDICIAL REVIEW
IN COMPARATIVE PERSPECTIVE

A CLOSER LOOK

Unlike the U.S. Constitution, most modern constitutions contain explicit provision for judicial review. Here are four good examples:

Republic of South Africa: "The Constitutional Court makes the final decision whether an Act of Parliament, a provincial Act or conduct of the President is constitutional, and must confirm any order of invalidity made by the Supreme Court of Appeal, a High Court, or a court of similar status, before that order has any force." *Constitution of the Republic of South Africa* (1996), Chapter 8, Sect. 167, para. (5)

Canada: "Anyone whose rights or freedoms, as guaranteed by this Charter, have been infringed or denied may apply to a court of competent jurisdiction to obtain such remedy as the court considers appropriate and just in the circumstances." *The Canadian Charter of Rights and Freedoms* (1982), Sect. 24 (1)

"The Constitution of Canada is the supreme law of Canada, and any law that is inconsistent with the provisions of the Constitution is, to the extent of the inconsistency, of no force or effect." *Ibid.*, Sect. 52 (1)

Germany: "The Federal Constitutional Court shall decide: (1) on the interpretation of this Basic Law in the event of disputes concerning the extent of the rights and duties of a supreme federal body or of other parties vested with rights of their own by this Basic Law or by the rules of a supreme federal body; . . . (4a) on complaints of unconstitutionality, which may be filed by any person who claims that one of his basic rights . . . has been violated by public authority." *Basic Law for the Federal Republic of Germany* (1949), Article 93

"(1) If a court considers that a statute on whose validity the court's decision depends is unconstitutional, the proceedings shall be stayed, and a decision shall be obtained . . . from the Federal Constitutional Court when this Basic Law is held to be violated." *Ibid.*, Article 100

Japan: "The Supreme Court is the court of last resort with power to determine the constitutionality of any law, order, regulation or official act." *The Constitution of Japan* (1947), Article 81

JUDICIAL ACTIVISM VERSUS JUDICIAL RESTRAINT

As the debate over the Warren Court suggests, since the 1960s judges and scholars have disagreed over the degree of creativity allowed in constitutional interpretation and over the role of courts in policymaking.

On one side of the debate are those who advocate **judicial activism,** a broader, more expansive interpretation of the Constitution, on the theory that it is a "living document" that needs to change with the times. After all, the Constitution was crafted in 1787 for a society that no longer exists, and either it must be amended con-

Impeach Earl Warren. Chief Justice Earl Warren was a former Republican governor of California appointed to the Court by President Dwight Eisenhower. To almost everyone's surprise, Warren led the Court during a particularly activist phase in the 1960s, which earned him the passionate opposition of many conservatives.

stantly to reflect changing societal conditions or the Court should be able to apply newer meanings of its words to fit contemporary society. Not to do so is to allow the Constitution to sink into irrelevance.

On the other side are those who advocate **judicial restraint.** They believe that the Constitution as the supreme law of the land should be interpreted narrowly, and that the Court's decisions should defer to the majority will as expressed through the democratic process. The task of lawmaking, they argue, belongs to the people's representatives in their legislature, not to the unelected judiciary.

Judicial restraint and judicial activism thus are concepts used to describe conflicting views about the proper role of courts in society. Four features are characteristic of judicial restraint. First, the Court is willing to let other branches and other levels of government decide issues, being careful not to usurp the authority of elected officials or views of the majority. Second, judicial restraint is marked by respect for the idea of **original intent,** that is, adherence to the ideas of the framers and ratifiers of the Constitution. Third, to practice judicial restraint means that courts will be bound by **precedent,** that is, the rule of law found in an earlier case that serves as a guide to the resolution of later cases. Precedent acts as a restraint in that it keeps courts from diverging significantly from historical or traditional interpretations of the law. Finally, judicial restraint steers courts away from "political questions"—issues that have historically been regarded as beyond the competence of courts and best left to the legislative and executive branches of government.

Judicial activists hold very different views about the proper role of the courts in society. It is incorrect to equate judicial activism with liberalism and judicial restraint with conservatism, even though most activist judges are liberal and most judges who practice judicial restraint are conservative. Indeed, there are judges who can best be described as "conservative judicial activists"; they try to advance a conservative political agenda through activist interpretations of the Constitution's meaning.

Whether their objectives are liberal or conservative, judges are considered activist if they (1) short-circuit the democratic process by deciding issues that have not been debated fully in the legislature; (2) replace the views of the legislature, as revealed in the plain meaning of the statute, with their own views about the social and economic effects of the legislation; (3) depart from precedent; and (4) attempt to address the most highly charged issues of the day, regardless of the reality that such issues might not be fit for the political process.

The tension between the values of judicial activism and judicial restraint is evident in *Griswold v. Connecticut* (1965), a case that challenged a state statute prohibiting the distribution of birth control information.[23] The suit was initiated by two members of the Planned Parenthood League of Connecticut who had been convicted of violating the Connecticut statute by giving information, instruction, and medical advice about contraception to married adults. The conviction was affirmed by the state's highest court.

On appeal, the U.S. Supreme Court reversed this decision by a 7-to-2 vote, holding that the statute was invalid because it infringed on a constitutionally protected "right to privacy." The challenge for Justice William O. Douglas and others in the majority was to justify the protection of a right, in this case the right to privacy, that is not expressly provided for in the Constitution. Justice Douglas did so by referring to rights that are implicit in, or peripheral to, other guarantees in the Bill of Rights. Although a right to privacy is not explicitly stated by the Constitution, he found protection for it in several constitutional provisions, including the Third Amendment's prohibition against the quartering of soldiers in any house in time of peace, the Fourth Amendment's protection of the "rights of the people to be secure in their persons, houses, papers, and effects," and the Fifth Amendment's prohibition against self-incrimination.

Justice Hugo Black, who wrote the dissenting opinion, was not convinced. "I like my privacy as well as the next one," he argued, "but I am nevertheless compelled to admit that government has a right to invade it unless prohibited by some specific constitutional provision." Black criticized the majority for their lack of judicial restraint, while Douglas defended their activism by recalling that this was not the first time the Court had recognized and protected a right that was not specifically mentioned in the Constitution.

PUBLIC OPINION AND THE SUPREME COURT

Complaints about the undemocratic nature of judicial power naturally arise when the Supreme Court's policymaking role expands. But history reveals that the Court has been more responsive to the public and has enjoyed greater support than one would assume. In his classic study of the relationship between public opinion (as reflected in the actions of the representatives of the people) and Court policy (as measured by the number of statutes declared unconstitutional), political scientist Robert Dahl found that the Court rarely gets very far out of line with popular opinion, and when it does, it does not do so for very long.[24] For Dahl judicial power is more democratic than it might seem. Judicial review is invoked rarely, he argues, and the Supreme Court acts most of the time to validate the majority's views and actions.

These studies of the relationship between public opinion and Supreme Court decisionmaking suggest at least three possible roles of the Court in the American system of government: trend-setter, trend-resister, and trend-follower. That is, the Court can lead the way, it can resist, or it can follow the general directions in public opinion on major issues.

Scholars believe that most of the time the Court acts as a trend-follower. In this regard, its function is to confer legitimacy on the policies established by the nation's lawmaking authorities. Although the Court may occasionally try to lead society down a more enlightened path, as it did in the area of race relations (*Brown v. Board of Education*), or to resist a measure passed by a temporary majority, as it did in upholding the rights of homosexuals (*Romer v. Evans*), history has shown that if the majority persists in its view, the Court will eventually capitulate. Thus, the Supreme Court may not be as undemocratic as its critics claim, and may not be the great champion of minority rights as many are inclined to believe.

CONCLUSION

The habit, observed by Tocqueville, of bringing social conflict into the legal arena is deeply embedded in American political culture. As a result, the courts have played an important role in the transformation of many aspects of American society. Since 1950 the Supreme Court's desegregation decisions, beginning with *Brown v. Board of Education* (1954); its criminal law decisions, as in *Mapp v. Ohio* (1961) and *Gideon v. Wainwright* (1963); its abortion decisions, beginning with *Roe v. Wade* (1973); and most recently its decision in *Romer v. Evans* (1996) on the status of homosexuals—all have influenced the political debate over the government's role in promoting improved race relations, law and order, gender equality, and the rights of other minorities. In each of these cases the Court has acted as a political as well as a judicial institution.

In fact, candidates for office at every level of government have had to respond to these decisions in one way or another, whether by voicing their agreement with the Court or by registering their disagreement and promising to promote change if elected. The Supreme Court has helped to establish public policy and will continue to help define and influence the political agenda for generations to come. In short, judicial politics is a dimension of American politics in general, another avenue for resolving the disputes that inevitably arise in a large and complex society.

SUMMARY

▶ Courts are as much political as legal institutions, as can be seen in the four functions they fulfill: social control, dispute settlement, social engineering, and regime maintenance.

▶ The judiciary consists of a dual system of state and federal courts, a structure that reflects the political system's principle of federalism.

▶ The process of advancing a case through the federal judiciary is an arduous one, with relatively few cases obtaining review by the Supreme Court. Should at least four of the nine justices agree to hear the case, the Court then holds oral argument, after which the justices discuss the case among themselves. In cases in which there is no unanimity, the respective sides produce majority and dissenting opinions that explain their differing perspectives. Sometimes a justice who votes with the majority will produce a concurring opinion, in which he or she offers a somewhat different perspective than the majority opinion.

▶ The professional qualifications of judicial nominees are important, but other factors, including political ones, also have an influence. Partisanship and ideological conflict help explain the occasional struggles over presidents' nominations to the Supreme Court.

▶ *Marbury v. Madison* (1803) established the power of the Supreme Court to declare unconstitutional laws or acts of the other branches or of the states. This doctrine, known as judicial review, has been an indispensable safeguard of democracy in the United States. Despite appearances, however, the Court rarely uses this power.

▶ The core of judicial power is interpretation of the law as it applies to real cases. There is significant disagreement over the degree of latitude judges should have in interpreting the Constitution. The debate pits those who promote judicial activism (that is, results-oriented decisionmaking) against those who promote judicial restraint (that is, judicial decisionmaking based on neutral principles of law), although this distinction is not always neat and clean.

▶ In describing the relationship between the Supreme Court and public opinion, the trend-following role best captures the work of the Court. This observation helps diminish the fear that the nation's highest court is out of step with the dominant views of society.

QUESTIONS FOR REVIEW AND DISCUSSION

1. Explain what we mean when we say that the judiciary is a political institution. Use examples.

2. Explain the process by which cases eventually rise to the level of Supreme Court review. What factors play a role in whether an appeal is heard by the Court?

3. What factors should be considered when a president nominates a person to the federal judiciary?

4. Define the terms *judicial activism* and *judicial restraint*. Which orientation should the Supreme Court adhere to when considering cases on which the Constitution is vague?

TERMS TO REMEMBER

amicus curiae	injunction	original intent
appeal	judicial activism	original jurisdiction
appellate jurisdiction	judicial restraint	precedent
briefs	judicial review	rule of four
concurring opinion	judiciary	writ of *certiorari*
consent decree	majority opinion	writ of *mandamus*
dissenting opinion		

WEB SOURCES

Project Hermes (www.law.cornell.edu/supct), developed by the Legal Information Institute of the Cornell Law School, makes the U.S. Supreme Court's opinions and rulings available to the public. This site also offers a collection of historically important decisions.

The United States Federal Judiciary site (www.uscourts.gov) is maintained by the Administrative Office of the U.S. Courts, and its function is to provide information about the judicial branch of the federal government.

Villanova School of Law (www.law.vill.edu/Fed-Ct/fedcourt.html) operates a site that contains links to the decisions of the U.S. Courts of Appeals and to the official homepages of four federal agencies that are relevant to the judiciary: Administrative Office of the U.S. Courts, U.S. Department of Justice, U.S. Sentencing Commission, and Federal Judicial Center.

SUGGESTED READINGS

Mark Tushnet, *Making Civil Rights Law: Thurgood Marshall and the Supreme Court, 1961–1991* (New York: Oxford University Press, 1996); Dennis Hutchinson, *The Man Who Once Was Whizzer White: A Portrait of Justice Byron White* (New York: Free Press, 1998). Two fine examples of biographies that examine the lives of Supreme Court justices. Both authors, former law clerks under their subjects, look at the justice both inside and outside of the Court.

The Supreme Court cases that become landmarks in American constitutional law are often the result of considerable human drama, which can make for fascinating reading. Journalist Anthony Lewis has written two of the very best: *Gideon's Trumpet* (New York: Penguin, 1964), an examination of *Gideon v. Wainwright*, the case in which a poor man successfully petitioned the Court to hear his appeal of a criminal conviction; and *Make No Law: The Sullivan Case and the First Amendment* (New York: Vintage, 1992), an examination of *New York Times v. Sullivan*, which established contemporary standards of freedom of the press. Another fine example is Richard Kluger, *Simple Justice: The History of Brown v. Board of Education and Black America's Struggle for Equality* (New York: Random House, 1977).

The inner workings of the Supreme Court always seem to have a mysterious quality. Two good behind-the-curtain looks at the Court are Bob Woodward and Scott Armstrong, *The Brethren: Inside the Supreme Court* (New York: Simon & Schuster, 1979), and Edward Lazarus, *Closed Chambers: The First Eyewitness Account of the Epic Struggles Inside the Supreme Court* (New York: Times Books, 1998).

Students interested in learning more about the federal judicial system and the Supreme Court in particular may want to see one or more of the following fine works: Henry J. Abraham, *The Judiciary: The Supreme Court in the Governmental Process*, 7th ed. (Boston, MA: Allyn & Bacon, 1989), Alexander Bickel, *The Least Dangerous Branch* (Indianapolis, IN: Bobbs-Merrill, 1962), Morton J. Horwitz, *The Warren Court and the Pursuit of Justice* (New York: Hill and Wang, 1998), and Robert G. McCloskey, *The American Supreme Court*, 2d ed., revised by Sanford Levinson (Chicago, IL: University of Chicago Press, 1994).

NOTES

1. *Penn Central Transportation Co. v New York City*, 438 US 104 (1978).

2. Henry R. Glick, "Judicial Innovation and Policy Re-Invention: The State Supreme Courts and the Right to Die," *Western Political Quarterly*, vol. 44 (1991), pp. 71–92.

3. The changes were included in the Antiterrorism Act (1996), Public Law 104–132.

4. J. Woodford Howard Jr., *Courts of Appeals in the Federal Judicial System: A Study of the Second, Fifth, and District of Columbia Circuits* (Princeton, NJ: Princeton University Press, 1981).

5. G. Alan Tarr and Mary Cornelia Aldis Porter, *State Supreme Courts in State and Nation* (New Haven, CT: Yale University Press, 1988).

6. Michael C. Tolley, *State Constitutionalism in Maryland* (New York: Garland Publishing, 1992), p. 142.

7. H. W. Perry, *Deciding to Decide: Agenda Setting in the United States Supreme Court* (Cambridge, MA: Harvard University Press, 1992).

8. Lyle Denniston, "School Bows in Prayer Case," *Baltimore Sun*, September 9, 1996, p. 1A.

9. *Cooper v Aaron*, 358 US 1 (1958).

10. Edward Lazarus, *Closed Chambers: The First Eyewitness Account of the Epic Struggles inside the Supreme Court* (1998), p. 33.

11. "The Supreme Court, 1997 Term," *Harvard Law Review*, vol. 112 (1998), p. 366.

12. Robert Bork, *The Tempting of America: The Political Seduction of the Law* (New York: Free Press, 1990), p. 279.

13. John A. Maltese Jr., *The Selling of Supreme Court Nominees* (Baltimore, MD: Johns Hopkins University Press, 1995).

14. Alexander Hamilton, James Madison, and John Jay, *The Federalist Papers*, Clinton Rossiter, ed. (New York: New American Library, 1961), p. 467.

15. *Ibid.*, p. 465.

16. *Marbury v Madison*, 5 US (1 Cranch) 137 (1803).

17. *Romer v Evans*, 517 US 620, at 633 (1996).

18. David M. O'Brien, *Storm Center: The Supreme Court in American Politics*, 2d ed. (New York: Norton, 1990), p. 60.

19. Alexis de Tocqueville, *Democracy in America*, ed. by J. P. Mayer and Max Lerner, trans. by George Lawrence (New York: Harper & Row, 1966), p. 248.

20. Letter from Felix Frankfurter to Hugo Black in 1939 (*Frankfurter Papers*, Library of Congress, Manuscript Division).

21. C. Neal Tate and Torbjorn Vallinder, eds., *The Global Expansion of Judicial Power* (New York: New York University Press, 1995).

22. Morton J. Horwitz, *The Warren Court and the Pursuit of Justice* (New York: Hill and Wang, 1998), p. vii.

23. *Griswold v Connecticut*, 381 US 479 (1965).

24. Robert Dahl, "Decisionmaking in a Democracy: The Supreme Court as a National Policymaker," *Journal of Public Law*, vol. 6 (1957), pp. 279–295.

PRIMARY SOURCE READINGS

ORAL ARGUMENTS, *ROE V. WADE*, 410 U.S. 113 (1973)
Argued: December 13, 1971

Roe v. Wade *is the landmark U.S. Supreme Court decision establishing a limited right to a legal abortion. What follows are excerpts from the oral arguments in that case.*

CHIEF JUSTICE BURGER: We will hear arguments in No. 18, *Roe against Wade*. Mrs. Weddington, you may proceed whenever you're ready.

MRS. SARAH WEDDINGTON, representing Jane Roe:
Mr. Chief Justice, and may it please the court: The instant case is a direct appeal from a decision of the United States District Court for the Northern District of Texas. The court declared the Texas abortion law to be unconstitutional for two reasons: First, that the law was impermissibly based; and, second, that it violated a woman's right to continue or terminate a pregnancy. . . . The Texas law in question permits abortions to be performed only in instances where it is for the purpose of saving the life of the woman. The case originated with the filing of two separate complaints, the first being filed on behalf of Jane Roe, an unmarried pregnant girl; and the second being filed on behalf of Jane and Mary Doe, a married couple. Jane Roe, the pregnant woman, had gone to several Dallas physicians seeking an abortion, but had been refused care because of the Texas law. She filed suit on behalf of herself and all those women who have in the past at that present time or in the future would seek termination of a pregnancy. In her affidavit she did state some of the reasons that she desired an abortion at the time she sought one. But, contrary to the contentions of appellee, she continued to desire the abortion. And it was not only at the time she sought the abortion that her desire was to terminate the pregnancy. . . .

Our Texas statute provides an abortion only when it is for the purpose of saving the life of the woman . . . in Texas, we tell the doctor that unless he can decide whether it's necessary for the purpose of saving her life, and for no other reason, that he is subject to criminal sanctions. I think it's important to note the range of problems that could be presented to a doctor. The court, for example, cited the instance of suicide—if a woman comes in alleging that she will commit suicide. Is it then necessary for him to do or can he do an abortion for the purpose of saving her life? Or, is that a situation where he has to have something more? I think all of those questions cannot be answered, at this point.

This brings up the married couple in our case. The woman in that case had a neurochemical condition. Her doctor had advised her not to get pregnant, and not to take the birth control pills. She was using alternative means of birth control, but she and her husband were fearful that she would become pregnant and that, although the neurochemical condition would impair her health, evidently her doctor did not feel that she would die if she continued the pregnancy. And certainly they were very concerned about the effects of the statute, and her physician seemed uncertain about its implications. The doctors in our State continue to feel that our law is vague. . . . And, instead, 728 women in the first nine months after the decision went to New York for an abortion. Texas women are coming here. It's so often the poor and the disadvantaged in Texas who are not able to escape the effect of the law. . . .

As to . . . there is an allegation that the question is moot since the woman has now had . . . has carried the pregnancy to term. And I think it is important to realize that there are several important aspects in which this case differs from the case that the Court might usually be presented. . . . But in this case, a progressing pregnancy does not suspend itself in order to give the courts time to act. Certainly Jane Roe brought her suit as soon as she knew she was pregnant. As soon as she had sought an abortion, and been denied, she came to Federal court. She came on behalf of a class of women. And I don't think there's any question but that women in Texas continue to desire abortions, and to seek them out outside our State. There was an absence of any other remedy. . . .

In Texas, the woman is the victim. The State cannot deny the effect that this law has on the women of Texas. Certainly there are problems regarding even the use of contraception. Abortion now, for a woman, is safer than childbirth. In the absence of abortions—or legal medically safe abortions—women often resort to the illegal abortions, which certainly carry risks of death, all the side effects such as severe infections, permanent sterility, all the complications that result. And, in fact, if the woman is unable to get either a legal abortion or an illegal abortion in our State, she can do a self-abortion, which is certainly, perhaps, by far the most dangerous. And that is no crime. . . .

Texas, for example, it appears to us, would not allow any relief at all, even in situations where the mother would suffer perhaps serious physical or mental harm. . . . If the pregnancy would result in the birth of a deformed or defective child, she has no relief. Regardless of the circumstances of conception, whether it was because of rape, incest, whether she is extremely immature, she has no relief. I think it's without question that pregnancy to a woman can completely disrupt her life. Whether she's unmarried; whether she's pursuing an education; whether she's pursuing a career; whether she has family problems; all of the problems of personal and family life, for a woman, are bound up in the problem of abortion. For example, in our State there are many schools where a woman is forced to quit if she becomes pregnant. . . . And that's true of some colleges in our State.

In the matter of employment, she often is forced to quit at an early point in her pregnancy. She has no provision for maternity leave. She cannot get unemployment compensation under our laws, because the laws hold that she is not eligible for employment, being pregnant, and therefore is eligible for no unemployment compensation. At the same time, she can get no welfare to help her at a time when she has no unemployment compensation and she's not eligible for any help in getting a job to provide for herself. There is no duty for employers to rehire women if they must drop out to carry a pregnancy to term. And, of course, this is especially hard on the many women in Texas who are heads of their own households and must provide for their already existing children.

And, obviously, the responsibility of raising a child is a most serious one, and at times an emotional investment that must be made, cannot be denied. So, a pregnancy to a woman is perhaps one of the most determinative aspects of her life. It disrupts her body. It disrupts her education. It disrupts her employment. And it often disrupts her entire family life. And we feel that, because of the impact on the woman, this certainly—in as far as there are any rights which are fundamental—is a matter which is of such fundamental and basic concern to the woman involved that she should be allowed to make the choice as to whether to continue or to terminate her pregnancy. . . .

JUSTICE STEWART: Mrs. Weddington, so far on the merits, you've told us about the important impact of this law, and you made a very eloquent policy argument against it. And I trust you are going to get to what provisions of the Constitution you rely on. Sometimes the Court . . . we would like to, sometimes but we cannot here be involved simply with matters of policy, as you know.

MRS. WEDDINGTON: Your Honors, in the lower court, as I'm sure you're aware, the court held that the right to determine whether or not to continue a pregnancy rested upon the Ninth Amendment—which, of course, reserves those rights not specifically enumerated to the Government, to the people. I think it is important to note . . . that at the time the Constitution was adopted there was no common law prohibition against abortions; that they were available to the women of this country. . . . I do feel that it is—that the Ninth Amendment is an appropriate place for the freedom to rest. I think the Fourteenth Amendment is equally an appropriate place, under the rights of persons to life, liberty, and the pursuit of happiness. I think that in as far as "liberty" is meaningful, that liberty to these women would mean liberty from being forced to continue the unwanted pregnancy. . . .

I think, inasfar as the Court has said that there is a penumbra that exists to encompass the entire purpose of the Constitution, that I think one of the purposes of the Constitution was to guarantee to the individual the right to determine the course of their own lives. Insofar as there was, perhaps, no compelling state interest—and we allege there is none in this case—that, there again, that the right fits within the framework of the previous decisions of this Court.

JUSTICE STEWART: What is the asserted State interest? Is there any legislative history on this statute?

MRS. WEDDINGTON: No, sir, Your Honor. No, sir, there is not. The only legislative history, of course, is that which is found in other states—which has been pointed out to the Court before—and, as Professor Means points out again, that these statutes were adopted for the health of the mother. Certainly, the Texas courts have referred to the woman as being the victim, and they have never referred to anyone else as being the victim. Concepts have certainly changed. I think it's important to realize that in Texas self-abortion is no crime. The woman is guilty of no crime, even though she seeks out the doctor; even though she consents; even though she participates; even though she pays for the procedure. She, again, is guilty of no crime whatsoever.

It's also interesting that in our statutes, the penalty for the offense of abortion depends on whether or not the consent of the woman was obtained prior to the procedure. It's double if you don't get her consent. . . . Obviously, in our State, the offense is not murder. It is an abortion, which carries a significantly lesser offense. There is no requirement of—even though the State, in its brief, points out the development of the fetus in an eight-week period, the same State, does not require any death certificate, or any formalities of birth. . . .

JUSTICE WHITE: What's your constitutional position there? . . .

MRS. WEDDINGTON: It is our position that the freedom involved is that of a woman to determine whether or not to continue a pregnancy. Obviously I have a much more difficult time saying that the State has no interest in late pregnancy.

JUSTICE WHITE: Why? Why is that?

MRS. WEDDINGTON: I think that's more the emotional response to a late pregnancy, rather than it is any constitutional. . . .

JUSTICE WHITE: Emotional response by whom?

MRS. WEDDINGTON: I guess by persons considering the issue outside the legal context. I think, as far as the State . . .

JUSTICE WHITE: Well, do you or don't you say that the constitutional—

MRS. WEDDINGTON: I would say the constitutional . . .

JUSTICE WHITE: right you insist on reaches up to the time of birth, or—

MRS. WEDDINGTON: The Constitution, as I read it . . . attaches protection to the person at the time of birth. Those persons born are citizens. The enumeration clause, we count those people who are born. The Constitution, as I see it, gives protection to people after birth.

JAY FLOYD, ESQ., Assistant Attorney General of Texas, represented Henry Wade and the State of Texas:
      Mr. Chief Justice, may it please the Court: Before I proceed to the original issue in this case. . . . I would like to bring to the Court's attention some grave matters concerning what has been referred to as the standing of the parties. The couple involved: they were a married couple—childless married couple. The only matter—evidence, or whatever—in the record concerning their contentions is contained in their first amended original petition. That is, that the woman would have difficulty if she became pregnant in carrying a child to childbirth. Further, that they were unprepared for parenthood. We submit to the Court that their cause of action is strictly based upon conjecture. Will they continue the marriage? Will her health improve? Will they then be, at some time in the future, prepared or unprepared for parenthood? There is no fear of prosecution by Mary Doe. . . . We feel that the lower court properly denied them standing. As to the unmarried pregnant female, a unique situation arises in: Is her action now moot? Of course if moot, there is no case or controversy. . . .

JUSTICE STEWART: How do you suggest, if you're right, how do you . . . what procedure would you suggest for any pregnant female in the State of Texas ever to get any judicial consideration of this constitutional claim?

MR. FLOYD: Your Honor, let me answer your question with a statement, if I may. I do not believe it can be done. There are situations in which, of course as the Court knows, no remedy is provided. Now I think she makes her choice prior to the time she becomes pregnant. That is the time of the choice. It's like, more or less, the first three or four years of our life we don't remember anything. But, once a child is born, a woman no longer has a choice, and I think pregnancy then terminates that choice. . . .

JUSTICE MARSHALL: What is Texas' interest? What is Texas' interest in the statute?

MR. FLOYD: Mr. Justice . . . The State—the State Court, Court of Criminal Appeals, held that the State had a compelling interest because of the protection of fetal life—of fetal life protection. They recognized the humanness of the embryo, or the fetus, and they said we have an interest in protecting fetal life. Whether or not that was the original intent of the statute, I have no idea.

JUSTICE STEWART: Yet, Texas does not attempt to punish a woman who herself performs an abortion on herself.

MR. FLOYD: That is correct, Your Honor. And the matter has been brought to my attention: Why not punish for murder, since you are destroying what you—or what has been said to be a human being? I don't know, except that I will say this. As medical science progresses, maybe the law will progress along with it. Maybe at one time it could be possible, I suppose, statutes could be passed. Whether or not that would be constitutional or not, I don't know.

JUSTICE STEWART: But we're dealing with the statute as it is. There's no state, is there, that equates abortion with murder? Or is there?

MR. FLOYD: There is none, Your Honor, except one of our statutes that if the mother dies, that the doctor shall be guilty of murder. . . .

JUSTICE MARSHALL: The Texas statute covers the entire period of pregnancy?

MR. FLOYD: Yes, it does, Mr. Justice. Yes. . . .

JUSTICE STEWART: You're saying, in answer to my brother Marshall's question—what is the interest of the State in this litigation; or, even, what is its purpose, its societal purpose—your answer was . . . the protection of fetal life? And I think you also said that that was not, perhaps, its original purpose.

MR. FLOYD: Well, I'm not sure of that. I . . .

JUSTICE STEWART: Well, it may be rather important. In a constitutional case of this kind, it becomes quite vital, sometimes, to rather precisely identify what the asserted interest of the state is.

MR. FLOYD: I think that original purpose, Mr. Justice, and the present prevailing purpose, may be the same in this respect. There have been statistics furnished to this Court in various briefs from various groups, and from medical societies of different groups of physicians and gynecologists, or whatever it may be. These statistics have not shown me, for instance—for example, that abortion is safer than normal childbirth. They have not shown me that there are not emotional problems that are very important, resulting from an abortion. The protection of the mother, at one time, may still be the primary—but the policy considerations, Mr. Justice, would seem to me to be for the State legislature to make a decision.

JUSTICE STEWART: Certainly that's true. Policy questions are for legislative and executive bodies, both in the State and Federal Governments. But we have here a constitutional question. And, in deciding it, it's important to know what the asserted interest of the State is in the enactment of this legislation.

MR. FLOYD: I am . . . and this is just from my—l speak personally, if I may, I would think that even when this statute was first passed, there was some concern for the unborn fetus.

JUSTICE STEWART: When was it enacted?

MR. FLOYD: 1859 was the original statute. This, I believe, was around 1900, 1907. . . .

JUSTICE STEWART: Before that there were no criminal abortion laws in Texas?

MR. FLOYD: As far as I know there were not, no. . . .

JUSTICE MARSHALL: You make no distinctions whether there's life there or not?

MR. FLOYD: We say there is life from the moment of impregnation.

JUSTICE MARSHALL: And do you have any scientific data to support that?

MR. FLOYD: Well we begin, Mr. Justice, in our brief, with the—the development of the human embryo, carrying it through the development of the fetus from about seven to nine days after conception.

JUSTICE MARSHALL: Well, what about six days?

MR. FLOYD: We don't know.

JUSTICE MARSHALL: But the statute goes all the way back to one hour?

MR. FLOYD: I don't . . . Mr. Justice, there are unanswerable questions in this field. . . . When does the soul come into the unborn—if a person believes in a soul—I don't know. I assume the appellants now are operating under the Ninth Amendment rights. There are allegations of First Amendment rights being violated. However, I feel there is no merit—this statute does not establish any religion; nor does it prohibit anyone from practicing of any part of any religious group. I see no merit in their contentions that it could possibly be under freedom of speech or press. . . . The other constitutional rights that the appellant speaks of, I think, are expressed in two manners: The individual, or marital right of privacy; and, secondly—or . . . or the right to choose whether or not to abort a child. Now, if the . . . those are out of the case, the marital privacy is out of the case. But be that as it may, neither individual nor marital privacy has been held to be absolute. We have legal search and seizure. We have the possession of illegal drugs; the practice of polygamy, and other matters. A parent, I do not believe or parents, cannot refuse to give their child some form of education. As far as the freedom over one's body is concerned, this is not absolute—the use of illicit drugs; the indecent exposure legislation; and, as Mr. Goldberg stated in the Griswold case, that adultery and fornication are constitutional beyond doubt.

JUSTICE STEWART: "Are constitutional"? Or do you mean laws against them are constitutional?

MR. FLOYD: The laws against them are constitutional. Now . . . there is nothing in the United States Constitution concerning birth, contraception, or abortion. Now, the appellee does not disagree with the appellants' statement that a woman has a choice. But, as we have previously mentioned, we feel that this choice is left up to the woman prior to the time she becomes pregnant. . . .

JUSTICE STEWART: Texas doesn't grant any exemption in the case of a rape, where the woman's pregnancy has resulted from rape—either statutory or otherwise—does it?

MR. FLOYD: There is nothing in our statute about that. Now, the procedure . . .

JUSTICE STEWART: And such a woman wouldn't have had a choice, would she?

MR. FLOYD: The procedure—and now I'm telling the Court something that's outside the record—as I understand, the procedure when a woman is brought in after a rape, is to try to stop whatever has occurred, immediately, by the proper procedure in the hospital. Immediately she's taken there, if she reports it immediately. But, no, there is nothing in the statute. Now as I previously informed the Court, the statistics—or the people who prepare the statistics, and the different statistics are . . . are not in conformity in connection with the medical aspects of abortion; that is, whether or not it's safer. There are some statistics that say it is and statistics that say it's not. It has been provided to this Court, the common law and the legislative history of abortion; and that the morality of abortion has been injected in various cases by various groups. We think these matters are matters of policy which can be properly addressed by the State legislature. We think that the consideration should be given to the unborn, and in some instances, a consideration should be given for the father, if he would be objective to abortion. . . .

CHIEF JUSTICE BURGER: Thank you. Thank you, Mrs. Weddington. Thank you, Mr. Floyd. The case is submitted.

CHALLENGES FOR AMERICAN DEMOCRACY

WHAT WOULD YOU DO?
FUNDING THE PUBLIC SCHOOLS
THE FLAG AND THE CONSTITUTION
DISPOSING OF LOW-LEVEL RADIOACTIVE WASTE
UNIVERSITY FUNDING FOR STUDENT GROUPS
WELFARE
PROVIDING HEALTH CARE TO ALL
REGULATING DIETARY SUPPLEMENTS
THE PURPOSE OF GOVERNMENT

THREE QUESTIONS FOR THE NEW CENTURY
WHAT KIND OF SOCIETY?
WHO HAS POWER?
THE ROLE OF THE UNITED STATES IN THE WORLD

THE HEALTH OF DEMOCRACY
A DECLINE IN SOCIAL CAPITAL?

OBJECTIVES

❑   To reexamine the themes of conflict and compromise

❑   To revisit some of the cases discussed in the previous chapters and ask:
What would you do? The answers to this question address the issue of the
purpose of government.

❑   To pose three questions confronting the nation as it enters the new century:
What is America? Who has power? What is the role of the United States in
the world?

❑   To discuss current concerns about the vitality of American democracy,
particularly the role of the citizen in participating in democratic processes

Citizen involvement at work. Members of a community group work on a plan for policing their neighborhood. Effective government involves more than elected officials, judges, and bureaucrats. It requires the active involvement of citizens at the grassroots level.

In this textbook we have examined conflict and compromise in American politics. We have seen that conflict is normal in any society. And, as James Madison stressed in *Federalist* No. 10, it is inevitable in a society with diverse interests and that guarantees freedom of speech, assembly, and the press.[1] So it is no surprise that those who study American politics usually begin by considering the nature of conflict in the political system and then proceed to try to understand how that system deals with conflict.

We also defined "politics" as the process of trying to transform conflict into compromise. The American political system—or any political system, for that matter—is a framework of processes and institutions designed to make living in a society possible. Of course, these processes and institutions don't always work, and we learn a great deal about the capacity of political processes and government institutions when conflicts fester for a long time or when compromises are not reached. But we should not forget that the political system *does* handle most conflicts in some way, even if the resolution settles only part of the conflict because trying to resolve the whole problem is too difficult.

We should not ignore the importance of compromise, even if it seems inadequate or disappointingly short of some ideal. Sometimes a compromise is a short-term step that keeps the discussion going, making possible further progress toward a greater, if more elusive goal. As we saw in the case of AmeriCorps in chapter 8, President Clinton did not get everything he wanted, but he got the program going. AmeriCorps survived and, at this writing six years after its inception, has even grown as many of its former critics dropped their opposition after observing its successes.[2]

To some readers, our focus on compromise might not sound very inspirational. After all, shouldn't politics be guided by universal goals such as equality, liberty, and justice? Of course it should. Otherwise we risk reducing politics to little more than squabbles between selfish individuals for their own material gain. As we saw in chapter 4, without a large dose of idealism, the extension of civil rights to minorities, women, and other previously excluded groups might never have happened. In fact, a lot of politics consists of striving to achieve ideals. As we discussed in chapter 2, in framing the U.S. Constitution the challenge was to give meaning to core beliefs of liberty, representative government, and individualism. The framers didn't necessarily succeed, but they tried. In the same way, we should remember that ideals such as justice and liberty are abstractions that we may never attain completely. As the framers saw, the important point is to keep trying, to keep moving toward those goals. Politics is the process by which we try to do so.

In this chapter we reassess the textbook's theme. We revisit some of the cases introduced in the previous chapters and ask you to think about what you would do to resolve them. We then look at three major questions facing Americans at the beginning of a new century. Finally, we pose the question: What is the role of the citizen in all this? That is, what role should *you* play in the American political system?

WHAT WOULD YOU DO?

We began each chapter with a case that involved some kind of conflict. In some cases the conflict was resolved, in others it was not. In this section we revisit a few of those conflicts, provide an update, and ask a question: What would *you* do?

FUNDING THE PUBLIC SCHOOLS

According to a survey, 86 percent of the students who entered college in September, 1998, had attended a public high school.[3] That includes most readers of this textbook. This fact alone underscores the importance of a high-quality public education. It is also a key to understanding the conflicts over how to pay for public schools.

As of April 1, 1999, the state of New Hampshire still had not figured out how to finance its public schools. As we saw in chapter 1, this problem arose when the state's supreme court ruled that New Hampshire's reliance on local property taxes to finance public education prevented poorer school districts from providing their children with the "adequate" level of education guaranteed by the state constitution. The court ordered the state to resolve the problem by April 1, 1999; after that date, school districts could no longer use local property taxes to pay for their operations.

The governor and state legislators in New Hampshire struggled over how to resolve this problem. A few conservatives wanted to remove the state constitution's guarantee of support for public education, making it entirely a local concern, but this proposal won few supporters. Many liberals advocated that the state replace the local property tax with statewide income tax, which they argued would be fairer to the less affluent. But New Hampshire has never had a state income tax, and its residents are famous for demanding that elected officials take "the pledge" never to seek one. Neither does the state have a statewide sales tax, because it wishes to attract shoppers from neighboring states. If the state will not or cannot rely on a broad income or sales tax to generate the funds necessary to pay for its public schools, how will it obtain the needed funds?

In late April, 1999, the Democratic governor and Republican state legislature came up with a compromise: a statewide property tax, combined with increases in cigarette and business profits taxes. Advocates of the compromise argued that the new system would reduce the tax burden on residents in less-affluent communities, but critics argued that it unfairly shifted the burden to residents in more-affluent communities. Others criticized keeping any type of property tax as the basis for funding, saying that income taxes were fairer to homeowners with lower incomes. However, elected officials from both parties defended the compromise as the best available solution for the time being. After all, the deadline had passed, and they had to do something.[4]

New Hampshire's experience is not unique, and again raises the question, How *should* we fund our schools? Should we leave it entirely up to each town, or should the state try to ensure relatively equal support for all schools? Or should this issue be dealt with by the federal government so that all Americans have access to high-quality public education?

Suppose that you are the governor of your state. Education is an important issue to your voters, and you were elected specifically to solve the problem. If you push for a statewide income or sales tax, you might lose the next election, but if you fail to solve the problem the schools might have to cut back considerably on programs for lack of funds. What would you do?

THE FLAG AND THE CONSTITUTION

In chapter 2 we examined the conflict over desecration of the American flag. In June, 1999, the U.S. House of Representatives once again passed a constitutional amendment by the required two-thirds vote to enable Congress to enact laws banning physical desecration of the flag. The matter is now before the Senate, where passage is uncertain. Two years earlier, the House had voted to approve such an amendment, but the measure did not pass in the Senate.

So the debate goes on. Many Americans want to make it a federal crime to burn or otherwise deface an American flag. Many others defend the right to burn or deface a flag, claiming that such an act is protected by the First Amendment guarantee of freedom of expression. For one side, the issue is patriotism; for the other side, it is individual freedom. Even those who support such an amendment know that writing a flag desecration law will be difficult. After all, the flag is used in all kinds of ways, from advertising to fashion. If burning a flag is wrong, is using it to sell automobiles right? What constitutes improper use of the flag?

Suppose that you are a new member of the House of Representatives, and the first vote you will cast is on a constitutional amendment to ban flag desecration. You aren't sure about the wisdom or practicality of this action. On the other hand, the Veterans of Foreign Wars in your district want you to support the amendment, and they are very vocal about the issue. The rest of your constituents don't seem very interested in the dispute, but you worry that you won't be able to defend your vote when you stand for reelection in two years. You could go along with the amendment and hope that it doesn't go very far, but you don't want to be cynical about the issue. What would you do?

DISPOSING OF LOW-LEVEL RADIOACTIVE WASTE

In chapter 3 we discussed the problem of low-level radioactive waste disposal. This isn't a sexy issue, to be sure, but it is an important one. As we explained, Congress passed a law enabling groups of states to create regional waste disposal programs, but few of the identified disposal sites had been constructed because of community fears about the possible environmental and health effects.

This resistance typifies what some call the NIMBY (Not In My Back Yard) Syndrome. Herein lies the dilemma: How can democratic government deal effectively with tough choices such as where to construct waste disposal sites, prisons, or residences for the mentally ill without undermining the rights of people living close to those facilities? After all, these facilities have to be located *somewhere*.

To political scientist Barry Rabe, it is wrong to blame any community for resisting such facilities. He says that local residents are reacting rationally to what they see as an unfair and often antidemocratic imposition of the larger society's unwanted burdens on their shoulders. Residents also might mistrust policymakers, because in the past state and federal governments have often placed unwanted facilities in poor or rural areas whose residents lacked the political influence to resist them. With this history in mind, Rabe argues that policymakers must involve citizens at earlier stages of the decisionmaking process. He concludes that those who govern must not only "respect and protect the political choices of their citizens but also must encourage and facilitate their participation in every dimension of the siting process and ultimate facility operation, thereby providing constant reassurance against the threat of exploitation."[5] Those who are most affected by the facility must have a greater say in what happens to them and their neighborhoods.

Suppose that your state is part of a multistate compact that proposes to construct a low-level radioactive waste disposal facility at the site of an empty factory just outside your town. Experts have testified that these materials shouldn't cause health or environmental problems if they are disposed of properly, but you aren't sure they are right. On the other hand, your town lost a lot of jobs when the old factory closed, and the new facility will employ at least 200 people. Those jobs will be good for the town's tax base and its schools, and they will keep a lot of your friends from moving away. But you are also concerned about the potential effects of this waste disposal site on your property and your childrens' health.

You and your neighbors are part of a citizens group that can have a lot of influence over whether this facility comes to your town. You want to do what is best for your family, your neighbors, and your friends. What would you do?

UNIVERSITY FUNDING FOR STUDENT GROUPS

As we saw in chapter 4, the Supreme Court tried to reconcile conflicting rights in the case of the Christian student group seeking funding from the University of Virginia. But its decision did not resolve a larger issue: whether students could block the use of their activity fees for groups or purposes that they opposed.

On March 30, 1999, the U.S. Supreme Court agreed to decide a case dealing with this issue. Three University of Wisconsin law students had sued the university to

Making tough decisions. Residents observe as members of a city council try to work out a solution to a pressing community need. In a democracy, the dilemma is how to resolve difficult common problems without imposing unfair burdens on any one group.

keep it from using any part of their student activity fees for groups whose orientations or views they opposed, in this case a gay and lesbian group, the campus women's center, an AIDS support network, and a group that opposed the death penalty. The U.S. Court of Appeals for the Seventh Circuit ruled in the students' favor, arguing that forcing public university students to subsidize groups whose views they oppose violates their First Amendment right to "freedom of belief." The university appealed, arguing that funding an array of groups assures a diversity of views, especially minority or unpopular ones, which, in turn, enhances students' educational experience.[6]

At the same time, the U.S. Court of Appeals for the Ninth Circuit ruled that the University of Oregon *could* use student activity fees to support the Oregon Student Public Interest Research Group, which advocates liberal views on environmental, consumer protection, and other policy issues. In this case, the court ruled, student activity funds were being used for educational purposes, because the organization used other funds to support more openly political activities such as lobbying state legislators.[7]

You pay a student activity fee. Some of that money goes into a fund that is used to support all types of student groups, some of which you might not support if given a choice. But the same can be said for other students whose fees pay for a group that you belong to. Without these funds, your group and many other student groups might not be able to survive, as most groups have difficulty getting enough students to pay dues and, except for a few politically connected organizations, it is difficult to generate support from sources outside the university.

The questions are many: Should students be able to prevent their fees from being used to support groups that they oppose? Who should decide which groups receive support? Should a college use student activity funds to support student groups at all? Is doing so essential to a well-rounded educational experience?

Suppose that you are on the student activities board and your task is to allocate funds to student groups. A group of students demands that your board deny funding for a controversial group, but the group insists that it has a right to the money. What would you do?

WELFARE

In chapter 5 we examined the politics behind the overhaul of the nation's welfare system. In particular, we saw that Congress replaced the federal Aid to Families with Dependent Children program (AFDC) with lump-sum grants to the states. The states would have a great deal of freedom to decide who was eligible for aid and for how long, what kinds of benefits they would receive, and in some cases, what jobs they would have to perform in return for the support.

The aim of welfare reform was to get people off welfare and into the labor force. Has it been achieved? As Table 12.1 shows, it is clear that welfare caseloads have dropped sharply. Some welfare recipients were dropped from the rolls as a result of rigid time limits or because they knew that the cutoff date was approaching. Some states have been aggressive in cutting welfare rolls, whereas others have been more flexible in dealing with welfare recipients, particularly those who have with disabilities or lack of skills such as the ability to read.[8]

It is less clear what has happened to those who are no longer on the rolls. Many, if not a majority, apparently found jobs. So in that sense welfare reform worked. Others walked away because they figured that the new rules weren't worth the benefits, or they were single mothers who decided that they would rather stay home and raise their children than place them in day care. They will rely on support from their families or from private charities. They left the rolls, but in some respect they made their own choices.

Yet others may have been scared away because they lack the skills necessary to deal with the new rules or because they suffer from emotional or mental disabilities that make them anxious about the new system. They may not function well in the highly competitive American society. They are the least likely to be able to find or hold a job, and they are the most likely to end up in homeless shelters, on the streets, in prison, or public hospitals, thereby straining the budgets of other government-sponsored programs.

Thus the dilemma: To what extent should a society care for its poorest or least-equipped citizens? The American political culture stresses individual moral strength and hard work as the keys to success, with the parallel attitude that failure is also personal. But even a wealthy society has its poor and those who seem unable to make it for one reason or another.

Suppose that you are a policy expert in the federal Department of Health and Human Services and the president has instructed your office to recommend changes in the nation's welfare policies. You want to encourage people to work, but you also recognize that not everyone will be able to make enough money to cover food, rent, clothes, and transportation, much less health care. You want single mothers to be able to take care of their children, but you don't want to encourage long periods of dependence on public support. You also don't want to be cruel, and you don't want innocent people to fall through the cracks. What would you do?

PROVIDING HEALTH CARE TO ALL

In chapter 7 we looked at President Clinton's inability to win congressional support for his comprehensive plan to reform the nation's health care system. In 1993, when

TABLE 12.1.   PERCENTAGE CHANGE IN WELFARE CASELOADS
SINCE ENACTMENT OF THE 1996 FEDERAL WELFARE
REFORM LAW

Idaho	−85	New Hampshire	−37
Wyoming	−84	North Dakota	−37
Wisconsin	−77	Kentucky	−35
Mississippi	−64	Pennsylvania	−35
West Virginia	−61	New Jersey	−34
Florida	−54	Montana	−33
South Carolina	−54	Nevada	−32
Colorado	−52	Hawaii	−31
Alabama	−48	Washington	−31
Georgia	−48	Illinois	−30
Kansas	−48	Maine	−30
Louisiana	−47	Utah	−28
Texas	−47	Iowa	−27
Arkansas	−44	California	−26
Maryland	−44	Connecticut	−26
Oregon	−44	Massachusetts	−26
South Dakota	−43	New York	−25
Ohio	−42	Vermont	−23
Tennessee	−42	Washington, D.C.	−22
Arizona	−41	New Mexico	−22
Delaware	−41	Alaska	−21
Oklahoma	−40	Indiana	−18
Michigan	−39	Minnesota	−17
North Carolina	−39	Nebraska	−6
Virginia	−38	Rhode Island	−4
Missouri	−37		

Source: Indicators of Welfare Dependence, Annual Report to Congress, U.S. Department of Health and Human Services, October 1998, p. A19.

Clinton took office, approximately 37 million nonelderly Americans, or about 17 percent of the entire population, lacked health insurance. Most of the uninsured were working people.[9] The elderly had health insurance through Medicare; the poor were covered under Medicaid.

Six years later more than 43 million nonelderly Americans, or 18 percent of the population, were without health insurance. As before, most of the uninsured work, but about half of them work for small companies that do not offer health care benefits.[10] What is more, the number of the uninsured is expected to rise, including people who have been forced off the welfare rolls, often into jobs with no health care benefits. Furthermore, most of the uninsured are adults, because in 1997 Clinton was able to persuade Congress to enact legislation that provides health insurance for children. So in some respects the nation was worse off in 1999 than in 1993.

Even for those with health insurance, there are still two issues that have not been resolved: choice and cost. Today more Americans belong to "managed care" systems such as health maintenance organizations, which try to control costs by placing limits on patients' ability to choose their doctors and on the range of procedures covered. Most Americans would like greater choice, especially if they develop chronic illnesses or need to undergo specialized procedures, but they usually cannot afford the extra costs of going to a specialist "outside the plan." At the same time, the health care industry is going through massive changes as hospitals and health maintenance organizations try to control costs through mergers and reductions in staffs. This also tends to reduce the choices available to patients.

The next president probably will have to tackle the problems of the nation's health care system that Clinton and Congress could not resolve. The issues remain the same: Should the United States ensure that all citizens have access to affordable health care? If so, what role should government play in fulfilling this goal?

Suppose that you have just been elected president. What would you do?

REGULATING DIETARY SUPPLEMENTS

As we saw in chapter 10, in the early 1990s the Food and Drug Administration tried to extend its regulatory authority to cover so-called "dietary supplements." However, in 1994 Congress passed the Dietary Supplement and Health Education Act, which prohibited the FDA from putting dietary supplements in the same category as prescription drugs. Thus, the FDA had limited authority to compel producers of dietary supplements to prove the effectiveness of their products or even to guarantee their safety.

In early 1999 the FDA asked manufacturers to cease selling dietary supplements containing the chemical gamma butyrolactone, or GBL. These products, sold under such names as Blue Nitro and RemForce, were promoted as muscle builders, sexual performance enhancers, and stress reducers.[11] However, the FDA said that products containing GBL have caused illness in scores of people and led to at least one death. GBL, the FDA warned consumers, is a powerful chemical that affects the central nervous system in ways that can lead to vomiting, seizures, and even unconsciousness. Moreover, GBL has been used in so-called "date-rape" drugs—with which victims are incapacitated, and then assaulted—and is even used in a commercial floor stripper.

The problem for the FDA was that it could regulate GBL if it was being sold in prescription drugs but, because of the 1994 law, it had little authority when the chemical was used in dietary supplements. The agency could not force the companies involved to remove their products or stop making them, nor could it regulate manufacturers' claims about the effectiveness or safety of their products. What is more, the FDA is now being forced to deal with the rapid increase in sales of supplements over the Internet, a medium that is almost entirely unregulated.

Consumers want to be able to buy new products, but they also want someone to guarantee the safety and effectiveness of those products. They don't want government to tell them what they can and cannot eat, drink, or put into their bodies, but they also want to keep harmful products off the market. They don't want "too much" government, but they want enough to keep them safe. Many companies that make and sell these products are leery of FDA oversight, but they also are worried that unscrupulous manufacturers that sell dangerous or ineffective products might give their industry a bad name and drive away customers.

Suppose that you are a member of a special commission created by the president and Congress to figure out how to deal with this problem. You know that it would be expensive to try to test every single product on the market, and you also know that it would be almost impossible to monitor sales. But people are getting sick, some have died, and everyone wants some kind of protection against dangerous or fraudulent products. What would you do?

THE PURPOSE OF GOVERNMENT

Go down the list of cases just discussed and think about your answers. You will probably see some patterns. Now try to generalize from your responses: In which situations do you believe government should play an active role, and in which situations do you believe government should do little or nothing? Where do you stand on cases (such as flag desecration or funding student groups) that might require a balance between the rights and liberties of some individuals and those of others? To what degree should government ensure health care for all or an adequate level of economic support for the poor? How much should government regulate consumer products such as dietary supplements? What role should citizens play in deciding how to distribute burdens such as low-level radioactive waste? How should government finance public education, and who decides how this money should be spent?

Don't be surprised if you haven't figured out answers to all of these problems. There aren't any easy answers. And don't be concerned if your views on some issues contradict your views on others, or conflict with your self-image as a liberal or a conservative. As we saw in chapter 5, that's a normal part of the process of political socialization. But think about your answers: They reflect your overall views on the proper role of government. And your views, along with those of your fellow students and citizens, will shape politics in the United States for generations to come.

THREE QUESTIONS FOR THE NEW CENTURY

The cases discussed in the previous section are important, but they pale in significance next to the three questions we examine in this section. The answers to these questions will shape the future of the nation and its system of government.

▶ What kind of society will we have?

▶ Who has power?

▶ What is the proper role of the United States in the world?

The first two questions have been debated throughout the nation's history. They were debated in the colonies before the War of Independence and by the framers of the Constitution in 1787. They were at the heart of the divisions that led to the Civil War, and they defined what it meant to be a liberal or a conservative. The last question is the newest: It didn't become a major issue until the 20th century, but the answer to it may have a major impact on the answers to the other two questions.

WHAT KIND OF SOCIETY?

The United States always has been a nation of immigrants, and each major wave of newcomers has changed the society in important ways. Today is no different. As we saw in chapter 1, since 1981, the nation has witnessed a wave of immigration unlike any since the beginning of the 20th century. A century ago, most of the newcomers were Europeans, particularly central and eastern Europeans, Russians, and Italians.[12] Today, immigrants are far more likely to hail from Latin America and Asia. And as before, these new waves of immigrants are changing American society, influencing its cuisine, language, religion, and customs.

Immigration is an ongoing dilemma for Americans, both for native-born citizens and for those newly arrived. On one hand, the United States has always been relatively open to newcomers. They provide inexpensive labor, especially in occupations that most native-born citizens avoid, and our history as an immigrant society makes it hard for us to close the door. On the other hand, those who are already citizens worry, even if only subconsciously, that each new wave of immigration might change the society in unexpected and possibly undesirable ways.

At the heart of this debate is the question, What does it mean to be an American? On one side of the debate are scholars such as Samuel Huntington. Huntington points out that previous waves of immigrants were absorbed into the prevailing European-dominated culture and adhered to the norms of the American political culture (discussed in chapter 1). As a result, he concludes, the United States has been able to avoid the ethnic and cultural conflicts that have torn apart nations such as Rwanda, Indonesia, and Yugoslavia, among others. But will non-Western immigrants also be assimilated? Or will the United States be plagued by the kinds of ethnic and cultural wars that afflict other countries? As Huntington puts it, "Will the de-Westernization of the United States, if it occurs, also mean its de-Americanization?"[13]

Huntington's view is shared by scholars who wonder whether the nation's core political beliefs will withstand the potent forces of race, ethnicity, culture, religion, and language that these new waves of immigrants bring with them. In particular, they worry that these newer immigrants will be less willing to become "American"—that they will be less willing than were earlier waves of Irish, Italian, Greek, or Polish immigrants to assimilate themselves into the society by learning English, becoming citizens, and taking part in democratic politics.[14]

Other observers are more optimistic about the newcomers and about the society's ability to adapt to new cultures. After all, they say, "American culture" has always been more diverse and more fluid than the society portrayed by social critics such as Huntington. Haven't generations of immigrants confronted the same con-

What kind of America? Faced with the ethnic, nationalist, and religious conflicts in other lands, many Americans worry about the effects of immigration on their own nation's political culture and institutions. Are these valid concerns, or are they simply newer variations on an old theme?

cerns? Didn't earlier generations worry about the effects on American culture of too many Italians or Poles, or too many Catholics? Worries about the impact of immigrants are nothing new. More important is the continued force of the ideals that motivate the newcomers. The desire to make a better life matters, as it always has. But so do the ideals that have always inspired those who came to these shores: life, liberty, and the pursuit of happiness.

Still, Huntington's argument is not easy to dismiss. In many ways, the picture of contemporary immigration is more complicated than the "huddled masses" portrayed in Emma Lazarus's poem (see chapter 1). Many contemporary immigrants are educated and highly skilled. For example, the U.S. government allows the nation's high technology companies to recruit foreign software engineers because of a shortage of Americans in these professions. As a result, many are content to retain their nationality because they don't need to become American citizens to enjoy economic self-sufficiency. For others, proximity to Mexico and other Latin American countries makes it easier to keep alive the dream of returning home, even if most do not. Indeed, unlike the days when immigration meant long and probably one-way sea voyages, air travel makes it easier for all contemporary immigrants to travel to and from their homelands. Given that mobility, committing one's loyalties to a single nation becomes all the more difficult.[15]

The impacts of these immigrants are not yet well understood. Even those analysts who do not share Huntington's philosophical views agree that the issue is an important one. As political scientists Louis DeSipio and Rodolfo O. de la Garza state in their study of immigration, "The success or failure of the political and social incorporation of today's immigrants depends in part on increased national attention not just to whom the United States admits but also to what the country offers these immigrants once they are here."[15]

Just what kind of America this will be is not yet clear.

WHO HAS POWER?

Inscribed on one wall of the Lincoln Memorial in Washington, D.C., is Lincoln's Gettysburg Address, which ends with these words, "that government of the people, by the people, for the people, shall not perish from the earth."

Government of the people, by the people, for the people. Isn't this the essence of democracy? Yet we have seen throughout this book that it isn't that simple. For one thing, the people do not govern directly. Instead, they elect others to represent them. As we saw in chapter 6, there is often a gap between what the people want and what government does: Many people aren't paying attention to issues; they aren't always clear about what they want; many do not vote; and elections sometimes send muddled messages to winners and losers alike. We also know that campaign spending affects election outcomes—even in referenda, where the link between voter preferences and policy outcomes is supposed to be clearest. It is often very unclear how much elections really matter and whose values they really reflect.

The question of power goes beyond elections, of course. Corporations have tremendous power, whether through their ability to spend money on election campaigns or because they employ thousands of people. Interest groups such as the National Rifle Association and the American Association of Retired Persons also can shape public policy, particularly on issues about which the general public isn't interested or well informed. Personal wealth makes a difference, too: Microsoft's Bill Gates probably has a lot more power than you do. Those who control mass media outlets, such as Fox Television's Rupert Murdoch or CNN's Ted Turner, have a tremendous capacity to shape public debate on issues. Those who occupy important positions in the bureaucracy, such as Alan Greenspan, chairman of the Federal Reserve Board, or who are members of the judicial system, such as Attorney General Janet Reno or the justices of the Supreme Court, can make decisions without widespread public input.

In short, the central problem of democratic government still holds: How much power do the people have? This wasn't an easy question back when Americans worked on farms and walked to the town square to debate politics and vote in local elections. The question is even more difficult in a world of increasing technological complexity and rapid economic and social change, one in which so much of daily life is influenced by huge corporations and massive media conglomerates, in which some problems are so technologically complex that average people feel inadequate to make decisions, and in which events in distant countries can have almost immediate impacts at home.[16]

Certainly, many citizens vote, and many participate in political activities (see Box 12.1). Those who govern often do care about public opinion, particularly on important issues. But we know that this connection isn't perfect, and in many situations the

BOX 12.1. PROJECT VOTE SMART

It didn't necessarily bother Richard Kimball that he lost his race to be elected to the U.S. Senate from Arizona. After all, someone has to lose. But Kimball was bothered by *how* he was defeated, and he came away from the experience convinced that the American electoral system had become corrupted by money and slick media campaigns. Moreover, Kimball felt that voters could not cut through the hype and get the kind of effective, unbiased information he felt was necessary for voters to make informed choices on election day.

Out of this sense of mission came Project Vote Smart, a citizens' information resource center founded by Kimball and established at Oregon State University in Corvallis, Oregon, in 1992. The original aim was to give average citizens a place where they could call a toll-free number and receive nonpartisan, unbiased information on candidates' backgrounds, views on issues, the sources of their campaign funds, and, once they are elected, their votes on legislation. PVS also would enable citizens to track legislation in Congress.

Kimball's vision, in his words, was to "turn the same slick, high technology used by candidates and elected officials around to the citizen's advantage instead. Allow each individual citizen to decide for himself or herself what information is important and then provide instant access to it. In our democracy no power is more decisive, no political weapon more potent, than dependable, accurate, factual information."

Project Vote Smart is unique in three ways. First, its board of directors, all of whom are politicians or community activists, come from all political stripes, and new board members cannot be seated unless they first bring with them another board member from the opposite party or political philosophy. This rule is meant to protect Vote Smart's nonpartisan standing. Funding comes from members' contributions and grants from foundations.

Second, Project Vote Smart is run almost entirely by college student interns and volunteers. One group operates the Vote Smart hotline, responding to caller questions and assisting members of the public and the media in finding information on candidates or issues. This program began at Oregon State and, in 1994, expanded by opening up a center at Northeastern University in Massachusetts, the home institution to the authors of this book. A second group is the National Intern Program, which to date has involved over 150 students from over 100 universities representing 46 states and 11 other nations. These interns, who receive some financial support, do most of the research that goes into PVS's database and Web site (www.vote-smart.org), which opened in 1995 and has become one of the most comprehensive sites devoted to politics on the Web.

Third, Vote Smart asks candidates to complete the National Political Awareness Test, a survey of their views on issues and their ideas for new programs or policies. It then puts the responses into its database, from which citizens are able to put together profiles of the candidates and their views. At first, few candidates would fill out the survey; they were particularly wary of answering questions about controversial issues. But widespread media coverage of the survey and of candidates who refused to answer it has led to higher response rates with each election cycle.

→

A CLOSER LOOK

Keeping a watchful eye. Project Vote Smart interns at work. Student interns develop databases and provide callers with nonpartisan information on candidates' records, views on issues, and sources of their campaign funds. Armed with such information, voters might be able to make more informed choices on election day.

By the 1998 election, PVS covered over 13,000 separate candidates for state and federal office and distributed over one million free copies of its *Voter's Self-Defense Manual*, a free guide to candidates' issue positions, sources of funding, and recent votes on legislation. Vote Smart also provides support to nearly 50,000 journalists with a *Vote Smart Web Yellow Pages*, an exhaustive guide to politics Web sites of all kinds, and *The Reporter's Sourcebook*, which contains brief essays on the issues expected to be important in the upcoming campaign as well as tips for how journalists can find out more information on these issues.

In 1999, Vote Smart took a radical step and moved its West Coast office from Corvallis to the Great Divide Ranch in Philipsburg, Montana, where the PVS staff and National Interns will work amidst the splendor of the mountains.

The purpose of Vote Smart is to help citizens make more informed choices at election time. Anyone can visit the PVS Web site or can call 1-800-VOTESMART and talk directly to student interns in Boston or Montana for research assistance—or for information on becoming an intern!

Source: Project Vote Smart (www.vote-smart.org).

The world's policeman? U.S. forces on the ground in Kosovo. With the end of the cold war between the United States and former Soviet Union, Americans are once again debating the degree to which they should be called on to resolve the world's conflicts. The answer is not neat and clean.

average individual might well wonder whether he or she has any say in what government does.

THE ROLE OF THE UNITED STATES IN THE WORLD

As we saw in chapter 9, President George Bush rallied Americans and a coalition of other nations in defense of Kuwait after it was occupied by the neighboring nation of Iraq. Two years later, Bush was defeated for reelection by Bill Clinton partly because so many voters thought Bush had spent too much of his time and energy on foreign policy and not enough on the economic needs of Americans.

Yet President Clinton found that for much of the time his job required him to focus on foreign policy. He tried to resolve longstanding conflicts between Israel and the Palestinians, between Catholics and Protestants in Northern Ireland, and between Greece and Turkey over the future of Cyprus, to mention just a few. The president also found himself using American armed forces for a greater range of purposes than he had expected—for example, to fight terrorism against Americans in Kenya, preserve a democratically elected government in Haiti, provide humanitarian relief in Somalia, and support peacekeeping efforts in parts of the former Yugoslavia. Indeed, in 1999 Clinton deployed American armed forces to take part in a multinational effort to force the leaders of Yugoslavia to end their repression of ethnic Albanians in the province of Kosovo.

Americans rightly wonder whether the United States can or should take on such an active global role. After all, why should we pay with money and blood to resolve ethnic conflicts half a world away? Didn't the United States do enough to defend freedom during the almost 50 years of the cold war? Didn't we spend enough money and lose enough lives in two world wars? Why should the United States try to solve the world's problems? Why should it worry about ethnic conflict in the Balkans or the economic health of Asian nations such as Thailand and Malaysia? Why can't we just worry about our own affairs? These are powerful arguments, particularly for a nation that has never been entirely comfortable with the role of "world policeman."

As journalist Thomas Friedman points out, however, we may have no choice but to accept this role. In many respects, he argues, the global spread of capitalist economic systems, the advent of the Internet, and increased mobility for individuals fit the American ideal of free markets and individual liberty, and in many ways Americans are in the best position to benefit from this new world system. "As the country that benefits most from global economic integration," Friedman continues, "we have the responsibility of making sure that this new system is sustainable."[17] American ideas, products, and cultural values pervade this new system, so the United States must take the lead in ensuring global stability and peace. Not all Americans will like this responsibility because the United States is destined to pay a disproportionate share of its costs, but we probably have no choice if we want to live in a world of peace, prosperity, democracy, and human rights for all.

This debate over the proper role of the United States in the world is important. As we know from our own history, and as the framers of the Constitution recognized, government sometimes is necessary to ensure social stability, guarantee the functioning of free markets, and protect the civil rights and civil liberties of those who are unpopular or left out. The same need holds true on a global scale. Regardless of the important roles played by the United Nations, the North Atlantic Treaty Organization (NATO), the World Bank, and other international organizations, there is probably still a need for a few nations to take the lead in keeping the peace and enforcing democratic ideals throughout the world. As the superpower, the United States automatically assumes this role—not always alone, but certainly in the lead.

THE HEALTH OF DEMOCRACY

We have examined three major questions facing the American political system at the beginning of the new century. But there is another question that is being debated by political scientists, philosophers, clergy, and politicians today: Is American democracy healthy?

As we have seen throughout this book, politics is the process of transforming conflict into compromise. We have seen that conflict is inevitable in a large and diverse society such as the United States. But compromise is not inevitable, as we know too well from our own history, not to mention that of other nations. If history is not enough to remind us of this fact, we need only to open the newspaper or watch the news on television.

Compromise is not inevitable. It takes a great deal of work, ingenuity, and desire. Left unresolved, conflicts can degenerate into bitterness and even open violence. Thus, we need a better understanding of how all this actually works. Throughout this book we have emphasized institutions and processes—how Congress makes laws, how the electoral system works, and so on—because they are the means by which we seek to manage conflict and turn it into something less dangerous and perhaps into something useful. Here, however, we turn a mirror on ourselves and ask: Do we have the kind of civic life necessary to make American democracy work?

Why do we turn our gaze on ourselves? The answer is that having the *forms* of democratic government is only a start. To make democracy work, the people must act as citizens. They must play an active role in maintaining democracy. This does not involve reforming the nation's core institutions, because the basic constitutional blueprint of the American system seems as workable as ever. Besides, changes in those institutions are unlikely to happen unless the nation finds itself in a severe crisis. Instead, making democracy work involves enhancing our *civic life*—that is, the way we connect to our political communities and participate in politics.

A DECLINE IN SOCIAL CAPITAL?

The question of how we can enhance civic life is an important one. Observers of American democracy going back to Alexis de Tocqueville have recognized a link between the health of a nation's *civil society*—defined here as the public activities of its citizens—and the health of democracy in that nation.

In 1996 political scientist Robert Putnam started a heated debate among political scientists and others interested in the health of democratic government by arguing that "the vibrancy of American civil society has notably declined over the past several decades."[18] That is, Putnam argued that he had observed a steady erosion in the nation's *social capital*, the "norms and networks of civic engagement" that students of politics believe are essential to the maintenance of a healthy democratic system of government.

Putnam's thesis is that societies develop by building various kinds of capital: physical capital such as factories, transportation systems, and communities; and human capital in the form of healthy and educated citizens. But the development of democracy depends on social capital in order to handle the conflicts that inevitably arise. This social capital is built up over decades, even centuries, as citizens work on issues of shared concern through a variety of formal institutions (such as a town meeting), informal associations (such as a community group dedicated to building a new town library), and even occasional communal activities such as a "walkathon" (see Box 12.2). The concept of social capital also encompasses belonging to civic associations such as the League of Women Voters or the Chamber of Commerce as well as norms such as trust in other members of the society and belief in the value of working out problems in a collaborative manner. This includes being willing to seek compromise.

Putnam argues, however, that the nation's social capital has eroded over the past 40 years. As evidence, he points to well-known trends: a decline in voter turnout; reduced participation in public meetings, political rallies, and community boards; decreased interest in news on politics; an apparent decrease in volunteering for charitable or civic purposes. Fewer people even donate blood. "By almost every measure," he says, "Americans' direct engagement in politics and government has fallen steadily and sharply over the last generation, despite the fact that average levels of education—the best individual-level predictor of political participation—has risen sharply

---

BOX 12.2.
WALKATHONS

WHAT DO YOU THINK?

Have you participated in a walkathon? In recent years, walkathons have become important fundraising events as well as publicity tools. The March of Dimes' Walk America, Walk for Hunger, AIDS Walk, and other such events are commonplace across America. In fact, in some cities there seems to be a walk of some kind every weekend in April and May! Thousands of walkers participate each year, and many more people provide pledges of financial support for each mile the walkers complete.

Walk America, sponsored by the March of Dimes, is one of the oldest and largest walkathons. In 1999, more than 1 million people in 1,500 communities around the country participated in the charity's Walk America, raising over $76 million. The Walk for Hunger in Boston is one of the largest single walkathon events, drawing more than 40,000 participants and raising approximately $3 million.

The popularity of walkathons has spawned other similar events: hopathons for children, danceathons for teenagers and young adults, bikeathons, and aerobathons. Compared to traditional $500-a-plate black-tie fundraising events, or lengthy telethons, walkathons and similar fundraising strategies provide a way for many more people to get involved in supporting a cause.

But are walkathons effective and meaningful forms of citizen participation? Supporters of walkathons argue "yes." Walkathons raise money for a host of important causes, and they involve both walkers and pledgers in supporting a cause. In addition, the publicity that accompanies a walkathon carries the message into many more homes.

However, walkathons have their critics. From this perspective, walkathons allow people to avoid confronting the true causes of and possible solutions to a social problem. Raising money to support a cause is important, but it shouldn't replace the hard work needed to truly address a problem. Walkathons allow people to avoid the tough jobs of lobbying for change and engaging in direct action to change public policies relating to hunger, AIDS, or other problems.

What do you think? Is a walkathon an important way to participate in the civic life of your community, or does it merely detract from more meaningful forms of participation needed to change public policies and address the problems we face?

Sources: Lena Williams, "New Charity Strategy: Get Up and Go," *New York Times*, May 7, 1995, p. A32; Elsa Brenner, "Cast of Thousands Raises Money for Dozens of Worthy Causes," *New York Times*, May 23, 1999, Section 14WC, p. 6.

---

throughout this period. Every year over the last decade or two, millions more have withdrawn from the affairs of their communities."[19]

Why is this happening? According to Putnam, explanations include the loosening bonds of community as people move more frequently for career purposes; the re-

Scenes from a mall. For many Americans, the commercial values embodied by the suburban mall have flourished at the expense of local communities and of active citizen involvement in public activities.

placement of neighbors with coworkers as the workplace becomes the focus of social life; a decline in membership in civic organizations such as the Chamber of Commerce, fraternal organizations such as the Kiwanis Club, and, as more women have entered the workforce, "women's groups" such as the League of Women Voters; the transformation of leisure from communal activities such as town picnics or city block parties to individual activities such as watching television or surfing the Internet.

To this list other observers might add the triumph of free markets and the related norms of individual liberty over the bonds created by family, church, and community. For example, most states once enforced "blue laws" that prohibited most commercial activity on Sunday, a day that was supposed to be used to go to church and spend time with the family. But over the past 40 years such laws have been overturned in the courts or eliminated by state governments as unwarranted restrictions on a merchant's right to be open on Sunday and an individual's right to shop if he or she wishes to do so. To some, the end of the blue laws meant greater individual freedom and an end to state-sponsored religious days; to others, it meant the triumph of market values over family and community.

Why is this apparent erosion in social capital a problem? Putnam argues that it erodes the fabric of social interaction and activism that is essential to the health of democracy. That is, by working together through a variety of formal institutions and informal associations, citizens learn to trust others, especially those unlike themselves, and find ways to get things done. In turn, successful collaborative efforts breed a sense of "public purposefulness," a greater sense of the common good and greater willingness to compromise.

Imagine two communities. One has strong community groups and a great deal of civic activity. The other has weak community groups and a much lower level of civic life, whether measured by voter turnout or by volunteering to flip pancakes at the annual fundraiser for the school band. Which of the two communities do you think will have more responsive government and more effective civic life? For that matter, which of the two would you rather live in? Researchers are beginning to understand the links between the character of civic life and the performance of government institutions; in this regard, it might not be too much to say that you get the kind of government you work for.

As Putnam points out, "In the established democracies, ironically, growing numbers of citizens are questioning the effectiveness of their public institutions at the very moment when liberal democracy has swept the battlefield, both ideologically and geopolitically."[20] Even with the end of the cold war, the demise of the Soviet Union, the apparent trend toward free market economic systems and democratic forms of government throughout the world, and a booming economy at home, Americans are turning their eyes toward their own political system and asking, "Is this system failing?"

Is it? Or is the problem a decline in the vibrancy of the nation's civil society? Perhaps, as Putnam and others suggest, the key to democratic government lies in cultivating the political attitudes that encourage the formation of civic associations and political participation that goes beyond an occasional trip to the voting booth. Voting is important, but the health of democracy ultimately depends on development of the social capital that makes elections mean something.

Other scholars dispute Putnam's thesis about erosion in the nation's social capital. They point to trends that might indicate what political scientist Michael Kryzanek calls a "renewal of American participation in civic life."[21] In particular, Kryzanek notes the following evidence:

More grassroots political activism. Voting rates may be down, but more Americans than ever are members of groups such as local environmental organizations, youth athletic associations, and self-help groups. Americans may have decided that voting is less effective than getting involved in more direct forms of participation, especially at the local level.

Increased use of referenda and initiatives. In the same vein, although voting for candidates may have dropped, reliance on "direct democracy" may have increased. That is, more people are relying on referenda to make direct changes in state and local laws. Citizens may wonder whether their votes for president make much difference, but they seem more certain that their votes on specific issues matter.

Talk radio and Internet chat rooms. Americans may spend less time in the town square talking about local politics, but many are calling into talk radio shows; others are spending hours debating one another over the Internet. Today's town square is cyberspace. The quality of the debate may be different, but it is nonetheless debate.

A rise in volunteering. Other observers dispute Putnam's assessment of a decrease in volunteering. They point to the success of AmeriCorps, Habitat for Humanity, the Atlanta Project (see Box 12.3), National Service Day, and other forms of civic participation as affirmation that the nation's social capital isn't as depleted as Putnam fears.

BOX 12.3.
JIMMY CARTER AND THE ATLANTA PROJECT

Jimmy Carter served as the 39th president of the United States from 1977 to 1981. To many Americans, Carter's presidency was noted most for its problems—high world oil prices, inflation, and, particularly, the lengthy period during which Iranian revolutionaries held American diplomats hostage. Carter's perceived weaknesses as a leader led to his defeat by Ronald Reagan in the election of 1980.

Whatever his image as a president, since leaving office Carter has established a global reputation as peacemaker and advocate for building communities from the ground up. Along with his wife, Rosalynn, Carter founded the Carter Center, a nonprofit organization based in Atlanta, Georgia, that brings people and resources together to promote peace and human rights, foster democracy and development, and fight poverty, hunger and disease throughout the world.

In October, 1991, the Carter Center launched a grassroots project to revitalize Carter's own backyard. The Atlanta Project was created to enable the city's neediest communities to gain access to the resources they need to address the problems that most concern them—poverty, inadequate health care and education, unemployment, homelessness, juvenile delinquency, crime and violence. The persistence of these problems, often after years of considerable federal and state government spending, suggested that new solutions were needed for some old problems.

In this regard, the Atlanta Project's overriding philosophy is that communities are able and willing to take responsibility for solving their own problems if only they have access to necessary resources, including financial support, expertise, and volunteers. To accomplish this task the Atlanta Project builds partnerships with major corporations, foundations, and universities in addressing some of the problems associated with poverty in Atlanta. It then connects these institutions and their resources to community leaders and volunteers to overcome what appear to be the intractable social problems associated with poverty.

The Atlanta Project (and others like it) thus focuses on building a community from the bottom up, not the top down. In the process, it is also working to strengthen that community's "social capital." In essence, the thousands of volunteers who give their time to the Atlanta Project's programs become "investors" in the future of their communities, commitments without which no community can thrive. The following are some examples of The Atlanta Project's activities:

→

Maybe Americans aren't joining the kinds of groups they joined in the past, but they may be focusing their energies where they expect direct results.

Are the trends Kryzanek refers to accurate? Even if they are, do they contribute to a healthy civil society? For example, are people really working actively in grassroots

---

A CLOSER LOOK

▶ *Immunization and Children's Health Initiatives.* In 1993, the Atlanta Project coordinated the largest childhood immunization campaign in the nation's history. More than 7,000 volunteers went door-to-door to collect data on children's health and to distribute educational materials, and nearly 16,000 children were vaccinated at immunization sites in a one-week period. A multicounty computer database was developed to track the health and immunization records of all youth in metropolitan Atlanta, which in turn led to improvements in preventative care.

▶ *Entrepreneurial Development Loan Fund.* Working with the Atlanta Chamber of Commerce and seven area financial institutions, the Atlanta Project established a $11.5 million loan fund to help new businesses receive funding and technical support where little such support had existed before. Obtaining capital for business development is especially difficult in low-income areas, and the project's efforts led to 70 loans to new businesses, which in turn created 130 new jobs and retained 233 existing jobs in Atlanta neighborhoods. These numbers might seem modest, but they marked a dramatic improvement in the homegrown employment prospects for local residents.

▶ *Projects for Children, Youth, and Families.* Working with the State of Georgia, the Atlanta Project developed programs to support the state's goals of improving the quality of life for children and families. These programs included after-school programs for middle school students that were designed to give teenagers an alternative to the streets; "welfare-to-work" programs to facilitate the often-difficult transition from dependence to independence; prekindergarten classes to enable these former welfare mothers to work without worrying about their children's care; and family health clinics that give poor people access to preventative health care.

The Atlanta Project is only one example of a community development group trying to bring together different groups and institutions in order to make a difference in America's communities.

Source: The Carter Center; http://www.emory.edu/CARTER_CENTER

---

organizations, or are they only writing checks for annual membership dues? The latter action lacks the element of personal interaction with others that helps foster norms of collaboration and compromise. Is a relatively anonymous contribution to a radio talk show or Internet chat room the same as face-to-face debate? These are questions worth asking.

Habitat for Humanity. Volunteers work together to help construct affordable housing for the less affluent, who themselves invest "sweat equity" into their new homes. By making home ownership more widespread, Habitat for Humanity hopes to stabilize poorer communities and nurture the emergence of citizen activism in local affairs.

CONCLUSION: WHAT DO YOU THINK?

Look around your hometown, and think about your high school days. Is Putnam right? Are the bonds of community so eroded and the spirit of civic participation so faint that democracy itself is endangered? Or do you see signs that the picture is brighter than the one Putnam paints?

Equally important, what *should* the role of the citizen in a democracy be? Is voting enough, or should citizens take a more active and direct role in their political system? What are the obstacles to achieving this ideal, or does it really matter? Is the average citizen so lacking in political power that government is entirely in the hands of the few? If so, is this a democracy anymore? What kind of country will the United States be 10, 20, or 30 years from now? Its system of government has endured many crises over many years, but can it survive or even be relevant in a world of global markets and the Internet?

These are hard questions, and the answers to them will affect your lives and the lives of your children. As we pointed out in chapter 1, the first task of citizenship is thinking and acting on politics. So, *what do you think?*

SUMMARY

▶ Conflict is natural in any society, but the ability and desire to seek compromise is not. It has to be cultivated and nurtured in every generation. Politics is the process of trying to transform conflict into compromise. The American political system is a framework of processes and institutions designed to make living in a society possible.

▶ Several cases first discussed in the previous chapters are revisited: financing public schools; flag desecration; disposing of low-level radioactive waste; funding for student groups; welfare reform; health care; regulating dietary supplements. In each case, the central issues are posed, followed by the question: What would you do? The answers to this question address the issue of the purpose of government.

▶ The United States faces three major questions as it enters the new century. First, with new waves of immigration during the 1990s, what kind of society will the United States be? Will newer waves of Asian, African, and Latin American immigrants adhere to the cultural ideals of the American society as did their European forebears? Second, in a system of government that dares to call itself a democracy, who really has power? Do the people govern, or is power so concentrated in the hands of major corporations that democracy is a hollow ideal? Third, what is the role of the United States in the world? Will Americans play an active part of the world community, or try to isolate themselves from it?

▶ The health of American democracy is a topic of debate among political scientists and others. Of particular concern is the apparent decline in social capital, in the webs of social attachments that breed democratic values, which is posed as a challenge to the continued maintenance of effective democratic government. Without informed and active citizens, democratic government may be more difficult to sustain.

QUESTIONS FOR REVIEW AND DISCUSSION

1. What is the proper role of government today? That is, what things should government do and what things shouldn't it do?

2. What role should the United States play in the contemporary world? What issues are in the nation's vital interests and in what cases should it intervene militarily?

3. What is the proper role of the citizen in American democracy today? Tomorrow?

WEB SOURCES

AmeriCorps (www.americorps.gov). Site operated by the Corporation for National Service, of which AmeriCorps is part. Contains everything you would want to know about the AmeriCorps program, in which 100,000 people participated its first five years (1993–1998). See also the Peace Corps (www.peacecorps.gov) for information on service opportunities in other countries.

Habitat for Humanity (www.habitat.org). Site operated by a nonprofit organization that mobilizes volunteers to help to build owner-occupied housing in poorer areas.

Points of Light Foundation (www.pointsoflight.org) and and Americas Promise (www.americaspromise.org/pol). Two organizations, the first inspired by former President George Bush and the second by General Colin Powell, former Chairman of the Joint Chiefs of Staff, that seek to promote volunteerism and citizen involvement in community service.

SUGGESTED READINGS

John W. Kingdon, *America the Unusual* (New York: St. Martin's Press, 1999). Government plays a more limited role in the United States than in other economically advanced nations, and Americans seems to expect less of it. Political scientist John Kingdon compares the role of government in several nations and asks, "Why is the United States different?" How did these differences come about, and what are their effects?

Benjamin Barber, *Jihad vs. McWorld: How Globalism and Tribalism are Reshaping the World* (New York: Ballantine Books, 1996); and Thomas L. Friedman, *The Lexus and the Olive Tree: Understanding Globalization* (New York: Farrar, Straus & Giroux, 1999). Two fascinating books that look at the forces of economic, technological, social, cultural, and political globalization affecting all nations and the role of the United States in the world. Barber, a political scientist, is pessimistic about the future of democratic politics in a world buffeted by consumer capitalism on one side and religious fundamentalism and ethnic tribalism on the other. Friedman, a journalist, sees many of the same dangers but expresses some optimism about that brave new world—and the need for American leadership in it.

Graham K. Wilson, *Only in America? The Politics of the United States in a Comparative Perspective* (Chatham, NJ: Chatham House, 1998). Political scientist Graham Wilson challenges the common assumption about "American exceptionalism," the view that the United States is unique, by looking at the social, economic, and political problems that affect all economically advanced societies, and how they seek to address those problems. In particular, Wilson argues, if you look beyond the obviously distinct aspects of American institutions of government you find that the United States has far more in common with nations such as Canada, France, Italy, and Japan than a focus on culture, language, or history might suggest.

NOTES

1. Alexander Hamilton, James Madison, and John Jay, *The Federalist Papers*, Clinton Rossiter, ed. (New York: New American Library, 1961), p. 79.

2. E. J. Dionne Jr., "A Meeting of Minds; Coming Together on AmeriCorps," *Washington Post*, March 5, 1999, p. A33.

3. Higher Education Research Institute as reported in "This Year's Freshmen: A Statistical Profile," *The Chronicle of Higher Education*, January 29, 1999, p. A47.

4. Thomas Oliphant, "Governor Shaheen's Savvy," *Boston Globe*, May 4, 1999, p. A21; editorial, "New Hampshire's Unfinished Work," *Boston Globe*, May 2, 1999, p. E6.

5. Barry G. Rabe, *Beyond NIMBY: Hazardous Waste Siting in Canada and the United States* (Washington, D.C.: Brookings Institution, 1994), p. 4.

6. Lyle Denniston, "High Court Will Hear College Activity-Fee Case," *The Baltimore Sun*, March 30, 1999, p. 3A.

7. "Student Fees and Speech," Editorial, *Washington Post*, March 19, 1999, p. A28.

8. Jonathan Walters, "Beyond the Welfare Clock," *Governing*, April, 1999, p. 24.

9. Haynes Johnson and David Broder, *The System: The American Way of Politics at the Breaking Point* (Boston: Little, Brown, 1996), pp. 61–62.

10. Jane Bryant Quinn, "The Invisible Uninsured," *Newsweek*, March 1, 1999, p. 49.

11. John Schwartz, "FDA Warns against Supplement; Recall Requested of Dietary Products with Chemical Suspected in Death," *Washington Post*, January 22, 1999, p. A2.

12. Louis DeSipio and Rodolfo O. de la Garza, *Making Americans: Remaking America* (Boulder, CO: Westview Press, 1998), pp. 18–21.

13. Samuel P. Huntington, "If Not Civilizations, What? Paradigms of the Post–Cold War World," in Huntington, et al., *Samuel Huntington's The Clash of Civilizations? The Debate* (New York: Norton, 1996), pp. 61–62.

14. See Arthur Schlesinger Jr., *The Disuniting of America: Reflections on a Multicultural Society* (New York: Norton, 1992).

15. DeSipio and de la Garza, *Making Americans: Remaking America*, p. 134.

16. See Benjamin Barber, "Electronic Democracy: The Implications of Technology," *Political Science Quarterly*, vol. 113, no. 4 (Winter 1999).

17. Thomas L. Friedman, "A Manifesto for the Fast World," *New York Times Magazine*, March 28, 1999, p. 43.

18. Robert D. Putnam, "Bowling Alone: America's Declining Social Capital," *Journal of Democracy*, vol. 6, no. 1 (January 1996), p. 65.

19. Ibid., p. 68.

20. Ibid., p. 77.

21. Michael J. Kryzanek, *Angry, Bored, Confused: A Citizen Handbook of American Politics* (Boulder, CO: Westview Press, 1999).

PRIMARY SOURCE READINGS

ANDREW CARNEGIE
"Wealth"

Andrew Carnegie (1835–1919) was born in Scotland and came to the United States with his family. The story of how Carnegie become a powerful industrialist (railroads, steel) is the stuff of American legend. So too was his decision to give away most of his fortune during his lifetime to public institutions such as libraries, pension funds for teachers, and grants to universities. In this excerpt, Carnegie explains his views.

> The problem of our age is the proper administration of wealth, so that the ties of brotherhood may still bind together the rich and poor in harmonious relationship. The conditions of human life have not only been changed, but revolutionized, within the past few hundred years. In former days there was little difference between the dwelling, dress, food, and environment of the chief and those of his retainers. . . . The contrast between the palace of the

millionaire and the cottage of the laborer with us today measures the change which has come with civilization.

This change, however, is not to be deplored, but welcomed as highly beneficial. It is well, nay, essential for the progress of the race, that the houses of some should be homes for all that is highest and best in literature and the arts, and for all the refinements of civilization, rather than that none should be so. Much better this great irregularity than universal squalor. . . .

Today the world obtains commodities of excellent quality at prices which even the generation preceding this would have deemed incredible. In the commercial world similar causes have produced similar results, and the race is benefited thereby. The poor enjoy what the rich could not before afford. What were the luxuries have become the necessaries of life. . . .

The price we pay for this salutary change is, no doubt, great. We assemble thousands of operatives in the factory, in the mine, and in the counting-house, of whom the employer can know little or nothing, and to whom the employer is little better than a myth. . . . Under the law of competition, the employer of thousands is forced into the strictest economies, among which the rates paid to labor figure prominently, and often there is friction between the employer and the employed, between capital and labor, between rich and poor. Human society loses homogeneity.

The price which society pays for the law of competition, like the price it pays for cheap comforts and luxuries, is also great; but the advantages of this law are also greater still, for it is to this law that we owe our wonderful material development, which brings improved conditions in its train. . . .

Having accepted these, it follows that there must be great scope for the exercise of special ability in the merchant and in the manufacturer who has to conduct affairs upon a great scale, That this talent for organization and management is rare among men is proved by the fact that it invariably secures for its possessor enormous rewards, no matter where or under what laws or conditions. . . . It is a law, as certain as any of the others named, that men possessed of this peculiar talent for affairs, under the free play of economic forces, must, of necessity, soon be in receipt of more revenue than can be judiciously expended upon themselves; and this law is as beneficial for the race as the others. . . .

The question then arises. . . . What is the proper mode of administering wealth after the laws upon which civilization is founded have thrown it into the hands of the few? . . .

There are but three modes in which surplus wealth can be disposed of. It can be left to the families of the decedents; or it can be bequeathed for public purposes; or, finally, it can be administered during their lives by its possessors. . . .

The first is the most injudicious. . . . Why should men leave great fortunes to their children? If this is done from affection, is it not misguided affection? Observation teaches that, generally speaking, it is not well for the children that they should be so burdened. Neither is it well for the state. Beyond providing for the wife and daughters moderate sources of income, and very moderate allowances indeed, if any, for the sons, men may well hesitate, for it is no longer questionable that great sums bequeathed oftener work more for the injury than for the good of the recipients. . . .

As to the second mode, that of leaving wealth at death for public uses, it may be said that this is only a means for the disposal of wealth, provided a man is content to wait until he is dead before it becomes of much good in the world. Knowledge of the results of legacies bequeathed is not calculated to inspire the brightest hopes of much posthumous good being accomplished. The cases are not few in which the real object sought by the testator is not attained, nor are they few in which his real wishes are thwarted. . . .

The growing disposition to tax more and more heavily large estates left at death is a cheering indication of the growth of a salutary change in public opinion. . . . Of all forms of taxation, this seems the wisest. Men who continue hoarding great sums all their lives, the proper use of which for the public ends would work good to the community, should be made to feel that the community, in the form of the state, cannot thus be deprived of its proper share. By taxing estates heavily at death the state marks its condemnation of the selfish millionaire's unworthy life. . . .

There remains, then, only one mode of using great fortunes; but in this we have the true antidote for the temporary unequal distribution of wealth, the reconciliation of the rich and the poor . . . in which the surplus wealth of the few will become, in the best sense, the property of the many, because administered for the common good, and this wealth, passing through the hands of the few, can be made a much more potent force for the elevation of our race than if it had been distributed in small sums to the people themselves. Even the poorest can be made to see this, and to agree that great sums gathered by some of their fellow-citizens and spent for public purposes, from which the masses reap the principal benefit, are more valuable to them than if scattered among them through the course of many years in trifling amounts. . . .

This, then, is held to be the duty of the man of Wealth: First, to set an example of modest, unostentatious living, shunning display or extravagance; to provide moderately for the legitimate wants of those dependent upon him; and after doing so to consider all surplus revenues which come to him simply as trust funds, which he is called upon to administer, and strictly bound as a matter of duty to administer in the manner which, in his judgment, is best calculated to produce the most beneficial results for the community—the man of wealth thus becoming the mere agent and trustee for his poorer brethren, bringing to their service his superior wisdom, experience, and ability to administer, doing for them better than they would or could do for themselves.

Source: North American Review, CXLVIII (June 1889), pp. 653–664.

GEORGE ORWELL
"Politics and the English Language"

The English writer George Orwell (1903–1950) is best known for his novels, Animal Farm *(1945) and* 1984 *(1949), in which attacked the enforced conformity and political repression he saw in Soviet Communism. In this essay (1946), Orwell looks more generally at how the use of language in politics can shape how people perceive of events or conditions. It is useful to apply Orwell's views to the language employed, both those in government, business, the media, and, even, in universities.*

In our time, political speech and writing are largely the defense of the indefensible. Things like the continuance of British rule in India, the Russian purges and deportations, the dropping of the atom bombs on Japan, can indeed be defended, but only by arguments which are too brutal for most people to face, and which do not square with the professed aims of political parties. Thus political language has to consist largely of euphemism, question-begging and sheer cloudy vagueness. Defenseless villages are bombarded from the air, the inhabitants driven out into the countryside, the cattle machine-gunned, the huts set on fire with incendiary bullets: this is called *pacification*. Millions of peasants are robbed of their farms and sent trudging along the roads with no more than they can carry: this is called *transfer of population* or *rectification of frontiers*. People are imprisoned for years without trial, or shot in the back of the neck or sent to die of scurvy in Arctic lumber camps: this is called *elimination of unreliable elements*. Such phraseology is needed if one wants to name things without calling up mental pictures of them. Consider for instance some comfortable English professor defending Russian totalitarianism. He cannot say outright, "I believe in killing off your opponents when you can get good results by doing so." Probably, therefore, he will say something like this:

> While freely conceding that the Soviet regime exhibits certain features which the humanitarian may be inclined to deplore, we must, I think, agree that a certain curtailment of the right to political opposition is an unavoidable concomitant of transitional periods, and that the rigors which the Russian people have been called upon to undergo have been amply justified in the sphere of concrete achievement. . . .

The great enemy of clear language is insincerity. When there is a gap between one's real and one's declared aims, one turns, as it were instinctively, to long words and exhausted idioms, like a cuttlefish squirting out ink. In our age there is no such thing as "keeping out of politics." All issues are political issues, and politics itself is a mass of lies, evasions, folly, hatred and schizophrenia. When the general atmosphere is bad, language must suffer. I should expect to find—this is a guess which I have not sufficient knowledge to verify—that the German, Russian and Italian languages have all deteriorated in the last ten or fifteen years as a result of dictatorship.

But if thought corrupts language, language can also corrupt thought. A bad usage can spread by tradition and imitation, even among people who should and do know better. The debased language that I have been discussing is in some ways very convenient. Phrases like a *not unjustifiable assumption*, *leaves much to be desired*, *would serve no good purpose*, *a consideration which we should do well to bear in mind*, are a continuous temptation, a packet of aspirins always at one's elbow. . . . This invasion of one's mind by ready-made phrases (*lay the foundations*, *achieve a radical transformation*) can only be prevented if one is constantly on guard against them, and every such phrase anesthetizes a portion of one's brain. . . .

What is above all needed is to let the meaning choose the word, and not the other way about. In prose, the worst thing one can do with words is to surrender them. When you think of a concrete object, you think wordlessly, and then, if you want to describe the thing you have been visualizing, you probably hunt about till you find the exact words that seem to fit it. When you think of something abstract you are more inclined to use words from the start, and unless you make a conscious effort to prevent it, the existing dialect will come rushing in and do the job for you, at the expense of blurring or even changing your meaning. Probably it is better to put off using words as long as possible and get one's meaning as clear as one can through pictures or sensations. Afterwards one can choose—not simply *accept*—the phrases that will best cover the meaning, and then switch round and decide what impressions one's words are likely to make on another person. This last effort of the mind cuts out all stale or mixed images, all prefabricated phrases, needless repetitions, and humbug and vagueness generally. . . .

If you simplify your English, you are freed from the worst follies of orthodoxy. You cannot speak any of the necessary dialects, and when you make a stupid remark its stupidity will be obvious, even to yourself. Political language—and with variations this is true of all political parties, from Conservatives to Anarchists—is designed to make lies sound truthful and murder respectable and to give an appearance of solidity to pure wind. One cannot change this all in a moment, but one can at least change one's own habits, and from time to time one can even, if one jeers loudly enough, send some worn-out and useless phrase—some *jackboot*, *Achilles' heel*, *hotbed*, *melting pot*, *acid test*, *veritable inferno* or other lump of verbal refuse—into the dustbin where it belongs.

APPENDIX

THE DECLARATION OF INDEPENDENCE

THE CONSTITUTION OF THE UNITED STATES

The Declaration of Independence

In Congress, July 4, 1776

The unanimous Declaration of the thirteen united States of America

When in the Course of human events, it becomes necessary for one people to dissolve the political bands which have connected them with another, and to assume among the powers of the earth, the separate and equal station to which the Laws of Nature and of Nature's God entitle them, a decent respect to the opinions of mankind requires that they should declare the causes which impel them to the separation.

We hold these truths to be self-evident, that all men are created equal, that they are endowed by their Creator with certain unalienable Rights, that among these are Life, Liberty and the pursuit of Happiness. That to secure these rights, Governments are instituted among Men, deriving their just Powers from the consent of the governed,—That whenever any Form of Government becomes destructive of these ends, it is the Right of the People to alter or to abolish it, and to institute new Government, laying its foundation on such principles and organizing its powers in such form, as to them shall seem most likely to effect their Safety and Happiness. Prudence, indeed, will dictate that Governments long established should not be changed for light and transient causes; and accordingly all experience hath shewn, that mankind are more disposed to suffer, while evils are sufferable, than to right themselves by abolishing the forms to which they are accustomed. But when a long train of abuses and usurpations, pursuing invariably the same Object evinces a design to reduce them under absolute Despotism, it is their right, it is their duty, to throw off such Government, and to provide new guards for their future security—Such has been the patient sufferance of these Colonies; and such is now the necessity which constrains them to alter their former Systems of Government.—The history of the present King of Great Britain is a history of repeated injuries and usurpations, all having in direct object the establishment of an absolute Tyranny over these States. To prove this, let facts be submitted to a candid world.

He has refused his Assent to Laws, the most wholesome and necessary for the public good.

He has forbidden his Governors to pass Laws of immediate and pressing importance, unless suspended in their operation till his Assent should be obtained; and when so suspended, he has utterly neglected to attend to them.

He has refused to pass other Laws for the accommodation of large districts of people, unless those people would relinquish the right of Representation in the Legislature, a right inestimable to them and formidable to tyrants only.

He has called together legislative bodies at places unusual, uncomfortable, and distant from the depository of their Public Records, for the sole purpose of fatiguing them into compliance with his measures.

He has dissolved Representative Houses repeatedly, for opposing with manly firmness his invasions on the rights of the people.

He has refused for a long time, after such dissolutions, to cause others to be elected; whereby the Legislative Powers, incapable of Annihilation, have returned to the People at large for their exercise; the State remaining in the mean time exposed to all the dangers of invasion from without, and convulsions within.

He has endeavoured to prevent the population of these States; for that purpose obstructing the Laws for Naturalization of Foreigners; refusing to pass others to encourage their migrations hither, and raising the conditions of new Appropriations of Lands.

He has obstructed the Administration of Justice, by refusing his Assent to Laws for establishing Judiciary Powers.

He has made Judges dependent on his Will alone, for the tenure of their offices, and the amount and payment of their salaries.

He has erected a multitude of New Offices, and sent hither swarms of Officers to harrass our People, and eat out their substance.

He has kept among us, in times of peace, Standing Armies without the Consent of our legislatures.

He has affected to render the Military independent of and superior to the Civil Power.

He has combined with others to subject us to a jurisdiction foreign to our constitution, and unacknowledged by our laws; giving his Assent to their Acts of pretended Legislation:

For Quartering large bodies of armed troops among us:

For protecting them, by a mock Trial, from Punishment for any Murders which they should commit on the Inhabitants of these States:

For cutting off our Trade with all parts of the world:

For imposing Taxes on us without our Consent:

For depriving us in many cases, of the benefits of Trial by Jury:

For transporting us beyond seas to be tried for pretended offences:

For abolishing the free system of English Laws in a neighbouring Province, establishing therein an Arbitrary government, and enlarging its Boundaries so as to render it at once an example and fit instrument for introducing the same absolute rule into these Colonies:

For taking away our Charters, abolishing our most valuable Laws, and altering fundamentally the forms of our Governments:

For suspending our own Legislature, and declaring themselves invested with power to legislate for us in all cases whatsoever.

He has abdicated Government here, by declaring us out of his Protection and waging War against us.

He has plundered our seas, ravaged our Coasts, burnt our towns, and destroyed the lives of our people.

He is at this time transporting large Armies of foreign Mercenaries to compleat the works of death, desolation and tyranny, already begun with circumstances of Cruelty and perfidy scarcely parallelled in the most barbarous ages, and totally unworthy the Head of a civilized nation.

He has constrained our fellow Citizens taken Captive on the high Seas to bear Arms against their Country, to become the executioners of their friends and Brethren, or to fall themselves by their Hands.

He has excited domestic insurrections amongst us, and has endeavoured to bring on the inhabitants of our frontiers, the merciless Indian Savages, whose known rule of warfare, is an undistinguished destruction of all ages, sexes and conditions.

In every stage of these Oppressions we have Petitioned for Redress in the most humble terms: Our repeated Petitions have been answered only by repeated injury. A Prince, whose character is thus marked by every act which may define a Tyrant, is unfit to be the ruler of a free people.

Nor have we been wanting in attention to our Brittish brethren. We have warned them from time to time of attempts by their legislature to extend an unwarrantable jurisdiction over us. We have reminded them of the circumstances of our emigration and settlement here. We have appealed to their native justice and magnanimity, and we have conjured them by the ties of our common kindred to disavow these usurpations, which, would inevitably interrupt our connections and correspondence. They too have been deaf to the voice of justice and of consanguinity. We must, therefore, acquiesce in the necessity, which denounces our Separation, and hold them, as we hold the rest of mankind, Enemies in War, in Peace Friends.

We, therefore, the Representatives of the united States of America, in General Congress, Assembled, appealing to the Supreme Judge of the world for the rectitude of our intentions, do, in the Name, and by Authority of the good People of these Colonies, solemnly publish and declare, That these United Colonies are, and of Right ought to be Free and Independent States; that they are absolved from all Allegiance to the British Crown, and that all political connection between them and the State of Great Britain, is and ought to be totally dissolved; and that as Free and Independent States, they have full Power to levy War, conclude Peace, contract Alliances, establish Commerce, and to do all other Acts and Things which Independent States may of right do.

And for the support of this Declaration, with a firm reliance on the protection of Divine Providence, we mutually pledge to each other our Lives, our Fortunes and our sacred Honor.

John Hancock	Wm. Paca
Button Gwinnett	Thos. Stone
Lyman Hall	Charles Carroll of Carrollton
Geo. Walton	George Wythe
Wm. Hooper	Richard Henry Lee
Joseph Hewes	Th. Jefferson
John Penn	Benja. Harrison
Edward Rutledge	Thos. Nelson, Jr.
Thos. Heyward, Junr.	Francis Lightfoot Lee
Thomas Lynch, Junr.	Carter Braxton
Arthur Middleton	Robt. Morris
Samuel Chase	Benjamin Rush

Benja. Franklin	Fras. Hopkinson
John Morton	John Hart
Geo. Clymer	Abra. Clark
Jas. Smith	Josiah Bartlett
Geo. Taylor	Wm. Whipple
James Wilson	Saml. Adams
Geo. Ross	John Adams
Caesar Rodney	Robt. Treat Paine
Geo. Read	Elbridge Gerry
Tho. Mckean	Step. Hopkins
Wm. Floyd	William Ellery
Phil. Livingston	Roger Sherman
Frans. Lewis	Samuel Huntington
Lewis Morris	Wm. Williams
Richd. Stockton	Oliver Wolcott
Jno. Witherspoon	Matthew Thornton

THE CONSTITUTION OF THE UNITED STATES

Preamble

We the People of the United States, in Order to form a more perfect Union, establish Justice, insure domestic Tranquility, provide for the common defence, promote the general Welfare, and secure the Blessings of Liberty to ourselves and our Posterity, do ordain and establish this Constitution forthe United States of America.

Article I.
Section 1—Legislative Powers; in whom vested.

All legislative Powers herein granted shall be vested in a Congress of the United States, which shall consist of a Senate and House of Representatives.

Section 2—House of Representatives, how and by whom chosen. Qualifications of a Representative. Representatives and direct taxes, how apportioned. Enumeration. Vacancies to be filled. Power of choosing officers, and of impeachment.

The House of Representatives shall be composed of Members chosen every second Year by the People of the several States, and the Electors in each State shall have the Qualifications requisite for Electors of the most numerous Branch of the State Legislature.

No Person shall be a Representative who shall not have attained to the Age of twenty five Years, and been seven Years a Citizen of the United States, and who shall not, when elected, be an Inhabitant of that State in which he shall be chosen.

Representatives and direct Taxes shall be apportioned among the several States which may be included within this Union, according to their respective Numbers, which shall be determined by adding to the whole Number of free Persons, including those bound to Service for a

Term of Years, and excluding Indians not taxed, three fifths of all other Persons (superseded by Amendment XIV, section 2.). The actual Enumeration shall be made within three Years after the first Meeting of the Congress of the United States, and within every subsequent Term of ten Years, in such Manner as they shall by Law direct. The Number of Representatives shall not exceed one for every thirty Thousand, but each State shall have at Least one Representative; and until such enumeration shall be made, the State of New Hampshire shall be entitled to chuse three, Massachusetts eight, Rhode Island and Providence Plantations one, Connecticut five, New York six, New Jersey four, Pennsylvania eight, Delaware one, Maryland six, Virginia ten, North Carolina five, South Carolina five and Georgia three.

When vacancies happen in the Representation from any State, the Executive Authority thereof shall issue Writs of Election to fill such Vacancies.

The House of Representatives shall chuse their Speaker and other Officers; and shall have the sole Power of Impeachment.

Section 3—Senators, how and by whom chosen. How Classified. Qualifications of a Senator. President of the Senate, his right to vote. President pro tem., and other officers of the Senate, how chosen. Power to try impeachments. When President is tried, Chief Justice to preside. Sentence.

The Senate of the United States shall be composed of two Senators from each State, *chosen by the Legislature thereof* (superseded by Amendment XVII, section 1) for six Years; and each Senator shall have one Vote.

Immediately after they shall be assembled in Consequence of the first Election, they shall be divided as equally as may be into three Classes. The Seats of the Senators of the first Class shall be vacated at the Expiration of the second Year, of the second Class at the Expiration of the fourth Year, and of the third Class at the Expiration of the sixth Year, so that one third may be chosen every second Year;*and if Vacancies happen by Resignation, or otherwise, during the Recess of the Legislature of any State, the Executive thereof may make temporary Appointments until the next Meeting of the Legislature, which shall then fill such Vacancies* (superseded by Amendment XVII, section 2).

No person shall be a Senator who shall not have attained to the Age of thirty Years, and been nine Years a Citizen of the United States, and who shall not, when elected, be an Inhabitant of that State for which he shall be chosen.

The Vice President of the United States shall be President of the Senate, but shall have no Vote, unless they be equally divided.

The Senate shall chuse their other Officers, and also a President pro tempore, in the absence of the Vice President, or when he shall exercise the Office of President of the United States.

The Senate shall have the sole Power to try all Impeachments. When sitting for that Purpose, they shall be on Oath or Affirmation. When the President of the United States is tried, the Chief Justice shall preside: And no Person shall be convicted without the Concurrence of two thirds of the Members present.

Judgment in Cases of Impeachment shall not extend further than to removal from Office, and disqualification to hold and enjoy any Office of honor, Trust or Profit under the United States: but the Party convicted shall nevertheless be liable and subject to Indictment, Trial, Judgment and Punishment, according to Law.

Section 4—Times, etc., of holding elections, how prescribed. One session each year.

The Times, Places and Manner of holding Elections for Senators and Representatives, shall be prescribed in each State by the Legislature thereof; but the Congress may at any time by Law make or alter such Regulations, except as to the Place of Chusing Senators.

The Congress shall assemble at least once in every Year, and such Meeting shall *be on the first Monday in December* (superseded by Amendment XX, section 2) unless they shall by Law appoint a different Day.

Section 5—Membership, quorum, adjournments, rules. Power to punish or expel. Journal. Time of adjournments, how limited, etc.

Each House shall be the Judge of the Elections, Returns and Qualifications of its own Members, and a Majority of each shall constitute a Quorum to do Business; but a smaller number may adjourn from day to day, and may be authorized to compel the Attendance of absent Members, in such Manner, and under such Penalties as each House may provide.

Each House may determine the Rules of its Proceedings, punish its Members for disorderly Behavior, and, with the Concurrence of two-thirds, expel a Member.

Each House shall keep a Journal of its Proceedings, and from time to time publish the same, excepting such Parts as may in their Judgment require Secrecy; and the Yeas and Nays of the Members of either House on any question shall, at the Desire of one fifth of those Present, be entered on the Journal.

Neither House, during the Session of Congress, shall, without the Consent of the other, adjourn for more than three days, nor to any other Place than that in which the two Houses shall be sitting.

Section 6—Compensation, privileges, disqualifications in certain cases.

The Senators and Representatives shall receive a Compensation for their Services, to be ascertained by Law, and paid out of the Treasury of the United States. They shall in all Cases, except Treason, Felony and Breach of the Peace, be privileged from Arrest during their Attendance at the Session of their respective Houses, and in going to and returning from the same; and for any Speech or Debate in either House, they shall not be questioned in any other Place.

No Senator or Representative shall, during the Time for which he was elected, be appointed to any civil Office under the Authority of the United States which shall have been created, or the Emoluments whereof shall have been increased during such time; and no Person holding any Office under the United States, shall be a Member of either House during his Continuance in Office.

Section 7—House to originate all revenue bills. Veto. Bill may be passed by two-thirds of each House, notwithstanding, etc., Bill, not returned in ten days, becomes a law. Provisions as to orders, concurrent resolutions, etc.

All bills for raising Revenue shall originate in the House of Representatives; but the Senate may propose or concur with Amendments as on other Bills.

Every Bill which shall have passed the House of Representatives and the Senate, shall, before it become a Law, be presented to the President of the United States; If he approve he shall sign it, but if not he shall return it, with his Objections to that House in which it shall have originated, who shall enter the Objections at large on their Journal, and proceed to reconsider it. If after such Reconsideration two thirds of that House shall agree to pass the Bill, it shall be sent, together with the Objections, to the other House, by which it shall likewise be reconsidered, and if approved by two thirds of that House, it shall become a Law. But in all such Cases the Votes of both Houses shall be determined by Yeas and Nays, and the Names of the Persons voting for and against the Bill shall be entered on the Journal of each House respectively. If any Bill shall not be returned by the President within ten Days (Sundays excepted) after it shall have been presented to him, the Same shall be a Law, in like Manner as if he had signed it, unless the Congress by their Adjournment prevent its Return, in which Case it shall not be a Law.

Every Order, Resolution, or Vote to which the Concurrence of the Senate and House of Representatives may be necessary (except on a question of Adjournment) shall be presented to the President of the United States; and before the Same shall take Effect, shall be approved by him, or being disapproved by him, shall be repassed by two thirds of the Senate and House of Representatives, according to the Rules and Limitations prescribed in the Case of a Bill.

Section 8—Powers of Congress.

The Congress shall have Power To lay and collect Taxes, Duties, Imposts and Excises, to pay the Debts and provide for the common Defence and general Welfare of the United States; but all Duties, Imposts and Excises shall be uniform throughout the United States;

To borrow money on the credit of the United States;

To regulate Commerce with foreign Nations, and among the several States, and with the Indian Tribes;

To establish an uniform Rule of Naturalization, and uniform Laws on the subject of Bankruptcies throughout the United States;

To coin Money, regulate the Value thereof, and of foreign Coin, and fix the Standard of Weights and Measures;

To provide for the Punishment of counterfeiting the Securities and current Coin of the United States;

To establish Post Offices and Post Roads;

To promote the Progress of Science and useful Arts, by securing for limited Times to Authors and Inventors the exclusive Right to their respective Writings and Discoveries;

To constitute Tribunals inferior to the supreme Court;

To define and punish Piracies and Felonies committed on the high Seas, and Offenses against the Law of Nations;

To declare War, grant Letters of Marque and Reprisal, and make Rules concerning Captures on Land and Water;

To raise and support Armies, but no Appropriation of Money to that Use shall be for a longer Term than two Years;

To provide and maintain a Navy;

To make Rules for the Government and Regulation of the land and naval Forces;

To provide for calling forth the Militia to execute the Laws of the Union, suppress Insurrections and repel Invasions;

To provide for organizing, arming, and disciplining the Militia, and for governing such Part of them as may be employed in the Service of the United States, reserving to the States respectively, the Appointment of the Officers, and the Authority of training the Militia according to the discipline prescribed by Congress;

To exercise exclusive Legislation in all Cases whatsoever, over such District (not exceeding ten Miles square) as may, by Cession of particular States, and the acceptance of Congress, become the Seat of the Government of the United States, and to exercise like Authority over all Places purchased by the Consent of the Legislature of the State in which the Same shall be, for the Erection of Forts, Magazines, Arsenals, dock-Yards, and other needful Buildings; And

To make all Laws which shall be necessary and proper for carrying into Execution the foregoing Powers, and all other Powers vested by this Constitution in the Government of the United States, or in any Department or Officer thereof.

Section 9—Provision as to migration or importation of certain persons. Habeas corpus, bills of attainder, etc. Taxes, how apportioned. No export duty. No commercial preference. Money, how drawn from Treasury, etc. No titular nobility. Officers not to receive presents, etc.

The Migration or Importation of such Persons as any of the States now existing shall think proper to admit, shall not be prohibited by the Congress prior to the Year one thousand eight hundred and eight, but a tax or duty may be imposed on such Importation, not exceeding ten dollars for each Person.

The privilege of the Writ of Habeas Corpus shall not be suspended, unless when in Cases of Rebellion or Invasion the public Safety may require it.

No Bill of Attainder or ex post facto Law shall be passed.

No capitation, or other direct, Tax shall be laid, unless in Proportion to the Census or Enumeration herein before directed to be taken (modified by Amendment XVI).

No Tax or Duty shall be laid on Articles exported from any State.

No Preference shall be given by any Regulation of Commerce or Revenue to the Ports of one State over those of another: nor shall Vessels bound to, or from, one State, be obliged to enter, clear, or pay Duties in another.

No Money shall be drawn from the Treasury, but in Consequence of Appropriations made by Law; and a regular Statement and Account of the Receipts and Expenditures of all public Money shall be published from time to time.

No Title of Nobility shall be granted by the United States: And no Person holding any Office of Profit or Trust under them, shall, without the Consent of the Congress, accept of any present, Emolument, Office, or Title, of any kind whatever, from any King, Prince or foreign State.

Section 10—States prohibited from exercise of certain powers.

No State shall enter into any Treaty, Alliance, or Confederation; grant Letters of Marque and Reprisal; coin Money; emit Bills of Credit; make any Thing but gold and silver Coin a Tender in Payment of Debts; pass any Bill of Attainder, ex post facto Law, or Law impairing the Obligation of Contracts, or grant any Title of Nobility.

No State shall, without the Consent of the Congress, lay any Imposts or Duties on Imports or Exports, except what may be absolutely necessary for executing it's inspection Laws: and the net Produce of all Duties and Imposts, laid by any State on Imports or Exports, shall be for the Use of the Treasury of the United States; and all such Laws shall be subject to the Revision and Controul of the Congress.

No State shall, without the Consent of Congress, lay any duty of Tonnage, keep Troops, or Ships of War in time of Peace, enter into any Agreement or Compact with another State, or with a foreign Power, or engage in War, unless actually invaded, or in such imminent Danger as will not admit of delay.

Article II.

Section 1—President: his term of office. Electors of President; number and how appointed. Electors to vote on same day. Qualifications of President. On whom his duties devolve in case of his removal, death, etc. President's compensation. His oath of office.

The executive Power shall be vested in a President of the United States of America. He shall hold his Office during the Term of four Years, and, together with the Vice-President chosen for the same Term, be elected, as follows:

Each State shall appoint, in such Manner as the Legislature thereof may direct, a Number of Electors, equal to the whole Number of Senators and Representatives to which the State may be entitled in the Congress: but no Senator or Representative, or Person holding an Office of Trust or Profit under the United States, shall be appointed an Elector.

The Electors shall meet in their respective States, and vote by Ballot for two persons, of whom one at least shall not lie an Inhabitant of the same State with themselves. And they shall make a List of all the Persons voted for, and of the Number of Votes for each; which List they shall sign and certify, and transmit sealed to the Seat of the Government of the United States, directed to the President of the Senate. The President of the Senate shall, in the Presence of the Senate and House of Representatives, open all the Certificates, and the Votes shall then be counted. The Person having the greatest Number of Votes shall be the President, if such Number be a Majority of the whole Number of Electors appointed; and if there be more than one who have such Majority, and have an equal Number of Votes, then the House of Representatives shall immediately chuse by Ballot one of them for President; and if no Person have a Majority, then from the five highest on the List the said House shall in like Manner chuse the President. But in chusing the President, the Votes shall be taken by States, the Representation from each State having one Vote; a quorum for this Purpose shall consist of a Member or Members from two-thirds of the States, and a Majority of all the States shall be necessary to a Choice. In every Case, after the Choice of the President, the Person having the greatest Number of Votes of the Electors shall be the Vice President. But if there should remain two or more who have equal Votes, the Senate shall chuse from them by Ballot the Vice-President (superseded by Amendment XII).

The Congress may determine the Time of chusing the Electors, and the Day on which they shall give their Votes; which Day shall be the same throughout the United States.

No person except a natural born Citizen, or a Citizen of the United States, at the time of the Adoption of this Constitution, shall be eligible to the Office of President; neither shall any Person be eligible to that Office who shall not have attained to the Age of thirty-five Years, and been fourteen Years a Resident within the United States.

In Case of the Removal of the President from Office, or of his Death, Resignation, or Inability to discharge the Powers and Duties of the said Office, the same shall devolve on the Vice President, and the Congress may by Law provide for the Case of Removal, Death, Resignation or Inability, both of the President and Vice President, declaring what Officer shall then act as President, and such Officer shall act accordingly, until the Disability be removed, or a President shall be elected (modified by Amendments XX and XXV).

The President shall, at stated Times, receive for his Services, a Compensation, which shall neither be increased nor diminished during the Period for which he shall have been elected, and he shall not receive within that Period any other Emolument from the United States, or any of them.

Before he enter on the Execution of his Office, he shall take the following Oath or Affirmation:

"I do solemnly swear (or affirm) that I will faithfully execute the Office of President of the United States, and will to the best of my Ability, preserve, protect and defend the Constitution of the United States."

Section 2—President to be Commander-in-Chief. He may require opinions of cabinet officers, etc., may pardon. Treaty-making power. Nomination of certain officers. When President may fill vacancies.

The President shall be Commander in Chief of the Army and Navy of the United States, and of the Militia of the several States, when called into the actual Service of the United States; he may require the Opinion, in writing, of the principal Officer in each of the executive Departments, upon any subject relating to the Duties of their respective Offices, and he shall have Power to Grant Reprieves and Pardons for Offenses against the United States, except in Cases of Impeachment.

He shall have Power, by and with the Advice and Consent of the Senate, to make Treaties, provided two thirds of the Senators present concur; and he shall nominate, and by and with the Advice and Consent of the Senate, shall appoint Ambassadors, other public Ministers and Consuls, Judges of the Supreme Court, and all other Officers of the United States, whose Appointments are not herein otherwise provided for, and which shall be established by Law: but the Congress may by Law vest the Appointment of such inferior Officers, as they think proper, in the President alone, in the Courts of Law, or in the Heads of Departments.

The President shall have Power to fill up all Vacancies that may happen during the Recess of the Senate, by granting Commissions which shall expire at the End of their next Session.

Section 3—President shall communicate to Congress. He may convene and adjourn Congress, in case of disagreement, etc. Shall receive ambassadors, execute laws, and commission officers.

He shall from time to time give to the Congress Information of the State of the Union, and recommend to their Consideration such Measures as he shall judge necessary and expedient; he may, on extraordinary Occasions, convene both Houses, or either of them, and in Case of Disagreement between them, with Respect to the Time of Adjournment, he may adjourn them to such Time as he shall think proper; he shall receive Ambassadors and other public Ministers; he shall take Care that the Laws be faithfully executed, and shall Commission all the Officers of the United States.

Section 4—All civil offices forfeited for certain crimes.

The President, Vice President and all civil Officers of the United States, shall be removed from Office on Impeachment for, and Conviction of, Treason, Bribery, or other high Crimes and Misdemeanors.

Article III.
Section 1—Judicial powers, Tenure. Compensation.

The judicial Power of the United States, shall be vested in one Supreme Court, and in such inferior Courts as the Congress may from time to time ordain and establish. The Judges, both of the supreme and inferior Courts, shall hold their Offices during good Behavior, and shall, at stated Times, receive for their Services a Compensation which shall not be diminished during their Continuance in Office.

Section 2—Judicial power; to what cases it extends. Original jurisdiction of Supreme Court; appellate jurisdiction. Trial by jury, etc. Trial, where.

The judicial Power shall extend to all Cases, in Law and Equity, arising under this Constitution, the Laws of the United States, and Treaties made, or which shall be made, under their Authority; to all Cases affecting Ambassadors, other public Ministers and Consuls; to all Cases of admiralty and maritime Jurisdiction; to Controversies to which the United States shall be a Party; to Controversies between two or more States; between a State and Citizens of another State; between Citizens of different States; between Citizens of the same State claiming Lands under Grants of different States, and between a State, or the Citizens thereof, and foreign States, Citizens or Subjects (modified by Amendment XI).

In all Cases affecting Ambassadors, other public Ministers and Consuls, and those in which a State shall be Party, the Supreme Court shall have original Jurisdiction. In all the other Cases before mentioned, the Supreme Court shall have appellate Jurisdiction, both as to Law and Fact, with such Exceptions, and under such Regulations as the Congress shall make.

Trial of all Crimes, except in Cases of Impeachment, shall be by Jury; and such Trial shall be held in the State where the said Crimes shall have been committed; but when not committed within any State, the Trial shall be at such Place or Places as the Congress may by Law have directed.

Section 3—Treason defined, Proof of, Punishment of.

Treason against the United States, shall consist only in levying War against them, or in adhering to their Enemies, giving them Aid and Comfort. No Person shall be convicted of Treason unless on the Testimony of two Witnesses to the same overt Act, or on Confession in open Court.

The Congress shall have power to declare the Punishment of Treason, but no Attainder of Treason shall work Corruption of Blood, or Forfeiture except during the Life of the Person attainted.

Article IV
Section 1—Each State to give credit to the public acts, etc., of every other state.

Full Faith and Credit shall be given in each State to the public Acts, Records, and judicial Proceedings of every other State. And the Congress may by general Laws prescribe the Manner in which such Acts, Records and Proceedings shall be proved, and the Effect thereof.

Section 2—Privileges of citizens of each State. Fugitives from justice to be delivered up. Persons held to service having escaped to be delivered up.

The Citizens of each State shall be entitled to all Privileges and Immunities of Citizens in the several States.

A Person charged in any State with Treason, Felony, or other Crime, who shall flee from Justice, and be found in another State, shall on demand of the executive Authority of the State from which he fled, be delivered up, to be removed to the State having Jurisdiction of the Crime.

No Person held to Service or Labour in one State, under the Laws thereof, escaping into another, shall, in Consequence of any Law or Regulation therein, be discharged from such Service or Labour, But shall be delivered up on Claim of the Party to whom such Service or Labour may be due (superseded by Amendment XIII).

Section 3—Admission of new States. Power of Congress over territory and other property.

New States may be admitted by the Congress into this Union; but no new States shall be formed or erected within the Jurisdiction of any other State; nor any State be formed by the Junction of two or more States, or parts of States, without the Consent of the Legislatures of the States concerned as well as of the Congress.

The Congress shall have Power to dispose of and make all needful Rules and Regulations respecting the Territory or other Property belonging to the United States;

and nothing in this Constitution shall be so construed as to Prejudice any Claims of the United States, or of any particular State.

Section 4—Republican form of government guaranteed. Each state to be protected.

The United States shall guarantee to every State in this Union a Republican Form of Government, and shall protect each of them against Invasion; and on Application of the Legislature, or of the Executive (when the Legislature cannot be convened) against domestic Violence.

Article V
Constitution: how amended; proviso.

The Congress, whenever two thirds of both Houses shall deem it necessary, shall propose Amendments to this Constitution, or, on the Application of the Legislatures of two thirds of the several States, shall call a Convention for proposing Amendments, which, in either Case, shall be valid to all Intents and Purposes, as part of this Constitution, when ratified by the Legislatures of three fourths of the several States, or by Conventions in three fourths thereof, as the one or the other Mode of Ratification may be proposed by the Congress; Provided that no Amendment which may be made prior to the Year One thousand eight hundred and eight shall in any Manner affect the first and fourth Clauses in the Ninth Section of the first Article; and that no State, without its Consent, shall be deprived of its equal Suffrage in the Senate.

Article VI
Certain debt, etc., declared valid. Supremacy of Constitution, treaties, and laws of the United States. Oath to support Constitution, by whom taken. No religious test.

All Debts contracted and Engagements entered into, before the Adoption of this Constitution, shall be as valid against the United States under this Constitution, as under the Confederation.

This Constitution, and the Laws of the United States which shall be made in Pursuance thereof; and all Treaties made, or which shall be made, under the Authority of the United States, shall be the supreme Law of the Land; and the Judges in every State shall be bound thereby, any Thing in the Constitution or Laws of any State to the Contrary notwithstanding.

The Senators and Representatives before mentioned, and the Members of the several State Legislatures, and all executive and judicial Officers, both of the United States and of the several States, shall be bound by Oath or Affirmation, to support this Constitution; but no religious Test shall ever be required as a Qualification to any Office or public Trust under the United States.

Article VII
What ratification shall establish Constitution.

The Ratification of the Conventions of nine States, shall be sufficient for the Establishment of this Constitution between the States so ratifying theSame.

Done in Convention by the Unanimous Consent of the States present the Seventeenth Day of September in the Year of our Lord one thousand seven hundred and Eighty seven and of the Independence of the United States of America the Twelfth. In Witness whereof We have hereunto subscribed our Names.

Go Washington, President and deputy from Virginia

New Hampshire: John Langdon, Nicholas Gilman

Massachusetts: Nathaniel Gorham, Rufus King

Connecticut: Wm Saml Johnson, Roger Sherman

New York: Alexander Hamilton

New Jersey: Wil Livingston, David Brearley, Wm Paterson, Jona. Dayton

Pensylvania: B Franklin, Thomas Mifflin, Robt Morris, Geo. Clymer, Thos FitzSimons, Jared Ingersoll, James Wilson, Gouv Morris

Delaware: Geo. Read, Gunning Bedford jun, John Dickinson, Richard Bassett, Jaco. Broom

Maryland: James McHenry, Dan of St Tho Jenifer, Danl Carroll

Virginia: John Blair, James Madison Jr.

North Carolina: Wm Blount, Richd Dobbs Spaight, Hu Williamson

South Carolina: J. Rutledge, Charles Cotesworth Pinckney, Charles Pinckney, Pierce Butler

Georgia: William Few, Abr Baldwin

Attest: William Jackson, Secretary

The Amendments

Amendment I—Religious establishment prohibited. Freedom of speech, of the press, and right to petition. *Ratified 12/15/1791.*
Congress shall make no law respecting an establishment of religion, or prohibiting the free exercise thereof; or abridging the freedom of speech, or of the press; or the right of the people peaceably to assemble, and to petition the Government for a redress of grievances.

Amendment II—Right to keep and bear arms. *Ratified December 15, 1791.*
A well regulated Militia, being necessary to the security of a free State, the right of the people to keep and bear Arms, shall not be infringed.

Amendment III—Conditions for quarters for soldiers. *Ratified December 15, 1791.*
No Soldier shall, in time of peace be quartered in any house, without the consent of the Owner, nor in time of war, but in a manner to be prescribed by law.

Amendment IV—Right of search and seizure regulated. *Ratified December 15, 1791.* The right of the people to be secure in their persons, houses, papers, and effects, against unreasonable searches and seizures, shall not be violated, and no Warrants shall issue, but upon probable cause, supported by Oath or affirmation, and particularly describing the place to be searched, and the persons or things to be seized.

Amendment V—Provisions concerning prosecution. Trial and punishment—private property not to be taken for public use without compensation. *Ratified December 15, 1791.*
No person shall be held to answer for a capital, or otherwise infamous crime, unless on a presentment or indictment of a Grand Jury, except in cases arising in the land or naval forces, or in the Militia, when in actual service in time of War or public danger; nor shall any person be subject for the same offense to be twice put in jeopardy of life or limb; nor shall be compelled in any criminal case to be a witness against himself, nor be deprived of life, liberty, or property, without due process of law; nor shall private property be taken for public use, without just compensation.

Amendment VI—Right to speedy trial, witnesses, etc. *Ratified December 15, 1791.*
In all criminal prosecutions, the accused shall enjoy the right to a speedy and public trial, by an impartial jury of the State and district wherein the crime shall have been committed, which district shall have been previously ascertained by law, and to be informed of the nature and cause of the accusation; to be confronted with the witnesses against him; to have compulsory process for obtaining witnesses in his favor, and to have the Assistance of Counsel for his defence.

Amendment VII—Right of trial by jury. *Ratified December 15, 1791.*
In suits at common law, where the value in controversy shall exceed twenty dollars, the right of trial by jury shall be preserved, and no fact tried by a jury, shall be otherwise re-examined in any Court of the United States, than according to the rules of the common law.

Amendment VIII—Excessive bail or fines and cruel punishment prohibited.
Ratified December 15, 1791.
Excessive bail shall not lie required, nor excessive fines imposed, nor cruel and unusual punishments inflicted.

Amendment IX—Rule of construction of Constitution. *Ratified December 15, 1791.*
The enumeration in the Constitution, of certain rights, shall not be construed to deny or disparage others retained by the people.

Amendment X—Rights of States under Constitution. *Ratified December 15, 1791.*
The powers not delegated to the United States by the Constitution, nor prohibited by it to the States, are reserved to the States respectively, or to the people.

Amendment XI—Judicial Powers construed. *Ratified February 7, 1795.*
The Judicial power of the United States shall not be construed to extend to any suit in law or equity, commenced or prosecuted against one of the United States by Citizens of another State, or by Citizens or subjects of any foreign State.

Amendment XII—Manner of choosing President and Vice-President. *Ratified June 15, 1804.*
The Electors shall meet in their respective States, and vote by ballot for President and Vice-President, one of whom, at least, shall not be an inhabitant of the same State with themselves; they shall name in their ballots the person voted for as President, and in distinct ballots the person voted for as Vice-President, and they shall make distinct lists of all persons voted for as President, and of all persons voted for as Vice-President and of the number of votes for each, which lists they shall sign and certify, and transmit sealed to the seat of the Government of the United States, directed to the President of the Senate;

The President of the Senate shall, in the presence of the Senate and House of Representatives, open all the certificates and the votes shall then be counted;

The person having the greatest number of votes for President, shall be the President, if such number be a majority of the whole number of Electors appointed; and if no person have such majority, then from the persons having the highest numbers not exceeding three on the list of those voted for as President, the House of Representatives shall choose immediately, by ballot, the President. But in choosing the President, the votes shall be taken by States, the representation from each State having one vote; a quorum for this purpose shall consist of a member or members from two-thirds of the States, and a majority of all the States shall be necessary to a choice. And if the House of Representatives shall not choose a President whenever the right of choice shall devolve upon them, before the fourth day of March next following, then the Vice-President shall act as President, as in the case of the death or other constitutional disability of the President.

The person having the greatest number of votes as Vice-President, shall be the Vice-President, if such number be a majority of the whole number of Electors appointed, and if no person have a majority, then from the two highest numbers on the list, the Senate shall choose the Vice-President; a quorum for the purpose shall consist of two-thirds of the whole number of Senators, and a majority of the whole number shall be necessary to a choice. But no person constitutionally ineligible to the office of President shall be eligible to that of Vice-President of the United States.

Amendment XIII—Slavery Abolished. *Ratified December 6, 1865.*
1. Neither slavery nor involuntary servitude, except as a punishment for crime whereof the party shall have been duly convicted, shall exist within the United States, or any place subject to their jurisdiction.
2. Congress shall have power to enforce this article by appropriate legislation.

Amendment XIV—Citizenship rights not to be abridged. *Ratified July 9, 1868.*

1. All persons born or naturalized in the United States, and subject to the jurisdiction thereof, are citizens of the United States and of the State wherein they reside. No State shall make or enforce any law which shall abridge the privileges or immunities of citizens of the United States; nor shall any State deprive any person of life, liberty, or property, without due process of law; nor deny to any person within its jurisdiction the equal protection of the laws.

2. Representatives shall be apportioned among the several States according to their respective numbers, counting the whole number of persons in each State, excluding Indians not taxed. But when the right to vote at any election for the choice of Electors for President and Vice-President of the United States, Representatives in Congress, the executive and judicial officers of a State, or the members of the Legislature thereof, is denied to any of the male inhabitants of such State, being twenty-one years of age, and citizens of the United States, or in any way abridged, except for participation in rebellion, or other crime, the basis of representation therein shall be reduced in the proportion which the number of such male citizens shall bear to the whole number of male citizens twenty-one years of age in such State.

3. No person shall be a Senator or Representative in Congress, or elector of President and Vice-President, or hold any office, civil or military, under the United States, or under any State, who, having previously taken an oath, as a member of Congress, or as an officer of the United States, or as a member of any State legislature, or as an executive or judicial officer of any State, to support the Constitution of the United States, shall have engaged in insurrection or rebellion against the same, or given aid or comfort to the enemies thereof. But Congress may by a vote of two-thirds of each House, remove such disability.

4. The validity of the public debt of the United States, authorized by law, including debts incurred for payment of pensions and bounties for services in suppressing insurrection or rebellion, shall not be questioned. But neither the United States nor any State shall assume or pay any debt or obligation incurred in aid of insurrection or rebellion against the United States, or any claim for the loss or emancipation of any slave; but all such debts, obligations and claims shall be held illegal and void.

5. The Congress shall have power to enforce, by appropriate legislation, the provisions of this article.

Amendment XV—Race no bar to voting rights. *Ratified February 3, 1870.*

1. The right of citizens of the United States to vote shall not be denied or abridged by the United States or by any State on account of race, color, or previous condition of servitude.

2. The Congress shall have power to enforce this article by appropriate legislation.

Amendment XVI—Income taxes authorized. *Ratified February 3, 1913.*
The Congress shall have power to lay and collect taxes on incomes, from whatever source derived, without apportionment among the several States and without regard to any census or enumeration.

Amendment XVII—United States Senators to be elected by popular vote. *Ratified April 8, 1913.*

The Senate of the United States shall be composed of two senators from each State, elected by the people thereof, for six years; and each Senator shall have one vote. The electors in each State shall have the qualifications requisite for electors of the most numerous branch of the State legislature.

When vacancies happen in the representation of any State in the Senate, the executive authority of such State shall issue writs of election to fill such vacancies: Provided, That the legislature of any State may empower the executive thereof to make temporary appointments until the people fill the vacancies by election as the legislature may direct.

This amendment shall not be so construed as to affect the election or term of any senator chosen before it becomes valid as part of the Constitution.

Amendment XVIII—Liquor prohibition amendment. *Ratified January 16, 1919; Repealed by Amendment XXI, December 5, 1933.*

1. After one year from the ratification of this article, the manufacture, sale, or transportation of intoxicating liquors within, the importation thereof into, or the exportation thereof from the United States and all territory subject to the jurisdiction thereof for beverage purposes is hereby prohibited.

2. The Congress and the several States shall have concurrent power to enforce this article by appropriate legislation.

3. This article shall be inoperative unless it shall have been ratified as an amendment to the Constitution by the legislatures of the several States, as provided in the Constitution, within seven years from the date of the submission hereof to the States by Congress.

Amendment XIX—Giving nationwide suffrage to women. *Ratified August 8, 1920.*

The right of citizens of the United States to vote shall not be denied or abridged by the United States or by any States on account of sex.

The Congress shall have power by appropriate legislation to enforce the provisions of this article.

Amendment XX—Terms of President and Vice President to begin on Jan. 20; those of Senators, Representatives, Jan. 3. *Ratified January 23, 1933.*

1. The terms of the President and Vice-President shall end at noon on the 20th day of January, and the terms of Senators and Representatives at noon on the 3d day of January, of the years in which such terms would have ended if this article had not been ratified; and the terms of their successors shall then begin.

2. The Congress shall assemble at least once in every year, and such meeting shall begin at noon on the 3d day of January, unless they shall by law appoint a different day.

3. If, at the time fixed for the beginning of the term of the President, the President-elect shall have died, the Vice-President-elect shall become President. If a President shall not have been chosen before the time fixed for the beginning of his term,

or if the President-elect shall have failed to qualify, then the Vice-President-elect shall act as President until a President shall have qualified; and the Congress may by law provide for the case wherein neither a President-elect nor a Vice-President-elect shall have qualified, declaring who shall then act as President, or the manner in which one who is to act shall be selected, and such person shall act accordingly until a President or Vice-President shall have qualified.

4. The Congress may by law provide for the case of the death of any of the persons from whom the House of Representatives may choose a President whenever the right of choice shall have devolved upon them, and for the case of the death of any of the persons from whom the Senate may choose a Vice-President whenever the right of choice shall have devolved upon them.

5. Sections 1 and 2 shall take effect on the 15th day of October following the ratification of this article.

6. This article shall be inoperative unless it shall have been ratified as an amendment to the Constitution by the legislatures of three-fourths of the several States within seven years from the date of its submission.

Amendment XXI—Repeal of Amendment XVIII. *Ratified December 5, 1933.*

1. The eighteenth article of amendment to the Constitution of the United States is hereby repealed.

2. The transportation or importation into any State, Territory, or possession of the United States for delivery or use therein of intoxicating liquors, in violation of the laws thereof, is hereby prohibited.

3. The article shall be inoperative unless it shall have been ratified as an amendment to the Constitution by conventions in the several States, as provided in the Constitution, within seven years from the date of the submission hereof to the States by the Congress.

Amendment XXII—Limiting Presidential terms of office. *Ratified February 27, 1951.*

1. No person shall be elected to the office of the President more than twice, and no person who has held the office of President, or acted as President for more than two years of a term to which some other person was elected President shall be elected to the office of the President more than once. But this Article shall not apply to any person holding the office of President when this Article was proposed by the Congress, and shall not prevent any person who May be holding the office of President, or acting as President, during the term within which this Article becomes operative from holding the office of President or acting as President during the remainder of such term.

2. This article shall be inoperative unless it shall have been ratified as an amendment to the Constitution by the legislatures of three-fourths of the several States within seven years from the date of its submission to the States by the Congress.

Amendment XXIII—Presidential vote for District of Columbia. *Ratified March 29, 1961.*

1. The District constituting the seat of government of the United States shall appoint in such manner as the Congress may direct: A number of electors of President and Vice-President equal to the whole number of Senators and Representatives in Congress to which the District would be entitled if it were a State, but in no event more than the least populous State; they shall be in addition to those appointed by the States, but they shall be considered, for the purposes of the election of President and Vice-President, to be electors appointed by a State; and they shall meet in the district and perform such duties as provided by the twelfth article of amendment.

2. The Congress shall have power to enforce this article by appropriate legislation.

Amendment XXIV—Barring poll tax in federal elections. *Ratified January 23, 1964.*

1. The right of citizens of the United States to vote in any primary or other election for President or Vice-President, for electors for President or Vice-President, or for Senator or Representative in Congress, shall not be denied or abridged by the United States or any State by reason of failure to pay any poll tax or other tax.

2. The Congress shall have power to enforce this article by appropriate legislation.

Amendment XXV—Presidential disability and succession. *Ratified February 10, 1967.*

1. In case of the removal of the President from office or of his death or resignation, the Vice-President shall become President.

2. Whenever there is a vacancy in the office of the Vice-President, the President shall nominate a Vice-President who shall take office upon confirmation by a majority vote of both Houses of Congress.

3. Whenever the President transmits to the President pro tempore of the Senate and the Speaker of the House of Representatives his written declaration that he is unable to discharge the powers and duties of his office, and until he transmits to them a written declaration to the contrary, such powers and duties shall be discharged by the Vice-President as Acting President.

4. Whenever the Vice-President and a majority of either the principal officers of the executive departments or of such other body as Congress may by law provide, transmit to the President pro tempore of the Senate and the Speaker of the House of Representatives their written declaration that the President is unable to discharge the powers and duties of his office, the Vice-President shall immediately assume the powers and duties of the office as Acting President.

Thereafter, when the President transmits to the President pro tempore of the Senate and the Speaker of the House of Representatives his written declaration that no inability exists, he shall resume the powers and duties of his office unless the Vice-President and a majority of either the principal officers of the executive department or of such other body as Congress may by law provide, transmit within four days to the President pro tempore of the Senate and the Speaker of the House of Representatives their written declaration that the President is unable to discharge the powers and duties of his office. Thereupon Congress shall decide the issue, assembling within forty-eight hours for that purpose if not in session. If the Congress, within twenty-one days after receipt of the latter written declaration, or, if Congress is not in session, within twenty-one days after Congress is required to assemble, determines by two-thirds vote of both Houses that the President is unable to discharge the powers and duties of his office, the Vice-President shall continue to discharge the same as Acting President; otherwise, the President shall resume the powers and duties of his office.

Amendment XXVI—Lowering voting age to 18 years. *Ratified July 1, 1971.*

1. The right of citizens of the United States, who are eighteen years of age or older, to vote shall not be denied or abridged by the United States or by any State on account of age.

2. The Congress shall have power to enforce this article by appropriate legislation.

Amendment XXVII—Congressional Pay. *Ratified May 7, 1992.*

No law, varying the compensation for the services of the Senators and Representatives, shall take effect, until an election of Representatives shall have intervened.

INDEX